THE MIDDLE LENGTH SAYINGS

MAJJHIMA-NIKĀYA

VOLUME II

Pali Text Society
TRANSLATION SERIES, NO. 30

THE COLLECTION OF THE MIDDLE LENGTH SAYINGS

(MAJJHIMA-NIKĀYA)

VOL. II

THE MIDDLE FIFTY DISCOURSES

(MAJJHIMAPAṆṆĀSA)

TRANSLATED FROM THE PALI BY

I. B. HORNER, M.A.

Associate of Newnham College, Cambridge
Translator of "The Book of the Discipline," volumes I-V

Published by
THE PALI TEXT SOCIETY · LONDON
Distributed by
ROUTLEDGE & KEGAN PAUL
LONDON & BOSTON
1975

First published *1957*

Reprinted *1970*

Reprinted *1975*

ISBN 0 7100 8217 7

Printed in Great Britain by
Unwin Brothers Limited, Old Woking, Surrey

CONTENTS

III. THE DIVISION ON WANDERERS (PARIBBĀJAKAVAGGA)

IV. THE ROYAL DIVISION (RĀJAVAGGA)

V. THE DIVISION ON BRAHMANS
(BRĀHMAṆAVAGGA)

INDEXES

TRANSLATOR'S INTRODUCTION

This volume contains a translation of the Middle (or Second) Fifty Discourses of the Majjhima-Nikāya. They are arranged, as are the First Fifty and the last Fifty (-two), in five Divisions (*vagga*) of ten Discourses each. But the assemblage of Discourses in the different Divisions and the naming of the Divisions are less complicated here than in either of the other Sections. For the assemblage and the naming are based in a concrete and factual way on five of the main segments of the population of the day. The Discourses that each Division contains therefore do not depend for their grouping on whether they go in pairs or are similes, for there are only two pairs (Nos. 63, 64 and 77, 79[1]) and only one *upama*-Discourse; nor are they collected according to the apparently more arbitrary plan of naming a Division after the Discourse placed first in it and then including the remaining nine Discourses for reasons that may be more or less clear or obscure to us. On the contrary, the Discourses here are referred to various groups of persons who went to make up a major part of the contemporary life of India: Householders, Monks, Wanderers, Royalty and Brahmans, all of deep interest to the Buddha's followers. By and large, but with exceptions, the ten Discourses assigned to each of the five Divisions of the Middle Fifty logically belong not only together but also to the Divisions in which they are placed, since in some manner, actual or narrative, each Division throughout contains material appropriate to its title.

No assessment could be complete however unless an investigation were made of material that might have been contained in these Divisions but which in fact occurs elsewhere. For example, are there Discourses to, for or about wanderers or royalty in some other Divisions than those called by either of these names? If the question is: are there other Discourses to, for or about monks, the answer is quite definitely and naturally in the affirmative. Even if some of these may lack the *Vinaya* flavour characteristic of a number of Discourses in the Monks' Division, monks nevertheless remain, both when carrying out the *Vinaya* rules and regulations, and

[1] On these (the Rāhulovāda Suttas and the Vacchagotta Suttas) see *M.L.S.* i, Intr. p. xiii.

when practising such other parts of the training as meditation, a chief centre of interest all through the Piṭakas.

Space does not permit in this Introduction of making any such assessment of other *Majjhima* Discourses that might have been placed among the Middle Fifty or of the reasons why they have not been so placed. It would have been ideal if each Division could have been furnished with its own foreword as is nearly every Discourse in *The Dialogues of the Buddha.*[1] Nor is there space to tabulate the names of places where Discourses are said to have been given, the names of those who gave them, or the names of those to whom they were spoken. Nor is it possible to discriminate between Discourses spontaneously given, those prompted by a statement that may have seemed shallow or untrue, those given in response to a question or an invitation to speak on a certain topic, or those that begin with Gotama or one of his disciples asking a question and then proceeding to develop some theme. As things are, the *Majjhima* is too long and its " rich variety " too great. This Introduction can therefore aim at being no more than a general and much compressed survey of a few out of the many striking situations, words and phrases recorded in these fifty Discourses which, stemming from India, " the very mother of religions," still shine and glow with vitality.

In the *Division on Householders* (Nos. 51-60), the first in this volume, all the Discourses except two (Nos. 57, 58) are either in whole or in part addressed to householders or are prompted by some remark or question attributed to a householder, *gahapati*. Three bear the names of householders in their titles (Nos. 54, 55, 56) and one (No. 52) that of a householder's town, although the parallel version at *A*. v. 342 is called after the man himself. One Discourse is named after a wanderer (No. 51); and the one named after a canine ascetic (No. 57) has no more to do with householders than has No. 58 which is named after a prince. In this Division no special charter for householders is found as in the *Sigālovādasuttanta* of the *Dīgha*. Dhamma is presented to them, neither curtailed nor adapted to their life in the world, nor made easier for them to undertake and practise than it is for monks (see especially Stas. Nos. 52, 53, 54). Nor can one say that the various leading topics occur here and nowhere else, since exhortations on the moral habits, sense-pleasures, feelings and

[1] Sacred Books of the Buddhists, vols. II, III, IV, translated by T. W. and C. A. F. Rhys Davids.

the four types of "tormentors" do in fact appear in other parts of the Nikāyas. For example, even the classification of the feelings by groups of increasing numbers, from 2 to 108 (Sta. No. 59) is also found at *S*. iv. 231f. Or again, Sta. No. 53, in which a precise meaning is ascribed to the compound *vijjā-caraṇa-sampanna*, has affinities with the *Ambaṭṭha-* and the *Sāmaññaphala-suttantas*.[1]

This compound, which may be rendered "possessed of knowledge and (right) conduct" (or, practice), is not only used as one of the many, and so far uncollected, epithets of the Buddha; it also stands for an achievement an ariyan disciple can win by strict training and self-control. The *Sekha-sutta* (No. 53) assigns a very definite connotation both to *caraṇa* and *vijjā*, as to a lesser extent does the *Ambaṭṭha-suttanta*, according to which *caraṇa* consists of fifteen factors, as noted briefly at *AA*. iii. 151, *SA*. i. 217, and more fully at *SA*. i. 219: possession of moral habit (*sīlasampanna*), guarding the doors of the senses, moderation in eating, intentness on vigilance or wakefulness, possession of the seven excellent things, acquirement at will and without trouble or difficulty of the four *jhāna* which are of the purest (or, highest) mentality and are abidings in ease here and now, *diṭṭhadhammasukhavihāra*. And *vijjā*, knowledge, is broken up into and specified as three kinds or branches represented by the verbs *anussarati*, *pajānāti* and *abhijānāti*.[2]

Two points here call for comment: (1) the term *diṭṭhadhamma-sukhavihāra*, which I have translated as "abiding in ease here and now," and which has been most variously rendered by English translators, is here as elsewhere applied solely to the four *jhāna* and to nothing but the *jhāna*. It is an appellation of these meditative states and of these only.

(2) The description of the ariyan disciple who is possessed of moral habit, *sīlasampanna*, shows him as one who is "moral" in more senses than that of observing the *sīlas*. But the opening word of this description, *sīlavant*, is doubtless intended to refer to this first and fundamentally necessary stage in the whole training. While the *Sāmaññaphalasuttanta*, §§43-62, says of the mastery of each of the major, middle and minor *sīla* that, in regard to the ariyan disciple "it is so of him in regard to moral habit," *idam pi' ssa hoti sīlasmiṁ*, the *Sekhasutta* says of the mastery of each of the fifteen factors of *caraṇa*, of which only the first is possession of moral habit but on a scale more expanded than is usual, that "this is so of him in regard

---

[1] *D*. Stas. Nos. 3 and 2 respectively.

[2] See *PED*. *s.v.* *vijjā*.

to conduct," *idam pi' ssa hoti caraṇasmiṁ*. The *Sāmaññaphala Sta.* therefore appears to supply something lacking in the *Sekha*, something perhaps already known and not necessary to repeat; but the *Sekha-sutta*, on the other hand, makes an advance over the *Sāmaññaphala* in that, having almost certainly assumed *idam pi' ssa hoti sīlasmiṁ*, it takes the ariyan disciple not only where *idam pi' ssa hoti caraṇasmiṁ* but also where, having successfully broken through the egg-shell of ignorance, *idam pi' ssa hoti vijjāya*, " this is so of him in regard to knowledge." By *vijjā* the threefold knowledge is meant: recollection of former habitations; comprehension that it is in accordance with *kamma* that beings, beheld with the purified *deva*-vision, pass hence and come to be elsewhere; and realisation that by the destruction of the *āsavā* the mind is freed.[1] It is by the ariyan disciple's recollection, comprehension and realisation (in these senses) that " it is so of him in regard to knowledge."

Jains are particularly mentioned in Stas. Nos. 56 and 58. In the long *Upāli-sutta* (No. 56) the householder of this name, who earlier had been a Jain adherent and supporter, became so much convinced by the arguments he heard the " recluse Gotama " put forward that three times he asked to become an *upāsaka*, a lay-devotee, and thus more closely knit to the fourfold community. On each occasion he was answered by the Lord exactly as was General Sīha[2] who had also begun as a follower of the Jains. This curious parallelism of question and answer which I find only on these two occasions inclines one to ask whether there may not be here some special formula in use now and again for accepting Jains, or Jains of a particular standing —" well-known men " perhaps. For, on the other hand, Vappa the Sakyan who had also been a disciple of the Jains appears to have become a lay-devotee simply by uttering the usual formula[3] once only, as was the general custom in force no matter from what stratum of society a man or woman came wanting to join the Buddha's community. Upāli's set of verses with which this Sutta concludes, all in eulogy of " this Lord whose disciple am I," is remarkable for the variety of its epithets, each pointing to some decisive quality or attainment of this " recluse, a human being, in his last body, a man."

A *Division on Monks* (Nos. 61-70) was no doubt necessary to give the right balance to the social picture evoked by the titles of the four other Divisions of the Middle Fifty. Otherwise, and considering the

---

[1] See below, p. 24. [2] *Vin.* i. 236 f.; *A.* iv. 185. [3] *A.* ii. 199-200.

multitude of Discourses throughout the *M*. that are addressed not only to monks but specially to them, why is there a Division on Monks at all? Or why, to form the Division, were these particular ten Discourses selected? It is true that at least four of them (Nos. 65, 66, 67, 70) contain a *Vinaya* element, but so do others for example No. 82 (and 104). All the Discourses in this Division are concerned with monks, and all the monks referred to were already ordained. This distinguishes them from Stas. Nos. 82 and 86, the former of which tells the story of the entry into the Order of monks of Raṭṭhapāla the young man of family, and the latter that of Aṅgulimāla the bandit. These two Discourses are respectively named after them. Except for these and six Discourses in the Division on Monks (Nos. 61-65 and No. 69) none other in the Middle Fifty takes a monk's name for its title, nor does any in the First Fifty, but there are some nine in the Final Fifty to do so. No. 66 is an *upama*-Sutta,[1] addressed to the monk Udāyin, but in the six *upama*-Discourses in the Third Division of the First Fifty, four were spoken to monks. The position of Discourse No. 66 is thus something of an anomaly. Discourse No. 67, having a place-name for title, and including one of the few recorded rebukes to Sāriputta,[2] was spoken to an Order of monks. No. 68, again with a place-name for title, was given to various young men of family, apparently very recently ordained, several of whom were later to become well-known and respected figures in the Order. No. 70, also called after a place, was addressed to Assaji and Punabbasuka, two of the six sectarian leaders of groups of monks, and who made their head-quarters at Kīṭāgiri.

The first two Discourses in the Division on Monks are reputed to have been addressed by Gotama to Rāhula, his son. No. 61, sometimes called the "criterion of Buddhist morality," is concerned with the need to reflect before doing a deed on whether it will harm oneself and others; and No. 62 is concerned with various forms of mind-development, *bhāvanā*. The next two Discourses are called the *Cūḷa-* and *Mahā-māluṅkyāputta-suttas*, although the *Mahā-* is addressed more specifically to Ānanda than to the monk Māluṅkyāputta. While the first member of this pair gives reasons why current speculative views have not been explained by the Tathāgata, in the latter the Teacher—after rebuking Māluṅkyāputta—spoke on the course and the practice to be followed for achieving escape,

---

[1] See *M.L.S.* Intr., p. xi.

[2] See below, p. xxvi.

nissaraṇa, from the five fetters, as far as the stage where the meditator, realising the impermanence of all the meditative planes he has so far mastered, focuses his mind instead on the "deathless element,"[1] the real, the excellent.

Discourse No. 65 is as interesting both for its simile of the Thoroughbred Colt and the ten respects in which this becomes, by training, *parinibbuta*,[2] as for its reference to the seven kinds of monks. All of these, from the one "freed both ways" to the one that "strives after faith," each of whom would "be a causeway for me across the mire," are more fully explained in Sta. No. 70.

No. 69 is reputed to have been spoken by Sāriputta to the monks at large. Taking the monk Gulissāni as the type of forest-dwelling monk, Sāriputta recommends what his behaviour should be when he returns to stay with his Order, or otherwise people will conclude that he was lax and self-indulgent when he was alone in the forest. And Sāriputta goes on to outline in positive terms the ways in which he should train himself in his solitude, and ends by advocating three forms of (Buddhist) *yoga*, yoking oneself to by earnest study. These are *yoga* devoted to *abhidhamma*[3] and *abhivinaya*; the peaceful Deliverances; and *uttarimanussadhamma*,[4] the mental states of men that have gone further (than the here-now) and the goal for the sake of which the forest-dwelling monk has gone forth.

Each Discourse in the *Division on Wanderers* (Nos. 71-80) is called after the wanderer, *paribbājaka*, to whom it was delivered, with the exception of No. 78 which was spoken to Pañcakaṅga the carpenter, a layman. But it was the outcome of a statement made by a wanderer; and his name, or rather his mother's, forms the title. It therefore has similarities with the naming and the opening of Sta. No. 51. That they are not placed in the same Division is as much of a puzzle as is the separation of the *Abhayarājakumāra-sutta* (No. 58) and the *Bodhirājakumāra-sutta* (No. 85), each named after a prince who never came to the throne.

This Division gives some indication of the behaviour and conversation of wanderers: sitting down and noisily shouting out *tiracchānakathā*, low, worldly talk, but all the same appreciating that

---

[1] For six further references to *amata-dhātu* see *PTC*. I, p. 230.

[2] *Cf. nibbāyeyya*, in the simile of the fires, at *M*. i. 487.

[3] See *B.D.* iii. Intr. p. x *ff*. and *PTC*. I, p. 216.

[4] See *Vin*. iii. 91, 92, iv. 25 (*B.D*. i. 159, 161, ii. 211) where this word is defined.

the disciples of Gotama like quietude; of their attitude towards Gotama, whether favourable or unfavourable; of the views that interested them; of what they wanted to learn of the Buddha's teaching; and of what they were taught of this, which amounted to a very full measure of the whole (see especially Sta. No. 77). An experienced wanderer was doubtless a capable listener and learner.

It is noteworthy that one of the very few occasions when nibbāna is, in the Middle Fifty Discourses, made in any way more important than as the final member of a stereotyped sequence, is in the *Māgandiya-sutta* (No. 75). This opens with the wanderer Māgandiya scoffing at the samaṇa Gotama and telling a brahman who was already favourably disposed towards the Lord and was expecting a visit from him, that it is but " a sorry sight to see the sleeping-place of the good Gotama, a destroyer of growth "—*bhūnahu*, certainly a word of deep contempt (*cf. Sn.* 664; *anariya bhūnahu pāpaka dukkatakāri purisanta . . . nerayika*), and translated by Lord Chalmers as " rigid repressionist," i.e. of the senses, which the wanderer appears to think should be given full scope. However Māgandiya claims no originality for this abusive term; instead he asserts that " it is told thus in a sutta of ours," *evaṁ hi no sutte ocarati*.

The word *bhūnahu* may be compared with that other misrepresentation of the Lord made by some recluses and brahmans when they say that " the samaṇa Gotama is a *venayika* (a perverter or leader away) who lays down the cutting off, annihilation and destruction of the essential being." *sato sattassa* (*M.* Sta. 22).[1] For when the word *venayika* is not being used in its Buddhist and therefore favourable sense, as it was used by Upāli in his great eulogy of the Lord (Sta. No. 56), it is not impossible to see between it and *bhūnahu* some basic similarity of intention, perhaps even enough to read into this latter archaic and etymologically uncertain word the meaning of " destroyer of beings," which to the wanderers would be but the natural outcome of destroying the senses. Their mistake would have been in thinking that Gotama taught destruction; what he taught was control of the sense-organs and the suppression of the fever of thirst for sensory impressions. Māgandiya then hears that, as it is possible to attain extra-sensory delight, there is no longer any reason to envy the man whose pleasures are merely " low," *hīna*, (illustrated by the similes of the lepers). Then comes the gentle

---

[1] At *M.* ii. 228 this speculative view is ascribed to " some recluses and brahmans."

persuasion (illustrated by the similes of the blind man) that the wanderers' interpretation of "health" and "nibbāna" lacks the ariyan vision. For, as the climax affirms, in order to know health and see nibbāna as the stopping of this whole mass of the ill that has been generated by grasping after "low" things, it is essential to follow a prescribed course. Otherwise one will go astray, will be defrauded, as was the blind man.

This reasoned talk was not lost upon Māgandiya. He uttered the Three Goings for Refuge and asked for ordination as a monk: When informed by the Lord that former members of other sects had first to undertake a four months' probation (*Vin.* i. 69), he, in common with Seniya the canine ascetic (Sta. No. 57) and Vacchagotta, another famous wanderer (No. 73), rather exaggeratedly asserted that he would undertake it for four years. They all however appear to have been ordained at once, and not long afterwards each became "one of the arahants." These three Discourses therefore have the added interest of using a *Vinaya* element to stress the fervour of a new adherent to the Order. That they record their corresponding episodes in exactly the same terms as one another is not unexpected.

Further, the *Māgandiya-sutta* is one of a number of narrations found in the Middle Fifty to tell of a spiritual evolution,[1] each more or less complete in itself and in little or no need of filling out from other contexts in the Piṭakas. It has been said already that this Discourse reveals that Gotama was known to the wanderers as *bhūnahu.* It also reveals that the first line of a two-lined verse was part of the wanderers' tradition. Against this, Gotama tells Māgandiya that both the lines were spoken by former Buddhas—and these, judging by canonical evidence, were perhaps never very far from his thoughts.[2] Although this two-lined verse may not be precisely a *dhammapada*, a footprint of Dhamma, a word used in this technical sense at *D.* iii. 229 and *A.* ii. 29 where the four *dhammapadāni* enumerated are said to be ancient, of long standing, traditional, it is nevertheless invested here with a great antiquity.

The Division on Wanderers is also noteworthy for the two occasions on which Naked Ascetics, *ājīvika*, are mentioned. One of these is when the wanderer Sandaka is recorded to speak of them as "children of a childless mother," because they have only three great leaders,

---

[1] Others are the stories of King Pasenadi (Stas. 86-89), Aṅgulimāla (No. 86), and Vacchagotta (Nos. 71-73).

[2] See e.g. Sta. No. 81.

niyyātaro, that is leaders out from *dukkha* and *saṁsāra*, and whom he names, in contradistinction to the large numbers of great leaders in this Dhamma and Discipline (Sta. No. 76).

The other reference to Naked Ascetics is when the wanderer Vacchagotta in one of his questions to the Lord (No. 71) draws the response from him that, although he recollects ninety-one kappas, he knows of only one Naked Ascetic to have attained heaven. In my note on p. 161 below I have drawn attention to the tradition that Vipassin, the first Buddha to have preceded Gotama when these Buddhas are reckoned as six, is said to have arisen in the world ninety-one kappas ago. Taken together, these two passages may suggest that it was not necessary for Gotama's recollection of former habitations to go back to ages remoter still, and that therefore when it is said of him, as of others too, that they recollect many a kappa of the world's re-formation and disintegration, this is not a deliberately gross factual exaggeration so much as symbolical language devised to indicate immense reaches of the past, the precision of which, except in the case of the Buddha, and this only in very few passages, would be of no material significance. Again, these two passages, if taken together, may be regarded as one more indication that the numbering of the preceding Buddhas as six is indeed earlier than their numbering as twenty-four. For, unless this were of subsequent growth, why does the Buddha Gotama here clearly speak of ninety-one kappas, a figure so curiously reminiscent of the alleged date of Vipassin's Buddhahood ? At *Jā*. i. 391 "I myself was that Naked Ascetic".

But any mere claims, not based on fact, to recollecting former habitations (referring to the past) or to comprehending that beings uprise according to kamma (referring to the future) have to be waved aside and the actuality of the Teaching that is Dhamma (referring to the present) grasped instead: "There *is* birth, *atth' eva jāti*, there is ageing and dying, there are grief, sorrow, suffering, lamentation and despair of which I lay down the suppression, *nighāta*, here and now" (*M*. i. 430). So, "Let be the past, let be the future. I will teach you Dhamma: if this is, that comes to be; from the arising of this, that arises; if this is not, that does not come to be; from the stopping of this, that is stopped "[1]—pregnant words uttered to the wanderer Sakuludāyin (*M*. ii. 32; *cf*. *M*. ii. 44), and by

---

[1] Mrs. Rhys Davids, in spite of her great appreciation of this "really universal statement" (on cause), rather misses its special application in *M*. Sta. 79 as the "now" between the past and the future; her "beginning" and "end" I find both too finite and too vague; see *K.S*. ii. Intr. p. xi.

imputation stressing the here-and-now as the principal concern of the ariyan disciple.

No royal person, in the First Fifty Discourses, figures in a story from the past, nor is any contemporary king or queen recorded to have been present when any one of these Discourses was spoken, the names of Bimbisāra, Pasenadi and Ajātasattu being used merely to give point to an argument. The *Royal Division* (Nos. 81-90), on the other hand, although having only two Discourses named after a royal personage (No. 83, after a king who reigned in the distant past, and No. 85 after a prince who never ascended the throne), yet brings in a fine array of kings and queens and princes and contains no Discourses from which a royal name is absent: Kiki, King of Kāsi in a story from the past (No. 81); Koravya, apparently a Kuru King (No. 82); Makhādeva, his unnamed son and his son's descendants down to King Nimi and his son Kaḷārajanaka, also in a story from the past (No. 83); Avantiputta, King of Madhurā, in a Discourse given after the *parinibbāna* (No. 84); Prince Bodhi (No. 85); King Pasenadi (Nos. 86-90) with his Queen Mallikā, their child and another consort in No. 87; with Viḍūḍabha, his son, in Nos. 87 and 90; and with Somā and Sakulā, said to have been other consoıts, in No. 90; and besides Pasenadi, there is a reference to Ajātasattu, a reigning king, in No. 88.

One of the most interesting aspects of the Royal Division is the cycle of Discourses (Nos. 86-89 and continuing into 90) in which Pasenadi's spiritual evolution can be traced until it reached a full development and maturity, that is to say in the faith and reliance that he came to repose in the Lord. In Sta. No. 86, primarily concerned with the regeneration and birth in the " ariyan birth," *ariyāya jātiyā*, of the dreaded bandit Aṅgulimāla, Pasenadi was " amazed " at the Lord's power to tame without stick or sword " him that I was unable to tame with stick and sword." In the next Discourse he chides Mallikā for her blind assumption, as he takes it to be, that if the Lord says a thing is so, then it is so. She sends a brahman to the Lord to ask him to confirm that he had indeed said that grief and sorrow are born of affection rather than bliss and happiness, as seemed more commonly thought. This the Lord does and he gives the brahman many examples to explain what he means. Mallikā adapts and particularises these to fit the circumstances of Pasenadi's life with such success that he is again filled with wonder and amazement, this time at the Lord's wisdom by means of which he penetrates and perceives so much. And so he tells Mallikā that he wishes to bathe ceremonially, a ritual that would purify him for three times uttering the solemn utterance: "Praise to that Lord, arahant, perfect Buddha." The king made this salutation at a distance, as did also on other occasions Brahmāyu the brahman (*M*. ii. 140) and the devout brahman lady Dhānañjānī, no doubt as a kind of charm or spell for averting ill-luck, once when she tripped or stumbled (Sta. No. 100).

In Sta. No. 88, Pasenadi's interest in the Buddha has obviously grown and, anxious to learn more about him, he visits Ānanda and puts some questions to him, for example: would the Lord engage in such conduct as was offensive to intelligent recluses and brahmans, and does he not praise getting rid of all unskilled states and acquiring all skilled ones? So much delighted was he with the well-chosen words with which Ānanda replied, that he persuaded this frugal-minded disciple to accept from him a piece of cloth that King Ajātasattu had sent as a present from over the border.

Neither Sta. No. 87 nor No. 88 records any meeting between the king and the Buddha. But it seems that all the time the former's faith and respect were building up to the great culmination recorded in Sta. No. 89, the *Dhammacetiya*. Here Pasenadi is recorded to have gone to visit the Lord and to greet him in the unusually devout but not unparalleled fashion of kissing and stroking his feet and then of twice pronouncing his own name: "I, revered sir, am Pasenadi, King of Kosala." On the Lord's asking him why he pays such deep respect to "this body" and displays such tokens of friendship (thus indicating that this form of greeting was not in general use) Pasenadi, in a long and reasoned reply supported by deductions he had made from his own observations of life around him, gave seven grounds for his great veneration for the Buddha, Dhamma and Saṅgha, in his eyes superior to anything the world has to offer as well as to anything that other recluses and brahmans appear to derive from the sects they favour. After he had left the Lord's presence, the Buddha succinctly summarised his eulogy as "testimonies to Dhamma," and exhorted the monks to learn and remember them, thus paying a signal compliment to the king.

At *A*. v. 65-66 Pasenadi is again recorded to greet the Lord in this same manner. But when the Lord asked him why he did so, he said it was to show his gratitude and thankfulness for which he had ten reasons.

In Sta. No. 90, Pasenadi asked not Ānanda but the Lord himself a number of questions: about omniscience, the purity of the four castes, *devas* and Brahmā, and he declared himself to be pleased and delighted with every explanation given to him. It therefore seems that his faith and reliance had come full circle.

Each of the ten Discourses in the *Division on Brahmans* (Nos. 91-100) is called after the name of a brahman. Parallel versions of Discourses Nos. 92 and 98 occur in the *Sn.*; and the chief material of No. 91, its core as it were, namely the enumeration of the Thirty-two Marks of a (or, the) Great Man, from a brahman point of view, also appears in other Discourses, for example in *Dīgha* Suttantas Nos. 14 and 30.

Some of these brahmans are represented as holding Gotama in great esteem as did also Keniya the matted hair ascetic. Saṅgārava, at first, was an exception. He was loyal to the brahmans and also ignorant of the Lord's moral habit and wisdom, but he was willing to meet him. Had the *Saṅgārava-sutta* been printed in full it would have been extremely long, for it contains "autobiographical" matter from the *Ariyapariyesana-sutta* and the *Mahāsaccaka-sutta*. It is a little disconcerting to find Saṅgārava, at the end of this tremendous dissertation, although commenting that "the good Gotama's striving has indeed been steadfast," hurrying on to ask him if there were *devas*. They had not been mentioned hitherto in the Discourse. And indeed, setting aside the stereotyped mention of them in such passages as "teacher of *devas* and men," there are very few other occasions in the Middle Fifty Discourses where they form a subject of conversation. One is in Sta. No. 90 where Pasenadi is recorded to ask the Lord whether there are *devas*, and if so whether they are returners or non-returners to this state of things, and where Viḍūḍabha is also recorded to ask Ānanda about the Devas of the Thirty-three. In Discourse No. 90, however, it would seem natural that, while the principal characters were waiting, rather uneasily, for the arrival of the brahman Sañjaya of the Ākāsa clan to tell them who it was that had brought a *kathāvatthu*, a point of controversy, point at issue or subject of conversation, into the palace,[1] they should speak of various matters. But in Sta. No. 100 I find the sudden introduction of this question about *devas* rather perplexing.

---

[1] In Discourse No. 87 we hear of another *kathāvatthu* filtering through into the palace.

It is interesting to see something of the relations that these brahmans had with others, thus: Brahmāyu, very old, wealthy, learned, venerated and himself full of veneration had Uttara, also learned in brahman lore, as pupil (No. 91); Sela had 300 brahman youths in his train, all of whom became ordained as monks by the Lord (No. 92); Assalāyana seems to have been at the beck and call of 500 brahmans who were staying at Sāvatthī on business (No. 93); Ghoṭamukha, Esukārin and Dhānañjāni appear to have been on their own (Nos. 94, 96, 97); an attempt was made by 500 brahmans who were staying at Opasāda to dissuade Caṅkī, who also lived there, from going to see Gotama (No. 95); Vāseṭṭha and Bhāradvāja, two brahman youths, were staying at Icchānaṅkala where many wealthy and distinguished brahmans were also staying (No. 98); Subha was staying in a householder's dwelling (No. 99); and Saṅgārava was living at Caṇḍalakappa as was also a brahman lady[1] of his acquaintance through whose intervention Saṅgārava met the Lord (No. 100). All these brahmans, as a result of the conversations they had with Gotama, either became lay-devotees or joined the Order of monks—all except Caṅkī. But Caṅkī, in the Discourse to which he gives his name, insisted that all the brahmans should go to visit Gotama, whose praises he sings at length and in a more factual way than Upāli, for it did not seem right to him that one of such immeasurable splendour, *vaṇṇa*, as the good Gotama should go to see the brahmans. When they arrived Gotama in fact addressed his Discourse principally to a brahman youth named Kāpaṭhika, also very learned, and who, after he had learnt a great deal about the way to awaken to truth and attain it, became a lay-devotee.

For the divergent views professed, *evaṁvādino evaṁdiṭṭhino*, by contemporary leaders of other sects, the Middle Fifty Discourses prove a mine of information. It is apparent that the compilers of the *M.* were well acquainted with these views; and also that the contact between Gotama and the other sects was close and living and on the whole friendly.

There is mention of the views attributed to the six most famous heretical leaders of other sects, Pūraṇa Kassapa and so on (Stas. Nos. 60, 69, 76, 77, etc.), and also of other divergent views less frequently cited in the Piṭakas, such as "there is (not) formlessness throughout," "there is (not) the stopping of becomings throughout" (No.

---

[1] It was this lady who tripped, see above, p. xix.

60); and " all is (not) pleasing to me, part is (not) pleasing to me " (No. 74). Again, we find Gotama refusing to explain any of the opposing views in another and an important set found throughout the Nikāyas: " the world is (not) eternal " down to " The Tathāgata both is and is not after dying, neither is nor is not after dying " (No. 63). He refused both because the living of the Brahma-faring has nothing to do with and does not depend on the explanation of such views, even as the life of a man pierced by an arrow could not be saved if, before allowing it to be extracted, he insisted on knowing such irrelevant details as its make, the kind of bow it was shot from or the kind of man who shot it (No. 63); and he refused because such views, wildernesses and fetters that they are, neither conduce to nibbāna nor do they yield any possible description of the Tathāgata. For, since he is freed from all denotation by the *khandha*, he cannot be " reckoned " by the four categories of " arising " after dying, and it is inept to attempt to do so.

Views held by recluses and brahmans indeed form part of the stock-in-trade of the *M*. In the Royal Division and that on Brahmans, however, various other matters come to the fore as ones in which brahmans were particularly interested: caste (in both Divisions), *mantras*, sacrifice (No. 99), the Thirty-two Marks of a Great Man, from the brahman point of view, and the " wealth " brahmans lay down as the typical wealth of each caste (No. 96). The Buddhist counter-assertions are that in freedom as against freedom members of each caste are on an exact level, for it is not caste in itself that is undesirable or to be done away with (which Gotama never tried to do), but the arrogant brahman claims. Members of all four castes are alike, for example, in that if one of their members turn thief or recluse, he is henceforth to be reckoned simply as " thief " or " recluse," his identification by caste being lost. The ariyan disciples also asserted that other brahman claims could be argued out of court (No. 99) or at best shown not to be the final means to an end but rather mental equipments for developing a mind that is without enmity or malevolence (No. 99); and they laid down that a man's wealth is the ariyan transcendental Dhamma, *ariyaṁ lokuttaraṁ dhammaṁ purisassa sandhanaṁ paññāpemi* (No. 96)—a " man's " be it noted, a general term beneath which monks and members of this caste or that alike lie buried. The final summing up is in Sta. No. 98=*Sn*. 650: " By deeds is one a brahman, by deeds no brahman."

Yet although, in terminology reminiscent of the Upanishads,

" there is the arising of a being from what has come to be, he arises according to what he does . . . creatures are heirs to deeds," *bhūtā bhūtassa upapatti hoti, yaṁ karoti tena upapajjati . . . kammadāyādā sattā* (No. 57), there is also the deed, *kamma*, which, neither dark nor bright and neither dark nor bright in results, is the highest of four types of deeds since it conduces to the destruction of deeds (No. 57). This is the deed that carries forward no fruits or reactions and which is therefore different in category from, but not inconsistent with such statements as " there is indeed cause " (*M*. i. 405). It is for professing this last belief that the one Naked Ascetic is said to have gone to heaven.[1]

I have already remarked on the two questions asked about *devas*, the one occurring in the Royal Division and the other in the Division on Brahmans, and also on the questions about caste that occur in the two Divisions (but also elsewhere). It is interesting, but perhaps quite without significance, to find other episodes that these two Divisions have in common. For example, each has a Discourse said to have been delivered after the *parinibbāna* (Nos. 84 and 94),[2] and each one in which the Buddha was greeted in a specially reverential way (Nos. 89 and 91). Thus, in Discourse No. 84 Avantiputta, rājā (chieftain or king) of Madhurā is so much impressed by Mahā-Kaccāna's arguments about the potentially equal purity of members of all four castes that, wishing to become an *upāsaka*, a lay-devotee, he utters the usual formula which by then must have been quite venerable: " Excellent, excellent. It is as if one might set upright . . ." and so on. But then, before asking to be accepted as " an *upāsaka* going for refuge from this day forth for as long as life lasts," which was also customary, he deviates from the norm by stating: " Thus I am going to the revered Kaccāna for refuge and to Dhamma and the Order of monks." To this Kaccāna objects: " But do not, sire, go for refuge to me. You must go for refuge only to that Lord to whom I have gone for refuge." Upon Avantiputta asking where this Lord is staying at present, Kaccāna replies that he has attained complete or final nibbāna, *parinibbuta*. Protesting that he would have gone even 100 *yojana* to see him had he heard that he was staying that distance away, Avantiputta concurs: " Since that Lord has now

---

[1] See above, p. xvii.

[2] Discourse No. 108 is also said to have been held after the *parinibbāna*.

attained final nibbāna, I am going for refuge to that Lord who has attained final nibbāna and to Dhamma and to the Order of monks."

In Discourse No. 94 the brahman Ghoṭamukha visits the monk Udena and hears from him a discourse about the four kinds of "tormentors."[1] He is impressed and wishes to become an *upāsaka*. This Discourse then proceeds precisely as does No. 84, except that the rājā and the brahman give different appellations to the Lord, no doubt in accordance with their own status in the world.

Mahā-kaccāna was a contemporary of the Buddha. This incident must therefore have taken place comparatively soon after the *parinibbāna*. There seems little information about Avantiputta, beyond *MA*. iii. 319 calling him *Avantiraṭṭhe rañño dhītāya putto*, and where this "king" perhaps means Pajjota (whom Kaccāna had established in the Buddhist teaching), Avantiputta being thus his grandson. Neither Ghoṭamukha nor Udena appears to be mentioned anywhere in the Pali Canon but here, and so we can only presume that they were contemporaneous with the Buddha and that no very long time had elapsed since the *parinibbāna* when this conversation between them was supposed to have taken place, or else Ghoṭamukha (as also Avantiputta) would already have heard of it.

These two Suttas provide enough evidence to show that, even as refuge was taken in the Buddha during his life-time, it must continue to be so taken after his death. No bhikkhu could regard himself as a refuge or allow others to do so. But he could accept into the community a person who wished to be an *upāsaka*. This point does not I think arise elsewhere in the *M*. than in these two Discourses, for on every other occasion where refuge was taken, it was the Lord himself who established the new person in his teaching and accepted him as an *upāsaka*. That is to say, there appears to be no record of any bhikkhu accepting an *upāsaka* into the community at a time when the Lord might have been staying some distance away, although seeing to it that he took his refuge in the Lord and not in the bhikkhu himself. There is no evidence for this, but one may none the less not unjustifiably imagine that it may sometimes have occurred. Responsibility to ordain candidates into the Order of monks was delegated by the Lord first to bhikkhus acting alone and then to the Saṁgha acting corporately (*Vin*. Mahāvagga I. 12 and 28). It would therefore seem not only possible, but it must

---

[1] See below, p. 5 *ff*.

have been necessary in the expanding community to allow bhikkhus, even if as individuals rather than as members of the Saṁgha, to accept a new *upāsaka*. These two Suttas show that this was at least the case after the *parinibbāna*.

I have already referred to the deep respect Pasenadi paid to the Lord on greeting him:[1] kissing and stroking his feet and pronouncing his own name, and to the fact that this was an unusual and an unusually devout form of salutation. It was one also adopted by Añña-Koṇḍañña (*S*. i. 193) when he came to see the Buddha after a long interval, twelve years according to the Commentary. And it was also adopted by two brahmans, not as a greeting on first approaching the Lord, but rather as a salutation, a form of acknowledgment of his greatness made during the course of a conversation with him. And almost immediately afterwards these two brahmans, Mānatthaddha at *S*. i. 177 and Brahmāyu in *M*. Sta. No. 91, asked to become an *upāsaka*, but not before the Lord had asked each of them to rise up (or, stand up, *uṭṭhehi* at *S*. i. 178, *uṭṭhaha* at *M*. ii. 145) and sit down in his own place (although, as far as the record goes Mānatthaddha had all the time been standing) "where your mind was first pleased with me." The two concourses that witnessed these scenes marvelled, the one that Mānatthaddha who greeted neither his mother nor father, teacher nor eldest brother should show such deep respect to the recluse Gotama; and the other at the great psychic power of the recluse Gotama in virtue of which the well-known and renowned Brahmāyu showed such veneration. That they did so provides additional evidence that this kind of salutation or greeting was rare and of a specially fervent kind.

The kissing of the feet and the pronouncing of one's own name go together, but appear to do so only when it is the Buddha who is evoking so great a respect; to members of other sects only the name was now and again pronounced (e.g. at *S*. i. 78, *Ud*. 65) and the rest of the greeting conveyed by the normal method of stretching forth the joined palms.

As far as the *M*. text goes, Brahmāyu pronounced his name once only, whereas Añña-Koṇḍañña, Pasenadi (twice) and Mānatthaddha are recorded each to have pronounced his own name twice. They all apostrophised the Lord in accordance with their own social status. So, apart from this small exception in Brahmāyu's case, and apart from Mānatthaddha not mentioning his status, the Pali tradition of

[1] See above, p. xix. This occurs in Sta. No. 89.

kissing the Lord's feet and pronouncing one's own name appears to be based on a regularised pattern which, besides appearing to denote some unusual excitation of feeling, certainly signifies a highly reverential and seldom used form of greeting and acknowledgment, far from being in common vogue.

In his Commentaries on the *M.* and *S.*, Buddhaghosa has nothing to say about kissing the Lord's feet. The kiss however establishes a living link, it is a "touch;" and although primarily intended to betoken a physical relationship, when regarded as a blessing or a salutation or a ceremonial greeting it takes on a ritual aspect. Bu., on the other hand, has an exegesis on *nāma*, name. Although this occurs once only (*SA.* i. 282) and although it might have done fuller justice to the inner and vital significance of the name[1] and the uttering of it, it yet does not lack in penetration, for it ends by saying: "So he (i.e. Añña-Koṇḍañña) makes known his name, thus closing for beings the path to the sorrowful ways and opening the path to heaven." As Bu. perceives, the pronouncing of the name is one of "the keys to power" by means of which one puts oneself into the power of someone else. For this reason names were sometimes kept secret[2] as was for example Anāthapiṇḍika's name Sudatta, known only to himself and his family.[3] So that, voluntarily to state one's own name is, as much of the world's literature testifies, an express acknowledgment of the faith and trust that one person unreservedly places in another.

The kiss and the pronouncement of the name are physical and spiritual actions which, when made together, indicate a very close bond of union, the prototype for which is the father-son relationship where, as some records of Indian thought show, over and above the physical paternity a spiritual paternity may also be presumed: "On returning from a journey he should 'touch' ('kiss') his head, saying: 'You, my son, originated from my limbs, you are born of my heart, you are indeed as myself' . . . and he therewith takes hold of his son by name . . . and says: 'By your name, my son, I kiss (touch) your head.'"[4]

These Middle Fifty Discourses also contain records of two rebukes administered by the Buddha to Sāriputta. There seems to be only

---

[1] "It is by his deathless name that Indra outlasts all generations of men," RV. 18. 7.

[2] Thus also warding off the threat of the evil eye.

[3] *Vin.* ii. 156, *VA.*

[4] *Kausītaki Upanishad* II, 11.

one other such occasion,[1] unless we count the *Sampasādaniya-suttanta*[2] where the Buddha, by asking Sāriputta whether he knew anything either of the past or the future Buddhas he had referred to, tried to curb his chief disciple's almost excessive glorification of the Teacher.

In the *Cātuma-sutta* (No. 67) the Lord had had to dismiss from his presence an extremely noisy Order of monks[3] that Sāriputta and Moggallāna had brought to see him. When they were allowed to return, the Lord asked Sāriputta what he had thought when the Order was sent away. His thoughts had been, he replied: "Now, the Lord, untroubled, can abide intent on abiding in ease here and now.[4] And we too, untroubled, can abide intent on abiding in ease here and now." But to have done so would have been a dereliction of his duty, *bhārabhāva*, to the Order of which he was in charge. So, the rebuke was: "Wait, Sāriputta, wait. Never let such a thought arise in you again." Moggallāna was then asked the same question. The first part of his answer was the same as the first part of Sāriputta's. But his second part, showing that he was aware of his responsibilities: "The venerable Sāriputta and I will now look after the Order of monks," was approved by the Lord, who added that either he could look after it or Sāriputta and Moggallāna could do so.

What then, in view of this statement made by the Teacher to Moggallāna, are we to make of his assertion to Devadatta[5] that he would not hand over the Order even to Sāriputta and Moggallāna, far less therefore to Devadatta? Is it possible that at that time he thought his chief disciples too old? He himself, according to Devadatta, was approaching the end of his life, although there may have been about eight years still to run before the *parinibbāna*.[6] Sāriputta however seems to have been well and active at the time of this episode as he was sent to Rājagaha to carry out an Act of Information against Devadatta. It is also true that Devadatta, in

---

[1] *Jā*. i. 161-2. [2] *D*. Sta. No. 28.

[3] Although they may have been "novices" as said at *DPPN*., p. 1110, n. 10, and see below, p. 129 n. 1, they are simply called *āgantukā*, in-comers, while the resident monks are called *nevāsikā*.

[4] See above, p. xi. [5] *Vin*. ii. 188.

[6] Devadatta's attempt to wrest the leadership of the Order away from Gotama is, in the *Vin*., sandwiched in between two other episodes, in the first of which Devadatta curries favour with Prince Ajātasattu, and in the second incites him to slay his father, Bimbisāra. He, however, abdicates in favour of his son. According to *Mhvs*. 11. 32 the Buddha died in the eighth year of Ajātasattu's reign.

telling Gotama that he is now worn, old and full of years, does not put in the final touch of saying that he is in the eighties, *asītika*. The absence of this word may be an indication that Gotama was actually not so old as his cousin could have wished, and was in all likelihood not more than in the seventies. Although it seems difficult to discover Sāriputta's age when he died and also the length of time by which he predeceased the Founder, he was probably the younger of the two as his mother appears to have been alive at the time of his death.[1]

On the other hand it is not impossible that the *Vinaya-bhāṇakas* and the *Majjhima-bhāṇakas*[2] followed somewhat different traditions concerning the possible leadership of the Order, the former holding that only Gotama could lead, and for that reason they attribute the formulation of practically every one of the *Vinaya* rules to him; and the latter holding that others also could look after the Order, as our *M.* context suggests, and as is borne out to some extent by the Discourses given by disciples and of which Gotama is recorded to have approved. However, this is a point that could only be substantiated by further research.

Again it is possible, and perhaps it is even probable, that the episodes recorded at *M.* i. 459 and *Vin.* ii. 188 refer to different Saṁghas. For saṁgha is not necessarily a comprehensive word for the whole Order of monks, and which indeed S. Dutt thinks was known as the Saṁgha of the four quarters.[3] It can also refer, and does often refer to this Order or that, each regarded as part of the whole and bound by the same rules and regulations, but marked off from one another by virtue of the residence of monks within this *sīmā* (boundary) or that. If this is so, then Sāriputta and Moggallāna might well have been regarded as the right disciples to be in charge of some particular Saṁgha, but not necessarily of another; and, accepting this hypothesis, the apparent contradiction between *M.* i. 459 and *Vin.* ii. 188 would be resolved.

Finally, the Buddha at the end of his life says, as recorded,[4] that it does not occur to a Tathāgata: "I, *ahaṁ*, will look after the (or, an) Order of monks." Again, therefore, this does not tally with his statement at *M.* i. 459 that either he or Sāriputta and Moggallāna could look after a (localised and particular ?) Order of monks. Whether the Buddha sometimes spoke as a man, the much tried but

---

[1] *SA.* iii. 213.

[2] *DA.* 15 says that the *Majjhima* was handed over to the school of Sāriputta.

[3] *Early Buddhist Monachism.*

[4] *D.* ii. 100.

ever valiant and selfless Leader and Founder of the whole Order, and whether he sometimes also spoke as Tathāgata, trackless, incon-numerable, freed from reckoning or designation by the five *khandha*,[1] is a point still requiring further investigation. Personally I incline to think there are grounds suggesting that he sometimes spoke as Tathāgata and, if so, this *Dīgha* passage would be such a case. Although the personal pronoun is frequently used for the sake of emphasis, I do not believe *ahaṁ* to be a key-word here—even a Buddha uses the conventional parlance of the world.[2] I believe the key-word is Tathāgata, one who has nothing more to do with the common difficulties of either a monastic or a secular world, and that it may here contain, although in a contrary sense, some hidden reference to part of the Bodhisatta's vows: "May I look after an Order of monks."[3] This is a vow, an aspiration for the future. The Tathāgata, on the other hand, is in every way accomplished, free of past, future and present, beyond all change and mutation and the relationships imposed by personality. Pali is a most precise instrument in many ways, and I believe that where a certain term is used it is for some definite reason and has something definite to convey. It is for us to "swelter at the task"[4] of regaining the wonderful precision of language the teachers and *bhāṇakas* of old knew so well how to employ.

The other occasion when, in these Middle Fifty Discourses, Sāriputta is recorded to have been rebuked (Sta. No. 97) was when he established the dying brahman Dhānañjāni in *hīne Brahmaloke*, "in the lesser, the Brahma-world," although there was something further to be done for him. It seems to me that since the attainment of the Brahma-world or of companionship with Brahmā is not the ultimate goal of the Brahma-farer who is the Dhamma-farer and even-farer, this alone is a sufficient reason for taking *hīne* and *Brahmaloke* in apposition to one another as though, while separate and the former not actually qualifying the latter,[5] they nevertheless belong to one another in Buddhist thought. The Brahma-world is less or lesser when compared with the goal set before the ariyan disciple. Therefore the rebuke was justified in that Sāriputta, missing a rare opportunity, had failed to lift up the brahman's

---

[1] *M.* i. 487, 488.

[2] *Cf. M.* i. 500, *yañ ca loke vuttaṁ tena voharati aparāmasaṁ.*

[3] E.g. *Mhvu.* i. 38, 238, 331.

[4] *Dhp.* 276.

[5] According to A. P. Buddhadatta, *Concise Pali-English Dictionary*, *hīna* is an adjective. *PED.* gives it as p.p. of *jahati*.

mind to heights it was probably able to encompass. If so, if Dhānañjāni had truly been capable of greater spiritual achievement had he been rightly taught, then it would seem that the brahman youth Subha Todeyyaputta (Sta. No. 99) was, on the contrary, not yet ready to go beyond instruction in the way to companionship with Brahmā. For this is the instruction he received from Gotama himself who propounded the usual method for gaining this companionship: the development of the four *brahmavihāra*. In the discipline for an ariyan the evidence goes to show that this did not have attainment of the Brahma-world as its goal as it did for brahmans.

A long article might be written to illustrate the high regard and esteem in which the Buddha held Sāriputta, his own (spiritual) son, *anujāta*, " who rolls on the Wheel of Dhamma set rolling by me."[1] One may therefore suppose that the Buddha, refusing to follow the wrong course of showing partiality, *chandâgati*, which with the other three *agati*, he often spoke against,[2] intended his rebukes to Sāriputta to intimate the pitfalls of his responsible position in the Order—as preceptor to Rāhula[3] and many another, as looking after an Order, and as friend and counsellor of brahmans—and hence to provide examples for right thought and behaviour and warnings against wrong for the men who came after.

The "rich variety of the Majjhima"—how true are not these words of the late F. L. Woodward.[4] It is long, it is thorough, many of its Discourses are complete in themselves, which, while meaning that a great deal may be learnt from any one of them, does not at all mean that they will not grow in depth and significance the more their affinities with other parts of the Piṭakas can be traced. Sometimes two or more existing versions are word for word alike; sometimes in contexts that are otherwise parallel interesting variations and divergencies are displayed; sometimes the conclusion that has been worked up to is quite different after an otherwise identical narrative; or, once some part of a story or dissertation has been told in more or less the same words it may at a certain point break off and proceed on different lines. If a concordance of the *M.* were made, the number of passages having parallel versions elsewhere and also the number of

---

[1] *M.* Sta. 92=*Sn.* 557.

[2] *Vin.* i. 283, *D.* iii. 182, *A.* i. 72 (and for further references see *B.D.* i. 313 n. 7).

[3] *Jā.* i. 161-2.

[4] *K.S.* iii. Intr. p. xiv.

times certain themes recur within the *M.* itself might cause some surprise.

In the Middle Fifty Discourses the overriding emphasis is perhaps laid on the *jhāna* or fine-material meditative stages; the *āyatana*, the immaterial or incorporeal meditative stages or planes culminating in the stopping of feeling and perceiving; and on the threefold knowledge, *tevijjā* (see e.g. Stas. Nos. 51, 52, 59, 64, 65, 66, 71, 77, 79, 99, 100). Discourse No. 51 gives the lead: it lays down the whole training for a monk from the arising of a Tathāgata in the world, through the young man of family being ordained a monk, then possessing himself of moral conduct, of control over his senses, of vigilance, mindfulness and clear consciousness, then purifying his mind of the five Hindrances after which he can acquire mastery in the four *jhāna*, and finally can direct his mind to the gaining of the three knowledges, *tevijjā*. This Discourse propounds all the parts of this process in standardised words found in other passages (cf. Stas. Nos. 55, 60, 61, 76, 79). All the time it is leading up to a climax which, appearing again elsewhere and always in the same stereotyped words (*cf.* Stas. Nos. 55, 60, 61, 94), is none the less striking or important for that. It is that, of the four "tormentors" (of each of which a number of the Discourses give a very full description), the last "tormentor," who in fact is a tormentor neither of himself nor of others, is he who, having fulfilled the training as set forth in these Discourses, is "here-now allayed, quenched, become cool, an experiencer of bliss that lives with self Brahma-become," *nicchāto nibbuto sītibhūto sukhapaṭisaṁvedī brahmabhūtena attanā viharati*. This is a description applied only but invariably to the non-tormentor. He has reached a summit. Harmlessness, *ahiṁsā*, was a living force, great in its results.[1]

This unravelling of the tangle which is man, beside whom animals are an open clearing (Sta. No. 51, *M.* i. 340-341), and this showing of the ordered way by which "this sure Dhamma" (No. 60, *M.* i. 401) leads on to the freeing of the mind from the three cankers of sense-pleasures, becoming and ignorance, this consequent assumption of a self that lives Brahma-become, is of the essence of and crucial to the Buddha's Teaching.

To dwell with self Brahma-become is, as these Middle Fifty Discourses make abundantly clear, an achievement superior to abiding in or dwelling in the *brahmavihāra*. Yet, if these, sublime as each

---

[1] *Cf.* S. i. 75, "let not the self-lover harm another."

one is, for the Lord abides in each one,[1] are placed against the wide background of his teaching, as in Sta. No. 52, it is to be expected for a monk that if he stand firm in the conviction that, like the *jhāna*, each of the *brahmavihāra* when regarded as a freedom of the mind, is (karmically) effected and thought out, *abhisaṅkhata abhisañcetayita*, impermanent and of the nature to cease (as one emerges from meditation), then, having sought for a " door to the deathless " so as to make himself safe, *attānaṁ sotthiṁ kātuṁ*, he may become an arahant or a non-returner. This is expressed by saying: " he attains the destruction of the cankers; but if he fails to do so then . . . by the destruction of the five fetters binding to this lower (shore), he is of spontaneous uprising, one who attains nibbāna there, not liable to return from that world." It is of interest to observe that while the *M.* uses the three associated words *arahant*, *sakadāgāmin* and *sotâpanna*, the technical term *anāgāmin*, non-returner, is not found at all and is represented only by its formula (e.g. in Stas. Nos. 52, 64, 68, 73).

A basic part of the training necessary to bring the goal into view—here mostly spoken of in terms of the threefold knowledge—is the turning away from and renunciation of sense-pleasures (Stas. Nos. 54, 59, 66, 67, 68, 75, 80, 99) together with the refusal to be entranced by sensory impacts or impingements. In place of sensory enjoyment and craving there should be a steady development of that equanimity and mindfulness wherein all grasping after the material things of the world is stopped entirely. Derived extra-sensorily, this other happiness which ensues is more peaceful and exquisite (e.g. Stas. Nos. 59, 79) than that due to the senses. It is not only pleasant feeling that belongs to happiness. On the contrary, as laid down by the Tathāgata, " whenever, wherever, whatever happiness is found, it belongs to happiness," *yattha yattha sukhaṁ upalabbhati yahiṁ yahiṁ tan-taṁ Tathāgato sukhasmiṁ paññāpeti* (Sta. No. 59). The renunciation of grasping after sense-pleasures is however but a foretaste of the unresting forward movement characteristic of meditation. In no stage in the *jhāna* or the *āyatana* should the meditator pause: " it is not enough, get rid of it, transcend it " (*M.* i. 455), and as he has been taught to do by the Parable of the Raft,[2] until he can enter and abide in the stopping of feeling and perceiving (*M.* i. 456) where he is free of all fetters, whether minute

---

[1] *brahmā mettavihārī . . . bhagavā hi mettavihārī*, *M.* i. 369.

[2] See *M.L.S.* i. 175 f.

or massive. Indeed, " faring along as instructed it will not be long before he (the aspirant, earnest and zealous in training) knows and sees of himself. Even so is deliverance from the direst bond—the bond of ignorance " (*M*. ii. 44).

I have to acknowledge with gratitude the debt I owe both to Mr. P. Mehta for reading the typescript, and to my colleague, Mr. J. J. Jones, translator of the *Mahāvastu*, for reading the proofs.

I. B. Horner.

London, 1955.

ABBREVIATIONS

A. = Anguttara-Nikāya.
AA. = Commentary on A.
Asl. = Atthasālinī.
B.D. = *Book of the Discipline.*
B.H.S. Dict. = *Buddhist Hybrid Sanskrit Dictionary* (Franklin Edgerton).
Budv. = Buddhavaṁsa.
C.P.D. = *Critical Pali Dictionary* (Dines Andersen and Helmer Smith).
Comy. = Commentary.
D. = Dīgha-Nikāya.
DA. = Commentary on D.
DhA. = Commentary on Dhp.
Dhp., or *Dh.* = Dhammapada.
Dhs. = Dhammasaṅgaṇi.
Dial. = *Dialogues of the Buddha.*
D.P.P.N. = *Dictionary of Pali Proper Names* (G. P. Malalasekera).
Expos. = *Expositor.*
Fur. Dial. = *Further Dialogues of the Buddha.*
G.S. = *Gradual Sayings.*
H.J.A.S. = *Harvard Journal of Asiatic Studies.*
I.H.Q. = *Indian Historical Quarterly.*
ItA. = Commentary on Iti.
Iti. = Itivuttaka.
Jā. = Jātaka.
J.P.T.S. = *Journal of the Pali Text Society.*
Khp. = Khuddakapāṭha.
KhpA. = Commentary on Khp.
K.S. = *Kindred Sayings.*
Kvu. = Kathāvatthu.
M. = Majjhima-Nikāya.
MA. = Commentary on M.
Mhvs. = Mahāvaṁsa.
Mhvu. = Mahāvastu.

Miln.	= Milindapañha.
Min. Anth.	= *Minor Anthologies of the Pali Canon.*
M.L.S.	= *Middle Length Sayings.*
Mppś.	= Mahāprajñāpāramitāśāstra (translated by Et. Lamotte).
Nd.	= Niddesa.
Netti.	= Nettipakaraṇa.
Nissag.	= Nissaggiya.
Pāc.	= Pācittiya.
P.E.D.	= *Pali-English Dictionary* (T. W. Rhys Davids and W. Stede).
P. Purity	= *Path of Purity.*
Pss. Breth.	= *Psalms of the Brethren.*
P.T.C.	= *Pali Tipiṭakaṁ Concordance* (F. L. Woodward, E. M. Hare, etc.).
Pṭs.	= Paṭisambhidāmagga.
PṭsA.	= Commentary on Pṭs.
Pug.	= Puggalapaññatti.
PvA.	= Commentary on Petavatthu.
RV.	= Rig-Veda.
S.	= Saṁyutta-Nikāya.
SA.	= Commentary on S.
S.B.E.	= *Sacred Books of the East.*
S.H.B.	= Simon Hewavitarne Bequest.
Sn.	= Suttanipāta.
SnA.	= Commentary on Sn.
Sta.	= Sutta.
Thag.	= Theragāthā.
ThagA.	= Commentary on Thag.
U.C.R.	= *University of Ceylon Review.*
Ud.	= Udāna.
UdA.	= Commentary on Ud.
Vbh.	= Vibhanga.
VbhA.	= Commentary on Vbh.
Vin.	= Vinaya-piṭaka.
VinA.	= Commentary on Vin.
Vism.	= Visuddhimagga.
VvA.	= Commentary on Vimānavatthu.

I. THE DIVISION ON HOUSEHOLDERS

(Gahapativagga)

51. DISCOURSE TO KANDARAKA[1]

(Kandarakasutta)

[**339**] THUS have I heard: At one time the Lord was staying near Campā on the bank of the Gaggarā lotus-pond together with a large Order of monks. Then Pessa, the son of an elephant-trainer, and the wanderer Kandaraka approached the Lord; when they had approached, Pessa, the son of the elephant-trainer, having greeted the Lord, sat down at a respectful distance. But the wanderer Kandaraka exchanged greetings with the Lord; having conversed in a friendly and courteous way, he stood at a respectful distance. As he was standing at a respectful distance the wanderer Kandaraka, having looked round at the Order of monks which became absolutely silent, spoke thus to the Lord:

"It is wonderful, good Gotama, it is marvellous, good Gotama, that is to say how the Order of monks has been led[2] properly by the good Gotama. And, good Gotama, those who in the long past were perfected ones, fully Self-Awakened Ones—did these Lords also have an equally excellent Order of monks that they led properly even as the Order of monks is now being led properly by the good Gotama? And, good Gotama, those who in the distant future will be perfected ones, fully Self-Awakened Ones—will these Lords also have an equally excellent Order of monks that they will lead properly even as the Order of monks is now being led properly by the good Gotama?"

"It is so, Kandaraka; it is so, Kandaraka. Those who, Kandaraka, in the long past were perfected ones, fully Self-Awakened Ones—these Lords had an equally excellent Order of monks that they led properly, even as the Order of monks is now being led properly by me. And those, Kandaraka, who in the distant future

---

[1] Kandaraka (whom *MA*. iii. 2 says was a clothed wanderer) asks only one question however; but the answer and the way Pessa takes this up lead on to the main topics: the ineffectiveness and cruelty of asceticism, and the disciple's development from the moment he acquires faith to his attainment of arahantship. The name of this Discourse might more suitably be rendered: "Discourse prompted by Kandaraka."

[2] *paṭipādita*, made to fare, to journey along.

will be perfected ones, fully Self-Awakened Ones—these Lords will have an equally excellent Order of monks that they will lead properly, even as the Order of monks is now being led properly by me. For there are, Kandaraka, monks in this Order of monks who are perfected ones, the cankers destroyed, who have lived the life, done what was to be done, shed the burden, attained their own goal, and who, by the utter destruction of the fetters of becoming, are freed by perfect profound knowledge. And there are, Kandaraka, monks in this Order of monks who are learners, undeviating in moral habit,[1] undeviating in conduct, intelligent, their ways of living intelligent, and these dwell with their minds well applied to the four applications of mindfulness. What four? As to this, Kandaraka, [**340**] a monk fares along contemplating the body in the body, ardent, clearly conscious (of it), mindful (of it), so as to control the covetousness and dejection in the world; he fares along contemplating the feelings in the feelings, ardent, clearly conscious (of them), mindful (of them), so as to control the covetousness and dejection in the world; he fares along contemplating the mind in the mind, ardent, clearly conscious (of it), mindful (of it), so as to control the covetousness and dejection in the world; he fares along contemplating the mental states in the mental states, ardent, clearly conscious (of them), mindful (of them), so as to control the covetousness and dejection in the world."[2]

When this had been said, Pessa, the son of an elephant-trainer, spoke thus to the Lord:

"It is wonderful, revered sir, it is marvellous, revered sir, that these four applications of mindfulness are so well laid down by the Lord for the purification of beings, for the overcoming of griefs and sorrows, for the going down of sufferings and miseries, for winning the right path, for realising nibbāna.[3] And, revered sir, we householders too, dressed in white, from time to time dwell with our minds well applied to the four applications of mindfulness.[4] As to this, revered sir, we fare along contemplating the body in the body . . . the feelings in the feelings . . . the mind in the mind . . . the mental states in the mental states, ardent, clearly

---

[1] *santata-sīla*. *Santata*, which *MA*. iii. 4 explains as *nirantara*, uninterrupted, means consistent, stable.

[2] See *M*. Sta. 10 (*M.L.S*. i. 83) and *D*. Sta. 22.

[3] As at *M.L.S*. i. 83.

[4] As they have various things to do for monks they cannot engage in the four applications of mindfulness all the time; but when they get an opportunity they are able to do so, *MA*. iii. 6.

conscious (of them), mindful (of them), so as to control the covetousness and dejection in the world. It is wonderful, revered sir, it is marvellous, revered sir, how the Lord knows the welfare and woe of beings while there is this human tangle, this human guile, this human treachery. For this[1], revered sir, is a tangle, that is to say human beings. But this, revered sir, is an open clearing, that is to say animals.[2] Now I, revered sir, am able to make an elephant under training so remember that, every time he is coming into Campā or leaving it, he will display all kinds of treachery, deceit, fraud, trickery. But, revered sir, those that are called our slaves or messengers or workpeople, they do one thing with their body, another in speech, and their thought is still other.[3] It is wonderful, revered sir, it is marvellous, revered sir, how the Lord knows the welfare and woe of beings while there is this human tangle, this human guile, this human treachery. For this, revered sir, is a tangle, that is to say human beings. But this, revered sir, is an open clearing, that is to say animals."

"It is so, Pessa, it is so, Pessa. [**341**] For this, Pessa, is a tangle, that is to say human beings. But this, Pessa, is an open clearing, that is to say animals. Pessa, these four kinds of persons are found in the world.[4] What four? As to this, Pessa, some person is a self-tormentor, intent on the practice of self-torment; as to this, Pessa, some person is a tormentor of others, intent on the practice of tormenting others; as to this, Pessa, some person is both a self-tormentor, intent on the practice of tormenting self, and a tormentor of others, intent on the practice of tormenting others; as to this, Pessa, some person is neither a self-tormentor, not intent on the practice of self-torment, nor a tormentor of others, not intent on the practice of tormenting others. He, neither a self-tormentor nor a tormentor of others, is here-now allayed, quenched, become cool, an experiencer of bliss[5] that lives with self Brahma-become. Of these four persons, Pessa, which appeals to your mind?"

"Now, revered sir, that person who is a self-tormentor, intent on the practice of self-torment—that person does not appeal to my mind. And, revered sir, that person who is a tormentor of others, intent on the practice of tormenting others—neither does

---

[1] Cited at *DhA*. i. 173. [2] All four-footed things, *MA*. iii. 7.

[3] *Cf*. *DhA*. i. 173.

[4] *Cf*. *M*. i. 411, ii. 159; *D*. iii. 234; *A*. ii. 205; *Pug*. 55.

[5] *MA*. iii. 10, the "blisses" (happinesses, eases) of meditation, the Ways, the fruits, nibbāna.

that person appeal to my mind. And, revered sir, that person who is a self-tormentor, intent on the practice of self-torment, and who is also a tormentor of others, intent on the practice of tormenting others—neither does that person appeal to my mind. But, revered sir, that person who is neither a self-tormentor, not intent on the practice of self-torment, nor a tormentor of others, not intent on the practice of tormenting others, he, neither a self-tormentor nor a tormentor of others, is here-now allayed, quenched, become cool, an experiencer of bliss that lives with self Brahma-become—this person appeals to my mind."

"But why, Pessa, do those three persons not appeal to your mind?"

"Revered sir, whatever person is a self-tormentor, intent on the practice of self-torment, he mortifies and torments himself[1] although he yearns for happiness and recoils from pain. Therefore this person does not appeal to my mind. And, revered sir, whatever person is a tormentor of others, intent on the practice of tormenting others, he mortifies and torments others although they yearn for happiness and recoil from pain. Therefore this person does not appeal to my mind. And, revered sir, whatever person is both a self-tormentor, intent on the practice of self-torment, and also a tormentor of others, intent on the practice of tormenting others, he mortifies and torments himself and others although they (all) yearn for happiness and recoil from pain. Therefore this person does not appeal to my mind. But, [**342**] revered sir, whatever person is neither a self-tormentor, intent on the practice of self-torment, nor a tormentor of others, intent on the practice of tormenting others, he, neither a self-tormentor nor a tormentor of others, is here-now allayed, quenched, become cool, an experiencer of bliss that lives with self Brahma-become. Therefore this person appeals to my mind. But, revered sir, we must be going, we are very busy, there is much to be done by us."

"You must do, Pessa, whatever you think it is now the right time for."

Then Pessa, the son of the elephant-trainer, having rejoiced in what the Lord had said, having given thanks, rising from his seat, having greeted the Lord, departed keeping his right side towards him. Soon after Pessa, the son of the elephant-trainer, had departed, the Lord addressed the monks, saying:

---

[1] *Cf. S.* iv. 337 *ff.*

"Monks, Pessa, the son of the elephant-trainer, is clever[1]; monks, Pessa, the son of the elephant-trainer, is of great wisdom. If, monks, Pessa, the elephant-trainer's son, had sat down for a moment whilst I had analysed the four kinds of persons for him in detail, he would have gained great good.[2] Nevertheless, even to some extent has Pessa, the elephant-trainer's son, gained great good."

"It is the right time for this, Lord,[3] it is the right time for this, Wellfarer—for the Lord to analyse these four persons in detail. When the monks have heard the Lord, they will remember."

"Well then, monks, listen, attend carefully, and I will speak."

"Yes, revered sir," these monks answered the Lord in assent. The Lord spoke thus:

"And which, monks, is the self-tormentor, intent on the practice of self-torment? In this case, monks, some person comes to be unclothed,[4] flouting life's decencies, licking his hands (after meals), not one to come when asked to do so, not one to stand still when asked to do so. He does not consent (to accept food) offered or specially prepared (for him) or (to accept) an invitation (to a meal). He does not accept (food) straight from a cooking-pot or pan, nor within the threshold, nor among the faggots, nor among the rice-pounders, nor when two people are eating, nor from a pregnant woman, nor from one giving suck, nor from one cohabiting with a man, nor from gleanings, nor from where a dog is standing by, nor where flies are swarming, nor fish, nor meat. He drinks neither fermented liquor nor spirits nor rice-gruel. He comes to be a one-house man or a one-piece man, or a two-house man or a two-piece man . . . or a seven-house man or a seven-piece man. He subsists on one little offering . . . and he subsists on seven little offerings. He takes food only once a day, [**343**] and once in two days . . . and once in seven days. Then he lives intent on such a practice as eating rice at regular fortnightly intervals. He is one feeding on potherbs or feeding on millet or on wild rice or on snippets of leather or on water-plants or on the red powder of rice husks or on the discarded scum of rice on the boil or on the flour of oil-

---

[1] Not in regard to these four categories of persons, but in regard to the four applications of mindfulness, *MA*. iii. 10.

[2] *mahatā atthena saṁyutto agamissa*. Siam. version has *abhavissa* for text's *agamissa*, and is supported by *MA*. iii. 10-11: *sotâpanno abhavissa*.

[3] *bhagavā*, as at *M*. i. 433.

[4] The remainder of this paragraph as at *M*. i. 77-78; *A*. ii. 205 *ff*. is similar to above from here to the end of this Discourse.

seeds or grass or cowdung. He is one who subsists on forest roots or fruits, eating the fruits that have fallen. He wears coarse hempen cloths and he wears mixed cloths or cerements or rags taken from the dust-heap or tree-bark fibre or antelope skins or strips of antelope skin or cloths of *kusa*-grass or cloths of bark or cloths of wood shavings or a blanket of human hair or he wears owls' feathers. He is one who plucks out the hair of his head and beard, intent on the practice of plucking out the hair of the head and beard; and he is one who stands upright, refusing a seat; and he is one who squats on his haunches, intent on the practice of squatting; and he is one for covered thorns, he makes his bed on covered thorns; and he lives intent on the practice of going down to the water to bathe three times in an evening. Thus in many a way does he live intent on the practice of mortifying and tormenting his body. Monks, this is called the person who is a self-tormentor, intent on the practice of self-torment.

And which, monks, is the person who is a tormentor of others, intent on the practice of tormenting others? In this case, monks, some person is a cattle-butcher, or pig-killer, fowler, deer-stalker, hunter, fisherman, thief, executioner, jailer, or (one of) those others who follow a bloody calling.[1] This is the person, monks, who is called a tormentor of others, intent on the practice of tormenting others.

And which, monks, is the person who is both a self-tormentor, intent on the practice of tormenting self, and also a tormentor of others, intent on the practice of tormenting others? In this case, monks, some person is a noble anointed king or a very rich brahman. He, having had a new conference hall[2] built to the east of the town, having had his head and beard shaved, having put on a shaggy skin, having smeared his body with ghee and oil, scratching his back with a deer-horn, enters the conference hall together with his chief consort and a brahman priest. Then he lies down to sleep on the bare grassy ground. The king lives on the milk from one udder of a cow that has a calf of like colour, [**344**] his chief consort lives on the milk from the second udder, the brahman priest lives on the milk from the third udder, the milk from the fourth udder they offer to the fire; the calf lives on what is over. He speaks thus: 'Let so many bulls be slain for the sacrifice, let so many steers . . .

---

[1] *Cf. A.* iii. 383.

[2] *santhāgāra. MA.* iii. 12 says *yaññasālā*, sacrificial hall.

heifers . . . goats . . . let so many rams be slain for the sacrifice, let so many trees be felled for the sacrificial posts, let so much *kusa*-grass be reaped for the sacrificial spot.'[1] Those who are called his slaves or messengers or workpeople, they, scared of the stick, scared of danger,[2] with tearful faces and crying, set about their preparations. This, monks, is called the person who is both a self-tormentor, intent on the practice of self-torment, and a tormentor of others, intent on the practice of tormenting others.

And which, monks, is the person who is neither a self-tormentor, not intent on the practice of self-torment, nor a tormentor of others, not intent on the practice of tormenting others, and who, neither a self-tormentor nor a tormentor of others, is here-now allayed, quenched, become cool, an experiencer of bliss that lives with self Brahma-become? In this case, monks, a Tathāgata arises in the world,[3] a perfected one, fully Self-Awakened One, endowed with (right) knowledge and conduct, well-farer, knower of the worlds, matchless charioteer of men to be tamed, teacher of *devas* and mankind, the Awakened One, the Lord. Having realised it by his own super-knowledge, he proclaims this world with its *devas*, Māras, Brahmās, creation with its recluses and brahmans, with its *devas* and men. With the meaning and the spirit he teaches *dhamma* that is lovely at the beginning, lovely in the middle, lovely at the ending; he proclaims the Brahma-faring wholly fulfilled and purified. A householder or a householder's son or one born in some respectable family hears that *dhamma*. When he has heard that *dhamma* he acquires faith in the Tathāgata. Possessed of this faith he has acquired, he reflects thus: 'Confined is this household life, a path of dust, while going forth is of the open air. Yet it is not easy for one who has lived in a house to fare the Brahma-faring completely fulfilled, completely purified, polished like a conch-shell. Yet suppose I were to have my hair and beard shaved, to don saffron robes, and go forth from home into homelessness?' After a time, getting rid of his mass of wealth, whether large or small, [**345**] getting rid of his circle of relations, whether large or small, having had his hair and beard shaved, having donned saffron robes, he goes forth from home into homelessness.

He, gone forth thus, being possessed of the way of life and the

---

[1] *D.* i. 141; *A.* ii. 207.

[2] *bhayatajjitā; cf. Dhp.* 188. *Tajjita* also means "spurred on by."

[3] From here to the end of this Discourse *cf. M.* i. 179 *ff.*; and see *M.L.S.* i. 235 *ff.* for notes.

training of monks, abandoning onslaught on creatures, is one that abstains from onslaught on creatures; stick and sword laid aside he dwells scrupulous, kindly, friendly and compassionate towards all living things and creatures. Abandoning the taking of what has not been given, he is one that abstains from taking what has not been given; taking (only) what is given, waiting for what is given, without stealing he dwells with self become pure. Abandoning unchastity, he is one that is chaste, keeping remote he is one that refrains[1] from dealings with women. Abandoning lying speech, he is one that abstains from lying speech, a truth-speaker, a bondsman to truth, trustworthy, dependable, no deceiver of the world. Abandoning slanderous speech, he is one that abstains from slanderous speech; having heard something here he is not one to repeat it elsewhere for (causing) variance among those people; or, having heard something elsewhere he is not one to repeat it here for (causing) variance among these people; concord is his pleasure, concord his delight, concord his joy, concord the motive of his speech. Abandoning harsh speech, he is one that abstains from harsh speech; whatever speech is gentle, pleasing to the ear, affectionate, going to the heart, urbane, pleasant to the manyfolk, agreeable to the manyfolk—he is one that utters speech like this. Abandoning frivolous chatter, he is one that abstains from frivolous chatter; he is a speaker at a right time, a speaker of fact, a speaker on the goal, a speaker on *dhamma*, a speaker on discipline, he speaks words that are worth treasuring, with an opportune simile,[2] discriminating, connected with the goal. He is one that abstains from what involves destruction to seed-growth, to vegetable growth. He is one that eats one meal a day, desisting at night, refraining from eating at a wrong time. He is one that abstains from watching shows of dancing, singing, music. He is one that abstains from using garlands, scents, unguents, adornments, finery. He is one that abstains from using high beds, large beds. He is one that abstains from accepting gold and silver. He is one that abstains from accepting raw grain . . . raw meat . . . women and girls . . . women slaves and men slaves . . . goats and sheep . . . fowl and swine . . . elephants, cows, horses, mares . . . fields and sites. He is one that abstains from the practice of sending or going on

---

[1] *virato.* I have translated the more frequent *paṭivirato* of this passage as " one that abstains."

[2] *sāpadesa*, explained at *DA*. i. 76 as *sa-upama*, *sakāraṇa*, with a simile, with a device (argument, supposition ?).

messages. He is one that abstains from buying and selling . . . from cheating with weights, bronzes and measures. [**346**] He is one that abstains from the crooked ways of bribery, fraud and deceit. He is one that abstains from maiming, murdering, manacling, highway robbery. He is contented with a robe to protect his body, with almsfood to sustain his stomach. Wherever he goes he takes these things with him as he goes. As a bird on the wing wherever it flies takes its wings with it as it flies, so a monk, contented with a robe to protect his body, with almsfood to sustain his stomach, wherever he goes takes these things with him as he goes. He, possessed of this ariyan body of moral habit, inwardly experiences the bliss of blamelessness.[1]

Having seen a material shape with the eye, he is not entranced by the general appearance, he is not entranced by the detail. If he dwell with this organ of sight uncontrolled, covetousness and dejection, evil unskilled states of mind might predominate. So he fares along controlling it, he guards the organ of sight, he achieves control over the organ of sight. Having heard a sound with the ear. . . . Having smelt a smell with the nose. . . . Having savoured a taste with the tongue. . . . Having felt a touch with the body. . . . Having cognised a mental object with the mind, he is not entranced by the general appearance, he is not entranced by the detail. If he dwell with this organ of mind uncontrolled, covetousness and dejection, evil unskilled states of mind might predominate. So he fares along controlling it, he guards the organ of mind, he achieves control over the organ of mind. He, possessed of this ariyan control over the sense-organs, inwardly experiences the bliss of being 'unaffected.'[2]

Whether he is setting out or returning, he is one who comports himself properly; whether he is looking down or looking round . . . whether he is bending back or stretching out (his arm) . . . whether he is carrying his outer cloak, his bowl, his robe . . . whether he is munching, drinking, eating, savouring . . . whether he is obeying

---

[1] *anavajjasukha.*

[2] *avyāsekasukha,* not sprinkled (with evil), not mixing with it. His control acts as a barrier to the flowing-in of impurity. At *M.L.S.* i. 227 I translated the compound as "unsullied well-being." I now think that the above translation better balances the "bliss of blamelessness" at the end of the preceding paragraph, and that the two compounds ending in *sukha* are intentional. "Unsullied well-being" at vol. i, p. 226 is an error and should read "bliss of blamelessness."

the calls of nature . . . whether he is walking, standing, asleep, awake, talking, silent, he is one who comports himself properly.

Possessed of this ariyan body of moral habit, possessed of this ariyan control over the sense-organs, and possessed of this ariyan mindfulness and clear consciousness, he chooses a remote lodging in a forest, at the root of a tree, on a mountain slope, in a wilderness, a hill-cave, a cemetery, a forest haunt, in the open air or on a heap of straw. Returning from alms-gathering after the meal, he sits down cross-legged holding the back erect, having made mindfulness rise up in front of him. **[347]** Having got rid of covetousness for the world, he lives with a mind devoid of coveting and purifies the mind of coveting. By getting rid of the taint of ill-will, he lives benevolent in mind; and, compassionate for the welfare of all creatures and beings, he purifies the mind of the taint of ill-will. By getting rid of sloth and torpor, he lives devoid of sloth and torpor; perceiving the light, mindful and clearly conscious, he purifies the mind of sloth and torpor. By getting rid of restlessness and worry, he lives calmly, the mind inwardly tranquillised, and he purifies the mind of restlessness and worry. By getting rid of doubt, he lives doubt-crossed; unperplexed as to states that are skilled, he purifies the mind of doubt.

" He, by getting rid of these five hindrances—defilements of the mind and weakening to intuitive wisdom—aloof from pleasures of the senses, aloof from unskilled states of mind, enters and abides in the first meditation, which is accompanied by initial thought and discursive thought, is born of aloofness and is rapturous and joyful. By allaying initial and discursive thought, the mind subjectively tranquillised and fixed on one point, he enters and abides in the second meditation, which is devoid of initial and discursive thought, is born of concentration and is rapturous and joyful. By the fading out of rapture, he dwells with equanimity, attentive and clearly conscious, and experiences in his person that joy of which the ariyans say: 'Joyful lives he who has equanimity and is mindful', and he enters and abides in the third meditation. By getting rid of joy, by getting rid of anguish, by the going down of his former pleasures and sorrows, he enters and abides in the fourth meditation, which has neither anguish nor joy, and which is entirely purified by equanimity and mindfulness.

Thus with the mind composed,[1] quite purified, quite clarified,

---

[1] *A*. ii. 211 omits this paragraph and the next.

without blemish, without defilement, grown soft and workable, stable, immovable, he directs his mind to the knowledge and recollection of former habitations. He recollects a variety of former habitations, thus: one birth, two births, three . . . four . . . five . . . ten . . . twenty . . . thirty . . . forty . . . fifty . . . a hundred . . . a thousand . . . a hundred thousand births, and many an eon of integration and many an eon of disintegration and many an eon of integration-disintegration: 'Such a one was I by name, having such and such a clan, such and such a colour, so was I nourished, such and such pleasant and painful experiences were mine, so did the span of life end. Passing from this, I came to be in another state where I was such a one by name, having such and such a clan, such and such a colour, so was I nourished, such and such pleasant and painful experiences were mine, [**348**] so did the span of life end. Passing from this, I arose here.' Thus he recollects divers former habitations in all their modes and detail.

With the mind composed thus, quite purified . . . fixed, immovable, he directs his mind to the knowledge of the passing hence and the arising of beings. With the purified *deva*-vision surpassing that of men, he sees beings as they pass hence or come to be; he comprehends that beings are mean, excellent, comely, ugly, well-going, ill-going, according to the consequences of deeds, and thinks: 'Indeed these worthy beings who were possessed of wrong conduct in body, speech and thought, scoffers at the ariyans, holding a wrong view, incurring deeds consequent on a wrong view—these, at the breaking up of the body after dying, have arisen in a sorrowful state, a bad bourn, the abyss, Niraya Hell. But these worthy beings who were possessed of good conduct in body, speech and thought, who did not scoff at the ariyans, holding a right view, incurring deeds consequent on a right view—these at the breaking up of the body after dying, have arisen in a good bourn, a heaven world.' Thus with the purified *deva*-vision surpassing that of men does he see beings as they pass hence, as they arise; he comprehends that beings are mean, excellent, comely, ugly, well-going, ill-going according to the consequences of deeds.

With the mind composed thus . . . fixed, immovable, he directs his mind to the knowledge of the destruction of the cankers. He comprehends as it really is: This is anguish, this the arising of anguish, this the stopping of anguish, this the course leading to the stopping of anguish. He comprehends as it really is: These are the cankers, this the arising of the cankers, this the stopping of the cankers, this the course leading to the stopping of the cankers. Knowing thus, seeing thus, his mind is freed from the canker of sense-pleasures and his mind is freed from the canker of becoming and his mind is freed from the canker of ignorance. In freedom the knowledge comes to be: I am freed; and he comprehends: Destroyed is birth, brought to a close the Brahma-faring, done is what was to be done, there is no more of being such or so.

This, monks, is called the person who is neither a self-tormentor intent on the practice of tormenting self, nor a tormentor of others intent on the practice of tormenting others. [**349**] He, neither a self-tormentor nor a tormentor of others, is here-now allayed, quenched, become cool, an experiencer of bliss that lives with self Brahma-become."

Thus spoke the Lord. Delighted, these monks rejoiced in what the Lord had said.

Discourse to Kandaraka:
The First

52. DISCOURSE TO A CITIZEN OF AṬṬHAKA

(Aṭṭhakanāgarasutta)[1]

THUS have I heard: At one time the venerable Ānanda was staying near Vesālī in Beluva hamlet.[2] Now at that time the householder Dasama of Aṭṭhaka had arrived in Pātaliputta on some business or other. Then the householder Dasama of Aṭṭhaka approached a monk in Cock's monastery[3]; having approached, having greeted that monk, he sat down at a respectful distance. As he was sitting down at a respectful distance the householder Dasama of Aṭṭhaka spoke thus to that monk: "Revered sir, where is the venerable Ānanda staying at present, for we are anxious to see the venerable Ānanda?"

"Householder, the venerable Ānanda is staying near Vesālī in Beluva hamlet."

---

[1] This Discourse is also at *A.* v. 342 *ff.*, and is there called Dasama Sutta, after the name of the householder. See the notes at *G.S.* v. 219 *ff.*

[2] On a slope of a hill to the south of Vesālī, *MA.* iii. 12=Comy. on *A.*

[3] *MA.* iii. 13 says it was made by a *seṭṭhi*, a rich man, banker or merchant, called Kukkuṭa (Cock).

Then the householder Dasama of Aṭṭhaka, having concluded his business in Pātaliputta, approached the venerable Ānanda in Beluva hamlet; having approached, having greeted the venerable Ānanda, he sat down at a respectful distance. As he was sitting down at a respectful distance, the householder Dasama of Aṭṭhaka spoke thus to the venerable Ānanda:

" Now is there, revered Ānanda, any one thing pointed out by that Lord who knows, who sees, perfected one, fully Self-Awakened One, whereby if a monk dwell diligent, ardent, self-resolute, his mind, not (yet) freed, is freed; or the cankers, not (yet) completely destroyed, go to complete destruction; or he attains the matchless security from the bonds, not (yet) attained?"

" There is one thing, householder, pointed out by that Lord . . . fully Self-Awakened One, [**350**] whereby if a monk dwell diligent, ardent, self-resolute, his mind not (yet) freed, is freed; and also the cankers, not (yet) completely destroyed, go to complete destruction; and, too, he attains the matchless security from the bonds, not (yet) attained."

" But what, revered Ānanda, is this one thing pointed out by the Lord . . . whereby if a monk dwell diligent . . . he attains the matchless security from the bonds, not (yet) attained?"

" As to this, householder, a monk, aloof from pleasures of the senses, aloof from unskilled states of mind, enters and abides in the first meditation, which is accompanied by initial thought and discursive thought, is born of aloofness and is rapturous and joyful. He reflects on this and comprehends: ' This first meditation is effected and thought out.[1] But whatever is effected and thought out, that is impermanent, it is liable to stopping.' Firm in this, he attains the destruction of the cankers. If he does not attain the destruction of the cankers, then by this attachment to *dhamma*, by this delight in *dhamma*, by the destruction of the five fetters binding to this lower (shore), he is of spontaneous uprising, one who attains nibbāna there, not liable to return from that world. This, householder, is one thing pointed out by the Lord . . . whereby, if a monk dwell diligent . . . he attains the matchless security from the bonds, not (yet) attained.

And again, householder, a monk, by allaying initial and discursive thought . . . enters on and abides in the second meditation. He reflects on this and comprehends: ' This second meditation is also effected and thought out . . . impermanent, it is liable to stopping.'

---

[1] *abhisaṅkhatam abhisañcetayitaṁ.*

Firm in this he attains destruction of the cankers . . . one who attains nibbāna there, not liable to return from that world. This too, householder, is one thing pointed out by that Lord . . . [**351**] . . . whereby if a monk dwell diligent . . . he attains the matchless security from the bonds, not (yet) attained.

And again, householder, a monk, by the fading out of rapture . . . enters and abides in the third meditation. He reflects on this and comprehends: 'This third meditation is also effected and thought out. But whatever is effected and thought out, that is impermanent, it is liable to stopping.' Firm in this . . . he attains the matchless security from the bonds, not (yet) attained.

And again, householder, a monk, by getting rid of joy, by getting rid of anguish, . . . enters and abides in the fourth meditation. He reflects on this and comprehends: 'This fourth meditation is also effected and thought out. But whatever is effected and thought out, that is impermenent, it is liable to stopping.' Firm in this . . . he attains the matchless security from the bonds, not (yet) attained.

And again, householder, a monk dwells having suffused the first quarter with a mind of friendliness; likewise the second, likewise the third, likewise the fourth; just so above, below, across; he dwells having suffused the whole world everywhere, in every way, with a mind of friendliness that is far-reaching, wide-spread, immeasurable, without enmity, without malevolence. He reflects on this and comprehends: 'This freedom of mind that is friendliness is also effected and thought out. But whatever is effected and thought out, that is impermanent, it is liable to stopping.' Firm in this . . . he attains the matchless security from the bonds, not (yet) attained.

And again, householder, a monk dwells having suffused the first quarter with a mind of compassion . . . with a mind of sympathetic joy . . . with a mind of equanimity; likewise the second, likewise the third, likewise the fourth; just so above, below, across; he dwells having suffused the whole world everywhere, in every way, with a mind of compassion . . . of sympathetic joy . . . of equanimity that is far-reaching, wide-spread, immeasurable, without enmity, without malevolence. He reflects on this and comprehends: 'This freedom of mind that is compassion . . . sympathetic joy . . . equanimity is also effected and thought out. But whatever is effected and thought out, that is impermanent, [**352**] it is liable to stopping.' Firm in this . . . he attains the matchless security from the bonds, not (yet) attained.

And again, householder, a monk, by wholly transcending perceptions of material shapes, by the going down of perceptions due to sensory impressions, by not reflecting on perceptions of multiformity, thinking 'Ether[1] is unending', entering on, abides in the plane of infinite ether. He reflects on this and comprehends: 'This attainment of the plane of infinite ether is also effected and thought out. But whatever is effected and thought out, that is impermanent, it is liable to stopping. Firm in this . . . he attains the matchless security from the bonds, not (yet) attained.

And again, householder, a monk, by wholly transcending the plane of infinite ether, thinking 'Consciousness is unending', entering on, abides in the plane of infinite consciousness. He reflects on this and comprehends: 'This attainment of the plane of infinite consciousness is also effected and thought out. What is effected and thought out, that is impermanent, it is liable to stopping.' Firm in this . . . he attains the matchless security from the bonds, not (yet) attained.

And again, householder, a monk, by wholly transcending the plane of infinite consciousness, thinking 'There is no-thing,' entering on, abides in the plane of no-thing. He reflects on this and comprehends: 'This attainment of the plane of no-thing is also effected and thought out. But whatever is effected and thought out, that is impermanent, it is liable to stopping.' Firm in this, he attains the destruction of the cankers. If he does not attain the destruction of the cankers, then by this attachment to *dhamma*, by this delight in *dhamma*, by the destruction of the five fetters binding to this lower (shore), he is of spontaneous uprising, one who attains nibbāna there, not liable to return from that world. This, householder, is one thing pointed out by that Lord who knows, who sees, perfected one, fully Self-Awakened One, whereby if a monk dwell diligent, ardent, self-resolute, his mind, not (yet) freed, is freed; and the cankers, not (yet) completely destroyed, go to complete destruction; and he attains the matchless security from the bonds, not (yet) attained."

When this had been said, the householder Dasama of Aṭṭhaka spoke thus to the venerable Ānanda: "Revered Ānanda, it is as though a man who was seeking for one opening to (some hidden) treasure were to come at one and the same time on eleven openings to the treasure. [**353**] Even so do I, revered sir, in seeking for one

---

[1] As I used "ether" for *ākāsa* in vol. i, I retain it in this volume, although "ether," for science, no longer means the substratum or ultimate matter out of which come all solids, liquids, gases, etc. Nor is *ākāsa* "space" in such contexts as the above; it is, however, as is *nibbāna*, in some sense an absolute, for neither of the two is born of *kamma*, of cause, or of nature, *Miln.* 268.

door to the deathless come to hear[1] at one and the same time of eleven doors to the deathless. And too, revered sir, it is like a man's house that has eleven doors; if his house were on fire he could make himself safe by any one of the doors. Even so can I, revered sir, make myself safe by any one of these eleven doors to the deathless. Now, revered sir, members of other sects will look about for a fee for the teacher, but why should not I pay honour to the venerable Ānanda ?"

Then the householder Dasama of Aṭṭhaka, having had the Order of monks that was at Pāṭaliputta and Vesālī gathered together, with his own hand served and satisfied them with sumptuous foods, solid and soft, and presented each monk with a separate pair of cloths; to the venerable Ānanda he presented a set of three robes and had a dwelling-place[2] that cost five hundred pieces built for the venerable Ānanda.

Discourse to a Citizen of Aṭṭhaka:
The Second

53. DISCOURSE FOR LEARNERS

(Sekhasutta)

THUS have I heard: At one time the Lord[3] was staying among the Sakyans near Kapilavatthu in Nigrodha's monastery. Now at that time a new conference hall had not long been built for the Sakyans of Kapilavatthu, and had never (yet) been occupied by a recluse or brahman or any human being. Then the Sakyans of Kapilavatthu approached the Lord; having approached, having greeted the Lord, they sat down at a respectful distance. As they were sitting down at a respectful distance, the Sakyans of Kapilavatthu spoke thus to the Lord:

" Lord, there is a new conference hall here, built not long ago for the Sakyans of Kapilavatthu, which has never (yet) been occupied by a recluse or brahman or any human being. Lord, let the Lord be the first to use it. When the Lord has used it first, the Sakyans

---

[1] *savanāya* (for the hearing of); *A*. v. 346 reads *sevanāya* (for entering in by), with v.l. *savanāya*.

[2] *MA*. iii. 16, says a *paṇṇasālā*, a leaf hut (or, hall).

[3] *S*. iv. 182-3. At *D*. iii. 207 *ff*. the scene is laid among the Mallas of Pāvā.

of Kapilavatthu will use it afterwards, and for a long time that will be for the welfare and happiness of the Sakyans of Kapilavatthu."[1]

[**354**] The Lord consented by becoming silent. Then the Sakyans of Kapilavatthu, having understood the Lord's consent, rising from their seats, having greeted the Lord, approached the conference hall keeping their right sides towards him. Having approached, having spread the conference hall with all the spreadings,[2] having got seats ready, having set out a water vessel, having hung up an oil lamp, they approached the Lord; having approached and greeted the Lord, they stood at a respectful distance. As they were standing at a respectful distance, the Sakyans of Kapilavatthu spoke thus to the Lord:

" Lord, the conference hall has been spread with all the spreadings, seats have been got ready, a water vessel set out, an oil lamp hung up. Let the Lord now do that for which he thinks it is the right time." When the Lord had dressed, taking his bowl and robe, he approached the conference hall together with an Order of monks; having approached, he washed his feet, entered the conference hall and sat down against the middle pillar, facing the east. The Order of monks also washed their feet, entered the conference hall and sat down against the western wall, facing the east with the Lord in front of them. The Sakyans of Kapilavatthu also washed their feet, entered the conference hall and sat down against the eastern wall, facing the west with the Lord in front of them. Then the Lord, having gladdened, roused, incited, delighted the Sakyans of Kapilavatthu with reasoned talk far into the night, addressed the venerable Ānanda,[3] saying:

" Ānanda, let there occur to you a learner's course[4] for the Sakyans of Kapilavatthu; my back is aching, I will stretch it."

---

[1] *Cf.* RV. VIII. 17. 14, " Strong pillar thou, Lord of the home !"

[2] *sabbasantharim santhāgāram santharitvā.* On *santhata*, p.p. of *santharati*, see *B.D.* ii. p. xxi *ff.*; and on v.ll. of *santharitvā* in this connection see *D.* iii, 208, *n.* 5. The reading should probably be *santharāpetvā* as in *D.*

[3] Ānanda was a learned expert in the three Piṭakas, and was able to speak of the three (parts of the) training by means of them: the Vinaya spoken for speaking of the higher morality, the Sutta-piṭaka for speaking of the higher thought, and the Abhidhamma-piṭaka for speaking of the higher wisdom, *MA*. iii. 28. These three branches of the whole training are all mentioned in this Discourse.

[4] *Sekho pāṭipado. Cf. A.* ii. 86 (*bhikkhu sekho hoti paṭipado,* and where it would seem that *pāṭi-* is " the more correct," *G. S.* ii. 96, *n.* 2), and *Iti.* p. 80, (*sāvako . . . pāṭipado pi sekho*).

"Yes, revered sir," the venerable Ānanda answered the Lord in assent. Then the Lord, having folded his outer robe into four, lay down on his right side in the lion posture, foot resting on foot, mindful, clearly conscious, reflecting on the thought of getting up again. Then the venerable Ānanda addressed Mahānāma the Sakyan[1], saying:

"Now, Mahānāma, a disciple of the ariyans is possessed of moral habit, he is one who guards the doors of the sense-organs, he is moderate in eating, intent on vigilance, possessed of the seven excellent things,[2] one who acquires at will,[3] without trouble, without difficulty, the four meditations which are of the purest mentality, abidings in ease here and now.[4] And how, [**355**] Mahānāma, is an ariyan disciple possessed of moral habit?[5] As to this, Mahānāma, an ariyan disciple is moral;[6] he lives controlled by the control of the Obligations, possessed of (right) behaviour and resort, seeing danger in the slightest faults; undertaking them rightly, he trains in the rules of training. It is thus, Mahānāma, that an ariyan disciple is possessed of moral habit.

And how, Mahānāma, is an ariyan disciple one who guards the doors of the sense-organs?[7] As to this, Mahānāma, an ariyan disciple, having seen a material shape with the eye, is not entranced by the general appearance, is not entranced by the detail. For if he dwell with the organ of sight uncontrolled, covetousness and dejection, evil unskilled states of mind, might predominate. So he fares along controlling it, he guards the organ of sight; he achieves control over the organ of sight. Having heard a sound with the ear . . . Having smelt a smell with the nose . . . Having savoured a taste with the tongue . . . Having felt a touch with the body . . . Having cognised a mental state with the mind, he is not entranced by the general

---

[1] *MA*. iii. 29 says he was chief and head of the company at that time.

[2] *saddhammehi; MA*. iii. 29 reads *sundaradhammehi sataṁ vā sappurisaṁ dhammehi*. *AA*. iv. explains *saddhammehi* by *suddhammehi*. With this paragraph *cf*. *A*. iv. 108 *f*.

[3] See *M*. i. 33.

[4] This phrase also at *A*. ii. 23, 36, etc. See *P.T.C.*, s.v. *abhicetasika*.

[5] *MA*. iii. 29 refers to the *Ākaṅkheyya Sutta* (*M*. Sta. 6), etc. See also *M*. Sta. 107.

[6] *sīlavant*. *Cf*. *Sāmaññaphalasuttanta*, §§ 43-62, each of which ends by saying: *idaṁ pi 'ssa hoti sīlasmiṁ*, a phrase to be compared with *idaṁ pi 'ssa hoti caraṇasmiṁ . . . vijjāya*, "this is so of him in regard to conduct . . . knowledge" on p. 24 below.

[7] *Cf*. *M*. i. 180 (*M.L.S*. i. 226).

appearance, is not entranced by the detail. If he dwell with the organ of mind uncontrolled, covetousness and dejection, evil unskilled states, might predominate. So he fares along controlling it, he guards the organ of mind; he achieves control over the organ of mind. It is thus, Mahānāma, that an ariyan disciple is one who guards the doors of the sense-organs.

And how, Mahānāma, is an ariyan disciple one who is moderate in eating?[1] As to this, Mahānāma, an ariyan disciple takes food reflecting carefully, not for fun or indulgence or personal charm or beautification, but just enough for maintaining this body and keeping it going, for keeping it unharmed, for furthering the Brahma-faring, with the thought: 'Thus will I crush out an old feeling, and I will not allow a new feeling to arise, and then there will be for me subsistence and blamelessness and abiding in comfort.' It is thus, Mahānāma, that an ariyan disciple is moderate in eating.

And how, Mahānāma, is an ariyan disciple intent on vigilance?[2] As to this, Mahānāma, an ariyan disciple during the day, while pacing up and down and while sitting down, cleanses his mind of obstructive mental states; during the first watch of the night, pacing up and down, sitting down, he cleanses his mind of obstructive mental states; during the middle watch of the night, he lies down on his right side in the lion posture, foot resting on foot, mindful, clearly conscious, reflecting on the thought of getting up again; during the last watch of the night, when he has risen, while pacing up and down, while sitting down, he cleanses his mind of obstructive mental states. It is thus, Mahānāma, that an ariyan disciple is intent on vigilance.

And how, Mahānāma, [**356**] is an ariyan disciple possessed of the seven excellent things?[3] As to this, Mahānāma, the ariyan disciple is of faith;[4] he has faith in the awakening of the Tathāgata, and thinks: He is indeed Lord, perfected one, fully Self-Awakened One, endowed with right knowledge and conduct, well-farer, knower of the world(s), matchless charioteer of men to be tamed, teacher of *devas* and men, the Awakened One, the Lord.

He comes to have shame; he is ashamed of wrong conduct in body, of wrong conduct in speech, of wrong conduct in thought, he is ashamed to fall into evil unskilled mental states.

He has fear of blame; he fears blame for wrong conduct in body . . . speech . . . thought, he fears blame for falling into evil unskilled mental states.

---

[1] As at *M.* i. 273. [2] As at *M.* i. 273.
[3] *Cf. M.* iii. 23; *D.* iii. 252, 282; *A.* iv. 108 *ff.* [4] *Cf. S.* v. 196.

He is one who has heard much, who remembers what he has heard, who stores up what he has heard. Those things, lovely in the beginning, lovely in the middle, lovely at the ending which, with the meaning and the spirit, declare the Brahma-faring wholly fulfilled, perfectly purified, such things are much heard by him, borne in mind, familiarised by speech, pondered over in the mind, well penetrated by right view.[1]

He dwells with stirred up energy[2] for getting rid of unskilled mental states, for acquiring skilled mental states, steadfast, firm in advance, persevering amid skilled mental states.

He is mindful,[3] possessed of the highest mindfulness and discrimination,[4] remembering, recollecting[5] what he has done and said long ago.

He is one of wisdom,[6] endowed with wisdom leading to (the cutting off of) rise and fall, with the ariyan penetration leading to the complete destruction of anguish. It is thus, Mahānāma, that an ariyan disciple is possessed of the seven excellent things.

And how, Mahānāma, is an ariyan disciple one who acquires at will, without trouble, without difficulty, the four meditations which are of the purest mentality, abidings in ease here and now ?[7] As to this, Mahānāma, an ariyan disciple, aloof from pleasures of the senses, aloof from unskilled states of mind, enters and abides in the first meditation, which is accompanied by initial thought and discursive thought, is born of aloofness and is rapturous and joyful. By allaying initial and discursive thought, with the mind subjectively tranquillised and fixed on one point, he enters and abides in the second meditation which is devoid of initial and discursive thought, is born of concentration and is rapturous and joyful . . . he enters and abides in the third meditation . . . the fourth meditation. It is thus, Mahānāma, that an ariyan disciple is one who acquires at will, without trouble, without difficulty, the four meditations which are of the purest mentality, abidings in ease here and now.

When, Mahānāma, an ariyan disciple is endowed with moral habit thus, is one who guards the doors of his sense-organs thus, is moderate in eating thus, is intent on vigilance thus, is endowed with the seven excellent things thus, [**357**] is one who acquires thus at will, without trouble, without difficulty, the four meditations which are of the

---

[1] *Cf. M.* iii. 11. [2] *Cf. M.* ii. 95, *S.* v. 197, *A.* iii. 11, iv. 3, *Ud.* 37.

[3] *Cf. S.* v. 197, *A.* iii. 11. [4] *nepakka*, see *Vbh.* 249.

[5] *MA.* iii. 30 distinguishes saying that *saritā* (remembering) is remembering once, *anussaritā* (recollecting) is remembering again and again.

[6] *Cf. M.* ii, 95. [7] *Cf. A.* ii. 22 *f.*, iii. 131, iv. 108 *ff.*

purest mentality, abidings in ease here and now, then he, Mahānāma, is called an ariyan disciple who is on a learner's course, possessed of (mental) soundness, he becomes one for successful breaking through,[1] he becomes one for self-awakening, he becomes one for winning the matchless security from the bonds. Mahānāma, it is as if there were eight or ten or a dozen hen's eggs, properly sat on, properly incubated, properly hatched by that hen; such a wish as this would not arise in that hen: 'O may my chicks, having pierced through the egg-shell with the point of the claw on their feet or with their beaks, break forth safely,' for these chicks were ones who were able to break forth safely having pierced the egg-shells with the point of the claw on their feet or with their beaks. Even so, Mahānāma, when an ariyan disciple is endowed with moral habit thus, is one who guards the doors of his sense-organs thus, is moderate in eating thus, is intent on vigilance thus, is endowed with the seven excellent things thus, is one who acquires thus at will, without trouble, without difficulty the four meditations which are of the purest mentality, abidings in ease here and now, then he, Mahānāma, is called an ariyan disciple who is on a learner's course, possessed of (mental) soundness, he becomes one for successful breaking through, he becomes one for self-awakening, he becomes one for winning the matchless security from the bonds. That ariyan disciple, Mahānāma, having come to this matchless purification through equanimity and mindfulness,[2] recollects a variety of former habitations, that is to say one birth, two births . . . Thus in all their mode and detail he recollects a variety of former habitations. This is his first breaking through as a chick's from the egg-shell.

Then this ariyan disciple, Mahānāma, having come to this matchless purification through equanimity and mindfulness, with the purified *deva*-vision surpassing that of men, sees beings as they are passing hence and uprising, mean, excellent, comely, ugly, well-going, ill-going . . . he comprehends beings according to the consequences of deeds. This is his second breaking through as a chick's from the egg-shell.

Then this ariyan disciple, Mahānāma, having come to this matchless purification through equanimity and mindfulness, by the destruction of the cankers having here-now realised by his own super-knowledge the freedom of mind and the freedom through intuitive wisdom that are cankerless, [**358**] enters and abides therein. This is his third breaking through as a chick's from the egg-shell.

---

[1] *I.e.* from ignorance to knowledge, from darkness to light. *Cf. M.* i. 104.

[2] In the fourth meditation. See also below, p. 31.

Whatever ariyan disciple, Mahānāma, is possessed of moral habit, this is so of him in regard to conduct.[1] And, Mahānāma, whatever ariyan disciple is guarded as to the doors of his sense-organs, this too is so of him in regard to conduct. And, Mahānāma, whatever ariyan disciple is moderate in eating . . . is intent on vigilance . . . is possessed of the seven excellent things . . . acquires at will, without trouble, without difficulty, the four meditations that are of the purest mentality, abidings in ease here and now, this too is so of him in regard to conduct. But, Mahānāma, whatever ariyan disciple in many a figure recollects his former habitations, that is to say one birth, two births . . . that is so of him in regard to knowledge.[2] And, Mahānāma, whatever ariyan disciple, by the purified *deva*-vision surpassing that of men, sees beings as they are passing hence and uprising, mean, excellent, comely, ugly, well-going, ill-going . . . who comprehends beings according to the consequences of deeds, this too is so of him in regard to knowledge. And, Mahānāma, whatever ariyan disciple, by the destruction of the cankers, having realised here and now by his own super-knowledge the freedom of mind and the freedom through wisdom that are cankerless, enters and abides therein, this too is so of him in regard to knowledge.[3] Mahānāma, this ariyan disciple is said to be possessed of knowledge and to be possessed of (right) conduct and to be possessed of knowledge and (right) conduct. And, Mahānāma, this verse was spoken by Brahmā Ever-Young:[4]

'The noble warrior is best among those people who value clan;
He who is possessed of knowledge and (right) conduct is the best of *devas* and men.'[5]

Mahānāma, this verse was rightly sung, not wrongly sung by Brahmā Ever-Young; it was rightly spoken, not wrongly spoken; it is connected with the goal, not connected with what is not the goal. It is approved by the Lord."

Then the Lord, having risen, addressed the venerable Ānanda,

---

[1] *caraṇa*. [2] *vijjā*. On *vijjācaraṇa* see *A*. ii. 163, v. 326 *f*.; and *Vism*. 202.

[3] *Cf*. the fifteen things (*dhammā*) given at *Vism*. 202 in its definition of *caraṇa*, "conduct," The implied idea of movement in the word *caraṇa* is also made explicit at *Vism*. 202: "these very fifteen things are those by which an ariyan disciple walks (*carati*, fares, moves) and goes to the deathless quarter." *Cf*. also the fifteen factors (*aṅga*) at *M*. i. 303, 304. The three knowledges are meant here according to *MA*. iii. 33, and also, as *Vism*. 202 notices, in the *Bhayabheravasutta* (*M*. Sta. 4), but eight are spoken of in the *Ambaṭṭhasutta* (*D*. i. 100). [4] Sanaṅkumāra. See *Chānd. Up*. Ch. VII.

[5] *D*. i. 99; iii. 97; *S*. i. 153, ii. 284; *A*. v. 327.

saying: " It is good, it is good, Ānanda; it is good that you, Ānanda, spoke on a learner's course to the Sakyans of Kapilavatthu."

[**359**] Thus spoke the venerable Ānanda, the Teacher approving. Delighted, the Sakyans of Kapilavatthu rejoiced in what the venerable Ānanda had said.

Discourse for Learners:
The Third

54. DISCOURSE TO POTALIYA

(Potaliyasutta)

THUS have I heard: At one time the Lord was staying near Aṅguttarāpa.[1] Āpaṇa[2] was a market town in Aṅguttarāpa. Then the Lord, having dressed in the morning, taking his bowl and robe, entered Āpaṇa for almsfood. When he had walked for almsfood in Āpaṇa and was returning from the alms-gathering after the meal, he approached a certain forest-thicket for the day-sojourn; and having plunged into that forest-thicket he sat down at the root of a tree. And the householder Potaliya,[3] who was constantly pacing up and down and roaming about on foot, fully dressed[4] and clothed,[4] with parasol and slippers, approached that forest-thicket; having plunged into that forest-thicket, he approached the Lord; having approached, he exchanged greetings with the Lord; having conversed in a friendly and courteous way, he stood at a respectful distance. Then the Lord spoke thus to the householder Potaliya as he was standing at a respectful distance: " There are seats, householder; if you wish, do sit down." When this had been said, the householder Potaliya thinking: " The recluse Gotama addresses me with the word ' householder ' ", angry, displeased, became silent. And a second time the Lord spoke thus to the householder Potaliya: " There are

---

[1] *MA*. iii. 34, Aṅga was a district. Not far north of the waters of the river Mahī, there was Uttarāpa. Aṅguttarāpa mentioned at *M*. i. 447, *Vin*. i. 243, *Sn*. p. 102.

[2] So called because it had many shops and bazaars, *MA*. iii. 37.

[3] He possibly became the wanderer Potaliya, of *A*. ii. 100 *f*.

[4] *nivāsa* and *pāvuraṇa* refer to putting on of different garments (or cloths), the former to the loin-cloth or under garment, and the latter to the shoulder-cloth or outer garment. *MA*. iii. 38 distinguishes between these two cloths (the attire of the ordinary Indian), and says the former had a long fringe.

seats, householder; if you wish, do sit down." And a second time the householder Potaliya thinking: "The recluse Gotama addresses me with the word 'householder'", angry, displeased, became silent. And a third time the Lord spoke thus to the householder Potaliya: "There are seats, householder; if you wish, do sit down." When this had been said, the householder Potaliya thinking: "The recluse Gotama addresses me with the word 'householder'", angry, displeased, spoke thus to the Lord:

"This, [**360**] good Gotama, is not proper, it is not suitable, that you should address me with the word 'householder.'"

"But you, householder, have all the characteristic marks and signs of a householder."

"But all relevant occupations have been abandoned by me, good Gotama, all avocations given up."

"But, householder, how have all occupations been abandoned by you, all avocations given up?"

"As to this, good Gotama, I handed over to my sons as their inheritance all that I had of wealth or grain or silver or gold. Without giving advice or blame in these matters I live on a minimum of food and covering.[1] This is how all occupations have been abandoned by me, good Gotama, all avocations given up."

"But what you, householder, call a giving up of avocations is one thing; but in the discipline for an ariyan the giving up of avocations is another thing."

"And what, revered sir, is the giving up of avocations in the discipline for an ariyan? It would be good, revered sir, if the Lord were to teach me *dhamma* as to that which is the giving up of avocations in the discipline for an ariyan."

"Well then, householder, listen, attend carefully and I will speak."

"Yes, revered sir," the householder Potaliya answered the Lord in assent. The Lord spoke thus:

"Householder, these eight things conduce to the giving up of avocations in the discipline for an ariyan.[2] What eight? Through no onslaught on creatures, onslaught on creatures should be got rid of; through taking what is given, taking what is not given should be got rid of; through speaking truth, lying speech should be got rid of; through unslanderous speech, slanderous speech should be got rid of; through non-covetise and greed, covetise and greed should be got rid of; through no angry fault-finding, angry fault-finding should be got

---

[1] *Cf. D.* i. 60. [2] *Cf. M.* iii. 29; *Vin.* iv. 2; *D.* iii. 232; *A.* ii. 246, iv. 307.

rid of; through no wrathful rage, wrathful rage should be got rid of; through no arrogance, arrogance should be got rid of. These are the eight things, householder, spoken of in brief, not explained in detail, that, in the discipline for an ariyan, conduce to the giving up of avocations."

"As to these eight things, revered sir, which are spoken of in brief, not explained in detail, and which, in the discipline for an ariyan, conduce to the giving up of avocations, it were good, revered sir, if the Lord out of compassion were to explain these eight things to me in detail."

"Well then, householder, listen, attend carefully and I will speak."

"Yes, revered sir," the householder Potaliya answered the Lord in assent. The Lord spoke thus:

[**361**] "When I said: 'Through no onslaught on creatures, onslaught on creatures should be got rid of'—in reference to what was this said? As to this, householder, an ariyan disciple reflects thus: 'I am faring along for getting rid of and abandoning those fetters of which onslaught on creatures might be a cause; for if I were to make onslaught on creatures, not only would self upbraid me as a result of making onslaught on creatures, but intelligent men (also) after scrutinising, would blame me[1] as a result of making onslaught on creatures; and at the breaking up of the body after dying a bad bourne would be expected as a result of making onslaught on creatures. This is indeed a fetter, this is a hindrance, that is to say onslaught on creatures. But for one who refrains from onslaught on creatures there are not those destructive and consuming cankers[2] that might arise as a result of making onslaught on creatures.' When I said: 'Through no onslaught on creatures, onslaught on creatures should be got rid of,' it was said in reference to this."

(*The other seven things are spoken of in exactly the same terms, pp.* **362, 363**.)

[**364**] "These, householder, are the eight things spoken of in brief, (now) explained in detail, that, in the discipline for an ariyan, conduce to the giving up of avocations. But not even yet in the

---

[1] *attā pi maṁ upavadeyya anuvicca viññū garaheyyuṁ; cf. A.* i. 57, iii. 255, 267-8, all reading *attā pi attānaṁ upavadati.* See *G.S.* i. 52, *n.* 3 on *anuvicca,* translated above as "scrutinising," following *MA.* iii. 40 which explains by *tulayitvā pariyogahetvā,* having weighed, having scrutinised (or examined).

[2] *MA.* iii. 40-42 states which single canker arises, or which two or which three arise, out of the total of four, for each one of the eight things so long as these have not been extirpated.

discipline for an ariyan is there an entire giving up in every way of all avocations."

"But how is it, revered sir, in the discipline for an ariyan there is an entire giving up in every way of all avocations? It were good, revered sir, if the Lord were to teach me *dhamma* as to how, in the discipline for an ariyan, there is an entire giving up in every way of all avocations."

"Well then, householder, listen, attend carefully and I will speak."

"Yes, revered sir," the householder Potaliya answered the Lord in assent. The Lord spoke thus:

"It is, householder, as if a dog, overcome by hunger and exhaustion[1] were to happen on a slaughtering place for cows, and the skilled cattle-butcher there or his apprentice were to fling him a bone, scraped and well scraped, fleshless, but with a smearing of blood. What do you think about this, householder? Could that dog, gnawing such a bone, scraped and well scraped, fleshless, but with a smearing of blood, appease his hunger and exhaustion?"

"No, revered sir. What is the reason for this? That bone, revered sir, is scraped and well scraped, fleshless, but although it has a smearing of blood, that dog would be worn out with fatigue or ever he got anything from it."

"Even so, householder, an ariyan disciple reflects thus: 'Pleasures of the senses have been likened to a skeleton[2] by the Lord, of much pain, of much tribulation, wherein is more peril.' And having seen this thus as it really is by means of perfect wisdom, having avoided[3] that which is equanimity in face of multiformity,[4] resting on multiformity, he develops that equanimity which is equanimity in face of uniformity, resting on uniformity, wherein all graspings after the material things of the world are stopped entirely.

And, householder, it is as if a vulture or kite or hawk seizing a lump of flesh were to fly upwards, and other vultures, kites and hawks following hard after it were to tear at it and pull it to pieces.[5] What do you think about this, householder? If that vulture or kite or

---

[1] *Cf. M.* i. 114.

[2] *Cf. M.* i. 130. For the following things to which pleasures of the senses are likened, see *B.D.* iii. 22 *f.* (*Vin.* iv. 134) and notes.

[3] *abhinivajjetvā*, as at *M.* i. 111; *D.* iii. 113.

[4] *Cf. M.* iii. 220. "Multiformity" consists of the five sensual qualities, "uniformity" of the four *jhānas*, *MA.* iii. 43.

[5] *Cf. Vin.* iii. 105; *S.* ii. 255.

hawk were not to let go quickly of that lump of flesh, would it, from that cause, come to death or pain like unto death ?"

" Yes, revered sir."

" Even so, householder, an ariyan disciple reflects thus: ' Pleasures of the senses have been likened to a lump of flesh[1] by the Lord, of much pain, of much tribulation, wherein is more peril.' [**365**] And having seen this thus as it really is by means of perfect wisdom, having avoided that which is equanimity in face of multiformity . . . he develops that equanimity which is equanimity in face of uniformity . . . material things of the world are stopped entirely.

And, householder, it is as though a man might come along bringing a blazing grass torch[2] against the wind. What do you think about this, householder ? If that man were not to let go quickly of that blazing grass torch, would it burn his hand or burn his arm or burn another part of his body so that, from that cause, he would come to death or pain like unto death ?"

" Yes, revered sir."

" Even so, householder, an ariyan disciple reflects thus: ' Pleasures of the senses have been likened by the Lord to a grass torch,[3] of much pain, of much tribulation, wherein is more peril.' And having seen this thus as it really is by means of perfect wisdon, having avoided . . . the material things of the world are stopped entirely.

And, householder, it is as if there might be a pit of glowing embers, deeper than a man's height, full of embers that were neither flaming nor smoking,[4] and a man might come along wanting to live, not wanting to die, wanting happiness, recoiling from pain; but two strong men, having grasped hold of his arms, might drag him towards that pit of glowing embers. What do you think about this, householder ? Would not that man twist his body this way and that ?"[5]

" Yes, revered sir. What is the reason for this ? Revered sir, that man realises: ' If I fall down into this pit of glowing embers, from that cause I will come to death or pain like unto death.' "

" Even so, householder, an ariyan disciple reflects thus: ' Pleasures of the senses have been likened by the Lord to a pit of glowing embers,[6] of much pain, of much tribulation, wherein is more peril.' And having seen this thus as it really is by means of perfect wisdom, having avoided . . . the material things of the world are stopped entirely.

---

[1] *Cf. M.* i. 145. [2] *Cf. M.* i. 128. [3] *Cf. S.* ii. 152.
[4] *Cf. M.* i. 74. [5] As at *M.* i. 507.
[6] *Cf. D.* iii. 283; *S.* iv. 188; *A.* iv. 224, v. 175; *Sn.* 396.

And, householder, it is as if a man might see in a dream delightful parks, delightful woods, delightful stretches of level ground and delightful lakes; but on waking up could see nothing. Even so, householder, an ariyan disciple reflects thus: 'Pleasures of the senses have been likened by the Lord to a dream, of much pain, of much tribulation, wherein is more peril.' And having seen this thus as it really is by means of perfect wisdom . . . the material things of the world are stopped entirely.

And, householder, it is as if a man, having borrowed[1] a loan of wealth, [**366**] a fashionable[2] vehicle and splendid jewels and ear-ornaments, might go forth into the bazaar, honoured for his loan of wealth, surrounded by it, so that people having seen him might say: 'This man is indeed wealthy, and undoubtedly wealthy men enjoy their wealth thus'; but the veritable owners, wherever they might see him, might take away what was theirs. What do you think about this, householder? Would that man have had enough of being other (than what he is)?"

"Yes, revered sir. What is the reason for this? It is, revered sir, that the veritable owners take away what is theirs."

"Even so, householder, an ariyan disciple reflects thus: 'Pleasures of the senses have been likened by the Lord to what is borrowed, of much pain, of much tribulation, wherein is more peril.' And having seen this thus as it really is by means of perfect wisdom . . . the material things of the world are stopped entirely.

And, householder, it is as if in a dense forest thicket not far from a village or a market town there might be a tree laden with ripe fruit, but with no fruit fallen to the ground; and a man might come along walking about and aiming at fruit, seeking for fruit, looking about for fruit; having plunged into that forest thicket, he might see that tree laden with ripe fruit, and it might occur to him: 'This tree is laden with ripe fruit, but no fruit has fallen to the ground. However, I know how to climb a tree. Suppose that I, having climbed this tree, should eat as much as I like and should fill my clothes?'[3] So he, having climbed that tree, might eat as much as he liked and might fill his clothes. Then a second man might come

---

[1] Or, begged, *yācitvā*. Trenckner suggests *yāceyya*, *M*. i. 574.

[2] *poroseyya*. *P.E.D.* rejects the derivation from *purisa*, as at *MA*. iii. 44, and says the word is derived from *pura*, a town. However, the text is corrupt here; see v.l. at *M*. i. 561, 574.

[3] *ucchaṅga*, used in a similar sense here and at *Vin*. i. 225. Probably meaning the man knotted his cloth garment so as to carry the fruit.

along walking about and aiming at fruit, seeking for fruit, looking about for fruit, and bringing a sharp axe. Having plunged into that forest thicket, he might see that tree laden with ripe fruit, and it might occur to him: ‘ This tree is laden with ripe fruit but no fruit has fallen to the ground. Now, I don’t know how to climb a tree, so suppose that I, having cut down this tree at the root, should eat as much as I like and should fill my clothes ?’ So he might cut down this tree at the root. What do you think about this, householder ? Unless he came down very quickly, would not that tree in falling crush the hand or the foot or another part of the body of that man who had first climbed the tree, [**367**] so that, from that cause he might come to death or to pain like unto death ?”

“ Yes, revered sir.”

“ Even so, householder, an ariyan disciple reflects thus: ‘ Pleasures of the senses have been likened by the Lord to the fruits of a tree, of much pain, of much tribulation, wherein is more peril.’ And having seen this thus as it really is by means of perfect wisdom, having avoided that equanimity which is multiformity, resting on multiformity, he develops that equanimity which is uniformity, resting on uniformity wherein all graspings after the material things of the world are stopped entirely.

This ariyan disciple, householder, who has come to this matchless purification through equanimity and mindfulness, recollects a variety of former habitations, that is to say one birth, two births . . . thus in all their mode and detail he recollects a variety of former habitations. This ariyan disciple, householder, who has come to this matchless purification through equanimity and mindfulness, with the purified *deva*-vision surpassing that of men, sees beings as they are passing hence and uprising, mean, excellent, comely, ugly, well-going, ill-going . . . comprehends beings according to the consequences of deeds. This ariyan disciple, householder, who has come to this matchless purification through equanimity and mindfulness, by the destruction of the cankers having here-now realised by his own super-knowledge the freedom of mind and the freedom through wisdom that are cankerless, enters and abides therein.

It is to this extent, householder, that in the discipline for an ariyan there is an entire giving up in every way of all avocations. What do you think about this, householder ? Do you behold in yourself a giving up of avocations such as is, in the discipline for an ariyan, an entire giving up in every way of all avocations ?”

“ Who am I, revered sir, that there is an entire giving up of all avocations in every way? I, revered sir, am far from the entire giving up in every way of all avocations according to the discipline for an ariyan. For hitherto we, revered sir, deemed wanderers belonging to other sects to be superior although they are inferior; although they are inferior we offered them food for superiors; although they are inferior we placed them in places for superiors. And we, revered sir, deemed monks to be inferior although they are superior; although they are superior we offered them food for inferiors; although they are superior we placed them in places for inferiors. But now we, revered sir, [**368**] will know that wanderers belonging to other sects, being inferior, are inferior; because they are inferior we will offer them food for inferiors; because they are inferior we will place them in places for inferiors. And we, revered sir, will know that monks, being superior, are superior; because they are superior we will offer them food for superiors; because they are superior we will place them in places for superiors. Indeed, revered sir, the Lord has inspired in me a recluse's regard for recluses, a recluse's satisfaction in recluses, a recluse's reverence for recluses. It is excellent, revered sir, it is excellent, revered sir. Revered sir, it is as if one might set upright what had been upset, or might disclose what what was covered, or show the way to one who had gone astray, or bring an oil-lamp into the darkness so that those with vision might see material shapes—even so in many a figure has *dhamma* been made clear by the Lord. I, revered sir, am going to the Lord for refuge and to *dhamma* and to the Order of monks. May the Lord accept me as a lay follower going for refuge from this day forth for as long as life lasts."

Discourse to Potaliya:
The Fourth

55. DISCOURSE TO JĪVAKA

(Jīvakasutta)

THUS have I heard: At one time the Lord was staying at Rājagaha in Jīvaka Komārabhacca's[1] Mango Grove. Then Jīvaka Komāra-

[1] See *Vin.* i. 71 *ff.*, 269 *ff.* Also *B.D.* iv. 381, *n.* 3. *MA.* iii. 45 says his name means "Prince-fed."

bhacca approached the Lord; having approached, having greeted the Lord, he sat down at a respectful distance. As he was sitting down at a respectful distance, Jīvaka Komārabhacca spoke thus to the Lord:

" This is what I have heard, revered sir: that they kill living creatures on purpose for the recluse Gotama, and that the recluse Gotama knowingly makes use of meat killed on purpose and specially provided for him. Those who speak thus, revered sir: ' They kill living creatures on purpose for the recluse Gotama, and the recluse Gotama knowingly makes use of meat killed on purpose and specially provided for him '—now, are these quoting the Lord's own words, revered sir, not misrepresenting the Lord with what is not fact, are they explaining in conformity with *dhamma*, and does no reasoned thesis[1] give occasion for contempt ?"[2]

[**369**] " Jīvaka, those who speak thus: ' They kill living creatures on purpose for the recluse Gotama, and the recluse Gotama knowingly makes use of meat killed on purpose and specially provided for him '—these are not quoting my own words, but are misrepresenting me with what is not true, with what is not fact. I, Jīvaka, say that in three cases meat may not be used: if it is seen, heard, suspected (to have been killed on purpose for a monk). In these three cases I, Jīvaka, say that meat may not be used. But I, Jīvaka, say that in three cases meat may be used: if it is not seen, heard, suspected (to have been killed on purpose for a monk).[3] In these three cases I, Jīvaka, say that meat may be used.

As to this, Jīvaka, a monk lives depending on a village or market town.[4] He dwells having suffused the first quarter with a mind of friendliness, likewise the second, likewise the third, likewise the fourth; just so above, below, across; he dwells having suffused the whole world everywhere, in every way, with a mind of friendliness that is far-reaching, wide-spread, immeasurable, without enmity, without malevolence. A householder or a householder's son, having approached him, invites him to a meal on the morrow. The monk accepts, Jīvaka, if he so desires. At the end of that night, having dressed in the early morning, taking his bowl and robe, he approaches

---

[1] *vādānuvāda* here; some texts read *vādānupāta*.

[2] *Cf. M.* i. 482, ii. 127, 222, iii. 77; *A.* i. 161; *D.* i. 161, iii. 115; *S.* ii. 33, 36, iii. 6, iv. 51, 340, 381, v. 6.

[3] *Cf. Vin.* i. 238, iii. 172.

[4] The next few paragraphs should be compared with *A.* i. 274 (Sutta 121); there are several interesting variations.

the dwelling of that householder or householder's son; having approached, he sits down on the appointed seat, and the householder or householder's son waits on him with sumptuous almsfood. It does not occur to him: 'Indeed it is good that a householder or a householder's son waits on me with sumptuous almsfood. O may a householder or a householder's son also wait on me in the future with similar sumptuous almsfood'—this does not occur to him. He makes use of that almsfood without being ensnared, entranced or enthralled by it, but seeing the peril in it, wise as to the escape. What do you think about this, Jīvaka? Is that monk at that time striving for the hurt of self or is he striving for the hurt of others or is he striving for the hurt of both?"

"Not this, revered sir."

"Is not that monk at that time, Jīvaka, eating food that is blameless?"

"Yes, revered sir. I had heard this, revered sir: Sublime is abiding in friendliness.[1] The Lord is seen as my witness for this, revered sir, for the Lord is abiding in friendliness."[1]

"Jīvaka, that attachment, that [**370**] aversion, that confusion through which there might be malevolence, these have been got rid of by the Tathāgata, cut off at the root, made like a palm-tree stump that can come to no further existence in the future. If this is the meaning of what you said, Jīvaka, I agree with you."

"This is the exact meaning of what I said, revered sir."

"As to this, Jīvaka, a monk lives depending on a village or market town. He dwells having suffused the first quarter with a mind of compassion . . . a mind of sympathetic joy . . . a mind of equanimity, likewise the second, likewise the third, likewise the fourth; just so above, below, across; he dwells having suffused the whole world everywhere, in every way, with a mind of equanimity that is far-reaching, wide-spread, immeasurable, without enmity, without malevolence. A householder or a householder's son, having approached him, invites him to a meal on the morrow . . .(*as above* ...) Is that monk at that time striving for the hurt of self or is he striving for the hurt of others or is he striving for the hurt of both?"

"Not this, revered sir."

"Is not that monk at that time, Jīvaka, eating food that is blameless?"

---

[1] *Brahmā mettāvihārī . . . bhagavā hi mettāvihārī. Cf. Sn.* 151, *Khp.* ix.: *brahmam etaṁ vihāram idha-m-āhu*, sublime is this abiding called here.

"Yes, revered sir. I had heard this, revered sir: Sublime is abiding in equanimity. The Lord is seen as my witness for this, revered sir, for the Lord is abiding in equanimity."

"Jīvaka, that attachment, that aversion, that confusion through which there might be annoyance, through which there might be dislike, through which there might be repugnance, these have been got rid of by the Tathāgata, cut off at the root, made like a palm-tree stump that can come to no further existence in the future. If this is the meaning of what you said, Jīvaka, I agree [**371**] with you."

"This is the exact meaning of what I said, revered sir."

"Jīvaka, he who kills a living creature on purpose for a Tathāgata or a Tathāgata's disciple stores up much demerit in five ways: In that, when he speaks thus: 'Go and fetch such and such a living creature,' in this first way he stores up much demerit. In that, while this living creature is being fetched it experiences pain and distress because of the affliction to its throat[1]—in this second way he stores up much demerit. In that, when he speaks thus: 'Go and kill that living creature'—in this third way he stores up much demerit. In that, while this living creature is being killed it experiences pain and distress, in this fourth way he stores up much demerit. In that, if he proffers to[2] a Tathāgata or a Tathāgata's disciple what is not allowable,[3] in this fifth way he stores up much demerit. He who, Jīvaka, kills a living creature on purpose for a Tathāgata or a Tathāgata's disciple stores up much demerit in these five ways."

When this had been said, Jīvaka Komārabhacca spoke thus to the Lord: "It is wonderful, revered sir, it is marvellous, revered sir. Indeed, revered sir, the monks eat food that is allowable; indeed, revered sir, the monks eat food that is blameless. It is excellent, revered sir, it is excellent, revered sir. . . . May the Lord accept me as a lay-disciple going for refuge from this day forth for as long as life lasts."

Discourse to Jīvaka:
The Fifth

---

[1] *galappavedhakena*. *MA*. iii. 51 says: *yottena gale bandhitvā kaḍḍhito galena pavedhentena* (v. l. *paveṭhiyamānena vā*): having secured (or, bound) it with a thong (or, strap) round its throat, it is dragged along with agony (or, terror) in its throat.

[2] *āsādeti*. *MA*. iii. 51 gives *khādāpetvā*, having made to eat.

[3] *akappiya*, such as various kinds of meat named at *MA*. iii. 51. Other unallowable kinds are given at *Vin*. i. 218-219.

56. DISCOURSE WITH UPĀLI

(Upālisutta)

THUS have I heard: At one time the Lord was staying near Nāḷandā in Pāvārika's[1] Mango Grove. Now at that time Nātaputta the Jain was residing in Nāḷandā with a large company of Jains. Then Dīghatapassin[2] the Jain, having walked in Nāḷandā for almsfood, returning from the alms-gathering after the meal, approached Pāvārika's Mango Grove and the Lord; [372] having approached, he exchanged greetings with the Lord; having conversed in a friendly and courteous way, he stood at a respectful distance. The Lord spoke thus to Dīghatapassin the Jain as he was standing at a respectful distance: "There are seats, Tapassin; if you wish, do sit down." When this had been said, Dīghatapassin the Jain, having taken a low seat, sat down at a respectful distance. The Lord spoke thus to Dīghatapassin the Jain as he was sitting down at a respectful distance:

"How many (kinds of) deeds, Tapassin, does Nātaputta the Jain lay down for the effecting of an evil deed, for the rolling on of an evil deed?"

"Friend Gotama, it is not the custom of Nātaputta the Jain to lay down 'deed, deed'; friend Gotama, it is the custom of Nātaputta the Jain to lay down 'wrong, wrong.'"[3]

"How many (kinds of) wrongs, Tapassin, does Nātaputta the

---

[1] He was a merchant who apparently sold mantles (*pāvāra*) in pairs. Hence he was also called Dussapāvārika, *MA*. iii. 52; *DA*. ii. 873; *SA*. iii. 207.

[2] This name means "The one of long austerity."

[3] *daṇḍa*, stem of a tree; stick and so penalty. *P.E.D.* says that in the above passage it is "(fig) a means of frightening, frightfulness, violence, teasing"; and under *mano-* it suggests "mind-punishment." Chalmers has "infliction"; H. Jacobi "torment" (*S.B.E.* xxii. p. 7); Neumann "Streich," blow (vol. ii, p. 54, *n.*). In the present context the word appears to mean affliction, injury, hurt, wrong done. Sometimes of course it means punishment or penalty. *Cf. Dhp.* 133 *paṭidaṇḍa*, retaliation, or exchange-blows. See Manu xii, 10: "That man is called a (true) *tridaṇḍin* in whose mind these three: control over his speech (*vāgdaṇḍa*), control over his thought (*manodaṇḍa*) and control over his body (*kāyadaṇḍa*) are firmly fixed." Here then *daṇḍa* appears to mean "restraint," which Monier-Williams gives for this passage. *MA*. iii. 52 says that the Jain idea is that *kāya-* and *vacī-daṇḍa* are without *citta* (present in *manodaṇḍa*), so that they just stir and sound like trees in the wind.

Jain lay down for the effecting of an evil deed, for the rolling on of an evil deed ?"

"Friend Gotama, Nātaputta the Jain lays down three (kinds of) wrongs for the effecting of an evil deed, for the rolling on of an evil deed, that is to say wrong of body, wrong of speech, wrong of mind."[1]

"But, Tapassin, is wrong of body one thing, wrong of speech another, wrong of mind another ?"

"Friend Gotama, wrong of body is one thing, wrong of speech another, wrong of mind another."

"But, Tapassin, of these three wrongs thus divided, thus particularised, which is the wrong that Nātaputta the Jain lays down as the more blamable in the effecting of an evil deed, in the rolling on of an evil deed ? Is it wrong of body or is it wrong of speech or is it wrong of mind ?"

"Friend Gotama, of these three wrongs thus divided, thus particularised, Nātaputta the Jain lays down that wrong of body is the more blamable in the effecting of an evil deed, in the rolling on of an evil deed; wrong of speech is not like it, wrong of mind is not like it."

"Do you say 'wrong of body,' Tapassin ?"

"I say 'wrong of body,' friend Gotama."

"Do you say 'wrong of body,' Tapassin ?"

"I say 'wrong of body,' friend Gotama."

"Do you say 'wrong of body,' Tapassin ?"

"I say 'wrong of body,' friend Gotama."

In this way did the Lord up to the third time pin down Dīghatapassin the Jain to this point of controversy.

[**373**] When this had been said, Dīghatapassin the Jain spoke thus to the Lord: "But, friend Gotama, how many (kinds of) wrongs do you lay down for the effecting of an evil deed, for the rolling on of an evil deed ?"

"Tapassin, it is not the custom of a Tathāgata to lay down 'wrong, wrong'; Tapassin, it is the custom for a Tathāgata to lay down 'deed, deed.'"

"But how many (kinds of) deeds do you lay down, friend Gotama, for the effecting of an evil deed, for the rolling on of an evil deed ?"

"I, Tapassin, lay down three (kinds of) deeds for the effecting of an evil deed, for the rolling on of an evil deed, that is to say deed of body, deed of speech, deed of mind."

---

[1] *Cf. SnA.* 63, *Nd.* ii. 293 where *daṇḍa*, a synonym for *duccarita*, wrong behaviour in body, speech and thought, afflicts and injures and brings to trouble and distress.

"But, friend Gotama, is deed of body one thing, deed of speech another, deed of mind another ?"

"Tapassin, deed of body is one thing, deed of speech another, deed of mind another."

"But, friend Gotama, of these three deeds thus divided, thus particularised, which deed do you lay down as the more blamable in the effecting of an evil deed, in the rolling on of an evil deed ? Is it deed of body or is it deed of speech or is it deed of mind ?"

"Tapassin, of these three deeds thus divided, thus particularised, I lay down that deed of mind is the more blamable in the effecting of an evil deed, in the rolling on of an evil deed; deed of body is not like it, deed of speech is not like it."

"Do you say 'deed of mind,' friend Gotama ?"

"I say 'deed of mind,' Tapassin."

"Do you say 'deed of mind,' friend Gotama ?"

"I say 'deed of mind,' Tapassin."

"Do you say 'deed of mind,' friend Gotama ?"

"I say 'deed of mind,' Tapassin."

In this way did Dīghatapassin the Jain, having up to the third time pinned down the Lord to the point of controversy, rising from his seat, approach Nātaputta the Jain.

Now at that time Nātaputta the Jain was sitting down together with a very large company of householders headed by Upāli of Bālaka village.[1] Nātaputta the Jain saw Dīghatapassin the Jain coming in the distance; having seen him, he spoke thus to Dīghatapassin the Jain "Well, where are you coming from, Tapassin, in the heat of the day ?"

"I, revered sir, am coming from the presence of the recluse Gotama."

"Now, did you, Tapassin, have any conversation together with the recluse Gotama ?"

[374] "Indeed, revered sir, I did have some conversation together with the recluse Gotama."

"On what topic, Tapassin, was there some conversation between you and the recluse Gotama ?"

Then Dīghatapassin the Jain told Nātaputta the Jain the whole of the conversation he had had with the Lord. When this had been said, Nātaputta the Jain spoke thus to Dīghatapassin the Jain:

"It is good, it is good, Tapassin, that the recluse Gotama was

---

[1] Bālakiniyā, see *D.P.P.N.*

answered thus by Dīghatapassin the Jain, an instructed disciple who understands aright the teacher's instruction. For how can an insignificant wrong of mind shine out in comparison with this important[1] wrong of body, since wrong of body itself is the more blamable in the effecting of an evil deed, in the rolling on of an evil deed—wrong of speech is not like it, wrong of mind is not like it."

When this had been said, Upāli the householder spoke thus to Nātaputta the Jain:

"Good, revered sir, is Tapassin, he is good, in that the recluse Gotama was answered thus by the revered Tapassin, an instructed disciple who understands aright the teacher's instruction. For how can an insignificant wrong of mind shine out in comparison with this important wrong of body since wrong of body itself is the more blamable in the effecting of an evil deed, in the rolling on of an evil deed—wrong of speech is not like it, wrong of mind is not like it. But, if you please, I am going, revered sir, I will refute the words of the recluse Gotama on this point of controversy. If the recluse Gotama pins me down as he pinned down the revered Tapassin, then as a strong man[2] who has taken hold of the fleece of a long-fleeced ram, might tug it towards him, might tug it backwards, might tug it forwards and backwards, even so will I, speech by speech, tug the recluse Gotama forwards, tug him backwards, tug him forwards and backwards. And even as a powerful distiller of spirituous liquor, having sunk his cask for the spirituous liquor in a deep pool of water, taking it by a corner might tug it forwards, might tug it backwards, might tug it forwards and backwards, even so will I, speech by speech, tug the recluse Gotama forwards, tug him backwards, tug him forwards and backwards. And even as a powerful drunkard of abandoned life, having taken hold of a hair-sieve at the corner, would shake it upwards, would shake it downwards, would toss it about, even so will I, speech by speech, [**375**] shake the recluse Gotama upwards, shake him downwards, toss him about. And even as a full-grown elephant, sixty years old, having plunged into a deep tank, plays at the game called the 'merry-washing,' even so methinks will I play the game of 'merry-washing' with the recluse Gotama. But, if you please, I am going, revered sir, I will refute the words of the recluse Gotama on this point of controversy."

"Go you, householder, refute the words of the recluse Gotama on

---

[1] *oḷārika*, here the opposite of *chava*, "insignificant"; explained by *mahanta*, "great," at *MA*. iii. 55.

[2] As at *M*. i. 228 for the following similes.

this point of controversy. For, householder, either I or Dīghatapassin the Jain or you could refute the words of the recluse Gotama."

When this had been said, Dīghatapassin the Jain spoke thus to Nātaputta the Jain: "I am not pleased, revered sir, that the householder Upāli should refute the words of the recluse Gotama. For the recluse Gotama is deceitful, revered sir, he knows the 'enticing device' by which he entices disciples of other sects."[1]

"It is impossible, Tapassin, it cannot come to pass that the householder Upāli should come to discipleship under the recluse Gotama. But this situation exists—that the recluse Gotama might come to discipleship under the householder Upāli. Go you, householder, refute the words of the recluse Gotama on this point of controversy. Either I, householder, could refute the recluse Gotama, or Dīghatapassin the Jain, or you." And a second time . . . And a third time did Dīghatapassin the Jain speak thus to Nātaputta the Jain: "I am not pleased. . . " . . . " . . . Either I, householder, could refute the recluse Gotama, or Dīghatapassin the Jain, or you."

"Very well, revered sir," and the householder Upāli, having answered Nātaputta the Jain in assent, rising from his seat, having greeted Nātaputta the Jain keeping his right side towards him, approached Pāvārika's Mango Grove [**376**] and the Lord; having approached, having greeted the Lord, he sat down at a respectful distance. As he was sitting down at a respectful distance, the householder Upāli spoke thus to the Lord: "Revered sir, did not Dīghatapassin the Jain come here?"

"Yes, householder, Dīghatapassin the Jain did come here."

"And did you, revered sir, have any conversation with Dīghatapassin the Jain?"

"Indeed, householder, I did have some conversation with Dīghatapassin the Jain."

"But on what topic did you, revered sir, have this conversation with Dīghatapassin the Jain?"

Then the Lord told the householder Upāli the whole of the conversation he had had with Dīghatapassin the Jain. When this had been said, the householder Upāli spoke thus to the Lord: "Good, revered sir, is Tapassin, he is good, in that the Lord was answered thus by Dīghatapassin the Jain, an instructed disciple who understands aright the teacher's instruction. For how can an insig-

---

[1] As at *A*. ii. 190.

nificant wrong of mind shine out in comparison with this important wrong of body, since wrong of body is itself the more blamable in the effecting of an evil deed, in the rolling on of an evil deed—wrong of speech is not like it, wrong of mind is not like it."

"If you, householder, were to speak as one grounded on the truth, there might be some conversation here."

"I, revered sir, will speak as one grounded on the truth. Let us have some conversation here."

"What do you think about this, householder? There might be a Jain here who, although sick, suffering, very ill, refuses cold water[1] and takes (only) warm water; not getting cold water, he might pass away. Now, householder, where is it that Nātaputta the Jain lays down that there is uprising for him?"

"Revered sir, there are *devas* called 'Mind attached.'[2] He uprises there. What is the reason for this? It is, revered sir, that when he passed away he was devoted to mind."

"Householder, householder! Take care how you explain, householder. Your earlier (remarks) do not tally with your later, nor your later with your earlier. And yet these words were spoken by you, householder: 'I, revered sir, will speak as one grounded on the truth. Let us have some conversation here.'"

"Although, revered sir, the Lord speaks thus, yet wrong of body is the more blamable in the effecting of an evil deed, in the rolling on of an evil deed—wrong of speech is not like it, wrong of mind is not like it."

"What do you think about this, **[377]** householder? There might be a Jain here who is controlled by the control of the fourfold watch:[3] he is wholly restrained in regard to water;[4] he is bent on warding off

---

[1] *MA*. iii. 57, "Jains are aware that there are conscious beings" in cold water.

[2] *Manosattā*; beings who depend on, hang on (*laggā, laggitā*) mind, *MA*. iii. 57; *satta* is here p.p. of *sajjati*.

[3] See *D*. i. 57; *Dial*. i. 75, *n*. 1. Referred to at *S*. i. 66. The Buddhist fourfold watch is given at *D*. iii. 48 *f*., *MA*. iii. 58; see *K.S*. i. 91.

[4] *sabba-vāri-vārito*. *MA*. iii. 58 gives two meanings: either *vārita-sabba-udaka*, he is restrained in regard to all water; or *sabbena pāpavāraṇena vārita-pāpo*, evil is restrained by the total warding off of evil. *DA*. i. 168, *SA*. i. 126-127 omit the second alternative, but speak of evil in connection with the three remaining "watches," controls or restraints, which read: *sabbavāri-yuto sabbavāridhuto sabbavāriphuṭo*. It would seem that *MA*. iii. 58 means "the total warding off of evil" of its second alternative to the first clause to include the use of (unfiltered) water, in which there would still be small living

all evil; he has shaken off all evil; he is permeated with the (warding off) of all evil—but while going out or returning he brings many small creatures to destruction. What result, householder, does Nātaputta the Jain lay down for him ?"

" Nātaputta the Jain, revered sir, lays down that, being unintentional, there is no great blame."

" But if he does intend it, householder ?"

" It is of great blame, revered sir."

" In what (division[1]), householder, does Nātaputta the Jain lay down 'intention' ?"

" In that of wrong of mind, revered sir."

" Householder, householder! Take care how you explain, householder. Your earlier (remarks) do not tally with your later nor your later with your earlier. And yet these words were spoken by you, householder: 'I, revered sir, will speak as one grounded on the truth. Let us have some conversation here.' "

" Although, revered sir, the Lord speaks thus, yet wrong of body is the more blamable in the effecting of an evil deed, in the rolling on of an evil deed—wrong of speech is not like it, wrong of mind is not like it."

" What do you think about this, householder ? Is this Nāḷandā rich and wealthy, crowded and populous ?"

" Yes, revered sir, this Nāḷandā is rich and wealthy, crowded and populous."

" What do you think about this, householder ? A man might come here with a drawn sword[2] and speak thus: 'In a moment, in a second, I will make all the living creatures in this Nāḷandā into one heap of flesh, one mass of flesh.' What do you think about this, householder ? Is that man able in one moment, one second, to make all the living creatures in this Nāḷandā into one heap of flesh, one mass of flesh ?"[3]

" Even ten men, revered sir, even twenty, thirty, forty men, even fifty men are not able in one moment, one second, to make all the

---

[1] *koṭṭhāsa*, *MA*. iii. 58. [2] *ukkhittāsika*, as at *S*. iv. 173.
[3] As at *M*. i. 404; *D*. i. 52.

---

things. A. L. Basham, *History of the Ājīvikas*, p. 16, translating: " He practices restraint with regard to water, he avoids all sin, by avoiding sin his sins are washed away, he is filled with the sense of all sin avoided," remarks that this is a " doubtful interpretation on the basis of Buddhaghosa." See also *Āyāraṅga Sutta*, I. 13 (translation at *S.B.E.* XXII).

living creatures in this Nāḷandā into one heap of flesh, one mass of flesh. How then can one insignificant man shine out at this ?"

"What do you think about this, householder ? A recluse or a brahman might come here, one of psychic power and attained to mastery of thought, and he might speak thus: 'I will reduce this Nāḷandā to cinders by one (act of) ill-will of mind.' What do you think about this, householder ? Is that recluse or brahman who is of psychic power and attained to mastery of thought, able to reduce this Nāḷandā to cinders by one (act of) ill-will of mind ?"

[**378**] "That recluse or brahman, revered sir, by one (act of) ill-will of mind is able to reduce even ten Nāḷandās to cinders, or even twenty, thirty, forty or fifty Nāḷandās. How then can one insignificant Nāḷandā shine out at this ?"

"Householder, householder ! Take care how you explain, householder. Your earlier (remarks) do not tally with your later, nor your later with your earlier. And yet these words were spoken by you, householder: 'I, revered sir, will speak as one grounded on the truth. Let us have some conversation here.' "

"Although, revered sir, the Lord speaks thus, yet wrong of body is the more blamable in the effecting of an evil deed, in the rolling on of an evil deed—wrong of speech is not like it, wrong of mind is not like it."

"What do you think about this, householder ? Have you heard that the (former) forests of Daṇḍaka,[1] Kālinga,[2] Mejjha[3] and Mātanga[4] became forests again ?"

"Yes, revered sir, I have heard that the (former) forests of Daṇḍaka, Kālinga, Mejjha and Mātanga became forests again."

"What do you think about this, householder ? Perhaps you have heard how it was that the (former) forests of Daṇḍaka, Kālinga, Mejjha and Mātanga became forests again ?"

"Yes, revered sir, I have heard that through (an act of) ill-will of mind on the part of seers the forests of Daṇḍaka, Kālinga, Mejjha and Mātanga became forests again."

"Householder, householder ! Take care how you explain, householder. Your earlier (remarks) do not tally with your later, nor your later with your earlier. And yet these words were spoken by you, householder: 'I, revered sir, will speak as one grounded on the truth. Let us have some conversation here.' "

---

[1] *Jā*. iii. 463, v. 133 *ff*., 267; *Miln*. 130.
[2] *Jā*. v. 144; *Miln*. 130.
[3] *Jā*. iv. 389, v. 267; *Miln*. 130.
[4] *Jā*. v. 114, 267; *Miln*. 130. Also known as Mejjhārañña; *cf*. *Jā*. iv. 388 *f*.

"I, revered sir, was pleased and satisfied[1] with the Lord's first illustration. But because I wanted to hear the Lord's diversified ways of putting questions,[2] I judged that I must make myself his adversary. It is excellent, revered sir; revered sir, it is excellent. As, revered sir, one might set upright what had been upset, or disclose what had been covered, or show the way to one who had gone astray, or bring an oil-lamp into the darkness so that those with vision might see material shapes—even so in many a figure has *dhamma* been made clear by the Lord. I, revered sir, am going to the Lord for refuge [**379**] and to *dhamma* and to the Order of monks. May the Lord accept me as a lay-disciple going for refuge from today forth for as long as life lasts."

"Now, householder, make a proper investigation. Proper investigation is right in the case of well-known men like yourself."[3]

"I, revered sir, am even exceedingly pleased and satisfied with that which the Lord has said to me: 'Now, householder, make a proper investigation . . . like yourself.' For if, revered sir, members of other sects had secured me as a disciple, they would have paraded a banner all round Nāḷandā, saying: 'The householder Upāli has joined our discipleship.' But then the Lord spoke to me thus: 'Now, householder, make a proper investigation. Proper investigation is right in the case of a well-known man like yourself.' So I, revered sir, for the second time am going to the Lord for refuge and to *dhamma* and to the Order of monks. May the Lord accept me as a lay-disciple going for refuge from today forth for as long as life lasts."

"For a long time, householder,[4] your family has been a well-spring to the Jains. You will bethink you to give alms to those that approach you?"

"I, revered sir, am even exceedingly pleased and satisfied that the Lord speaks to me thus: 'For a long time . . . to those that approach you?' I have heard, revered sir, that the recluse Gotama speaks thus: 'Gifts should be given to me only, not to others should gifts be given. Gifts should be given to my disciples only, not to the disciples of others should gifts be given. What is given to me is alone of great fruit, what is given to others is not of great fruit. What is given to my disciples is alone of great fruit, what is given to the disciples of others is not of great fruit.' But then the Lord urged

---

[1] Following passage also at *D.* ii. 352.

[2] *pañhapaṭibhāna*, as at *M.* i. 83.

[3] As at *Vin.* i. 236; *A.* iv. 185.

[4] Following passage at *Vin.* i. 236 *f.* (Sīha the general). And see *Dial.* i. 177, *n.* 3 for further references.

upon me giving to the Jains also. Indeed, revered sir, we shall know the right time for that. So I, revered sir, for the third time am going to the Lord for refuge and to *dhamma* and to the Order of monks. May the Lord accept me as a lay disciple going for refuge from today forth for as long as life lasts."

Then the Lord talked a progressive talk[1] to the householder Upāli, that is to say talk on giving, talk on moral habit, talk on heaven; he explained the peril, the vanity, the depravity of pleasures of the senses, the advantage in renouncing them. When the Lord knew that the mind of the householder Upāli [**380**] was ready, malleable, devoid of the hindrances, uplifted, pleased, then he explained to him that teaching on *dhamma* which the Awakened Ones have themselves discovered: ill, uprising, stopping, the Way. And as a clean cloth without black specks will easily take dye, even so, as the householder Upāli was (sitting) there on that very seat, *dhamma*-vision, dustless, stainless, arose to him that: whatever is of the nature to uprise, all that is of the nature to stop. Then the householder Upāli, as one who had seen *dhamma*, attained to *dhamma*, known *dhamma*, plunged into *dhamma*, who had crossed over doubt, put away uncertainty, who had attained without another's help to full confidence in the Teacher's instruction, spoke thus to the Lord: "Now, I, revered sir, must be going, I am very busy, there is much to be done."

"You, householder, must now do that for which you think it is the right time."

Then the householder Upāli, having rejoiced in what the Lord had said, having given thanks, rising from his seat, having greeted the Lord keeping his right side towards him, approached his own dwelling; having approached, he said to the door-keeper:

"Today, good door-keeper, I am closing the door to men and women Jains; but the door is open to the Lord's monks, nuns, men and women lay-disciples. If any Jain comes you should speak thus to him: 'Stand still, sir, do not enter. Today the householder Upāli has come to discipleship under the recluse Gotama; the door is closed to Jain men and women, but the door is open to the Lord's monks, nuns, men and women lay-disciples. If you, sir, need almsfood, stand still just where you are and they will bring it to you here.'"

"Very well, sir," the door-keeper answered the householder Upāli in assent.

Then Dīghatapassin the Jain heard that the householder Upāli

[1] As at *Vin.* i. 15-16, etc. See *B.D.* iv. 23, *n.* 1 for further references.

had come to discipleship under the recluse Gotama. Then Dīghatapassin the Jain approached Nātaputta the Jain; having approached, he spoke thus to Nātaputta the Jain: "I have heard, revered sir, that the householder Upāli has come to discipleship under the recluse Gotama."

"This is impossible, Tapassin, it cannot come to pass that the householder Upāli should come to discipleship under the recluse Gotama; but this situation exists: that the recluse Gotama might come to discipleship under the householder Upāli."

[**381**] And a second time . . . And a third time did Dīghatapassin the Jain speak thus to Nātaputta the Jain: "I have heard, revered sir, that the householder Upāli has come to discipleship under the recluse Gotama."

"This is impossible, Tapassin, it cannot come to pass that the householder Upāli should come to discipleship under the recluse Gotama; but this situation exists: that the recluse Gotama might come to discipleship under the householder Upāli."

"If you please, revered sir, I am going to find out whether or not the householder Upāli has come to discipleship under the recluse Gotama."

"Do go, Tapassin, and find out whether or not the householder Upāli has come to discipleship under the recluse Gotama."

Then Dīghatapassin the Jain approached the dwelling of the householder Upāli. The door-keeper saw Dīghatapassin the Jain coming in the distance; seeing him, he spoke thus to Dīghatapassin the Jain: "Stand still, revered sir, do not enter. Today the householder Upāli has come to discipleship under the recluse Gotama; the door is closed to Jain men and women, but the door is open to the Lord's monks, nuns, men and women lay-disciples. If you, revered sir, need almsfood, stand still just where you are and they will bring it to you here."

Having said: "Friend, I am not in need of almsfood," having turned back again, he approached Nātaputta the Jain; having approached, he spoke thus to Nātaputta the Jain: "It is quite true, revered sir, that Upāli the householder has come to discipleship under the recluse Gotama. As to that, I did not agree with you, revered sir, and I said: 'I am not pleased, revered sir, that the householder Upāli should refute the words of the recluse Gotama. For the recluse Gotama is deceitful, revered sir, he knows the 'enticing device' by which he entices disciples of other sects.' Now, revered sir, your householder Upāli has been enticed by the recluse Gotama by the 'enticing device.'"

"This is impossible, Tapassin, it cannot come to pass that the householder Upāli should have come to discipleship under the recluse Gotama; but this situation exists: that the recluse Gotama might come to discipleship under the householder Upāli." And a second time . . . And a third time Dīghatapassin the Jain spoke thus to Nātaputta the Jain: "It is quite true, revered sir, that the householder Upāli has come to discipleship under the recluse Gotama. [**382**] As to that, I did not agree with you, revered sir, and I said: 'I am not pleased, revered sir, that the householder Upāli should refute the words of the recluse Gotama . . .' . . . Now, revered sir, your householder Upāli has been enticed by the recluse Gotama by the 'enticing device.'"

"This is impossible, Tapassin, it cannot come to pass that the householder Upāli should come to discipleship under the recluse Gotama; but this situation exists: that the recluse Gotama might come to discipleship under the householder Upāli. But if you please, Tapassin, I am going to find out for myself whether or not the householder Upāli has come to discipleship under the recluse Gotama."

Then Nātaputta the Jain together with a great company of Jains approached the dwelling of the householder Upāli. The door-keeper saw Nātaputta the Jain coming in the distance; seeing him, he spoke thus to Nātaputta the Jain: "Stand still, revered sir, do not enter. Today the householder Upāli has come to discipleship under the recluse Gotama; the door is closed to Jain men and women, but the door is open to the Lord's monks, nuns, men and women lay-disciples. If you, revered sir, need almsfood, stand still just where you are and they will bring it to you here."

"Well then, good door-keeper, approach the householder Upāli; having approached, speak thus to the householder Upāli: 'Revered sir, Nātaputta the Jain is standing outside the porch of the door together with a large company of Jains, and he wishes to see you.'"

"Very good, revered sir," and the door-keeper, having answered Nātaputta the Jain in assent, approached the householder Upāli; having approached, he spoke thus to the householder Upāli: "Revered sir, Nātaputta the Jain . . . wishes to see you."

"Well then, good door-keeper, make ready seats in the middle hall with a door."[1]

[1] *MA*. iii. 93 says that if a house has seven porches the middle one is the fourth; if five porches the middle one is the third; if three porches, then the second porch with a door is called the middle hall with a door. *Cf.* below, p. 256.

"Yes, revered sir," and the door-keeper, having answered the householder Upāli in assent, having made ready seats in the middle hall with a door, approached the householder Upāli; having approached, he spoke thus to the householder Upāli: "Those seats, revered sir, have been made ready in the middle hall with a door. Do now that for which you think it is the right time."

Then the householder Upāli [**383**] approached the middle hall with a door; having approached and having sat down there on the chief and best, the choicest and finest seat, he summoned the door-keeper, and said: "Well now, good door-keeper, approach Nātaputta the Jain; having approached, speak thus to Nātaputta the Jain: 'The householder Upāli, revered sir, says: Do come in if you wish, revered sir.'"

"Very good, revered sir," and the door-keeper having answered the householder Upāli in assent, approached Nātaputta the Jain; having approached, he spoke thus to Nātaputta the Jain: "The householder Upāli, revered sir, says: 'Do come in if you wish, revered sir.'" Then Nātaputta the Jain together with the large company of Jains approached the middle hall with a door.

Then the householder Upāli, who was there first, saw Nātaputta the Jain coming in the distance; having seen him and gone out to meet him, having with his upper cloth dusted the chief and best, the choicest and finest seat, having taken possession of it, he sat down on it himself; and now when he himself had sat down on the chief and best, the choicest and finest seat, he spoke thus to Nātaputta the Jain: "There are seats, revered sir; do sit down if you wish."

When this had been said, Nātaputta the Jain spoke thus to the householder Upāli: "You, householder, are out of your mind; you, householder, are idiotic. Saying: 'I, revered sir, will refute the recluse Gotama', and having gone (to him), you have returned enmeshed in a great verbal tangle.[1] Householder, as a man, a gelder, having gone away, might return with removed testicles, or as a man, a gouger, having gone away, might return with removed eyeballs, even so did you, householder, saying: 'I, revered sir, will refute the recluse Gotama,' having gone (to him), return enmeshed in a great verbal tangle. You, householder, were enticed by the 'enticing device' of the recluse Gotama."

"Auspicious, revered sir, is this 'enticing device,' lovely, revered sir, is this 'enticing device.' If, revered sir, my dear kith and kin

---

[1] *vādasaṅghāṭapaṭimukka*. *Cf. taṇhāsaṅghāṭapaṭimukka* at *M*. i. 271.

could be enticed by this 'enticing,' for long it would be for the welfare and happiness of my dear kith and kin. And, revered sir, if all nobles could be enticed by this 'enticing,' for long it would be for the [384] welfare and happiness of all nobles also. And, revered sir, if all brahmans . . . all merchants . . . all workers could be enticed by this 'enticing,' for long it would be for the welfare and happiness of all workers also. And, revered sir, if the world, with its *devas*, its Māras, its Brahmās, creation with its recluses and brahmans, its *devas* and men, could be enticed by this 'enticing,' for long it would be for the welfare and happiness of this world with its *devas*, its Māras, its Brahmās, of creation with its recluses and brahmans, its *devas* and men. Well then, revered sir, I will make you a parable, for by a parable some intelligent persons here understand the meaning of what has been said.[1]

Once upon a time, revered sir, a certain brahman, worn, old, full of years, had a young brahman wife, pregnant and nearing her confinement. Then, sir, that young brahman woman spoke thus to that brahman: 'Go you, brahman, having bought a young male monkey at a shop, bring him along so that he can be a playmate for my little boy.' When this had been said, revered sir, that brahman spoke thus to that young brahman woman: 'Wait, my dear, until you have given birth. If you, my dear, give birth to a little boy, then having bought a young male monkey at that shop, I will bring him along so that he can be a playmate for your little boy. But if you, my dear, give birth to a little girl, having bought a young female monkey at that shop, I will bring her along so that she can be a playmate for your little girl.' And a second time . . . And a third time that young brahman woman spoke thus to that brahman: 'Go you, brahman, having bought a young male monkey at that shop, bring him along so that he can be a playmate for my little boy.' Then, revered sir, that brahman, being passionately in love with that young brahman woman, having bought a young male monkey at that shop, and having brought him back, spoke thus to that young brahman woman: 'My dear, this is the young male monkey, bought for you at that shop, [385] and who has come to be a playmate for your little boy.' When this had been said, revered sir, that young brahman woman said to that brahman: 'Do you go, brahman, and taking that young male monkey, approach Rattapāṇi, the dyer's son; having approached, speak thus to Rattapāṇi, the dyer's son: Good

[1] As at *M.* i. 148.

Rattapāṇi, I want this young male monkey dyed a daubed yellow colour, thoroughly pressed all round,[1] and made smooth on each side.' Then, revered sir, that brahman, being passionately in love with that young brahman woman, taking that young male monkey, approached Rattapāṇi, the dyer's son; having approached, he spoke thus to Rattapāṇi, the dyer's son: 'Good Rattapāṇi, I want this young male monkey dyed a daubed yellow colour, thoroughly pressed all round, and made smooth on each side.'

When this had been said, Rattapāṇi, the dyer's son, spoke thus to that brahman: 'Yes, sir, this young male monkey can take colouring, but he can't take pressing or smoothing.' Even so, revered sir, is this doctrine[2] of the foolish Jains, for it takes colouring from fools but not from the wise[3], it does not take (kindly) to examination, it does not take (kindly) to smoothing. Then, revered sir, after a time that brahman, taking a new pair of garments, approached Rattapāṇi, the dyer's son; having approached, he spoke thus to Rattapāṇi, the dyer's son: 'Good Rattapāṇi, I want this new pair of garments dyed a daubed yellow colour, thoroughly pressed all round, and made smooth on each side.' When this had been said, Rattapāṇi, the dyer's son, spoke thus to that brahman: 'Yes, sir, this new pair of garments of yours can take the colouring and it can take the pressing and it can take the smoothing.' Even so, revered sir, is the doctrine of this Lord, perfected one, fully Self-Awakened One, for it takes its colouring from the wise, not from fools, and it takes (kindly) to examination and it takes (kindly) to smoothing."

"Householder, this company including the rulers know thus: Upāli the householder is a disciple of Nātaputta the Jain. Householder, whose disciple do we understand you to be?" When this had been said, the householder Upāli, rising from his seat, having arranged his upper cloth over one shoulder, [**386**] having saluted the Lord with joined palms, spoke thus to Nātaputta the Jain: "Well then, revered sir, hear whose disciple I am:

Of the wise,[4] whose confusion is gone, whose mental barrenness
is split asunder,[5] who has won to victory,

---

[1] Said of a robe, below, and at *S.* ii. 282.

[2] *vāda.*

[3] *MA.* iii. 95 says that neither the doctrine of the Jains nor another useless way of speaking is liked in the (Mahā-) Bhārata and the Rāmâyana, and so on.

[4] *dhīra. MA.* iii. 96 equates this with *paṇḍicca, paṇḍita.*

[5] *Cf. M.* Sta. 16.

Who is without ill,[1] of very even mind, of grown moral habit,
of lovely wisdom,
The 'All-within,'[2] the stainless—of this Lord the disciple am I.

Of him who has no doubts, rejoicing, the material things of the
world renounced,[3] of joyful sympathy,
Who is a recluse, a human being, in his last body, a man,
The peerless, the dustless—of this Lord the disciple am I.

Of him who is sure, skilled, the leader away,[4] the excellent
charioteer,
The matchless, the shining, of no incertitude,[5] bringing light,
Breaking pride, the hero[6]—of this Lord the disciple am I.

Of the noblest of men, immeasurable, deep,[7] won to knowledge,[8]
Bringer of security, a knower[9], on *dhamma* standing, self-
controlled,
Who has gone beyond attachment, who is freed—of this Lord
the disciple am I.

Of the supreme one,[10] whose lodgings are remote, who has
destroyed the fetters, who is freed,
Who speaks amiably, who is purified, the flag laid low,[11] pas-
sionless,
Tamed, without impediments[12]—of this Lord the disciple am I.

---

[1] *anigha*. *MA*. iii. 96 says *niddukkha; cf. Jā*. iii. 443; *PvA*. 230; *DhA*. iii. 454; *UdA*. 370. A different explanation is given at *SnA*. i. 25.

[2] *vessantara*, occurring also at *It*. p. 32 (*vissantara*). *MA*. iii. 96 explains as "poised, having crossed the unevenness (v.l. *visa*, poison) of passion, etc." See *Min. Anth*. II. 139, *n*. 1.

[3] *vantalokāmisa*, as at *Dhp*. 378. The *lokāmisa* are identified at *MA*. iii. 97 with *kāmaguṇa*, as in the *Nivāpasutta* (*M*. Sta. 25).

[4] *venayika*, the averter, or diverter of passions, etc., or as at *MA*. iii. 97 the one who disciplines beings. Used in a derogatory sense of "the recluse Gotama" at *M*. i. 140.

[5] *nikkaṅkha*, as at *S*. ii. 84. [6] *vīra*. *MA*. iii. 97 reads *viriya*, energy.

[7] *Cf*. *M*. i. 487 where the Tathāgata is deep (or unfathomable) and immeasurable as the great ocean.

[8] *monapattassā ti ñāṇaṃ pattassa*, *MA*. iii. 97.

[9] *veda*. This may mean that he is Knowledge itself. *MA*. iii. 97 says *vedo vuccati ñāṇaṃ*.

[10] *nāga*, supreme in his solitude, far from evil; *cf*. *S*. i. 28.

[11] *pannadhaja; cf*. *M*. i. 139, *A*. iii. 84. One whose fight is over.

[12] *nippapañca; cf*. *Dh*. 254; *M*. i. 65.

Of the seventh seer,[1] trust gone,[2] of threefold wisdom, Brahma-attained,[3]
Washen, skilled in the lines,[4] tranquil, who discovered knowledge.
Breaker of the citadel, Sakka[5]—of this Lord the disciple am I.

Of the pure one, whose self is developed, who has attained the attainable,[6] the expounder,
The one with recollection, whose vision is clear,[7] not bent on passion,[8] without hatred,
Impassible, attained to mastery—of this Lord the disciple am I.

---

[1] *MA.* iii. 97 says that of the six seers (Buddhas) who have arisen since Vipassin, he is the seventh. *Cf. Sn.* 356; *S.* i. 192; *Thag.* 1240. *Fur. Dial.* i. 277, *n.* refers us to *Dīgha* Sutta 14 for a pioneer list of seven Buddhas "amplified later (*Jā.* i. 44) by inventing eighteen extra predecessors for Gotama, so that he became the twenty-fifth." *Cf. SnA.* i. 351 and *Budv.*

[2] *Sn.* 957. *Cf.* "Go not by hearsay" in the discourse to the Kālāmas.

[3] *Brahmapattassa. Cf. D.* iii. 84, *It.* p. 57, etc., *brahmabhūta.*

[4] *Cf. D.* i. 88; *A.* i. 163; *M.* ii. 133 where the word *padaka* occurs among the items of a brahman's knowledge. *MA.* iii. 98 says, "having supplied the syllables, he is skilled in making verses and lines (*pada*)." On *pada,* a line, see *B.D.* ii. 190 *f.* where it refers to a line of *dhamma;* and as such I take it here. But I also suggest that *padaka* has a reference to the Tathāgata's footprints as in *M.* Sutta 27.

[5] *purindada Sakka. MA.* iii. 98 takes these as separate terms, the former meaning the bestower of the gift of *dhamma;* and the latter "able, strong, capable" (*samattha*) which of course is one meaning of *sakka.* But *purindada* is also an epithet of Sakka, and Sakka=Indra. *Cf. S.* i. 230 where *purindada* is explained as "giver from town to town." A. K. Coomaraswamy, *Hinduism and Buddhism,* p. 76 says "insofar as the Buddha's 'life' and deeds are described, it is the doings of Brahma as Agni and Indra that are being retold," and see *loc. cit. n.* 256, where A. K. C. says that "in *M.* i. 386 the Buddha seems to be addressed as Indra." At *Budv.* xvi. 9 the Buddha says that in the time of the Buddha Dhammadassin he was Sakka *purindada.* See also C. E. Godage, *The Place of Indra in Early Buddhism,* p. 49: Purindada is a distortion of Vedic Puraṃdara (fort-shatterer), when the clouds were fortresses. To shatter the clouds means to obtain the life-giving rains (*cf. RV.* I. 102. 7). Siva (Rudra) is Tripurântaka, he who puts an end to the three towns (built in the earth, the middle space and the firmament by a tyrant-demon, *asura*). See *Indo-Aryan Mythology,* vol. I, pp. 34, 248, 353, 376, 379, 384.

[6] *pattipatta,* as at *Sn.* 536; *It.* p. 32. *MA.* iii. 98, "who has attained those excellent things that must be attained, *pattabbā.*"

[7] *Cf. Sn.* 349; *A.* iv. 244, *vipassin.*

[8] Both *P.E.D.* and *C.P.D.* translate *anabhinata* as above. *MA.* iii. 98 explains by *arahatta.*

Of him who has gone to the highest, the meditator, inwardly unobstructed,[1] cleansed,
The unattached, the unaiming,[2] the aloof, the attainer of the highest,
The crossed over, the helper across—of this Lord the disciple am I.

Of the calmed, the one of extensive wisdom, of great wisdom, without greed,[3]
The Tathāgata, the Well-farer, incomparable person, unequalled,
The confident, the accomplished—of this Lord the disciple am I.

Of the cutter off of craving, the Awakened One, obscurity gone,[4] unstained,
Worthy of offerings, the *yakkha*,[5] the best of persons, beyond measure,[6]
Great, attained to the height of glory—of this Lord the disciple am I."

"But when were these splendours of the recluse Gotama collected[7] by you, householder ?"

"Revered sir, it as if there were a great heap of flowers, of different flowers,[8] [387] which a clever garland-maker or his apprentice might string into a variegated garland; even so, revered sir, this Lord has many splendours, many hundreds of splendours. And who, revered sir, would not give praise[9] to one deserving praise ?"

---

[1] *ananugatantara*. *MA*. iii. 98 refers this to the unobstruction of the mind by the *kilesas*.

[2] *appahīna*. No comment at *MA*. iii. 98. *C.P.D.* refers the word in this passage to *appaṇihita*, aimless, not bent on anything; and *s.v. appabhīta* (not terrified) gives this as Siamese conjecture (?) for the *appahīna* of this passage. I think the corruption, whatever it is, is due to a confusion of thought between (1) being unattached (to pleasures) and not aiming at them or directing the mind towards them, and (2) not being terrified, because of being aloof from them.

[3] *I.e.* without greed for the five sensory pleasures.

[4] *vītadhūma*, without smoke.

[5] spirit, as in *Sn*. 478, 876, *yakkhassa suddhi*, "the cleansing of the spirit."

[6] *atula*, which cannot be weighed, imponderable.

[7] *saññūḷha*; *cf*. *D*. ii. 267. [8] *Cf*. *Miln*. 347.

[9] "Splendour" and "praise" are both *vaṇṇa*.

But because Nātaputta the Jain could not bear the eulogy of the Lord, then and there hot blood issued from his mouth.[1]

Discourse with Upāli:
The Sixth

57. DISCOURSE ON THE CANINE ASCETIC
(Kukkuravatikasutta)

THUS have I heard: At one time the Lord was staying among the Koḷiyans; the market town of the Koḷiyans was called Haliddavasana.[2] Then Puṇṇa, a Koḷiyan who was a bovine ascetic,[3] and Seniya who was an unclothed canine ascetic,[4] approached the Lord; having approached, Puṇṇa the Koḷiyan who was the bovine ascetic, after greeting the Lord, sat down at a respectful distance. But Seniya the unclothed canine ascetic, having exchanged greetings with the Lord and conversed in a friendly and courteous way, sat down at a respectful distance doubling up like a dog.[5] As he was sitting down at a respectful distance, Puṇṇa the Koḷiyan, the bovine ascetic, spoke thus to the Lord:

---

[1] *MA.* iii. 99-100 says that he fell down, was taken outside the town on a litter and then on to Pāvā, where he died, for few beings are able to live after discharging blood. According to the tradition here, Nigaṇṭha Nātaputta predeceased Gotama. *M.* Sta. 104 and *D.* Sta. 29, 33 all also agree that he died at Pāvā while Gotama was alive, but they do not agree upon where Gotama was at the time of Nātaputta's death.

[2] At the time when it was building people wore golden coloured garments, *haliddavatthanivatthā*, to celebrate the "lunar mansion." *Vasana* means both a garment and a habitation. The name Haliddavasana occurs also at *S.* v. 115.

[3] *govatika.* Having undertaken the "cow-practice," *go-vata,* putting a horn on his head and tying on a tail, he went about grazing with cows, *MA.* iii. 100.

[4] *kukkuravatika,* having undertaken the "dog-practice," he did everything done by a dog. See *D.* iii. 6-7 for the habits of Korakkhattiya, the unclothed canine ascetic.

[5] *MA.* iii. 100, like a dog, *sunakha,* in his master's presence. Having scratched the ground with his two feet he sits down hunched, and greets the Lord by saying, "I will do what a dog does"; then having scratched the ground with his two hands, shaking his head, he says *bhun bhun,* and doubling in his hands and feet, he sits down like a dog.

" Revered sir, this Seniya, an unclothed canine ascetic, is a doer of things hard to do—he eats lying on the ground, a canine practice which has been carried out in full by him for a long time. What is his bourn,[1] what his future state ?"

" Enough, Puṇṇa, let this be, do not ask me this." And a second time . . . And a third time Puṇṇa the Koḷiyan, the bovine ascetic, spoke thus to the Lord: " Revered sir, this Seniya, an unclothed canine ascetic, is a doer of things hard to do—he eats lying on the ground, a canine practice which has been carried out in full by him for a long time. What is his bourn, what his future state ?"

" Although I, Puṇṇa, did not really countenance your (question) and said: ' Enough, Puṇṇa, let this be, do not ask me this,' nevertheless I will explain to you. Here, Puṇṇa, someone develops the canine practice completely and constantly, he develops the canine habits[2] completely and constantly, he develops the canine mentality completely [**388**] and constantly, he develops the canine behaviour[3] completely and constantly. Having developed the canine practice . . . the canine habits . . . the canine mentality . . . the canine behaviour completely and constantly, he, on the breaking up of the body after dying, arises in companionship with dogs. But if he should have a view like this: ' I, through this habit or practice or austerity or chastity,[4] will become a *deva*[5] or a (lesser) *deva* '[6]—that is a wrong view on his part. I, Puṇṇa, say that there is one of two bourns for one of wrong view: either Niraya Hell or animal birth. So it is, Puṇṇa, that the canine practice, on prospering, leads to companionship with dogs, on failing, to Niraya Hell."

When this had been said, Seniya the unclothed canine ascetic cried out and burst into tears. Then the Lord spoke thus to Puṇṇa the Koḷiyan, the bovine ascetic:

" I did not countenance this (question) of yours, Puṇṇa, (so) I said: ' Enough, Puṇṇa, let this be, do not ask me this.' "

" I, revered sir, am not crying because the Lord speaks thus about me. It is, revered sir, because this canine practice has been carried

---

[1] *gati*, going, destination, karmic course.

[2] *kukkurasīla*. *MA*. iii. 101 explains as *kukkurācāra*.

[3] *kukkurākappa*, in standing, walking, sitting, lying down, baring the teeth on seeing actual dogs.

[4] So explained at *MA*. iii. 101. *Brahmacariya* is also the higher life.

[5] A Sakka or Suyāma, etc.

[6] A certain *deva* in the second or third position. For *devaññatara*, *cf*. *S*. iv. 180, *A*. iv. 461.

out in full by me for a long time. Revered sir, this Puṇṇa the Koḷiyan is a bovine ascetic, and the bovine practice has been carried out in full by him for a long time. What is his bourn, what his future state ?'

"Enough, Seniya, let this be, do not ask me this." And a second time . . . And a third time Seniya the unclothed canine ascetic spoke thus to the Lord: "Revered sir, this Puṇṇa the Koḷiyan is a bovine ascetic, and the bovine practice has been carried out in full by him for a long time. What is his bourn, what his future state ?"

"Although, Seniya, I did not really countenance your (question) and said: 'Enough, Seniya, let this be, do not ask me this,' nevertheless I will explain to you. Here, Seniya, someone develops the bovine practice completely and constantly, he develops the bovine habits completely and constantly, he develops the bovine mentality completely and constantly, he develops the bovine behaviour completely and constantly. Having developed the bovine practice . . . the bovine habits . . . the bovine mentality . . . the bovine behaviour completely and constantly, he, on the breaking up of the body after dying, arises in companionship with cattle. But if [**389**] he should have a view like this: 'I, through this habit or practice or austerity or chastity, will become a *deva* or a (lesser) *deva* '—that is a wrong view on his part. I, Seniya, say that there is one of two bourns for one of wrong view: either Niraya Hell or animal birth. So it is, Seniya, that the bovine practice, on prospering, leads to companionship with cattle, on failing, to Niraya Hell."

When this had been said, Puṇṇa the Koḷiyan, the bovine ascetic, cried out and burst into tears. Then the Lord spoke thus to Seniya, the unclothed canine ascetic:

"I did not countenance this (question) of yours, Seniya, (so) I said: 'Enough, Seniya, let this be, do not ask me this.' "

"I, revered sir, am not crying because the Lord speaks thus about me. It is, revered sir, because this bovine practice has been carried out in full by me for a long time. Revered sir, I have trust[1] in the Lord thus: The Lord is able so to teach *dhamma* that I might give up this bovine practice, and Seniya the unclothed canine ascetic might give up that canine practice."

"Well then, Puṇṇa, listen, pay careful attention, and I will speak."

"Yes, revered sir," Puṇṇa the Koḷiyan, the bovine ascetic, answered the Lord in assent. The Lord spoke thus:

---

[1] *pasanna*, satisfaction, pleasure, approval, appreciation.

"Puṇṇa, these four (kinds of) deeds[1] are made known by me, having realised them by my own super-knowledge. What four? There is, Puṇṇa, the deed that is dark, dark in result. There is, Puṇṇa, the deed that is bright, bright in result. There is, Puṇṇa, the deed that is dark and bright, dark and bright in result. There is, Puṇṇa, the deed that is not dark (and) not bright, neither dark nor bright in result, the deed that conduces to the destruction of deeds.[2]

And what, Puṇṇa, is the deed that is dark, dark in result? As to this, Puṇṇa, someone effects[3] an activity of body[4] that is harmful, he effects an activity of speech that is harmful, he effects an activity of mind that is harmful. He, having effected an activity of body that is harmful . . . activity of speech that is harmful, having effected an activity of mind that is harmful, arises in a world that is harmful. Because he has uprisen in a world that is harmful, harmful sensory impingements assail him. He, being assailed by harmful sensory impingements, experiences a harmful feeling, without exception painful, even as do creatures [**390**] in Niraya Hell. In this way,[5] Puṇṇa, there is the uprising of a being from what has come to be[6]; he uprises according to what he does[7]; when he has uprisen sensory impingements assail him. So I speak thus, Puṇṇa: Creatures are heirs to deeds.[8] This, Puṇṇa, is called the deed that is dark, dark in result.

And what, Puṇṇa, is the deed that is bright, bright in result? As to this, Puṇṇa, someone effects an activity of body that is harmless . . . an activity of speech . . . an activity of mind that is harmless. He, having effected an activity of body . . . an activity of speech . . . an activity of mind that is harmless, arises in a world that is harmless. Because he has uprisen in a world that is harmless, harmless sensory impingements assail him. He, being assailed by harmless sensory impingements, experiences a harmless feeling, without exception pleasant, even as do the Ever-Radiant *devas*. In this way, Puṇṇa, there is the uprising of a being from what has come

---

[1] See *A.* ii. 230 *ff.*, and *G.S.* ii. 238 *f.*; *cf. D.* iii. 230, *Netti.* 98, 159, *Asl.* 89.

[2] On the Jains' mistaken conception of the importance and consequences of this, see *M.* i. 93.

[3] *abhisaṅkharoti.* *Cf. A.* i. 122 *f.*, ii. 230.

[4] *kāyasaṅkhāra.* *Cf. M.* i. 301; and see *M.L.S.* i. Intr. p. xxiv.

[5] This sentence and the next are omitted at *A.* ii. 230, but occur at *A.* v. 289 *ff.*

[6] *bhūtā bhūtassa upapatti hoti.*

[7] *Cf. Chānd. Up.* 5. 10. 7; *Bṛhad. Up.* 4. 4. 5.

[8] *Cf. A.* iii. 72, 186, v. 289.

to be; he uprises according to what he does; when he has uprisen sensory impingements assail him. So I speak thus, Puṇṇa: Creatures are heirs to deeds. This, Puṇṇa, is called the deed that is bright, bright in result.

And what, Puṇṇa, is the deed that is dark and bright, dark and bright in result? As to this, Puṇṇa, someone effects an activity of body that is harmful and harmless . . . an activity of speech . . . an activity of mind that is harmful and harmless. He, having effected an activity of body . . . an activity of speech . . . an activity of mind that is harmful and harmless, arises in a world that is harmful and harmless. Because he has uprisen in a world that is harmful and harmless, harmful and harmless sensory impingements assail him. He, being assailed by harmful and harmless sensory impingements, experiences a feeling that is harmful and harmless, partially pleasant and painful, even as do men and some *devas* and some in the sorrowful state.[1] In this way, Puṇṇa, there is the uprising of a being from what has come to be; he uprises according to what he does; when he has uprisen sensory impingements assail him. So I speak thus, Puṇṇa: Creatures are heirs to deeds.[2] This, Puṇṇa, is called the deed that is dark and bright, dark and bright in result.

[391] And what, Puṇṇa, is the deed that is not dark (and) not bright, neither dark nor bright in result, the deed that conduces to the destruction of deeds? Where, Puṇṇa, there is the will[3] to get rid of that deed that is dark, dark in result, and the will to get rid of that deed that is bright, bright in result, and the will to get rid of that deed that is dark and bright, dark and bright in result, this, Puṇṇa, is called the deed that is not dark (and) not bright, neither dark nor bright in result, the deed that conduces to the destruction of deeds. These, Puṇṇa, are the four (kinds of) deeds made known by me, having realised them by my own super-knowledge."

When this had been said, Puṇṇa the Koḷiyan, the bovine ascetic, spoke thus to the Lord: "It is excellent, revered sir, it is excellent, revered sir. It is as if, revered sir . . . May the Lord accept me as a lay-disciple going for refuge from this day forth for as long as life lasts."

But Seniya the unclothed canine ascetic spoke thus to the Lord: "It is excellent, revered sir, it is excellent, revered sir. It is as if, revered sir, one might set upright what had been upset, or might

---

[1] *Cf. M.* i. 73, of those of spontaneous uprising.

[2] This paragraph, except the first and last sentences, is quoted at *Kvu.* 522.

[3] *cetanā.*

disclose what was covered, or show the way to one who had gone astray, or bring an oil-lamp into the darkness so that those with vision might see material shapes—even so in many a figure has *dhamma* been made clear by the Lord. Thus I, revered sir, am going to the Lord for refuge and to *dhamma* and to the Order of monks. Revered sir, may I receive the going forth in the Lord's presence, may I receive ordination ?"

" Seniya, if a former member of another sect wishes for the going forth in this *dhamma* and discipline, wishes for ordination, he undertakes probation for four months[1]; at the end of the four months the monks, if they so decide, may let him go forth, may ordain him into the status of a monk; but even here differences among individuals are known to me."[2]

" If, revered sir, former members of other sects, wishing for the going forth in this *dhamma* and discipline, wishing for ordination, undertake probation for four months, and if at the end of the four months the monks, if they so decide, let them go forth, ordain them into the status of a monk, then will I undertake probation for four years[3]; at the end of the four years the monks, if they so decide, may let me go forth, may ordain me into the status of a monk." But Seniya, the unclothed canine ascetic, received the going forth in the Lord's presence, he received ordination.[4]

Soon after he was ordained the venerable Seniya, dwelling alone, aloof, [**392**] diligent, ardent, self-resolute, in no long time having realised here-now by his own super-knowledge that matchless culmination of the Brahma-faring for the sake of which young men of family rightly go forth from home into homelessness, entering on it, abided in it. And he knew: Destroyed is birth, brought to a close the Brahma-faring, done is what was to be done, there is no more of being such or so. So was the venerable Seniya one of the perfected ones.

Discourse on the Canine Ascetic:
The Seventh

---

[1] Laid down at *Vin.* i. 69. See also *M.* i. 494, 512; *D.* i. 176; *S.* ii. 21; *Sn.* p. 101-102.

[2] One meriting probation but not another, *MA.* iii. 106; *VinA.* v. 990. For as *SnA.* ii. 436 (citing *Vin.* i. 71) points out, the fire-worshipping matted hair ascetics are exempt from the four months' probation.

[3] The same willingness to undertake probation for four years, instead of the four prescribed months, is manifested *e.g.* by Vacchagotta at *M.* i. 494, and Māgandiya at *M.* i. 512.

[4] *MA.* iii. 106 says that the Lord thought that Seniya, on account of his

58. DISCOURSE TO PRINCE ABHAYA

(Abhayarājakumārasutta)

THUS have I heard: At one time the Lord was staying near Rājagaha in the Bamboo Grove at the squirrels' feeding place. Then Prince Abhaya[1] approached Nātaputta the Jain; having approached, having greeted Nātaputta the Jain, he sat down at a respectful distance. Nātaputta the Jain spoke thus[2] to Prince Abhaya as he was sitting down at a respectful distance: " Come you, Prince, refute the recluse Gotama so that a lovely reputation goes forth about you to the effect that the recluse Gotama, of such great psychic power, of such great majesty, was refuted by Prince Abhaya."

" But how can I, revered sir, refute the recluse Gotama who is of such great psychic power, of such great majesty ?"

" Come you, Prince, approach the recluse Gotama; having approached, speak thus to the recluse Gotama: ' Now, revered sir, could a Tathāgata utter a speech that is disliked by others, disagreeable to them ?' If the recluse Gotama on being questioned by you thus should answer: ' Prince, a Tathāgata could utter a speech that is disliked by others, disagreeable to them,' then you should speak to him thus: ' But then, where is the difference, revered sir, between you and an average person ? For an average person could also utter a speech that is disliked by others, disagreeable to them.' But if the recluse Gotama, on being questioned thus by you, should answer: ' Prince, a Tathāgata could not utter a speech **[393]** that is disliked by others, disagreeable to them,' then you should speak to him thus: ' Then how is it, revered sir, that when Devadatta was told by you: " Devadatta is doomed to a sorrowful way[3] (after death),

---

[1] Son of King Bimbisāra. [2] *Cf. S.* iv. 323.

[3] *āpāyika*, a man in " Misery." These and the following three expressions are also found at *Vin.* ii. 202, *It.* p. 85, *A.* iii. 402, iv. 160, etc. *Cf. Vin. Texts* iii. 262, *n.* 3.

---

keen desire, did not merit probation. But he was not ordained (by the Lord himself) by the *ehi bhikkhu* formula; he was " received " or allowed to go forth by a monk acting on the Lord's instructions, and then brought into the Lord's presence.

Devadatta is doomed to Niraya Hell, Devadatta is fixed for a *kalpa*,[1] Devadatta is incurable,"[2] Devadatta was angry and displeased with you for these words?' Prince, the recluse Gotama, on being asked this double-edged question[3] by you will neither be able to spew out nor swallow down[4] (the puzzle). Just like an iron hook stuck in a man's throat that he can neither spew out nor swallow down, even so, Prince, the recluse Gotama, on being asked this double-edged question by you, will neither be able to spew out nor swallow down (the puzzle)."

"Very well, revered sir," and Prince Abhaya having answered Nātaputta the Jain in assent, rising from his seat, having greeted Nātaputta the Jain keeping his right side towards him, approached the Lord; having approached, having greeted the Lord, he sat down at a respectful distance. After looking at the sun, it occurred to Prince Abhaya as he was sitting down at a respectful distance: "It is not the right time today to refute the Lord, but tomorrow I, in my own house, will refute the Lord," and he spoke thus to the Lord: "Revered sir, may the Lord consent to take a meal with me on the morrow with three others?"[5] The Lord consented by becoming silent. Then Prince Abhaya, having understood the Lord's consent, rising from his seat, having greeted the Lord, departed keeping his right side towards him. Then the Lord, at the end of that night, having dressed in the early morning, taking his bowl and robe, approached Prince Abhaya's dwelling; having approached, he sat down on the appointed seat. Then Prince Abhaya with his own hand served and satisfied the Lord with sumptuous solid and soft

---

[1] *kappaṭṭha*, endures for an eon in these states (Misery and Hell), incapable of winning out of them to happier births during this eon, *kappa*.

[2] *atekiccha*. Mrs. Rhys Davids, *G.S.* iii. p. xiv refers to *atekiccha* as having "the fearful implication, possibly monkish, of a Buddhist hell that is unending," or, as *MA*. iii. 108 says, *buddhasahassena*, while a thousand Buddhas come and go. Certainly the Hell, for Devadatta, endures as long as the *kalpa*, but the *kalpa*, as in Hindu philosophy, is regarded as subject to "involution," absorption, rest, before it evolves or manifests again—and endlessly again. Only the major, almost symbolical events are repeated in each *kalpa;* the details vary, so after this *kalpa* Devadatta is no longer doomed to states of misery and Hell.

[3] *Cf. Miln.* 108, 162; *K.S.* iv. 229, *n.*, "the horns of a dilemma."

[4] *Cf. Miln.* 5.

[5] *attacatuttho*, himself as the fourth, as at *M.* iii. 145, *A.* iii. 36. *MA.* iii. 109 says Abhaya did not ask more in case they quarrelled, nor did he ask them individually lest he was reproached for miserliness, but he compromised by asking three with Gotama as the fourth.

foods. Then when the Lord had eaten and had withdrawn his hand from the bowl, Prince Abhaya, taking a low seat, sat down at a respectful distance. Prince Abhaya, sitting down at a respectful distance, spoke thus to the Lord:

" Now, revered sir, could a Tathāgata utter a speech disliked by others, disagreeable to them?"

" Is not this one-sided,[1] Prince?"

" At this point, revered sir, the Jains have lost."[2]

" Why do you speak thus, Prince: **[394]** ' At this point, revered sir, the Jains have lost'?"

" Now, I, revered sir, approached Nātaputta the Jain; having approached, having greeted Nātaputta the Jain, I sat down at a respectful distance. Nātaputta the Jain spoke thus to me, revered sir, as I was sitting down at a respectful distance: ' Come you, Prince, refute the recluse Gotama . . . (*as above*) . . . Just like an iron hook stuck in a man's throat that he can neither spew out nor swallow down, even so, Prince, the recluse Gotama, on being asked this double-edged question by you, will neither be able to spew out nor swallow down (the puzzle).' "

At that time an innocent little baby boy was lying on its back[3] on Prince Abhaya's knees. Then the Lord spoke thus to Prince Abhaya: " What **[395]** do you think about this, Prince? If this boy owing to your carelessness or that of his nurse were to put a stick or stone into his mouth, what would you do for him?"

" I would get it out, revered sir. And if I, revered sir, were not able to get it out at once, then taking hold of his head with my left hand, crooking a finger, I would get it out with my right hand, even though it were with blood. What is the reason for this? Revered sir, I have compassion for the boy."

" Even so, Prince, whatever speech the Tathāgata knows to be not fact, not true, not connected with the goal, and that is not liked by others, disagreeable to them, that speech the Tathāgata does not utter. And whatever speech a Tathāgata knows to be fact, true, but not connected with the goal, and not liked by others, disagree-

---

[1] *ekaṁsena.* No doubt referring to the two-edged question the Jains planned to ask Gotama so as to trip him up. *Cf. ekaṁsavādo* at *M.* ii. 197.

[2] *anassuṁ*, are frustrated. *MA.* iii. 109 says *naṭṭhā*, lost, destroyed, perished. The meaning is that in view of this counter-question of Gotama's, the Jains are already defeated as the further questions they had devised would now be meaningless.

[3] *Cf. A.* iii. 6. For the opening phrase, *cf. M.* i. 324, ii. 24.

able to them, neither does the Tathāgata utter that speech. And whatever speech the Tathāgata knows to be fact, true, connected with the goal, but not liked by others, disagreeable to them, the Tathāgata is aware of the right time for explaining that speech. Whatever speech the Tathāgata knows to be not fact, not true, not connected with the goal, but that is liked by others, agreeable to them, that speech the Tathāgata does not utter. And whatever speech the Tathāgata knows to be fact, true, but not connected with the goal, yet liked by others, agreeable to them, neither does the Tathāgata utter that speech. And whatever speech the Tathāgata knows to be fact, true, connected with the goal, and liked by others, agreeable to them, the Tathāgata is aware of the right time for explaining that speech. What is the reason for this? It is, Prince, that the Tathāgata has compassion for creatures."

"Revered sir, if those who are learned nobles and learned brahmans and learned householders and learned recluses approach the Tathāgata and ask him a question they have constructed—has the Lord already reflected in his mind on this, thinking: 'Whoever, having approached me, questions me like this, then, asked thus, I will answer them thus,' or does (the answer) occur to a Tathāgata immediately?"[1]

"Well then, Prince, I will ask you a question in return. As it may please you, so may you answer it. What do you think about this, Prince? Are you skilled in the various parts of a chariot?"

"Yes, revered sir, I am skilled in the various parts of a chariot."

"What do you think about this, Prince? If those who have approached you should ask thus: 'What is the name of this particular part of the chariot?' would you have already [**396**] reflected on this in your mind, thinking: 'If those who have approached me should ask thus, then I will answer them thus,' or would (the answer) occur to you immediately?"

"Because, revered sir, I am a renowned charioteer, skilled in the various parts of a chariot, all the particular parts of a chariot are fully known to me, so (the answer) would occur to me immediately."

"Even so, Prince, if those who are learned nobles and learned brahmans and learned householders and learned recluses approach the Tathāgata and ask him a question they have constructed, (the answer) occurs to the Tathāgata immediately. What is the reason

---

[1] *ṭhānaso*, both on the spot (*ṭhānuppattika*) and at that moment (*taṁ khaṇaṁ*). It means "without an interval or a cause (of change), at once, immediately, spontaneously, impromptu." *P.E.D.*

for this? It is, Prince, that the constitution of *dhamma*[1] is fully penetrated by the Tathāgata, and because of his full penetration of the constitution of *dhamma* (the answer) occurs to the Tathāgata immediately."

When this had been said, Prince Abhaya spoke thus to the Lord: "It is excellent, revered sir, it is excellent, revered sir. It is as if one might set upright what had been upset, or might disclose what had been covered, or show the way to one who had gone astray, or bring an oil-lamp into the darkness so that those with vision might see material shapes, even so is *dhamma* made clear in many a figure by the Lord. I, revered sir, am going to the Lord for refuge and to *dhamma* and to the Order of monks. May the Lord accept me as a lay-disciple going for refuge from this day forth for as long as life lasts."

Discourse to Prince Abhaya:
The Eighth

59. DISCOURSE ON MUCH TO BE EXPERIENCED

(Bahuvedaniyasutta)

THUS have I heard: At one time the Lord was staying near Sāvatthī in the Jeta Grove in Anāthapiṇḍika's monastery. Then[2] Fivetools,[3] the carpenter, approached the venerable Udāyin[4]; having approached, having greeted the venerable Udāyin, he sat down at a respectful distance. As he was sitting down at a respectful distance, Fivetools, the carpenter, spoke thus to the venerable Udāyin:

---

[1] The word *dhammadhātu*, as the ultimate principle or own-nature, own-being, self-nature, of *dhamma* occurs also at *D*. ii. 8. It is explained at *MA*. iii. 113 as *dhammasabhāva*. At *S*. ii. 143, *Netti*. 64, *Vism*. 486 it would seem to be used in the sense of mental state considered as an irreducible element, *cf*. *Dhs*. 67, 69, *Vbh*. 87, 89. For a more detailed discussion of the Buddha's "power of immediate response," see A. K. Coomaraswamy, *Some Pali Words, H.J.A.S.*, vol. IV, No. 2, July 1939, p. 188.

[2] As at *S*. iv. 223 *ff*.

[3] See *K.S*. iv. 149, n. 2. Pañcakaṅga also found at *M*. ii. 23, iii. 144. His five tools are enumerated at *MA*. iii. 114 and *SA*. iii. 79.

[4] *MA*. iii. 114 calls him *paṇḍita-Udāyitthera*, the learned Elder Udāyin.

" Now, revered Udāyin, how many feelings are spoken of by the Lord ?"

" Three, householder,[1] are the feelings that are spoken of by the Lord: pleasant feeling, painful feeling, feeling that is neither painful nor pleasant. [**397**] These, householder, are the three feelings spoken of by the Lord."

" Revered Udāyin, three feelings are not spoken of by the Lord. Two feelings are spoken of by the Lord: pleasant feeling, painful feeling. Revered sir, that feeling which is neither painful nor pleasant, *that* is spoken of by the Lord as belonging to exquisite happiness."

And a second time the venerable Udāyin spoke thus to Fivetools, the carpenter: " Householder, two feelings are not spoken of by the Lord; three feelings are spoken of by the Lord: pleasant feeling, painful feeling, feeling that is neither painful nor pleasant. These, householder, are the three feelings spoken of by the Lord."

And a second time Fivetools the carpenter spoke thus to the venerable Udāyin: " Revered Udāyin, three feelings are not spoken of by the Lord . . . *that* is spoken of by the Lord as belonging to exquisite happiness."

And a third time the venerable Udāyin spoke thus to Fivetools the carpenter:

" Householder, two feelings are not spoken of by the Lord . . . These, householder, are the three feelings spoken of by the Lord."

And a third time Fivetools the carpenter spoke thus to the venerable Udāyin: " Revered Udāyin, three feelings are not spoken of by the Lord. Two feelings are spoken of by the Lord: pleasant feeling, painful feeling. Revered sir, that feeling which is neither painful nor pleasant, *that* is spoken of by the Lord as belonging to exquisite happiness." So neither was the venerable Udāyin able to convince Fivetools the carpenter, nor was Fivetools the carpenter able to convince the venerable Udāyin.

Now, the venerable Ānanda overheard this conversation between the venerable Udāyin and Fivetools the carpenter. Then the venerable Ānanda approached the Lord; having approached, having greeted the Lord, he sat down at a respectful distance. Seated at a respectful distance, the venerable Ānanda told the Lord the whole of the conversation between the venerable Udāyin and Fivetools the

---

[1] *S.* iv. 223 *f.* reads *thapati,* carpenter, for *Majjhima's gahapati,* householder.

carpenter as far as it went.[1] When this had been said, the Lord spoke thus to the venerable Ānanda:

" Although, Ānanda, Udāyin's classification[2] was right, Fivetools the carpenter disagreed; and although Fivetools the carpenter's classification was right, Udāyin disagreed. Ānanda, two feelings[3] are spoken of by me [**398**] according to (one) classification, and three feelings[4] are spoken of by me according to (one) classification, and five feelings[5] . . . and six feelings[6] . . . and eighteen feelings[7] . . . and thirty-six feelings[8] . . . and one hundred and eight feelings[9] are spoken of by me according to (one) classification. Thus, Ānanda, is *dhamma* taught by me according to classification. As *dhamma* is taught by me thus, Ānanda, according to classification, of those who will not accede to, approve of or accept what has been well said, well spoken by each other, this is to be expected: that they will live wrangling, quarrelsome, disputatious, wounding one another with the weapons of the tongue.[10] Thus, Ānanda, is *dhamma* taught by me according to classification. As *dhamma* is taught by me thus, Ānanda, according to classification, of those who will accede to, approve of and accept what has been well said, well spoken by each other, this is to be expected: that they will live all together on friendly terms and harmonious as milk and water blend, regarding one another with the eye of affection.[11]

Ānanda, there are these five strands of sense-pleasures.[12] What are the five ? Material shapes cognisable by the eye, agreeable, pleasant, liked, enticing, connected with sensual pleasures, alluring. Sounds cognisable by the ear . . . Smells cognisable by the nose . . .

---

[1] *yāvatako, cf. M.* i. 374.

[2] *pariyāya*, explained by *kāraṇa* at *MA.* iii. 114.

[3] Bodily and mental, *MA.* iii. 114 quoting *S.* iv. 231.

[4] The three beginning with pleasant (feeling), *MA.* iii. 114 quoting *S.* iv. 232.

[5] The five *indriyas*, beginning with that which is pleasant, *MA.* iii. 114 quoting *S.* iv. 232; *cf.* also *S.* v. 207.

[6] Six sensory impingements, by way of the doors (of the senses), beginning with the eye, *MA.* iii. 114 quoting *S.* iv. 232.

[7] The six ways of attending to material shape founded on happiness, the six founded on grief, the six founded on indifference (or, equanimity).

[8] The six forms of happiness connected with the household life, the six connected with renunciation; the six forms of misery connected with the household life, the six with renunciation; the six " indifferences " of a householder, the six of renunciation, *MA.* iii. 114 quoting *S.* iv. 232.

[9] In the past, the future and in the present: each thirty-six feelings. *Cf.* the 18, 36 and 108 " thoughts " at *A.* ii. 212.

[10] *Cf. Ud.* 67, etc. [11] As at *M.* i. 206. [12] As at *M.* i. 85, 92, 454.

Tastes cognisable by the tongue . . . Touches cognisable by the body, agreeable, pleasant, liked, enticing, connected with sensual pleasures, alluring. These, Ānanda, are the five strands of sense-pleasures. Whatever happiness, whatever joy, Ānanda, arises in consequence of these five strands of sense-pleasures, it is called happiness in sense-pleasures.

Whoever, Ānanda, should speak thus: 'This is the highest happiness and joy that creatures experience'—this I cannot allow on his part. What is the reason for this? There is, Ānanda, another happiness more excellent and exquisite than that happiness.[1] And what, Ānanda, is this other happiness more excellent and exquisite than that happiness? Here, Ānanda, a monk, aloof from pleasures of the senses, aloof from unskilled states of mind, enters and abides in the first meditation that is accompanied by initial thought and discursive thought, is born of aloofness and is rapturous and joyful. This, Ānanda, is the other happiness that is more excellent and exquisite than that happiness.

Whoever, Ānanda, should speak thus: 'This is the highest happiness and joy that creatures experience'—this I cannot allow on his part [**399**]. What is the reason for this? There is, Ānanda, another happiness more excellent and exquisite than that happiness. And what, Ānanda, is this other happiness more excellent and exquisite than that happiness? Here, Ānanda, a monk, by allaying initial thought and discursive thought, his mind inwardly tranquillised and fixed on one point, enters and abides in the second meditation which is devoid of initial and discursive thought, is born of concentration, and is rapturous and joyful. This, Ānanda, is the other happiness that is more excellent and exquisite than that happiness.

Whoever, Ānanda, should speak thus . . . And what, Ānanda, is this other happiness more excellent and exquisite than that happiness? Here, Ānanda, a monk, by the fading out of rapture, abides with equanimity, attentive and clearly conscious, and he experiences in his person that happiness of which the ariyans say: 'Joyful lives he who has equanimity and is mindful.' And entering on the third meditation he abides in it. This, Ānanda, is the other happiness that is more excellent and exquisite than that happiness.

Whoever, Ānanda, should speak thus . . . And what, Ānanda, is this other happiness more excellent and exquisite than that happiness? Here, Ānanda, a monk, by getting rid of happiness and

[1] *Cf. M.* i. 247.

by getting rid of anguish, by the going down of his former pleasures and sorrows, enters and abides in the fourth meditation which has neither anguish nor happiness, and which is entirely purified by equanimity and mindfulness. This, Ānanda, is the other happiness that is more excellent and exquisite than that happiness.

Whoever, Ānanda, should speak thus . . . And what, Ānanda is this other happiness more excellent and exquisite than that happiness? Here, Ānanda, a monk, by wholly transcending perceptions of material shapes, by the going down of perceptions due to sensory impressions, by not attending to perceptions of difference, thinking: 'Ether is unending,' enters and abides in the plane of infinite ether. This, Ānanda, is the other happiness that is more excellent and exquisite than that happiness.

Whoever, Ānanda, should speak thus . . . And what, Ānanda, is this other happiness more excellent and exquisite than that happiness? Here, Ānanda, a monk, by wholly transcending the plane of infinite ether and thinking: 'Consciousness is unending,' enters and abides in the plane of infinite consciousness. This, Ānanda, is the other happiness that is more excellent and exquisite than that happiness.

Whoever, Ānanda, should speak thus . . . And what, Ānanda, is this other happiness more excellent and exquisite than that happiness? Here, Ānanda, a monk, by wholly transcending the plane of infinite consciousness, and thinking: 'There is no thing,' enters and abides in the plane of no-thing. This, Ānanda, is the other happiness that is more excellent and exquisite than that happiness.

[**400**] Whoever, Ānanda, should speak thus . . . And what, Ānanda, is this other happiness more excellent and exquisite than that happiness? Here, Ānanda, a monk, by wholly transcending the plane of no-thing, enters and abides in the plane of neither-perception-nor-non-perception. This, Ānanda, is the other happiness that is more excellent and exquisite than that happiness.

Whoever, Ānanda, should speak thus: 'This is the highest happiness and joy that creatures experience'—this I cannot allow on his part. What is the reason for this? There is, Ānanda, another happiness more excellent and exquisite than that happiness. And what, Ānanda, is this other happiness more excellent and exquisite than that happiness? Here, Ānanda, a monk, by wholly transcending the plane of neither-perception-nor-non-perception, enters and abides in the stopping of perceiving and feeling. This,

Ānanda, is the other happiness that is more excellent and exquisite than that happiness.

But the situation occurs, Ānanda, when wanderers belonging to other sects may speak thus: 'The recluse Gotama speaks of the stopping of perceiving and feeling, and lays down that this belongs to happiness. Now what is this, now how is this?' Ānanda, wanderers belonging to other sects who speak thus should be spoken to thus: 'Your reverences, the Lord does not lay down that it is only pleasant feeling that belongs to happiness; for, your reverences, the Tathāgata lays down that whenever, wherever, whatever happiness is found it belongs to happiness.' "

Thus spoke the Lord. Delighted, the venerable Ānanda rejoiced in what the Lord had said.

Discourse on Much to be Experienced:
The Ninth

60. DISCOURSE ON THE SURE

(Apaṇṇakasutta)

THUS have I heard: At one time the Lord, walking on tour among the Kosalans together with a large Order of monks,[1] arrived at the brahman village of the Kosalans named Sālā. The brahman householders of Sālā heard: " It is said that the recluse Gotama, the son of the Sakyans, gone forth from the Sakyan family, and walking on tour among the Kosalans [**401**] together with a large Order of monks, has reached Sālā, and that a lovely reputation has gone forth about the Lord Gotama thus: 'The Lord is perfected, wholly Self-awakened, endowed with (right) knowledge and conduct, well-farer, knower of the worlds, incomparable charioteer of men to be tamed, teacher of *devas* and men, the Awakened One, the Lord. He makes known this world with the *devas*, with Māra, with Brahmā, creation with its recluses and brahmans, its *devas* and men, having realised them by his own super-knowledge. He teaches *dhamma* that is lovely at the

---

[1] Down to where the Lord begins to speak is the same as at *M.* i. 285.

beginning, lovely in the middle, lovely at the ending, with the spirit and the letter; he proclaims the Brahma-faring wholly fulfilled, quite purified. It were good to see perfected ones like this.' "

Then the brahman householders of Sālā approached the Lord; some, having approached, having greeted the Lord, sat down at a respectful distance; some exchanged greetings with the Lord and having conversed in a friendly and courteous way, sat down at a respectful distance; some, having saluted the Lord with joined palms, sat down at a respectful distance; some, having made known their names and clans in the Lord's presence, sat down at a respectful distance; some, becoming silent, sat down at a respectful distance. As they were sitting down at a respectful distance, the Lord spoke thus to the brahman householders of Sālā:

" Have you, householders, some satisfactory teacher in whom your faith is grounded ?"

" We have no satisfactory teacher, revered sir, in whom our faith is grounded."

" If you, householders, have no satisfactory teacher, then taking up this sure[1] *dhamma* you should practise it. For, householders, sure is *dhamma*; rightly undertaken, it will long be for your welfare and happiness. And what, householders, is this sure *dhamma* ?

There are, householders, some recluses and brahmans who speak thus and are of these views[2]: ' There is no (result of) gift, there is no (result of) offering, no (result of) sacrifice; there is no fruit or ripening of deeds well done or ill done; there is not this world, there is not a world beyond; there is no (benefit from serving) mother or father; there are no spontaneously arising beings; there are not in the world recluses and brahmans who are faring rightly, proceeding rightly, and who proclaim this world and a world beyond, having realised them by their own super-knowledge.' But, householders, there are [**402**] some recluses and brahmans who speak in direct opposition to these recluses and brahmans, and who say this: ' There is (result of) gift, there is (result of) offering, there is (result of) sacrifice; there is fruit and ripening of deeds well done and ill done; there is this world, there is a world beyond; there is (benefit from serving) mother and father; there are spontaneously uprising beings; there are in the world recluses and brahmans who are faring rightly, proceeding rightly, and who proclaim this world and a world beyond,

---

[1] *apaṇṇaka*. *Cf. A.* i. 113, ii. 76 (*apaṇṇakatā paṭipadā*), and see notes at *G.S.* i. 97, ii. 85.

[2] As at *M.* i. 287.

having realised them by their own super-knowledge.' What do you think about this, householders? Do not these recluses and brahmans speak in direct opposition to one another?"[1]

"Yes, revered sir."

"As to this, householders, of those recluses and brahmans who speak thus and are of these views: 'There is no (result of) gift . . . having realised them by their own super-knowledge,' this is to be expected for them: Having laid aside these three good things: right conduct of body, right conduct of speech, right conduct of thought, and taking up these three bad things: wrong conduct of body, wrong conduct of speech, wrong conduct of thought, they practise them. What is the reason for this? It is that these worthy recluses and brahmans do not see the peril in wrong things, the vanity, the defilement, nor the advantage, allied to purity, of renouncing them for the good things. And because there is indeed a world beyond, the view of anyone that there is not a world beyond is a false view of his. As there is indeed a world beyond, if anyone has the conception that there is not a world beyond, it is a false conception of his. As there is indeed a world beyond, if anyone utters the speech: 'There is not a world beyond,' it is a false speech of his. As there is indeed a world beyond, if anyone says that there is not a world beyond, he makes mock of those perfected ones who are knowers of a world beyond. As there is indeed a world beyond, if he convinces others that there is not a world beyond, that convincing of his is against true *dhamma*, and because of that convincing which is against true *dhamma*, he is exalting himself and disparaging others. Indeed, before his good morality is got rid of, bad morality is set up. And this false view, false conception, false speech, the mocking of the ariyans, the convincing which is against true *dhamma*, the exalting of oneself, the disparaging of others—these are a variety of evil, unskilled states that arise thus because of false view.

[**403**] Hereupon,[2] householders, an intelligent man reflects thus: 'If there is not a world beyond, this worthy individual at the breaking up of the body will make himself safe;[3] but if there is a world beyond, this worthy individual at the breaking up of the body after dying, will arise in a sorrowful way, a bad bourn, the downfall, Niraya Hell. But if it be granted that there is not a world beyond, if this is a true speech of these recluses and brahmans,

---

[1] As at *D.* i. 1.

[2] *MA.* iii. 117 "among the views of those recluses and brahmans."

[3] *sotthim attānaṁ karissati.* *MA.* iii. 117 does not explain. *Cf. M.* i. 353.

then the worthy individual is condemned here and now by intelligent persons who say: 'Of bad moral habit is the individual, of false view, he holds the theory of " There is not ".'[1] But if there is indeed a world beyond, thus is there defeat[2] in two ways for this worthy individual: inasmuch as he is condemned here and now by intelligent persons, and inasmuch as at the breaking up of the body after dying he will uprise in a sorrowful way, a bad bourn, the downfall, Niraya Hell. Thus this sure *dhamma* has been undertaken imperfectly by him, he has applied himself one-sidedly,[3] he is neglecting the skilled stance.[4]

Hereupon, householders, of those recluses and brahmans who speak thus and are of these views: ' There is (result of) gift, . . . having realised them by their own super-knowledge,' this is to be expected of them: Having laid aside these three bad things: wrong conduct of body, wrong conduct of speech, wrong conduct of thought, and taking up these three good things: right conduct of body, right conduct of speech, right conduct of thought, they practise them. What is the reason for this ? It is that these worthy recluses and brahmans see the peril, the vanity, the defilement in wrong things, and the advantage, allied to purity, of renouncing them for states that are good. And because there is indeed a world beyond, the view of anyone that there is a world beyond is a right view of his. As there is indeed a world beyond, if anyone has the conception[5] that there is a world beyond it is a right conception[6] of his. As there is indeed a world beyond, if anyone utters the speech: ' There is a world beyond,' it is a right speech of his. As there is indeed a world beyond, if anyone says that there is a world beyond, he does not make mock of those perfected ones who are knowers of the world beyond. As there is indeed a world beyond, if he convinces others that there is a world beyond, [**404**] that convincing of his is according to true *dhamma*, and because of this convincing which is in accordance with true *dhamma*, he does not exalt just himself, he does not disparage others. Indeed, before his bad morality is got rid of, good morality is set up. And this right view, right conception, right speech, this non-mocking of the ariyans, the convincing which is in accordance with true *dhamma*, the non-exalting of self, the non-disparaging of others

---

[1] *natthikavāda*, a " there-is-not-ist."

[2] *kaliggaha*, the losing throw at dice.

[3] Intent on his own theory.

[4] *ṭhāna*, occasion, situation, position.

[5] *saṅkappeti*.

[6] *sammāsaṅkappa*. See table of attempts to translate this word at Mrs. Rhys Davids, *Sakya*, p. 85.

—these are a variety of good states that arise because of right view.

Hereupon, householders, an intelligent man reflects thus: 'If there is a world beyond, this worthy individual at the breaking up of the body after dying will arise in a good bourn, a heaven world. But if it be granted that there is not a world beyond, if this is a true speech of these recluses and brahmans, then this worthy individual is praised here and now by intelligent persons who say: 'Of good moral habit is the individual, of right view, he holds the theory of "There is."'[1] But if there is indeed a world beyond, thus is there victory[2] in two ways for this worthy individual: inasmuch as he is praised here and now by intelligent persons, and inasmuch as at the breaking up of the body after dying he will uprise in a good bourn, a heaven world. Thus this sure *dhamma* has been undertaken perfectly by him, he has applied himself two-sidedly,[3] he is neglecting the unskilled stance.

There are, householders, some recluses and brahmans who speak thus and are of these views:[4] 'From doing,[5] from making (another) do, from mutilating, from making (another) mutilate, from threatening, from making (another) threaten, from causing grief, from tormenting, from torturing, from making (another) torture, from making onslaught on creatures, from taking what is not given, from house-breaking, from plundering, from robbery, from waiting in ambush, from going after other men's wives, from lying speech—from acting (thus) evil is not done. If anyone with a discus having an edge sharp as a razor should make the creatures of this earth into one mass of flesh, into one heap of flesh, from that source there is not evil, there is not the perpetuating[6] of evil. And if anyone should go to the south bank of the Ganges[7] slaying and striking, mutilating, making (others) mutilate, threatening, making (others) threaten, from that source there is not evil, there is not the perpetuating of evil. And if he should go to the north bank of the Ganges[8] giving,

---

[1] He is an Affirmationist, a "there-is-ist," *atthikavāda*.

[2] *kaṭaggaha*, the winning throw at dice.

[3] *MA*. iii. 118, intent on his own theory and that of others.

[4] As at *M*. i. 516; *S*. iii. 208; at *D*. i. 52 attributed to Pūraṇa Kassapa.

[5] *MA*. iii. 118, "with the hand."

[6] *āgama*, the handing down, tradition; *cf*. *āgatāgama* as at *Vin*. iv. 158: one to whom the tradition has been handed down.

[7] People here are rough and cruel, *MA*. iii. 119.

[8] People here have faith and are believing, devoted to the Buddha, *dhamma* and the Order.

making (others) give, offering, making (others) offer, from that source there is not merit, there is not the perpetuating of merit. There is no merit from giving, from taming oneself, from restraining oneself, from truth-speaking, there is not the perpetuating of merit.' Householders, some recluses and brahmans speak in direct opposition to these recluses and brahmans, [**405**] they speak thus: 'From doing, from making (another) do . . . from lying . . . from acting (thus) evil is done. If any one with a discus having an edge sharp as a razor should make the creatures of this earth into one heap of flesh, one mass of flesh, from that source there is evil, there is the perpetuating of evil. And if anyone should go to the south bank of the Ganges slaying and striking . . . from that source there is evil, there is the perpetuating of evil. And if he should go to the north bank of the Ganges giving, making (others) give . . . from that source there is merit, there is the perpetuating of merit. There is merit from giving, from taming oneself, from restraining oneself, from truth-speaking, there is the perpetuating of merit.' What do you think about this, householders? Do not these recluses and brahmans speak in direct opposition to one another?"

"Yes, revered sir."

"Hereupon, householders, of those recluses and brahmans who speak thus and hold these views: 'From doing, from making (another) do . . . there is not the perpetuating of merit,' this is to be expected for them: Having laid aside these three good things: right conduct of body, right conduct of speech, right conduct of thought, and taking up these three bad things: wrong conduct of body, wrong conduct of speech, wrong conduct of thought, they practise them. What is the reason for this? It is that these worthy recluses and brahmans do not see the peril in wrong things, the vanity, the defilement, nor the advantage, allied to purity, of renouncing them for the good things. And because there is indeed effective action,[1] the view of anyone that there is not effective action is a false view of his. As there is indeed effective action, if anyone has the conception that there is not effective action it is a false conception of his. As there is indeed effective action, if anyone utters the speech: 'There is not effective action,' it is a false speech of his. As there is indeed effective action, if anyone says there is not effective action he is making a mock of those perfected ones who profess effective action.[2] As there is indeed effective action, if he convinces others that there

---

[1] *kiriya*, doing, fulfilment, so a complete act, *i.e.* act and its effect(s).

[2] *kiriyavāda*.

is not effective action, that convincing of his is against true *dhamma*, and because of that convincing which is against true *dhamma*, he is exalting himself and disparaging others. Indeed, before his good morality is got rid of, bad morality is set up. [**406**] And this false view, false conception, false speech, the mocking of the ariyans, the convincing which is against true *dhamma*, the exalting of oneself, the disparaging of others—these are a variety of evil, wrong states that arise because of false view.

Hereupon, householders, an intelligent man reflects thus: 'If there is not effective action, this worthy individual at the breaking up of the body will make himself safe; but if there is effective action, this worthy individual at the breaking up of the body after dying will arise in a sorrowful way, a bad bourn, the downfall, Niraya Hell. But if it be granted that there is not effective action, if this is a true speech of these worthy recluses and brahmans, then the worthy individual is condemned here and now by intelligent persons who say: "Of bad moral habit is the individual, of false view, he professes ineffective action."[1] But if there is indeed effective action, there is thus defeat in two ways for this worthy individual: inasmuch as he is condemned here and now by intelligent persons, and inasmuch as at the breaking up of the body after dying he will uprise in a sorrowful way, a bad bourn, the downfall, Niraya Hell. This sure *dhamma* has thus been undertaken imperfectly by him, he has applied himself one-sidedly, he is neglecting the skilled stance.

Hereupon, householders, those recluses and brahmans who speak thus and hold these views: 'From doing, from making (another) do . . . there is the perpetuation of merit,' this is to be expected for them: Having laid aside these three bad things: wrong conduct of body, wrong conduct of speech, wrong conduct of thought, and taking up these three good things: right conduct of body, right conduct of speech, right conduct of thought, they practise them. What is the reason for this? It is that these worthy recluses and brahmans see the peril in wrong things, the vanity, the defilement, and the advantage, allied to purity, of renouncing them for states that are good. And because there is indeed effective action, the view of anyone that

---

[1] *akiriyavāda.* *Cf.* *D.* i. 53, *akiriyaṁ vyākāsi,* and *A.* i. 286 where the view *n'atthi kammaṁ n'atthi kiriyaṁ n'atthi viriyaṁ* is ascribed to Makkhali Gosāla. See also E. J. Thomas, *Hist. Bud. Thought,* p. 72. A. K. Coomaraswamy, *Some Pali Words, H.J.A.S.,* vol. 4, No. 2, p. 119 appears to confuse *akiriya* with *akaraṇiya.*

there is effective action is a right view of his. And as there is indeed effective action, if anyone has the conception that there is effective action, it is a right conception of his. And as there is indeed effective action, if anyone utters the speech: 'There is effective action,' it is a right speech of his. And as there is indeed effective action, if anyone says that there is effective action, he is not making a mock of those perfected ones who hold the theory of effective action. As there is indeed effective action, if he convinces others that there is effective action, that convincing of his is according to true *dhamma*, [**407**] and because of this convincing which is in accordance with true *dhamma*, he is not exalting himself, he is not disparaging others. Indeed before his bad morality is got rid of, good morality is set up. And this right view, right conception, right speech, the non-mocking of the ariyans, the convincing which is in accordance with true *dhamma*, the non-exalting of self, the non-disparagement of others —these are a variety of good states which arise because of right view.

Hereupon, householders, an intelligent man reflects thus: 'If there is effective action, this worthy individual at the breaking up of the body after dying will arise in a good bourn, a heaven world. But if it be granted that there is not effective action, if this is a true speech of these worthy recluses and brahmans, then this worthy individual is praised here and now by intelligent persons who say: 'Of good moral habit is the individual, of right view, he professes effective action. If there is indeed effective action, thus is there victory in two ways for this worthy individual: inasmuch as he is praised here and now by intelligent persons, and inasmuch as at the breaking up of the body after dying he will uprise in a good bourn, in a heaven world. Thus this sure *dhamma* has been undertaken perfectly by him, he has applied himself two-sidedly, he is neglecting the unskilled stance.

There are, householders, some recluses and brahmans who speak thus and are of these views:[1] 'There is no cause, no reason for the defilement of creatures, creatures are defiled without cause, without reason. There is no cause, no reason for the purification of creatures, creatures are purified without cause, without reason. There is not strength, there is not energy, there is not human vigour, there is not human effort; all creatures,[2] all breathing things, all beings, all

---

[1] Also given at *S.* iii. 210. At *D.* i. 53 they are ascribed to Makkhali Gosāla.

[2] *MA.* iii. 120=*DA.* i. 161 says creatures, *sattā*, are camels, oxen, donkeys, etc.; "breathers," *pāṇā*, are those who have one or two faculties; beings,

living things are without power, without strength, without energy, bent[1] by fate,[2] chance,[3] and nature[4], they experience pleasure and pain[5] amid the six classes[6].' But, householders, there are some recluses and brahmans who speak in direct opposition to these recluses and brahmans, and who say this: 'There is cause, there is reason for the defilement of creatures, creatures are defiled with cause, with reason. There is cause, there is reason for the purification of creatures, creatures are purified with cause, with reason. There is strength, there is energy, there is human vigour, there is human effort; all creatures, all breathing things, all beings, all living things are not (so) without power, without strength, without energy that they are bent by fate, chance and nature, that they experience pleasure and pain amid the six classes. What do you think about this, householders? [**408**] Do not these recluses and brahmans speak in direct opposition to one another?"

"Yes, revered sir."

"Hereupon, householders, those recluses and brahmans who speak thus and are of these views: 'There is no cause, there is no reason ... amid the six classes,' this is to be expected for them: Having laid aside the three good things: right conduct of body, right conduct of speech, right conduct of thought, and taking up these three bad things: wrong conduct of body, wrong conduct of speech, wrong conduct of thought, they practise them. What is the reason for this? It is that these worthy recluses and brahmans do not see the peril in wrong things, the vanity, the defilement, nor the advantage, allied to purity, in renouncing them for the good things. And because there is indeed cause, the view of anyone that there is not cause is a

---

[1] *pariṇatā*, also meaning changed, ripened, matured.

[2] *niyati*, a word, as used by Makkhali Gosāla, implying determination, necessity. See B. M. Barua, *Pre-Buddhistic Indian Philosophy*, p. 310; and A. L. Basham, *History and Doctrines of the Ājīvikas*, p. 224.

[3] *saṅgati*, meeting together, here of events over which the being has no power or control, see B. M. Barua, *op. cit.*, p. 311; Basham, *op. cit.*, p. 225.

[4] *bhāva=sabhāva*, *MA*. iii. 120, character, nature, disposition. See Barua, *op. cit.*, p. 311; Basham, *op. cit.*, p. 226.

[5] See comment at *Sūtrakṛtāṅga*, I. i. 2. 4.

[6] Of beings. The divisions to which Gosāla's expression has reference are of colours: black, blue (or green), red, yellow, white, and intensely white. Typical members of the classes are given at *MA*. iii. 121. *Cf. D.* iii. 250; *A*. iii. 383; *G.S.* iii. 273, and see B. M. Barua, *op. cit.* p. 309.

---

bhūtā, are those enclosed in eggs or membraneous sheaths; living things, *jīvā*, are rice, wheat, etc. See *Dial.* i. 71, n. 2.

false view of his. As there is indeed cause, if anyone has the conception that there is not cause it is a false conception of his. As there is indeed cause, if anyone utters the speech: 'There is not cause,' it is a false speech of his. As there is indeed cause, if anyone says there is not cause, he makes mock of those perfected ones who profess that there is cause. As there is indeed cause, if he convinces others that there is not cause, this convincing of his is against true *dhamma*, and because of this convincing which is against true *dhamma*, he is exalting himself and disparaging others. Indeed, before his good morality is got rid of, bad morality is set up. And this false view, false conception, false speech, the mocking of the ariyans, the convincing which is against true *dhamma*, the exalting of oneself, the disparaging of others—these are a variety of evil, wrong states that arise thus because of false view.

Hereupon, householders, an intelligent man reflects thus: 'If there is not cause, this worthy individual at the breaking up of the body will make himself safe; but if there is cause, this worthy individual at the breaking up of the body after dying will arise in a sorrowful way, a bad bourn, the downfall, Niraya Hell. But if it be granted that there is not cause, if this is a true speech of these recluses and brahmans, then this worthy individual is condemned here and now by intelligent persons who say: "Of bad moral habit is the individual, of false view, he professes that there is not cause." But if there is indeed cause, thus there is defeat in two ways for this worthy individual: [**409**] inasmuch as he is condemned here and now by intelligent persons, and inasmuch as on the breaking up of the body after dying he will arise in a sorrowful way, a bad bourn, the downfall, Niraya Hell. This sure *dhamma* has thus been imperfectly undertaken by him, he has applied himself one-sidedly, he is neglecting the skilled stance.

Hereupon, householders, those recluses and brahmans who speak thus and are of these views: 'There is cause, there is reason . . . amid the six classes,' this is to be expected for them: Having laid aside these three bad things: wrong conduct of body, wrong conduct of speech, wrong conduct of thought, and taking up these three good things: right conduct of body, right conduct of speech, right conduct of thought, they practise them. What is the reason for this? It is that these worthy recluses and brahmans see the peril in wrong things, the vanity, the defilement, the advantage, allied to purity, of renouncing them for good states. And because there is indeed cause, the view of anyone that there is cause is a right view of his.

As there is indeed cause, if anyone has the conception that there is cause it is a right conception of his. As there is indeed cause, if anyone utters the speech: 'There is cause,' it is a right speech of his. As there is indeed cause, if anyone says that there is cause, he does not make mock of those perfected ones who hold the theory of cause. As there is indeed cause, if he convinces others that there is cause, this convincing of his is in accordance with true *dhamma*, and because of this convincing which is in accordance with true *dhamma*, he does not exalt himself, does not disparage others. Indeed, before his bad morality is got rid of, good morality is set up. And this right view, right conception, right speech, the non-mocking of the ariyans, the convincing which is in accordance with true *dhamma*, the non-exalting of self, the non-disparaging of others—these are a variety of good states that arise because of right view.

Hereupon, householders, an intelligent man reflects thus: 'If there is indeed cause, this worthy individual at the breaking up of the body after dying will arise in a good bourn, a heaven world. But if it be granted that there is not cause, if this is a true speech of these worthy recluses and brahmans, then this worthy individual is praised here and now by intelligent persons who say: 'Of good moral habit is the individual, of right view, he professes that there is cause.' If there is indeed [**410**] cause, thus is there victory in two ways for this worthy individual: inasmuch as he is praised here and now by intelligent persons, and inasmuch as on the breaking up of the body after dying he will arise in a good bourn, a heaven world. Thus this sure *dhamma* has been undertaken perfectly by him, he has applied himself two-sidedly, he is neglecting the unskilled stance.

There are, householders, some recluses and brahmans who speak thus and are of this view: 'There is not formlessness throughout.'[1] But, householders, there are some recluses and brahmans who are in direct opposition to these recluses and brahmans, and who say this: 'There is formlessness throughout.' What do you think about this, householders? Do not these recluses and brahmans speak in direct opposition to one another?"

"Yes, revered sir."

"Hereupon, householders, an intelligent man reflects thus: 'Those worthy recluses and brahmans who speak thus and are of this view: "There is not formlessness throughout"—this is not seen by

---

[1] *n'atthi sabbaso āruppā ti. MA.* iii. 122 says there is not a Brahma-world that is formless throughout (or in every way).

me. And those worthy recluses and brahmans who speak thus and are of this view: " There is formlessness throughout "—this is not known by me. And if I, not knowing, not seeing, were to take up one side and define it, saying: " This is the truth, all else is falsehood," this would not be suitable in me. If this is a true saying of these worthy recluses and brahmans who speak thus and are of this view: " There is not formlessness throughout," then this situation occurs that surely my uprising will be there where are those *devas* that have form and are made by mind.[1] But if this is a true saying of those worthy recluses and brahmans who speak thus and are of this view: " There is formlessness throughout," then this situation occurs that surely my uprising will be there where are those *devas* that are formless, made from perceiving.[2] Concerning what has form, taking up the stick is to be seen, and taking up the sword, quarrel, dispute, contention, strife, slander, lying speech.[3] But there is not this in what is formless throughout.' So, by reflecting thus, he is one faring along precisely for the disregard of material shapes, for detachment (concerning them) and for their stopping.

There are, householders, some recluses and brahmans who speak thus and are of this view: ' There is not the stopping of becomings[4] throughout.' But, householders, there are some recluses and brahmans who speak in direct opposition to those recluses and brahmans and who say this: ' There is **[411]** the stopping of becomings throughout.' What do you think about this, householders ? Do not these recluses and brahmans speak in direct opposition to one another ?"

" Yes, revered sir."

" Hereupon, householders, an intelligent man reflects thus: ' Those worthy recluses and brahmans who speak thus and are of this view: " There is not the stopping of becomings throughout "—this is not seen by me. But those worthy recluses and brahmans who speak thus and are of this view: " There is the stopping of

---

[1] *manomayā*. *MA*. iii. 122 explains by *jhānacittamayā*, made by thought in meditation.

[2] *saññāmayā*. *MA*. iii. 122 says *arūpajjhānasaññāya saññāmayā*, made by perception in the perception in the meditation on formlessness.

[3] Sequence as at *M*. i. 110.

[4] *MA*. iii. 123 says that *bhavanirodha* (the stopping of becoming or becomings) is nibbāna, as does *S*. ii. 117, *A*. v. 9. I take *bhava*, in *bhavanirodha*, as a plural to fit the plural *bhavānaṁ* at the end of this clause, see p. 81 below. Reference is no doubt intended to the three becomings, *kāmabhava*, *rūpa-* and *arūpabhava*.

becomings throughout "—this is not known by me. And if I, not knowing, not seeing, were to take up one side and define it, saying: " This is the truth, all else is falsehood"—this would not be suitable in me. If this is a true saying of those worthy recluses and brahmans who speak thus and are of this view: " There is not the stopping of becomings throughout," then this situation occurs that surely my uprising will be there where are those *devas* who are formless, made from perceiving. But if this is a true saying of those worthy recluses and brahmans who speak thus and are of this view: " There is the stopping of becomings throughout," then this situation occurs: that I will attain nibbāna here-now. If this is a true saying of those worthy recluses and brahmans who speak thus and are of this view: " There is not the stopping of becomings throughout," this view of theirs is close to attachment, close to the fetters, close to delight, close to cleaving, close to grasping. But if this is a true saying of those worthy recluses and brahmans who speak thus and are of this view: " There is the stopping of becomings throughout," this view of theirs is close to detachment, close to the absence of the fetters, close to the absence of delight, close to the absence of cleaving, close to the absence of grasping.'[1] Through reflecting thus he is one faring along precisely for the disregard of becomings, for detachment (concerning them), and for their stopping.

Householders, there are these four kinds of persons existing in the world.[2] What four? Here, householders, some person is a tormentor of self, intent on the practice of self-torment. Here, householders, some person is a tormentor of others, intent on the practice of tormenting others. Here, householders, some person is both a self-tormentor, intent on the practice of tormenting self, and a tormentor of others, intent on the practice of tormenting others. Here, householders, some person is neither a self-tormentor intent on the practice of self-torment, nor a tormentor of others intent on the practice of tormenting others. He, [**412**] neither a self-tormentor nor a tormentor of others, is here-now allayed, quenched,

---

[1] *Cf. M.* i. 498.

[2] As in the *Kandaraka Sutta, M.* Sta. No. 51. *MA.* iii. 124 says that the five types of persons who hold the views: There is not, there is no efficient action, there is no cause, there is not formlessness, there is not stopping—become as it were three persons here; and the five who hold the opposite views of There is, etc., become as it were one person, namely the fourth kind. It must therefore be supposed that Bu. thought of the first group as comprising tormentors of self, of others and of both. The second " group " held the right views and are non-tormentors.

become cool, an experiencer of bliss that lives with self Brahma-become.

And which, householders, is the self-tormentor, intent on the practice of self-torment ? In this case, householders, some person comes to be unclothed, flouting life's decencies, licking his hands (after meals) . . . (*as in the* Kandarakasutta[1]) . . . Thus in many a way does he live intent on the practice of mortifying and tormenting his body. Householders, this person is called a self-tormentor, intent on the practice of self-torment.

And which, householders, is the tormentor of others, intent on the practice of tormenting others ? In this case, householders, some person is a cattle-butcher,[2] or pig-killer, fowler . . . or one of those others who follow a bloody calling. This is the person, householders, who is called a tormentor of others, intent on the practice of tormenting others.

And which, householders, is the person who is a self-tormentor, intent on the practice of self-torment, and also a tormentor of others, intent on the practice of tormenting others ? In this case, householders, some person is a noble anointed king or a very rich brahman . . . [3] . . . Those who are called his slaves or messengers or work-people, they, scared of danger, with tearful faces and crying, set about their preparations. This, householders, is called the person who is a self-tormentor, intent on the practice of self-torment and also a tormentor of others, intent on the practice of tormenting others.

And which, householders, is the person who is neither a self-tormentor intent on the practice of self-torment, nor a tormentor of others intent on the practice of tormenting others, and who, neither a self-tormentor nor a tormentor of others, is here-now allayed, quenched, become cool, an experiencer of bliss that lives with self Brahma-become ? In this case, householders, a Tathāgata arises in the world[4] . . . **[413]** . . . Destroyed is birth, brought to a close the Brahma-faring, done is what was to be done, there is no more of being such or so. This, householders, is called the person who is neither a self-tormentor, not intent on the practice of tormenting self, nor a tormentor of others, not intent on the practice of tormenting others, and who, neither a self-tormentor nor a tormentor of others, is here-now allayed, quenched, become cool, an experiencer of bliss that lives with self Brahma-become."

---

1 *M.* i. 342.
2 *M.* i. 343.
3 *M.* i. 343-344.
4 *M.* i. 344-349.

When this had been said, the brahman householders of Sālā spoke thus to the Lord: " Excellent, good Gotama; good Gotama, it is excellent. It is as if, good Gotama, one might set upright what had been upset . . . even so in many a figure has *dhamma* been made clear by the good Gotama. We are going to the revered Gotama for refuge and to *dhamma* and to the Order of monks. May the good Gotama accept us as lay-disciples going for refuge from this day forth for as long as life lasts."

Discourse on the Sure:
The Tenth

Division on Householders:
The First

II. THE DIVISION ON MONKS

(Bhikkhuvagga)

61. DISCOURSE ON AN EXHORTATION TO RĀHULA AT AMBALAṬṬHIKA

(Ambalaṭṭhikā-Rāhulovādasutta)[1]

[414] THUS have I heard: At one time the Lord was staying near Rājagaha in the Bamboo Grove at the squirrels' feeding place. At that time the venerable Rāhula[2] was staying at Ambalaṭṭhikā. Then the Lord, emerging from solitary meditation towards evening, approached Ambalaṭṭhikā and the venerable Rāhula. Then the venerable Rāhula saw the Lord coming in the distance; seeing him, he made ready a seat and water for (washing) the feet. The Lord sat down on the seat made ready; as he was sitting down he bathed his feet. And the venerable Rāhula, having greeted the Lord, sat down at a respectful distance.

Then the Lord, having put a little quantity of water that was left over into a water-vessel, addressed the venerable Rāhula, saying: "Do you, Rāhula, see this little quantity of water that is left over and that is put into the water-vessel?"

"Yes, revered sir."

"Even so, Rāhula, little is the recluseship of those who have no shame at intentional lying." Then the Lord, having thrown away that little quantity of water, addressed the venerable Rāhula, saying: "Do you, Rāhula, see this little quantity of water that has been thrown away?"

"Yes, revered sir."

"Even so, Rāhula, thrown away is the recluseship of those who have no shame at intentional lying." Then the Lord, having overturned that water-vessel, addressed the venerable Rāhula,

---

[1] This Discourse is mentioned in the Bhābrū Rock Edict of Asoka as among those that all monks, nuns, men and women lay followers should hear often and reflect upon.

[2] See *DPPN.*, *s.v.* Ambalaṭṭhikārāhulovādasutta. *MA.* iii. 126 and *AA.* i. 258 say that at this time Rāhula had been a *sāmaṇera* for seven years. At *A.* i. 24 he is called chief of those anxious for training. His verses are at *Thag.* 295-298.

saying: "Do you, Rāhula, see this water-vessel that has been overturned ?"

" Yes, revered sir."

" Even so, Rāhula, overturned is the recluseship of those who have no shame at intentional lying." Then the Lord, having turned upright that water-vessel, addressed the venerable Rāhula, saying: " Do you, Rāhula, see this water-vessel that is empty, void ?"

" Yes, revered sir."

" Even so, Rāhula, void and empty is the recluseship of those who have no shame at intentional lying. Rāhula, it is like[1] a king's bull-elephant whose tusks are as long as a plough-pole,[2] massive,[3] finely bred,[4] whose home is the battle-field,[5] and who, when going forth to battle, uses[6] his forelegs, uses his hindlegs, uses the forepart of his body, uses the hindpart of his body, uses his head, uses his ears, uses his tusks and uses his tail, [**415**] protecting only his trunk.[7] Thereupon it occurs to the mahout: ' This king's bull-elephant whose tusks are as long as a plough-pole . . . protects only his trunk. This king's bull-elephant has not thrown away his life.'[8] But when, Rāhula, the king's bull-elephant whose tusks are as long as a plough-pole . . . uses his forelegs . . . uses his tail and uses his trunk, it thereupon occurs to the mahout: ' This king's bull-elephant . . . uses his tail and uses his trunk. This king's bull-elephant has thrown away his life, there is nothing to be done now for the king's bull-elephant.' Even so, Rāhula, of anyone for whom there is no shame at intentional lying, of him I say that there is no evil he cannot do. Wherefore, for you, Rāhula, ' I will not speak a lie, even for fun '[9]—this is how you must train yourself, Rāhula.

" What do you think about this, Rāhula ? What is the purpose of a mirror ?"

" Its purpose is reflection, revered sir."

" Even so, Rāhula, a deed is to be done with the body (only) after

---

[1] As at *M.* i. 450. [2] As at *Vin.* i. 353.

[3] Explained at *MA.* iii. 127 as *abhivaḍḍhito ārohasampanno.*

[4] *abhijāta* as at *A.* iii. 158, also of a king's elephant.

[5] *A.* iii. 158. [6] *kammaṁ karoti,* with the instrumental case.

[7] He puts it in his mouth, *MA.* iii. 128.

[8] Literally, the life of the king's bull-elephant has not been thrown away (or, abandoned, given up, *apariccattaṁ*).

[9] *MA.* iii. 125 says he (the Buddha) thought that young boys say things both proper and improper, and are called *piyamusāvādā* (fond of lying) for they say they saw something when they did not, or did not see it when they did.

repeated reflection; a deed is to be done with speech . . . with the mind (only) after repeated reflection.

If you, Rāhula, are desirous of doing a deed with the body, you should reflect on that deed of your body, thus: 'That deed which I am desirous of doing with the body is a deed of my body that might conduce to the harm of self and that might conduce to the harm of others and that might conduce to the harm of both; this deed of body is unskilled, its yield is anguish, its result is anguish.' If you, Rāhula, reflecting thus, should find, 'That deed which I am desirous of doing with the body is a deed of my body that would conduce to the harm of self and to the harm of others and to the harm of both; this deed of body is unskilled, its yield is anguish, its result is anguish' —a deed of body like this, Rāhula, is certainly[1] not to be done by you. [**416**] But if you, Rāhula, while reflecting thus, should find, 'That deed which I am desirous of doing with the body is a deed of my body that would conduce neither to the harm of self nor to the harm of others nor to the harm of both; this deed of body is skilled, its yield is happy, its result is happy'—a deed of body like this, Rāhula, may be done by you.

While you, Rāhula, are doing this deed with the body, you should reflect thus on this self-same deed of body, 'Is this deed that I am doing with the body a deed of my body that is conducing to the harm of self and to the harm of others and to the harm of both? Is this deed of body unskilled, its yield anguish, its result anguish?' If you, Rāhula, while reflecting thus should find, 'This deed that I am doing with the body is a deed of my body that is conducing to the harm of self . . . others . . . both; this deed of body is unskilled, its yield is anguish, its result is anguish'—you, Rāhula, should avoid a deed of body like this. But if you, Rāhula, while reflecting thus, should find, 'This deed that I am doing with the body is a deed of my body that is not conducing to the harm of self . . . of others . . . of both; this deed of body is skilled, its yield is happy, its result happy' —you, Rāhula, could repeat[2] a deed of body like this.

And when you, Rāhula, have done a deed with the body you should reflect on this self-same deed of body thus: 'Was this deed that I did with the body a deed of my body that conduced to the harm of self and to the harm of others and to the harm of both?

---

[1] *sasakkaṁ*, as at *M*. i. 514. *MA*. iii. 128 explains by *ekaṁsena*=surely, definitely, certainly.

[2] *anupadajjeyyāsi*. *MA*. iii. 128 gives *upathambheyyāsi punappunaṁ kareyyāsi*.

Was this an unskilled deed of body, its yield anguish, its result anguish?' If you, Rāhula, while reflecting thus, should find, 'This deed that I did with the body was a deed of my body that conduced to the harm of self . . . others . . . both; this deed of body was unskilled, its yield anguish, its result anguish'—such a deed of your body, Rāhula, should be confessed, disclosed, declared to the Teacher or to intelligent Brahma-farers so that, confessed, disclosed and declared, it would induce restraint in the future. [**417**] But if you, Rāhula, while reflecting thus, should find, 'This deed that I did with the body was a deed of my body that conduced neither to the harm of self nor of others nor of both; it was a skilled deed of body, its yield happy, its result happy'—because of it you, Rāhula, may abide in zest and rapture training yourself day and night in states that are skilled.

If you, Rāhula, are desirous of doing a deed with speech . . . with mind . . . (*repeat the paragraphs concerned with a* deed with the body *but reading* deed with speech *and then* deed with the mind) . . . [**418**] . . . [**419**] . . . training yourself day and night in states that are skilled.

[**420**] All those recluses and brahmans, Rāhula, who in the long past purified a deed of body, purified a deed of speech, purified a deed of mind, did so (only) after repeated reflection. And all those recluses and brahmans, Rāhula, who in the distant future will purify a deed of body, will purify a deed of speech, will purify a deed of mind, will do so (only) after repeated reflection. And all those recluses and brahmans, Rāhula, who in the present are purifying a deed of body, are purifying a deed of speech, are purifying a deed of mind, are doing so (only) after repeated reflection. Wherefore, Rāhula, thinking: 'We will purify a deed of body after repeated reflection, we will purify a deed of speech after repeated reflection, we will purify a deed of mind after repeated reflection'—this is how you must train yourself, Rāhula."

Thus spoke the Lord. Delighted, the venerable Rāhula rejoiced in what the Lord had said.

Discourse on an Exhortation to Rāhula at Ambalaṭṭhikā:
The First

62. GREATER DISCOURSE ON AN EXHORTATION TO RĀHULA

(Mahā-Rāhulovādasutta)

THUS have I heard: At one time the Lord was staying near Sāvatthī in the Jeta Grove in Anāthapiṇḍika's monastery. Then the Lord, having dressed in the morning, taking his bowl and robe, entered Sāvatthī for almsfood. The venerable Rāhula, [421] having also dressed in the morning, taking his bowl and robe followed close after the Lord. Then the Lord, having looked round, addressed the venerable Rāhula, saying:

"Whatever, Rāhula, is material shape, past, future, present, subjective or objective, gross or subtle, low or excellent, distant or near, all material shape should be seen as it really is by means of perfect intuitive wisdom thus: 'This is not mine, this am I not, this is not my self.'"

"Only material shape, Lord, only material shape, Well-farer?"

"Material shape, Rāhula, and feeling, Rāhula, and perception, Rāhula, and the habitual tendencies, Rāhula, and consciousness, Rāhula."

Then the venerable Rāhula thought: "Who indeed today, when he has been exhorted with an exhortation face to face with the Lord, could enter a village for almsfood?" And turning back from there, he sat down cross-legged at the root of a tree, holding his back erect and arousing mindfulness in front of him. Then the venerable Sāriputta saw the venerable Rāhula sitting down cross-legged at the root of the tree, holding his back erect and arousing mindfulness in front of him; and seeing him, he addressed the venerable Rāhula, saying: "Develop the (mind-) development[1] that is mindfulness on in-breathing and out-breathing, Rāhula. Mindfulness on in-breathing and out-breathing, Rāhula, if developed and made much of is of great fruit, of great advantage." Then the venerable

[1] *bhāvanaṁ bhāvehi.*

Rāhula, emerging from solitary meditation towards evening, approached the Lord; having approached, having greeted the Lord, he sat down at a respectful distance. As he was sitting down at a respectful distance, the venerable Rāhula spoke thus to the Lord:

"Revered sir, how if mindfulness on in-breathing and out-breathing is developed and made much of is it of great fruit, of great advantage?"

"Whatever,[1] Rāhula, is hard, solid, is internal, referable to an individual and derived therefrom, that is to say: the hair of the head, the hair of the body, nails, teeth, skin, flesh, sinews, bones, marrow of the bones, kidney, heart, liver, pleura, spleen, lungs, intestines, mesentery, stomach, excrement, or whatever other thing is hard, solid, is internal, referable to an individual and derived therefrom, this, Rāhula, is called the internal element of extension. Whatever is an internal element of extension and whatever is an external element of extension, just these are the element of extension. By means of perfect intuitive wisdom it should be seen of this as it really is, thus: This is not mine, this am I not, this is not my self. [**422**] Having seen it thus as it really is by means of perfect intuitive wisdom, he disregards the element of extension, he cleanses his thought of the element of extension.

And what, Rāhula, is the liquid element? The liquid element may be internal, it may be external. And what, Rāhula, is the internal liquid element? Whatever is liquid, fluid, is internal, referable to an individual and derived therefrom, that is to say: bile, phlegm, pus, blood, sweat, fat, tears, serum, saliva, mucus, synovial fluid, urine or whatever other thing is liquid, fluid, is internal, referable to an individual and derived therefrom, this, Rāhula, is called the internal liquid element. Whatever is an internal liquid element and whatever is an external liquid element, just these are the liquid element. By means of perfect intuitive wisdom it should be seen of this as it really is, thus: This is not mine, this am I not, this is not my self. Having seen this thus as it really is by means of perfect intuitive wisdom, he disregards the liquid element, he cleanses his thought of the liquid element.

And what, Rāhula, is the element of heat? The heat element may be internal, it may be external. And what, Rāhula, is the

---

[1] Down to the end of "the element of motion," *cf. M.* Sta. 28. For notes, see *M.L.S.* i. 231 *ff. Cf. A.* ii. 164, and see *G.S.* ii. 171, *n.* 1.

internal heat element? Whatever is heat, warmth, is internal, referable to an individual and derived therefrom, such as by whatever one is vitalised, by whatever one is consumed, by whatever one is burnt up, and by whatever one has munched, drunk, eaten and tasted that is properly transformed (in digestion), or whatever other thing is heat, warmth, is internal, referable to an individual and derived therefrom, this, Rāhula, is called the internal heat element. Whatever is an internal element of heat and whatever is an external element of heat, just these are the element of heat. By means of perfect intuitive wisdom it should be seen of this as it really is, thus: This is not mine, this am I not, this is not my self. Having seen this thus as it really is by means of perfect intuitive wisdom, he disregards the heat element, he cleanses his thought of the heat element.

And what, Rāhula, is the element of motion? The element of motion may be internal, it may be external. And what, Rāhula, is the internal element of motion? Whatever is motion, wind, is internal, referable to an individual and derived therefrom, such as winds going upwards, winds going downwards, winds in the abdomen, winds in the belly, winds that shoot across the several limbs, in-breathing, out-breathing, or whatever other thing is motion, wind, is internal, referable to an individual and derived therefrom, this, Rāhula, is called the internal element of motion. Whatever is an internal element of motion and whatever is an external element of motion, just these are the element of motion. By means of perfect intuitive wisdom it should be seen of this as it really is, thus: This is not mine, this am I not, this is not my self. Having seen this thus as it really is [**423**] by means of perfect intuitive wisdom, he disregards the element of motion, he cleanses his thought of the element of motion.

And what, Rāhula, is the element of space?[1] The element of space may be internal, it may be external. And what, Rāhula, is the internal element of space? Whatever is space, spacious, is internal, referable to an individual and derived therefrom, such as the auditory and nasal orifices, the door of the mouth and that by which one swallows what is munched, drunk, eaten and tasted, and where this remains, and where it passes out of (the body) lower down, or whatever other thing is space, spacious, is internal, referable to an

[1] *ākāsadhātu* does not occur in Sta. 28, but in Stas. 112, 115, 140 *viññāṇa-dhātu* is added to the five mentioned above, as also at *D.* iii. 247, *A.* i. 176. See also *Dhs.* 638.

individual and derived therefrom, this, Rāhula, is called the internal element of space. Whatever is an internal element of space and whatever is an external element of space, just these are the element of space. By means of perfect intuitive wisdom it should be seen of this as it really is, thus: This is not mine, this am I not, this is not my self. Having seen this thus as it really is by means of perfect intuitive wisdom, he disregards the element of space, he cleanses his thought of the element of space.

Develop the (mind-) development that is like the earth,[1] Rāhula. For, from developing the (mind-) development that is like the earth, Rāhula, agreeable and disagreeable sensory impressions that have arisen, taking hold of your thought, will not persist. As, Rāhula, people cast what is clean on to the earth and what is unclean and ordure and urine and spittle and pus and blood, and yet the earth is not troubled thereby nor worried or disgusted, even so do you, Rāhula, develop the (mind-) development that is like the earth. For, from developing the (mind-) development that is like the earth, Rāhula, agreeable and disagreeable sensory impressions that have arisen, taking hold of your thought, will not persist.

Develop the (mind-) development that is like water, Rāhula. For, from developing the (mind-) development that is like water, Rāhula, agreeable and disagreeable sensory impressions that have arisen, taking hold of your thought, will not persist. As, Rāhula, people wash what is clean in water and what is unclean and wash away ordure and urine and spittle and pus and blood, and yet the water is not troubled thereby nor worried or disgusted, [**424**] even so do you, Rāhula, develop the (mind-) development that is like water. For, from developing . . . will not persist.

Develop the (mind-) development that is like fire,[2] Rāhula. For, from developing the (mind-) development that is like fire, Rāhula, agreeable and disagreeable sensory impressions that have arisen, taking hold of your thought, will not persist. As, Rāhula, fire burns what is clean and what is unclean and ordure and urine and spittle and pus and blood, and yet the fire is not troubled thereby nor

---

[1] Earth, water, fire, wind, *ākāsa* are in Pali the same for the words rendered above respectively: extension, liquid (or cohesion), heat, motion, space. For a note on *ākāsa*, see above, p. 17, *n*. 1. *Cf. Thag*. 1014 where Sāriputta says of himself that he is like earth, water, fire in that he is neither attached to nor revolted by (sensory impingements); and *A*. iv. 394 *f*. where he tells the Lord that he abides with his mind like the first four of these elements.

[2] *Cf. Miln*. 385.

worried or disgusted, even so do you, Rāhula, develop the (mind-) development that is like fire. For, from developing . . . will not persist.

Develop the (mind-) development that is like wind, Rāhula. For, from developing the (mind-) development that is like wind, Rāhula, agreeable and disagreeable sensory impressions that have arisen, taking hold of your thought, will not persist. As, Rāhulla, the wind blows upon what is clean and what is unclean and upon ordure and urine and spittle and pus and blood, and yet the wind is not troubled thereby nor worried or disgusted, even so do you, Rāhula, develop the (mind-) development that is like wind. For, from developing . . . will not persist.

Develop the (mind-) development that is like air, Rāhula. For, from developing the (mind-) development that is like air, Rāhula, agreeable and disagreeable sensory impressions that have arisen, taking hold of your thought, will not persist. As, Rāhula, the air does not repose anywhere, even so do you, Rāhula, develop the (mind-) development that is like air. For, from developing the (mind-) development that is like air, Rāhula, agreeable and disagreeable sensory impressions that have arisen, taking hold of your thought, will not persist.[1]

Develop the (mind-) development that is friendliness,[2] Rāhula. For, from developing the (mind-) development that is friendliness, Rāhula, that which is malevolence will be got rid of. Develop the (mind-) development that is compassion, Rāhula. For, from developing the (mind-) development that is compassion, Rāhula, that which is harming will be got rid of. Develop the (mind-) development that is sympathetic joy, Rāhula. For, from developing the (mind-) development that is sympathetic joy, Rāhula, that which is dislike[3] will be got rid of. Develop the (mind-) development that is equanimity, Rāhula. For, from developing the (mind-) development that is equanimity, Rāhula, that which is sensory reaction will be got rid of. Develop the (mind-) development that is

---

[1] These last two sentences are quoted at *Miln.* 388.

[2] For this and the following five kinds of mental development, *cf.* the six *nissaranīyā dhātuyo* (elements from which there is escape) at *D.* iii. 247-250, a passage which shows interesting similarities as well as variations in respect of the six " developments " of the *M.* passage above.

[3] *arati*, aversion, fretting. *MA.* iii. 140 explains *arati* as *arati pantasenāsanesu c'eva adhikusalesu dhammesu ca ukkaṇṭhitā* (aversion from, or dislike of, remote lodgings as well as longing for (fretting after) highly skilled *dhammā* (items, mental states ?).

on the foul, Rāhula. For, from developing the (mind-) development that is on the foul, Rāhula, that which is attachment will be got rid of.[1] Develop the (mind-) development that is perception of impermanence, Rāhula. [**425**] For, from developing the (mind-) development that is perception of impermanence, Rāhula, that which is the conceit 'I am'[2] will be got rid of.

Develop the (mind-) development that is mindfulness of in-breathing and out-breathing, Rāhula. Mindfulness of in-breathing and out-breathing, Rāhula, is of great fruit, of great advantage. And how, Rāhula, if mindfulness of in-breathing and out-breathing is developed, how, if it is made much of, is it of great fruit, of great advantage?

As to this, Rāhula, a monk who is forest-gone[3] or gone to the root of a tree or gone to an empty place, sits down cross-legged, holding his back erect, arousing mindfulness in front of him. Mindful he breathes in, mindful he breathes out. Breathing in a long (breath) he comprehends, 'I am breathing in a long (breath)'; or breathing out a long (breath) he comprehends, 'I am breathing out a long (breath)'; or breathing in a short (breath) he comprehends, 'I am breathing in a short (breath)'; or breathing out a short (breath) he comprehends, 'I am breathing out a short (breath).' He trains himself thinking: 'I shall breathe in experiencing the whole body'; he trains himself thinking: 'I shall breathe out experiencing the whole body.' He trains himself thinking: 'I shall breathe in tranquillising the activity of the body'; he trains himself thinking, 'I shall breathe out tranquillising the activity of the body.'

He trains himself thinking 'I shall breathe in experiencing rapture'; he trains himself thinking, 'I shall breathe out experiencing rapture.' He trains himself thinking, 'I shall breathe in . . . out experiencing happiness . . . I shall breathe in . . . out experiencing the activity of thought . . . tranquillising the activity of thought . . . experiencing thought . . . rejoicing in thought . . . concentrating thought . . . freeing thought.' He trains himself thinking, 'I shall breathe in . . . out beholding impermanence . . . beholding dispassion . . . beholding stopping . . . beholding casting away.'

---

[1] *Cf. A.* iv. 46.

[2] *asmimāna*; *cf. M.* i. 139. It is the pride due to thinking, 'I am in material shapes, and so on.'

[3] With the following *cf. M.* i. 56. All the terms, to the end of this Discourse, are explained in *Vism.*, Ch. VIII.

Mindfulness of in-breathing and out-breathing if developed thus, Rāhula, if made much of thus, is of great fruit, of great advantage. When, Rāhula, mindfulness of in-breathing and out-breathing has been developed thus, [**426**] has been made much of thus, then those which are the last in-breaths and out-breaths are also stopped only when they are known, not when they are unknown."[1]

Thus spoke the Lord. Delighted, the venerable Rāhula rejoiced in what the Lord had said.

Greater Discourse on an Exhortation to Rāhula:
The Second

63. LESSER DISCOURSE TO MĀLUṄKYĀ (PUTTA)

(Cūḷa-Māluṅkyasutta)[2]

THUS have I heard: At one time the Lord was staying near Sāvatthī in the Jeta Grove in Anāthapiṇḍika's monastery. Then a reasoning of mind arose to the venerable Māluṅkyāputta[3] as he was meditating in solitary seclusion, thus: "Those (speculative) views that are not explained, set aside and ignored by the Lord: The world is eternal, the world is not eternal, the world is an ending thing, the world is not an ending thing; the life-principle is the same as the body, the life-principle is one thing, the body another; the Tathāgata[4] is after dying, the Tathāgata is not after dying, the Tathāgata both is and is not after dying, the Tathāgata neither is nor is not after dying—the Lord does not explain these to me. That the Lord does not explain these to me does not please me, does not satisfy me, so I, having approached the Lord, will question him on the matter. If

[1] *Vism.* 291 *f.* gives some explanation of the meaning of *ye pi te carimakā assāsapassāsā te pi viditā va nirujjhanti no aviditā.*

[2] Referred to at *Miln.* 144.

[3] Two sets of verses are ascribed to him in *Thag*: 399-404 (ver. 404 speaking of drawing out the arrow, or dart, *salla*, see below, p. 99), and 794-817. For further references see *DPPN.*

[4] *MA.* iii. 141 explains *tathāgata* by *satta*, being; *cf. MA.* ii. 117. At *UdA.* 340 *tathāgata* is explained by *attā*.

the Lord will explain to me either that the world is eternal or that the world is not eternal or that the world is an ending thing . . . or that the Tathāgata neither is nor is not after dying, then will I fare the Brahma-faring under the Lord. But if the Lord will not explain to me either that the world is eternal or that the world is not eternal . . . or that the Tathāgata neither is nor is not after dying, then will I, disavowing the training, revert to secular life."

[**427**] Then the venerable Māluṅkyāputta, emerging from solitary meditation towards evening, approached the Lord; having approached, having greeted the Lord, he sat down at a respectful distance. As he was sitting down at a respectful distance, the venerable Māluṅkyāputta spoke thus to the Lord: " Now, revered sir, as I was meditating in solitary seclusion, a reasoning of mind arose to me thus: ' Those (speculative) views that are not explained, set aside, ignored by the Lord: The world is eternal . . . or that the Tathāgata neither is nor is not after dying, then will I, disavowing the training, revert to secular life.' If the Lord knows that the world is eternal, let the Lord explain to me that the world is eternal. If the Lord knows that the world is not eternal, let the Lord explain to me that the world is not eternal. If the Lord does not know whether the world is eternal or whether the world is not eternal, then, not knowing, not seeing, this would be honest, namely to say: ' I do not know, I do not see.' If the Lord knows that the world is an ending thing . . . (*repeated in the case of each view as above*) . . . [**428**] . . . If the Lord does not know whether the Tathāgata neither is nor is not after dying, then, not knowing, not seeing, this would be honest, namely to say: ' I do not know, I do not see.' "

" But did I ever speak thus to you, Māluṅkyāputta: ' Come you, Māluṅkyāputta, fare the Brahma-faring under me and I will explain to you either that the world is eternal or that the world is not eternal . . . or that the Tathāgata neither is nor is not after dying ?"

" No, revered sir."

" Or did you speak thus to me: ' I, revered sir, will fare the Brahma-faring under the Lord if the Lord will explain to me either that the world is eternal or that the world is not eternal . . . or that the Tathāgata neither is nor is not after dying '?"

" No, revered sir."

" So it is agreed, Māluṅkyāputta, that neither did I say: ' Come you, Māluṅkyāputta, fare the Brahma-faring under me and I will explain to you either that the world is eternal or that the world is not eternal . . . or that the Tathāgata neither is nor is not after dying ';

and that neither did you say: 'I, revered sir, will fare the Brahma-faring under the Lord if the Lord will explain to me either that the world is eternal . . . or that the Tathāgata neither is nor is not after dying.' This being so, foolish man, who are you that you are disavowing ?[1]

Whoever, Māluṅkyāputta, should speak thus: 'I will not fare the Brahma-faring under the Lord until the Lord explains to me whether the world is eternal or whether the world is not eternal . . . or whether the Tathāgata neither is nor is not after dying' [**429**]—this man might pass away, Māluṅkyāputta, or ever this was explained to him by the Tathāgata. Māluṅkyāputta, it is as if a man were pierced by an arrow that was thickly smeared with poison and his friends and relations, his kith and kin, were to procure a physician and surgeon.[2] He might speak thus: 'I will not draw out this arrow until I know of the man who pierced me whether he is a noble or brahman or merchant or worker.' He might speak thus: 'I will not draw out this arrow until I know the name and clan of the man who pierced me.' He might speak thus: 'I will not draw out this arrow until I know of the man who pierced me whether he is tall or short or middling in height.' He might speak thus: 'I will not draw out this arrow until I know of the man who pierced me whether he is black or deep brown or golden skinned.' He might speak thus: 'I will not draw out this arrow until I know of the man who pierced me to what village or market town or town he belongs.' He might speak thus: 'I will not draw out this arrow until I know of the bow from which I was pierced whether it was a spring-bow[3] or a cross-bow.' He might speak thus: 'I will not draw out this arrow until I know of the bow-string from which I was pierced whether it was of swallow-wort or of reed or sinew or hemp or a tree.'[4] He might speak thus: 'I will not draw out this arrow until I know of the shaft by which I was pierced whether it was of reeds of this kind or that.'[5] He

---

[1] As at *D.* iii. 3. *Ko santo kaṁ paccācikkhasi* might also mean: being whom what are you disavowing ?

[2] As at *M.* ii. 216, 256.

[3] This is a tentative translation of *cāpa; cf. capala*, wavering, trembling, quivering. The word *cāpâtikhiṇā* occurs at *Dhp.* 156.

[4] *khīrapaṇṇiṁ*, Eulotropis gigantea, a tree whose leaves contain milky sap, as the Pali name indicates.

[5] Two kinds are mentioned: *yadi vā kacchaṁ yadi vā ropimaṁ.* On the two kinds of *kaccha* mentioned at *MA.* iii. 142 (mountain and river) *cf. SnA.* 33. *Ropimaṁ* is explained at *MA.* iii. 142 as: making an arrow (or, reed) taken from a thicket of (*sara-*) reeds.

might speak thus: 'I will not draw out this arrow until I know of the shaft from which I was pierced what kind of feathers it had: whether those of a vulture or heron or hawk or peacock or some other bird.'[1] He might speak thus: 'I will not draw out this arrow until I know of the shaft from which I was pierced with what kind of sinews it was encased: whether those of a cow or buffalo or deer or monkey.'[2] He might speak thus: 'I will not draw out this arrow until I know of the arrow by which I was pierced whether it was an (ordinary) arrow or some other kind of arrow.'[3] [**430**] Māluṅkyāputta, this man might pass away or ever this was known to him. In the same way, Maluṅkyāputta, whoever should speak thus: 'I will not fare the Brahma-faring under the Lord until the Lord explains to me either that the world is eternal or that the world is not eternal . . . or that the Tathāgata neither is nor is not after dying,' this man might pass away, Māluṅkyāputta, or ever it was explained to him by the Tathāgata.

The living of the Brahma-faring, Māluṅkyāputta, could not be said to depend on the view that the world is eternal. Nor could the living of the Brahma-faring, Māluṅkyāputta, be said to depend on the view that the world is not eternal. Whether there is the view that the world is eternal or whether there is the view that the world is not eternal, there *is* birth, there is ageing, there is dying, there are grief, sorrow, suffering, lamentation and despair, the suppression[4] of which I lay down here and now. (*The same is repeated for each of the other speculative views: that the world is an ending thing, not an ending thing; that the life-principle and the body are the same and that they are different; that after dying the Tathāgata is, is not, both is and is not, neither is nor is not*) . . . [**431**] . . . The living of the Brahma-faring, Māluṅkyāputta, could not be said to depend on the view that the Tathāgata both is and is not after dying. The living of the Brahma-faring, Māluṅkyaputta, could not be said to depend on the view that the Tathāgata neither is nor is not after dying. Whether there is the view that the Tathāgata both is and is not after dying, or whether, Māluṅkyāputta, there is the view that the Tathāgata neither is nor is not after dying, there *is* birth,

---

[1] A specific kind of bird is mentioned, *sithilahanu*.

[2] *semhāra*, meaning conjectural, *PED*; but *MA*. iii. 142 gives *makkaṭa*.

[3] Together with *salla*, a usual word for arrow or dart, the text mentions five other kinds: *khurappa, vekaṇḍa, nārāca, vacchadanta, karavīrapatta*. Not one is commented upon at *MA*. iii. 142.

[4] *nighāta*, the destruction, overthrow, striking down.

there is ageing, there is dying, there are grief, sorrow, suffering, lamentation and despair, the suppression of which I lay down here and now.

Wherefore, Māluṅkyāputta, understand as not explained what has not been explained by me, and understand as explained what has been explained by me. And what, Māluṅkyāputta, has not been explained by me? That the world is eternal has not been explained by me, Māluṅkyāputta; that the world is not eternal . . . that the world is an ending thing . . . that the world is not an ending thing . . . that the life-principle and the body are the same . . . that the life-principle is one thing and the body another thing . . . that after dying the Tathāgata is . . . is not . . . both is and is not . . . neither is nor is not has not been explained by me, Māluṅkyāputta. And why, Māluṅkyāputta, has this not been explained by me? It is because it is not connected with the goal, is not fundamental to the Brahma-faring, and does not conduce to turning away from, nor to dispassion, stopping, calming, super-knowledge, awakening nor to nibbāna. Therefore it has not been explained by me, Māluṅkyāputta. And what has been explained by me, Māluṅkyāputta? 'This is anguish' has been explained by me, Māluṅkyāputta. 'This is the arising of anguish' has been explained by me. 'This is the stopping of anguish' has been explained by me. 'This is the course leading to the stopping of anguish' has been explained by me. And why, Māluṅkyāputta, has this been explained by me? It is because it is connected with the goal, is fundamental to the Brahma-faring, and conduces to turning away from, to dispassion, stopping, calming, super-knowledge, awakening and nibbāna. Therefore it has been explained by me. Wherefore, [**432**] Māluṅkyāputta, understand as not explained what has not been explained by me, and understand as explained what has been explained by me."

Thus spoke the Lord. Delighted, the venerable Māluṅkyāputta rejoiced in what the Lord had said.

Lesser Discourse to Māluṅkyā(putta):
The Third

64. GREATER DISCOURSE TO MĀLUṄKYĀ(PUTTA)

(Mahā-Māluṅkyasutta)

THUS have I heard: At one time the Lord was staying near Sāvatthī in the Jeta Grove in Anāthapiṇḍika's monastery. Then the Lord addressed the monks, saying: "Monks." "Revered one," these monks answered the Lord in assent. The Lord spoke thus:

"Do you, monks, remember that I taught you about the five fetters binding to the lower (shore)?" When this had been said, the venerable Māluṅkyāputta spoke thus to the Lord: "Yes, I, revered sir, remember that the Lord taught that there are five fetters binding to the lower (shore)."

"But do you, Māluṅkyāputta, remember it as it was spoken by me when I taught you about the five fetters binding to the lower (shore)?"

"I, revered sir, remember that the Lord taught that false view of own body[1] is a fetter binding to the lower (shore). I, revered sir, remember that perplexity . . . clinging to rites and customs . . . desire for sense-pleasures . . . malevolence is a fetter binding to the lower (shore). It is thus that I, revered sir, remember the five fetters binding to the lower (shore) as taught by the Lord."

"And about whom do you, Māluṅkyāputta, remember that I thus taught the five fetters binding to the lower (shore)? Would not wanderers belonging to other sects chide[2] you with the simile of the baby?[3] For, Māluṅkyāputta, if there were not 'own body' for an innocent baby boy lying on his back, [433] whence could there arise for him the view of 'own body'? A leaning to the view of 'own body' indeed lies latent in him. Māluṅkyāputta, if there were not 'things'[4] for an innocent baby boy lying on his back,

---

[1] *sakkāya*. *Cf. M.* i. 300.

[2] *iminā taruṇūpamena upārambhena upārambhissanti* (the last word so corrected at *M.* i. 574 from *upārambhissati* of the text, and so reading at *M.* i. 433).

[3] *Cf. M.* i. 459.

[4] *dhammā*, things, phenomena; mental states, objects or contents of thought or consciousness.

whence could there arise for him perplexity about things? A leaning to perplexity indeed lies latent in him. Māluṅkyāputta, if there were not 'habits'[1] for an innocent baby boy lying on his back, whence could there arise for him clinging to rites and customs? A leaning to clinging to rites and customs indeed lies latent in him. Māluṅkyāputta, if there were not 'sense-pleasures' for an innocent baby boy lying on his back, whence could there arise for him desire for sense-pleasures among the sense-pleasures? A leaning to attachment to sense-pleasures indeed lies latent in him. Māluṅkyāputta, if there were not 'beings' for an innocent baby boy lying on his back, whence could there arise for him malevolence towards beings? A leaning to malevolence indeed lies latent in him. Now, Māluṅkyāputta, would not wanderers belonging to other sects chide you with this simile of the baby?"

When this had been said, the venerable Ānanda spoke thus to the Lord: "Lord, this is the time, Well-farer, this is the time that the Lord might teach (us) about the five fetters binding to the lower (shore). When the monks have heard the Lord they will remember."

"Well then, Ānanda, listen, attend carefully, and I will speak."

"Yes, revered sir," the venerable Ānanda answered the Lord in assent. The Lord spoke thus:

"Herein, Ānanda, an uninstructed ordinary person, taking no count of the pure ones, unskilled in the *dhamma* of the pure ones, untrained in the *dhamma* of the pure ones; taking no count of the true men, unskilled in the *dhamma* of the true men, untrained in the *dhamma* of the true men, lives with his mind obsessed by false view as to 'own body,' overcome by false view as to 'own body,' and he does not comprehend the escape,[2] as it really is, from the false view of 'own body' that has arisen. That false view of his of 'own body,' resistant, not dispelled, is a fetter binding to the lower (shore). He lives with his mind obsessed by perplexity . . . He lives with his mind obsessed by clinging to rites and customs . . . He lives with his mind obsessed by attachment to sense-pleasures . . . [**434**] . . . He lives with his mind obsessed by malevolence, overcome by malevolence, and he does not comprehend the escape, as it really is, from the malevolence that has arisen. That malevolence of his, resistant, not dispelled, is a fetter binding to the lower (shore).

But, Ānanda, an instructed disciple of the pure ones, taking count

---

[1] *sīlā*. [2] *MA*. iii. 144 says that the escape from false view is nibbāna.

of the pure ones, skilled in the *dhamma* of the pure ones, trained in the *dhamma* of the pure ones; taking count of the true men, skilled in the *dhamma* of the true men, trained in *dhamma* of the true men, does not live with his mind obsessed by false view as to 'own body,' overcome by false view as to 'own body,' and he comprehends the escape, as it really is, from the false view of 'own body' that has arisen. That false view of his of 'own body' is got rid of with the leaning[1] towards it. He does not live with his mind obsessed by perplexity . . . He does not live with his mind obsessed by clinging to rites and customs . . . He does not live with his mind obsessed by attachment to sense-pleasures . . . He does not live with his mind obsessed by malevolence, overcome by malevolence, and he comprehends the escape as it really is from the malevolence that has arisen. That malevolence of his is got rid of with the leaning towards it.

Whatever, Ānanda, is the way, whatever the course for getting rid of the five fetters binding to the lower (shore)—that one could know or see or get rid of the five fetters binding to the lower (shore) irrespective of that way, that course—this situation does not occur. Just as this situation does not occur, Ānanda, that without having cut off the bark of a great, stable and pithy tree, without having cut out the softwood, there can be no cutting out of the pith,[2] even so, Ānanda, whatever is the way, whatever the course for getting rid of the five fetters binding to the lower (shore)—that one could know or see or get rid of the five fetters binding to the lower (shore) irrespective of this way, this course—this situation does not occur.

But, Ānanda, whatever is the way, whatever the course for getting rid of the five fetters binding to the lower (shore) [**435**]—that one could know or see or get rid of the five fetters binding to the lower (shore) because of that way, that course—this situation occurs. Just as this situation occurs, Ānanda, that having cut off the bark of a great, stable and pithy tree, having cut out the softwood, there can be a cutting out of the pith, even so, Ānanda, whatever is the way, whatever the course for getting rid of the five fetters binding to the lower (shore)—that one could know or see or get rid of the five fetters binding to the lower (shore) because of this way, this course—this situation occurs. It is as if, Ānanda, the river Ganges were full of

---

[1] *sânusayā*. *MA*. iii. 144 says, in effect, that the fetter and the "leaning" are the same.

[2] *MA*. iii. 145 says cutting off the bark is like attaining, cutting out the softwood is like insight, cutting out the pith is like the Way.

water, overflowing, so that a crow could drink from it, and a feeble man should come along, thinking: 'Having cut across the stream of the river Ganges, using my arms, I am going safely beyond,' yet he would not be able, having cut across the stream of the river Ganges and using his arms, to go safely beyond. Even so, Ānanda, whoever while *dhamma* is being taught to him for the stopping of 'own body' does not rejoice, is not pleased and composed, he is not freed,[1] even as this is to be understood of that feeble man. But, Ānanda, if the river Ganges were full of water, overflowing, so that a crow could drink from it, and a strong man should come along, thinking: 'Having cut across the stream of the river Ganges, using my arms, I am going safely beyond,' he would be able, having cut across the stream of the river Ganges and using his arms, to go safely beyond. Even so, Ānanda, whoever while *dhamma* is being taught to him for the stopping of 'own body' rejoices, is pleased and composed, he is freed, even as this is to be understood of that strong man.

And what, Ānanda, is the way, what the course for getting rid of these five fetters binding to the lower (shore)? Here, Ānanda, a monk, by aloofness from 'clinging,'[2] by getting rid of unskilled states of mind, by allaying every bodily impropriety, aloof from pleasures of the senses, aloof from unskilled states of mind, enters and abides in the first meditation which is accompanied by initial thought and discursive thought, is born of aloofness and is rapturous and joyful. Whatever is there of material shape, feeling, perception, the habitual tendencies, consciousness—he beholds these things as impermanent, suffering, as a disease, an imposthume, a dart, a misfortune, an affliction, as other, as decay, empty, not-self.[3] He

---

[1] *Cf. M.* i. 186, where the *na vimuccati* of above reads *adhimuccati*, is set on, intent on, and which Trenckner says (*M.* i. 566) he should have adopted here. But I think *na vimuccati* (and *vimuccati* a little lower) are certainly right here, for to cross over is to be freed. Moreover at *M.* i. 186 *adhimuccati* is part of the sequence of verbs all referring to the same subject, whereas above *na vimuccati* is not. Thus the compilers were right to vary the last of the four verbs in these two contexts however much the first three are identical.

[2] *upadhi* is the basis, attachment or bond tying one to birth and continued existence.

[3] As at *M.* i. 500; *A.* iv. 422-423; *cf. A.* ii. 128, and for notes on this paragraph see *G.S.* iv. 284, 285. It is said at *MA.* iii. 146 that the suffering-mark is sixfold, the impermanence-mark twofold (with 'decay,' *palokata*) and the not-self-mark threefold: other, empty, not-self.

turns his mind from these things;[1] and when he has turned his mind from these things [**436**] he focuses his mind on the deathless element, thinking: 'This is the real,[2] this the excellent,[3] that is to say the tranquillising of all the activities, the casting out of all clinging, the destruction of craving, dispassion, stopping, nibbāna.'[4] If he is steadfast therein, he achieves destruction of the cankers; if he does not achieve destruction of the cankers, then through his attachment to *dhamma*, his delight in *dhamma*, through his utter destruction of the five fetters binding to the lower (shore), he is of spontaneous uprising, one who attains nibbāna there, not liable to return from that world. This, Ānanda, is the way, this the course for getting rid of the five fetters binding to the lower (shore).

And again, Ānanda, a monk, by allaying initial and discursive thought, with the mind subjectively tranquillised and fixed on one point, enters and abides in the second meditation which is devoid of initial and discursive thought, is born of concentration and is rapturous and joyful . . . the third meditation . . . enters and abides in the fourth meditation. Whatever is there of material shape, feeling, perception, the habitual tendencies, consciousness . . . (*as above*) . . . not liable to return from that world. This, Ānanda, is the way, this the course for getting rid of the five fetters binding to the lower (shore).

And again, Ānanda, a monk, by wholly transcending perceptions of material shapes, by the going down of perceptions due to sensory impressions, by not reflecting on perceptions of variety, thinking, 'Ether is unending,' enters and abides in the plane of infinite ether. Whatever is there of feeling, perception, the habitual tendencies, consciousness . . . (*as above*) . . . not liable to return from that world.

And again, Ānanda, a monk, by wholly transcending the plane of infinite ether, thinking, 'Consciousness is unending,' enters and abides in the plane of infinite consciousness . . . by wholly transcending the plane of infinite consciousness, thinking, 'There is no thing,' enters and abides in the plane of no-thing. Whatever is there of feeling, perception, the habitual tendencies, consciousness —he beholds these things as impermanent, suffering, as a disease, an imposthume, a dart, a misfortune, an affliction, as other, as decay, empty, not-self. He turns his mind from these things; and when he

---

[1] *MA*. iii. 146, from the five *khandhas* all of which have the threefold mark.

[2] *santa* is both 'real' and 'peace.'

[3] As at *M*. ii. 235, 263; *A*. iv. 423, v. 8, 110, 320, 322, 354 *ff*.

[4] As at *M*. i. 136.

has turned his mind from these things, he focuses his mind on the deathless element, thinking, 'This is the real, this the excellent, that is to say the tranquillising of all the activities, the casting out of all clinging, the destruction of craving, dispassion, stopping, nibbāna.' If he is steadfast therein, [**437**] he achieves destruction of the cankers; if he does not achieve destruction of the cankers, then through his attachment to *dhamma*, his delight in *dhamma*, through his utter destruction of the five fetters binding to the lower (shore), he is of spontaneous uprising, one who attains nibbāna there, not liable to return from that world. This, Ānanda, is the way, this the course for getting rid of the five fetters binding to the lower (shore)."

"If this, revered sir, is the way, this the course for getting rid of the five fetters binding to the lower (shore), then how is it that some monks here are those who have freedom of mind while others are those who have freedom through intuitive wisdom ?"[1]

"As to this, I, Ānanda, say that there is a difference in their faculties."[2]

Thus spoke the Lord. Delighted, the venerable Ānanda rejoiced in what the Lord had said.

Greater Discourse to Māluṅkyā(putta)
The Fourth

65. DISCOURSE TO BHADDĀLI

(Bhaddālisutta)

THUS have I heard: At one time the Lord was staying near Sāvatthī in the Jeta Grove in Anāthapiṇḍika's monastery. While he was

---

[1] *MA*. iii. 147-8: If when a monk goes after calm, one-pointedness of mind is to the forefront—this monk is called freed in mind; but if wisdom is to the forefront—such a monk is called freed through wisdom. When one goes after insight, if wisdom is to the forefront, such a monk is called freed through wisdom; if his one-pointedness of mind is to the forefront, he is called freed in mind. The two chief disciples attained arahantship with calm and insight to the forefront; Sāriputta was freed through wisdom and Moggallāna was freed in mind.

[2] *indriya*. On the various groups, see *PED*. The Comy. here does not explain. *Cf. M*. i. 453.

there the Lord addressed the monks, saying: " Monks." " Revered one," these monks answered the Lord in assent. The Lord spoke thus:

" I, monks, partake of my food at one session.[1] Partaking of my food at one session, I, monks, am aware of good health and of being without illness and of buoyancy and strength and living in comfort. Come, do you too, monks, partake of your food at one session. Partaking of your food at one session, you too, monks, will be aware of good health, of being without illness, of bouyancy and strength and living in comfort."

When this had been said, the venerable Bhaddāli spoke thus to the Lord: " I, revered sir, am not capable[2] of eating my food at one session; revered sir, if I ate my food at one session, I might have scruples,[3] I might have misgivings."

" Well then, you, Bhaddāli, having eaten one portion there where you were invited, having taken another portion away, might eat that too; so [**438**] could you, Bhaddāli, eating thus, keep yourself going."

" I, revered sir, am not capable of eating in this fashion; even eating so, revered sir, I might have scruples, I might have misgivings."

Then the venerable Bhaddāli, while a rule of training was being laid down by the Lord,[4] while the Order of monks was undertaking the training, made known his inability. Then the venerable Bhaddāli did not see the Lord face to face for an entire three months because he was one who did not carry out in full the training under the Teacher's instruction.

Now at that time a number of monks were making up robe-material for the Lord, and they said: " When the Lord's robe-material is settled,[5] he will set out on a three months tour." Then the venerable Bhaddāli approached these monks; having approached, he exchanged greetings with these monks; having conversed in a

---

[1] As at *M*. i. 124.

[2] *na ussahāmi*, I am not able, or, I do not dare.

[3] *kukkucca* is scrupulous doubting, doubting whether one is doing right. Bhaddāli says he wonders if he could or could not fare the Brahma-faring for the whole of his life if he ate thus. He had been a crow in a former birth, and because crows are great eaters he had the nickname of Mahāchātaka, Great Eater, *MA*. iii. 148 *f*.

[4] According to *MA*. iii. 149 this was the rule forbidding eating at the wrong time (given at *Vin*. iv. 85).

[5] *niṭṭhita*. See *Vin*. iii. 195 *ff*., and *B.D*. ii. 4, *n*. 5.

friendly and courteous way, he sat down at a respectful distance. These monks spoke thus to the venerable Bhaddāli as he was sitting down at a respectful distance:

" Reverend Bhaddāli, this robe-material is being made up for the Lord. When the robe-material is settled, the Lord will set out on a three months tour. Please, reverend Bhaddāli, pay careful attention to this opportunity,[1] lest later it is more difficult for you."

" Yes, your reverences," and the venerable Bhaddāli, having answered these monks in assent, approached the Lord; having approached, having greeted the Lord, he sat down at a respectful distance. As he was sitting down at a respectful distance, the venerable Bhaddāli spoke thus to the Lord:

" Revered sir, a transgression has overcome me, foolish, misguided and wrong that I was, inasmuch as I made known an inability when a rule of training was being laid down by the Lord and when the Order of monks was undertaking the training. Revered sir, may the Lord acknowledge the transgression as a transgression for the sake of restraint in the future."

" Indeed, Bhaddāli, a transgression overcame you, foolish, misguided and wrong that you were, inasmuch as while a rule of training was being laid down by me and while the training was being undertaken by the Order of monks, you made known your inability.

At that time this was not realised by you, Bhaddāli: The Lord is staying near Sāvatthī and the Lord will know of me that the monk named Bhaddāli is not one that carries out in full the training under the Teacher's instruction.[2] At that time this was not realised by you, Bhaddāli. Nor at that time was this realised by you, Bhaddāli: A number [**439**] of monks who have come to Sāvatthī for the rains will also know of me that the monk named Bhaddāli is not one that carries out in full the training under the Teacher's instruction. At that time this was not realised by you either, Bhaddāli. Nor at that time was this realised by you, Bhaddāli: A number of nuns who have come to Sāvatthī for the rains will also know of me . . . a number of layfollowers who are living in Sāvatthī . . . a number of women layfollowers who are living in Sāvatthī will also know of me that the monk named Bhaddāli is not one that carries out in full the training under the Teacher's instruction. At that time this was not realised by you either, Bhaddāli. Nor at that time was this realised by you,

---

[1] *desaka*. *MA*. iii. 149 has the v.l. *dosaka* and explains by *okāsa aparādha*, occasion (permission) and fault.

[2] Quoted at *DA*. 32, *VA*. i. 107, *UdA*. 19, *Asl*. 57.

Bhaddāli: A number of recluses and brahmans belonging to other sects who have come to Sāvatthī for the rains will also know of me that the monk named Bhaddāli, a disciple and an elder under the recluse Gotama, is not one that carries out in full the training under the Teacher's instruction. At that time this was not realised by you either, Bhaddāli."

"Revered sir, a transgression has overcome me, foolish, misguided and wrong that I was . . . may the Lord acknowledge the transgression as a transgression for the sake of restraint in the future."

"Indeed, Bhaddāli, a transgression overcame you, foolish, misguided and wrong that you were, inasmuch as while a rule of training was being laid down by me and while the training was being undertaken by the Order of monks, you made known your inability.

What do you think about this, Bhaddāli? There might be a monk here, freed both ways,[1] to whom I might speak thus: 'Come you, monk, be a causeway for me across the mire.' Would he make a causeway of himself[2] or would he twist his body in another (direction), or would he say No?"

"Not this, revered sir."

"What do you think about this, Bhaddāli? There might be a monk here, freed through intuitive wisdom . . . a mental realiser[3] . . . won to view . . . freed through faith . . . who strives after *dhamma* . . . who strives after faith,[4] and to whom I might speak thus: 'Come you, monk, be a causeway for me across the mire.' Would he make a causeway of himself, or would he twist his body in another (direction), or would he say No?"

"Not this, revered sir."

"What do you think about this, Bhaddāli? At that time were

---

[1] See *M.* i. 477 (and below, p. 151). This and the other six terms (freed through intuitive wisdom down to the one who strives after faith) occur also at *M.* i. 477-479 and at *A.* i. 73-74, iv. 10; *D.* iii. 105, 253-254; *Pug.* 14-15; and with three others at *A.* v. 23.

[2] *saṅkameyya.* *Cf. Jā.* iii. 373, *attānaṁ saṅkamaṁ katvā.*

[3] *kāyasakkhin.* See *M.* i. 478. *Cf. A.* i. 118 *f.* on this and the next two terms, and where it is said it is difficult to decide which is the most excellent. *MA.* iii. 189=*AA.* ii. 190 says the *kāyasakkhin* first attains *jhāna* and later realises stopping and nibbāna. *M.* i. 478=*Pug.* 14, 73 describes him as "a person who abides having attained the (eight) Deliverances *kāyena* (through mind? while in the body?) and some of whose cankers are destroyed if he has seen by means of right wisdom." He should be compared with the person who is freed both ways and the one freed by means of wisdom.

[4] *Cf.* the strivers after *dhamma* and after faith at *M.* i. 226.

you, Bhaddāli, freed both ways [**440**] or freed through intuitive wisdom or a mental realiser or one that had won to view or one freed through faith or one striving after *dhamma* or one striving after faith ?"

"Not this, revered sir."

"At that time were not you, Bhaddāli, empty, void, fallen short ?"[1]

"Yes, revered sir. Revered sir, a transgression overcame me, foolish, misguided, wrong that I was, inasmuch as I made known an inability while a rule of training was being laid down by the Lord and while the training was being undertaken by the Order of monks. May the Lord acknowledge the transgression as a transgression for the sake of restraint in the future."

"Indeed, Bhaddāli, a transgression overcame you, foolish, misguided and wrong that you were, inasmuch as while a rule of training was being laid down by me, and while the training was being undertaken by the Order of monks, you made known an inability. But since you, Bhaddāli, see the transgression as a transgression and confess it according to the rule,[2] we acknowledge it for you. For, Bhaddāli, in the discipline for an ariyan, this is growth: whoever, seeing a transgression as a transgression, confesses according to the rule, he comes to restraint in the future.

Herein, Bhaddāli, some monk is not one that carries out[3] in full the Teacher's instruction. It occurs to him: 'Suppose I were to resort to a remote lodging—to a forest, to the root of a tree, a mountain slope, a wild place, a hill cave, a cemetery, a woodland thicket, the open air, a heap of straw—I should probably realise conditions of further-men, the excellent knowledge and insight befitting the ariyans.' So he resorts to a remote lodging—to a forest, to the root of a tree . . . a heap of straw. As he is staying aloof in this way the Teacher upbraids him, and when they have examined him his learned fellow Brahma-farers upbraid him, and *devatās* upbraid him, and the self upbraids the self. He, upbraided by the Teacher, and upbraided by his learned fellow Brahma-farers after they have examined him, and upbraided by *devatās*, and the self upbraided by the self, does not realise conditions of further-men, the excellent knowledge and insight befitting the ariyans. What is

---

[1] *MA*. iii. 152 says "empty and void because of lack of inner development of the qualities of ariyans."

[2] *Cf. Vin*. i. 315, ii. 126, 192, iv. 18-19, etc. See *PTC*. s.v. *accaya*.

[3] Probably, *sikkhāya*, the training, should be inserted here as it occurs in all the corresponding passages in this Discourse.

the reason for this ? It is thus, Bhaddāli, since he is not one that carries out in full the training under the Teacher's instruction.[1]

But, Bhaddāli, there is some monk here who fully carries out the training under the Teacher's instruction. It occurs to him: 'If I were to resort to a remote lodging—to a forest, to the root of a tree, a mountain slope, a wild place, a hill cave, a cemetery, a woodland thicket, the open air, [**441**] a heap of straw, I should probably realise conditions of further-men, the excellent knowledge and insight befitting the ariyans.' So he resorts to a remote lodging—to a forest, to the root of a tree . . . a heap of straw. As he is staying aloof in this way neither the Teacher upbraids him, nor, after they have examined him, do his learned fellow Brahma-farers upbraid him, nor do *devatās* upbraid him, nor does the self upbraid the self. He, neither upbraided by the Teacher, nor upbraided by his learned fellow Brahma-farers after they have examined him, nor upbraided by *devatās*, nor the self upbraided by the self, realises conditions of further-men, the excellent knowledge and insight befitting the ariyans. He, aloof from pleasures of the senses, aloof from unskilled states of mind, enters and abides in the first meditation which is accompanied by initial thought and discursive thought, is born of aloofness and is rapturous and joyful. What is the reason for this ? It is thus, Bhaddāli, for one who fully carries out the training under the Teacher's instruction.

And again, Bhaddāli, the monk, by allaying initial and discursive thought, the mind subjectively tranquillised and fixed on one point, enters and abides in the second meditation which is devoid of initial and discursive thought, is born of concentration and is rapturous and joyful. What is the reason for this ? It is thus, Bhaddāli, for one who fully carries out the training under the Teacher's instruction.

And again, Bhaddāli, the monk, by the fading out of rapture, dwells with equanimity, attentive and clearly conscious and he experiences in his person that joy of which the ariyans say: 'Joyful lives he who has equanimity and is mindful,' and he enters and abides in the third meditation. What is the reason for this ? It is thus, Bhaddāli, for one who fully carries out the training under the Teacher's instruction.

And again, Bhaddāli, the monk, by getting rid of joy, by getting rid of anguish, by the going down of his former pleasures and sorrows, enters and abides in the fourth meditation, which has neither joy

---

[1] *Cf. S.* v. 378.

nor anguish and which is entirely purified by equanimity and mindfulness. What is the reason for this? It is thus, Bhaddāli, for one who fully carries out the training under the Teacher's instruction.

He, with his mind thus composed, quite purified, quite clarified[1] . . . directs his mind to the knowledge and recollection of former habitations . . . Thus he recollects a variety of former habitations in all their modes and details. What is the reason for this? It is thus, [**442**] Bhaddāli, for one who fully carries out the training under the Teacher's instruction.

He, with his mind thus composed, quite purified . . . directs his mind to the knowledge of the passing hence and arising of beings . . . Thus with the purified *deva*-vision surpassing that of men does he see beings as they pass hence, as they arise; he comprehends that beings are mean, excellent, comely, ugly, well-going, ill-going according to the consequences of deeds. What is the reason for this? It is thus, Bhaddāli, for one who fully carries out the training under the Teacher's instruction.

He, with his mind thus composed, quite purified, quite clarified . . . directs his mind to the knowledge of the destruction of the cankers. He comprehends as it really is: This is anguish . . . He comprehends as it really is: This is the course leading to the stopping of anguish. He comprehends as it really is: These are the cankers . . . He comprehends as it really is: This is the course leading to the stopping of the cankers. Knowing this thus, seeing this thus, his mind is freed from the canker of sense-pleasures and his mind is freed from the canker of becoming and his mind is freed from the canker of ignorance. In freedom the knowledge comes to be: I am freed; and he comprehends: Destroyed is birth, brought to a close the Brahmafaring, done is what was to be done, there is no more of being such or so. What is the reason for this? It is thus, Bhaddāli, for one who fully carries out the training under the Teacher's instruction."

When this had been said, the venerable Bhaddāli spoke thus to the Lord: "What is the cause, revered sir, what the reason why they constantly[2] take action[3] against some monk here? What is the

---

[1] For this passage, down to 'there is no more of being such or so,' see above, p. 12 *ff*.

[2] *pavayha pavayha*, urgent, pressing, constantly. *MA*. iii. 153 says: Having constantly reproved him for even trifling faults. *Cf*. *M*. iii. 118.

[3] *kāraṇaṁ karonti*. This probably means the juridical action that the Saṁgha (Order) has power to employ. Similarly below, *adhikaraṇa*, "legal

cause, revered sir, what the reason why they do not constantly take similar action against some other monk here ?"

" As to this, Bhaddāli, some monk is a constant offender, full of offences.[1] On being spoken to by the monks he shelves the question by asking another, he answers off the point, he evinces anger and ill-will and discontent,[2] he does not conduct himself properly, is not subdued, does not mend his ways,[3] and does not say: ' What can I do to please the Order ?' Therefore, Bhaddāli, it occurs to the monks: ' This monk, your reverences, is a constant offender, full of offences. On being spoken to by the monks he shelves the question . . . and does not say: " What can I do to please the Order ?" [**443**] It were good if the venerable ones were to investigate this monk in such a way that this legal question of his should not be settled quickly.' So, Bhaddāli, the monks investigate this monk in such a way that this legal question of his is not settled quickly.

But, Bhaddāli, some monk is a constant offender, full of offences. He, on being spoken to by the monks does not shelve the question by asking another, he does not answer off the point, he does not evince anger and ill-will and discontent, he conducts himself properly, is subdued, mends his ways, and he says: ' What can I do to please the Order ?' Therefore, Bhaddāli, it occurs to the monks: ' This monk, your reverences, is a constant offender . . . and he says: " What can I do to please the Order ?" It were good if the venerable ones were to investigate this monk in such a way that this legal question of his should be settled quickly.' So, Bhaddāli, the monks investigate this monk in such a way that this legal question of his is settled quickly.

Then, Bhaddāli, some monk here is an occasional offender, he is not full of offences. But he, on being spoken to by the monks shelves the question by asking another, he answers off the point, he evinces anger and ill-will and discontent, he does not conduct himself properly, is not subdued, does not mend his ways, and he does not say: ' What can I do to please the Order ?' Therefore, Bhaddāli, it occurs to the monks: ' This monk, your reverences, is an occasional offender, he is not full of offences . . . he does not say: " What can

---

[1] *āpattibāhula*, as at *Vin.* i. 321, 330, 332.

[2] *Cf. M.* i. 99, 250; *Vin.* iv. 135.

[3] As at *Vin.* i. 49.

---

question " refers only to the four types of these that the Saṁgha is able to deal with. They are treated of in detail at *Vin.* ii. 88 *ff.*, and come under " ecclesiastical " jurisdiction only, having nothing to do with a secular court of justice.

I do to please the Order ?" It were good if the venerable ones were to investigate this monk in such a way that this legal question of his should not be settled quickly.' So, Bhaddāli, the monks investigate this monk in such a way that [**444**] this legal question of his is not settled quickly.

But, Bhaddāli, some monk is an occasional offender, he is not full of offences. He, on being spoken to by the monks does not shelve the question by asking another, he does not answer off the point, he does not evince anger and ill-will and discontent, he conducts himself properly, is subdued, mends his ways, and he says: 'What can I do to please the Order ?' Therefore, Bhaddāli, it occurs to the monks: 'This monk, your reverences, is an occasional offender, he is not full of offences . . . he says: "What can I do to please the Order ?" It were good if the venerable ones were to investigate this monk in such a way that this legal question of his should be settled quickly.' So, Bhaddāli, the monks investigate this monk in such a way that this legal question of his is settled quickly.

In this connection, Bhaddāli, some monk is going along with only a little faith, with only a little regard.[1] Therefore, Bhaddāli, it occurs to the monks: 'This reverend monk is going along with only a little faith, only a little regard. If we constantly take action against this monk, be careful lest even that little faith of his, even that little regard, deteriorate.' Bhaddāli, it is like a man with only one eye[2]—his friends and acquaintances, his kith and kin would take care of that one eye so that that one eye of his did not deteriorate, thinking: 'Take care lest that one eye of his deteriorates.' Even so, Bhaddāli, some monk goes along with only a little faith, only a little regard. Therefore, Bhaddāli, it occurs to the monks: 'This reverend monk is going along with only a little faith . . . be careful lest even that little faith of his, even that little regard, deteriorate'.

This, Bhaddāli, is the cause, this the reason why they constantly take action against some monk here. But, Bhaddāli, this is the cause, this the reason why they do not constantly take similar action against some (other) monk here."

"What is the cause, revered sir, what the reason why there were formerly fewer [**445**] rules of training but more monks who were established in profound knowledge ? And what is the cause, revered sir, what the reason why there are now more rules of training but fewer monks who are established in profound knowledge ?"

---

[1] *pema*, affection or regard.

[2] Lit., "like the eye of one man."

"It is thus, Bhaddāli: When beings are deteriorating, when true *dhamma* is vanishing away, there are more rules of training and fewer monks established in profound knowledge. Not until some conditions which cause cankers appear here in the Order[1] does the Teacher, Bhaddāli, lay down a rule of training for disciples.[1] But when, Bhaddāli, some conditions which cause cankers appear here in the Order, then the Teacher lays down a rule of training for disciples so as to ward off those very conditions which cause cankers. Not until the Order has arrived at greatness,[2] Bhaddāli, do some conditions which cause cankers appear here in the Order. But when, Bhaddāli, the Order has arrived at greatness, then some conditions which cause cankers appear here in the Order, and then the Teacher lays down a rule of training for disciples so as to ward off those very conditions which cause cankers. Not until the Order has arrived at the height of gain[3] . . . at the height of fame[4] . . . at much learning[5] . . . at long standing,[6] Bhaddāli, do some conditions which

---

[1] *Cf. Vin.* iii. 10.

[2] *mahatta,* a considerable size. *MA.* iii. 155-156 says that when the Order has become large, *mahantabhāva,* then the lodgings do not suffice for the elders, those of middle standing and the newly ordained monks. So conditions causing cankers arise in regard to the lodgings. The rules of training laid down for an Order attained to largeness are (1) "whatever monk should lie down to sleep with one who is not ordained, there is a pācittiya offence" (Pāc. 5. *Vin.* iv. 16), and (2) "Whatever nun should ordain every year, there is a pācittiya. . . . (3) Whatever nun should ordain two (probationers) in one year, there is a pācittiya offence" (Nuns' Pāc. 72, 73, *Vin.* iv. 336, 337).

[3] *lābhagga. Vin.* iii. 10 reads *lābhaggamahatta;* see *B.D.* i. 19, n. 1. The conditions causing cankers to arise when the Order has arrived at the height of gains or acquisitions are controlled by Pāc. 41 (*Vin.* iv. 92, cited at *MA.* iii. 156): "Whatever monk should with his own hand give solid or soft food to an unclothed ascetic or to a male or female wanderer, there is a pācittiya offence."

[4] *yasagga.* Not at *Vin.* iii. 10. For this stage in the Order's deterioration the 51st Pāc. (*Vin.* iv. 110) was laid down: "in drinking strong drinks and intoxicants, there is a pācittiya offence," cited at *MA.* iii. 156. *Cf. lābhagga-yasaggappattā* of the Bodhisatta's mother at *Jā.* i. 51.

[5] At this stage there are misunderstandings, and people explain the Teacher's instruction by what is against *dhamma* and against *vinaya. MA.* iii. 156 cites *Vin.* iv. 135-139, which include the "perverse or wrong views" ascribed to the monk Ariṭṭha and the novice Kandaka (Pāc. 68, 70).

[6] *rattaññuta.* Here, as in the other cases, the reference is to the members of the Order rather than to the Order as a whole. So, here the meaning is "when those who have gone forth for a long time know how many nights it is since they first went forth." *MA.* iii. 157 refers to Upasena Vaṅganta-putta's offence in ordaining his pupil when he himself was only of one year's

cause cankers appear here in the Order. But when, Bhaddāli, the Order has arrived at long standing, then some conditions which cause cankers appear in the Order, and then the Teacher lays down a rule of training for disciples so as to ward off those very conditions which cause cankers.

You were few at the time when I, Bhaddāli, taught you the disquisition on *dhamma*—the Parable of the Thoroughbred Colt. Do you, Bhaddāli, remember ?"

"No, revered sir."

"To what cause do you attribute this, Bhaddāli ?"

"It is that I, revered sir, for a long time was not one who carried out in full the training under the Teacher's instruction."

"This was not the only cause or reason, Bhaddāli. For, for a long time, Bhaddāli, I have known your mind with my mind (and I knew): While *dhamma* is being taught by me this foolish man does not listen to *dhamma* with ready ear, applying himself, paying attention, concentrating with all his mind.[1] However, I, Bhaddāli, will teach you the disquisition on *dhamma*—the Parable of the Thoroughbred Colt. Listen to it, attend carefully, [**446**] and I will speak."

"Yes, revered sir," the venerable Bhaddāli answered the Lord in assent. The Lord spoke thus:

"Bhaddāli, as a skilled horse-trainer,[2] having received a beautiful thoroughbred, first of all makes it get used to the training in respect of wearing the bit; while it is getting used to the training in respect of wearing the bit, whatever the contortions, capers, struggles[3] while it is getting used to a training it was not used to before, yet because of the continual training, the gradual training it is brought to perfection[4] in that respect. When, Bhaddāli, the beautiful thoroughbred

---

[1] *Cf. M.* i. 325. [2] *Cf. M.* iii. 2.

[3] *Cf. M.* i. 234 for these words where they are applied to Saccaka the Jain because of his inconsistent statements.

[4] *parinibbāyati*, or, is perfected, perfectly trained, dompted or extinguished in regard to its former restlessness, etc.

---

standing—he had seen monks being ordained when they were less than ten years' standing. So, "One of less than ten years' standing should not be ordained" (*Vin.* i. 59), and "One should not be ordained by an ignorant, inexperienced (monk) . . . I allow monks to be ordained by an experienced, capable (monk) if they are of ten years' standing or of more than ten years' standing" (*Vin.* i. 60). As *MA.* iii. 157 remarks two rules of training are laid down to cover the time of reaching "long-standing."

is perfected[1] in that respect by the continual training, the gradual training, the horse-trainer makes it get used to a further training in respect of wearing the harness. While it is getting used to the training in respect of wearing the harness . . . because of the gradual training it is brought to perfection in that respect. When, Bhaddāli, the beautiful thoroughbred is perfected in that respect by the continual training, the gradual training, the horse-trainer makes it get used to a further training in respect of going straight on[2], in respect of (running in) a circle,[3] in respect of its hoofs,[4] in respect of galloping, of neighing,[5] of the "royal trick,"[6] the "royal acrobatic feat,"[7] in respect of matchless speed, of matchless swiftness, of matchless manners. While it is getting used to the training in matchless speed, matchless swiftness, matchless manners, whatever the contortions, capers, struggles while it is getting used to a training it was not used to before, yet because of the continual training, the gradual training it is brought to perfection in each respect. When, Bhaddāli, the beautiful thoroughbred is perfected in each respect, the horse-trainer provides it further with a gloss and shine.[8] Bhaddāli, a beautiful thoroughbred, when endowed with these ten qualities,[9] becomes worthy of a king, a royal treasure, and it is reckoned as an attribute of royalty. Even so, Bhaddāli, if a monk is endowed with ten qualities, he is worthy of offerings, worthy of hospitality, worthy of gifts, to be saluted with joined palms, an unsurpassed field of merit for the world. With what ten? Herein, Bhaddāli, a monk is endowed with an adept's right view, he is endowed with an adept's right thought, he is endowed with an adept's

---

[1] *parinibbuta.*

[2] *anukkama.* *MA.* iii. 156 appears to explain that the trainer gives the four feet a hit with a knife so that the horse raises them. Childers, s.v. *anukkama,* gives "regular succession, order." The idea seems to be that the horse is trained to raise all its four feet the same distance from the ground.

[3] *maṇḍale,* in a ring or circle. *MA.* iii. 158 says that if someone is sitting on the horse's back he can pick up a weapon that has fallen to the ground; for the sake of doing this he makes the horse go in a circle. *Cf. Mhvs.* xxiii. 73 where a horse was made to gallop *maṇḍale,* "in a circle."

[4] *khurakāya.* The horse is trained to go along on the tips of its hoofs so that no sound is heard, *MA.* iii. 159.

[5] Important in battle.

[6] *rājaguṇa.* *PED.* says "a trick of a circus horse"; according to *MA.* iii. 159 it is some trick of plunging into water.

[7] *rājavaṁsa.* *Cf. vaṁsa . . . ghaṭikā* at *D.* i. 6.

[8] *vaṇṇiya ca valiya ca.* Meaning is not clear. The Comy. says nothing.

[9] Three at *A.* i. 244; four at *A.* ii. 113. *Cf. A.* i. 284, ii. 116, 170.

right speech, he is endowed with an adept's right action, he is endowed with an adept's right mode of livelihood, he is endowed with an adept's right endeavour, [**447**] he is endowed with an adept's right mindfulness, he is endowed with an adept's right concentration, he is endowed with an adept's right knowledge, he is endowed with an adept's right freedom. Bhaddāli, if a monk is endowed with these ten qualities, he is worthy of offerings, worthy of hospitality, worthy of gifts, to be saluted with joined palms, an unsurpassed field of merit for the world."

Thus spoke the Lord. Delighted, the venerable Bhaddāli rejoiced in what the Lord had said.

Discourse to Bhaddāli:
The Fifth

66. DISCOURSE ON THE SIMILE OF THE QUAIL

(Laṭukikopamasutta)

THUS have I heard: At one time the Lord was staying near Aṅguttarāpa. Āpaṇa[1] was the name of a market town in Aṅguttarāpa. Then the Lord, having dressed in the morning, taking his bowl and robe, entered Āpaṇa for almsfood. When he had walked for almsfood and was returning from the almsgathering after the meal, he approached a forest-thicket for the day-sojourn. When he had plunged into that forest-thicket, he sat down at the root of a tree for the day-sojourn. And the venerable Udāyin also, having dressed in the morning, and taking his bowl and robe, entered Āpaṇa for almsfood. When he had walked for almsfood and was returning from the almsgathering after the meal, he approached that same forest-thicket for the day-sojourn. When he had plunged into that forest-thicket, he sat down at the root of a tree for the day-sojourn. Then while the venerable Udāyin was in private seclusion a reasoning arose in his mind thus:

---

[1] *Potaliya Sutta*, *M*. i. 359, was preached here.

"Indeed our Lord is a remover of many painful things, indeed our Lord is a bringer of many pleasant things, indeed our Lord is a remover of many unskilled things, indeed our Lord is a bringer of many skilled things."[1] Then the venerable Udāyin, emerging from his seclusion towards evening, approached the Lord; having approached, having greeted the Lord, [**448**] he sat down at a respectful distance. As he was sitting down at a respectful distance, the venerable Udāyin spoke thus to the Lord:

"While I, revered sir, was in private seclusion, a reasoning arose in my mind thus: 'Indeed our Lord is a remover of many painful things . . . indeed our Lord is a bringer of many skilled things.' We, revered sir, used to eat in the evening and in the morning and during the day—at a wrong time.[2] Revered sir, the Lord at that time addressed the monks, saying: 'Please do you, monks, give up eating at this wrong time, during the day.' I was depressed because of this, revered sir, I was sorry, and thought: 'The Lord speaks of our giving up that sumptuous food, solid and soft, which the believing householders give us during the day—at the wrong time, and the Well-farer speaks of our rejecting it.' Those of us, revered sir, who look to the Lord with regard and respect and modesty and fear of blame, gave up such food as this (given) during the day, at the wrong time. Then we, revered sir, used to eat in the evening as well as in the morning. It was at this time that the Lord addressed the monks, saying: 'Please do you, monks, give up eating at this wrong time, during the night.' I was depressed because of this, revered sir, I was sorry, and thought: 'The Lord speaks of our giving up that which is reckoned as the more sumptuous of these two meals, and the Well-farer speaks of our rejecting it.' Once upon a time, revered sir, a certain man, having obtained some curry during the day, spoke thus: 'Come, let us put this aside, and in the evening we will enjoy it all together.' All cooking, revered sir, is at night, there is little during the day. But those of us, revered sir, who look to the Lord with regard and respect and modesty and fear of blame, gave up such food as this (given) at night, at the wrong time. Once upon a time, revered sir, when the monks were walking for almsfood in the dense darkness of the night,[3] they would walk into a pool at the entrance to a village, and they would fall into the dirty pool near

---

[1] Quoted at *Kvu.* 528.

[2] See *Vin.* iv. 85, and *B.D.* ii. 335, n. Pāc. 37 makes it an offence to eat after noon has passed until the next sunrise. See *M.* i. 474.

[3] *rattandhakāratimisāya; cf. D.* iii. 85, *Pug.* 30.

the village, and they would blunder into a thorny hedge, and they would blunder into a sleeping cow, and they would meet with young men,[1] both those who had committed a crime and those who had not, and women would solicit them[2] against true *dhamma*. Once upon a time I, revered sir, used to walk for almsfood in the dense darkness of the night, and a certain woman saw me during a lightning flash as she was washing a bowl,[3] and terrified at seeing me, she uttered a scream of horror: 'How terrible for me, indeed there is a demon after me.'[4] This said, I, revered sir, said to this woman: 'Sister, I am not a demon, I am a monk [**449**] standing for almsfood.' She said, 'The monk's father must be dead, the monk's mother must be dead[5]—it were better for you, monk, to have your belly cut out with a sharp butcher's knife than to walk for almsfood for the sake of your belly in the dense darkness of the night.' When I remember this, revered sir, it occurs to me: 'Indeed our Lord is the remover of many painful things, indeed our Lord is the bringer of many pleasant things, indeed our Lord is the remover of many unskilled things, indeed our Lord is the bringer of many skilled things.' "

" But even so, Udāyin, some foolish persons here, on being told by me: 'Give this up,' speak thus: 'But what of this trifling insignificant matter? This recluse lays too much emphasis on (exertion).'[6] But they do not give it up and they cause dissatisfaction to be nursed against me and against those monks who desire the training. This[7] becomes for them,[8] Udāyin, a strong bond, a stout bond, a solid bond, a bond that does not rot away, a thick log of wood.[9] Udāyin, as a quail, a little hen bird,[10] because she is caught in a trap of creepers, comes[11] to slaughter there or to captivity or dying; so that, Udāyin, if any one should say: 'That quail, a little hen bird, because she is caught in a trap of creepers comes to slaughter there or to captivity, or dying, yet for her it is a bond of no strength,

---

[1] *MA*. iii. 164 explains *māṇava*, as is often the case, by *cora*, thief.

[2] *Cf*. Pāc. 6 (*Vin*. iv. 17 *ff*.).

[3] Quoted at *DA*. 34.

[4] As at *Vin*. ii. 115.

[5] *bhikkhussa ātu māri bhikkhussa mātu māri*. According to Trenckner (*M*. i. 567) the text "no doubt purports to make the woman speak a sort of patois."

[6] *adhisallikhati;* as at *A*. i. 236. See *G.S*. i. 217, *n*. 1, and Neumann, vol. i. 22, n. *MA*. iii. 165 explains by *atisallekhati ativāyāmaṁ karoti*.

[7] This trifling matter.

[8] The foolish people.

[9] *thūla kaḷiṅgara*. *MA*. iii. 166 says it is like a great piece of wood tied to their throats. *Cf*. *S*. ii. 268, *Dhp*. 41.

[10] *Cf*. *D*. i. 91.

[11] *āgameti=upeti*, *MA*. iii. 166.

a weak bond, a bond that rots away, a pithless bond '—would anyone speaking thus, Udāyin, be speaking rightly ?"

"No, revered sir. That quail, a little hen bird, revered sir, because she is caught in a trap of creepers, comes to slaughter there or to captivity, or dying, since for her it is a strong bond, a stout bond, a solid bond, a bond that does not rot away, a thick log of wood."

"Even so, Udāyin, some foolish persons here, on being told by me, 'Give this up,' speak thus: 'But what of this trifling insignificant matter ? This recluse lays too much emphasis on (exertion),' and they do not give it up and they cause dissatisfaction to be nursed against me and against those monks who desire the training. This is for them, Udāyin, a strong bond, a stout bond, a solid bond, a bond that does not rot away, a thick log of wood.

But, Udāyin, some young men of family here, on being told by me, 'Give this up,' [**450**] speak thus: 'But what of this trifling insignificant matter to be given up and of whose giving up the Lord speaks to us, and of whose rejection the Well-farer speaks to us ?' And they give it up and they do not cause dissatisfaction to be nursed against me or against those monks who desire the training. These, giving that up, are unconcerned, unruffled, dependent on others, with a mind become as a wild creature's.[1] This for them, Udāyin, is a bond of no strength, a weak bond, a bond that rots away, a pithless bond. Udāyin, it is like[2] a king's bull-elephant whose tusks are as long as a plough-pole, who is massive, finely bred, whose home is the battle-field and who, if bound with a stout leather bond,[3] having easily twisted his body, having burst those bonds tearing them asunder, goes away as he pleases. Now, Udāyin, if anyone should speak thus: 'That king's bull-elephant whose tusks are as long as a plough-pole . . . and who, if bound with a stout leather bond, having easily twisted his body, having burst those bonds tearing them asunder, goes away as he pleases; yet for him it was a strong bond, a stout bond, a solid bond, a bond that does not rot away, a thick log of wood '—would anyone speaking thus, Udāyin, be speaking rightly ?"

"No, revered sir. That king's bull-elephant, revered sir, whose tusks are as long as a plough-pole . . . and who if bound with a stout leather bond, having easily twisted his body, having burst those bonds tearing them asunder, goes away as he pleases, because for

---

[1] As at *Vin.* ii. 184. See *B.D.* v. 259 for notes.

[2] As at *M.* i. 414.

[3] *Cf. A.* ii. 33; *S.* iii. 85.

him it is a bond of no strength, a weak bond, a bond that rots away, a pithless bond."

"Even so, Udāyin, some young men of family here, on being told by me, 'Give this up,' speak thus: 'But what of this trifling insignificant matter to be given up and of whose giving up the Lord speaks to us and of whose rejection the Well-farer speaks to us?" And they give it up and they do not cause dissatisfaction to be nursed against me or against those monks who desire the training. These, giving that up, are unconcerned, unruffled, dependent on others, with a mind become as a wild creature's. This for them, Udāyin, is a weak bond, a bond of no strength, a bond that rots away, a pithless bond.

And, Udāyin, it is like a man, poor, needy, destitute,[1] who has one little tumbledown[2] hovel,[3] open to the crows, unlovely to see, one tumbledown pallet, unlovely to see, his [**451**] grain and store-room in one jar, unlovely to see, his one wife unlovely to see. He might see a monk in a monastery, his hands and feet properly washed, who, after eating a delicious meal, was sitting in the cool shade intent on the higher thought. It might occur to him: 'Indeed, recluseship is pleasant, indeed recluseship is healthy. Suppose that I, having cut off my hair and beard, having donned saffron robes, should go forth from home into homelessness?' But he might not be able to bring himself to give up his one little tumbledown hovel . . . his one wife, unlovely to see, and to go forth from home into homelessness, having cut off his hair and beard and having donned saffron robes. Now, Udāyin, if anyone should speak thus: 'That man, bound by those bonds is unable, giving up his one little tumbledown hovel . . . his one wife, unlovely to see, to go forth from home into homelessness, having cut off his hair and beard and having donned saffron robes, because for him it is a bond of no strength, a weak bond, a bond that rots away, a pithless bond —would anyone speaking thus, Udāyin, be speaking rightly?' "

"No, revered sir. That man, bound by those bonds, is not able to give up his one little tumbledown hovel . . . his one wife, unlovely to see, and to go forth from home into homelessness, having cut off his hair and beard and having donned saffron robes, because for him it is a strong bond, a stout bond, a solid bond, a bond that does not rot away, a thick log of wood."

"Even so, Udāyin, some foolish persons here, on being told by me,

---

[1] These three terms at *M.* ii. 178, *A.* iii. 351-2. [2] As at *M.* i. 80.

[3] *agāraka. MA.* iii. 167 says *khuddakageha*, little house.

'Give this up,' speak thus: 'But what of this trifling insignificant matter? This recluse lays too much emphasis on (exertion).' And they do not give it up and they cause dissatisfaction to be nursed against me and against those monks who desire the training. This is for them, Udāyin, a strong bond, a stout bond, a solid bond, a bond that does not rot away, a thick log of wood.

"And, Udāyin, it is like a householder or his son, rich, [**452**] of great wealth, of great possessions, with a mass of abundant gold ornaments,[1] a mass of abundant corn, a mass of abundant fields, with a mass of abundant raiment, with a mass of abundant wives, a mass of abundant men slaves, a mass of abundant women slaves. He might see a monk in a monastery, his hands and feet properly washed, who, after eating a delicious meal, was sitting in the cool shade intent on the higher thought. It might occur to him: 'Indeed recluseship is pleasant, indeed recluseship is healthy. Suppose that I, having cut off my hair and beard, having donned saffron robes, should go forth from home into homelessness?' And he might be able to bring himself to give up his mass of abundant gold ornaments, his mass of abundant corn . . . his mass of abundant women slaves, and to go forth from home into homelessness, having cut off his hair and beard and having donned saffron robes. If anyone should speak thus, Udāyin: 'That householder or his son, bound by those bonds, is able to give up his mass of abundant gold ornaments, his mass of abundant fields, his mass of abundant raiment, his mass of abundant wives, his mass of abundant men slaves, his mass of abundant women slaves, and having cut off his hair and beard and having donned saffron robes, to go forth from home into homelessness, because for him it was a strong bond, a stout bond, a solid bond, a bond that does not rot away, a thick log of wood'—would any one speaking thus, Udāyin, be speaking rightly?"

"No, revered sir. That householder or householder's son, revered sir, bound by those bonds, is able to give up his mass of abundant gold ornaments, his mass of abundant corn . . . his mass of abundant women slaves, and to go forth from home into homelessness, having cut off his hair and beard and donned saffron robes, because for him that was a bond of no strength, a weak bond, a bond that rots away, a pithless bond."

"Even so, Udāyin, some young men of family here, on being told by me, 'Give this up,' speak thus: 'But what of this trifling insig-

---

[1] *nikkhagaṇa*.

nificant matter to be given up and of whose giving up the Lord speaks to us and of whose rejection the Well-farer speaks to us ?' And they give it up and they do not cause dissatisfaction to be nursed against me or against those monks who desire the training. These, [**453**] giving that up, are unconcerned, unruffled, dependent on others, with a mind become as a wild creature's. This for them, Udāyin, is a bond of no strength, a weak bond, a bond that rots away, a pithless bond.

Udāyin, these four types of persons are found existing in the world. What four ? As to this, Udāyin, a certain person is faring along towards the getting rid of clinging,[1] towards the casting out of clinging. But while he is faring along towards the getting rid of clinging, towards the casting out of clinging, memories and thoughts[2] belonging to clinging beset him. He gives in to them, he does not get rid of them, he does not dispel them, he does not make an end of them, he does not send them to destruction. I, Udāyin, say that this person is fettered,[3] not unfettered. What is the reason for this ? Differences in faculties in this person are known to me, Udāyin.

And here, Udāyin, some person is faring along towards the getting rid of clinging, towards the casting out of clinging. But while he is faring along towards the getting rid of clinging, towards the casting out of clinging, memories and thoughts belonging to clinging beset him. He does not give in to them, he gets rid of them, he dispels them, he makes an end of them, he sends them to destruction. But I say that this person is also fettered, Udāyin, not unfettered. What is the reason for this ? Differences in faculties in this person are known to me, Udāyin.

And some person here, Udāyin, is faring along towards the getting rid of clinging, towards the casting out of clinging. While he is faring along towards the getting rid of clinging, towards the casting out of clinging, from confusion in mindfulness memories and thoughts belonging to clinging at times beset him. Slow, Udāyin, is the arising of mindfulness, and then he gets rid of it quickly, dispels it, makes an end of it, sends it to destruction. Udāyin, it is as if a man were to let two or three drops of water fall into an iron pot that had been heated all day long. Slow, Udāyin, is the falling of the drops of water, but they would be quickly destroyed and consumed. Even so, Udāyin, some person here is faring along towards the getting rid

---

[1] *upadhi*, a residual basis remaining for a new birth.

[2] *sarasaṅkappa*, as at *M*. iii. 89, 132, *S*. iv. 76, 190. [3] *saṁyutta*.

of clinging, towards the casting out of clinging. While he is faring along towards the getting rid of clinging, towards the casting out of clinging, from confusion in mindfulness memories and thoughts belonging to clinging at times beset him. Slow, Udāyin, is the arising of mindfulness, and then he gets rid of it quickly, dispels it, makes an end of it, sends it to destruction. I, Udāyin, say that this person is also fettered, not unfettered. [**454**] What is the reason for this ? Differences in faculties in this person are known to me, Udāyin.

But some person here, Udāyin, thinking, 'Clinging is the root of anguish,' and having understood it so, he is without clinging, freed by the destruction of clinging. I, Udāyin, say that this person is unfettered, not fettered. What is the reason for this ? Differences in faculties in this person are known to me, Udāyin.

There are these five strands of sense-pleasures,[1] Udāyin. What five ? Material shapes cognisable by the eye, agreeable, pleasant, liked, enticing, connected with sensual pleasures, alluring. Sounds cognisable by the ear . . . Smells cognisable by the nose . . . Tastes cognisable by the tongue . . . Touches cognisable by the body, agreeable, pleasant, liked, enticing, connected with sensual pleasures, alluring. These, Udāyin, are the five strands of sense-pleasures. Whatever happiness, whatever joy, Udāyin, arises in consequence of these five strands of sense-pleasures, it is called a happiness of sense-pleasures that is a vile happiness, the happiness of an average person, an unariyan happiness. It should not be pursued, developed or made much of. I say of this happiness that it is to be feared. In this connection, Udāyin, a monk, aloof from the pleasures of the senses, aloof from unskilled states of mind, enters and abides in the first meditation which is accompanied by initial thought and discursive thought, is born of aloofness, and is rapturous and joyful. By allaying initial and discursive thought, with the mind subjectively tranquillised and fixed on one point, he enters and abides in the second meditation which is devoid of initial and discursive thought, is born of concentration, and is rapturous and joyful . . . he enters and abides in the third meditation . . . the fourth meditation. This is called the happiness of renunciation, the happiness of aloofness, the happiness of tranquillity, the happiness of self-awakening.[2] It should be pursued, developed and made much of. I say of this happiness that it is not to be feared.

---

[1] As at *M.* i. 85.

[2] These four 'happinesses,' *sukha*, occur also at *A.* iv. 341-342.

As to this, Udāyin, a monk, aloof from pleasures of the senses . . . enters and abides in the first meditation which is . . . rapturous and joyful. I, Udāyin, say that this is in the unstable.[1] And what is in the unstable there ? That very initial and discursive thought that is not stopped there—this is in the unstable there. As to this, Udāyin, a monk, by allaying initial and discursive thought . . . enters and abides in the second meditation which is . . . rapturous and joyful. I, Udāyin, say that this too is in the unstable. And what is in the unstable there ? That very rapture and joy that are not stopped there—these are in the unstable there. As to this, Udāyin, a monk, by the fading out of rapture, dwells with equanimity, attentive and clearly conscious . . . and enters and abides in the third meditation. I, Udāyin, say that this too is in the unstable. And what is in the unstable there ? That very happiness in equanimity [**455**] that is not stopped there—this is in the unstable there. As to this, Udāyin, a monk, by getting rid of happiness and by getting rid of anguish . . . enters and abides in the fourth meditation which . . . is entirely purified by equanimity and mindfulness. I, Udāyin, say that this is in the stable.

As to this, Udāyin, a monk, aloof from pleasures of the senses . . . enters and abides in the first meditation . . . which is rapturous and joyful. I, Udāyin, say, 'This is not enough,' I say, 'Get rid of it,' I say, 'Transcend it.' And what, Udāyin, is its transcending ? As to this, Udāyin, a monk, by allaying initial and discursive thought . . . enters and abides in the second meditation. This is its transcending. But I, Udāyin, again say, 'This is not enough,' I say, 'Get rid of it,' I say, 'Transcend it.' And what is its transcending ? As to this, Udāyin, a monk, by the fading out of rapture . . . enters and abides in the third meditation. This is its transcending. But I, Udāyin, again say, 'This is not enough,' I say, 'Get rid of it,' I say, 'Transcend it.' And what is its transcending ? As to this, Udāyin, a monk, by getting rid of happiness . . . enters and abides in the fourth meditation. This is its transcending. But I, Udāyin, again say, 'This is not enough,' I say, 'Get rid of it,' I say, 'Transcend it.' And what is its transcending ? As to this, Udāyin, a monk, by wholly transcending perception of material shapes, by the going down of perception due to sensory impressions, by not attending to perception of variety, thinking, 'Ether is unending,' enters and abides in the plane of

---

[1] *iñjitasmiṁ*, what can be stirred or moved. *Cf. S.* i. 109: there is no instability in the wholly freed Buddhas. *Cf.* also *S.* iv. 202, *Sn.* 750.

infinite ether. This is its transcending. But I, Udāyin, again say, 'This is not enough,' I say, 'Get rid of it,' I say, 'Transcend it.' And what is its transcending? As to this, Udāyin, a monk, by wholly transcending the plane of infinite ether, thinking, 'Consciousness is unending,' enters and abides in the plane of infinite consciousness. This is its transcending. But I, Udāyin, again say, 'This is not enough,' I say, 'Get rid of it,' I say, 'Transcend it.' And what is its transcending? As to this, Udāyin, a monk, by wholly transcending the plane of infinite consciousness, thinking, 'There is not anything,' enters and abides in the plane of no-thing. This is its transcending. But I, Udāyin, again say, 'This is not enough,' I say, 'Get rid of it,' I say, 'Transcend it.' And what is its transcending? As to this, Udāyin, a monk, by wholly transcending the plane of no-thing, enters and abides in the plane of neither-perception-nor-non-perception. [**456**] This is its transcending. But I, Udāyin, again say, 'This is not enough,' I say, 'Get rid of it,' I say, 'Transcend it.' And what is its transcending? As to this, Udāyin, a monk, by wholly transcending the plane of neither-perception-nor-non-perception, enters and abides in the stopping of perception and feeling. This is its transcending. It is for this that I, Udāyin, speak even of the getting rid of the plane of neither-perception-nor non-perception. Now do you, Udāyin, see any fetter, minute or massive, of the getting rid of which I have not spoken to you?"[1]

"No, revered sir."

Thus spoke the Lord. Delighted, the venerable Udāyin rejoiced in what the Lord had said.

Discourse on the Simile of the Quail:
The Sixth

67. DISCOURSE AT CĀTUMĀ

(Cātumasutta)

THUS have I heard: At one time the Lord was staying near Cātumā in the Myrobalan Grove. Now at that time at least five hundred

[1] Quoted at *MA*. ii. 109 in explanation of "even (right) states of mind are to be got rid of," as said at end of the Parable of the Raft.

monks,[1] with Sāriputta and Moggallāna[2] at their head had arrived at Cātumā to see the Lord, and there was a loud noise, a great noise as these incoming monks were exchanging greetings with the resident monks, while lodgings were being prepared and bowls and robes were being put away. Then the Lord addressed the venerable Ānanda, saying: " What, Ānanda, is this loud noise, this great noise, which seems like that of fisherfolk when hauling in a catch ?"

" Revered sir, these monks, at least five hundred, with Sāriputta and Moggallāna at their head have arrived at Cātumā to see the Lord, and while the incoming monks are exchanging greetings with the resident monks, while lodgings are being prepared and bowls and robes are being put away, there is a loud noise, a great noise."

" Well then, Ānanda, in my name summon these monks, saying: 'The Teacher is summoning the venerable ones.' "

" Yes, revered sir," and the venerable Ānanda, having answered the Lord in assent, approached these monks; having approached, he spoke thus to these monks: " The Teacher is summoning the venerable ones."

" Yes, your reverence," and these [**457**] monks, having answered the venerable Ānanda in assent, approached the Lord; having approached, having greeted the Lord, they sat down at a respectful distance. The Lord spoke thus to these monks as they were sitting down at a respectful distance: " Do not you, monks, think that the loud noise, the great noise is like that of fisherfolk when hauling in a catch ?"

" Revered sir, at least five hundred monks with Sāriputta and Moggallāna at their head have arrived at Cātumā to see the Lord, and while . . . bowls and robes are being put away, there is a loud noise, a great noise."

" Go away, monks, I dismiss you, you should not stay near me."

" Very well, revered sir," and these monks having answered the Lord in assent, having greeted the Lord keeping their right sides towards him, having packed away their lodgings, departed taking their bowls and robes.

---

[1] This passage also occurs at *Ud.* 24-25, where Yasoja is at the head of 500 monks, but the episode is there placed at Sāvatthī. These monks were perhaps only recently ordained, and that is why the two chief disciples were in charge of them. *MA.* iii. 172 speaks of them as *kulaputtā*, as though hardly recognising their passage to monk's status. But with this compare the first speech ascribed to the Lord in the next Discourse where he refers to those who have gone forth both as young men of family and as monks.

[2] No epithet 'venerable' here.

Now at that time the Sakyans of Cātumā were assembled in the conference hall on some business or other. The Sakyans of Cātumā saw these monks coming in the distance; having seen them, they approached these monks; having approached, they spoke thus to these monks: " Now, where are you, venerable ones, going ?"

" Friends, the Order of monks has been dismissed by the Lord."

" Well then, venerable ones, sit down for a moment; perhaps we could reconcile the Lord."

" Very well, friends," these monks answered the Sakyans of Cātumā in assent. Then the Sakyans of Cātumā approached the Lord; having approached, having greeted the Lord, they sat down at a respectful distance. As they were sitting down at a respectful distance, the Sakyans of Cātumā spoke thus to the Lord:

" Revered sir, let the Lord rejoice the Order of monks, let the Lord greet the Order of monks. Revered sir, even as the Order of monks was helped previously by the Lord, so let the Lord help the Order of monks now. There are here,[1] revered sir, new monks, not long gone forth, quite recently come into this *dhamma* and discipline. Not getting a chance to see the Lord, there may be faltering[2] for them, there may be vicissitudes.[3] Even, revered sir, as there may be faltering and vicissitudes for young seeds if they do not get water, even so, revered sir, there are here [**458**] new monks, not long gone forth, quite recently come into this *dhamma* and discipline; if they do not get a chance to see the Lord, there may be faltering for them, there may be vicissitudes. And even, revered sir, as there may be faltering, as there may be vicissitudes for a young calf that does not see its mother, so, revered sir, there are here new monks, not long gone forth, quite recently come into this *dhamma* and discipline. Not seeing the Lord, there may be faltering for them, there may be vicissitudes. Revered sir, let the Lord rejoice the Order of monks, let the Lord greet the Order of monks. Revered sir, even as the Order of monks was helped previously by the Lord, so let the Lord help the Order of monks now."

Then Brahmā Sahampati,[4] knowing by mind the reasoning in the Lord's mind, as a strong man might stretch forth his bent arm or

---

[1] *Cf. S.* iii. 91.

[2] *aññathatta,* " otherness." See *M.* i. 448 (" depression "), ii. 51, and *S.* iii. 91-92.

[3] *vipariṇāma,* change, falling away.

[4] The persuasions of Brahmā Sahampati and the Sakyans of Cātumā are referred to at *Miln.* 209 *f.*

might bend back his outstretched arm, even so, vanishing from the Brahma-world he appeared before the Lord. Then Brahmā Sahampati, arranging his outer robe over one shoulder, saluting the Lord with joined palms, spoke thus to the Lord: "Revered sir, let the Lord rejoice the Order of monks . . . (*repeat as for the Sakyans of Cātumā*) . . . Revered sir, even as the Order of monks was helped previously by the Lord, [**459**] so let the Lord help the Order of monks now."

The Sakyans of Cātumā and Brahmā Sahampati were able to reconcile the Lord by the analogy of the seeds and the analogy of the young[1] (calf). Then the venerable Moggallāna the Great addressed the monks, saying: "Arise, your reverences, pick up your bowls and robes, the Lord has been reconciled by the Sakyans of Cātumā and by Brahmā Sahampati with the analogy of the seeds and the analogy of the young (calf)."

"Yes, your reverence," and these monks, having answered the venerable Moggallāna the Great in assent, rising from their seats, taking their bowls and robes, approached the Lord; having approached, having greeted the Lord, they sat down at a respectful distance. The Lord spoke thus to the venerable Sāriputta as he was sitting down at a respectful distance:

"What did you, Sāriputta, think when the Order of monks was dismissed by me?"

"When the Order of monks was dismissed by the Lord, I, revered sir, thought: 'The Lord is now unconcerned, he will abide intent on abiding in ease here and now.[2] We too, unconcerned now, will abide intent on abiding in ease here and now.'"

"Do you wait, Sāriputta, do you wait, Sāriputta. Sāriputta, never let such a thought arise in you again."[3] Then the Lord addressed the venerable Moggallāna the Great, saying:

"What did you, Moggallāna, think when the Order of monks was dismissed by me?"

"When the Order of monks was dismissed by the Lord, I, revered sir, thought: 'The Lord is now unconcerned, he will abide intent on

---

[1] *taruṇūpama*, as at *M*. i. 432, of a young baby.

[2] Except for the tense, these words are identical with Devadatta's at *Vin*. ii. 188.

[3] According to *MA*. iii. 176, the Elder did not know his duty (*bhārabhāva*), which was, as was Moggallāna's, to the Order of monks—as shown by the latter's answer; therefore he was commended for it. It is not often that Sāriputta is rebuked by Gotama, but see *M*. ii. 195, and Intr. p. xxvi.

abiding in ease here and now. I and the venerable Sāriputta will now lead the Order of monks.' "

" It is good, Moggallāna, it is good. For either I, Moggallāna, could lead the Order of monks, or Sāriputta and Moggallāna."[1]

Then the Lord addressed the Order of monks, saying: " Monks, these four perils for one going down to the water[2] are to be expected. What four ? Peril of waves, peril of crocodiles,[3] peril of whirlpools, peril of fierce fishes.[4] These are the four perils to be expected for one going down to the water. Similarly, monks, four perils are to be expected for some persons here who have gone forth from home into homelessness in this *dhamma* and discipline. [**460**] What four ? Peril of waves, peril of crocodiles, peril of whirlpools, peril of fierce fishes.

And what, monks, is the peril of waves ? Here, monks, some young man of family, gone forth from home into homelessness through faith, thinks: ' Although I am oppressed by birth, ageing, dying, by grief, sorrow, suffering, lamentation and despair, oppressed by anguish, overcome by anguish, yet perhaps some ending of this whole mass of anguish may be seen.' His fellow Brahma-farers exhort and instruct him who has thus gone forth: ' Thus should you go out, thus should you return, thus should you look in front, thus should you look round, thus should you bend out (your arm), thus should you bend it back, thus should you carry your outer cloak, your bowl and robe.' If it occurs to him: ' While I was formerly in the household state, we used to exhort and instruct others, but these who seem like our sons, who seem like our grandsons, think that they should exhort and instruct us '—then, disavowing the training, he returns to the low life of the world. This one, monks, who disavows the training and returns to the low life of the world is called one who is scared by the peril of waves. ' The peril of waves,' monks, is a synonym for angry wrath.[5]

And what, monks, is the peril of crocodiles ? Here, monks, some young man of family who has gone forth from home into homelessness through faith, thinks: ' Although I am oppressed by birth . . .

---

[1] At *D.* ii. 100, Gotama tells Ānanda that it does not occur to a Tathāgata: ' I will lead the Order of monks.' At *Vin.* ii. 188 he tells Devadatta he would not hand over (*na nissajjeyyaṁ*) the Order of monks even to Sāriputta and Moggallāna. See Intr. p. xxvii.

[2] *Cf. A.* ii. 123 *ff.*

[3] Referred to at *Thig.* 502.

[4] Referred to among the many perils or fears, *bhaya*, at *Miln.* 196.

[5] Another synonym for this is given at *M.* i. 144.

yet perhaps some ending of this whole mass of anguish may be seen.' His fellow Brahma-farers exhort and instruct him who has thus gone forth: 'This can be eaten[1] by you, this cannot be eaten by you, this can be partaken of by you, this cannot be partaken of by you, this can be savoured by you, this cannot be savoured by you, this can be drunk by you, this cannot be drunk by you; you should eat what is allowable, you should not eat what is not allowable, you should partake of what is allowable, you should not partake of what is not allowable, you should savour what is allowable, you should not savour what is not allowable, you should drink what is allowable, you should not drink what is not allowable; you should eat at the right time, you should not eat at the wrong time, you should partake of at the right time, you should not partake of at the wrong time, you should savour at the right time, you should not savour at the wrong time, you should drink at the right time, you should not drink at the wrong time.' If it occurs to him **[461]** 'Formerly when I was in the household state we ate what we liked, we did not eat what we did not like, we partook of what we liked, we did not partake of what we did not like, we savoured what we liked, we did not savour what we did not like, we drank what we liked, we did not drink what we did not like; we ate what was allowable and we ate what was not allowable, we partook of what was allowable and we partook of what was not allowable, we savoured what was allowable and we savoured what was not allowable, we drank what was allowable and we drank what was not allowable; we ate at the right time and we ate at the wrong time, we partook of at the right time and we partook of at the wrong time, we savoured at the right time and we savoured at the wrong time, we drank at the right time and we drank at the wrong time. But when those householders who have faith give us sumptuous foods, solid and soft, at a wrong time, during the day, it seems as if they are putting restraint over the mouth'[2]—and disavowing the training, he returns to the low life of the world. This one, monks, who disavowing the training, returns to the low life of the world, is called one who is scared by the peril of crocodiles. 'The peril of crocodiles,' monks, is a synonym for gluttony.

And what, monks, is the peril of whirlpools? Here, monks, some young man of family who has gone forth from home into homeless-

---

[1] *khāditabbaṁ*, referring to eating solid food, and *bhuñjitabbaṁ* (partake of) to eating soft food.

[2] *mukhāvaraṇaṁ karonti*. *Āvaraṇa* is a prohibition, interdiction, obstruction, covering.

ness through faith, thinks: 'I am oppressed by birth . . . but perhaps some ending can be seen of this whole mass of anguish.' He, gone forth thus, having dressed in the morning, taking his bowl and robe, enters a village or market town for almsfood unguarded as to his body, unguarded as to his speech,[1] mindfulness not set up, the sense-organs uncontrolled. He there sees a householder or a householder's son indulging in and provided with the five strands of sense-pleasures, and finding delight in them. If it occurs to him; 'Formerly while we were in the household state, indulging in and provided with the five strands of sense-pleasures, we found delight in them. As there is wealth in my home, it is possible both to enjoy wealth and to do meritorious things,' he, disavowing the training, returns to the low life of the world. This one, monks who, disavowing the training, returns to the low life of the world, is called one who is scared of the peril of whirlpools. 'The peril of whirlpools,' monks, is a synonym for the five strands of sense-pleasures.

And what, monks, is the peril of fierce fishes? Here, monks, [**462**] some young man of family who has gone forth from home into homelessness through faith, thinks: 'I am oppressed by birth . . . but perhaps some ending to this whole mass of anguish can be seen.' He, gone forth thus, having dressed in the morning, taking his bowl and robe, enters a village or a market town for almsfood unguarded in his body, unguarded in his speech, mindfulness not set up, the sense-organs uncontrolled. He sees a woman there[2] who is improperly dressed or improperly clothed. When he has seen that woman who is improperly dressed or improperly clothed, passion corrupts his mind, and with his mind corrupted by passion, disavowing the training he returns to the low life of the world. This one, monks, who disavowing the training, returns to the low life of the world, is called one who is scared by the peril of fierce fishes. 'The peril of fierce fishes,' monks, is a synonym for women.

These monks, are the four perils to be expected for some persons here who have gone forth from home into homelessness in this *dhamma* and discipline."

Thus spoke the Lord. Delighted, these monks rejoiced in what the Lord had said.

Discourse at Cātumā:
The Seventh

---

[1] *A*. ii. 125 inserts (rightly) *arakkhitena cittena*, unguarded as to his thought.
[2] *Cf*. *S*. ii. 231, 271; *A*. iii. 95.

68. DISCOURSE AT NAḶAKAPĀNA

(Naḷakapānasutta)[1]

THUS have I heard: At one time the Lord was staying among the Kosalans near Naḷakapāna[2] in the Judas-tree Grove.[3] Now at that time many well known young men of family had gone forth from home into homelessness through faith in the Lord: the venerable Anuruddha[4] and the venerable Nandiya and the venerable Kimbila and the venerable Bhagu[5] and the venerable Kuṇḍadhāna[6] and the venerable Revata and the venerable Ānanda, and many other well known young men of family. Now at that time the Lord [**463**] was sitting in the open surrounded by an Order of monks. Then the Lord addressed the monks concerning these young men of family, saying: "Those young men of family, monks, who have gone forth from home into homelessness through faith in me—I hope, monks, that these monks are finding delight in the Brahma-faring?" When he had spoken thus, these monks became silent. And a second time . . . and a third time the Lord addressed the monks concerning these young men of family, saying: "Those young men of family, monks, who have gone forth from home into homelessness through faith in me—I hope, monks, that these monks are finding delight in the Brahma-faring?" And a third time these monks became silent.

Then it occurred to the Lord: "Now, suppose that I were to question these young men of family themselves?" Then the Lord addressed the venerable Anuruddha, saying: "I hope that you, Anuruddhas,[7] are finding delight in the Brahma-faring?"

"Certainly we, revered sir, are finding delight in the Brahma-faring."

---

[1] *Cf. Jā.* No. 20 which describes how the Bodhisatta, as a monkey, taught his followers to drink water through a hollow reed; referred to at *MA.* iii. 178.

[2] *Cf. A.* v. 122, 125.

[3] *Palāsavana. MA.* iii. 180 says that *palāsa* is *kiṃsuka,* "strange." *PED.* gives Butea frondosa. The Palāsajātaka is at *Jā.* iii. 23. *Cf.* also the simile of the *kiṃsuka* at *S.* iv. 193.

[4] For some of the following names see *M.* i. 205, 212, iii. 155; *Vin.* ii. 128.

[5] His verses are at *Thag.* 271-274. See *Vin.* i. 350.

[6] His verses are at *Thag.* 15. He has a place among the *etad aggas* at *A.* i. 24.

[7] For use of plural, Anuruddhā, see *M.L.S.* i. 257, *n.* 4.

"It is good, it is good, Anuruddhas. This is fitting in you, Anuruddhas, who are young men of family gone forth from home into homelessness through faith, that you should find delight in the Brahma-faring. Yet while you, Anuruddhas, possessed of radiant youth, in the prime of your lives, with coal-black hair, might be enjoying the pleasures of the senses, you, Anuruddhas, although possessed of radiant youth, in the prime of your lives, with coal-black hair, have nevertheless gone forth from home into homelessness. But you, Anuruddhas, are neither those that have gone forth from home into homelessness on the suggestion of kings[1] nor those who have gone forth from home into homelessness on the suggestion of thieves . . . nor because of debt . . . nor through fear,[2] nor are you those that have gone forth from home into homelessness because of having lost the means of livelihood. Yet was it not with the thought: 'Although I am oppressed by birth, ageing, dying, by grief, sorrow, suffering, lamentation and despair, oppressed by anguish, beset by anguish, yet perhaps some ending of this whole mass of anguish may be seen,' that you, Anuruddhas, have gone forth from home into homelessness through faith?"

"Yes, revered sir."

"And when, Anuruddhas, a young man of family has gone forth thus, what is there to be done by him? Anuruddhas, aloof from pleasures of the senses, aloof from unskilled states of mind, if he does not win joy and happiness or something more peaceful than that,[3] then coveting persists in obsessing his mind, and malevolence persists in obsessing his mind, and sloth and torpor . . . and restlessness and worry . . . and doubt . . . [**464**] and discontent . . . and apathy persists in obsessing his mind. Aloof, Anuruddhas, from pleasures of the senses, aloof from unskilled states of mind, he does not win joy and happiness or something more peaceful than that. Anuruddhas, aloof from pleasures of the senses, aloof from unskilled states of mind, if he wins joy and happiness and something more peaceful than that, then coveting does not persist in obsessing his mind, and

[1] *Cf. Iti.* § 91; *S.* iii. 93; *Miln.* 32. If a king or thieves to whom someone has done a wrong catch him, they say: 'If you will go forth, you can be free,' *MA.* iii. 180.

[2] If he is scared by a certain peril or fear (*bhaya*)—of a king and so forth, he goes forth. *SA.* ii. 302 gives the "perils" as those regarding kings, thieves, hunger, illness and debt.

[3] *MA.* iii. 181 says that if at this stage he does not win joy and so on, then he does not win the more peaceful happiness of the two following *jhāna* and the four ways.

malevolence . . . and sloth and torpor . . . and restlessness and worry . . . and doubt . . . and discontent . . . and apathy does not persist in obsessing his mind. Aloof, Anuruddhas, from pleasures of the senses, aloof from unskilled states of mind, he wins joy and happiness and something more peaceful than that.

What do you think about me, Anuruddhas ? That those cankers which have to do with the defilements,[1] with again-becoming, which are fearful, whose result is anguish, making for birth, ageing and dying in the future—that these have not been got rid of by the Tathāgata, and that therefore the Tathāgata, having considered[2], pursues one thing; having considered, endures another thing; having considered, avoids another thing; having considered, controls another thing ?"[3]

"We, revered sir, do not think this of the Lord, that those cankers which have to do with the defilements, with again-becoming . . . making for birth, ageing and dying in the future—that these have not been got rid of by the Tathāgata, and that therefore the Tathāgata, having considered, pursues one thing; having considered, endures another thing; having considered, avoids another thing; having considered, controls another thing. We, revered sir, think this of the Lord, that those cankers that have to do with the defilements, with again-becoming . . . making for birth, ageing and dying in the future —that these have been got rid of by the Tathāgata, and that therefore the Tathāgata, having considered, pursues one thing; having considered, endures another thing; having considered, avoids another thing; having considered, controls another thing."

"It is good, it is good, Anuruddhas.[4] Those cankers of the Tathāgata that had to do with the defilements, with again-becoming, that were fearful, whose result was anguish, making for birth, ageing and dying in the future—these have been got rid of, cut off at the root, made like a palm-tree stump that can come to no further existence in the future. Even, Anuruddhas, as a palm-tree whose crown is cut off can come to no further growth, so, Anuruddhas, those cankers of the Tathāgata that had to do with the defilements . . . can come to no further existence in the future. Therefore the Tathāgata, having considered, pursues one thing; having considered, endures another thing; having considered, avoids another thing; having considered, controls another thing.

---

[1] As at *M*. i. 250. [2] *sankhāya*, as at *A*. ii. 143.

[3] *Cf*. *M*. i. 7 for these ways of dealing with the cankers. These four phrases are used in connection with the four *apassena* at *D*. iii. 224.

[4] This paragraph also at *M*. i. 250.

What do you think about this, Anuruddhas ? Beholding what special purpose does the Tathāgata explain the uprisings in which are disciples who have deceased and passed away, saying: 'Such a one has uprisen in one, such a one has uprisen in another[1] ?' "

[**465**] "Things for us, revered sir, are rooted in the Lord, have the Lord for conduit, the Lord for arbiter. It were good indeed, revered sir, if the meaning of this speech of the Lord's were explained; having heard the Lord, the monks would remember."[2]

"Anuruddhas, the Tathāgata does not have the purpose[3] of defrauding people nor the purpose of cajoling people nor the purpose of gains, honour, fame and material advantages, nor the thought: 'Let people know me thus '[4] when he explains the uprisings in which are disciples who have deceased and passed away, saying: 'Such a one has uprisen in one, such a one has uprisen in another.' But there are, Anuruddhas, young men of family who have faith and are of great enthusiasm,[5] of great joyousness and who, having heard this, focus their minds on suchness.[6] Anuruddhas, this will be for their weal and happiness for a long time.

In this case, Anuruddhas, a monk hears: 'The monk so and so has passed away; it is declared by the Lord that he is established in profound knowledge.' If a venerable one has himself seen or has heard by hearsay that the venerable one was of such moral habit and that the venerable one was of such mentality[7] and that the venerable one was of such wisdom and that the venerable one was such an abider and that the venerable one was freed thus, he, while recollecting his faith and moral habit and learning and giving up and wisdom, focusses his mind on suchness. It is thus, Anuruddhas, that there is abiding in comfort for a monk.

In this case, Anuruddhas, a monk hears: 'The monk so and so has passed away; it is declared by the Lord that by the utter destruction of the five fetters binding to this lower (shore), he is of spontaneous generation, one that has attained nibbāna there, not liable to return from that world.' If a venerable one has himself seen or has heard

---

[1] *Cf. D.* ii. 200. [2] As at *M.* i. 310. [3] *Cf. Iti.* § 35, 36; *A.* ii. 26.

[4] *MA.* iii. 182, "the multitude will know me thus, a lovely report will go forth about me among the multitude."

[5] *uḷāravedā*, *MA.* iii. 182 saying *mahantatuṭṭhino.*

[6] *tathattāya*, the state of being so; but possibly here meaning that they imitate the monks who have died.

[7] *evaṁdhammo.* Here *dhamma*, between *sīla* and *paññā*, seems to take the place of the more usual *samādhi* or *citta*, and so means having (right) mental objects.

by hearsay that the venerable one was of such moral habit . . . of such mentality . . . of such wisdom . . . was such an abider . . . was freed thus, he, while recollecting his faith and . . . wisdom, focusses his mind on suchness. It is thus too, Anuruddhas, that there is abiding in comfort for a monk.

In this case, Anuruddhas, a monk hears: 'The monk so and so has passed away; it is declared by the Lord that by the utter destruction of the three fetters, by the reduction of attachment, aversion and confusion, he is a once-returner who, having come back once only to this world, will make an end of anguish.' If a venerable one has himself seen or has heard by hearsay that the venerable one was of such moral habit . . . was freed thus, he, while recollecting his faith and . . . wisdom, focusses his mind on suchness. [**466**] It is thus too, Anuruddhas, that there is abiding in comfort for a monk.

In this case, Anuruddhas, a monk hears: 'The monk so and so has passed away; it is declared by the Lord that by the utter destruction of the three fetters he is a stream-attainer, not liable to the Downfall, assured, bound for enlightenment.' If a venerable one has himself seen or has heard by hearsay that the venerable one was of such moral habit . . . of such mentality . . . of such wisdom . . . was such an abider . . . was freed thus, he, while recollecting his faith and moral habit and learning and giving up and wisdom, focusses his mind on suchness. It is thus, Anuruddhas, that there is abiding in comfort for a monk.

In this case, Anuruddhas, a nun hears: 'The nun so and so has passed away; it is declared of her by the Lord that she is established in profound knowledge.' If that sister has herself seen or has heard by hearsay that that sister was of such moral habit . . . mentality . . . wisdom . . . such an abider . . . was freed thus, she, while recollecting her faith and moral habit and learning and giving up and wisdom, focusses her mind on suchness. It is thus, Anuruddhas that there is abiding in comfort for a nun.

In this case, Anuruddhas, a nun hears: 'The nun so and so has passed away; it is declared of her by the Lord that by the utter destruction of the five fetters binding to this lower (shore), she is of spontaneous generation, one that has attained nibbāna there, not liable to return from that world . . . It is declared of her by the Lord that by the utter destruction of the three fetters, by the reduction of attachment, aversion, confusion, she is a once-returner who, having come back once only to this world, will make an end of anguish . . . It is declared of her by the Lord that by the utter destruction of the three fetters she is a stream-attainer, not liable to the Downfall, assured, bound for enlightenment.' [**467**] If that sister has herself seen or has heard by hearsay that that sister was of such moral habit . . . was freed thus, she, while recollecting her faith . . . and wisdom, focusses her mind on suchness. It is thus, Anuruddhas, that there is abiding in comfort for a nun.

In this case, Anuruddhas, a layfollower hears: 'The layfollower so and so has passed away; it is declared of him by the Lord that by the utter destruction of the five fetters binding to this lower (shore), he is of spontaneous generation, one that has attained nibbāna there, not liable to return from that world . . . It is declared of him by the Lord that by the utter destruction of the three fetters, by the reduction of attachment, aversion, confusion, he is a once-returner who, having come back once only to this world, will make an end of anguish . . . It is declared of him by the Lord that by the utter destruction of the three fetters, he is a stream-attainer, not liable to the Downfall, assured, bound for enlightenment.' If that layfollower has himself seen or has heard by hearsay that that layfollower was of such moral habit . . . was freed thus, he, while recollecting his faith . . . and wisdom, focusses his mind on suchness. It is thus, Anuruddhas, that there is abiding in comfort for a layfollower.

In this case, Anuruddhas, a laywoman follower hears, 'The laywoman follower so and so has passed away; it is declared of her by the Lord that by the utter destruction of the five fetters binding to this lower (shore), she is of spontaneous generation, one that has attained nibbāna there, not liable to return from that world . . . [**468**] . . . It is declared of her by the Lord that by the utter destruction of the three fetters, by the reduction of attachment, aversion, confusion, she is a once-returner who, having come back cnce only to this world, will make an end of anguish . . . It is declared of her by the Lord that by the utter destruction of the three fetters, she is a stream-attainer, not liable to the Downfall, assured, bound for enlightenment.' If that sister has herself seen or has heard by hearsay that that sister was of such moral habit and that that sister was of such mentality and that that sister was of such wisdom and that sister was such an abider and that sister was freed thus, she, while recollecting her faith and moral habit and learning and giving up and wisdom, focusses her mind on suchness. It is thus, Anuruddhas, that there is abiding in comfort for a laywoman follower.

The Tathāgata, Anuruddhas, does not have the purpose of defrauding people nor the purpose of cajoling people nor the purpose of gains, honour, fame and material advantages, nor the thought: 'Let people know me thus' when he explains the uprising in which are disciples who have deceased and passed away, saying: 'Such and such a one has uprisen in one, such a one has uprisen in another.' But there are, Anuruddhas, young men of family who have faith and are of great enthusiasm, of great joyousness, and who, having heard this, focus their minds on suchness. Anuruddhas, this will be for their weal and happiness for a long time."

Thus spoke the Lord. Delighted, the venerable Anuruddha rejoiced in what the Lord had said.

Discourse at Naḷakapāna:
The Eighth

69. DISCOURSE ON GULISSĀNI

(Gulissānisutta)

[469] THUS have I heard: At one time the Lord was staying near Rājagaha in the Bamboo Grove at the squirrels' feeding place. At that time a monk named Gulissāni, forest-gone, uncouth in his habits, had arrived in the midst of an Order on some business or other. Thereupon the venerable Sāriputta addressed the monks concerning the monk Gulissāni, saying:

"Your reverences, a monk who is forest-gone and who comes back to an Order and is staying with an Order, should be deferential and respectful towards his fellow Brahma-farers. If, your reverences, a monk who is forest-gone comes back to an Order and is staying with an Order, and is not deferential and respectful towards his fellow Brahma-farers, there will be those who speak about him and say: 'What is the good of this venerable one who is forest-gone and who lives alone in the forest doing as he pleases but who is not deferential and respectful towards his fellow Brahma-farers?'—there will be those who speak about him. Therefore a monk who is forest-gone and who has come back to an Order and is staying with an Order should be deferential and respectful towards his fellow-Brahma-farers.

Your reverences, a monk who is forest-gone and who comes back to an Order and is staying with an Order, should be skilled about the seats, thinking: 'I will sit down not encroaching on[1] (the space intended for) monks who are elders, nor will I keep newly ordained monks from a seat.'[2] If, your reverences, a monk who is forest-gone comes back to an Order and is staying with an Order, and is not skilled about the seats, there will be those who speak about him and say: 'What is the good of this venerable one who is forest-gone and who lives alone in the forest doing what he pleases but who does not even know the rule about decent conduct?'—there will be those who speak about him. Therefore a monk who is forest-gone and who has come back to an Order and is staying with an Order should be skilled about the seats.

Your reverences, a monk who is forest-gone and who comes back to an Order and is staying with an Order, should not enter a village too early nor return[3] during the day. If, your reverences, a monk who is forest-gone comes back to an Order and is staying with an Order, and enters a village too early and returns during the day, there will be those who speak about him and say: 'What is the good of this venerable one who is forest-gone and who lives alone in the forest doing as he pleases but who enters a village too early and returns during the day?'—there will be those who speak about him. Therefore a monk who is forest-gone and who comes back to an Order and is staying with an Order should not enter a village too early and should not return during the day.

Your reverences, a monk who is forest-gone . . . is staying with an Order, should not **[470]** call upon families before a meal or after a meal.[4] If, your reverences, a monk who is forest-gone comes back to an Order and is staying with an Order, and calls upon families before a meal or after a meal, there will be those who will speak about him and say: 'Is not this walking at a wrong time frequently practised by this venerable one who is forest-gone, living alone in the forest doing as he pleases, and does not he also boast about it to one who is in the Order?'—there will be those who speak about him.

---

[1] *Vin.* iv. 43; *cf. Vin.* ii. 88. [2] *Cf. Vin.* i. 47.

[3] *I.e.* to the monastery. See Pācittiya 85 (*Vin.* iv. 164 *ff.*), and Nuns' Pācittiya 17 (*Vin.* iv. 274).

[4] See Pācittiya 46 (*Vin.* iv. 99 *f.*).

Therefore a monk who is forest-gone and who comes back to an Order and is staying with an Order should call upon families neither before a meal nor after a meal.

Your reverences, a monk who is forest-gone and who comes back to an Order and is staying with an Order, should not be proud or inconsiderate.[1] If, your reverences, a monk who is forest-gone comes back to an Order and is staying with an Order, is proud and inconsiderate, there will be those who speak about him and say: 'Is not this pride and inconsiderateness frequently practised by this venerable one who is forest-gone, living alone in a forest doing as he pleases, and does not he also boast about it to one who is in the Order ?'—there will be those that speak about him. Therefore a monk who is forest-gone and who comes back to an Order and is staying with an Order should not be proud and inconsiderate.

Your reverences, a monk who is forest-gone . . . and is staying with an Order, should not be scurrilous or of loose talk.[1] If, your reverences, a monk who is forest-gone . . . and is staying with an Order, is scurrilous and of loose talk, there will be those who speak about him and say: 'What is the good of this venerable one who is forest-gone, living alone in a forest doing as he pleases, but who is scurrilous and of loose talk ?'—there will be those who speak about him. Therefore a monk who is forest-gone . . . and is staying with an Order should not be scurrilous or of loose talk.

Your reverences, a monk who is forest-gone . . . and is staying with an Order, should be of pleasant speech,[2] a friend of the lovely.[2] If, your reverences, a monk who is forest-gone . . . and is staying with an Order, is of wrong speech,[3] a friend of the evil,[2] there will be those who speak about him and say: 'What is the good of this venerable one who is forest-gone, living alone in a forest doing as he pleases, but who is of wrong speech, a friend of the evil ?'—there will be those who speak about him. Therefore a monk who is forest-gone . . . and is staying with an Order should be of pleasant speech, a friend of the lovely.

Your reverences, a monk who is forest-gone should be guarded as to the doors of his sense-organs. If, your reverences, a monk who is forest-gone is not guarded as to the doors of his sense-organs, there will be those who speak about him and say: 'What is the good of this venerable one who is forest-gone, living alone

[1] *Cf. M.* i. 32. [2] *See M.* i. 43.

[3] *dubbaca* can also mean "difficult to speak to," see *Vin.* ii¹. *M.* i. 43.

in a forest doing as he pleases, [471] but who is not guarded as to the doors of his sense-organs?'—there will be those who speak about him. Therefore a monk who is forest-gone should be guarded as to the doors of his sense-organs.

Your reverences, a monk who is forest-gone should be moderate in eating. If, your reverences, a monk who is forest-gone is not moderate in eating, there will be those who speak about him and say: 'What is the good of this venerable one who is forest-gone, living alone in a forest doing as he pleases, but who is not moderate in eating?'—there will be those who speak about him. Therefore a monk who is forest-gone should be moderate in eating.

Your reverences, a monk who is forest-gone should be intent on vigilance. If, your reverences, a monk who is forest-gone is not intent on vigilance, there will be those who speak about him and say: 'What is the good of this venerable one who is forest-gone, living alone in a forest doing as he pleases, but who is not intent on vigilance?'—there will be those who speak about him. Therefore a monk who is forest-gone should be intent on vigilance.

Your reverences, a monk who is forest-gone should put forth energy. If, your reverences, a monk who is forest-gone is lazy, there will be those who speak of him and say: 'What is the good of this venerable one who is forest-gone, living alone in a forest doing as he pleases, but who is lazy?'—there will be those who speak about him. Therefore a monk who is forest-gone should put forth energy.

Your reverences, a monk who is forest-gone should arouse mindfulness. If, your reverences, a monk who is forest-gone is of muddled mindfulness, there will be those who speak about him and say: 'What is the good of this venerable one who is forest-gone, living alone in a forest doing as he pleases, but who is of muddled mindfulness?'—there will be those who speak about him. Therefore a monk who is forest-gone should arouse mindfulness.

Your reverences, a monk who is forest-gone should have concentration. If, your reverences a monk who is forest-gone has not concentration, there will be those who speak about him and say: 'What is the good of this venerable one who is forest-gone, living alone in a forest doing as he pleases, but who has not concentration?'—there will be those who speak about him. Therefore a monk who is forest-gone should have concentration.

Your reverences, a monk who is forest-gone should have wisdom. If, your reverences, a monk who is forest-gone is poor in wisdom, there will be those who [472] speak about him and say: 'What is the good of this venerable one who is forest-gone, living alone in a forest doing as he pleases, but who is poor in wisdom?'—there will be those who speak about him. Therefore a monk who is forest-gone should have wisdom.

Your reverences, earnest study[1] in Further-Dhamma, in Further-Discipline[2] should be made by a monk who is forest-gone. Your reverences, there are those who will question a monk who is forest-gone on Further-Dhamma and Further-Discipline. If, your reverences, a monk who is forest-gone, on being asked a question on Further-Dhamma, on Further-Discipline, does not succeed (in answering it), there will be those who speak about him and say: 'What is the good of this venerable one who is forest-gone, living alone in a forest doing as he pleases, but who, on being asked a question on Further-Dhamma, on Further-Discipline, does not succeed (in answering it)?'—there will be those who speak about him. Therefore earnest study should be made in Further-Dhamma, in Further-Discipline by a monk who is forest-gone.

Your reverences, earnest study should be made by a monk who is forest-gone concerning those that are the peaceful Deliverances[3] and are incorporeal having transcended material shapes. There are, your reverences, those who will question a monk who is forest-gone about those that are the peaceful Deliverances and are incorporeal having transcended material shapes. If, your reverences, a monk who is forest-gone, on being asked a question about those that are the peaceful Deliverances and are incorporeal having transcended material shapes, does not succeed (in answering it), there will be those who speak about him and say: 'What is the good of this venerable one who is forest-gone, living alone in a forest doing as he pleases, but who, on being asked a question about those that are the peaceful Deliverances and are incorporeal having transcended material shapes, does not succeed (in answering it)?'—there will be those who speak about him. Therefore earnest study should be

---

[1] *yoga*, earnest application, a closing in on a subject until, in modern parlance, you have made it yours, are at one with it, "yoked" to it.

[2] *abhidhamma abhivinaya; cf. A.* i. 288 *ff. MA.* iii. 185 takes these as the Piṭakas; to the former it specially adds the *Dhammahadayavibhaṅga* (*Vbh.* 401). See *Asl.* p. 24: *abhidhamme duppaṭipanno dhammacittam atidhāvanto acinteyyāni pi cinteti, tato cittavikkhepaṁ pāpuṇāti;* translated at *Expos.* i. 31: "The bhikkhu who is ill-trained in the Abhidhamma makes his mind run to excess in metaphysical abstractions and thinks of the unthinkable. Consequently he gets mental distraction."

[3] See the eight *vimokha* at *D.* ii. 70, 71; also below, p. 152 *ff.*

made by a monk who is forest-gone concerning those that are the peaceful Deliverances and are incorporeal having transcended material shapes.

Your reverences, earnest study in states of further-men should be made by a monk who is forest-gone. There are, your reverences, those who will question a monk who is forest-gone about states of further-men. If, your reverences, a monk who is forest-gone, on being asked a question about states of further-men, does not succeed (in answering it), there will be those who speak about him and say: 'What is the good of this venerable one who is forest-gone, living alone in a forest doing as he pleases, but who does not even know the goal for the sake of which he has gone forth ?'—there will be those who speak about him. Therefore earnest study in states of further-men should be made by a monk who is forest-gone."

This said, the venerable Moggallāna the Great spoke thus to the venerable Sāriputta: "Reverend Sāriputta, are these things to be taken up and practised only by a monk who is forest-gone or [**473**] also by one staying near a village ?"

"These things, reverend Moggallāna, are certainly to be taken up and practised by a monk who is forest-gone, all the more[1] by one staying near a village."

Discourse on Gulissāni:
The Ninth

70. DISCOURSE AT KĪṬĀGIRI

(Kīṭāgirisutta)

THUS have I heard: At one time the Lord was walking on tour in Kāsi together with a large Order of monks. While he was there the Lord addressed the monks, saying: "I, monks, do not eat a meal at night. Not eating a meal at night, I, monks, am aware of good health[2] and of being without illness and of buoyancy and strength and living in comfort. Come, do you too, monks, not eat a meal at

[1] *pag-eva*, also meaning "much less," and *a fortiori*. It might here mean "in consequence also," suggesting that the village dweller should emulate the one who practises the austerity, *dhutaṅga*, of the forest dweller, since this was the original type of austere mode of living.

[2] As at *M*. i. 437.

night. Not eating a meal at night, you too, monks, will be aware of good health and of being without illness and of buoyancy and strength and living in comfort."

"Yes, revered sir," these monks answered the Lord in assent. Then the Lord, walking on tour in Kāsi, in due course arrived at Kīṭāgiri, a market town in Kāsi. Then the Lord stayed at Kīṭāgiri, the market town in Kāsi. Now at that time the monks named Assaji and Punabbasuka[1] were residing in Kīṭāgiri. Then several monks approached the monks Assaji and Punabbasuka; having approached, they spoke thus to them: "The Lord, your reverences, does not eat a meal at night, nor does the Order of monks; and because, your reverences, they do not eat a meal at night they are aware of good health and of being without illness and of buoyancy and strength and living in comfort. Come, do you too, your reverences, not eat a meal at night. Not eating a meal at night, you too, your reverences, will be aware of good health and of being without illness and of buoyancy and strength and living in comfort." **[474]** When this had been said, the monks Assaji and Punabbasuka spoke thus to these monks:

"We, your reverences, eat in the evening as well as in the morning and during the day—at the wrong time.[2] But although we eat in the evening as well as in the morning and during the day—at the wrong time—we are aware of good health and of being without illness and of buoyancy and strength and living in comfort. Why should we, giving up the things of the present,[3] run after those of the future?[4] We will eat in the evening as well as in the morning and during the day—at the wrong time."

So because these monks were unable to convince the monks Assaji and Punabbasuka, they approached the Lord; having approached, having greeted the Lord, they sat down at a respectful distance. As they were sitting down at a respectful distance, these monks spoke

---

[1] Two of the six sectarian leaders of groups of monks; names of the six leaders given at *MA*. iii. 186-7, *Jā*. ii. 387. These two, whose headquarters were at Kīṭāgiri, are mentioned at *e.g. Vin*. ii. 9 *ff*., 171, iii. 81, 178 *f*. See *B.D*. i. 314, *n*. 2.

[2] See *M*. i. 448 (above, p. 120).

[3] *sandiṭṭhika*, what can be seen and realised, a word used in the usual description of *dhamma*.

[4] *kālika*, involving time, so: not immediate. *MA*. iii. 187 explains as *anāgate kāle pattabbam ānisaṁsaṁ*, advantages to be obtained at a future time. The opposite, *akālika*, is another word used in the usual description of *dhamma*.

thus to the Lord: " Now we, revered sir, approached the monks Assaji and Punabbasuka; having approached, we spoke thus to the monks Assaji and Punabbasuka: ' The Lord, your reverences, does not eat a meal at night, nor does the Order of monks . . . and living in comfort.' When this had been said, revered sir, the monks Assaji and Punabbasuka spoke thus to us: ' We, your reverences, eat in the evening . . . at the wrong time.' It is because we, revered sir, were not able to convince the monks Assaji and Punabbasuka that we are telling this matter to the Lord."

Then the Lord summoned a certain monk, saying: " Come you, monk, in my name summon the monks Assaji and Punabbasuka, saying: ' The Teacher is summoning the venerable ones.' "

" Yes, revered sir," and this monk, having answered the Lord in assent, approached the monks Assaji and Punabbasuka; having approached, he spoke thus to the monks Assaji and Punabbasuka: " The Teacher is summoning the venerable ones."

" Yes, your reverence," and the monks Assaji and Punabbasuka, having answered that monk in assent, approached the Lord; having approached, having greeted the Lord, they sat down at a respectful distance. As they were sitting down at a respectful distance, the Lord spoke thus to the monks Assaji and Punabbasuka:

" Is it true, as is said, monks, that several monks, having approached you, spoke thus: ' The Lord, your reverences, does not eat a meal at night, nor does the Order of monks; and because, your reverences, they do not eat a meal at night they are aware of good health and of being without illness and of buoyancy and strength and living in comfort. Come, do you too, your reverences, not eat a meal at night. Not eating a meal at night, you too, your reverences, [**475**] will be aware of good health . . . and living in comfort.' It is said that when this had been said, monks, you spoke thus to those monks: ' We, your reverences, eat in the evening as well as in the morning and during the day—at the wrong time. But although we eat in the evening as well as in the morning and during the day—at the wrong time—we are aware of good health and of being without illness and of buoyancy and strength and living in comfort. Why should we, giving up the things of the present, run after those of the future ? We will eat in the evening as well as in the morning and during the day—at the wrong time.' "

" Yes, revered sir."

" Did you, monks, ever understand that *dhamma* was taught thus by me: Whatever an individual experiences—be it pleasant or painful or neither painful nor pleasant—unskilled states decline in him, skilled states grow much ?"

"No, revered sir."

"Did not you, monks, understand that *dhamma* was taught thus by me: For anyone here feeling a pleasant feeling of one kind[1] unskilled states[2] grow much, skilled states decline, but for anyone here feeling a pleasant feeling of another kind[1] unskilled states decline, skilled states grow much; for anyone here feeling a painful feeling of one kind unskilled states grow much, skilled states decline, but for anyone here feeling a painful feeling of another kind unskilled states decline, skilled states grow much; for anyone here feeling a feeling that is neither painful nor pleasant of one kind unskilled states grow much, skilled states decline, but for anyone here feeling a feeling that is neither painful nor pleasant of another kind unskilled states decline, skilled states grow much."

"Yes, revered sir."

"It is good, monks. If this, monks, had not been understood by me, if it had not been seen, known, realised, apprehended by means of wisdom that: For anyone here feeling a pleasant feeling of one kind unskilled states grow much, skilled states decline—could I, monks, not understanding it thus, say: Get rid of pleasant feeling of this kind[3]—and would this have been suitable in me, monks ?"

"No, revered sir."

"But, monks, since this has been understood by me, seen, known, realised and apprehended by means of wisdom that: For anyone here feeling a pleasant feeling of one kind unskilled [**476**] states grow much, skilled states decline—therefore I say: Get rid of pleasant feeling of this kind.

And if this, monks, had not been understood by me, if it had not been seen, known, realised, apprehended by means of wisdom that: For anyone here feeling a pleasant feeling of another kind unskilled states decline, skilled states grow much— could I, monks, not understanding it thus, say: Entering on pleasant feeling of this (other) kind,[4] abide in it—and would this have been suitable in me, monks ?"

"No, revered sir."

---

[1] *evarūpa*. [2] *dhammā*.

[3] Reference is here being made to the six types of pleasure of the worldly life; *cf. S.* iv. 232; *Vbh.* 381.

[4] The pleasant states not to be got rid of are the six ways of getting pleasure through renunciation, *S.* iv. 232.

" But, monks, since this has been understood by me, seen, known, realised and apprehended by means of wisdom that: For anyone here feeling a pleasant feeling of this other kind unskilled states decline, skilled states grow much—therefore I say: Entering on pleasant feeling of this (other) kind, abide in it.

And if this, monks, had not been understood by me, if it had not been seen, known, realised, apprehended by means of wisdom that: For anyone here feeling a painful feeling of one kind . . . a feeling that is neither painful nor pleasant of one kind unskilled states grow much, skilled states decline—could I, monks, not understanding it thus, say: Get rid of feeling that is neither painful nor pleasant of this kind—and would this have been suitable in me, monks ?

" No, revered sir."

" But, monks, since this has been understood by me, seen, known, realised and apprehended by means of wisdom that: For anyone here feeling a feeling that is neither painful nor pleasant of this kind unskilled states grow much, skilled states decline—therefore I say: Get rid of feeling that is neither painful nor pleasant of this kind.

And if this, monks, had not been understood by me, if it had not been seen, known, realised, apprehended by means of wisdom that: For anyone here feeling a feeling that is neither painful nor pleasant of another kind unskilled states decline, skilled states grow much—could I, monks, not understanding it thus, say: Entering on a feeling that is neither painful nor pleasant of this other kind, abide in it—and would this have been suitable in me ?"

" No, revered sir."

" But, monks, since this has been understood by me, seen, known, realised and apprehended by means of wisdom that: For anyone here feeling a feeling that is neither painful nor pleasant of this other kind, unskilled states decline, skilled states grow much—therefore I say [**477**]: Entering on a feeling that is neither painful nor pleasant of this (other) kind, abide in it.

I, monks, do not say of all monks that there is something to be done through diligence; yet, I, monks, do not say of all monks that there is not something to be done through diligence. Monks, those monks who are perfected ones, canker-waned, who have lived the life, done what there was to be done, laid down the burden, who have attained their own goal, the fetters of becoming utterly destroyed, who are freed by right profound knowledge, of monks such as these I do not say, monks, that there is something to be done through diligence. What is the reason for this ? It has (already) been done by these through diligence, these could not become negligent. But, monks, those monks who are learners, not attained to perfection,[1] but who live striving for the incomparable security from the bonds, of monks such as these I say, monks, that there is something to be done through diligence. What is the reason for this? Even while these venerable ones are resorting to suitable lodgings, associating with lovely friends, and are themselves controlling their sense-organs, having realised here and now by their own super-knowledge that matchless goal of the Brahma-faring for the sake of which young men of family rightly go forth from home into homelessness, entering on it, they could abide in it. So I, monks, beholding this fruit of diligence for these monks, say that there is something to be done through diligence.

Monks, there are the seven (types of) persons existing in the world. What seven?[2] The one who is freed both ways, the one freed by means of intuitive wisdom, the mental realiser, the one won to view, the one freed by faith, the striver after *dhamma*, the striver after faith.

And which, monks, is the person who is freed both ways?[3] As to this, monks, some person is abiding, having apprehended[4] with the

---

[1] As at *M*. i. 4.

[2] As at *M*. i. 439. *Cf. Vism*. 659 where these seven "ariyan persons" are given in a different order.

[3] *ubhatobhāgavimutta*. *Cf. M*. i. 439: *D*. ii. 71; *A*. i. 74, iv. 453; *Pug*. 14, 72, 73. At *MA*. iii. 188, *DA*. ii. 514, iii. 889 it is said that he is freed *rūpakāyato* (from the body, or, class, *kāya=nikāya*, of material shape, *i.e.* body) through the incorporeal attainments, and *nāmakāyato* (from the class of mind, mental aggregates) through the Way. This kind of freedom is therefore from *nāma* and *rūpa*, also the view of *SnA*. ii. 594, *AA*. iv. 207. It does not mean "freed through heart and intellect" as sometimes stated, *e.g. Fur. Dial*. i. 313. *MA*. iii. 188, *DA*. iii. 889 say: emerging one by one from the four incorporeal attainments, having mastered the (volitional) activities (*saṅkhārā*: of body, speech and thought), emerging from the cessation of the four attainments of arahantship, he has attained arahantship and is a non-returner—in this way it is fivefold. *DA*. ii. 514 says: emerging from the planes of infinite ether and so on, he has attained arahantship and is a non-returner, and emerging from cessation he has attained arahantship. It is fivefold. *DA*. ii. 514 also cites *Sn*. 1074, which speaks of *nāma-kāya-vimutto*, freed from the class of "name" (mind), or, freed from name and body? This explanation, attributed to Cūḷa-Sumana, an Elder of Ceylon, and recorded at *DA*. ii. 514, is supposed to be the most authoritative interpretation.

[4] *phassitvā*, with v. ll. *phusitvā, phussitvā*; at *MA*. i. 162 it is said *nāmakāyena phusitvā; pāpuṇitvā adhigantvā ti vuttaṁ hoti*, having apprehended with (through, or while in) the psycho-physical compound (taking *kāya* as equal to *rūpa*), having mastered, having won. *Cf. A*. ii. 87, etc.

person[1] those peaceful Deliverances[2] which are incorporeal[3] having transcended material shapes;[4] and having seen by means of wisdom his cankers are utterly destroyed. This, monks, is called the person who is freed both ways. I, monks, do not say of this monk that there is something to be done through diligence. What is the reason for this ? It has been done by him through diligence, he could not become negligent.

And which, monks, is the person who is freed by means of intuitive wisdom ? As to this, monks, some person is abiding without having apprehended with the person those peaceful Deliverances which are incorporeal having transcended material shapes; yet, having seen by means of wisdom his cankers are utterly destroyed.[5] This, monks, is called [**478**] the person who is freed by means of intuitive wisdom. I, monks, do not say of this monk that there is something to be done through diligence. What is the reason for this ? It has been done by him through diligence, he could not become negligent.

And which, monks, is the person who is a mental-realiser ?[6] As to this, monks, some person is abiding, having apprehended with the person those peaceful Deliverances which are incorporeal having transcended material shapes; and having seen by means of wisdom some (only) of his cankers are utterly destroyed. This, monks, is called the person who is a mental-realiser. I, monks, say of this monk that there is something to be done through diligence. What is

---

[1] *kāyena,* which would appear to mean the *rūpakāya* and the *nāmakāya,* see p. 151, n. 3 above, and *SnA.* ii. 594.

[2] These number eight, see *D.* ii. 70-71. At *MA.* i. 162 it is said that "peaceful" (or "calm," *santa*) is because there is peace in regard to the factors, *aṅga,* as well as in regard to the object of meditation; while *vimokkha* means freed from opposing *dhammā* and intent on the object of meditation or thought.

[3] In respect of the object of thought and resultant (thought) they are devoid of material shapes, *MA.* i. 162.

[4] Having transcended (or, passed beyond) in the *jhāna* on material spheres, *MA.* i. 162.

[5] *Pug.* 14, 73; quoted at *MA.* iii. 188, *DA.* ii. 512; *cf. A.* iv. 453.

[6] *kāyasakkhin.* See *M.* i. 439, *Pug.* 14, 73. At *MA.* iii. 189 it is said that he realises that which is apprehended; whoever first realises a *jhāna*-realisation afterwards realises stopping, nibbāna. So, having begun with stream-attainment, he goes on to arahantship. *Cf. A.* iv. 451 and *AA.* iv. 206 which says "because the first *jhāna* is realised by means of this *nāmakāya,* therefore in this way (*pariyāyena*) he is called a *kāyasakkhin.*" For *kāya* meaning the three mental factors (presumably referring to the *khandhas* of feeling, perception and the *saṅkhāras,* as at *Dhs.* 40) see *P. Purity,* 806, *n.* 2, and *Expos.* i. 199.

the reason for this ? Even while this venerable one is resorting to suitable lodgings, associating with lovely friends, and is himself controlling his sense-organs, having realised here and now by his own super-knowledge that matchless goal of the Brahma-faring for the sake of which young men of family rightly go forth from home into homelessness, entering on it he might abide in it. So I, monks, beholding this fruit of diligence for this monk, say that there is something to be done through diligence.

And which, monks, is the person who has won to view ?[1] As to this, monks, some person is abiding without having apprehended with the person those peaceful Deliverances which are incorporeal having transcended material shapes; yet, having seen by means of wisdom some of his cankers are utterly destroyed, and those things proclaimed by the Tathāgata are fully seen by him through intuitive wisdom and fully practised.[2] This, monks, is called the person who has won to view. I, monks, say of this monk that there is something to be done through diligence. What is the reason for this ? Even while this venerable one is resorting to suitable lodgings . . . he might abide in it. So I, monks, beholding this fruit of diligence for this monk, say that there is something to be done through diligence.

And which, monks, is the person who is freed by faith ?[3] As to this, monks, some person is abiding without having apprehended with the person those peaceful Deliverances which are incorporeal having transcended material shapes; yet, having seen by means of wisdom some of his cankers are utterly destroyed, and his faith in the Tathāgata is settled, genuine, established.[4] This, monks, is called the person who is freed through faith. I, monks, say of this monk that there is something to be done through diligence. What is the reason for this ? Even while this venerable one is resorting to suitable [**479**] lodgings . . . entering on it he might abide in it. So I, monks, beholding this fruit of diligence for this monk, say that there is something to be done through diligence.

And which, monks, is the person who is striving for *dhamma* ?[5]

---

[1] *diṭṭhipatta*. *MA*. iii. 189 quotes *M*. ii. 38=*Pug*. 15=43 *ff*. which are all passages that speak of comprehending the four Truths of anguish as they really are. [2] *Pug*. 15. See *A*. iv. 363 on the power, *bala*, of wisdom.

[3] See *Sn*. 1146: by faith you shall be free.

[4] *Pug*. 15 differs, giving the same interpretation for this person as for the preceding, while saying that they differ.

[5] *dhammânusārin*. *Pug*. 15 again differs. *Cf*. *M*. i. 142; *S*. iii. 225, 228. He and the next are stream-attainers. *MA*. iii. 190=*DA*. 890 says *dhammo ti paññā*, *dhamma* is wisdom.

As to this, monks, some person is abiding without having apprehended with the person those peaceful Deliverances which are incorporeal having transcended material shapes; but (although) he has seen by means of wisdom, his cankers are not (yet) utterly destroyed; and those things proclaimed by the Tathāgata are (only) moderately approved of[1] by him by means of intuitive wisdom, although he has these states, namely the faculty of faith, the faculty of energy, the faculty of mindfulness, the faculty of concentration, the faculty of wisdom.[2] This, monks, is called the person who is striving for *dhamma*. I, monks, say of this monk that there is something to be done through diligence. What is the reason for this? Even while this venerable one is resorting to suitable lodgings . . . entering on it he might abide in it. So I, monks, beholding this fruit of diligence for this monk, say that there is something to be done through diligence.

And which, monks, is the person striving after faith?[3] As to this, monks, some person is abiding without having apprehended with the person those peaceful Deliverances which are incorporeal having transcended material shapes; yet, having seen by means of wisdom his cankers are not utterly destroyed; but if he has enough faith in the Tathāgata, enough regard,[4] then he will have these things, that is to say the faculty of faith, the faculty of energy, the faculty of mindfulness, the faculty of concentration, the faculty of wisdom. This, monks, is called the person who is striving after faith. I, monks, say of this monk that there is something to be done through diligence. What is the reason for this? Even while this venerable one is resorting to suitable lodgings, associating with lovely friends, and is himself controlling his sense-organs, having realised here and now through his own super-knowledge that matchless goal of the Brahma-faring for the sake of which young men of family rightly go forth from home into homelessness, entering on it he might abide in it. So I, monks, beholding this fruit of diligence for this monk, say that there is something to be done through diligence.

I, monks, do not say that the attainment of profound knowledge comes straightaway; nevertheless, monks, the attainment of profound knowledge comes by a gradual training, a gradual doing, a gradual course. [**480**] And how, monks, does the attainment of profound knowledge come by means of a gradual training, a gradual

---

[1] *Mattaso nijjhānaṃ khamanti; cf. S.* iii. 228, v. 377; *A.* iv. 241.

[2] On these five faculties, or cardinal virtues, see *S.* v. 199.

[3] *Pug.* 15 differs. *Cf. M.* i. 142.

[4] *Cf. S.* v. 377.

doing, a gradual course? As to this, monks, one who has faith draws close;[1] drawing close, he sits down near by;[2] sitting down near by he lends ear; lending ear he hears *dhamma*; having heard *dhamma* he remembers it; he tests the meaning of the things he has borne in mind; while testing the meaning the things are approved of; there being approval of the things desire[3] is born; with desire born he makes an effort; having made the effort he weighs it up; having weighed it up he strives; being self-resolute he realises with his person the highest truth itself and, penetrating it by means of wisdom, he sees.[4] But, monks, had there not been that faith, there would not have been, monks, that drawing close; there would not have been, monks, that sitting down near by; there would not have been, monks, that lending ear; there would not have been, monks, that hearing of *dhamma*; there would not have been, monks, that remembering of *dhamma*; there would not have been, monks, that testing of the meaning; there would not have been, monks, that approval of the things; there would not have been, monks, that desire; there would not have been, monks, that effort; there would not have been, monks, that striving. Monks, you are on a wrong track, you are on a false track, monks. How very far, monks, have not these foolish persons strayed from this *dhamma* and discipline.

There is a fourfold exposition, monks, the meaning of which, when it is recited, an intelligent man could soon understand by means of wisdom. I will recite it to you, monks, you will understand it from me."

"Who are we, revered sir, and who are the knowers of *dhamma*?"

"Monks, even a teacher who sets store on material things,[5] is an heir to material things, and lives in association with material things—why, even to him, this kind of higgling and haggling does not apply,

---

[1] *MA*. iii. 193 says that "he goes near (or, into the presence of) a teacher." The following passage also occurs at *M*. ii. 173.

[2] *payirupāsati*, can also mean to pay respects to someone, to visit someone. *MA*. iii. 193=426 says "he sits down in the presence of," *santike*. *Cf*. *AA*. ii. 196.

[3] *chanda*. *MA*. iii. 193 calls this desire for what is skilled, *kusalachanda*.

[4] *Cf*. *A*. ii. 115. At *MA*. iii. 193 it is said that "he realises the truth of nibbāna *nāmakāyena*, by means of the class of name; and that 'by means of wisdom' means he sees, having pierced by means of the wisdom of the Way which is connected with *nāmakāya*." *Kāyena*, "with the person", would seem to mean the very opposite of "through the medium of his bodily senses" as at *Fur. Dial*. i. 338.

[5] That is, a teacher who is "outside" the Buddhist fold.

that (his followers) will or will not do this or that according as they like it or not. So what has this to do with the Tathāgata who lives dissociated from material things? For a disciple who has faith in the Teacher's instruction and lives in unison with it, monks, it is a principle[1] that: 'The Teacher is the Lord, a disciple am I; the Lord knows, I do not know.'[2] For a disciple who has faith in the Teacher's instruction and lives in unison with it, monks, the Teacher's instruction is a furthering in growth,[3] giving strength.[4] For a disciple who has faith in the Teacher's instruction and lives in unison with it, monks, [481] it is a principle that: 'Gladly[5] would I be reduced to skin and sinews and bone and let my body's flesh and blood[6] dry up if there came to be a vortex of energy so that that which is not (yet) won might be won by human strength, by human energy, by human striving.' For a disciple who has faith in the Teacher's instruction and lives in unison with it, monks, one of two fruits is to be expected: profound knowledge here and now, or, if there is any basis (for rebirth remaining), the state of no-return."

Thus spoke the Lord. Delighted, these monks rejoiced in what the Lord had said.

Discourse at Kīṭāgiri:
The Tenth

Division on Monks:
The Second

---

[1] *anudhamma*, a (right) method; in accordance with *dhamma*.

[2] Here, according to *MA*. iii. 194: "The Lord knows the advantages in eating only once a day; I do not. But, because of my faith, I will eat only one meal a day, giving up eating three times daiiy."

[3] *rumhaniya*. [4] *ojavant*; *MA*. iii. 194 says *sinehavant*.

[5] As at *A*. i. 50; *S*. ii. 28.

[6] *MA*. iii. 194 says that thus the application to the skin, sinews, bones, and the flesh and blood constitutes a fourfold energy. But the "fourfold exposition" is more likely to refer to the disciple who has faith. Nor is there anything here about the four truths (*MA*. iii. 193).

III. THE DIVISION ON WANDERERS

(Paribbājakavagga)

71. DISCOURSE TO VACCHAGOTTA ON THE THREEFOLD KNOWLEDGE

(Tevijja-Vacchagottasutta)

THUS have I heard: At one time the Lord was staying near Vesālī in the Great Grove in the hall of the Gabled House. Now at that time the wanderer Vacchagotta[1] was living in Ekapuṇḍarīka,[2] the wanderers' park. Then the Lord, having dressed in the morning, taking his bowl and robe, entered Vesālī for almsfood. But it occurred to the Lord: "It is still too early to walk for almsfood in Vesālī. Suppose I were to approach Ekapuṇḍarīka, the wanderers' park, and Vacchagotta the wanderer?" Then the Lord approached Ekapuṇḍarīka, the wanderers' park, and Vacchagotta the wanderer. The wanderer Vacchagotta saw the Lord coming in the distance and seeing him, he spoke thus to the Lord: "Revered sir, let the Lord come; revered sir, there is a welcome for the Lord; revered sir, it is long since the Lord made the opportunity to come here; revered sir, let the Lord sit down, this is the appointed seat." The Lord sat down on the appointed seat, and Vacchagotta the wanderer, [482] having taken a low seat, sat down at a respectful distance. As he was sitting down at a respectful distance, the wanderer Vacchagotta spoke thus to the Lord:

"Revered sir, I have heard: The recluse Gotama is all knowing,[3] all seeing; he claims all-embracing knowledge-and-vision, saying: 'Whether I am walking or standing still or asleep or awake, knowledge-and-vision is permanently and continuously before me.' Revered sir, those who speak thus: The recluse Gotama is all knowing, all seeing; he claims all-embracing knowledge-and-vision, saying:

---

[1] *Cf. A.* i. 160; *S.* iii. 257 *ff.*, iv. 391 *ff.* Verses are ascribed to him at *Thag.* 112. His spiritual evolution is told in this and the two following Discourses, and very briefly at *ThagA.* i. 235.

[2] *MA.* iii. 195=*DA.* ii. 416 says *puṇḍarīka* is a white mango tree. A solitary one (*eka*) grew in this wanderers' park. This park is not to be confused with the *ekapuṇḍarīka uyyāna* of *M.* i. 252.

[3] Said of Nātaputta at *M.* i. 92-93.

'Whether I am walking or standing still or asleep or awake, knowledge-and-vision is permanently and continuously before me'—revered sir, I hope that these[1] are speaking of the Lord in accordance with what has been said and are not misrepresenting the Lord with what is not fact, but are explaining in accordance with *dhamma*, and that no one of his fellow *dhamma*-men, of this way of speaking, gives grounds for reproach?"

"Vaccha, those who speak thus: the recluse Gotama is all knowing, all seeing; he claims all-embracing knowledge-and-vision, saying: 'Whether I am walking or standing still or asleep or awake, knowledge-and-vision is permanently and continuously before me'—these are not speaking of me in accordance with what has been said, but they are misrepresenting me with what is untrue, not fact."

"Expounding in what way, revered sir, would we be speaking in accordance with what has been said, and would not be misrepresenting the Lord with what is not fact, but would be explaining in accordance with *dhamma* so that no fellow *dhamma*-man, of the same way of speaking, could give grounds for reproach?"

"Vaccha, expounding: 'The recluse Gotama is a threefold-knowledge man,' you would be one who speaks in accordance with what has been said by me, you would not be misrepresenting me with what is not fact, you would be explaining in accordance with *dhamma*, and no fellow *dhamma*-man of this way of speaking could give grounds for reproach. For I, Vaccha, whenever I please recollect a variety of former habitations, that is to say one birth, two births . . . [2] thus do I recollect divers former habitations in all their modes and details. And I, Vaccha, whenever I please, with the purified *deva*-vision surpassing that of men . . . see beings as they pass hence and come to be; I comprehend that beings are mean, excellent, comely, ugly, well-going, ill-going according to the consequences of deeds. And I, Vaccha, by the destruction of the cankers, having realised here and now by my own super-knowledge the freedom of mind and the freedom through wisdom that are cankerless, entering thereon, abide therein. Vaccha, expounding that the recluse Gotama is a threefold-knowledge man, [**483**] you would be one who speaks in accordance with what has been said by me, you would not be misrepresenting me with what is not fact, you would be explaining in accordance with *dhamma*, and no

---

[1] *Cf. A.* i. 161, ii. 31, iii. 4; *S.* ii. 33, 36, iii. 6.

[2] *Cf. M.* i. 22.

fellow *dhamma*-man of this way of speaking could give grounds for reproach."

When this had been said, Vacchagotta the wanderer spoke thus to the Lord:

"Good Gotama, is there any householder who, not getting rid of the householder's fetter(s),[1] at the breaking up of the body is an end-maker of ill?"

"There is not any householder, Vaccha, who, not getting rid of the householder's fetter(s), at the breaking up of the body is an end-maker of ill."

"But is there, good Gotama, any householder who, not getting rid of the householder's fetter(s), at the breaking up of the body attains heaven?"

"Not just one hundred, Vaccha, nor two hundred, nor three, four or five hundred, but far more are those householders who, not getting rid of the householder's fetter(s), at the breaking up of the body attain heaven."

"Now, good Gotama, is there any Naked Ascetic who at the breaking up of the body is an end-maker of ill?"

"There is not, Vaccha, any Naked Ascetic who at the breaking up of the body is an end-maker of ill."

"But is there then, good Gotama, any Naked Ascetic who at the breaking up of the body attained heaven?"

"Although I, Vaccha, recollect ninety-one eons,[2] I do not know of any Naked Ascetic who attained heaven, except one; and *he* professed *kamma*, he professed operative *kamma*."[3]

---

[1] Probably meaning his wife, children and servants.

[2] At *D.* ii. 2 Gotama is reputed to say that the Buddha Vipassin arose in the world ninety-one eons, *kappa*, ago. This context mentions six Buddhas preceding Gotama; of these Vipassin is the first. I suggest that our *M.* passage may have a hidden reference to the fact that Gotama's recollection of his previous lives, or "habitations," goes back to Vipassin's time; and that, since from *D.* ii. 2 and *M.* i. 483 it does not appear to go back to the times of the other Buddhas who preceded Vipassin, is perhaps contributory evidence that the number of these was of later growth; see *e.g.* E. J. Thomas, *Life of Buddha*, p. 27. See Intr. p. xvii.

[3] *so p'āsi kammavādī kiriyavādī. MA.* iii. 196 says that if he was the former he could not avoid being the latter. A. L. Basham, *Hist. of the Ājīvikas*, p. 135 says he was in consequence of these views "not an orthodox follower of Makkhali Gosāla." *Cf. Vin.* i. 71: *kammavādino ete kiriyavādino*, said of the matted hair ascetics who, for this very reason, were to be privileged not to undergo the prescribed four months' probation for members of other sects before they were ordained as monks. *Cf.* also *A.* i. 287.

"This being so, good Gotama, that fold of the sects[1] is empty even in regard to attaining heaven."

"This being so, Vaccha, that fold of the sects is empty even in regard to attaining heaven."

Thus spoke the Lord. Delighted, the wanderer Vacchagotta rejoiced in what the Lord had said.

Discourse to Vacchagotta on the Threefold Knowledge:
The First

72. DISCOURSE TO VACCHAGOTTA ON FIRE

(Aggi-Vacchagottasutta)

THUS have I heard: At one time the Lord was staying near Sāvatthī in the Jeta Grove in Anāthapiṇḍika's monastery. Then the wanderer Vacchagotta approached the Lord; [**484**] having approached, he exchanged greetings with the Lord; having conversed in a friendly and courteous way, he sat down at a respectful distance. As he was sitting down at a respectful distance, the wanderer Vacchagotta spoke thus to the Lord:

"Now, good Gotama, is the revered Gotama of this view: 'The world is eternal,[2] this is indeed the truth, all else is falsehood'?"

"I, Vaccha, am not of this view: 'The world is eternal, this is indeed the truth, all else is falsehood.'"

"Then good Gotama, is the revered Gotama of this view: 'The world is not eternal, this is indeed the truth, all else is falsehood'?"

"I, Vaccha, am not of this view: 'The world is not eternal, this is indeed the truth, all else is falsehood.'"

"Now, good Gotama, is the revered Gotama of this view: 'The world is an ending thing, this is indeed the truth, all else is falsehood'?"

"I, Vaccha, am not of this view: 'The world is an ending thing, this is indeed the truth, all else is falsehood.'"

---

[1] *titthāyatana*, as at *Vin.* i. 60, 69, ii. 279, iv. 217; *A.* i. 173. See *B.D.* iii. 167, *n.* 2.

[2] *Cf. S.* iv. 391 *ff.*, where Vacchagotta is recorded to put all the following questions to Moggallāna; *cf. S.* iii. 257 *ff.*

"Then, good Gotama, is the revered Gotama of this view: 'The world is not an ending thing, this is indeed the truth, all else is falsehood'?"

"I, Vaccha, am not of this view: 'The world is not an ending thing, this is indeed the truth, all else is falsehood.'"

"Now, good Gotama, is the revered Gotama of this view: 'The life-principle and the body are the same, this is indeed the truth, all else is falsehood'?"

"I, Vaccha, am not of this view: 'The life-principle and the body are the same, this is indeed the truth, all else is falsehood.'"

"Then, good Gotama, is the revered Gotama of this view: 'The life-principle is one thing, the body another, this is indeed the truth, all else is falsehood'?"

"I, Vaccha, am not of this view: 'The life-principle is one thing, the body another, this is indeed the truth, all else is falsehood.'"

"Now, good Gotama, is the revered Gotama of this view: 'The Tathāgata is after dying, this is indeed the truth, all else is falsehood'?"

"I, Vaccha, am not of this view: 'The Tathāgata is after dying, this is indeed the truth, all else is falsehood.'"

"Then, good Gotama, is the revered Gotama of this view: 'The Tathāgata is not after dying, this is indeed the truth, all else is falsehood'?"

"I, Vaccha, am not of this view: 'The Tathāgata is not after dying . . . falsehood.'"

"Now, good Gotama, is the revered Gotama of this view: 'The Tathāgata both is and is not after dying, this is indeed the truth, all else is falsehood'?"

[**485**] "I, Vaccha, am not of this view: 'The Tathāgata both is and is not after dying . . . falsehood.'"

"Then, good Gotama, is the revered Gotama of this view: 'The Tathāgata neither is nor is not after dying, this is indeed the truth, all else is falsehood'?"

"I, Vaccha, am not of this view: 'The Tathāgata neither is nor is not after dying, this is indeed the truth, all else is falsehood.'"

"Now, good Gotama, the revered Gotama, on being asked whether he is of the view: 'The world is eternal, this is indeed the truth, all else is falsehood.' says: 'I, Vaccha, am not of this view: The world is eternal . . . all else is falsehood.' But, good Gotama, the revered Gotama, on being asked whether he is of the view: 'The world is not eternal . . .' . . . on being asked whether he is of the view: 'The

Tathāgata both is and is not after dying . . .' . . . on being asked whether he is of the view: 'The Tathāgata neither is nor is not after dying, this is indeed the truth, all else is falsehood,' says: 'I, Vaccha, am not of the view: The Tathāgata neither is nor is not after dying, this is indeed the truth, all else is falsehood.' What is the peril the revered Gotama beholds that he thus does not approach any of these (speculative) views ?"

"Vaccha, to think that 'the world is eternal'—this is going to a (speculative) view,[1] holding a view, the wilds of views, the wriggling of views, the scuffling of views, the fetter of views; it is accompanied by anguish, distress, misery, fever; it does not conduce to turning away from, nor to dispassion, stopping, calming, super-knowledge, awakening, nor to nibbāna. Vaccha, to think that 'the world is not eternal' . . . to think that 'the world is an ending thing' . . . to think that 'the world is not an ending thing' . . . to think that 'the life-principle and the body are the same' . . . to think that 'the life-principle is one thing, the body another' . . . to think that 'the Tathāgata is after dying' . . . **[486]** to think that 'the Tathāgata is not after dying' . . . to think that 'the Tathāgata both is and is not after dying' . . . to think that 'the Tathāgata neither is nor is not after dying'—this, Vaccha, is going to a (speculative) view, holding a view, the wilds of views, the wriggling of views, the scuffling of views, the fetter of views; it is accompanied by anguish, distress, misery, fever; it does not conduce to turning away from, nor to dispassion, stopping, calming, super-knowledge, awakening, nor to nibbāna. I, Vaccha, beholding that this is a peril, thus do not approach any of these (speculative) views."

"But does the good Gotama have any (speculative) view ?"

"Vaccha, going to 'speculative view'—this has been got rid of by the Tathāgata. But this, Vaccha, has been seen by the Tathāgata: 'Such is material shape, such is the arising of material shape, such the going down of material shape; such is feeling . . . perception . . . such are the habitual tendencies . . . such is consciousness, such is the arising of consciousness, such the going down of consciousness.' Therefore I say that by the destruction, dispassion, stopping, giving up, casting out of all imaginings,[2] all supposings, all latent pride that

---

[1] *Cf. M.* i. 8, 431. Since the Tathāgata knows and comprehends, he does not hold any speculative view; see below. In this paragraph I have mostly translated *diṭṭhi* as view, but speculative view is meant.

[2] *maññita. MA.* iii. 198 gives three: craving, false views, pride, as does *SA.* ii. 363. *Vbh.* 390 gives nine. *Cf. S.* iv. 21-22.

'I am the doer, mine is the doer,' a Tathāgata is freed without clinging."

"But, good Gotama, where does a monk arise whose mind is freed thus?"

"'Arise,' Vaccha, does not apply."

"Well then, good Gotama, does he not arise?"

"'Does not arise,' Vaccha, does not apply."

"Well then, good Gotama, does he both arise and not arise?"

"'Both arises and does not arise,' Vaccha, does not apply."

"Well then, good Gotama, does he neither arise nor not arise?"

"'Neither arises nor does not arise,' Vaccha, does not apply."

"But, good Gotama, on being asked where does a monk arise, whose mind is freed thus, you say: '"Arise," Vaccha, does not apply.' Well then, good Gotama, on being asked if he does not arise, you say: '"Does not arise," Vaccha, does not apply.' Well then, good Gotama, on being asked whether he both arises and does not arise, you say: '"Arises and does not arise," Vaccha, does not apply.' Well then, good Gotama, on being asked whether he neither arises nor does not arise, you say: '"Neither arises nor does not arise," Vaccha, does not apply.' [**487**] I am at a loss on this point, good Gotama, I am bewildered, and that measure of satisfaction I had from former conversation with the good Gotama—even that have I now lost."

"You ought to be at a loss, Vaccha, you ought to be bewildered. For, Vaccha, this *dhamma* is deep, difficult to see, difficult to understand, peaceful, excellent, beyond dialectic, subtle, intelligible to the wise; but it is hard for you who are of another view, another allegiance, another objective, of a different observance, and under a different teacher.[1] Well then, Vaccha, I will now question you in return. Answer as it pleases you. What do you think about this, Vaccha? If a fire were blazing in front of you would you know: This fire is blazing in front of me?"

"Good Gotama, if a fire were blazing in front of me I should know: This fire is blazing in front of me."

"But if, Vaccha, someone were to question you thus: This fire that is blazing in front of you—what is the reason that this fire is blazing?—what would you, Vaccha, reply when questioned thus?"

"If, good Gotama, someone were to question me thus: This fire that is blazing in front of you—what is the reason that this fire is

---

[1] As at *M*. ii. 43; *D*. i. 87, iii. 35.

blazing?—I, good Gotama, on being questioned thus would reply thus: This fire that is blazing in front of me—this fire is blazing because of a supply[1] of grass and sticks."

"If that fire that was in front of you, Vaccha, were to be quenched,[2] would you know: This fire that was in front of me has been quenched?"

"If, good Gotama, that fire that was in front of me were to be quenched, I would know: This fire that was in front of me has been quenched."

"But if someone were to question you thus, Vaccha: That fire that was in front of you and that has been quenched—to which direction has that fire gone from here, to the east or west or north or south? On being questioned thus, what would you, Vaccha, reply?"

"It does not apply, good Gotama. For, good Gotama, that fire blazed because of a supply of grass and sticks, yet from having totally consumed this and from the lack of other fuel, being without fuel it is reckoned to be quenched."

"Even so, Vaccha, that material shape by which one recognising the Tathāgata might recognise him—that material shape has been got rid of by the Tathāgata, cut off at the root, made like a palm-tree stump that can come to no further existence and is not liable to arise again in the future. Freed from denotation by material shape is the Tathāgata, Vaccha, he is deep, immeasurable, unfathomable as is the great ocean. 'Arises' does not apply, 'does not arise' does not apply, [**488**] 'both arises and does not arise' does not apply, 'neither arises nor does not arise' does not apply. That feeling . . . That perception . . . Those habitual tendencies . . . That consciousness by which one recognising the Tathāgata might recognise him—that consciousness has been got rid of by the Tathāgata, cut off at the root, made like a palm-tree stump that can come to no further existence and is not liable to arise again in the future. Freed from denotation by consciousness is the Tathāgata, Vaccha, he is deep, immeasurable, unfathomable as is the great ocean. 'Arises' does not apply, 'does not arise' does not apply, 'both arises and does not arise' does not apply, 'neither arises nor does not arise' does not apply."

When this had been said, the wanderer Vacchagotta spoke thus to the Lord: "Good Gotama, it is like a great sāl-tree not far from a village or market town whose branches and foliage might be dis-

---

[1] *upādāna*, fuel, supply; grasping, attachment.

[2] *nibbāyeyya*, were to be extinguished, put out, quenched.

solved because of their impermanence, whose bark and young shoots might be dissolved, whose softwood might be dissolved, so that after a time the branches and foliage gone, the bark and young shoots gone, the softwood gone, clear of them it would be established on the pith.[1] It is excellent, good Gotama, excellent, good Gotama. It is as if, good Gotama, one might set upright what had been upset, or disclose what had been covered, or might show the way to one who had gone astray, [**489**] or bring an oil-lamp into the darkness so that those with vision might see material shapes—even so, in many a figure has *dhamma* been made clear by the revered Gotama. I am going to the revered Gotama for refuge and to *dhamma* and to the Order of monks. May the revered Gotama accept me as a lay-follower going for refuge from this day forth for as long as life lasts."

Discourse to Vacchagotta on Fire:
The Second

73. GREATER DISCOURSE TO VACCHAGOTTA

(Mahā-Vacchagottasutta)

THUS have I heard: At one time the Lord was staying near Rājagaha in the Bamboo Grove at the squirrels' feeding place. Then the wanderer Vacchagotta approached the Lord; having approached, he exchanged greetings with the Lord; having conversed in a friendly and courteous way, he sat down at a respectful distance. As he was sitting down at a respectful distance, the wanderer Vacchagotta spoke thus to the Lord:

" It is a long time since I had a conversation with the good Gotama.[2] It were good if the revered Gotama were to teach me in brief what is skilled and what is unskilled."

" I, Vaccha, could teach you what is skilled and what is unskilled

---

[1] *suddho assa sāre patiṭṭhito,* as at *M.* i. 31-32. *Cf. M.* Stas 29, 30; also *M.* i. 434.

[2] *MA.* iii. 199-200 points out that the two foregoing Discourses were spoken to him, also the Avyāvaṭa Saṁyutta (*S.* iv. 391 *ff.*) and a discourse in the *Ang.* (*A.* v. 193). While it is reasonably clear that the two foregoing Discourses were in fact spoken to Vacchagotta before this " Greater " one, we have no idea of the length of time that separated any of them.

in brief; and I, Vaccha, could teach you what is skilled and what is unskilled in full. But I, Vaccha, will teach you what is skilled and what is unskilled in brief. Listen to it, attend carefully, and I will speak."

"Yes, sir," the wanderer Vacchagotta answered the Lord in assent. The Lord spoke thus:

"Greed, Vaccha, is unskill, absence of greed is skill. Aversion, Vaccha, is unskill, absence of aversion is skill. Confusion, Vaccha, is unskill, absence of confusion is skill. These are the three things that are unskilled, Vaccha, the three that are skilled. Then, Vaccha, onslaught on creatures[1] is unskill, restraint from onslaught on creatures is skill. Taking what has not been given, Vaccha, is unskill, restraint from taking what has not been given is skill. Wrong conduct in regard to sense-pleasures, Vaccha, is unskill, restraint from wrong conduct in regard to sense-pleasures is skill. Lying speech, Vaccha, is unskill, restraint from lying speech is skill. Slanderous speech, Vaccha, [**490**] is unskill, restraint from slanderous speech is skill. Harsh speech, Vaccha, is unskill, restraint from harsh speech is skill. Frivolous chatter, Vaccha, is unskill, restraint from frivolous chatter is skill. Covetousness, Vaccha, is unskill, absence of covetousness is skill. Malevolence, Vaccha, is unskill, absence of malevolence is skill. Wrong view, Vaccha, is unskill, right view is skill.[2] These are the ten things that are unskilled, Vaccha, and the ten that are skilled. When craving, Vaccha, has been got rid of by a monk, cut off at the root, made like a palm-tree stump that can come to no further existence in the future, he is a monk who is a perfected one, canker-waned, who has lived the life, done what was to be done, laid down the burden, attained his own goal, the fetters of becoming quite destroyed, freed by right profound knowledge."

"Let be the good Gotama. Has the good Gotama even one monk who is a disciple and who, by the destruction of the cankers, having realised here and now by his own super-knowledge the freedom of mind and the freedom through intuitive wisdom that are cankerless, entering on them is abiding in them?"

"Not merely a hundred, Vaccha, nor two hundred, three hundred, four hundred nor five hundred, but far more are those monks, disciples of mine, who, by the destruction of the cankers, having realised here and now by their own super-knowledge the freedom of

---

[1] *Cf. M.* i. 285-286; *D.* i. 4.

[2] This sentence is quoted at *Kvu.* 505.

mind and the freedom through intuitive wisdom that are cankerless, entering on them are abiding in them."

"Let be the good Gotama, let be the monks. But has the good Gotama even one nun who is a disciple and who, by the destruction of the cankers, having realised here and now by her own super-knowledge the freedom of mind and the freedom through intuitive wisdom that are cankerless, entering on them is abiding in them?"

"Not merely a hundred, Vaccha, nor two, three, four or five hundred, but far more are those nuns, disciples of mine, who, by the destruction of the cankers, having here and now realised by their own super-knowledge the freedom of mind and the freedom through intuitive wisdom that are cankerless, entering on them are abiding in them."

"Let be the good Gotama, let be the monks, let be the nuns. But has the good Gotama even one layfollower who is a disciple, a householder clothed in white, a Brahma-farer who, by the utter destruction of the five fetters binding to this lower (shore) is of spontaneous uprising, one who has attained nibbāna there and is not liable to return from that world?"

"Not merely a hundred, Vaccha, nor . . . five hundred, but far more are those layfollowers, disciples of mine, householders clothed in white, Brahma-farers, who by the utter destruction of the five fetters binding to this lower (shore), [**491**] are of spontaneous uprising, those who have attained nibbāna there and are not liable to return from that world."

"Let be the good Gotama, let be the monks, let be the nuns, let be the lay-followers who are householders clothed in white, Brahma-farers. But has the good Gotama even one layfollower who is a disciple, a householder clothed in white, and who, (though) an enjoyer of sense-pleasures, is a doer of the instruction, one who accepts the exhortation, who has crossed over doubt and, perplexity gone, fares in the Teacher's instruction, won to conviction, not relying on others?"[1]

"Not merely a hundred, Vaccha, nor . . . five hundred, but far more are those layfollowers, disciples of mine, householders clothed in white, and who, (though) enjoyers of sense-pleasures are doers of the instruction, those who accept the exhortation, who have crossed over doubt and, perplexity gone, fare in the Teacher's instruction, won to conviction, not relying on others."

---

[1] As at *M.* i. 235.

"Let be the good Gotama, let be the monks, let be the nuns, let be the layfollowers who are householders clothed in white, Brahma-farers, let be the layfollowers who are householders clothed in white, enjoyers of sense-pleasures. But has the good Gotama even one woman layfollower who is a disciple, a householder clothed in white, a Brahma-farer who, by the utter destruction of the five fetters binding to this lower (shore), is of spontaneous uprising, one who has attained nibbāna there and is not liable to return from that world?"

"Not merely a hundred, Vaccha, nor . . . five hundred, but many more are those women layfollowers, disciples of mine, householders clothed in white, Brahma-farers who, by the utter destruction of the five fetters binding to this lower (shore), are of spontaneous uprising, those who have attained nibbāna there and are not liable to return from that world."

"Let be the good Gotama, let be the monks, let be the nuns, let be the layfollowers who are householders clothed in white, Brahma-farers, let be the layfollowers who are householders clothed in white, enjoyers of sense-pleasures, let be the women layfollowers who are householders clothed in white, Brahma-farers. But has the good Gotama even one woman layfollower who is a disciple, a householder clothed in white, and who, (though) an enjoyer of sense-pleasures, is a doer of the instruction, one who accepts the exhortation, who has crossed over doubt and, perplexity gone, fares in the Teacher's instruction, won to conviction, not relying on others?"

"Not merely a hundred, Vaccha, nor two, three, four or five hundred, but many more are those women layfollowers, disciples of mine, householders clothed in white, and who, (though) enjoyers of sense-pleasures, are doers of the instruction, those who accept the exhortation, who have crossed over doubt and, perplexity gone, fare in the Teacher's instruction, won to conviction, not relying on others."

"If, good Gotama, the revered Gotama had himself undertaken this *dhamma* but the monks had not undertaken it, [**492**] then this Brahma-faring would have been incomplete as to this factor. But because the revered Gotama has undertaken this *dhamma* and the monks have undertaken it as well, so is this Brahma-faring complete as to this factor. If, good Gotama, the revered Gotama had himself undertaken this *dhamma* and the monks had undertaken it as well, but not the nuns, then this Brahma-faring would have been incomplete as to this factor. But because the revered Gotama has undertaken this *dhamma* and the monks and the nuns have undertaken it as well, so is this Brahma-faring complete as to this factor. If, good

Gotama, the revered Gotama had himself undertaken this *dhamma* and the monks and the nuns had undertaken it as well, but not the layfollowers who are householders clothed in white, Brahma-farers, then this Brahma-faring would have been incomplete as to this factor. But because the revered Gotama has undertaken this *dhamma* and the monks and the nuns and the layfollowers who are householders clothed in white, Brahma-farers, have undertaken it as well, so is this Brahma-faring complete as to this factor. If, good Gotama, the revered Gotama had himself undertaken this *dhamma* and the monks and the nuns and the layfollowers who are householders clothed in white, Brahma-farers, had undertaken it as well, but not the layfollowers who are householders clothed in white, enjoyers of sense-pleasures, then this Brahma-faring would have been incomplete as to this factor. But because the revered Gotama has undertaken this *dhamma*, and the monks and the nuns and the layfollowers who are householders clothed in white, Brahma-farers, and the layfollowers who are householders clothed in white, enjoyers of sense-pleasures, have undertaken it as well, so is this Brahma-faring complete as to this factor. If, good Gotama, the revered Gotama had himself undertaken this *dhamma* and the monks and . . . the layfollowers who are householders clothed in white, enjoyers of sense-pleasures, had undertaken it as well, but not the women lay followers who are householders clothed in white, Brahma-farers, [**493**] then this Brahma-faring would have been incomplete as to this factor. But because the revered Gotama has undertaken this *dhamma*, and the monks and the nuns and the layfollowers who are householders clothed in white, Brahma-farers, and the layfollowers who are householders clothed in white, enjoyers of sense-pleasures, and the women layfollowers who are householders clothed in white, Brahma-farers, have undertaken it as well, so is this Brahma-faring complete as to this factor. If, good Gotama, the revered Gotama had himself undertaken this *dhamma* and the monks and . . . the women layfollowers who are householders clothed in white, Brahma-farers, had undertaken it as well, but not the women layfollowers who are householders clothed in white, enjoyers of sense-pleasures, then the Brahma-faring would have been incomplete as to this factor. But because the revered Gotama has undertaken this *dhamma*, and the monks and the nuns and the layfollowers who are householders clothed in white, Brahma-farers, and the layfollowers who are householders clothed in white, enjoyers of sense-pleasures, and the women layfollowers who are householders clothed in white, Brahma-farers, and the women layfollowers who are householders clothed in white, enjoyers of sense-pleasures, have undertaken it as well, so is this Brahma-faring complete as to this factor.

Good Gotama, as the river Ganges,[1] sliding towards the sea, tending towards the sea, inclining towards the sea, stands knocking at[2] the sea, even so this company of the good Gotama, comprising householders and those that have gone forth,[3] sliding towards nibbāna, tending towards nibbāna, inclining towards nibbāna, stands knocking at nibbāna. It is excellent, good Gotama, excellent, good Gotama. It is as if, good Gotama, one might set upright what had been upset, or disclose what had been covered, or might show the way to one that had gone astray, or bring an oil-lamp into the darkness so that those with vision might see material shapes—even so in many a figure is *dhamma* made clear by the revered Gotama. I am going to the revered Gotama for refuge and to *dhamma* and to the Order of monks. May I receive the going forth in the good Gotama's presence, may I receive ordination."

[**494**] " Vaccha, if a former member of another sect[4] wishes for the going forth in this *dhamma* and discipline, wishes for ordination, he undertakes probation for four months; at the end of the four months the monks, if they so decide, may let him go forth, may ordain him into the status of a monk; but even here differences among individuals are known to me."

" If, revered sir, former members of other sects, desiring the going forth in this *dhamma* and discipline, desiring ordination, undertake probation for four months, and at the end of the four months the monks, if they so decide, let them go forth, ordain them into the status of a monk, then will I undertake probation for four years; at the end of the four years the monks, if they so decide, may let me go forth, may ordain me into the status of a monk." But the wanderer Vacchagotta received the going forth in the Lord's presence, he received ordination.

Not long after the venerable Vacchagotta was ordained, half a month after he was ordained, he approached the Lord; having approached, having greeted the Lord, he sat down at a respectful distance. As he was sitting down at a respectful distance, the venerable Vacchagotta spoke thus to the Lord:

---

[1] *Cf. S.* v. 39-40.

[2] *āhacca tiṭṭhati,* stands knocking or striking at. *Cf. S.* ii. 43, 45, 58, 80, *amatadvāram āhacca tiṭṭhati.*

[3] *parisā sagahaṭṭhapabbajitā; cf. Vin.* i. 115.

[4] As at *M.* i. 391, 512.

"Revered sir, I have attained as much as can be attained by a learner's knowledge, a learner's lore.[1] Let the Lord teach me some further *dhamma*."[2]

"Well then, do you, Vaccha, develop two things further: calm and vision. If these two things: calm and vision, are developed further, Vaccha, they will conduce to the penetration of a variety of elements.[3]

If you, Vaccha, should wish like this: 'May I experience[4] the various forms of psychic power: having been one may I be manifold, having been manifold may I be one; manifest or invisible may I go unhindered through a wall, through a rampart, through a mountain as if through air; may I plunge into the earth and shoot up again as if in water; may I walk upon the water without parting it as if on the ground; sitting cross-legged, may I travel through the air like a bird on the wing; with my hand may I rub and stroke this moon and sun although they are of such mighty power and majesty; and even as far as the Brahma-world may I have power in respect of my person' —you will achieve what may be realised here and there[5] so long as there is the objective.[6]

If you, Vaccha, should wish like this: 'May I, [**495**] with the purified *deva*-hearing surpassing that of men, hear both (kinds of) sounds—*deva*-like ones and human ones, whether they be far or near' —you will achieve what may be realised here and there, so long as there is the objective.

If you, Vaccha, should wish like this: 'May I know intuitively by mind the minds of other beings, of other individuals, so that I may know intuitively of a mind that is full of attachment . . . aversion . . . confusion, that it is full of attachment . . . aversion . . . confusion; or of a mind that is without attachment . . . aversion . . . confusion, that it is without attachment . . . without aversion . . . without confusion; or that I may know intuitively of a mind that is contracted that it is contracted, or of a mind that is distracted that it is distracted, or of a mind that has become great that it has become great, or of a mind that has not become great that it has not become great, or of a

---

[1] *vijjā*. *MA*. iii. 201 quotes *Dhs*. 1016, 1400, *katame ca dhammā sekhā?* and says non-returning was attained.

[2] *uttariṁ dhammaṁ*. [3] *dhātu*. [4] With the following *cf*. *M*. i. 34.

[5] *tatra tatr' eva sakkhibhabbataṁ pāpuṇissasi*.

[6] *sati sati āyatane*, quoted at *DA*. 125. *MA*. iii. 202, iv. 146 explain by *kāraṇe*. *Cf*. *Jā*. i. 251, *anāyatane akāraṇe*. *Āyatana* seems almost to be cause, right object, objective, inducement or sufficient reason. Same expression is used at *M*. iii. 96, *A*. iii. 27.

mind with (some other mental state) superior to it that it has (some other mental state) superior to it, or of a mind that has no (other mental state) superior to it that it has no (other mental state) superior to it, or of a mind that is composed that it is composed, or of a mind that is not composed that it is not composed, or of a mind that is freed that it is freed, or of a mind that is not freed that it is not freed '—you will achieve what may be realised here and there, so long as there is the objective.

If you, Vaccha, should wish like this: 'May I recollect (my) manifold former habitations, that is to say one birth, two births, three . . . four . . . five . . . ten . . . twenty . . . thirty . . . forty . . . fifty . . . a hundred . . . a thousand . . . a hundred thousand births, many an eon of integration, many an eon of disintegration, many an eon of integration-disintegration; such a one was I by name, having such and such a clan, such and such a colour, so was I nourished, such and such pleasant and painful experiences were mine, so did the span of life end. Passing from this, I came to be in another state where such a one was I by name, having such and such a clan, such and such a colour, so was I nourished, such and such pleasant and painful experiences were mine, so did the span of life end. Passing from this I arose here. Thus I recollect (my) divers former habitations in all their modes and detail '—you will achieve what may be realised here and there, so long as there is the objective. [**496**] If you, Vaccha, should wish like this: 'With the purified *deva*-vision surpassing that of men, may I behold beings as they pass hence or come to be—mean, excellent, comely, ugly, in a good bourn, in a bad bourn according to the consequences of deeds; may I comprehend: Indeed these worthy beings were possessed of wrong conduct in body, speech and thought, they were scoffers at the ariyans, holding a wrong view, incurring deeds consequent on a wrong view—these, at the breaking up of the body after dying, have arisen in a sorrowful state, a bad bourn, the abyss, Niraya Hell. But these worthy beings who were possessed of right conduct in body, speech and thought, who were not scoffers at the ariyans, holding a right view, incurring deeds consequent on a right view—these at the breaking up of the body after dying, have arisen in a good bourn, a heaven world. Thus with the purified *deva*-vision surpassing that of men may I behold beings as they pass hence, as they come to be, may I comprehend that they are mean, excellent, comely, ugly, in a good bourn, in a bad bourn according to the consequences of deeds '—you will achieve what may be realised here and there, so long as there is the objective.

If you, Vaccha, should wish like this: 'By the destruction of the cankers, having realised here and now by my own super-knowledge the freedom of mind and the freedom through intuitive wisdom that are cankerless, entering thereon, may I abide therein'—you will achieve what may be realised here and there, so long as there is the objective."

Then the venerable Vacchagotta, having rejoiced in what the Lord had said, having given thanks, rising from his seat, having greeted the Lord, departed keeping his right side towards him. Then the venerable Vacchagotta, having soon realised here and now through his own super-knowledge that incomparable goal of the Brahma-faring for the sake of which young men of family rightly go forth from home into homelessness, entering on it, abided in it. And he understood: Destroyed is birth, brought to a close is the Brahma-faring, done is what was to be done, there is no more of being such or so. And the venerable Vacchagotta became one of the perfected ones.[1]

Now at that time a number of monks were going to see the Lord. The venerable Vacchagotta saw these monks coming in the distance; having seen them, he approached these monks; having approached, he spoke thus to these monks:

[**497**] "But now, where are you venerable ones going?"

"We are going to see the Lord, your reverence."

"Well then, in my name let the venerable ones salute the Lord's feet with their heads, saying, 'Revered sir, the monk Vacchagotta salutes the Lord's feet with his head,' and then say: 'The Lord is waited on[2] by me, the Well-farer is waited on by me.'"

"Yes, your reverence," these monks answered the venerable Vacchagotta in assent. Then these monks approached the Lord; having approached, having greeted the Lord, they sat down at a respectful distance. As they were sitting down at a respectful distance these monks spoke thus to the Lord:

"Revered sir, the venerable Vacchagotta salutes the Lord's feet with his head and speaks thus: 'The Lord is waited on by me, the Well-farer is waited on by me.'"

"Monks, by a reasoning of mind I already knew the mind of the monk Vacchagotta: of threefold knowledge is the monk Vacchagotta, of great psychic power, of great majesty. And *devatās* also

---

[1] His verse is at *Thag.* 112.

[2] *paricinṇa; cf. S.* iv. 57; *Thag.* 178, 604, 687, 792, 891.

told me this matter:[1] 'Of threefold knowledge is the monk Vacchagotta, revered sir, he is of great psychic power, of great majesty.'"

Thus spoke the Lord. Delighted, these monks rejoiced in what the Lord had said.

Greater Discourse to Vacchagotta:
The Third

74. DISCOURSE TO DĪGHANAKHA

(Dīghanakhasutta)[2]

THUS have I heard: At one time the Lord was staying near Rājagaha on Mount Vulture Peak in the Boar's Cave.[3] Then the wanderer Dīghanakha[4] approached the Lord; having approached, he exchanged greetings with the Lord; having conversed in a friendly and courteous way, he stood at a respectful distance.[5] As he was standing at a respectful distance, the wanderer Dīghanakha spoke thus to the Lord:

"I, good Gotama, speak thus, I am of this view: All[6] is not pleasing to me."

"This view of yours, Aggivessana:[7] All is not pleasing to me—does this view of yours not please you?"

---

[1] *MA*. iii. 202 explains by *tesaṁ guṇānaṁ lābhī devatā: devatās* are the recipients of (or, are possessed of, or, are psychically intuitive of) these qualities; *cf. DA*. 120. It is possible that in such contexts *devatā* stands for a mental or psychical faculty.

[2] *Cf. DA*. 418, 882, *DhA*. i. 96, *SA*. i. 122, ii. 63, 234, etc., where this Sutta is referred to as *Vedanāpariggahanasuttanta*.

[3] This cave, Sūkarakhatā, is also mentioned at *S*. v. 233. *SA*. iii. 249 gives the same account of it as does *MA*. iii. 203.

[4] Sāriputta's nephew.

[5] *MA*. iii. 203 says that he stood at a respectful distance because the Elder (Sāriputta) was standing fanning the Lord, as below, p. 180.

[6] *MA*. iii. 204 explains "all," *sabbaṁ*, for Dīghanakha as all uprisings and re-linkings, for to this extent he is an annihilationist. Gotama, however, takes "all" in its literal sense.

[7] *Cf. M*. i. 229 *f*., 238 *ff*. and *M*. iii. 128 *f*. for this epithet.

"If this view were pleasing to me, good Gotama, this would be like it too, that [498] would be like it too.[1]"

"Now, Aggivessana, when those, the majority in the world, speak thus: 'This would be like it too, that would be like it too'—they do not get rid of that very view, and they take up another view.[2] Now, Aggivessana, when those, the minority in the world, speak thus: 'This would be like it too, that would be like it too'—they get rid of that very view and do not take up another view.

There are, Aggivessana, some recluses and brahmans who speak thus and are of this view: 'All is pleasing to me.' There are, Aggivessana, some recluses and brahmans who speak thus and are of this view: 'All is not pleasing to me.' There are, Aggivessana, some recluses and brahmans who speak thus and are of this view: 'Part is pleasing to me, part is not pleasing to me.' As to this, Aggivessana, those recluses and brahmans who speak thus and are of this view: 'All is pleasing to me'—this view of theirs is close to[3] attachment, close to the fetters, close to delight, close to cleaving, close to grasping. As to this, Aggivessana, those recluses and brahmans who speak thus and are of this view: 'All is not pleasing to me'—this view of theirs is close to detachment, close to the absence of fetters, close to the absence of delight, close to the absence of cleaving, close to the absence of grasping."

When this had been said, the wanderer Dīghanakha spoke thus to the Lord: "The good Gotama is complimentary to my view, the good Gotama is very complimentary to my view."

"As to this, Aggivessana, those recluses and brahmans who speak thus and are of this view: 'Part is pleasing to me, part is not pleasing to me'—that which in this view is pleasing to them is close to attachment, close to the fetters . . . close to grasping. But that which in this view is not pleasing to them is close to detachment, close to the absence of fetters . . . close to the absence of grasping.

Concerning those recluses and brahmans, Aggivessana, who speak thus and are of this view: 'All is pleasing to me,' if a learned man be there who reflects thus: 'If I were to express this view of mine: "All is pleasing to me," and, obstinately holding to it and adhering to it,[4] were to say: "This is indeed the truth, all else is falsehood" —there would be for me dispute with two (view-holders): both with whatever recluse or brahman speaks thus and is of this view: "All

---

[1] That is, "pleasing" too.

[2] *MA.* iii. 205 distinguishes these views as annihilationism and eternalism.

[3] As at *M.* i. 411.

[4] As at *M.* i. 130, 257.

is not pleasing to me," and with whatever recluse or brahman speaks thus and [**499**] is of this view: " Part is pleasing to me, part is not pleasing to me "—there would be dispute for me with these two. If there is dispute there is contention; if there is contention there is trouble; if there is trouble there is vexation.'[1] So he, beholding this dispute and contention and trouble and vexation for himself, gets rid of that very view and does not take up another view. Thus is the getting rid of these views, thus is the casting out of these views.

As to this, Aggivessana, those recluses and brahmans who speak thus and are of this view: 'All is not pleasing to me'—if a learned man be there who reflects thus: ' If I were to express this view of mine that: " All is not pleasing to me," and, obstinately holding to it and adhering to it, were to say: " This is the very truth, all else is falsehood," there would be for me dispute with two (view-holders): both with whatever recluse or brahman speaks thus and is of this view: " All is pleasing to me," and with whatever recluse or brahman speaks thus and is of this view: " Part is pleasing to me, part is not pleasing to me "—there would be dispute for me with these two. If there is dispute there is contention, if there is contention there is trouble, if there is trouble there is vexation.' So he, beholding this dispute and contention and trouble and vexation for himself, gets rid of that very view and does not take up another view. Thus is the getting rid of these views, thus is the casting out of these views.

As to this, Aggivessana, those recluses and brahmans who speak thus and are of this view: ' Part is pleasing to me, part is not pleasing to me '— if a learned man be there who reflects thus: ' If I were to express this view of mine: " Part is pleasing to me, part is not pleasing to me," and, obstinately holding to it and adhering to it, were to say: " This is the very truth, all else is falsehood," there would be for me dispute with two (view-holders): both with whatever recluse or brahman speaks thus and is of this view: " All is pleasing to me," and with whatever recluse or brahman speaks thus and is of this view: " All is not pleasing to me "—there would be dispute for me with these two. If there is dispute there is contention, if there is contention there is trouble, if there is trouble there is vexation.' So he, beholding this dispute and contention and trouble and vexation for himself, gets rid of that very view and does not take up another view. Thus is the getting rid of these views, thus is the casting out of these views.

---

[1] There is no indication whether the thoughts of the learned man stop here or at the end of the previous sentence.

[**500**] But this body, Aggivessana, which has material shape, is made up of the four great elements, originating from mother and father, nourished on gruel and sour milk, of a nature to be constantly rubbed away, pounded away, broken up and scattered,[1] should be regarded as impermanent, suffering, as a disease, an imposthume, a dart, a misfortune, an affliction, as other, as decay, empty, not-self.[2] When he regards this body as impermanent, suffering, as a disease, an imposthume, a dart, a misfortune, an affliction, as other, as decay, empty, not-self, whatever in regard to body is desire for body, affection for body, subordination to body, this is got rid of.

There are these three feelings, Aggivessana: pleasant feeling, painful feeling, feeling that is neither painful nor pleasant. At the time, Aggivessana, when one feels a pleasant feeling, at that time one feels neither a painful feeling nor does one feel a feeling that is neither painful nor pleasant. At the time, Aggivessana, when one feels a painful feeling, at that time one feels neither a pleasant feeling nor does one feel a feeling that is neither painful nor pleasant. At the time, Aggivessana, when one feels a feeling that is neither painful nor pleasant, at that time one feels neither a pleasant feeling nor does one feel a painful feeling. Pleasant feelings, Aggivessana, are impermanent, compounded, generated by conditions, liable to destruction, liable to decay, liable to fading away, liable to stopping.[3] And painful feelings . . . And, Aggivessana, feelings that are neither painful nor pleasant are impermanent, compounded, generated by conditions, liable to destruction, liable to decay, liable to fading away, liable to stopping. Seeing it thus, Aggivessana, an instructed disciple of the ariyans turns away from pleasant feelings and he turns away from painful feelings and he turns away from feelings that are neither painful nor pleasant; turning away he is dispassionate, being dispassionate he is freed,[4] in freedom the knowledge comes to be that he is freed and he comprehends: 'Destroyed is birth, brought to a close is the Brahma-faring, done is what was to be done, there is no more of being such or so.' A monk whose mind is freed thus, Aggivessana, does not concur with

---

[1] As at *M.* i. 144.

[2] As at *M.* i. 435.

[3] *Cf. D.* iii. 275, "the escape from what has become, is composite, originating from conditions, is its stopping"; and see *S.* ii. 26 which enumerates the things that, arising from cause, are impermanent, etc.; *cf. A.* v. 187.

[4] *Cf. S.* ii. 94, 125, iv. 2- 86; also *S.* iii. 46, 189; *A.* v. 3.

anyone, he does not dispute with anyone.[1] He makes use of the common phrases of the world without adhering to them."[2]

Now at that time the venerable Sāriputta [**501**] was standing behind the Lord, fanning the Lord. Then it occurred to the venerable Sāriputta: "The Lord speaks to us of getting rid of these things and those by means of super-knowledge,[3] the Well-farer speaks to us of casting out these things and those by means of super-knowledge." While the venerable Sāriputta was reflecting on this, his mind was freed from the cankers without clinging. But to the wanderer Dīghanakha there arose the stainless, spotless vision of *dhamma*, that whatever is of the nature to arise all that is of the nature to stop. Then the wanderer Dīghanakha, having seen *dhamma*, attained *dhamma*, known *dhamma*, plunged into *dhamma*, having crossed over doubt, having put away uncertainty, attaining without another's help to full confidence in the Teacher's instruction,[4] spoke thus to the Lord:

"It is excellent, good Gotama, excellent, good Gotama. It is, good Gotama, as if one might set upright what had been upset, or might disclose what had been covered, or point out the Way to one who had gone astray, or might bring an oil-lamp into the darkness so that those with vision might see material shapes—even so in many a figure has *dhamma* been made clear by the good Gotama. I am going to the revered Gotama for refuge and to *dhamma* and to the Order of monks. May the revered Gotama accept me as a layfollower going for refuge from today forth for as long as life lasts."

Discourse to Dīghanakha:
The Fourth

---

[1] *Cf. S.* iii. 138. *MA.* iii. 208 says he does not concur with the eternalists nor dispute with the partial-eternalists.

[2] *Cf. S.* i. 14; *D.* i. 202, quoted at *MA.* iii. 208.

[3] *MA.* iii. 208 says "he talked about the getting rid of the eternal having known through super-knowledge the eternalism of these things and those; he speaks of getting rid of the partially eternal through super-knowledge as to annihilation, as to partial eternalism; he speaks of getting rid of material shape through super-knowledge as to material shape".

[4] As at *Vin.* i. 12.

75. DISCOURSE TO MĀGANDIYA

(Māgandiyasutta)

THUS have I heard: At one time the Lord was staying among the Kurus—the market town of the Kurus was called Kammāssadhamma—on a spreading of grass in the fire-room[1] of a brahman of the Bhāradvāja clan. Then the Lord, having dressed early in the morning, taking his bowl and robe, entered Kammāssadhamma for almsfood. Having walked in Kammāssadhamma for almsfood, returning from his alms-gathering after the meal, having plunged into a forest thicket, he sat down at the root of a tree for the day-sojourn.

[**502**] Then the wanderer Māgandiya, who was constantly pacing up and down and roaming about on foot, approached the fire-room of the brahman of the Bhāradvāja clan. The wanderer Māgandiya saw the spreading of grass made ready in the fire-room of the brahman of the Bhāradvāja clan; seeing it, he spoke thus to the brahman of the Bhāradvāja clan: "For whom is this spreading of grass laid down in the good Bhāradvāja's fire-room? It seems like a recluse's sleeping place."

"Māgandiya, there is the recluse Gotama, son of the Sakyans, gone forth from the Sakyan clan, and about this revered Gotama a lovely reputation has gone abroad thus: He is indeed the Lord, perfected one, fully Self-Awakened One, endowed with right knowledge and conduct, knower of the worlds, Well-farer, incomparable trainer of men to be tamed, teacher of *devas* and men, the Awakened One, the Lord. That sleeping place is ready for this good Gotama."

"Indeed, good Bhāradvāja, we are seeing a poor sight in seeing the sleeping place of the good Gotama, the destroyer of growth."[2]

---

[1] *MA*. iii. 209, in the agnihotra-hall.

[2] *bhūnahuno. MA*. iii. 211: *hatavaḍḍhino mariyādakārakassa . . . vaḍḍhi-hato mariyādakārako*, a killer of growths, the maker of stringent controls (or, rules); and it explains by saying that Māgandiya holds that there should be development and growth in all the six sense-spheres, while the Lord holds that there should be restraint of them, and *MA*. cites verses at *Miln*. 167. The word *bhūnahu* occurs at *Sn*. 664, in voc. (*SnA*. 479: *bhūtihanaka vuddhi-nāsaka*) and at *Jā*. v. 266, in the plural. See *JāA*. v. 272: *te isīnam ativattāro attano vaḍḍhiyā hatattā bhūnahuno. Cf. Miln*. 314, *bhūtahacca*, citing the above *M*. passage. Chalmers translates *bhūnahu* as "rigid repressionist," *i.e.* of the

" Mind what you say,[1] Māgandiya, mind what you say, Māgandiya. For many learned nobles and learned brahmans and learned householders and learned recluses have great faith in this good Gotama, and are trained in the ariyan right path, in *dhamma*, in what is skilled."[2]

" If we could only see that revered Gotama face to face, Bhāradvāja, face to face would we say to him: ' The recluse Gotama is a destroyer of growth.' What is the reason for this ? It is handed down thus in a discourse of ours."

" If it is not disagreeable to the good Māgandiya, I will tell this to the recluse Gotama."

" It is of no consequence if the good Bhāradvāja should tell him just what has been said."

Then the Lord, with purified *deva*-hearing surpassing that of men, heard this conversation between the brahman of the Bhāradvāja clan and the wanderer Māgandiya. Then the Lord, emerging from solitary meditation towards evening, approached the fire-room of the brahman of the Bhāradvāja clan; having approached, he sat down on the spreading of grass that was ready. Then the brahman of the Bhāradvāja clan approached the Lord; having approached, he exchanged greetings with the Lord; and having conversed in a friendly and courteous way, he sat down at a respectful distance. As the brahman of the Bhāradvāja clan was sitting down at a respectful distance, the Lord spoke thus to him:

" There was some conversation, Bhāradvāja, between you and the wanderer Māgandiya [**503**] concerning this same grass spreading."

When this had been said the brahman Bhāradvāja, greatly moved and startled, spoke thus to the Lord: " But this was the very thing I wanted to tell the good Gotama, but the revered Gotama anticipated me."

But this conversation between the Lord and the brahman of the Bhāradvāja clan was interrupted when the wanderer Māgandiya, who was constantly pacing up and down and roaming about on foot, approached the Lord in the fire-room of the brahman of the Bhāradvāja clan; having approached, he exchanged greetings with the Lord; having conversed in a friendly and courteous way, he sat down

---

[1] As at *Vin.* ii. 186.

[2] *ariye ñaye dhamme kusale.* *Cf. M.* ii. 181, 197, *A.* i. 69, *D.* ii. 151. *MA.* iii. 211 says: *parisuddhe kāraṇe dhamme anavajje.*

---

senses, which the wanderer thinks should be given full scope. See above Intr. p. xv.

at a respectful distance. As the wanderer Māgandiya was sitting down at a respectful distance, the Lord spoke thus to him:[1]

"Māgandiya, the eye delights in material shapes, is delighted by material shapes, rejoices in material shapes; it is tamed, watched, guarded and controlled by a Tathāgata, and he teaches *dhamma* for its control. Was it on account of this, Māgandiya, that you said: 'The recluse Gotama is a destroyer of growth'?"

"Just on account of this did I say, good Gotama: 'The recluse Gotama is a destroyer of growth.' What is the reason for this? It is handed down thus in a discourse of ours."

"The ear, Māgandiya, delights in sounds . . . the nose in smells . . . the tongue in tastes . . . the body in touches . . . the mind, Māgandiya, delights in mental states, is delighted by mental states, rejoices in mental states; it is tamed, watched, guarded, controlled by a Tathāgata, and he teaches *dhamma* for its control. Was it on account of this, Māgandiya, that you said: 'The recluse Gotama is a destroyer of growth'?"

"Just on account of this, good Gotama, did I say: 'The recluse Gotama is a destroyer of growth.' What is the reason for this? It is handed down thus in a discourse of ours."

"What do you think about this, Māgandiya? Suppose someone [**504**] who formerly revelled in material shapes cognisable by the eye—agreeable, pleasant, liked, enticing, connected with sensual pleasure, alluring—after a time, having known the coming to be and passing away of material shapes and the satisfaction and the peril of them and the escape (from them) as it really is, getting rid of craving for material shapes, suppressing the fever for material shapes, should dwell devoid of thirst, his mind inwardly calmed. What have you, Māgandiya, to say of him?"

"Nothing, good Gotama."

"What do you think about this, Māgandiya? Suppose someone who formerly revelled in sounds cognisable by the ear . . . in smells cognisable by the nose . . . in tastes cognisable by the tongue . . . in touches cognisable by the body—agreeable, pleasant, liked, enticing, connected with sensual pleasure, alluring—after a time, having known the coming to be and passing away of touches and the satisfaction and the peril of them and the escape (from them) as it really is, getting rid of the craving for touches, suppressing the fever for

---

[1] *MA*. iii. 213 says it is said that the Lord told the wanderer not to speak to him, and began teaching *dhamma* at once.

touches, should dwell devoid of thirst, his mind inwardly calmed. What have you, Māgandiya, to say of him?"

"Nothing, good Gotama."

"Now I, Māgandiya, when I was formerly a householder, endowed and provided with the five strands of sense-pleasures, revelled in them—in material shapes cognisable by the eye, agreeable, pleasant . . . in sounds cognisable by the ear . . . in smells cognisable by the nose . . . in tastes cognisable by the tongue . . . in touches cognisable by the body, agreeable, pleasant, liked, enticing, connected with sensual pleasures, alluring. I had three palaces, Māgandiya, one for the rains, one for the cold weather, one for the hot weather. I, Māgandiya, during the four months of the rains being delighted in the palace for the rains by women musicians,[1] did not come down from that palace. But after a time, having known the coming to be and passing away of sense-pleasures and the satisfaction and the peril of them and the escape as it really is, getting rid of the craving for sense-pleasures, suppressing the fever for sense-pleasures, I dwelt devoid of thirst, my mind inwardly calmed. I saw other beings not yet devoid of attachment to sense-pleasures who were pursuing sense-pleasures (although) they were being consumed by craving for sense-pleasures, burning with the fever for sense-pleasures. I did not envy them: I had no delight therein. What was the reason for this? It was, Māgandiya, that there is this delight which, apart from pleasures of the senses, apart from unskilled states of mind, **[505]** stands firm on reaching[2] a *deva*-like happiness. Delighting in this delight,[3] I do not envy what is low,[4] I have no delight therein.

Māgandiya, it is like a householder or a householder's son, rich, of great wealth, of many possessions who, endowed and provided with the five strands of sense-pleasures, might revel in them—in material shapes cognisable by the eye, agreeable, pleasant . . . in sounds cognisable by the ear . . . in smells cognisable by the nose . . . in tastes cognisable by the tongue . . . in touches cognisable by the body, agreeable, pleasant, liked, enticing, connected with sensual pleasures,

---

[1] *MA*. iii. 215-6 says there were women everywhere; they were not only musicians, but door-keepers and barbers.

[2] *samadhiggayha tiṭṭhati* as at *M*. ii. 25; *S*. i. 86; *Iti*. p. 16. *Samadhigaṇhāti* appears to mean to reach, acquire, and also to distinguish (see *MA*. iii. 268 where it is glossed by *visesetvā*).

[3] *MA*. iii. 216 says the delight of attaining the fruit of the fourth meditation.

[4] *hīnassa*. *MA*. iii. 217 gives *hīnajanasukha* and also the five strands of human sense-pleasures.

alluring. He, having behaved well in body, having behaved well in speech, having behaved well in thought, at the breaking up of the body after dying, might arise in a good bourn, a heaven world, in companionship with the Devas of the Thirty-Three. Surrounded there in the Nandana Grove by a throng of nymphs, he, endowed and provided with the five *deva*-like strands of pleasures of the senses, might revel in them. He might see a householder or a householder's son endowed and provided with the five strands of sense-pleasures. What do you think about this, Māgandiya? Would that young *deva*, surrounded by a throng of nymphs in the Nandana Grove, endowed and provided with the five *deva*-like strands of sense-pleasures and revelling in them—would he envy that householder or householder's son or their five strands of human sense-pleasures, and revert to human sense-pleasures?"

"No, good Gotama. What is the reason for this? It is that *deva*-like sense-pleasures are more wonderful and excellent than human sense-pleasures."

"Even so did I, Māgandiya, when I was formerly a householder, endowed and provided with the five strands of sense-pleasures, revel in them—in material shapes cognisable by the eye, agreeable, pleasant . . . in sounds cognisable by the ear . . . in smells cognisable by the nose . . . in tastes cognisable by the tongue . . . in touches cognisable by the body, agreeable, pleasant, liked, enticing, connected with sensual pleasure, alluring. But after a time, having known the coming to be and passing away of sense-pleasures and the satisfaction and peril of them and the escape as it really is, getting rid of the craving for sense-pleasures, suppressing the fever for sense-pleasures, I dwelt devoid of thirst, my mind inwardly calmed. I saw other beings not yet devoid of attachment to sense-pleasures who were pursuing sense-pleasures (although) they were being consumed by the craving for sense-pleasures, [**506**] burning with the fever for sense-pleasures. I did not envy them; I had no delight therein. What was the reason for this? It was, Māgandiya, that there is this delight which, apart from pleasures of the senses, apart from unskilled states of mind, stands firm on reaching a *deva*-like happiness. Delighting in this delight, I do not envy what is low, I have no delight therein.

Māgandiya, it is like a leper, a man with his limbs all ravaged and festering,[1] and who, being eaten by vermin, tearing his open sores

---

[1] *Cf. S.* iv. 198.

with his nails, might scorch his body over a charcoal pit; his friends and acquaintances, his kith and kin might procure a physician and surgeon[1]; that physician and surgeon might make up a medicine; he, taking that medicine, might be freed of that leprosy, he might be well, at ease, independent, his own master, going wherever he liked.[2] He might see another leper, a man with his limbs all ravaged and festering, and who . . . might scorch his body over a charcoal pit. What do you think about this, Māgandiya ? Would that man envy that other leper man his charcoal pit or his course of medicine ?"

" No, good Gotama. What is the reason for this ? It is, good Gotama, that if there is illness, there is something to be done through medicine ; but if there is not illness there is nothing to be done through medicine."

" Even so did I, Māgandiya, when I was formerly a householder, endowed and provided with the five strands of sense-pleasures, revel in them . . . But after a time . . . I do not envy what is low, I have no delight therein.

[**507**] Māgandiya, it is like a leper . . . he might be well, at ease, independent, going wherever he liked. Two strong men, taking hold of him by his arms, might drag him towards a charcoal pit. What do you think about this, Māgandiya ? Would not that man twist his body this way and that ?"[3]

" Yes, good Gotama. What is the reason for that ? It is, good Gotama, that contact with the fire is painful, for it is both exceedingly hot and afflicting."

" What do you think about this, Māgandiya ? Is it only now that contact with the fire is painful and both exceedingly hot and afflicting, or was contact with that fire also painful before and both exceedingly hot and afflicting ?"

" It is both now, good Gotama, that contact with the fire is painful, exceedingly hot and afflicting, and also before that contact with that fire was painful, exceedingly hot and afflicting. Yet, good Gotama, this leper, a man with his limbs all ravaged and festering, being eaten by vermin, tearing his open sores with his nails, his sense-organs injured,[4] might, from the painful contact with the fire, receive a change of sensation and think it pleasant."

" Even so, Māgandiya, far into the past contact of sense-pleasures

---

[1] As at *M*. i. 429, ii. 216.
[2] *M*. ii. 216.
[3] As at *M*. i. 365.
[4] *upahatindriya*.

is painful, exceedingly hot and afflicting, far into the future too . . . and also now in the present contact of sense-pleasures is painful, exceedingly hot and afflicting. But those beings, Māgandiya, not yet devoid of attachment to pleasures of the senses, who are being consumed by the craving for sense-pleasures and burning with the fever for sense-pleasures, their sense-organs injured, may, from painful contact with sense-pleasures themselves, receive a change of sensation and think it pleasant.

Māgandiya, it is like a leper, a man with his limbs all ravaged and festering, and who, being eaten by vermin, tearing his open sores with his nails, scorches his body over a charcoal pit. But the more, Māgandiya, this leper, a man with his limbs . . . scorches his body over a charcoal pit, the more those open sores of his [**508**] become septic and evil-smelling and putrefying and there is only a sorry relief and satisfaction to be had from scratching the open sores. Even so, Māgandiya, do beings who are not yet devoid of attachment to sense-pleasures, while being consumed by the craving for sense-pleasures and burning with the fever for sense-pleasures, pursue sense-pleasures; and the more these beings who are not yet devoid of attachment to sense-pleasures . . . pursue them, the more their craving for sense-pleasures increases, the more they burn with the fever for sense-pleasures, and moreover there is only a sorry relief and satisfaction to be had from the five strands of sense-pleasures.

What do you think about this, Māgandiya ? Have you ever seen or heard of a king or a king's chief minister who, endowed and provided with the five strands of sense-pleasure—revelling in them —and who had neither got rid of the craving for sense-pleasures nor suppressed the fever for sense-pleasures, dwelt or is dwelling or will dwell devoid of thirst, his mind inwardly calmed ?"

" No, good Gotama."

" It is good, Māgandiya. Neither have I seen or heard of this, that a king or a king's chief minister . . . his mind inwardly calmed. But, Māgandiya, whatever recluses and brahmans, dwelt or are dwelling or will dwell, devoid of thirst, with a mind inwardly calmed, all these, having known the coming to be and passing away of these same sense-pleasures, their satisfaction and peril and the escape as it really is, on getting rid of the craving for sense-pleasures, suppressing the fever for sense-pleasures, dwelt or are dwelling or will dwell devoid of thirst, with a mind inwardly calmed."

Then the Lord at that time uttered this solemn utterance:

"*Health*[1] *is the highest gain, nibbāna the highest bliss;*
And of Ways, the Eightfold leads to deathlessness, to security."[2]

When this had been said, the wanderer Māgandiya spoke thus to the Lord:

"It is marvellous, good Gotama, it is wonderful, good Gotama, how well this is spoken by the good Gotama:

[**509**] '*Health is the highest gain, nibbāna the highest bliss.*'

For I too, good Gotama, have heard of this as having been spoken by earlier teachers of teachers of the wanderers:

'*Health is the highest gain, nibbāna the highest bliss.*'

So that this agrees, good Gotama."

"But as to what you heard, Māgandiya, as having been spoken by earlier teachers of teachers of the wanderers:

'*Health is the highest gain, nibbāna the highest bliss,*'

what is that health, what is that nibbāna ?"

When this had been said, the wanderer Māgandiya stroked his own limbs with his hands and said: "This is that health, good Gotama, this is that nibbāna. For I, good Gotama, am at present in good health, I have no disease at all."

"Māgandiya, it is like[3] a man blind from birth who could not see dark or bright shapes, nor green, yellow, red or crimson shapes, who could not see what is even or uneven, who could not see the stars, who could not see the moons and suns. If he should hear a man with vision saying: 'Indeed it is pleasing to have a lovely, unstained, pure white cloth,' he would walk about searching for a white (cloth). But some man might deceive him with a greasy grimy coarse robe, saying: "My good man, this is a lovely, unstained, pure white cloth,' and he might take it; having taken it, he might put it on; having put it on, he might, in his pride, utter a cry of pride: 'Indeed it is pleasing to have a lovely, unstained, pure white cloth.' What do you think about this, Māgandiya ? If that man, blind from birth, had known and seen, would he have taken that greasy grimy

---

[1] *MA*. iii. 218, for those who get wealth and fame and sons from (reciting) verses health is not the highest gain—yet it is higher than these. But for anyone who has the happiness of meditation or the Way or the fruits, there is no bliss higher than nibbāna.

[2] *Cf. Dhp.* 204.

[3] As at *M*. ii. 201.

coarse robe; having taken it, would he have put it on; having put it on, would he, in his pride, have uttered the cry of pride: 'Indeed it is pleasing to have a lovely, unstained, pure white cloth'? Or was it from faith in the man with vision?"

"Not knowing, good Gotama, not seeing, that man, blind from birth, might take a greasy grimy coarse robe; having taken it he might put it on; having put it on, he might, in his pride, utter a cry of pride: **[510]** 'Indeed it is pleasing to have a lovely, unstained, pure white cloth.' It was from faith in the man with vision."

"Even so, Māgandiya, wanderers belonging to other sects are blind, they are without vision;[1] not knowing health, not seeing nibbāna, they yet speak this verse:

'*Health is the highest gain, nibbāna the highest bliss.*'

But, Māgandiya, this verse was uttered in days gone by by perfected ones, fully Self-awakened Ones:

'*Health is the highest gain, nibbāna the highest bliss;*
And of Ways, the Eightfold leads to deathlessness, to security.'

This has now come down gradually to the ordinary people. And although, Māgandiya, this body has become an ill, an imposthume, a barb, a misery and a disease, yet of this body that has become an ill, an imposthume, a barb, a misery and a disease, *you* say: 'This is that health, this is that nibbāna.' So you have not that ariyan vision, Māgandiya, by which you might know health, might see nibbāna."

"I have reliance thus in the good Gotama that he could so teach me *dhamma* that I might know health, might see nibbāna."

"Māgandiya, it is like a man blind from birth who could not see . . . the moons and suns. His friends and acquaintances, kith and kin, might procure a physician and surgeon; that physician and surgeon might make up a medicine, but fail to provide him with eyes with it or clarify his eyes. What do you think about this, Māgandiya? Would that doctor feel much trouble and anxiety?"

"Yes, good Gotama."

"Even so, Māgandiya, if I were to teach you *dhamma*: This is that health, this is that nibbāna—you would not know that health, would not see that nibbāna. It would be a trouble to me, it would be a vexation to me."

[511] "I have reliance thus in the good Gotama that he could so teach me *dhamma* that I might know health, might see nibbāna."

---

[1] Said of Pokkharasāti at *M*. ii. 202.

"Māgandiya, it is like a man blind from birth who could not see dark or bright shapes . . .[1]. . . But some man might deceive him with a greasy grimy coarse robe, saying: 'My good man, this is a lovely, unstained, pure white cloth,' and he might take it; having taken it, he might put it on. His friends and acquaintances, his kith and kin might procure a physician and surgeon; that physician and surgeon might make up a medicine for him, emetics,[2] purgatives, collyrium (for the eyes), ointments, the nose-treatment.[3] Because of that medicine he might regain his vision,[4] might clarify his eyes. But with the regaining of his vision he might get rid of that desire and attachment to that greasy grimy coarse robe, and he might regard that man as no friend, might even regard him as an enemy and consider depriving him of life, thinking: 'For a long time indeed I have been defrauded, deceived, and cheated by this man with a greasy grimy coarse robe who said: "My good man, this is a lovely, unstained, pure white cloth."'

Even so, Māgandiya, if I were to teach you *dhamma*, saying: 'This is that health, this is that nibbāna,' you might know health, might see nibbāna. With the arising of your vision, you might get rid of that desire and attachment to the five groups of grasping, and this might even occur to you: 'For a long time indeed I have been defrauded, deceived and cheated by this mind for, grasping, I grasped after material shape itself . . . after feeling itself . . . after perception itself . . . after the habitual tendencies themselves; grasping, I grasped after consciousness itself. Conditioned by grasping after this, there was becoming for me; conditioned by becoming, birth; conditioned by birth, old age and dying, grief, sorrow, suffering, lamentation and despair **[512]** came into being. Thus is the origin of this whole mass of anguish.'"

"I have reliance thus in the good Gotama that he could so teach me *dhamma* that I could rise from this seat, not blind."

"Well then, Māgandiya, do you consort with true men; if you, Māgandiya, consort with true men, then will you, Māgandiya, hear true *dhamma*; if you, Māgandiya, hear true *dhamma* then will you, Māgandiya, fare along in accordance with *dhamma*; if you, Māgandiya, fare along in accordance with *dhamma*, then

---

[1] As above, p. 188. [2] The following list also occurs at *D.* i. 12.

[3] As at *Vin.* i. 204.

[4] *cakkhūni uppādeyya,* he might acquire eyes, make them arise. So, in this paragraph *cakkhuppādā* is translated as "the regaining of his vision" and in the next as "the arising of your vision."

will you, Māgandiya, know for yourself, then will you see for yourself that: 'These ills are imposthumes, barbs—but ills, imposthumes, barbs can be stopped here without remainder; from the stopping of grasping after this, there is the stopping of becoming for me; from the stopping of becoming, the stopping of birth; from the stopping of birth, old age and dying, grief, sorrow, suffering, lamentation and despair are stopped. Thus is the stopping of this whole mass of anguish.' "

When this had been said, Māgandiya the wanderer spoke thus to the Lord:

" It is excellent, good Gotama, excellent, good Gotama. It is, good Gotama, as if one might set upright what had been upset, or might disclose what had been covered, or point out the way to one who had gone astray, or might bring an oil-lamp into the darkness so that those with vision might see material shapes—even so in many a figure has *dhamma* been made clear by the good Gotama. I am going to the revered Gotama for refuge and to *dhamma* and to the Order of monks. May I receive the going forth in the revered Gotama's presence, may I receive ordination."

" Māgandiya, if a former member of another sect wishes for the going forth in this *dhamma* and discipline, wishes for ordination, he undertakes probation for four months.[1] At the end of the four months the monks, if they so decide, may let him go forth, may ordain him into the status of a monk; but even here differences among individuals are known to me."

" If, revered sir, former members of other sects, wishing for the going forth in this *dhamma* and discipline, wishing for ordination, undertake probation for four months, and if at the end of the four months the monks, if they so decide, let them go forth, ordain them into the status of a monk, then will I undertake probation for four years; at the end of the four years the monks, if they so decide, may let me go forth, may ordain me into the status of a monk." [**513**] But the wanderer Māgandiya received the going forth in the Lord's presence, he received ordination.

Soon after he was ordained the venerable Māgandiya, dwelling alone, aloof, diligent, ardent, self-resolute, in no long time having realised here and now by his own super-knowledge that matchless goal of the Brahma-faring for the sake of which young men of family rightly go forth from home into homelessness, entering on it, abided

---

[1] As above, p. 59.

in it. And he knew: "Destroyed is birth, brought to a close the Brahma-faring, done is what was to be done, there is no more of being such or so." So was the venerable Māgandiya one of the perfected ones.

Discourse to Māgandiya:
The Fifth

76. DISCOURSE TO SANDAKA

(Sandakasutta)

THUS have I heard: At one time the Lord was staying near Kosambī in Ghosita's monastery. Now at that time the wanderer Sandaka was staying in the Fig Tree[1] Cave with a great company of wanderers, with at least five hundred wanderers. Then the venerable Ānanda, emerging from solitude towards evening, addressed the monks, saying: "Come, your reverences, we will go to Devakaṭa Pool so as to see the Cave."

"Yes, your reverence," these monks answered the venerable Ānanda in assent. Then the venerable Ānanda, together with many monks, approached Devakaṭa Pool. Now at that time the wanderer Sandaka was sitting down with the great company of wanderers shouting out with a loud noise, a great noise, talking various kinds of inferior talk,[2] that is to say talk on kings, thieves, great ministers, armies, fears, battles, food, drink, clothes, beds, garlands, scents, relations, vehicles, villages, market towns, towns, the country, women, heroes, streets, wells, those departed before, talk of diversity, speculation about the world, speculation about the sea, **[514]** talk about becoming or not becoming thus or thus. The wanderer Sandaka saw the venerable Ānanda coming in the distance; seeing him, he called his own company to order, saying:

"Good sirs, let there be little noise; do not, good sirs, make a noise; this is a disciple of the recluse Gotama who is coming—the recluse Ānanda. For as long as disciples of the recluse Gotama have

---

[1] Pilakkha, probably *ficus infectoria*. See *Vin.* iv. 35. *MA.* iii. 220 says there was a tree of this kind at the entrance to the Cave.

[2] As at *Vin.* iv. 164. See *B.D.* iii. 82 *f.* for references and notes on the various kinds of talk.

been staying near Kosambī the recluse Ānanda has been among them. These venerable ones wish for little noise, they are trained to little noise, they are praisers of little noise. So he may consider approaching if he knows that this is a company of little noise." Then these wanderers fell silent. Then the venerable Ānanda approached the wanderer Sandaka. The wanderer Sandaka spoke thus to the venerable Ānanda:

"Let the revered Ānanda come, there is a welcome for the revered Ānanda; it is long since the revered Ānanda made this opportunity,[1] that is to say for coming here. Let the revered Ānanda sit down, this seat is ready." Then the venerable Ānanda sat down on the seat that was ready. And the wanderer Sandaka, having taken a low seat, sat down at a respectful distance. Then the venerable Ānanda spoke thus to the wanderer Sandaka as he was sitting down at a respectful distance:

"What is the talk for which you are now gathered together here, Sandaka? And what was your talk that was interrupted?"[2]

"Let be that talk, good Ānanda, for which we are now gathered together here. It will not be difficult for the good Ānanda to hear this talk later. It were good if some *dhamma*-talk belonging to his own teacher were to occur to the revered Ānanda himself."

"Well then, Sandaka, listen, attend carefully and I will speak."

"Yes, sir," the wanderer Sandaka answered the venerable Ānanda in assent. The venerable Ānanda spoke thus:

"Sandaka, these four ways of living a non-Brahma-faring have been pointed out by this Lord who knows and sees, perfected one, fully Self-Awakened One; and four comfortless Brahma-farings have been pointed out in which an intelligent man could certainly not live a Brahma-faring, or, if living it, could not gain success in the right path, in *dhamma*, in what is skilled."

"And what, good Ānanda, are these four ways of living a non-Brahma-faring that have been pointed out by the Lord . . . fully Self-Awakened One, in which [**515**] an intelligent man could certainly not live a Brahma-faring, or, if living it, could not gain success in the right path, in *dhamma*, in what is skilled?"

"As to this, Sandaka, some teacher speaks thus and is of this view:[3] 'There is no (result of) gift, no (result of) sacrifice; there is no

---

[1] *Cf. M.* i. 326, 481.

[2] As at *M.* ii. 1-2; *D.* i. 2; *Ud.* 11, 31.

[3] Ascribed to Ajita Kesakambalin at *D.* i. 55; *cf.* also *M.* i. 287, 402, *S.* iii. 206. See translation and notes by A. L. Basham in his ***History and Doctrines of the Ājīvikas***, London, 1951, p. 15.

fruit or ripening of deeds well done or ill done; there is not this world, there is not a world beyond; there is not (benefit from serving) mother or father; there are no beings of spontaneous uprising; there are not in the world recluses and brahmans who are faring rightly, proceeding rightly, and who proclaim this world and a world beyond, having realised them by their own super-knowledge. This man is derived from the four great elements so that, when he passes away, the earthy part of his body returns and relapses to earth, the fluid part to water, the hot part to heat, the windy part to wind, and his sense-organs pass over into the ether. Four men, with a bier as the fifth,[1] go along taking the corpse; as far as the cemetery they make known his characteristics.[2] His bones become pigeon-grey. Offerings end as ashes. It is imbeciles who speak of giving. It is vain, lying, empty talk on their part who profess to say: There is.[3] Fools and wise alike are annihilated and destroyed at the breaking up of the body; after dying they are not.'

Wherefore, Sandaka, an intelligent man reflects thus: 'This worthy teacher speaks thus and is of this view: "There is no (result of) gift . . . after dying they are not." If this is a true word of this good teacher, then what is done herein[4] is without my doing it, what is lived herein is without my living it. Moreover both of us are herein on an exact level in attaining recluseship, although I do not say: "We will both be annihilated and destroyed at the breaking up of the body; after dying we will not be." It is excessive of this good teacher to be naked, shaven, to practise squatting on his heels, to pluck out the hair of his head and beard, while I am living in a house surrounded and supported by sons, delighting in Kāsi's sandal-wood perfumes, decked with garlands, scents and unguents, enjoying the use of gold and silver.[5] For in a future state I will be on an exact level in wayfaring[6] as this good teacher. Knowing what, seeing what, should I fare the Brahma-faring under this teacher?' He, realising that this is a way of living a non-Brahma-faring, goes away uninterested in this Brahma-faring.

This, Sandaka, is the first way of living a non-Brahma-faring that

---

[1] Four men each take a leg of the bier, and so the bier as well.

[2] *padāni.*

[3] *atthikavāda*, affirmatists, "there-is-ists." Here *MA*. iii. 227 takes the theory to refer to there being fruit of giving.

[4] *ettha*. *MA*. iii. 228: in this recluses' *dhamma*.

[5] *Cf*. *A*. iii. 391, iv. 281; *Ud*. 65.

[6] *Cf*. *A*. iii. 347, v. 139.

has been pointed out by this Lord who knows and sees, perfected one, fully Self-Awakened One, (a way) in which an intelligent man could certainly not [**516**] live a Brahma-faring or, if living it, could not gain success in the right path, in *dhamma*, in what is skilled.

And again, Sandaka, some teacher here speaks thus and is of this view:[1] 'From doing, from making (another) do, from mutilating, from making (another) mutilate . . . from that source there is not merit, there is not the perpetuating of merit. There is no merit from giving, from taming, from restraining, from truth-speaking, there is not the perpetuating of merit.'

Wherefore, Sandaka, an intelligent man reflects thus: 'This worthy teacher speaks thus and is of this view: "From doing, from making (another) do . . . there is not the perpetuating of merit." If this is a true word of this good teacher, then what is done herein is without my doing it, what is lived herein is without my living it. Moreover both of us are herein on an exact level in attaining recluseship, although I do not say: "Evil will not be done by the deeds of both." It is excessive of this good teacher . . . Knowing what, seeing what, should I fare the Brahma-faring under this teacher ?' He, realising that this is a way of living a non-Brahma-faring, goes away uninterested in this Brahma-faring.

This, Sandaka, is the second way of living a non-Brahma-faring . . . could not gain success in the right path, in *dhamma*, in what is skilled.

And again, Sandaka, some teacher here speaks thus and is of this view:[2] 'There is no cause, no reason for the defilement of creatures . . .[**517**]. . . they experience pleasure and pain amid the six classes.'

Wherefore, Sandaka, an intelligent man reflects thus: 'This worthy teacher speaks thus and is of this view: "There is no cause, no reason for the defilement of creatures . . . they experience pleasure and pain amid the six classes." If this is a true word of this good teacher, then what is done herein is without my doing it, what is lived herein is without my living it. Moreover both of us are herein on an exact level in attaining recluseship, although I do not say: "We will both be purified without cause, without reason." It is excessive of this good teacher . . . Knowing what, seeing what, should I fare the Brahma-faring under this teacher ?' He, realising that

---

[1] As at *M.* i. 404; see above, p. 73. Also at *S.* iii. 208.

[2] As at *M.* i. 407; see above, p. 76. Also at *S.* iii. 210.

this is a way of living a non-Brahma-faring, goes away uninterested in this Brahma-faring.

This, Sandaka, is the third way of living a non-Brahma-faring . . . could not gain success in the right path, in *dhamma*, in what is skilled.

And again, Sandaka, some teacher here speaks thus and is of this view:[1] 'These seven classes are not made or caused to be made, they are not created or caused to be created, they are barren (of results), standing stable as a mountain, stable as a pillar,[2] they do not move or change or injure one another, they are unable to affect one another's pleasure or pain or pleasure-and-pain. What are the seven? Earth,[3] water, heat, wind, pleasures, pains, life-principles—these seven.[4] These seven classes are not made or caused to be made, they are not created . . . they are unable to affect one another's pleasure of pain or pleasure-and-pain. Herein there is neither slayer nor one that makes another slay,[5] neither hearer[6] nor one that makes another hear, neither knower[6] nor one that makes another know. Even he who cuts off (another's) head with a sharp sword deprives no one of life, for the sword merely penetrates the gap between the seven classes. There are these fourteen hundred thousand chief kinds of birth,[7] and sixty hundred and six hundred. There are five hundred karmas[8] and (another) five karmas[9] and (another) three karmas.[10] There is a karma[11] and half a karma.[12] There are sixty-two practices, sixty-two sub-divisions (in a great kalpa[13]), six classes

---

[1] At *D.* i. 56 ascribed to Pakudha Kaccāyana. See also *S.* iii. 211.

[2] As at *D.* i. 14.

[3] *paṭhavikāya*. *MA.* iii. 229 says that this is just earth or the aggregation of earth; and so for the other "elements."

[4] *M.* here reads *satt' ime* as against *sattame*, "as the seventh" of *D.* i. 56.

[5] *Cf. Iti.* p. 22=*Jā.* iv. 71=*Miln.* 402.

[6] At *A.* iv. 196 these are among the eight qualities fitting one to go on a message.

[7] For a discussion of these terms down to "great kalpas," see A. L. Basham, *op. cit.*, p. 240 *ff.* The following view is ascribed to Makkhali Gosāla at *D.* i. 53-54.

[8] *kammuno*. *MA.* iii. 230: all shown to be useless.

[9] *MA.* iii. 230=*DA.* 162: the five controlling faculties, or sense-organs, *indriya*.

[10] Of body, speech and thought, *MA.* iii. 230.

[11] Of body and speech, *MA.* iii. 230.

[12] Of thought, *MA.* iii. 230.

[13] *MA.* iii. 230: "in each kalpa there are 64 sub-divisions, *antarakappa*. But because he does not know the other two, he (Makkhali Gosāla) speaks thus."

of mankind,[1] eight stages in (the life of a) man,[2] forty-nine hundred modes of livelihood, forty-nine hundred wanderers,[3] [**518**] forty-nine hundred nāga-dwellings,[4] twenty hundred faculties, thirty hundred Niraya Hells, thirty-six places where dust collects, seven births where there is consciousness,[5] seven births where there is no consciousness,[6] seven kinds of production where there are joints in the stalk,[7] seven kinds of *devas*,[8] seven kinds of men,[9] seven kinds of demons, seven lakes, seven knots,[10] seven (greater) mountains, seven hundred (smaller) mountains, seven (great) dreams,[11] seven hundred (lesser) dreams. There are 84,000 great kalpas in which both fools and the wise, when they have run on and circled on, will make an end of anguish. It is useless to say: 'I, by this moral practice or habit or austerity or Brahma-faring[12] will bring an unmatured karma to maturity,[13] or gradually exhaust karma already matured.'[14] This is

---

[1] *chaḷ-abhijātiyo. Cf.* the corresponding theory of Pūraṇa Kassapa at *A.* iii. 383. See also *D.* iii. 250. Referred to at *M.* i. 407 as *chass-evâbhijāti*, as at *M.* ii. 222. The black class includes, according to *MA.* iii. 121, *DA.* 162, *SA.* ii. 343 butchers, hunters, fishermen, robbers, etc.; the blue includes monks and some wanderers; the red, Jains and wearers of one cloth only; the yellow, householders and disciples of unclothed ascetics; the white includes Nanda, Vaccha, Saṅkicca (*MA.* iii. 121), or it includes Naked Ascetics, men and women (*DA.* 162=*SA.* ii. 343); the radiant class includes Naked Ascetics (*MA.* iii. 121), or Nanda Vaccha, Kisa Saṅkicca, Makkhali Gosāla (*DA.* 162= *SA.* ii. 343).

[2] *MA.* iii. 230-231: babyhood, playtime, stage of investigation, standing erect, learning time, recluseship, victory (*jina*, explained by *jānanakāla*, time of knowing) and prostrate time, *pannabhūmi* (translated at *K.S.* iii. 171, *n.* 2 as "attainment," reading *pattabhūmi*, a suggested v.l. at *SA.* ii. 343).

[3] Unclothed ascetics—the white; Nanda Vaccha, Saṅkicca (*MA.* iii. 121), or Naked Ascetics, men and women (*DA.* 162=*SA.* ii. 343); the radiant, Naked Ascetics (*MA.* iii. 121), or Nanda Vaccha, Kisa Saṅkicca, Makkhali Gosāla (*DA.* 162=*SA.* ii. 343).

[4] *nāgāvāsa*, explained by *nāgamaṇḍala* at *MA.* iii. 231, circles or groups of nāgas.

[5] The *Comys* say camels, cows, donkeys, goats, cattle, deer, buffaloes.

[6] The *Comys* say rice, barley, wheat, beans, millet and two other kinds of grain.

[7] Sugar-cane, bamboo, reeds, etc.

[8] The *Comys* here say that seven stands for "many."

[9] Meaning "endless."

[10] *pavuṭā*, see *PED.*, *s.v.* *MA.* iii. 232, *ganṭhikā*. *Le Canon Pali bouddhique*, vol. I, fasc. i, p. 48 does not translate. The meaning is really unknown.

[11] Five dreams of Gotama given at *A.* iii. 240, *Jā.* i. 69.

[12] *I.e.* of unclothed or other ascetics.

[13] This is what a wise man might say.

[14] This is what the fool might say; but he goes on (in saṁsāra) after he has passed the time at which this was said, *MA.* iii. 233.

not so. Happiness and pain are measured out (as) in a bushel; circling on has its limits fixed; there is not decline and growth, there is not high degree or low.[1] Indeed, just as a ball of thread, when thrown down, unwinds itself as it rolls,[2] even so will fools and the wise alike, when they have run on and circled on, make an end of anguish.'

Wherefore, Sandaka, an intelligent man reflects thus: 'This worthy teacher speaks thus and is of this view: "These seven classes . . . will make an end of anguish." If this is a true word of this good teacher, then what is done herein is without my doing it, what is lived herein is without my living it. Moreover both of us are on an exact level in attaining recluseship, although I do not say: "When we have both run on and circled on we will make an end of anguish." It is excessive of this good teacher to be naked, shaven . . . seeing what, should I fare the Brahma-faring under this teacher?' He, realising that this is a way of living a non-Brahma-faring, goes away uninterested in that Brahma-faring.

This, Sandaka, is the fourth way of living a non-Brahma-faring that has been pointed out by this Lord who knows and sees, perfected one, fully Self-Awakened One, and in which an intelligent man could certainly not live a Brahma-faring, or, if living it, could not gain success in the right path, in *dhamma*, in what is skilled.

These, Sandaka, are the four ways of living a non-Brahma-faring that have been pointed out by this Lord who knows and sees, perfected one, fully Self-Awakened One, [**519**] and in which an intelligent man could certainly not live a Brahma-faring, or, if living it, could not gain success in the right path, in *dhamma*, in what is skilled."

"It is wonderful, good Ānanda, it is marvellous, good Ānanda, that although there are these four ways of living a non-Brahma-faring, they have been pointed out by this Lord who knows and sees, perfected one, fully Self-Awakened One, as those in which an intelligent man could certainly not live a Brahma-faring, or, if living it, could not gain success in the right path, in *dhamma*, in what is skilled. But now, good Ānanda, what are these four comfortless Brahma-farings that have been pointed out by this Lord who knows and sees, perfected one, fully Self-Awakened One, and in which an intelligent man certainly could not live a Brahma-faring, or, if living

---

[1] saṁsāra does not decline for the wise man or grow for the fool, *MA*. iii. 233.

[2] It goes on unwinding itself for the length of the thread, *MA*. iii. 233.

it, could not gain success in the right path, in *dhamma*, in what is skilled ?"

"As to this, Sandaka, some teacher, all-knowing,[1] all-seeing, claims all-embracing knowledge-and-vision, saying: 'Whether I am walking or standing still or asleep or awake, knowledge-and-vision is constantly and perpetually before me.' He enters an empty place, and he does not obtain almsfood, and a dog bites him, and he encounters a fierce elephant, and he encounters a fierce horse, and he encounters a fierce bullock, and he asks a woman and a man their name and clan, and he asks the name of a village or a market town and the way. He, being one who asks,[2] 'How was this ?' answers, 'I had to enter an empty place, therefore I entered; I had to obtain no almsfood, therefore I obtained none; (someone) had to be bitten by a dog, therefore I was bitten by one; (someone) had to encounter a fierce elephant, horse and bullock, therefore I encountered them; (someone) had to ask a woman and a man their name and clan, therefore I asked; (someone) had to ask the name of a village and market town and the way, therefore I asked.'

Whereupon, Sandaka, an intelligent person reflects thus: 'This revered teacher, all-knowing, all-seeing . . . therefore I asked.' Having realised that this Brahma-faring is comfortless, he goes away uninterested in this Brahma-faring.

This, Sandaka, is the first comfortless Brahma-faring that has been pointed out by this Lord who knows and sees, perfected one, fully Self-Awakened One, and [**520**] in which an intelligent man certainly could not live a Brahma-faring, or, if living it, could not gain success in the right path, in *dhamma*, in what is skilled.

And again, Sandaka, some teacher here depends on report,[3] holds to report for his 'truths,' he teaches *dhamma* according to report,[4] according to hearsay and tradition, according to the authority of the collections.[5] If a teacher, Sandaka, depends on report, holds to report for his 'truths,' he remembers (part) well and he remembers (part) badly, and is both right and wrong. Wherefore, Sandaka, an intelligent person reflects thus: 'This worthy teacher depends on report . . . and wrong.' Having realised that this Brahma-faring is comfortless, he goes away uninterested in this Brahma-faring.

---

[1] As at *M*. i. 92-93, ii. 31; *A*. i. 220.

[2] Being omniscient, why did he ask ? *MA*. iii. 233.

[3] *M*. ii. 211.

[4] *A*. i. 189, 195, ii. 91.

[5] *piṭaka; cf. M*. ii. 169.

This, Sandaka, is the second comfortless Brahma-faring . . . *dhamma*, in what is skilled.

And again, Sandaka, some teacher here is a reasoner and investigator;[1] he teaches *dhamma* on a system of his own devising, beaten out by reasoning and based on investigation. If, Sandaka, a teacher is a reasoner and investigator, part is well reasoned and part is badly reasoned, and is both right and wrong. Wherefore, Sandaka, an intelligent person reflects thus: 'This worthy teacher is a reasoner and investigator . . . and wrong.' Having realised that this Brahma-faring is comfortless, he goes away uninterested in this Brahma-faring.

This, Sandaka, is the third comfortless Brahma-faring . . . *dhamma*, in what is skilled.

And again, Sandaka, some teacher here is stupid and confused;[2] because of his stupidity and confusion, on being asked a question on this or that [**521**] he falls into equivocation, into eel-wriggling,[3] 'It is not thus for me,[4] it is not so for me, it is not otherwise for me, I do not say it is not, I do not say it is not not.' Wherefore, Sandaka, an intelligent person reflects thus: 'This worthy teacher is stupid and confused . . . I do not say that it is not not.' Having realised that this Brahma-faring is comfortless, he goes away uninterested in this Brahma-faring.

This, Sandaka, is the fourth comfortless Brahma-faring that has been pointed out by this Lord who knows and sees, perfected one, fully Self-Awakened One, and in which an intelligent man could certainly not live a Brahma-faring, or, if living it, could not gain success in the right path, in *dhamma*, in what is skilled.

These, Sandaka, are the four comfortless Brahma-farings that have been pointed out by this Lord . . . could not gain success in the right path, in *dhamma*, in what is skilled."

"It is wonderful, good Ānanda, it is marvellous, good Ānanda, that these four comfortless Brahma-farings have been pointed out by this Lord who knows and sees, perfected one, fully Self-Awakened One, as those in which an intelligent man could certainly not live a Brahma-faring or, if living it, could not gain success in the right path, in *dhamma*, in what is skilled. Good Ānanda, what does this Teacher teach, what does he profess whereby an intelligent man

---

[1] *Cf. M.* i. 68; *D.* i. 16.

[2] *Cf. D.* i. 27.

[3] On *amarāvikkhepa* see *D.* i. 24 *ff.*

[4] On these answers in a particular context see *D.* i. 27.

could certainly live a Brahma-faring and, living it, could gain success in the right path, in *dhamma*, in what is skilled ?"

" As to this, Sandaka, a Tathāgata arises in the world, a perfected one, a fully Self-Awakened One, endowed with knowledge and right conduct, well-farer, knower of the worlds, matchless charioteer of men to be tamed, teacher of *devas* and men, an Awakened One, a Lord. He (. . . *as in* Kandaraka Sutta, *M.*i. 344-347 . . .) having got rid of these five hindrances—defilements of the mind and weakening to intuitive wisdom—aloof from pleasures of the senses, aloof from unskilled states of mind, enters and abides in the first meditation, which is accompanied by initial thought and discursive thought, is born of aloofness and is rapturous and joyful. If a disciple attains such lofty eminence under this Teacher, [**522**] an intelligent person could certainly live that Brahma-faring and, living it, could gain success in the right path, in *dhamma*, in what is skilled. And again, Sandaka, a monk, by allaying inital and discursive thought . . . enters and abides in the second meditation . . . the third . . . the fourth meditation. If a disciple attains such lofty eminence . . . could gain success in the right path, in *dhamma*, in what is skilled.

Thus with the mind composed (. . . *as in* Kandaraka Sutta, *M.*i. 347-349) . . . he comprehends: Destroyed is birth, brought to a close the Brahma-faring, done is what was to be done, there is no more of being such or so. If a disciple attains such lofty eminence under this Teacher, an intelligent person could certainly live that Brahma-faring and, living it, could gain success in the right path, in *dhamma*, in what is skilled."

" But, good Ānanda, could that monk who is a perfected one, the cankers destroyed, who has lived the life, done what was to be done, laid down the burden, attained his own goal, the fetters of becoming utterly destroyed, freed by perfect profound knowledge—[**523**] could he enjoy pleasures of the senses ?"

" Whatever monk, Sandaka, is a perfected one[1] . . . freed by perfect profound knowledge, he cannot become one to transgress[2] five points:[3] a monk whose cankers are destroyed cannot become one intentionally to deprive a living creature of life . . . to take what has not been given, as it were by theft . . . to indulge in sexual intercourse . . . to speak a deliberate lie . . . to enjoy pleasures of the senses in

---

[1] As at *A.* iv. 369-370.

[2] *ajjhācaritum*, to practise (wrongly), to commit.

[3] *Cf. D.* iii. 133, 235.

regard to what was stored[1] as he did formerly when in the household state. Sandaka, whatever monk is a perfected one . . . freed by perfect profound knowledge he cannot become one to transgress these five points."

"But, good Ānanda, if a monk is one perfected . . . freed by perfect profound knowledge, then, whether he is walking or standing still or asleep or awake is the knowledge-and-vision constantly and perpetually present that his cankers are destroyed?"

"Well then, Sandaka, I will make you a simile, for by a simile some intelligent persons here understand the meaning of what has been said. Sandaka, it is like a man whose hands and feet have been cut off; whether he is walking or standing still or asleep or awake, constantly and perpetually are his hands and feet as though cut off; and moreover while he is reflecting on it, he knows: 'My hands and feet have been cut off.' Even so, Sandaka, whatever monk is a perfected one, the cankers destroyed, who has lived the life, done what was to be done, laid down the burden, attained his own goal, the fetters of becoming utterly destroyed, freed by perfect profound knowledge, for him whether he is walking or standing still or asleep or awake, the cankers are as though destroyed; and moreover while he is reflecting on it, he knows: 'My cankers are destroyed.'"

"How many great leaders,[2] good Ānanda, are there in this *dhamma* and discipline?"

"Not merely a hundred, nor two, three, four or five hundred, but far more are those who are great leaders in this *dhamma* and discipline."

"Wonderful, good Ānanda, marvellous, good Ānanda; there can be no extolling of their own *dhamma* nor disparaging of the *dhamma* of others; but both the teaching of *dhamma* in its (whole) extent[3] and so **[524]** many great leaders can be seen. On the other hand, these Naked Ascetics are children of a childless mother, they both extol themselves and disparage others, and they show only three great leaders, namely Nanda Vaccha, Kisa Saṅkicca and Makkhali Gosāla."[4]

Then the wanderer Sandaka addressed his own company, saying: "Let the good sirs fare forth; the living of the Brahma-faring is

---

[1] *sannidhikārakaṁ*. *Cf.* Pāc. 38 (*Vin.* iv. 86-87), and see *B.D.* ii. 339, *n.* 1; and also *G.S.* iv. 245, *n.* 8.

[2] *niyyātāro*.

[3] *āyatane* can also mean "practice."

[4] Mentioned at *M.* i. 238.

under the recluse Gotama, although it is not easy for us now to give up gains, honours, fame."

It was in this way that the wanderer Sandaka sent his own company into the Lord's Brahma-faring.

Discourse to Sandaka:
The Sixth[1]

77. GREATER DISCOURSE TO SAKULUDĀYIN

(Mahā-Sakuludāyisutta)

THUS have I heard: At one time the Lord was staying near Rājagaha in the Bamboo Grove at the squirrels' feeding place.[2] Now at that time a number of very celebrated wanderers, such as Anugāra,[3] Varadhara and the wanderer Sakuludāyin, and other celebrated wanderers, were staying in the wanderers' park at the peacocks' feeding place. Then the Lord, having dressed in the morning, taking his bowl and robe, entered Rājagaha for almsfood. Then it occurred to the Lord: "It is too early to walk for almsfood in Rājagaha. Suppose I were to approach the wanderers' park, the peacocks' feeding place and the wanderer Sakuludāyin?" Then the Lord approached the peacocks' feeding place in the wanderers' park. Now at that time the wanderer Sakuludāyin was sitting down with the great company of wanderers shouting out with a loud noise, a great noise, talking various kinds of inferior talk . . . [2] . . .[4] The Lord spoke thus to the wanderer Sakuludāyin as he was sitting down at a respectful distance:

"What is the talk for which you are now gathered together here, Udāyin? And what was your talk that was interrupted?"

---

[1] Here ends Trenckner, *Majjhima-Nikāya*, vol. I.

[2] *Cf. M.* Sta. 79.

[3] *MA.* iii. 235 calls him Annabhāra. A wanderer of this name is referred to at *A.* ii. 29, 176, with the other two mentioned above.

[4] As in the *Sandaka Sutta*, above, p. 192. For Sandaka read Sakuludāyin, and for Ānanda read the Lord.

"Let be that talk, revered sir, for which we are now gathered together here. It will not be difficult for the Lord to hear this talk later. Some time ago,[1] revered sir, when divers members of other sects, recluses and brahmans, were gathered together and were sitting down in the debating hall,[2] this chance conversation arose: 'Indeed it is profitable for the people of Aṅga-Magadha, indeed it is well gotten by the people of Aṅga-Magadha that these leaders in religious life, heads of companies, heads of groups, teachers of groups, well known, famous founders of sects, held in high repute by the many-folk,[3] have come to Rājagaha for the rains-residence. This Pūraṇa Kassapa is the head of a company, head of a group, the teacher of a group, he is well known, the famous founder of a sect, held in high repute by the manyfolk; he has come to Rājagaha for the rains-residence. This Makkhali Gosāla too . . . This Ajita of the hair-blanket too . . . This Pakudha Kaccāyana too . . . This Sañjaya Belaṭṭhi's son too—This Nātaputta the Jain too is the head of a company, head of a group, the teacher of a group, [**3**] he is well known, the famous founder of a sect, held in high repute by the manyfolk; he too has come to Rājagaha for the rains-residence. This recluse Gotama too is the head of a company, head of a group, the teacher of a group, he is well known, the famous founder of a sect, held in high repute by the manyfolk; he too has come to Rājagaha for the rains-residence. Now of these lords, heads of companies, heads of groups, teachers of groups, well known, famous founders of sects, held in high repute by the manyfolk, which is revered, respected, esteemed, honoured by disciples? And how do disciples, revering and respecting, live in dependence?'

Some of those who were there spoke thus: 'This Pūraṇa Kassapa is the head of a company, head of a group . . . held in high repute by the manyfolk. But he is not revered, respected, esteemed, honoured by disciples, nor do disciples, revering and respecting him, live in dependence on Pūraṇa Kassapa. Once upon a time Pūraṇa Kassapa was teaching *dhamma* to an innumerable assembly. But a certain disciple of his let it be heard: "Do not, good sirs, ask Pūraṇa Kassapa about this matter; he does not know about it, *we* know about it. Ask us about this matter, we can explain it to the good sirs." Once upon a time Pūraṇa Kassapa, with outstretched arms

---

[1] *purimāni divasāni purimatarāni*, as at *M.* ii. 31.

[2] *kutūhalasālā; cf. D.* i. 179, *S.* iv. 398.

[3] As at *M.* i. 198. The Tathāgata is honoured in this sense by wise people, *MA.* iii. 236.

and wailing, did not get the chance (to say[1]): "Let the good sirs be quiet; do not, good sirs, make a noise. These are not asking the good sirs, they are asking us, we will explain to them." Then many of Pūraṇa Kassapa's disciples, having refuted him, on seceding,[2] said: "You do not understand[3] this *dhamma* and discipline, I understand this *dhamma* and discipline. How can you understand this *dhamma* and discipline? You are faring along wrongly, I am faring along rightly. There is sense in what I say, no sense in what you say. You said at the end what should have been said at the beginning, and said at the beginning what should have been said at the end. Your method is reversed,[4] you are refuted,[5] you are caught out,[6] go away and think out your words,[7] or unravel them if you can." So Pūraṇa Kassapa is not revered, respected, esteemed, honoured by disciples, nor do disciples, revering and respecting, live in dependence on Pūraṇa Kassapa. On the contrary, Pūraṇa Kassapa is reviled with abuse for his behaviour.'[8]

[4] Some spoke thus: 'This Makkhali Gosāla too . . . This Ajita of the hair blanket too . . . This Pakudha Kaccāyana too . . . This Sañjaya Belaṭṭhi's son too . . . This Nātaputta the Jain too is the head of a company, head of a group . . . is not revered, respected, esteemed, honoured by disciples, nor do disciples, revering and respecting, live in dependence on Nātaputta the Jain. On the contrary, Nātaputta the Jain is reviled with abuse for his behaviour.'

Some spoke thus: 'This recluse Gotama is the head of a company, head of a group, the teacher of a group, he is well known, the famous founder of a sect, held in high repute by the manyfolk. He is revered, respected, esteemed, honoured by disciples; and disciples, revering and respecting the recluse Gotama, live in dependence on him. Once upon a time the recluse Gotama was teaching *dhamma* to an innumerable assembly. Then a certain disciple of the recluse Gotama coughed. A fellow Brahma-farer touched him with his knee and said: [5] "Let the venerable one be quiet; let the venerable one make no noise. The Teacher, our Lord, is teaching *dhamma*."

---

[1] *na labhati.* Chalmers: "remonstrated."

[2] Some became householders, some came into this teaching, *MA.* iii. 237.

[3] *Cf.* following with *D.* i. 8, *S.* iii. 12.

[4] *aviciṇṇan te viparāvattaṁ.*

[5] *āropito te vādo.* *Cf. Vin.* i. 60, *S.* i. 160.

[6] *niggahīto 'si.*

[7] *cara vādappamokkhāya.* *Cf. itivādappamokkhânisaṁsa* at *M.* i. 133, *S.* v. 73, *A.* ii. 26.

[8] *akkuṭṭho dhammakkosena.* *MA.* iii. 237 says that *dhamma* is *sabhāva*, nature, disposition, behaviour.

At the time when the recluse Gotama was teaching *dhamma* to an innumerable assembly, there was the sound neither of expectoration nor of coughing among his disciples.[1] Any group of people who were waiting were ready for him, thinking: "We will hear that *dhamma* that the Lord will teach us." It is as though a man at a crossing on a high road might press out a little pure honey,[2] and any group of people who were waiting might be ready for him. Even so at the time when the recluse Gotama was teaching *dhamma* to an innumerable assembly, there was the sound neither of expectoration nor of coughing among his disciples. Any group of people who were waiting were ready for him, thinking: "We will hear that *dhamma* that the Lord will teach us." And those disciples of the recluse Gotama who, quarrelling with fellow Brahma-farers and disavowing the training, return to the secular life, even these are speakers in praise of the Teacher, they are speakers in praise of *dhamma* and speakers in praise of the Order. They censure only themselves, they do not censure others, but say: "It is we ourselves that are unfortunate, it is we that are of little merit, in that we, although we have gone forth thus in this *dhamma* and discipline that are well taught, are unable for as long as life lasts to fare the Brahma-faring wholly complete, wholly purified." These, becoming monastery attendants or lay-disciples, live undertaking the five rules of training. Thus it is that the recluse Gotama is revered, respected, esteemed, honoured by disciples, and that disciples, revering and respecting the recluse Gotama, live in dependence on him.' "

"But how many things do you behold in me, Udāyin, for which my disciples revere, respect, esteem and honour me, and revering and respecting, live in dependence (on me)?"

"I, revered sir, behold five things for which disciples revere . . . honour the Lord, and, revering and respecting, live in dependence. What are the five? Revered sir, the Lord eats little and speaks in praise of eating little. That the Lord eats little and speaks in praise of eating little, this is the first thing that I, revered sir, behold in the Lord for which disciples revere . . . honour the Lord, and . . . live in dependence.

[**6**] And again, revered sir, the Lord is contented with any kind of robe-material and speaks in praise of content with any kind of robe-material. This is the second thing . . . for which disciples revere . . . honour the Lord, and . . . live in dependence.

---

[1] *Cf. M.* ii. 122.

[2] *Cf. D.* iii. 85.

And again, revered sir, the Lord is contented with any kind of almsfood and speaks in praise of content with any kind of almsfood. This is the third thing . . . for which disciples revere . . . honour the Lord, and . . . live in dependence.

And again, revered sir, the Lord is contented with any kind of lodgings and speaks in praise of content with any kind of lodgings. This is the fourth thing that I behold . . . for which disciples revere . . . honour the Lord, and . . . live in dependence.

And again, revered sir, the Lord is aloof[1] and speaks in praise of aloofness. That the Lord is aloof and speaks in praise of aloofness, this is the fifth thing that I, revered sir, behold in the Lord for which disciples revere, respect, esteem and honour the Lord and, revering and respecting, live in dependence.

These, revered sir, are the five things I behold in the Lord for which disciples revere . . . honour the Lord and, revering and respecting, live in dependence."

" 'The recluse Gotama eats little and speaks in praise of eating little '—if it were for this, Udāyin, that disciples would revere, respect, esteem and honour me and, revering and respecting, would live in dependence, there *are* disciples of mine, Udāyin, who live on a saucer of food and on half a saucer of food and on a fruit of the vilva tree and on half a fruit of the vilva tree. [7] But I, Udāyin, sometimes eat to the full of this bowl, and I eat more than that.[2] 'The recluse Gotama eats little and speaks in praise of eating little ' —if it were for this, Udāyin, that disciples would revere . . . and honour me and, revering and respecting, would live in dependence, it would not be, Udāyin, those of my disciples who live on a saucer of food and on half a saucer of food and on a fruit of the vilva tree and on half a fruit of the vilva tree who would revere, respect, esteem and honour me for this behaviour[3] (of mine) and, revering and respecting, would live in dependence.

'The recluse Gotama is content with any kind of robe-material and speaks in praise of content with any kind of robe-material'—if it were for this, Udāyin, that disciples would revere. . . and honour me and, revering and respecting, would live in dependence, there *are* disciples of mine, Udāyin, who are wearers of rag-robes taken from a dust-heap, and who wear robes that are worn thin; collecting shreds of

---

[1] *MA*. iii. 238 says the wanderer means no more than aloof in body, but the Lord is aloof with the three forms of aloofness (*cf*. *Vism*. 140, *SnA*. 299, 516, *DA*. 169, *MA*. ii. 143, *Asl*. 164).

[2] *Cf*. *Miln*. 213, *Vism*. 170. [3] *dhammena*. See above, p. 205, *n*. 8.

cloth from a cemetery, a rubbish heap or shop and having made up an outer cloak, they wear it. I, Udāyin, sometimes wear householders' robe-material, strengthening it if it is worn thin with thread from the white gourd. 'The recluse Gotama is content with any kind of robe-material and speaks in praise of content with any kind of robe-material'—if it were for this, Udāyin, that disciples would revere . . . and honour me and, revering and respecting, would live in dependence, it would not be, Udāyin, those of my disciples who are wearers of rag-robes taken from a dust-heap, and who wear robes that are worn thin; or those who, collecting shreds of cloth from a cemetery, a rubbish heap or shop and who, having made up an outer cloak, wear it, who would revere, respect, esteem, honour me for this behaviour (of mine) and, revering and respecting, would live in dependence.

'The recluse Gotama is content with any kind of almsfood and speaks in praise of content with any kind of almsfood'—if it were for this, Udāyin, that disciples would revere . . . and honour me and, revering and respecting, would live in dependence, there *are* disciples of mine, Udāyin, who eat only what is received into the begging bowl,[1] who walk on an uninterrupted alms-round, pleased with scraps of food;[2] these, having gone in amid the houses, even if offered a seat do not consent (to accept it). But I, Udāyin, sometimes eat where I am invited: rice, rice-gruel, [8] rice from which the black grains have been removed,[3] a variety of curries, a variety of condiments. 'The recluse Gotama is content with any kind of almsfood and speaks in praise of content with any kind of almsfood'—if it were for this, Udāyin, that disciples would revere . . . and honour me and, revering and respecting, would live in dependence, it would not be, Udāyin, those of my disciples who eat only what is received into the begging-bowl, who walk on an uninterrupted alms-round, pleased with scraps of food, and who, having gone in amid the houses, even if offered a seat do not consent (to accept it), who would revere . . . and honour me for this behaviour (of mine) and, revering and respecting, would live in dependence.

'The recluse Gotama is content with any kind of lodging and speaks in praise of content with any kind of lodging'—if it were for this, Udāyin, that disciples would revere . . . and honour me and, revering and respecting, would live in dependence, there *are* disciples

---

[1] *Cf. Vism.* 66, 67.

[2] *ucchepake vate rata. MA.* iii. 240, reading *va te*, has *bhatte* as a variant reading.

[3] *Cf. D.* i. 105.

of mine, Udāyin, who live at the roots of trees, in the open air, and who for eight months do not go under a roof. But I, Udāyin, sometimes stay in gabled houses, smeared inside and out, sheltered from the winds, having door-bolts that fasten and windows that close. 'The recluse Gotama is content with any kind of lodging and speaks in praise of content with any kind of lodging'—if it were for this, Udāyin, that disciples would revere . . . and honour me and, revering and respecting, would live in dependence, it would not be, Udāyin, those of my disciples who live at the roots of trees, in the open air, and who for eight months do not go under a roof, who would revere . . . and honour me for this behaviour (of mine) and, revering and respecting, would live in dependence.

'The recluse Gotama is aloof and speaks in praise of aloofness'—if it were for this, Udāyin, that disciples would revere, respect, esteem and honour me and, revering and respecting, would live in dependence, there *are* disciples of mine, Udāyin, who have gone to remote lodgings in the forest and who, having plunged into remote lodgings in forest and jungle, stay there; these return to the midst of the Order every half-month for the recitation of the Obligations.[1] But I, Udāyin, sometimes stay crowded round by monks and nuns, men and women lay-disciples, by kings and kings' chief ministers, by leaders and disciples of other sects. 'The recluse Gotama is aloof and speaks in praise of aloofness'—**[9]** if it were for this, Udāyin, that disciples would revere . . . and honour me and, revering and respecting, would live in dependence, it would not be, Udāyin, those of my disciples who have gone to remote lodgings in the forest and who, having plunged into remote lodgings in forest and jungle, stay there, but who return to the midst of the Order every half-month for the recitation of the Obligations, who would revere . . . and honour me for this behaviour (of mine) and, revering and respecting, would live in dependence.

It is thus, Udāyin—for these five ways of behaving—that disciples do not revere, respect, esteem and honour me and, revering and respecting, live in dependence.

But there are, Udāyin, five other things for which disciples revere . . . and honour me and, revering and respecting, live in dependence. What are the five? As to this, Udāyin, disciples of mine admire the higher morality, and think: 'The recluse Gotama is of moral habit, he is possessed of the most excellent body of moral habit.' Inas-

---

[1] *pātimokkha.*

much, Udāyin, as disciples of mine admire the higher morality, and think: 'The recluse Gotama is of moral habit, he is possessed of the most excellent body of moral habit'—this is the first thing, Udāyin, for which disciples of mine revere . . . and honour me and, revering and respecting, live in dependence.

And again, Udāyin, disciples of mine admire the surpassing knowledge-and-vision, and think: 'When the recluse Gotama says: I know, I see—it is because he does know, does see. The recluse Gotama teaches *dhamma* from super-knowledge, not without super-knowledge; the recluse Gotama teaches *dhamma* that has a causal basis[1], not without a causal basis; the recluse Gotama teaches *dhamma* that is convincing,[2] not unconvincing.' Inasmuch, Udāyin, as disciples of mine admire the surpassing knowledge-and-vision, and think: 'When the recluse Gotama says . . . teaches *dhamma* that is convincing, not unconvincing'—this is the second thing, Udāyin, for which [**10**] disciples of mine revere . . . and honour me and, revering and respecting, live in dependence.

And again, Udāyin, disciples of mine admire the higher wisdom, and the situation does not occur when they think: 'The recluse Gotama is wise; he is endowed with the most excellent body of wisdom. (Yet) he will not see (in advance) a future way of speech[3] nor will he refute with *dhamma*[4] a present opposed teaching that is rightly (to be) refuted.' What do you think about this, Udāyin? Could disciples of mine, knowing thus, seeing thus, interrupt a chance conversation?"

"No, revered sir."

"It is not I, Udāyin, that expect instruction from disciples; on the contrary, it is the disciples themselves that expect instruction from me.[5] So that, Udāyin, the situation does not occur when disciples

---

[1] *Cf. A.* i. 276, cited at *Kvu.* 561. *Cf. Mhvs.* iii. 51. *Sanidāna* is explained at *MA.* iii. 241 as *sappaccaya;* for the teaching is causal: *sahetukam pana taṁ desanaṁ katvā.*

[2] *sappāṭihāriya,* explained at *MA.* iii. 241 as *sakāraṇa.* See *G.S.* i. 254, *n.* 3, and *CPD.* s.v. *appāṭihāriya,* "not convincing, without arguments." The meaning is perhaps: he teaches a reliable *dhamma; cf. D.* ii. 104. See also *appāṭihīrakata* at *D.* i. 193, 239, "witless" or "unreliable."

[3] *vādapatha,* perhaps "line of argument."

[4] *saha dhammena,* explained at *MA.* iii. 242 as *sakāraṇena. Cf. MA.* iii. 241: *sakāraṇaṁ* in explanation of *sappāṭihāriyaṁ.* Therefore *saha dhammena* may mean here: with convincing arguments, or sound argument, *i.e.* well presented.

[5] *Cf. Vin.* ii. 187: "disciples do not protect me in regard to knowledge-and-vision and I do not expect protection from disciples as regards this."

of mine who admire the higher wisdom think: 'He would neither see (in advance) a future way of speech nor would he refute with *dhamma* a present opposed teaching that is rightly (to be) refuted.' This is the third thing, Udāyin, for which disciples of mine revere . . . and honour me and, revering and respecting, live in dependence.

And again, Udāyin, those disciples of mine who are beset by some anguish, overwhelmed by anguish, having approached me, ask about the ariyan truth of anguish. On being asked by them about the ariyan truth of anguish, I explain. I bend my mind to the answer to their question. They ask me about the ariyan truth of the uprising of anguish, of the stopping of anguish, of the course leading to the stopping of anguish. On being asked by them about the ariyan truth leading to the stopping of anguish, I explain. I bend my mind to the answer to their question. This is the fourth thing, Udāyin, [11] for which disciples of mine revere . . . and honour me and, revering and respecting, live in dependence.

And again, Udāyin, a course has been pointed out by me for disciples, practising which disciples of mine develop the four applications of mindfulness.[1] Herein, Udāyin, a monk fares along contemplating the body in the body, ardent, clearly conscious (of it), mindful (of it), so as to control the covetousness and dejection in the world . . . the feelings in the feelings . . . the mind in the mind . . . he fares along contemplating mental objects in mental objects, ardent, clearly conscious (of them), mindful (of them), so as to control the covetousness and dejection in the world. As to this, many of my disciples abide attained to accomplishment and to going beyond through super-knowledge.[2]

And again, Udāyin, a course has been pointed out by me for disciples, practising which disciples of mine develop the four right strivings.[3] Herein, Udāyin, a monk generates desire, he endeavours, stirs up energy, exerts his mind and strives for the non-arising of evil unskilled states of mind that have not arisen . . . for the getting rid

---

[1] See *M*. Sta. 10.

[2] *abhiññāvosānapāramippatta*, as at *A*. iii. 9; *cf*. *M*. ii. 211. Lamotte, *Mppś*. ii. 701 says: *pāra* . . . veut dire 'l'autre rive'; *mi* veut dire . . . 'arriver à.' So, *pāramī*, *pāramitā*, means that having realised perfection or excellence, one then arrives beyond on the Further Shore=*amata* (deathlessness) and nibbāna. *Cf*. *MA*. iii. 453 which uses the compound *nibbānappatta*. The Beyond, or Further Shore, is where there is no reaction to sensory impingement, where "all is still" (*Sn*. 920); the gaining of such a state is a fruit of intense meditative exercises.

[3] As at *A*. ii. 15, 256, etc.

of evil unskilled states of mind that have arisen . . . for the arising of skilled states of mind that have not arisen . . . for the maintenance, preservation, increase, maturity, development and completion of skilled states of mind that have arisen. As to this, many of my disciples abide attained to accomplishment and to going beyond through super-knowledge.

And again, Udāyin, a course has been pointed out by me for disciples, practising which disciples of mine develop the four bases of psychic power.[1] Herein, Udāyin, a monk cultivates the basis of psychic power that is possessed of concentration of intention with activities of striving . . . that is possessed of concentration of energy with activities of striving . . . that is possessed of concentration of consciousness with activities of striving . . . that is possessed of concentration of investigation with activities of striving. As to this, many of my disciples abide attained to accomplishment and to going beyond through super-knowledge.

And again, Udāyin, a course has been pointed out by me for disciples, practising which disciples of mine develop the five controlling faculties.[2] Herein, [**12**] Udāyin, a monk develops the controlling faculty of faith, leading to tranquillity, leading to awakening; he develops the controlling faculty of energy . . . of mindfulness . . . of concentration . . . he develops the controlling faculty of wisdom, leading to tranquillity, leading to awakening. As to this, many of my disciples abide attained to accomplishment and to going beyond through super-knowledge.

And again, Udāyin, a course has been pointed out by me for disciples, practising which disciples of mine develop the five powers. Herein, Udāyin, a monk develops the power of faith, leading to tranquillity, leading to awakening; he develops the power of energy . . . the power of mindfulness . . . the power of concentration . . . he develops the power of wisdom, leading to tranquillity, leading to awakening. As to this, many of my disciples abide attained . . . through super-knowledge.

And again, Udāyin, a course has been pointed out by me for disciples, practising which disciples of mine develop the seven limbs

---

[1] As at *M*. i. 103 (*M.L.S*. i. 147).

[2] *Cf*. *S*. v. 227, etc. On *indriya*, see *PED*. They correspond to the five powers (immediately below). *Indriya* appears to be connected with Vedic Indra, Pali *inda*, lord, ruler. The five would therefore seem to be not so much "moral faculties" (*B.H.S.D.*) as ruling faculties, controlling forces, controls, but I have elsewhere, in this translation, rendered *saṁvara* by "control," esp. *pātimokkhasaṁvara*.

of awakening.[1] Herein, Udāyin, a monk develops mindfulness as a limb of awakening and which is dependent on aloofness, dependent on dispassion, dependent on stopping, ending in renunciation; he develops investigation of *dhamma* as a limb of awakening . . . energy . . . rapture . . . serenity . . . concentration . . . even-mindedness as a limb of awakening and which is dependent on aloofness, dependent on dispassion, dependent on stopping, ending in renunciation. As to this, many of my disciples abide attained . . . through super-knowledge.

And again, Udāyin, a course has been pointed out by me for disciples, practising which disciples of mine develop the ariyan eightfold Way. Herein, Udāyin, a monk develops perfect view, he develops perfect intention . . . perfect speech . . . perfect action . . . perfect mode of livelihood . . . perfect endeavour . . . perfect mindfulness . . . perfect concentration. As to this, many of my disciples abide attained . . . through super-knowledge.

And again, Udāyin, a course has been pointed out by me for disciples, practising which disciples of mine develop the eight Deliverances.[2] Being in the fine-material sphere, he sees material shapes; this is the first deliverance. Not perceiving material shape internally he sees external material shapes; this is the second deliverance. By thinking of the Fair,[3] he is intent on it; this is the third deliverance. [13] By passing quite beyond perceptions of material shapes, by the going down of perceptions of sensory reactions, by not attending to perceptions of variety, thinking: 'Ether is unending,' entering on the plane of infinite ether, he abides in it; this is the fourth deliverance. By passing quite beyond the plane of infinite ether, thinking: 'Consciousness is unending,' entering on the plane of infinite consciousness, he abides in it; this is the fifth deliverance. By passing quite beyond the plane of infinite consciousness, thinking: 'There is not anything,' entering on the plane of no-thing, he abides in it; this is the sixth deliverance. By passing quite beyond the plane of no-thing, entering on the plane of neither-perception-nor-non-perception, he abides in it; this is the seventh deliverance. By passing quite beyond the plane of neither-perception-nor-non-perception, entering on the stopping of perception and feeling, he abides in it; this is the eighth deliverance. As

---

[1] *Cf. M.* i. 11 (*M.L.S.* i. 15).

[2] See *D.* ii. 70.

[3] By concentrating in meditation on the perfectly pure and bright colours as the objects of *kasiṇa* (for *kasiṇa*, see below, p. 215). Also, according to *MA.* iii. 256=*DA.* 513, quoting *Pṭs.* ii. 39, by way of the four *brahmavihāras.*

to this, many of my disciples abide attained to accomplishment and to going beyond through super-knowledge.

And again, Udāyin, a course has been pointed out by me for disciples, practising which disciples of mine develop the eight spheres of mastery.[1] Perceiving material shape internally, one sees external material shapes, small, comely, ugly, and he is one perceiving thus: 'Having mastered them, I know, I see'; this is the first sphere of mastery. Perceiving material shape internally, another sees external material shapes, illimitable, comely, ugly, and he is one perceiving thus: 'Having mastered them, I know, I see'; this is the second sphere of mastery. Not perceiving material shape internally, another sees external material shapes, small, comely, ugly, and he is one perceiving thus: 'Having mastered them, I know, I see'; this is the third sphere of mastery. Not perceiving material shape internally, another sees external material shapes, illimitable, comely, ugly, and he is one perceiving thus: 'Having mastered them, I know, I see'; this is the fourth sphere of mastery. Not perceiving material shape internally, another sees external material shapes that are blue-green,[2] blue-green in colour, blue-green in appearance, reflecting blue-green. As the flax blossom is blue-green, blue-green in colour, blue-green in appearance, reflecting blue-green; or again, as that fine muslin of Benares, of delicate finish on both sides, is blue-green . . . reflecting blue-green, even so anyone who, not perceiving material shape internally, sees external material shapes that are blue-green, blue-green in colour, blue-green in appearance, reflecting blue-green, is one perceiving thus: 'Having mastered them, I know, I see'; this is the fifth [14] sphere of mastery. Not perceiving material shape internally, another sees external material shapes that are yellow, yellow in colour, yellow in appearance, reflecting yellow. As the *kaṇṇikāra* blossom is yellow . . . or again, as that fine muslin of Benares, of delicate finish on both sides, is yellow . . . even so anyone . . . perceiving thus: 'Having mastered them, I know, I see'; this is the sixth sphere of mastery. Not perceiving material shape inter-

---

[1] *abhibhāyatana*; see *D.* ii. 110, *A.* i. 40, iv. 305, etc.; also see *Dhs.* §204 and *Bud. Psych. Ethics*, note on §204.

[2] These colours: blue-green, yellow, red, white, refer to personal colours: blue-green (or dark blue) to the hair or bile, etc.; yellow to skin or soles and palms, etc.; red to the flesh or blood or tongue, etc.; white to the bones or teeth or nails. These stages of meditative mastery are called *parikamma* (at *e.g.* *MA.* iii. 257), "preparatory," *i.e.* to attainment-concentration, *appanā-samādhi*.

nally, another sees external material shapes that are red, red in colour, red in appearance, reflecting red. As the *bandhujīvaka* blossom is red . . . or again, as that fine muslin of Benares, of delicate finish on both sides, is red . . . even so anyone . . . is one perceiving thus: ' Having mastered them, I know, I see '; this is the seventh sphere of mastery. Not perceiving material shape internally, another sees external material shapes that are white, white in colour, white in appearance, reflecting white. As the morning star is white, white in colour, white in appearance, reflecting white, or again, as that fine muslin of Benares, of delicate finish on both sides, is white, white in colour, white in appearance, reflecting white, even so anyone who, not perceiving material shape internally, sees external material shapes that are white, white in colour, white in appearance, reflecting white, is one perceiving thus: ' Having mastered them, I know, I see '; this is the eighth sphere of mastery. As to this, many of my disciples abide attained to accomplishment and to going beyond through super-knowledge.

And again, Udāyin, a course has been pointed out by me for disciples, practising which disciples of mine develop the ten spheres of the devices.[1] One is aware of the earth-device above, below, across, undivided, illimitable; another is aware of the water-device . . . another of the fire-device . . . another of the wind-device . . . another of the blue-green device . . . another of the yellow device . . . another of the red device . . . another of the white device . . . another of the space device . . . another [**15**] of the consciousness device above, below, across, undivided, illimitable. As to this, many of my disciples abide attained . . . through super-knowledge.

And again, Udāyin, a course has been pointed out by me for disciples, practising which disciples of mine develop the four meditations. Herein, Udāyin, a monk, aloof from pleasures of the senses, aloof from unskilled states of mind, enters and abides in the first meditation which is accompanied by initial thought and discursive thought, is born of aloofness, and is rapturous and joyful. He drenches,[2] saturates, permeates, suffuses this very body with the rapture and joy that are born of aloofness; there is no part of his whole body that is not suffused with the rapture and joy that are

[1] *kasiṇāyatana*. As at *A*. v. 46. See *G.S.* v. 31, *n*. 1, and *Vism*. 97, 110. The *kasiṇa* are purely external devices used in meditation exercises to produce and develop concentration and attain the four *jhāna*.

[2] This exposition of the four meditations with the similes has occurred at *M*. i. 276-278 (*M.L.S.* i. 330 *f*.); and see *D*. i. 73 *ff*.

born of aloofness. Udāyin, as a skilled bath-attendant or his apprentice, having sprinkled bath-powder into a bronze vessel, might knead it together with drops of water until the ball of lather has taken up moisture, is drenched with moisture, suffused with moisture inside and out, but there is no oozing—even so, Udāyin, does a monk drench, saturate, permeate, suffuse this very body with the rapture and joy that are born of aloofness; there is no part of his whole body that is not suffused with the rapture and joy that are born of aloofness.

And again, Udāyin, a monk, by allaying initial and discursive thought . . . enters and abides in the second meditation which is . . . born of concentration and is rapturous and joyful. He drenches, saturates, permeates, suffuses this very body with the rapture and joy that are born of concentration; there is no part of his whole body that is not suffused with the rapture and joy that are born of concentration. Udāyin, as a pool of water with water welling up within it, but which has no inlet for water from the eastern . . . western . . . northern . . . or from the southern side, [**16**] and even if the god did not send down showers upon it from time to time, yet a current of water having welled up in that pool would drench, saturate, permeate, suffuse that pool with cool water; there would be no part of that pool that was not suffused with cool water—even so, Udāyin, does a monk drench, saturate . . . there is no part of his whole body that is not suffused with the rapture and joy that are born of concentration.

And again, Udāyin, a monk, by the fading out of rapture . . . enters and abides in the third meditation. He drenches, saturates, permeates, suffuses this very body with the joy that has no rapture; there is no part of his whole body that is not suffused with the joy that has no rapture. In a pond of white . . . red . . . or blue lotuses, some white, red or blue lotuses are born in the water, grow up in the water, never rising above the surface but flourishing beneath it—as these from their roots to their tips are drenched, saturated, permeated, suffused by cool water—even so, Udāyin, does a monk drench, saturate . . . there is no part of his whole body that is not suffused with the joy that has no rapture.

And again, Udāyin, a monk by getting rid of joy and by getting rid of anguish, by the going down of his former pleasures and sorrows, enters and abides in the fourth meditation which has neither anguish nor joy, and which is entirely purified by equanimity and mindfulness. He, having suffused this very body with a mind that is utterly pure, utterly clean, comes to be sitting down; there is no part of his whole body that is not suffused with a mind that is utterly pure, utterly clean. Udāyin, a man might be sitting down who has clothed himself including his head with a white cloth. Even as there would be no part of his whole body not suffused with the white cloth, so, Udāyin, when a monk is sitting down having suffused this very body with a mind that is utterly pure, utterly clean, there is no part of his whole body [17] that is not suffused by a mind that is utterly pure, utterly clean. As to this, many of my disciples abide attained to accomplishment and to going beyond through super-knowledge.

And again, Udāyin, a course has been pointed out by me for disciples, practising which disciples of mine comprehend thus: 'This body of mine, having material shape, made of the four great elements, originated from mother and father, nourished on gruel and sour milk, is of a nature to be constantly rubbed away, pounded away, broken up and scattered,[1] but this consciousness of mine is fastened there, bound there.[2] Udāyin, as an emerald jewel,[3] of lovely water, well cut into eight facets, translucent, flawless, having all good qualities, might be strung on a thread, blue-green or yellow or red or white or orange-coloured; and a man with vision, having put it in his hand, might reflect: 'This emerald jewel . . . is strung on a thread, blue-green . . . or orange-coloured'—even so, Udāyin, a course has been pointed out by me for disciples, practising which disciples of mine know[4] thus: 'This body of mine . . . is of a nature to be constantly rubbed away . . . and scattered, but this consciousness[5] is fastened there, bound there.' As to this, many of my disciples abide attained . . . through super-knowledge.

And again, Udāyin, a course has been pointed out by me for disciples, practising which disciples of mine from this body (mentally) produce (another) body, having material shape, mind-made,[6] having all its major and minor parts, not deficient in any sense-organ.[7] As, Udāyin, a man might draw an arrow from a reed[8] and might think

---

[1] *Cf. M.* i. 144.

[2] As at *D.* i. 76.

[3] *Cf. M.* ii. 33, iii. 121; *D.* i. 76, ii. 13, etc. See *PTC.*, s.v. *aṭṭhaṁsa.*

[4] Above, *pajānanti,* "comprehend"; here *jānanti,* "know."

[5] *me,* "of mine," not in the text here although it is above.

[6] *manomaya* as at *Dhp.* 1, 2. *MA.* iii. 263 explains: *manena nibbattitaṁ.*

[7] As at *D.* i. 77; *cf.* also *D.* i. 34, 186, 195.

[8] *Dial.* i. 88, *n.* 2 notes that "this old simile has occurred already in the Śatapatha-Brāhmaṇa IV, 3, 3, 16." The other notes at *Dial.* i. 88 should also be consulted. A. K. Coomaraswamy, *Some Pali Words,* p. 166, says that

thus: 'This is the reed, this the arrow, the reed is one thing, the arrow another; it is from the reed that the arrow has been drawn'; or again, Udāyin, as a man might draw a sword from the scabbard and might think thus: 'This is the sword, this the scabbard, the sword is one thing, the scabbard another; it is from the scabbard that the sword has been drawn'; or again, [18] Udāyin, as a man might take a snake out of the slough and might think thus: 'This is the snake, this the slough, the snake is one thing, the slough another; it is from the slough that the snake has been taken out'—even so, Udāyin, a course has been pointed out by me for disciples, practising which my disciples from this body (mentally) produce (another) body . . . not deficient in any sense-organ. As to this many of my disciples abide attained to accomplishment and to going benond through super-knowledge.

And again, Udāyin, a course has been pointed out by me for disciples, practising which disciples of mine experience the various forms of psychic power;[1] having been one they become manifold; having been manifold they become one; manifest or invisible they go unhindered through a wall, through a rampart, through a mountain as if through air; they plunge into the ground and up again as if in water; they walk upon the water without parting it as if on the ground; sitting cross-legged they travel through the air like a bird on the wing; and with their hands they rub and stroke this moon and sun which are of such power and majesty, and even as far as the Brahma-world they have power with the person. As, Udāyin, a skilled potter or potter's apprentice from properly prepared clay could make whatever shaped clay vessel he wished; or as a skilled ivory-worker or ivory-worker's apprentice from properly prepared ivory could make whatever shaped ivory vessel he wished; or as a skilled goldsmith or goldsmith's apprentice from properly prepared gold could make whatever shaped gold vessel he wished—even so, Udāyin, a course has been pointed out by me for disciples, practising which disciples of mine experience the various forms of psychic power . . . [19] . . . and even as far as the Brahma-world

---

[1] As at *M.* i. 34, etc. All these are psychic powers of the spirit. The Brahma-world is no doubt the highest world of mentality and mental activity, and where the meditator is unhindered by reaction to sense-impressions.

---

when the fletcher goes to the *muñja* marshes, what he pulls out is for him the arrow and what he leaves behind is the plant. The point of all these similes is that what is pulled out resembles what it is pulled out from.

they have power with the person. As to this, many of my disciples abide attained to accomplishment and to going beyond through super-knowledge.

And again, Udāyin, a course has been pointed out by me for disciples, practising which disciples of mine through the purified *deva*-element of hearing surpassing that of men, hear both sounds: the *deva*-like and the human, those that are distant and those that are near. As, Udāyin, a powerful conch-blower could, without trouble, inform the four quarters, even so, Udāyin, a course has been pointed out by me for disciples, practising which disciples of mine through the purified *deva*-element of hearing . . . hear both sounds . . . and those that are near. As to this, many of my disciples abide . . . through super-knowledge.

And again, Udāyin, a course has been pointed out by me for disciples, practising which disciples of mine comprehend with the mind the minds of other beings, of other individuals[1]; they comprehend the mind with attachment as a mind with attachment; they comprehend the mind without attachment as a mind without attachment; they comprehend the mind with aversion as a mind with aversion; they comprehend the mind without aversion as a mind without aversion . . . the mind with confusion as a mind with confusion . . . the mind without confusion as a mind without confusion . . . the mind that is contracted as a mind that is contracted . . . the mind that is distracted as a mind that is distracted . . . the mind that has become great as a mind that has become great . . . the mind that has not become great as a mind that has not become great . . . the mind with (some other mental state) superior to it as a mind with (some other mental state) superior to it . . . the mind with no (other mental state) superior to it as a mind with no (other mental state) superior to it . . . the mind that is composed as a mind that is composed . . . the mind that is not composed as a mind that is not composed . . . the mind that is freed as a mind that is freed . . . the mind that is not freed as a mind that is not freed. Udāyin, it is like a woman or a man, young and of tender years, fond of adornment, who, regarding the reflection of (her or his) own face in a perfectly pure and perfectly clean mirror or in a bowl of clear water would, if it had a mole on it, know that it had, [**20**] and if not, would know that it had not.[2] Even so, Udāyin, a course has been pointed out by me for disciples, practising which disciples of mine comprehend with the

---

[1] As at *M.* i. 34, 39, etc.

[2] As at *D.* i. 80.

mind the mind of other beings, of other individuals; they comprehend the mind with attachment as a mind with attachment . . . the mind that is not freed as a mind that is not freed. As to this, many of my disciples abide . . . through super-knowledge.

And again, Udāyin, a course has been pointed out by me for disciples, practising which disciples of mine recollect a variety of former habitations,[1] that is to say: one birth, two births . . . three . . . four . . . five . . . ten . . . twenty . . . thirty . . . forty . . . fifty . . . a hundred . . . a thousand . . . a hundred thousand births, and many an eon of integration and many an eon of disintegration and many an eon of integration-disintegration. 'Such a one was I by name, having such and such a clan, such and such a colour, so was I nourished, such and such pleasant and painful experiences were mine, so did the span of life end. Passing from this, I came to be in another state where such a one was I by name, having such and such a clan, such and such a colour, so was I nourished, such and such pleasant and painful experiences were mine, so did the span of life end. Passing from this, I arose here.' Thus they recollect divers former habitations in all their mode and detail. Udāyin, it is like[2] a man who might go from his own village to another village, and who from that village might go to another village and from that village might return to his own village. This might occur to him: 'I went from my own village to a certain other village where I stood thus, sat down thus, spoke thus, was silent thus; and from that village I went to another village where too [21] I stood thus . . . was silent thus; then from that village I returned to my own village.' Even so, Udāyin, a course has been pointed out by me for disciples, practising which disciples of mine recollect a variety of former habitations, that is to say: one birth, two births . . . thus they recollect divers former habitations in all their mode and detail. As to this, many of my disciples abide . . . through super-knowledge.

And again, Udāyin, a course has been pointed out by me for disciples, practising which disciples of mine with the purified *deva*-vision surpassing that of men, see beings as they are passing hence and coming to be,[3] and they comprehend that beings are mean, excellent, comely, ugly, well-going, ill-going, according to the consequences of deeds and they think: 'Indeed these worthy beings who were possessed of wrong conduct in body . . . speech . . . thought, scoffers at the ariyans, holding a wrong view, incurring deeds

---

[1] As at *M*. i. 22, etc. [2] As at *M*. i. 278. [3] As at *M*. i. 22, etc.

consequent on a wrong view—these at the breaking up of the body after dying, have arisen in a sorrowful state, a bad bourn, the abyss, Niraya Hell. But these worthy beings who were possessed of good conduct in body . . . speech . . . thought, who did not scoff at the ariyans, holding a right view, incurring deeds consequent on a right view—these at the breaking up of the body after dying, have arisen in a good bourn, a heaven world.' Thus with the purified *deva*-vision surpassing that of men do they see beings as they are passing hence and coming to be, and they comprehend that beings are mean, excellent, comely, ugly, well-going, ill-going according to the consequences of deeds. It is as if,[1] Udāyin, there might be two houses with doors, and if a man with vision were standing there between them he might see people entering and leaving the houses, visiting and strolling about. Even so, Udāyin, a course has been pointed out by me for disciples, practising which disciples of mine with the purified *deva*-vision surpassing that of men see beings as they are passing hence and coming to be and they comprehend that beings are mean, excellent, comely, ugly, well-going, ill-going according to the consequences of deeds. As to this, many of my disciples abide . . . through super-knowledge.

[22] And again, Udāyin, a course has been pointed out by me for disciples, practising which disciples of mine by the destruction of the cankers, having realised here-now through their own super-knowledge the freedom of mind and the freedom through intuitive wisdom that are cankerless, enter and abide therein. Udāyin, it is like[1] a pure, limpid, serene pool of water where, if a man with vision were standing on the bank, he might see oysters and shells, and gravel and pebbles, and shoals of fish moving about and keeping still. It might occur to him: 'This pool of water is pure, limpid, serene, here these oysters and shells, and the gravel and pebbles, and shoals of fish are moving about and keeping still.' Even so, Udāyin, a course has been pointed out by me for disciples, practising which disciples of mine by the destruction of the cankers, having realised here-now through their own super-knowledge the freedom of mind and the freedom through wisdom that are cankerless, enter and abide therein. As to this, many of my disciples abide attained to accomplishment and to going beyond through super-knowledge.

This, Udāyin, is the fifth thing for which disciples of mine revere, respect, esteem and honour me and, revering and respecting, live in dependence.

---

[1] As at *M*. i. 279.

These, Udāyin, are the five things for which disciples of mine revere, respect, esteem and honour me and, revering and respecting, live in dependence."

Thus spoke the Lord. Delighted, the wanderer Sakuludāyin rejoiced in what the Lord had said.

Greater Discourse to Sakuludāyin:
The Seventh

78. DISCOURSE TO SAMAṆAMAṆḌIKĀ ('S SON)

(Samaṇamaṇḍikāsutta)

THUS have I heard: At one time the Lord was staying near Sāvatthī in the Jeta Grove in Anāthapiṇḍika's monastery. Now at that time the wanderer Uggāhamāna, Samaṇamaṇḍikā's son, was staying in the One Hall, set round with a row of *tinduka* trees,[1] in Mallikā's park which was intended for discussion,[2] [23] together with a company of wanderers numbering at least three hundred.[3] Then early one morning the carpenter Pañcakaṅga left Sāvatthī so as to see the Lord. Then it occurred to Pañcakaṅga the carpenter: "It is not yet the right time to see the Lord. The Lord has withdrawn. Nor is it the season to see the monks who are developing their minds.[4] The monks who are developing their minds have withdrawn. Suppose that I were to approach Mallikā's park, which is intended for discussion, the One Hall, set round with a row of *tinduka* trees, and Uggāhamāna the wanderer, Samaṇamaṇḍikā's son?"[5] Then

---

[1] *MA*. iii. 266 says that the One Hall, *ekasālā*, was surrounded by rows of *tinduka* and *timbaru* trees. At first there was only the one hall, and although later many more were built for the wanderers, such as Poṭṭhapāda and others, the name of One Hall was retained.

[2] *samayappavādake*. *MA*. iii. 266 says this is an *ārāma*, a park, where brahmans, Jains, unclothed wanderers and so on meet together to discuss and to state their opinions. *Samayappavādaka* is therefore a descriptive epithet of the park that Mallikā had made for the wanderers, and not "the debating hall" as such.

[3] This sentence is also at *D*. i. 178.

[4] *manobhāvaniyā bhikkhū*, as at *M*. iii. 261; *S*. iii. 1; *Miln*. 129.

[5] Although Uggāhamāna always receives this full title in this Discourse, for the sake of brevity I shall refer to him as Uggāhamāna only.

Pañcakaṅga the carpenter approached Mallikā's park . . . and Uggāhamāna. At that time Uggāhamāna was sitting down with a great company of wanderers shouting out with a loud noise, a great noise[1] . . . talk about becoming or not becoming thus or thus. Uggāhamāna saw the carpenter Pañcakaṅga coming in the distance; seeing him, he called his own company to order, saying:

"Good sirs, let there be little noise; do not, good sirs, make a noise; this is a disciple of the recluse Gotama who is coming—the carpenter Pañcakaṅga. For as long as white-frocked householders, disciples of the recluse Gotama, have been staying at Sāvatthī, the carpenter Pañcakaṅga has been among them. These venerable ones wish for little noise, they are trained to little noise, they are praisers of little noise. So, if he knows that this is a company of little noise, he may consider approaching." Then these wanderers fell silent.

Then Pañcakaṅga the carpenter approached Uggāhamāna; having approached he exchanged greetings with Uggāhamāna; [24] having conversed in a friendly and courteous way, he sat down at a respectful distance. Uggāhamāna spoke thus to Pañcakaṅga the carpenter as he was sitting down at a respectful distance:

"I, carpenter, lay down that an individual who is endowed with four qualities is abounding in skill, of the highest skill, an unconquerable recluse attained to the utmost attainments. With what four? As to this, carpenter, he does no evil deed with his body, he speaks no evil speech, he intends no evil intention, he leads no evil mode of livelihood. I lay down, carpenter, that if an individual is endowed with these four qualities he is abounding in skill, of the highest skill, an unconquerable recluse attained to the utmost attainments."

But the carpenter Pañcakaṅga neither rejoiced in what Uggāhamāna had said nor scoffed. Neither rejoicing nor scoffing, rising from his seat, he departed, thinking: "I will discover the meaning of what was said in the Lord's presence." Then Pañcakaṅga the carpenter approached the Lord; having approached, having greeted the Lord, he sat down at a respectful distance. As he was sitting down at a respectful distance Pañcakaṅga the carpenter told the Lord the whole of the conversation he had had with Uggāhamāna. This said, the Lord spoke thus to Pañcakaṅga the carpenter:

"This being so, carpenter, then according to the speech of Uggāhamāna a young baby boy lying on its back[2] would be of

---

[1] As in Suttas 76, 77, see above, pp. 192, 203. [2] *Cf. M.* i. 394.

abounding skill, of the highest skill, an unconquerable recluse attained to the utmost attainments. For, carpenter, a young baby boy lying on its back does not think of its own body.[1] How then could it do an evil deed with its body, except for a little kicking about? A young baby boy . . . does not think of its own voice. How then could it utter an evil speech, except for a little crying? A young baby boy . . . does not think about its own intention. How then could it intend an evil intention, except for a little excitement?[2] A young baby boy, carpenter, lying on its back does not think of its own mode of livelihood. How then [25] could it lead an evil mode of livelihood, except for taking its mother's milk? This being so, carpenter, then according to the speech of Uggāhamāna a young baby boy lying on its back would be of abounding skill . . . attained to the utmost attainments.

Now I, carpenter, lay down that an individual, endowed with four qualities, is neither of abounding skill nor of the highest skill nor is he an unconquerable recluse attained to the utmost attainments; and that these moreover merely distinguish[3] a young baby boy lying on its back. With what four? As to this, carpenter, he does no evil deed with his body, he utters no evil speech, he intends no evil intention, he leads no evil mode of livelihood. I, carpenter, lay down that if an individual is endowed with these four qualities he is neither abounding in skill, nor of the highest skill, nor an unconquerable recluse attained to the utmost attainments; and that these moreover merely distinguish a young baby boy lying on its back.

I, carpenter, lay down that an individual, endowed with ten qualities, is abounding in skill, of the highest skill, an unconquerable recluse attained to the utmost attainments. I say it is to be understood for him,[4] carpenter, that these[5] are unskilled moral habits. I say it is to be understood for him, carpenter, that hence-originating are unskilled moral habits. I say it is to be understood for him, carpenter, that here unskilled moral habits are stopped without remainder. I say it is to be understood for him, carpenter, that

---

[1] *kāyo ti pi na hoti*. *MA*. iii. 267 says it does not know the difference between its own body and those of others.

[2] It cries or laughs according to whether it has come from Niraya Hell or a deva-world, *MA*. iii. 268.

[3] *samadhiggayha tiṭṭhati*, see above, p. 184, *n*. 2.

[4] *tahaṁ*, a locative of *ta*.

[5] This and the next two sentences begin respectively with *ime, ito, idha*.

faring along thus, he is faring along for the stopping of unskilled moral habits. I say it is to be understood for him, carpenter, that these are skilled moral habits . . . I say it is to be understood for him, carpenter, that here skilled moral habits are stopped without remainder. I say it is to be understood for him, carpenter, that faring along thus, he is faring along for the stopping of skilled moral habits. I say it is to be understood for him, carpenter, that these are unskilled intentions . . . [**26**] I say it is to be understood for him, carpenter, that faring along thus, he is faring along for the stopping of skilled intentions.

And which, carpenter, are the unskilled moral habits ? Unskilled deed of body, unskilled deed of speech, evil mode of livelihood—these, carpenter, are called unskilled moral habits. And how, carpenter, do these unskilled moral habits originate ? Their origination is spoken of too. It should be answered that the origination is in the mind.[1] Which mind ? For the mind is manifold, various, diverse. That mind[2] which has attachment, aversion, confusion—originating from this are unskilled moral habits. But where,[3] carpenter, are these unskilled moral habits stopped without remainder ? Their stopping is spoken of too. As to this, carpenter, a monk, getting rid of wrong conduct in body, develops right conduct in body; getting rid of wrong conduct in speech, he develops right conduct in speech; getting rid of wrong conduct in thought, he develops right conduct in thought; getting rid of a wrong mode of livelihood, he leads his life with a right mode of livelihood. It is thus that these unskilled moral habits are stopped without remainder. And faring along in what way, carpenter, is he faring along for the stopping of unskilled moral habits ? As to this, carpenter, a monk generates desire,[4] he endeavours, stirs up energy, exerts his mind and strives for the non-arising of evil unskilled states of mind that have not arisen . . . for the getting rid of evil unskilled states of mind that have arisen . . . for the arising of skilled states of mind that have not arisen . . . for the maintenance, preservation, increase, maturity, development and completion of skilled states of mind that have

---

[1] *citta.*

[2] I think the reading here should be *yaṁ cittaṁ* (instead of *sacittaṁ*) as in the paragraph below on the skilled moral habits.

[3] *kuhiṁ.* *MA.* iii. 269 says *katamaṁ ṭhānaṁ pāpuṇitvā*, having achieved which stage ?—the stage of stream-attainment, or which ? The answer is immediately given, and its conclusion: 'It is here . . .' means, according to *MA.* iii. 269, in the fruit of stream-attainment.

[4] As at *M.* ii. 11.

arisen. Faring along thus, [27] carpenter, he is faring along for the stopping of unskilled moral habits.

And which, carpenter, are the skilled moral habits? Skilled deed of body, skilled deed of speech; and I, carpenter, say that included in moral habit is entire purity of mode of livelihood. These, carpenter, are called skilled moral habits. And how, carpenter, do these skilled moral habits originate? Their origination is spoken of too. It should be answered that the origination is in the mind. Which mind? For the mind is manifold, various, diverse. That mind which is devoid of attachment, devoid of aversion, devoid of confusion — originating from this are the skilled moral habits. And where, carpenter, are these skilled moral habits stopped without remainder? Their stopping is spoken of too. As to this, carpenter, a monk is of moral habit and has no addition to make to moral habit,[1] and he comprehends that freedom of mind, that freedom through intuitive wisdom as they really are. Herein[2] are these skilled moral habits of his stopped without remainder. And faring along in what way, carpenter, is he faring along for the stopping of skilled moral habits? As to this, carpenter, a monk generates desire, he endeavours, stirs up energy, exerts his mind and strives for the non-arising of evil unskilled states of mind that have not arisen . . . for the maintenance, preservation, increase, maturity, development and completion of skilled states of mind that have arisen. Faring along thus, carpenter, he is faring along for the stopping of skilled moral habits.

And which, carpenter, are unskilled intentions? Intention for sense-pleasures, intention for malevolence, intention for harming. These, carpenter, are called unskilled intentions. And how, carpenter, do these unskilled intentions originate? Their origination is spoken of too. It should be answered that their origination is in perception. Which perception? For perception is many, various, diverse: perception of sense-pleasures, perception of malevolence, perception of harming—originating from these are unskilled intentions. But where, carpenter, are these unskilled intentions stopped without remainder? Their stopping is spoken of too. As to this, carpenter, a monk, aloof from pleasures of the

---

[1] *sīlavā hoti no ca sīlamayo.* *VvA.* 10 adduces six meanings of the word *maya,* and as an example of the sixth gives *dānamaya, sīlamaya,* in the sense of adding a syllable for the sake of completeness. But *MA.* iii. 270 says *no ca sīlamayo* means that, being possessed of moral habit, there is nothing further than this to be done.

[2] *yattha*: in the fruit gf arahantship, *MA.* iii. 270.

senses, [**28**] . . . enters and abides in the first meditation. Herein are these unskilled intentions stopped without remainder. And faring along in what way, carpenter, is he faring along for the stopping of unskilled intentions ? As to this, carpenter, a monk generates desire, he endeavours, stirs up energy, exerts his mind and strives for the non-arising of evil unskilled states of mind that have not arisen . . . for the maintenance, preservation, increase, maturity, development and completion of skilled states of mind that have arisen. Faring along thus, carpenter, he is faring along for the stopping of unskilled intentions.

And which, carpenter, are skilled intentions ? Intention for renunciation, intention for non-malevolence, intention for non-harming. These, carpenter, are called skilled intentions. And how, carpenter, do these skilled intentions originate ? Their origination is spoken of too. It should be answered that their origination is in perception. Which perception ? For perception is many, various, diverse: perception of renunciation, perception of non-malevolence, perception of non-harming—originating from these are skilled intentions. But where, carpenter, are these skilled perceptions stopped without remainder ? Their stopping is spoken of too. As to this, carpenter, a monk, allaying initial and discursive thought . . . enters and abides in the second meditation. Herein are these skilled intentions stopped without remainder. And faring along in what way, carpenter, is he faring along for the stopping of skilled intentions ? As to this, carpenter, a monk generates desire, he endeavours, stirs up energy, exerts his mind and strives for the non-arising of evil unskilled states of mind that have not arisen . . . for the maintenance, preservation, increase, maturity, development and completion of skilled states of mind that have arisen. Faring along thus, carpenter, he is faring along for the stopping of skilled intentions.

And endowed with what ten qualities do I, carpenter, lay down that an individual [**29**] is abounding in skill, of the highest skill, an unconquerable recluse attained to the utmost attainments ? As to this, carpenter, a monk is endowed with the perfect view of an adept, he is endowed with the perfect intention of an adept . . . the perfect speech . . . the perfect action . . . the perfect mode of livelihood . . . the perfect endeavour . . . the perfect mindfulness . . . the perfect concentration . . . the perfect knowledge of an adept, he is endowed with the perfect freedom of an adept. I, carpenter, lay down that an individual, endowed with these ten qualities, is abounding in skill, of the highest skill, an unconquerable recluse attained to the highest attainments."

Thus spoke the Lord. Delighted, Pañcakaṅga the carpenter rejoiced in what the Lord had said.

Discourse to Samaṇamaṇḍikā ('s son):
The Eighth

79. LESSER DISCOURSE TO SAKULUDĀYIN

(Cūḷa-Sakuludāyisutta)

THUS have I heard: At one time the Lord was staying near Rājagaha in the Bamboo Grove at the squirrels' feeding place. Now at that time the wanderer Sakuludāyin was living in the wanderers' park at the peacocks' feeding place together with a large company of wanderers. Then the Lord, having dressed in the morning, taking his bowl and robe, entered Rājagaha for almsfood[1] . . . [**30**] ". . . And what was your talk that was interrupted ?"

"Let be that talk, revered sir, for which we are now gathered together here. It will not be difficult for the Lord to hear this talk later. When I, Lord, am not near this company, then this company is sitting down talking a variety of inferior talk. But when I, Lord, am near this company, then this company is sitting down gazing at my face, saying: 'We will listen to whatever *dhamma* the recluse Udāyin speaks to us.' But when, Lord, [**31**] the Lord is near this company, then I and this company are alike sitting down gazing at the Lord's face, and saying: 'We will listen to whatever *dhamma* the Lord speaks to us.'"

"Well then, Udāyin, let something occur to you here so that you can speak it to me."

"Some time ago, revered sir, one who was all-knowing, all-seeing, claiming all-embracing knowledge-and-vision, said: 'Whether I am walking or standing still or asleep or awake, knowledge-and-vision is constantly and perpetually before me.'[2] He, on being asked a

---

[1] As in Sta. 77; and *cf*. Stas. 76, 78. [2] As at *M*. i. 519.

question by me concerning the past, shelved the question by (asking) another, answered off the point and evinced temper and ill-will and sulkiness.[1] It was because of this, revered sir, that rapture arose in me respecting the Lord, and I thought: 'Ah, indeed it is the Lord, ah, indeed it is the Well-farer that is skilled in these matters.' "

" But who was this, Udāyin, that all-knowing, all-seeing, claiming all-embracing knowledge-and-vision, said: 'Whether I am walking or standing still or asleep or awake, knowledge-and-vision is constantly and perpetually before me,' and who, on being asked a question by you . . . evinced temper and ill-will and sulkiness ?"

" Revered sir, it was Nātaputta the Jain."

" Udāyin, whoever could recollect a variety of former habitations, that is to say: one birth, and two births . . . and could recollect thus in all their mode and detail a variety of former habitations, either he could ask me a question concerning the past or I could ask him a question concerning the past; either he could turn his mind to answering my question concerning the past or I could turn my mind to answering his question concerning the past. Udāyin, whoever could with the purified *deva*-vision surpassing that of men behold beings as they are passing hence and coming to be, mean, excellent, comely, ugly, well-going, ill-going . . . could comprehend creatures according to the consequences of deeds, either he could ask me a question concerning the future [**32**] or I could ask him a question concerning the future; either he could turn his mind to answering my question concerning the future or I could turn my mind to answering his question concerning the future.

Wherefore, Udāyin, let be the past, let be the future. I will teach you *dhamma*: If this is, that comes to be; from the arising of this, that arises; if this is not, that does not come to be; from the stopping of this, that is stopped."

" But I, revered sir, even to the extent that I have realised this individuality of mine, am not able to recollect it with its mode and detail. How then should I recollect a variety of former habitations, that is to say one birth, and two births . . . and say that I recollect a variety of former habitations in all their mode and detail, like the Lord ? Then I, revered sir, do not even see a mud-sprite[2] at present. How then should I with the purified *deva*-vision surpassing that of men behold beings as they are passing hence and coming to be . . . comprehend beings according to the consequences of deeds, like the

---

[1] *Cf. M.* i. 250.

[2] *paṁsupisācaka.*

Lord ? So that when, revered sir, the Lord spoke thus to me: 'Let be the past, let be the future. I will teach you *dhamma*: If this is, that comes to be; from the arising of this, that arises; if this is not, that does not come to be; from the stopping of this, that is stopped' —then that is not abundantly clear to me. Nevertheless I, revered sir, could satisfy the Lord's mind with an explanation of the question that belongs to our own teachers."

"What do your own teachers say, Udāyin ?"

"Revered sir, our own teachers speak thus: 'This is the highest lustre,[1] this is the highest lustre.'"

"But when your own teachers speak thus to you, Udāyin: 'This is the highest lustre, this is the highest lustre,' which is this highest lustre ?"

"Revered sir, there is no other lustre superior to or more excellent than this lustre, it is the highest lustre."

"But which is this lustre, Udāyin, than which there is no other lustre superior or more excellent ?"

[**33**] "Revered sir, there is no other lustre superior to or more excellent than that lustre, it is the highest lustre."

"You would be long in expanding this, Udāyin. You say: 'Revered sir, there is no other lustre superior to or more excellent than this lustre, it is the highest lustre,' but you do not point to this lustre. Udāyin, it is as though a man should say:[2] 'Whoever is the belle of this countryside, I want her, I desire her.' Another man might say to him 'My good man, do you know whether this belle of the countryside whom you want and desire is a noble maiden or a brahmin or a merchant or a worker ?' Asked this, he would say: 'No.' The other might say to him: 'My good man, do you know the name or the clan of this belle of the countryside whom you want and desire . . . whether she is tall or short or of medium height, or dark or brown or sallow; or what village or market town or what town she belongs to ?' Asked this, he might say: 'No.' The other might speak to him thus: 'My good man, do you want and desire her whom you know not, see not ?' Asked this, he might say: 'Yes.' What do you think about this, Udāyin ? This being so, surely that man's irresponsible talk[3] does not prosper him ?"

---

[1] *Cf.* the following with *M.* ii. 40. *Vaṇṇa* is a word of several meanings, such as colour, caste, beauty, appearance, praise.

[2] As at *D.* i. 241.

[3] *appāṭihīrakata bhāsita*, as at *M.* ii. 41, *D.* i. 193, 239, 242, 244. *MA.* iii. 273 explains as *anniyānika amūlaka niratthaka*, what does not lead onwards, is groundless and without a goal. *Cf. appāṭihāriya* at *M.* ii. 9.

"Certainly, revered sir, this being so, that man's irresponsible talk does not prosper him."

"But even so do you, Udāyin, say: 'Revered sir, there is no other lustre superior to or more excellent than this lustre, it is the highest lustre.' But you do not point to this lustre."

"Revered sir, as an emerald jewel,[1] of lovely water, well cut into eight facets, if placed on a pale piece of cloth shines and gleams and glows—of such a lustre is the hale self[2] after dying."

"What do you think about this, Udāyin? Of these two lustres, which is the surpassing and more excellent: that emerald jewel, of lovely water, cut into eight facets that, if placed on a pale piece of cloth [**34**] shines and gleams and glows; or some glow-worm or fire-fly in the dense darkness of the night?"

"Why, revered sir, of these two lustres, the surpassing and more excellent is the glow-worm or fire-fly in the dense darkness of the night."

"What do you think about this, Udāyin? Of these two lustres, which is the surpassing and more excellent: the glow-worm or fire-fly in the dense darkness of the night or an oil-lamp in the dense darkness of the night?"

"Why, revered sir, the oil-lamp."

"What do you think about this, Udāyin? Of these two lustres, which is the surpassing and more excellent: the oil-lamp in the dense darkness of the night or a great blaze of fire in the dense darkness of the night?"

"Why, revered sir, the great blaze of fire in the dense darkness of the night."

"What do you think about this, Udāyin? Of these two lustres, which is the surpassing and more excellent: the great blaze of fire in the dense darkness of the night or the morning star in a clear cloudless sky towards dawn?"

"Why, revered sir, the morning star in a clear cloudless sky towards dawn is the surpassing and more excellent of these two lustres."

"What do you think about this, Udāyin? Of these two lustres, which is the surpassing and more excellent: the morning star in a clear cloudless sky towards dawn or the moon at its zenith[3] in

---

[1] *Cf. M.* ii. 17.

[2] *Cf. M.* ii. 228. *MA.* iii. 273 says it is said that at the time of dying the self shines as though in the world of the Subhakiṇha *devas.*

[3] *abhido. MA.* iii. 274 says: *gaganamajjhe . . . majjhantike.*

a clear cloudless sky at midnight on an Observance day, a fifteenth ?"

"Why, revered sir, on an Observance day, a fifteenth, the moon at its zenith in a clear cloudless sky at midnight."

[**35**] "What do you think about this, Udāyin ? Of these two lustres, which is the surpassing and more excellent: the moon at its zenith in a clear cloudless sky at midnight on an Observance day, a fifteenth, or the sun at its zenith in a clear cloudless sky at noonday in the last month of the rains in the autumn ?"

"Why, revered sir, the sun at its zenith in a clear cloudless sky at noonday in the last month of the rains in the autumn is of these two lustres the surpassing and more excellent."

"Greater than these are those many *devas*, Udāyin, who do not share in[1] the brilliance of these moons and suns—that I comprehend. But then I do not say: 'There is no other lustre superior to or more excellent than this lustre.' But you, Udāyin, although the lustre of a glow-worm or a fire-fly is feebler and poorer, say it is the highest lustre. And you do not point to that lustre."

"The Lord has settled the talk, the Well-farer has settled the talk."

"But why do you, Udāyin, speak thus: 'The Lord has settled the talk, the Well-farer has settled the talk' ?"

"Revered sir, our own teachers speak thus: 'This is the highest lustre, this is the highest lustre.' But these teachers of ours, revered sir, on being questioned, cross-questioned and pressed for reasons by the Lord, are empty, void and have fallen short."[2]

"But, Udāyin, is there a world that is exclusively happy ? Is there a reasoned course[3] for realising a world that is exclusively happy ?"

"Revered sir, our own teachers speak thus: 'There is a world that is exclusively happy; there is a reasoned course for realising a world that is exclusively happy.'"

"And which, Udāyin, is this reasoned course for realising a world that is exclusively happy ?"

"As to this, revered sir, someone, giving up onslaught on creatures, abstains from onslaught on creatures; giving up taking what has not been given, he abstains from taking what has not been given; giving up wrong conduct in regard to sense-pleasures, he abstains from wrong conduct in regard to sense-pleasures; [**36**] giving up lying

---

[1] *nānubhonti*, not to share in, draw on or derive from. [2] As at *M*. i. 233.
[3] *ākāravatī paṭipadā*. *Cf*. *ākāravatī saddhā*, a reasoned faith, at *M*. i. 320.

speech, he abstains from lying speech; or he lives undertaking a certain asceticism.[1] This, revered sir, is a reasoned course for realising a world that is exclusively happy."

"What do you think about this, Udāyin? At the time when, giving up onslaught on creatures, he abstains from onslaught on creatures, is the self at that time exclusively happy or is it happy and sorrowful?"

"It is happy and sorrowful, revered sir."

"What do you think about this, Udāyin? At the time when giving up taking what has not been given . . . giving up wrong conduct in regard to sense-pleasures . . . at the time when, giving up lying speech, he abstains from lying speech, is the self at that time exclusively happy or is it happy and sorrowful?"

"It is happy and sorrowful, revered sir."

"What do you think about this, Udāyin? At the time when he lives undertaking some asceticism, is the self at that time exclusively happy or is it happy and sorrowful?"

"It is happy and sorrowful, revered sir."

"What do you think about this, Udāyin? Is not then the course for realising a world that is exclusively happy one that is both happy and sorrowful?"

"The Lord has settled this talk, the Well-farer has settled this talk."

"But why do you, Udāyin, speak thus: 'The Lord has settled this talk, the Well-farer has settled this talk'?"

"Revered sir, our own teachers speak thus: 'There is a world that is exclusively happy, there is a reasoned course for realising a world that is exclusively happy.' But these teachers of ours, revered sir, on being questioned, cross-questioned and pressed for reasons by the Lord, are empty, void, and have fallen short. But, revered sir, is there a world that is exclusively happy? Is there a reasoned course for realising a world that is exclusively happy?"

[37] "There is indeed, Udāyin, a world that is exclusively happy. There is a reasoned course for realising a world that is exclusively happy."

"And which, revered sir, is this reasoned course for realising a world that is exclusively happy?"

"As to this, Udāyin, a monk, aloof from pleasures of the senses . . . enters and abides in the first meditation; by the allaying of initial and discursive thought . . . he enters and abides in the second

[1] *tapoguṇa*.

meditation . . . he enters and abides in the third meditation. This, Udāyin, is that reasoned course for realising a world that is exclusively happy."

"But this, revered sir, is not a reasoned course for realising a world that is exclusively happy. For the world that is exclusively happy might have been already realised."

"Indeed, Udāyin, a world that is exclusively happy could not have been already realised. For this is itself the reasoned course for realising a world that is exclusively happy."

When this had been said, the wanderer Sakuludāyin's company shouted out with a loud noise, a great noise: "We have heard to here from our own teachers, we have heard to here from our own teachers. We comprehend nothing more beyond this." Then the wanderer Sakuludāyin, having quietened those wanderers, spoke thus to the Lord:

"But when could that world which is exclusively happy be realised, revered sir?"

"As to this, Udāyin, a monk, by getting rid of joy . . . enters and abides in the fourth meditation. As many as are the *devatās* that have uprisen in a world that is exclusively happy, he remains and talks and falls into conversation with these *devatās*. Indeed, Udāyin, a world that is exclusively happy might have been already realised."

"Now, revered sir, is it not for realising this world that is exclusively happy that monks fare the Brahma-faring under the Lord?"

"No, Udāyin, it is not for the sake of realising this world that is exclusively happy that monks fare the Brahma-faring under me. There simply are, Udāyin, other things superior and more excellent for the sake of realising which monks fare the Brahma-faring under me."

[38] "But what, revered sir, are these things superior and more excellent, for the sake of realising which monks fare the Brahma-faring under the Lord?"

"As to this, Udāyin, a Tathāgata arises in the world, perfected one, fully Self-Awakened One, endowed with (right) knowledge and conduct, Well-farer, knower of the worlds, matchless charioteer of men to be tamed, teacher of *devas* and men, the Awakened One, the Lord . . .[1] . . . He, by getting rid of these five hindrances—defilements

---

[1] As in *M*. Sta. 27 (see *M.L.S.* i. 223 *ff.*), and *M*. Sta. 51. *M*. ii. 38 does not repeat.

of the mind and weakening to intuitive wisdom—aloof from pleasures of the senses . . . enters and abides in the first meditation. This is a thing, Udāyin, superior and more excellent, for the sake of realising which monks fare the Brahma-faring under me. And again, Udāyin, a monk, by allaying initial and discursive thought . . . enters and abides in the second meditation . . . the third meditation . . . the fourth meditation. This too is a thing, Udāyin, superior and more excellent, for the sake of realising which monks fare the Brahma-faring under me. Thus with the mind composed, quite purified, quite clarified, without blemish, without defilement, grown soft and workable, fixed, immovable, he directs his mind to the knowledge and recollection of former habitations . . .[1] . . . Thus he recollects divers former habitations in all their mode and detail. This too is a thing, Udāyin, for the sake of realising which monks fare the Brahma-faring under me. With the mind composed thus, quite purified . . . immovable, he directs his mind to the knowledge of the passing hence and coming to be of beings . . . he comprehends that beings are mean, excellent, comely, ugly, well-going, ill-going according to the consequences of deeds. This too is a thing, superior and more excellent, Udāyin, for the sake of realising which monks fare the Brahma-faring under me. With the mind composed thus, quite purified . . . immovable, he directs his mind to the knowlege of the destruction of the cankers. He comprehends as it really is: 'This is anguish' . . . 'This is the uprising of anguish' . . . 'This is the stopping of anguish . . . 'This is the course leading to the stopping of anguish.' He comprehends as it really is: 'These are the cankers' . . . [**39**] 'This is the arising of the cankers' . . . 'This is the stopping of the cankers' . . . 'This is the course leading to the stopping of the cankers.' Of him who knows thus, sees thus, the mind is freed from the canker of sense-pleasures and the mind is freed from the canker of becoming and the mind is freed from the canker of ignorance. In freedom the knowledge comes to be that he is freed, and he comprehends: 'Destroyed is birth, brought to a close the Brahma-faring, done is what was to be done, there is no more of being such or so.' This too is a thing, superior and more excellent, Udāyin, for the sake of realising which monks fare the Brahma-faring under me. These, Udāyin, are the things, superior and more excellent, for the sake of realising which monks fare the Brahma-faring under me."

When this had been said, the wanderer Sakuludāyin spoke thus to

---

[1] See *M.L.S.* i. 28.

the Lord: " It is excellent, revered sir, excellent, revered sir. It is as if, revered sir, one might set upright what had been upset, or might disclose what was covered, or point out the way to one who had gone astray, or might bring an oil-lamp into the darkness so that those with vision might see material shapes—even so in many a figure is *dhamma* made clear by the Lord. I, revered sir, am going to the Lord for refuge and to *dhamma* and to the Order of monks. May I, revered sir, receive the going forth in the Lord's presence, may I receive ordination ?"

When this had been said the company of the wanderer Sakuludāyin spoke thus to him: " Do not, good Udāyin, fare the Brahma-faring under the recluse Gotama; do not, good Udāyin, having been a teacher, live as a pupil. As what was once a good water-pot might spring a leak, so would be this performance of the good Udāyin. Do not, good Udāyin, fare the Brahma-faring under the recluse Gotama; do not, good Udāyin, having been a teacher, live as a pupil."

It was thus that the company of the wanderer Sakuludāyin made for the wanderer Sakuludāyin a stumbling-block in (the way of) the Brahma-faring under the Lord.[1]

Lesser Discourse to Sakuludāyin:
The Ninth

80. DISCOURSE TO VEKHANASSA

(Vekhanassasutta)

[**40**] THUS have I heard: At one time the Lord was staying near Sāvatthī in the Jeta Grove in Anāthapiṇḍika's monastery. Then the wanderer Vekhanassa[2] approached the Lord; having approached,

---

[1] *MA.* iii. 275 says because he did not obtain the going forth they made this disturbance; and that later (*i.e. anāgate*, in the future), in the time of Asoka, he became the thera called Assagutta (see *Miln.* 6 *ff.*, *VbhA.* 272, *Asl.* 419) who was topmost of abiders in (the meditation on) friendliness, even extending a mind of friendliness to animals. It is because the Buddha knew that this would be so that he taught *dhamma* to Sakuludāyin.

[2] *MA.* iii. 277 says he was the teacher of Sakuludāyin (of Stas. 77 and 79). Wishing to find out why his pupil had been defeated by Gotama, and to defeat him himself on the question of the highest lustre, he went the forty-five *yojanas* from Rājagaha to Sāvatthī.

he greeted the Lord; and having conversed in a friendly and courteous way, he stood at a respectful distance. As he was standing at a respectful distance, the wanderer Vekhanassa uttered a solemn utterance in the Lord's presence: "This is the highest lustre, this is the highest lustre."

"But why do you, Kaccāna,[1] speak thus: 'This is the highest lustre, this is the highest lustre?' Which is this highest lustre?"

"Good Gotama, there is no other lustre superior to or more excellent than this lustre, it is the highest lustre."

"But which, Kaccāna, is this lustre than which there is no other lustre superior or more excellent?"

"Good Gotama, there is no other lustre superior to or more excellent than this lustre, it is the highest lustre."

"You would be long in expanding this, Kaccāna. You say: 'Good Gotama, there is no other lustre superior to or more excellent than this lustre, it is the highest lustre.' But you do not point to this lustre. Kaccāna, it is as though a man should say: 'Whoever is the belle of this countryside, I want her, I desire her' . . .[2] **[41]** . . . **[42]** . . . Greater than these are those many *devas*, Kaccāna, who do not share in the brilliance of these moons and suns—that I comprehend. But then I do not say: 'There is no other lustre superior to or more excellent than this lustre.' But you, Kaccāna, although this lustre of a glow-worm or a fire-fly is feebler and poorer, say it is the highest lustre. And you do not point to that lustre.

These five, Kaccāna, are the strands of sense-pleasures.[3] Which five? Material shapes cognisable by the eye, agreeable, pleasant, liked, enticing, connected with sensual pleasures, alluring. Sounds cognisable by the ear . . . Smells cognisable by the nose . . . Tastes cognisable by the tongue . . . Touches cognisable by the body, **[43]** agreeable, pleasant, liked, enticing, connected with sensual pleasures, alluring. These, Kaccāna, are the five strands of sense-pleasures. Whatever happiness, Kaccāna, whatever pleasure arises in consequence of these five strands of sense-pleasure, this is called happiness in sense-pleasures. Thus, because of sense-pleasures there is happiness in sense-pleasures; from happiness in sense-pleasures the topmost happiness in sense-pleasures[4] is there accounted topmost."

When this had been said, the wanderer Vekhanassa spoke thus to

---

[1] Kaccāna (or Kaccāyana) was the name of a *gotta*, a family or clan. Presumably therefore Vekhanassa belonged to this clan.

[2] Exactly as in the preceding Discourse, above, p. 230.

[3] As at *M*. i. 85.

[4] *MA*. iii. 277 calls this nibbāna.

the Lord: " It is wonderful, good Gotama, it is marvellous, good Gotama. So far this is well spoken by the good Gotama: ' Because of sense-pleasures there is happiness in sense-pleasures; from happiness in sense-pleasures the topmost happiness in sense-pleasures is there accounted topmost.' "

" Hard is this for you to understand, Kaccāna—sense-pleasures, or the happiness in sense-pleasures, or the topmost happiness in sense-pleasures—you who are of another view, another allegiance, another objective, of a different observance and under a different teacher.[1] But those monks, Kaccāna, who are perfected ones, the cankers destroyed, who have lived the life, done what was to be done, shed the burden, who have attained their own goal, the fetters of becoming utterly destroyed, and who are freed by perfect profound knowledge—these would know: sense-pleasures, or the happiness in sense-pleasures, or the topmost happiness in sense-pleasures."

When this had been said, the wanderer Vekhanassa, angry and displeased, scorning even the Lord, despising even him, saying[2] even of him: " The recluse Gotama shall be disgraced," spoke thus to the Lord: " But it is just that there are here some recluses and brahmans who, not knowing the past, not seeing the future, yet claim: ' Destroyed is birth, brought to a close the Brahma-faring, done is what was to be done, there is no more of being such or so.' This speech of theirs proves merely ridiculous, worthless, empty, void."[3]

" This censure is only just, Kaccāna, for those recluses and brahmans who, not knowing the past, [**44**] not seeing the future, yet claim: ' Destroyed is birth . . . there is no more of being such or so.' But, Kaccāna, let be the past, let be the future.[4] Let there come an intelligent man, guileless, honest, straight, and who says: ' I instruct, I teach *dhamma*.[5] Faring along as instructed it will not be long before (some man) of himself will know, of himself will see.' Even so, indeed, is deliverance from the direst bond—that is from the bond of ignorance. Kaccāna, it is like a young baby boy lying on his

---

[1] As at *M*. i. 487.

[2] *vadamāno*. This passage is also found at *M*. ii. 200, *D*. i. 90; at the latter the reading is *upavadamāno*, insulting.

[3] *Cf. D*. i. 240.

[4] As at *M*. ii. 32. *MA*. iii. 278 says Gotama said this because the wanderer had no knowledge of former habitations making it suitable to talk about the past; and no knowledge of the *deva*-vision making it suitable to talk about the future.

[5] As at *Vin*. i. 9, where the sentence is attributed to Gotama himself.

back and bound around his neck with a fivefold swaddling, it might be with swaddlings of thread. As he grows up and develops his faculties he would be released from those swaddlings, and in the absence of swaddlings he would know: 'I am released.' Even so, Kaccāna, let there come intelligent man, guileless, honest, straight . . . Even so, indeed, is deliverance from the direst bond—that is from the bond of ignorance."

When this had been said, the wanderer Vekhanassa spoke thus to the Lord: "It is excellent, good Gotama, excellent, good Gotama . . . May the revered Gotama accept me as a lay-disciple going for refuge from today forth for as long as life lasts."

Discourse to Vekhanassa:
The Tenth

Division on Wanderers:
The Third

IV. THE ROYAL DIVISION

(Rājavagga)

81. DISCOURSE ON GHAṬIKĀRA

(Ghaṭīkārasutta)

[**45**] THUS have I heard: At one time[1] the Lord was walking on tour among the Kosalans together with a large Order of monks. Then the Lord, turning aside from the road, smiled (when he came to a) certain place. Then it occurred to the venerable Ānanda: "What is the cause, what the reason that the Lord is smiling? Not without motive do Tathāgatas smile." Then the venerable Ānanda, having arranged his robe over one shoulder, having saluted the Lord with joined palms, spoke thus to the Lord: "Now, revered sir, what is the cause, what the reason that the Lord is smiling? Not without motive do Tathāgatas smile."

"Once upon a time, Ānanda, in this district there was a village township called Vebhaḷiṅga, prosperous and wealthy and crowded with people. And, Ānanda, the Lord Kassapa, perfected one, fully Self-Awakened One, lived depending on the village township of Vebhaḷiṅga. At that time, Ānanda, the monastery of the Lord Kassapa[2] . . . was here. At that time, Ānanda, the Lord Kassapa . . . instructed an Order of monks while he was seated here."

Then the venerable Ānanda, having laid down an outer cloak folded into four, spoke thus to the Lord: "Well then, revered sir, let the Lord sit down. This self-same piece of ground will (then) have been made use of by two perfected ones, fully Self-Awakened Ones." Then the Lord sat down on an appointed seat. As he was seated the Lord spoke thus to the venerable Ānanda:

"Once upon a time, Ānanda, in this district (*as above*) . . . [**46**] the Lord Kassapa . . . instructed an Order of monks while he was seated here. And, Ānanda, in the village township of Vebhaḷiṅga the potter named Ghaṭīkāra was a supporter—the chief supporter—of the Lord Kassapa . . . And, Ānanda, a brahman youth named

[1] *Cf. A.* iii. 214-215 for the opening of this Discourse. For the whole episode, told with some interesting variations, see *Mhvu.* i. 317 *ff.* (*Mhvu.* Translation i. 265 *ff.* in *S.B.B.*).

[2] All references in this Discourse to "the Lord Kassapa" are followed by the terms "perfected one, fully Self-Awakened One." I have omitted this full designation for reasons of space.

Jotipāla[1] was a friend—a dear friend—of the potter Ghaṭīkāra. Then, Ānanda, the potter Ghaṭīkāra addressed the brahman youth Jotipāla, saying: 'Let us go, dear Jotipāla, we will approach the Lord Kassapa . . . so as to see him. A sight of this Lord, perfected one, fully Self-Awakened One, would be greatly prized by me.' When this had been said, Ānanda, the brahman youth Jotipāla spoke thus to the potter Ghaṭīkāra: 'Yes, dear Ghaṭīkāra, but of what use is it to see this little shaveling recluse ?'

And a second time . . . And a third time, Ānanda, did Ghaṭīkāra the potter speak thus to the brahman youth Jotipāla: 'Let us go, dear Jotipāla, we will approach the Lord Kassapa . . .'. . . 'Yes, dear Ghaṭīkāra, but of what use is it to see this little shaveling recluse ?'

'Well then, dear Jotipāla, taking a back-scratcher and bath-powder, we will go to the river to bathe.' Ānanda, the brahman youth Jotipāla answered the potter Ghaṭīkāra in assent, saying: 'Yes, dear.'

Then, Ānanda, the potter Ghaṭīkāra and the brahman youth Jotipāla, taking a back-scratcher and bath-powder, went to the river to bathe. Then, Ānanda, the potter Ghaṭīkāra spoke thus to the brahman youth Jotipāla: 'This, dear Jotipāla, is near the monastery of the Lord Kassapa . . . Let us go, dear Jotipāla, we will approach the Lord Kassapa . . . so as to see him. A sight of this Lord, perfected one, fully Self-Awakened One, would be greatly prized by me.' When this had been said, Ānanda, the brahman youth Jotipāla spoke thus to the potter Ghaṭīkāra: 'Yes, dear Ghaṭīkāra, but [47] of what use is it to see this little shaveling recluse ?'

And a second time . . . And a third time, Ānanda, did Ghaṭīkāra the potter speak thus to the brahman youth Jotipāla: 'This, dear Jotipāla, is near the monastery of the Lord Kassapa . . . A sight of this Lord, perfected one, fully Self-Awakened One, would be greatly prized by me.' And a third time, Ānanda, did the brahman youth Jotipāla speak thus to the potter Ghaṭīkāra: 'Yes, dear Ghaṭīkāra, but of what use is it to see this little shaveling recluse ?'

Then, Ānanda, the potter Ghaṭīkāra, having laid hold of the brahman youth Jotipāla by the waist-band, spoke thus: 'This, dear

---

[1] At *D.* ii. 230 called the son of the brahman Govinda. At *Jā.* i. 43 called the Bodhisatta; see also the end of this Discourse. *Cf. Budv.* xxv. 10 *ff.*, *Miln* 221 *ff.* Also see the point of controversy at *Kvu.* 286 as to whether the Bodhisatta was a Brahma-farer and following the (right) method at the time of the Buddha Kassapa.

Jotipāla, is near the monastery of the Lord Kassapa . . . Let us go, dear Jotipāla, we will approach the Lord Kassapa so as to see him. A sight of this Lord, perfected one, fully Self-Awakened One, would be greatly prized by me.' Then, Ānanda, the brahman youth Jotipāla, having disengaged his waist-band, spoke thus to the potter Ghaṭīkāra: 'Yes, dear Ghaṭīkāra, but of what use is it to see this little shaveling recluse?' Then, Ānanda, the potter Ghaṭīkāra, having laid hold of the brahman youth Jotipāla by the hair—he had just performed an ablution of his head—spoke thus: 'This, dear Jotipāla, is near the monastery of the Lord Kassapa . . . Let us go . . . A sight of this Lord, perfected one, fully Self-Awakened One, would be greatly prized by me.'

Then, Ānanda, it occurred to the brahman youth Jotipāla: 'Indeed it is wonderful, indeed it is marvellous, that this potter Ghaṭīkāra, being of lowly birth, should lay hold of my hair although I have performed an ablution of my head,' and should think: 'Indeed this[1] surely cannot be insignificant.' He spoke thus to the potter Ghaṭīkāra: 'Is it really necessary,[2] dear Ghaṭīkāra?' 'It is really necessary, dear Jotipāla, most surely [48] a sight of this Lord, perfected one, fully Self-Awakened One, would be greatly prized by me.'

'Well then, dear Ghaṭīkāra, let go (of my hair); we will get along.'

Then, Ānanda, the potter Ghaṭīkāra and the brahman youth Jotipāla approached the Lord Kassapa . . . When they had approached, Ghaṭīkāra the potter greeted the Lord Kassapa . . . and sat down at a respectful distance. But the brahman youth Jotipāla exchanged greetings with the Lord Kassapa . . . and having conversed in a friendly and courteous way, he sat down at a respectful distance. And, Ānanda, as the potter Ghaṭīkāra was sitting down at a respectful distance, he spoke thus to the Lord Kassapa . . .: 'Revered sir, this brahman youth Jotipāla is my friend—my dear friend. Let the Lord teach him *dhamma*.' Then, Ānanda, the Lord Kassapa . . . gladdened, roused, incited, delighted the potter Ghaṭīkāra and the brahman youth Jotipāla, with talk on *dham-*

---

[1] "This going (*gamana*) of ours (to visit the Lord) cannot be insignificant or small; it will be great," *MA*. iii. 281. The text here may be slightly confused, see *v. ll.* at *M*. ii. 47. But all the time Jotipāla was more and more coming over to the idea of visiting the Lord Kassapa.

[2] *yāvetadohi pi*. *MA*. iii. 281 gives the meaning as *yāvetaparamaṁ*, and the sense as: In order to go there, is all this exertion necessary: from pleading, seizing hold of my waist-band and letting it go, and then to the length of taking hold of my hair?

ma.[1] Then, Ānanda, the potter Ghaṭīkāra and the brahman youth Jotipāla, gladdened, roused, incited, delighted by the Lord Kassapa's . . . talk on *dhamma*, having rejoiced in what the Lord Kassapa . . . had said, having given thanks and risen from their seats, greeting the Lord Kassapa . . . they departed keeping their right sides towards him.

Then, Ānanda, the brahman youth Jotipāla spoke thus to the potter Ghaṭīkāra: 'How is it that you, dear Ghaṭīkāra, on hearing this *dhamma*, do not go forth from home into homelessness ?'

'But, dear Jotipāla, do you not know that I look after my blind and ageing parents ?'

'Well then, dear Ghaṭīkāra, *I* will go forth from home into homelessness.'

Then, Ānanda, the potter Ghaṭīkāra and the brahman youth Jotipāla approached the Lord Kassapa . . .; [**49**] having approached and having greeted the Lord Kassapa . . . they sat down at a respectful distance. And, Ānanda, as Ghaṭīkāra the potter was sitting down at a respectful distance, he spoke thus to the Lord Kassapa . . .: 'Revered sir, this brahman youth Jotipāla is my friend—my dear friend. May the Lord let him go forth.' Ānanda, Jotipāla the brahman youth received the going forth in the presence of the Lord Kassapa[2] . . ., he received the ordination. Then, Ānanda, not long after the brahman youth Jotipāla had received ordination—half a month after his ordination—the Lord Kassapa . . ., having stayed at Vebhaḷiṅga for as long as he found suitable, set out on tour for Benares; walking on tour, in due course he arrived at Benares.

While he was there, Ānanda, the Lord Kassapa . . . stayed near Benares at Isipatana in the deer-park. Ānanda, Kikī, the king of Kāsi, heard that the Lord Kassapa . . . had arrived at Benares and was staying near Benares at Isipatana in the deer-park. Then, Ānanda, Kikī, the king of Kāsi, having had many lovely vehicles harnessed, having mounted a lovely vehicle, set off for Benares with the many lovely vehicles and with great royal pomp so as to see the Lord Kassapa . . . For as long as the ground was possible for a vehicle he went in the vehicle, then having dismounted from it, he approached the Lord Kassapa . . . on foot; having approached and having greeted the Lord Kassapa . . . he sat down at a respectful distance. Ānanda, as Kikī, the king of Kāsi, was sitting down at a respectful distance, the Lord Kassapa . . . roused, incited, gladdened

---

[1] *MA.* iii. 282 says that this was concerned with the attainment of mindfulness.

[2] *MA.* iii. 282 says that Bodhisattas go forth in the presence of Buddhas.

and delighted him with talk on *dhamma*. Then, Ānanda, Kikī, the king of Kāsi, roused . . . delighted by the Lord Kassapa . . . with talk on *dhamma*, spoke thus to the Lord Kassapa . . .:

[50] 'Revered sir, may the Lord consent to a meal with me on the morrow together with the Order of monks.' Ānanda, the Lord Kassapa consented by becoming silent. Then, Ānanda, Kikī the king of Kāsi, having understood the Lord Kassapa's consent, rising from his seat and greeting the Lord Kassapa, departed keeping his right side towards him. Then, Ānanda, towards the end of that night when Kikī, the king of Kāsi, had had sumptuous foods, solid and soft, prepared in his own dwelling: dry yellow rices,[1] various curries, the black grains removed, and various condiments, he had the time announced to the Lord Kassapa, saying: 'It is time, revered sir, the meal is ready.'

Then, Ānanda, the Lord Kassapa, having dressed in the morning, taking his bowl and robe, approached the dwelling of Kikī, the king of Kāsi; having approached, he sat down on the appointed seat together with the Order of monks. Then, Ānanda, Kikī, the king of Kāsi, with his own hand served and satisfied with sumptuous foods, solid and soft, the Order of monks with the Awakened One at its head. Then, Ānanda, when the Lord Kassapa had eaten and had withdrawn his hand from the bowl, Kikī, the king of Kāsi, taking a low seat, sat down at a respectful distance. As he was sitting down at a respectful distance, Kikī, the king of Kāsi spoke thus to the Lord Kassapa: 'Revered sir, may the Lord consent to (accept) my rains-residence in Benares; there will be suitable support for the Order.'

'No, sire, I have (already) consented to (accept) a rains-residence.' And a second time . . . And a third time, Ānanda, did Kikī, the king of Kāsi, speak thus to the Lord Kassapa . . .: 'Revered sir, may the Lord consent to (accept) my rains-residence in Benares; there will be suitable support for the Order.'

'No, sire, I have (already) consented to (accept) a rains-residence.'

Then, Ānanda, Kikī, the king of Kāsi thought: 'The Lord Kassapa [51] . . . does not consent to (accept) my rains-residence in Benares,' and he was depressed and grieved.[2] Then, Ānanda, Kikī, the king of Kāsi, spoke thus to the Lord Kassapa . . .: 'Then, have you, revered sir, some other supporter than me?'

'There is, sire, a village township called Vebhaḷiṅga. There is a

---

[1] *paṇḍumuṭikassa sālino.* *MA.* iii. 283 says: *muṭake katvā sukkhāpitassa rattasālino. Tassa kira sālino vappakālato paṭṭhāya ayam parīhāro.*

[2] As at *M.* i. 448, 457.

potter there called Ghaṭīkāra; he is my supporter—the chief supporter. But you, sire, think: The Lord Kassapa . . . does not consent to (accept) my rains-residence in Benares, and you are depressed and grieved. This is not so with the potter Ghaṭīkāra and nor can it be so. For, sire, the potter Ghaṭīkāra has gone to the Awakened One for refuge, he has gone to *dhamma* for refuge, he has gone to the Order for refuge. Ghaṭīkāra, the potter, sire, is restrained from onslaught on creatures, restrained from taking what has not been given, restrained from wrong enjoyment of sense-pleasures, restrained from lying speech, restrained from occasions of sloth engendered by strong drink and spirits. Ghaṭīkāra the potter, sire, is possessed of unwavering confidence in the Awakened One . . . in *dhamma* . . . the Order, he is possessed of moral habits that are dear to the ariyans. Ghaṭīkāra the potter, sire, doubts not about anguish . . . the uprising of anguish . . . the stopping of anguish, he doubts not about the course leading to the stopping of anguish. Ghaṭīkāra the potter, sire, is a one-meal-man, a Brahma-farer, virtuous, lovely in character. Ghaṭīkāra the potter, sire, is one who has laid aside jewels and wrought gold, who is without gold and silver. Ghaṭīkāra the potter, sire, does not dig the earth either with a spade or with his own hand; willingly he makes a vessel from the soil of a bank that is crumbling or scratched out by rats and dogs, and he speaks thus: "He that likes, if he lays down fragments of husked rice here, fragments of kidney-beans, fragments of chick-peas, may take whatever he likes."[1] Ghaṭīkāra the potter, sire, looks after his blind [**52**] ageing parents. Ghaṭīkāra the potter, sire, by the destruction of the five fetters binding to this lower (shore), is of spontaneous uprising, he attains final nibbāna there, he is not liable to return from that world.

At one time I, sire, was staying in the village township of Vebhaḷiṅga. Then I, sire, having dressed in the morning, taking my bowl and robe, approached the parents of the potter Ghaṭīkāra; having approached, I spoke thus to the parents of the potter Ghaṭīkāra: "Now, where has this potter[2] gone?" "Revered sir, your supporter has gone out, saying: Now, having taken conjey from the pot, having taken curry from the cauldron, enjoy them."

---

[1] *MA*. iii. 284-5 says he does not trade in the vessels he has fired. But once people know they can take what they like, they bring him useful materials from the forest.

[2] *bhaggava; cf. Kumbhakārajātaka*, and see *PED*. This that "seems to have been a generic name for all potters" is here not "a special form of address," as suggested in *DPPN*.

Then I, sire, having taken conjey from the pot, having taken curry from the cauldron, enjoyed them, and rising up from my seat I departed. Then, sire, Ghaṭīkāra the potter approached his parents; having approached, he spoke thus to his parents: " Who is it that, having taken conjey from the pot, having taken curry from the cauldron and having enjoyed them, is going away ?" " It is the Lord Kassapa . . ., dear, that, having taken conjey . . . is going away." Then, sire, it occured to Ghaṭīkāra the potter: " Indeed it is a gain for me, indeed it is well gotten by me that the Lord Kassapa . . . has such trust in me." Then, sire, joy and happiness did not leave Ghaṭīkāra the potter for half a month or his parents for seven days.

At one time I, sire, was staying in this very village township of Vebhaḷiṅga. Then I, sire, having dressed in the morning . . . (*as above*) . . . spoke thus to the parents of the potter Ghaṭīkāra: " Now, where has this potter gone ?" " Revered sir, your supporter has gone out, saying: Now, having taken boiled rice from the pan, having taken curry from the cauldron, enjoy them." Then I, sire, having taken boiled rice from the pan, having taken curry from the cauldron, [**53**] enjoyed them, and rising up from my seat I departed. Then, sire, the potter Ghaṭīkāra approached his parents . . . (*as above, reading;* having taken boiled rice from the pan, having taken curry from the cauldron) . . . Then, sire, joy and happiness did not leave the potter Ghaṭīkāra for half a month or his parents for seven days.

At one time I, sire, was staying in this very village township of Vebhaḷiṇga. At that time the hut leaked. So I, sire, addressed the monks, saying: " Go, monks, and find out if there is grass in the dwelling of Ghaṭīkāra the potter." When this had been said, sire, the monks spoke thus to me: " There is no grass, revered sir, in the dwelling of Ghaṭīkāra the potter, but his house has a grass roof." " Go, monks, and strip the grass from the house of Ghaṭīkāra the potter." Then, sire, these monks stripped the grass from the house of Ghaṭīkāra the potter. Then, sire, the parents of Ghaṭīkāra the potter spoke thus to the monks: " Who are they that are stripping the grass from the house ?" " Sister," the monks said, " the Lord Kassapa's hut is leaking." " Take it, revered sirs, take it, my honourable friends."[1] Then, sire, Ghaṭīkāra the potter approached his parents; having approached, he spoke thus to his parents: " Who are they that have stripped the grass from the house ?" " Monks,

---

[1] *bhadramukha*, as at *M*. ii. 210; *S*. i. 74. In translating the word thus, I follow the note at *K.S*. i. 100.

dear; the hut of the Lord Kassapa . . . is leaking." Then, sire, it occurred to Ghaṭīkāra the potter: "Indeed it is a gain for me, indeed it is well gotten by me that the Lord Kassapa . . . has such trust in me." Then, sire, joy and happiness did not leave the potter Ghaṭīkāra [**54**] for half a month or his parents for seven days. Then, sire, for a whole three months[1] that house stood with its roof open to the sky, but it did not rain into it. Such a one, sire, is Ghaṭīkāra the potter.'

'It is a gain, revered sir, it is well gotten, revered sir, by Ghaṭīkāra the potter in whom the Lord has such trust.'

Then, Ānanda, Kikī, the king of Kāsi, sent as many as five hundred cartloads of husked rice to Ghaṭīkāra the potter, dry yellow rices and suitable curries.[2] Then, Ānanda, these king's men, having approached Ghaṭīkāra the potter, spoke thus: 'These five hundred cartloads of husked rice, revered sir, have been sent to you by Kikī, the king of Kāsi, with dry yellow rices and suitable curries. Accept them, revered sir.' 'The king is very busy, there is much to be done. I am quite satisfied since this is for me from the king.'

It may be, Ānanda, that this will occur to you: 'Now, at that time the brahman youth Jotipāla was someone else.' But this, Ānanda, should not be thought of in this way. I, at that time, was Jotipāla the brahman youth."

Thus spoke the Lord. Delighted, the venerable Ānanda rejoiced in what the Lord had said.

Discourse on Ghaṭīkāra:
The First

82. DISCOURSE WITH RAṬṬHAPĀLA

(Raṭṭhapālasutta)

THUS have I heard: At one time the Lord, walking on tour among the Kurus together with a large Order of monks arrived at the market

[1] *MA*. iii. 286 says that the Lord had already passed one of the four months of the rains before he sent for the grass thatch.

[2] These were to be for him and the Order of monks for three months, *MA*. iii. 287.

town of the Kurus called Thullakoṭṭhita. The brahmans and householders of Thullakoṭṭhita heard: "Indeed the recluse Gotama, the son of the Sakyans, gone forth from the Sakyan family, [**55**] walking on tour among the Kurus together with a large Order of monks has arrived at Thullakoṭṭhita. A lovely report about the revered Gotama has gone forth thus: 'This Lord is perfected, wholly Self-Awakened, endowed with (right) knowledge and conduct, well-farer, knower of the worlds, incomparable charioteer of men to be tamed, teacher of *devas* and men, the Awakened One, the Lord. He makes known this world with the *devas*, with Māra, with Brahmā, creation with its recluses and brahmans, its *devas* and men, having realised them by his own super-knowledge. With the meaning and the spirit he teaches *dhamma* that is lovely in the beginning, lovely in the middle, lovely at the ending; he proclaims the Brahma-faring wholly fulfilled, quite purified. It were good to see perfected ones like this.'"

Then the brahmans and householders of Thullakoṭṭhita approached the Lord; having approached, some, having greeted the Lord, sat down at a respectful distance; some exchanged greetings with the Lord, and having conversed in a friendly and courteous way, sat down at a respectful distance; some, having saluted the Lord with joined palms, sat down at a respectful distance; some, having made known their names and clans in the Lord's presence, sat down at a respectful distance; some, becoming silent, sat down at a respectful distance. As the brahmans and householders of Thullakoṭṭhita were sitting down at a respectful distance, the Lord gladdened, roused, incited and delighted them with a talk on *dhamma*.

Now at that time a young man of family named Raṭṭhapāla,[1] the son of a leading family in that very Thullakoṭṭhita, was sitting down in this assembly. Then it occurred to Raṭṭhapāla, the young man of family:[2] "In so far as I understand *dhamma* taught by the Lord, it is no easy matter for one living in a house to fare the Brahma-faring completely fulfilled, completely pure and polished like a conch-shell. Suppose that I, having cut off hair and beard, having donned saffron garments, should go forth from home into homelessness?"

Then the brahmans and householders of Thullakoṭṭhita, gladdened, roused, incited and delighted by the Lord's talk on *dhamma*, rejoicing

[1] At *A.* ii. 24 called chief of those gone forth from faith.

[2] The story of Raṭṭhapāla's efforts to be ordained and of the events immediately following is very similar to the story of Sudinna at *Vin.* iii. 12 *ff.* There are also some interesting variations.

in what the Lord had said and giving thanks for it, [**56**] rising from their seats and greeting the Lord, departed keeping their right sides towards him. And not long after the brahmans and householders of Thullakoṭṭhita had departed, Raṭṭhapāla, the young man of family, approached the Lord; having approached, having greeted the Lord, he sat down at a respectful distance; sitting down at a respectful distance, he spoke thus to the Lord:

"In so far as I, revered sir, understand *dhamma* taught by the Lord, it is no easy matter for one living in a house to fare the Brahma-faring completely fulfilled, completely pure and polished like a conch-shell. I wish, revered sir, having cut off hair and beard, having donned saffron garments, to go forth from home into homelessness. May I, revered sir, receive the going forth in the Lord's presence, may I receive ordination."

"But have you, Raṭṭhapāla, your parents, consent for going forth from home into homelessness?"

"I have not, revered sir, the consent of my parents for going forth from home into homelessness."

"Raṭṭhapāla, Tathāgatas do not allow (one[1]) to go forth without the consent of the parents."

"I, revered sir, will do whatever is necessary so that my parents will consent to my going forth from home into homelessness."

Then Raṭṭhapāla, the young man of family, having greeted the Lord keeping his right side towards him, rising from his seat approached his parents; having approached, he spoke thus to his parents:

"Mother and father, in so far as I understand *dhamma* taught by the Lord, it is no easy matter for one living in a house to fare the Brahma-faring completely fulfilled, completely pure, and polished like a conch-shell. I wish, having cut off hair and beard, having donned saffron garments, to go forth from home into homelessness. Consent to my going forth from home into homelessness."

When this had been said, the parents of Raṭṭhapāla, the young man of family, spoke thus to him: "You, dear Raṭṭhapāla, are our only child, dear and beloved, you live in comfort and are well cared for; you, dear Raṭṭhapāla, do not know anything of suffering. Come you, dear Raṭṭhapāla, eat [**57**] and drink and amuse yourself; eating, drinking and amusing yourself, you can enjoy diverting yourself with sense-pleasures and doing meritorious things. We do not consent

---

1 *puttaṁ*, of *Vin.* iii. 12 (and *cf. Vin.* i. 83) is omitted here, perhaps because Raṭṭhapāla was at this time rather more than a child.

that you should go forth from home into homelessness. If you were to die we should be desolate without you. How could we, while you are living, consent to your going forth from home into homelessness?"

And a second time . . . And a third time Raṭṭhapāla, the young man of family, spoke thus to his parents: "Mother and father, in so far as I understand *dhamma* . . . Consent to my going forth from home into homelessness." And a second . . . And a third time the parents of Raṭṭhapāla, the young man of family, spoke thus to him: "You, dear Raṭṭhapāla, are our only child . . . How could we, while you are living, consent to your going forth from home into homelessness?"

Then Raṭṭhapāla, the young man of family, not receiving his parents' consent, lay down there on the bare ground and said: "Here will there be death for me or going forth."

[**58**] Then the parents of Raṭṭhapāla, the young man of family, spoke thus to him: "You, dear Raṭṭhapāla, are our only child, dear and beloved, you live in comfort and are well cared for; you, dear Raṭṭhapāla, do not know anything of suffering. Get up, dear Raṭṭhapāla, eat and drink and amuse yourself; eating, drinking, amusing yourself you can enjoy diverting yourself with sense-pleasures and doing meritorious things. We do not consent that you should go forth from home into homelessness. If you were to die we should be desolate without you. How could we, while you are living, consent to your going forth from home into homelessness?"

When this had been said, Raṭṭhapāla, the young man of family, was silent. And a second . . . And a third time the parents of Raṭṭhapāla, the young man of family, spoke thus to him: "You, dear Raṭṭhapāla, are our only child . . . How could we, while you are living, consent to your going forth from home into homelessness?" And a second . . . And a third time Raṭṭhapāla, the young man of family, was silent.

Then the parents of Raṭṭhapāla, the young man of family, approached his friends; having approached, they spoke thus to them: "This Raṭṭhapāla, the young man of family, is lying down on the bare ground, dears, and saying: 'Here will there be death for me or going forth.' Come, dears, approach Raṭṭhapāla, the young man of family; having approached, speak thus to him: 'You, good Raṭṭhapāla, are your parents' only child, dear and beloved, you live in comfort and are well cared for; you, good Raṭṭhapāla, do not know anything of suffering. Get up, good Raṭṭhapāla, eat and drink and amuse yourself; eating, drinking and amusing yourself, you can enjoy diverting yourself with sense-pleasures and doing meritorious things. Your parents do not consent that you should go forth from home into homelessness. If you were to die your parents would be desolate [**59**] without you. How can they, while you are living, consent to your going forth from home into homelessness ?' "

Then the friends of Raṭṭhapāla, the young man of family, having answered his parents in assent, approached Raṭṭhapāla, the young man of family; and having approached, they spoke thus to him: " You, good Raṭṭhapāla, are your parents' only child . . . How can they, while you are living, consent to your going forth from home into homelessness ?" When this had been said, Raṭṭhapāla, the young man of family, was silent. And a second. . . And a third time did the friends of Raṭṭhapāla, the young man of family, speak thus to him: " You, good Raṭṭhapāla, are your parents' only child . . . How can they, while you are living, consent to your going forth from home into homelessness ?" And a second . . . And a third time, Raṭṭhapāla, the young man of family, was silent.

Then the friends of Raṭṭhapāla, the young man of family, approached his parents; and having approached, they spoke thus to them: " Mother and father, this Raṭṭhapāla, the young man of family, is lying on the bare ground there saying: ' Here will there be death for me or going forth.' [**60**] If you do not consent that Raṭṭhapāla, the young man of family, should go forth from home into homelessness, he will die there. But if you consent to his going forth from home into homelessness, after he has gone forth you may see him again. If Raṭṭhapāla, the young man of family, does not enjoy the going forth from home into homelessness, what alternative will there be for him ? He will come back here. Consent to the going forth from home into homelessness of Raṭṭhapāla, the young man of family."

" We consent, dears, to the going forth from home into homelessness of Raṭṭhapāla, the young man of family. But after he has gone forth, he must come and see us."

Then the friends of Raṭṭhapāla, the young man of family, approached him; and having approached, they spoke thus to him: " You, good Raṭṭhapāla, are your parents' only child, dear and beloved, you live in comfort and are well cared for; you, good Raṭṭhapāla, do not know anything of suffering. Get up, eat and drink and amuse yourself; eating, drinking and amusing yourself, you can enjoy diverting yourself with sense-pleasures and doing meritorious things. Your parents have consented to your going forth from home into homelessness, but after you have gone forth you must see your parents."

Then Raṭṭhapāla, the young man of family, having got up and regained his strength, approached the Lord; having approached, having greeted the Lord, he sat down at a respectful distance. As he was sitting down at a respectful distance, Raṭṭhapāla, the young man of family, spoke thus to the Lord: " I, revered sir, have my parents' consent for the going forth from home into homelessness. May the Lord let me go forth." Raṭṭhapāla, the young man of family, received the going forth in the Lord's presence, he received ordination.

Not long after the venerable Raṭṭhapāla had been ordained—half a month after he had been ordained—the Lord, having stayed for as long as he found suitable in Thullakoṭṭhita, set out on tour for Sāvatthī; and in due course, walking on tour, he arrived at Sāvatthī. While he was there [**61**] the Lord stayed near Sāvatthī in the Jeta Grove in Anāthapiṇḍika's monastery. Then the venerable Raṭṭhapāla, dwelling alone, aloof, diligent, ardent, self-resolute, having soon realised here and now by his own super-knowledge that incomparable goal of the Brahma-faring for the sake of which young men of family rightly go forth from home into homelessness, entering on it, he abided in it. And he knew: " Destroyed is birth, brought to a close the Brahma-faring, done is what was to be done, there is no more of being such or so." And the venerable Raṭṭhapāla was one of the perfected ones.

Then the venerable Raṭṭhapāla approached the Lord; having approached, having greeted the Lord, he sat down at a respectful distance. As he was sitting down at a respectful distance, the venerable Raṭṭhapāla spoke thus to the Lord: " I want, revered sir, to see my parents, if the Lord allows me."

Then the Lord with his mind carefully reflected on the venerable Raṭṭhapāla's reasoning of mind. When the Lord knew that it was impossible for the venerable Raṭṭhapāla, throwing off the training, to return to the secular life, then the Lord spoke thus to the venerable Raṭṭhapāla: " Do now, Raṭṭhapāla, that for which you think it is the right time."

Then the venerable Raṭṭhapāla, rising from his seat, having greeted the Lord keeping his right side towards him, having packed away his bedding, set out on tour for Thullakoṭṭhita taking his bowl and robe; and in due course, walking on tour, he arrived at Thullakoṭṭhita.

While he was there, the venerable Raṭṭhapāla stayed near Thullakoṭṭhita in the deer-park of the Kuru king. Then the venerable Raṭṭhapāla, dressing in the morning, taking his bowl and robe, entered Thullakoṭṭhita for almsfood; while he was walking on an uninterrupted round for almsfood, he approached his own parents' house. Now at that time the venerable Raṭṭhapāla's father was having his hair combed in the middle hall which had a door.[1] He saw the venerable Raṭṭhapāla coming in the distance, and seeing him, he spoke thus: " Our only son, dear and beloved, has gone forth among these shaveling recluses." [**62**] And the venerable Raṭṭhapāla received neither alms nor a refusal[2] at his own father's house; all he received was abuse.

Now at that time the woman slave of the venerable Rāṭṭhapāla's relations wanted to throw away the previous evening's barley-gruel. But the venerable Raṭṭhapāla spoke thus to her: " If that, sister, is to be thrown away, put it here in my bowl." Then as the woman slave of the venerable Raṭṭhapāla's relations was putting the previous evening's barley-gruel into his bowl she recognised his hands and feet and voice. So the woman slave of the venerable Raṭṭhapāla's relations approached his mother, and having approached, she spoke thus to her: " If it please you, madam, you should know that the young master Raṭṭhapāla is back."

" Now then, if you speak the truth, you are a freed woman." Then the venerable Raṭṭhapāla's mother approached his father; and having approached, she spoke thus to his father: " If it please you, householder, you should know that Raṭṭhapāla, the young man of family, is indeed back."

Now at that time the venerable Raṭṭhapāla was eating the previous evening's barley-gruel in a room provided for the purpose.[3] Then the venerable Raṭṭhapāla's father approached him; having approached, he spoke thus to him: " Can it be, dear Raṭṭhapāla,

---

[1] *MA*. iii. 295 says: at the porch of the door in the middle of a house with seven porched doors. See above, p. 47.

[2] A refusal would mean that without waiting longer the bhikkhu could pass on to the next house; and might receive the necessary alms there.

[3] *kuḍḍaṁ nissāya*. Perhaps " leaning against a wall." But *MA*. iii. 297 says " in that district there were halls in benefactors' houses, where seats were prepared and vessels of water, and where those who had gone forth sat down and ate when they were walking for alms. . . . For those who have gone forth do not sit down to eat in unsuitable places as do beggars." The exact meaning of *kuḍḍa* (v.l. *kuṭṭa, kuḍḍa-* and *kuṭṭamūla*) in this passage is however not clear.

that you are eating last evening's barley-gruel? Surely, dear Raṭṭhapāla, you should come into your own home?"

"Where, householder, is there a home for us who have gone forth from home into homelessness? We are houseless ones, householder. I did come [**63**] to your home, householder; but I received neither alms there nor a refusal; all I received was abuse."

"Come, dear Raṭṭhapāla, we will go to the house."

"No, householder, I have done with eating for today."

"Well then, dear Raṭṭhapāla, consent to a meal on the morrow."

The venerable Raṭṭhapāla consented by becoming silent. And when the venerable Raṭṭhapāla's father had understood that he had consented, he went up to his own dwelling; and having gone there, he had a great heap made of gold coins and gold, and having had them hidden with screens, he summoned the venerable Raṭṭhapāla's former wives, and said: "Come you, daughters-in-law, adorn yourselves with the adornments adorned with which you used to be dear to Raṭṭhapāla, the young man of family, and beloved by him." And towards the end of that night the venerable Raṭṭhapāla's father, having had sumptuous foods, solid and soft, prepared in his own dwelling, had the time announced to the venerable Raṭṭhapāla, saying: "It is time, dear Raṭṭhapāla, the meal is ready." Then the venerable Raṭṭhapāla, having dressed in the morning, taking his bowl and robe, approached his own father's dwelling; having approached, he sat down on the seat made ready. And the venerable Raṭṭhapāla's father, having had that heap of gold coins and gold uncovered, spoke thus to the venerable Raṭṭhapāla:

"This, dear Raṭṭhapāla, is your mother's wealth, the other is your father's, the other your paternal grandfather's.[1] It is possible, dear Raṭṭhapāla, both to enjoy riches and do meritorious things. Come you, dear [**64**] Raṭṭhapāla, throwing off the training and returning to the secular life, enjoy riches and do meritorious things."

"If you, householder, would do my bidding, having loaded this heap of gold coins and gold into wagons, and then having had it brought down, you would have it dropped in the middle stream of the river Ganges. What is the reason for this? It is from that source, householder, that there will arise for you grief, sorrow, suffering, lamentation and despair."

Taking hold of his feet, the venerable Raṭṭhapāla's former wives

---

[1] *pitāmahaṁ*, perhaps more exactly "ancestors'."

then spoke thus to him: " Now, young master, of what kind are those nymphs for whose sake you fare the Brahma-faring ?"

" We, sisters, do not fare the Brahma-faring for the sake of nymphs."

Saying, " The young master Raṭṭhapāla addresses us with the word ' sisters,' " they fell down fainting just there. Then the venerable Raṭṭhapāla spoke thus to his father:

" If you would give food, householder, give it; but do not annoy us."

" Eat, dear Raṭṭhapāla, the meal is ready." Then the venerable Raṭṭhapāla's father with his own hand served and satisfied the venerable Raṭṭhapāla with sumptuous food, solid and soft. And when the venerable Raṭṭhapāla had eaten and had withdrawn his hand from the bowl, standing he spoke these verses:[1]

" See[2] the pranked-out puppet-shape,[3] a mass of sores, a congeries,[4]
afflicted, much thought of,[5] for which there is never stability.

See the pranked-out form with jewels and rings,
the bones sheathed in skin, resplendent with the clothes,

The feet dyed with lac, the face with powder smeared—
enough for delusion of a fool, but not for the quester of the Beyond.

[**65**] Hair braided eightfold, eyes with collyrium smeared—
enough for delusion of a fool, but not for the quester of the Beyond.

Like a new collyrium-box, embossed, is the foul body, adorned—
enough for delusion of a fool, but not for the quester of the Beyond.

The trapper set a snare; the deer touched not the net.
Having eaten the crop, we go while the deer-catchers lament."

---

[1] Verses as at *Thag.* 769-774, there also ascribed to Raṭṭhapāla. The remainder of his verses are at *M.* ii. 72-74 (*Thag.* 776-788), with the exception of *Thag.* ver. 775, 789-793 which occur only there.

[2] This verse also occurs at *Dhp.* 147, being spoken, according to *DhA.* iii. 104 on account of Sirimā, the beautiful courtesan of Rājagaha.

[3] *bimba*, a shape, image; *cf. S.* i. 134. *MA.* iii. 301=*DhA.* iii. 109= *ThagA.* explain by *attabhāva*.

[4] *samussitaṁ*. *MA.* iii. 302 says that, with 300 bones, held together by 900 sinews, smeared with 900 lumps of flesh, it is built up (*ussita*, erected?) on every side.

[5] *bahusaṁkappaṁ*, by others.

After the venerable Raṭṭhapāla had spoken these verses while he was standing, he approached the deer-park of the Kuru king;[1] having approached, he sat down for the day-sojourn at the root of a tree.

Then the Kuru king addressed a trapper,[2] saying: "Clear a pleasure-ground, good trapper, in the deer-park; we will go to see the lovely ground."

"Yes, sire," and when the trapper had answered the Kuru king in assent, he saw, while he was clearing the deer-park, the venerable Raṭṭhapāla sitting down for the day-sojourn at the root of a tree; on seeing him, he approached the Kuru king, and having approached, he spoke thus to him;

"Sire, the deer-park is cleared; but there is the young man of family, Raṭṭhapāla, the son of a leading family near this very Thullakoṭṭhita, and whom you have constantly praised, sitting at the root of a tree for the day-sojourn."

"Well then, good trapper, no more now today of the pleasure-ground, but we will now at once pay respects to the revered Raṭṭhapāla," and when he had said: "Give away all the solid and soft food that has been prepared," he had many lovely vehicles harnessed, and having mounted a lovely vehicle, he set forth from Thullakoṭṭhita in great royal pomp with the many lovely vehicles so as to see the venerable Raṭṭhapāla. Having gone by vehicle for as far as the ground was passable, and having then descended from the vehicle, with his princely train he approached the venerable Raṭṭhapāla on foot; having approached, [**66**] he exchanged greetings with the venerable Raṭṭhapāla; and having conversed in a friendly and courteous way, he stood at a respectful distance. As he was standing at a respectful distance, the Kuru king spoke thus to the venerable Raṭṭhapāla:

"Let the revered Raṭṭhapāla sit down here on the elephant-rug."[3]

---

[1] *rājā Koravyo,* It is not clear whether Koravya was his personal name or a generic name of the king of the Kurus. See *DPPN.* s.v. Korabya.

[2] *migava.* *MA.* iii. 304 says this is the name of the keeper of the pleasaunce. If so, his name was derived from his occupation. The same word has already occurred in the first line of the last verse above, and there in no way seems to be a proper name. Chalmers translates as "huntsman." As a proper name *migava* is not included in *DPPN.* Moreover, in Pali, a proper name is usually further defined to show who the person was: brahman, householder, king and so on.

[3] As at *M.* ii. 113. Had the word *hatthatthara* not been translated as "clump of flowers" by Chalmers, it would have needed no comment. As it is,

"No, sire; you sit down, I am sitting on a seat of my own." The Kuru king sat down on the prepared seat; while he was sitting down the Kuru king spoke thus to the venerable Raṭṭhapāla:

"Good Raṭṭhapāla, there are these four kinds of loss followed by which some (men) here, having cut off hair and beard, having donned saffron garments, go forth from home into homelessness. What are the four? Loss through old age, loss through illness, loss of wealth, loss of relations. And what, good Raṭṭhapāla, is loss through old age? As to this, good Raṭṭhapāla, someone is worn, old, full of years, has lived his span and is at the close of his life. He reflects thus: 'I am now worn, old, full of years, I have lived my span and am at the close of my life, so it is not easy for me to acquire wealth not already acquired or to use to advantage the wealth already acquired. Suppose that I, having cut off hair and beard, having donned saffron garments, should go forth from home into homelessness?' So he that is followed by this loss through old age, having cut off hair and beard, having donned saffron garments, goes forth from home into homelessness. Good Raṭṭhapāla, this is called loss through old age. But the revered Raṭṭhapāla is still young, endowed with the coal-black hair of radiant youth, in his early prime, and there is none of this loss through old age for the revered Raṭṭhapāla. What has the good Raṭṭhapāla known or seen or heard that he has gone forth from home into homelessness?

And what, good Raṭṭhapāla, is loss through illness? As to this, good Raṭṭhapāla, someone is ill, in pain, grievously ill. He reflects thus: 'I am now ill, in pain, grievously ill, so it is not easy for me to acquire wealth not already acquired or to use to advantage the wealth already acquired. [**67**] Suppose . . . (*as above*) . . .' So he that is followed by this loss through illness . . . goes forth from home into homelessness. Good Raṭṭhapāla, this is called loss through illness. But the revered Raṭṭhapāla is still free from illness, not ailing, possessed of a good digestion that is neither too cold nor too hot, and there is none of this loss through illness for the revered Raṭṭhapāla. What has the good Raṭṭhapāla known or seen or heard that he has gone forth from home into homelessness?

And what, good Raṭṭhapāla, is loss of wealth? As to this, good

---

it must be noticed that at *Vin.* i. 192, *D.* i. 7, *A.* i. 181 it is in a sequence with *assatthara rathatthara*, horse-rug, chariot-rug, and therefore appears to be elephant-rug. *MA.* iii. 305 says that a thin "elephant-rug" filled with flowers (? *bahalapuppho*) having been folded double, is spread and indicated (*abhilakkhita*, distinguished) for it would not be suitable to sit on it uninvited.

Raṭṭhapāla, someone is rich, of great possessions, very wealthy, but gradually these riches of his diminish. He reflects thus: 'Formerly I was rich, of great possessions, very wealthy, but gradually these riches of mine have diminished, so it is not easy for me to acquire wealth . . . (*as above*) . . .' So he that is followed by this loss of wealth . . . goes forth from home into homelessness. Good Raṭṭhapāla, this is called loss of wealth. But the revered Raṭṭhapāla is the son of a leading family in this very Thullakoṭṭhita, and there is none of this loss of wealth for the revered Raṭṭhapāla. What has the good Raṭṭhapāla known or seen or heard that he has gone forth from home into homelessness?

And what, good Raṭṭhapāla, is loss of relations? As to this, good Raṭṭhapāla, someone has many friends and acquaintances, kith and kin, but gradually these relations of his diminish. He reflects thus: 'Formerly I had many friends and acquaintances, kith and kin, but gradually these relations of mine have diminished, so it is not easy for me to acquire wealth . . . (*as above*) . . .' **[68]** So he that is followed by this loss of relations, having cut off hair and beard, having donned saffron garments, goes forth from home into homelessness. Good Raṭṭhapāla, this is called loss of relations. But the revered Raṭṭhapāla has many friends and acquaintances, kith and kin, in this very Thullakoṭṭhita, and there is none of this loss of relations for the revered Raṭṭhapāla. What has the good Raṭṭhapāla known or seen or heard that he has gone forth from home into homelessness?

These, good Raṭṭhapāla, are the four kinds of loss followed by which some (men) here, having cut off hair and beard, having donned saffron garments, go forth from home into homelessness. But there are none of these for the revered Raṭṭhapāla. What has the good Raṭṭhapāla known or seen or heard that he has gone forth from home into homelessness?"

"There are, sire, four expoundings of *dhamma* expounded by the Lord who knows, who sees, perfected one, fully Self-Awakened One; because I have known and seen and heard these I have gone forth from home into homelessness. What are the four? The first expounding of *dhamma* expounded by the Lord . . . fully Self-Awakened One is that: 'The instable world is brought to an end.'[1] Because I have known and seen and heard this I have gone forth

---

[1] *Upanīyati loko addhuvo.* On *upanīyati*, to be led, driven, to be carried on or away, see *K.S.* i. 4, *n.* 1.

from home into homelessness. The second expounding of *dhamma* expounded by the Lord . . . fully Self-Awakened One is that: 'The world is no refuge, no guard' . . . The third expounding of *dhamma* expounded by the Lord . . . fully Self-Awakened One is that: 'The world is not one's own, one must go leaving everything.' . . . The fourth expounding of *dhamma* expounded by the Lord who knows, who sees, perfected one, fully Self-Awakened One is that: 'The world lacks and is unsatisfied, a slave to craving.' Because I have known and seen and heard this I have gone forth from home into homelessness. These, sire, are the four expoundings of *dhamma* expounded by the Lord who knows, who sees, perfected one, fully [**69**] Self-Awakened One; because I have known and seen and heard these I have gone forth from home into homelessness."

"The good Raṭṭhapāla says: 'The instable world is brought to an end.' But how is the meaning of this saying to be understood, good Raṭṭhapāla?"

"What do you think about this, sire? Were you, at the age of twenty or twenty-five, expert in (handling) an elephant and a horse and a chariot and a bow and a sword, strong of leg and arm, able[1] and proficient in warfare?"

"I, good Raṭṭhapāla, at the age of twenty or twenty-five, was expert in (handling) an elephant and a horse and a chariot and a bow and a sword, I was strong of leg and arm, able and proficient in warfare; methinks I was sometimes inspired; I saw none equal to myself in strength."

"What do you think about this, sire? Are you still so strong in leg and arm, able and proficient in warfare?"

"No, good Raṭṭhapāla, I am now worn, old, full of years, I have lived my span and am at the close of my life—round eighty years of age. Sometimes, good Raṭṭhapāla, when I want to take a step in one direction I step in another."[2]

"It was in reference to this, sire, that the Lord who knows, who sees, perfected one, fully Self-Awakened One, said: 'The instable

---

[1] Reading *alamatto* with the text, other versions and *MA*. iii. 307 against one tentative v.l. and *PED*. which read, as in other contexts, *alamattho*. The meaning in each case however seems to be *samattho* (as also at *DA*. 660), to which at *MA*. iii. 307 is added *attabhāvo*, the individual. *Samattha-atta-bhāva* would therefore mean: "the individual is sufficient unto himself," self-reliant, self-sufficient, which also could be taken as a meaning of *alam-atta*, "self is enough."

[2] *Cf*. *DhA*. i. 7 *mahallakassa* . . . *hatthapādā anassavā honti*, an old man's arms and legs are disobedient.

world is brought to an end.' Because I have known and seen and heard this I have gone forth from home into homelessness."

"It is wonderful, good Raṭṭhapāla, it is marvellous, good Raṭṭhapāla, that this was so well spoken by the Lord who knows, who sees, perfected one, fully Self-Awakened One, that: 'The instable world is brought to an end.' For, good Raṭṭhapāla, the instable world is brought to an end. Now, good Raṭṭhapāla, in this royal family are squadrons of elephants and squadrons of horses and squadrons of chariots and squadrons of infantry which, if we were in distress, **[70]** would defend us.[1] The good Raṭṭhapāla says: 'The world is no refuge, no guard.' But how is the meaning of this saying to be understood, good Raṭṭhapāla?"

"What do you think about this, sire? Have you any chronic illness?"

"I have a chronic illness of wind, good Raṭṭhapāla. Sometimes friends and acquaintances, kith and kin stand round me, saying: 'Now the Kuru king will pass away, now the Kuru king will pass away.'"

"What do you think about this, sire? Would you be able to say to friends and acquaintances, kith and kin: 'Let the good friends and acquaintances, kith and kin, ease my pain, let them all share this feeling so that I could experience a more buoyant feeling?' Or do you have to experience that feeling alone?"

"I, good Raṭṭhapāla, am not able to say to friends and acquaintances, kith and kin: . . . (*as above*) . . . So I have to experience that feeling alone."

"It was in reference to this, sire, that the Lord who knows, who sees, perfected one, fully Self-Awakened One, said: 'The world is no refuge, no guard.' Because I have known and seen and heard this, I have gone forth from home into homelessness."

"It is wonderful, good Raṭṭhapāla, it is marvellous, good Raṭṭhapāla, that this was so well spoken by the Lord who knows, who sees, perfected one, fully Self-Awakened One, that: 'The world is no refuge, no guard.' For, good Raṭṭhapāla, the world is no refuge, no guard. Now, Raṭṭhapāla, in this royal family is an abundance of gold coins and gold, both in the ground and above it.[2] The good

---

[1] *pariyodhāya vattissanti*. *Cf. S.* i. 72-73 where the Buddhist view is given: that however many squadrons might guard (*rakkhanti*) a person, yet *attā* (self) is not guarded by them, *tesam arakkhito attā*; for theirs is merely an outer guard, not an inner.

[2] *vehāsaṭṭha* (with v.l. *vehāsagata*) as at *Vin.* iii. 48. See *B.D.* i. p. 79, *n.* 6 for further references.

Raṭṭhapāla says: 'The world is not one's own, one must go leaving everything.' But how is the meaning of this saying to be understood, good Raṭṭhapāla?"

"What do you think about this, sire? Although you at present [71] divert yourself endowed with and possessed of the five strands of sense-pleasures, will you hereafter be able to say: 'Even so am I diverting myself endowed with and possessed of these same five strands of sense-pleasures?' Or will others come into this wealth while you go on according to *kamma*?"

"Although I at present, dear Raṭṭhapāla, divert myself . . . I will not hereafter be able to say: 'Even so am I diverting myself endowed with and possessed of these same five strands of sense-pleasures.' So others will come into this wealth while I go on according to *kamma*."

"It was in reference to this, sire, that the Lord who knows, who sees, perfected one, fully Self-Awakened One, said: 'The world is not one's own, one must go leaving everything.' Because I have known and seen and heard this, I have gone forth from home into homelessness."

"It is wonderful, good Raṭṭhapāla, it is marvellous, good Raṭṭhapāla, that this was so well spoken by the Lord who knows, who sees, perfected one, fully Self-Awakened One, that: 'The world is not one's own, one must go leaving everything.' For, good Raṭṭhapāla, the world is not one's own, one must go leaving everything. Now, the good Raṭṭhapāla says: 'The world lacks and is unsatisfied, a slave to craving.' But how is the meaning of this saying to be understood, good Raṭṭhapāla?"

"What do you think about this, sire? Is the Kuru you dwell in as master,[1] prosperous?"

"Yes, good Raṭṭhapāla, the Kuru I dwell in as master is prosperous."

"What do you think about this, sire? If a trustworthy, reliable man were to come to you here from the east and having approached you should say: 'If it please you, sire, you should know that I am coming from the east, and have seen a great country there, rich, prosperous, thronged with people; there were many squadrons of elephants there, squadrons of horses, squadrons of chariots, squadrons of infantry; there is much ivory there, much gold both unwrought

---

[1] *ajjhāvasati*. *Cf. Jā.* vi. 273, where koravya is explained as Kururaṭṭhavāsika, a dweller in the Kuru kingdom.

and wrought, many women are there. And it is possible to conquer it with such and such a force. Conquer it, sire.' What would you do ?"

[72] "When I had conquered it, good Raṭṭhapāla, I should dwell in it as master."

"What do you think about this, sire ? If a trustworthy, reliable man were to come to you here from the west . . . the north . . . the south, and having approached you, should say: . . . (*as above, reading* west, north, south, *for* east) . . . What would you do ?"

"When I had conquered it, good Raṭṭhapāla, I should dwell in it as master."

"It was in reference to this, sire, that the Lord who knows, who sees, perfected one, fully Self-Awakened One, said: 'The world lacks and is unsatisfied, a slave to craving.' Because I have known and seen and heard this, I have gone forth from home into homelessness."

"It is wonderful, good Raṭṭhapāla, it is marvellous, good Raṭṭhapāla, that this was so well spoken by the Lord who knows, who sees, perfected one, fully Self-Awakened One, that: 'The world lacks and is unsatisfied, a slave to craving.' For, good Raṭṭhapāla, the world lacks, it is unsatisfied, it is a slave to craving."

The venerable Raṭṭhapāla said this; having said this, he further spoke thus:[1]

"I see men of wealth in the world—
acquiring property, from delusion they give not away;
out of greed a hoard of wealth they make,
and hanker sorely after more sense-pleasures.

A king, having forcibly conquered the earth,
inhabiting a land with the ocean its confines,
not satisfied with this side of the sea
hankers after the sea's further side too.

[73] Kings and full many another man
come to their dying their cravings not gone;

[1] In the following unmetrical rendering, I have attempted to be more exactly literal than either Mrs. Rhys Davids or Lord Chalmers. Otherwise I would have followed one or other of these beautiful versions, the former to be found in *Pss. Breth.*, and the latter in *Fur. Dial.* ii., and both of which I have found very helpful.

as those that still lack they put off the body;
yet in the world is no satisfaction in sense-pleasures.[1]

Letting down their hair, kinsmen bewail him
and say: ' Alas, he is not undying.'
Bearing him wrapped in a shroud,
kindling a pyre, they cremate him then.

Being prodded by stakes, he burns
in the one garment, riches got rid of.
Not to one who is dying are kinsfolk a refuge
any more than are friends or intimates here.

Heirs carry off his wealth;
but the being goes on according to *kamma*.
Wealth does not follow him who is dying,
nor child or wife, nor wealth or kingdom.

Long life is not gained from wealth,
nor is old age banished by property.
' For brief is this life,' the wise say,
non-eternal, subject to change.

Rich and poor feel the touch,[2]
fool and wise are touched alike.
But the fool, as though struck down by folly, prostrate lies,
while the wise, touched by the touch, trembles not.

Wherefore better than wealth is wisdom
by which one here secures accomplishment.[3]
Not being accomplished in this becoming or that,[4]
they do evil deeds from delusion.

---

[1] Meaning, I think, that they cannot be satiated.

[2] *phusanti phassaṁ*, *i.e.* they touch the touch, namely of dying, *maraṇa-phassa*, *MA*. iii. 308.

[3] *I.e.* arahantship.

[4] *bhavâbhavesu*, explained at *MA*. iii. 308 as " in low and excellent becomings," and at *ThagA*. as *mahantâmantesu bhavesu*. *Bhavâbhava* also occurs at *Sn*. 1060, 1068; and at *ThīgA*. 71, *saṁsaranto bhavâbhave;* it means in the various becomings. *Cf*. *phalâphala*, a variety, or all kinds, of fruit.

He comes to a womb and to another world,
being bound to *saṁsāra*,[1] in a successive (round);
one of little wisdom, having faith in him,
comes to a womb and to another world.

[74] As a thief of evil nature, caught in the act
of breaking in, is ruined[2] by his own *kamma*,
so the race, of evil nature, is hereafter,
in another world, ruined by its own *kamma*.

Divers sweet, delightful sense-pleasures
in various ways disturb the mind;
having seen the peril in sense-pleasures,
I, O sire, have therefore gone forth.

As fruits from the tree, so fall men,
both young and old, on the break up of the body.
Having seen[3] this too, I have gone forth, sire.
Better indeed is sure recluseship."

Discourse with Raṭṭhapāla:
The Second

83. DISCOURSE ON MAKHĀDEVA[4]

(Makhādevasutta)

THUS have I heard: At one time the Lord was staying near Mithilā in Makhādeva's Mango Grove.[5] Then the Lord smiled (when he

---

[1] *saṁsāram āpajja*, undergoes, experiences, produces *saṁsāra*. *Cf. S.* i. 37, 38, *satto saṁsāram āpādi*.

[2] *haññati*, is struck, hit, killed, destroyed.

[3] In answer to the king's questions, put in the narrative part of this Discourse, Raṭṭhapāla now tells him what he has seen and heard to make him go forth.

[4] *Cf. Makhādevajātaka*, No. 9, and *Nimijātaka*, No. 541.

[5] This Grove was originally planted by Makhādeva, and although other kings replaced trees that had died, the Grove was known by its early name, *MA*. iii. 309.

came to a) certain place. Then it occurred to the venerable Ānanda: "What is the cause, what the reason that the Lord is smiling? Not without motive do Tathāgatas smile." Then the venerable Ānanda, having arranged his robe over one shoulder, having saluted the Lord with joined palms, spoke thus to the Lord: "Now, revered sir, what is the cause, what the reason that the Lord is smiling? Not without motive do Tathāgatas smile."[1]

"Once upon a time, Ānanda, in this very Mithilā there was a king named Makhādeva, a *dhamma*-man, a king under *dhamma*, firm in *dhamma*, a great king who fared by *dhamma* among brahmans and householders, townsfolk and countryfolk, and who observed the Observance on the fourteenth, [75] fifteenth and eighth days of the half-month.[2] Then, Ānanda, at the end of many years, many hundreds of years, many thousands of years, King Makhādeva addressed his barber, saying: 'When, good barber, you see grey hairs growing on my head, then you may tell me.' Ānanda, the barber answered King Makhādeva in assent, saying, 'Yes, sire.' Then, Ānanda, at the end of many years, many hundreds of years, many thousands of years, the barber saw grey hairs growing on King Makhādeva's head. Seeing that, Ānanda, he spoke thus to King Makhādeva: 'Death's messengers[3] have appeared to his majesty; grey hairs are to be seen growing on his head.'

'Well then, good barber, when you have pulled out those grey hairs properly with the tweezers, place them on my fingers.'

'Yes, your majesty.' And when, Ānanda, the barber had answered King Makhādeva in assent, he pulled out the grey hairs properly with the tweezers and placed them on King Makhādeva's fingers. And, Ānanda, King Makhādeva, having given the boon of a village to the barber, had the prince who was his eldest son summoned and spoke thus:

'Dear Prince, Death's messengers have appeared to me; grey hairs are to be seen growing on my head. Human sense-pleasures

---

[1] *Cf. M.* Sta. 81.

[2] At *Vin.* i. 101 it is recorded that wanderers belonging to other sects gathered together on these days so as to speak *dhamma*. Buddhist monks were then allowed (by the Lord) to do the same, and a new ruling was subsequently introduced allowing them to recite the Pātimokkha, or Observance (recently devised by the Teacher) once in every half-month. *Vin.* i. 104. (See *B.D.* iv. 130 *ff.*).

[3] *devadūtā*. *MA.* iii. 310 says "the *deva* is death (*maccu*); his messengers are *devadūtā*." *Cf. Devadūta-Sutta, M.* Sta. No. 130; and *Devadūtavagga* at *A.* i. 132 *ff.*

have been enjoyed by me; it is now time to seek *deva*-like sense-pleasures. Come you, dear Prince, rule this kingdom. For I, having cut off my hair and beard, having donned saffron garments, will go forth from home into homelessness. And now, dear Prince, when you too see grey hairs growing on your head, then, having given the boon of a village to the barber, having handed over the kingdom properly to the prince who is your eldest son, having cut off your hair and beard, having donned saffron garments, you should go forth from home into homelessness. This lovely custom founded by me you should maintain; do not you be the last man after me. Dear Prince, while two persons exist and there is a breaking of such a lovely custom, whichever of these (breaks it) he is the last man.[1] So I, dear Prince, speak thus to you: This lovely [**76**] custom founded by me you should maintain; do not you be the last man after me.'

Then, Ānanda, King Makhādeva, having given the boon of the village to the barber, having handed over the kingdom properly to the prince who was his eldest son, having in this very Makhādeva Mango Grove cut off his hair and beard, having donned saffron garments, went forth from home into homelessness. He dwelt, having suffused the first quarter with a mind of friendliness, likewise the second, likewise the third, likewise the fourth; just so above, below, across; he dwelt having suffused the whole world everywhere, in every way, with a mind of friendliness that was far-reaching, wide-spread, immeasurable, without enmity, without malevolence. He dwelt having suffused the first quarter with a mind of compassion . . . sympathetic joy . . . equanimity . . . that was far-reaching, wide-spread, immeasurable, without enmity, without malevolence. But, Ānanda, King Makhādeva had played at boys' sports[2] for 84,000 years, had ruled as a viceroy[3] for 84,000 years, and had ruled as a king for 84,000 years; for 84,000 years, gone forth from home into homelessness in this very Makhādeva Mango Grove, he fared the Brahma-faring. He, having developed the four Brahma-abidings, was one who at the breaking up of the body after dying reached the Brahma-world.

And, Ānanda, at the end of many years, many hundreds of years, many thousands of years, King Makhādeva's son addressed his barber . . . (*as above, reading* King Makhādeva's son *throughout*) . . . [**77**] . . . [**78**] He, having developed the four Brahma-abidings, was

[1] Chalmers has " he who breaks it is the last of the line."

[2] *Cf.* with Mahāsudassana at *D.* ii. 196.

[3] See *A.* iii. 154 on making vice-royalty one's aim.

one who at the breaking up of the body after dying reached the Brahma-world.

And then, Ānanda, King Makhādeva's sons' descendants who succeeded him, after 84,000 years as nobles, having in this very Makhādeva Mango Grove cut off their hair and beards, having donned saffron garments, went forth from home into homelessness. These dwelt having suffused the first quarter with a mind of friendliness . . . These, having developed the four Brahma-abidings, were those who at the breaking up of the body after dying reached the Brahma-world.

Nimi was the last of these kings, a *dhamma*-man, a king under *dhamma*, firm in *dhamma*, a great king who fared by *dhamma* among brahmans and householders, townsfolk and countryfolk, and who observed the Observance on the fourteenth, fifteenth and eighth days of the half-month.

Once upon a time, Ānanda, when the Devas of the Thirty-Three [**79**] were sitting down gathered together in the Sudhammā debating hall, this chance talk arose: 'Indeed it is a gain for the Videhas,[1] indeed it is well gotten by the Videhas in that their king Nimi is a *dhamma*-man, a king under *dhamma*, firm in *dhamma*, a great king who fares by *dhamma* among brahmans and householders, townsfolk and countryfolk, and who observes the Observance on the fourteenth, fifteenth and eighth days of the half-month.'

Then, Ānanda, Sakka, the lord of *devas*, addressed the Devas of the Thirty-Three: saying; 'Do you, good sirs, want to see King Nimi?'

'We, good sir, want to see King Nimi.'

At that time King Nimi, keeping an Observance day, having washed his head on that Observance day—a fifteenth day—was sitting down on an upper terrace of his palace. Then, Ānanda, as a strong man might stretch out his bent arm or might bend back his outstretched arm, so did Sakka, the lord of *devas*, disappearing from the Devas of the Thirty-Three, appear before King Nimi. Then, Ānanda, Sakka, the lord of *devas*, spoke thus to King Nimi: 'It is a gain for you, sire, it is well gotten by you, sire. Sire, the Devas of the Thirty-Three are sitting down in the Sudhammā debating hall, praising you and saying: Indeed it is a gain for the Videhas . . . (*as above*) . . . of the half-month. Sire, the Devas of the Thirty-Three are anxious to see you, so I, sire, will send you a chariot harnessed

---

[1] Mithilā was the capital of Videha.

with a thousand thoroughbreds; sire, you should mount the *deva*-like vehicle without hesitation.'

Ānanda, King Nimi consented by becoming silent. Then, Ānanda, Sakka, the lord of *devas*, summoned the charioteer Mātali and said: 'Come you, good Mātali, having harnessed a chariot with a thousand thoroughbreds, and having approached King Nimi, speak thus: "This chariot, harnessed with a thousand thoroughbreds, has been sent to you by Sakka, the lord of *devas*. Sire, you should mount the *deva*-like **[80]** vehicle without hesitation." '

'So be it, your honour.' And, Ānanda, Mātali the charioteer, having answered Sakka, the lord of *devas*, in assent, having harnessed a chariot with a thousand thoroughbreds and having approached King Nimi, spoke thus: 'This chariot, sire, harnessed with a thousand thoroughbreds, has been sent to you by Sakka, the lord of *devas*; sire, you should mount the *deva*-like vehicle without hesitation. And, moreover, sire, by which (route) do I conduct you[1]—that by which evil deeds undergo the ripening of evil deeds or that by which lovely deeds undergo the ripening of lovely deeds[2]?'

'Conduct me by both, Mātali.' So, Ānanda, the charioteer Mātali brought King Nimi to the Sudhammā debating hall. And, Ānanda, Sakka, the lord of *devas*, saw King Nimi approaching from the distance; seeing him, he spoke to King Nimi: 'Come, sire, you are welcome, sire. Sire, the Devas of the Thirty-Three are sitting down in the Sudhammā debating hall praising you, and saying: Indeed it is a gain for the Videhas . . . (*as above*) . . . of the half-month. Sire, the Devas of the Thirty-Three are anxious to see you. Rejoice, sire, among the Devas with a *deva's* majesty.'

'Enough, good sir; let me return to Mithilā itself where I will fare by *dhamma* among brahmans and householders, townsfolk and countryfolk and will observe the Observance on the fourteenth, fifteenth and eighth days of the half-month.'

Then, Ānanda, Sakka, the lord of *devas*, summoned the charioteer Mātali and said: 'Come you, good Mātali, having harnessed a chariot with a thousand thoroughbreds, take King Nimi back to Mithilā itself.'

---

[1] *katamena taṁ nemi*. In the *Nimijātaka* (*Jā*. vi. 104), where the whole episode is given in much greater detail, the reading is *kena taṁ nemi maggena*. For the one road goes to Niraya Hell and the other to a *deva*-world.

[2] Perhaps "doers of evil deeds and doers of lovely deeds" should be understood. In spite of Bu.'s verse in *Vism*. that the deed exists but not the doer of it, at *MA*. iii. 316 he says *pāpakammantā pāpakānaṁ kammānaṁ vipākaṁ paṭisaṁvediyanti*, "doers of evil undergo the ripening of evil deeds."

'So be it, your honour.'[1] And, Ānanda, Mātali the charioteer, having answered Sakka, the lord of *devas*, in assent, harnessed a chariot with a thousand thoroughbreds and took King Nimi back to Mithilā itself. While he was there, Ānanda, King Nimi fared by *dhamma* among brahmans and householders, townsfolk and countryfolk, and [**81**] he observed the Observance on the fourteenth, fifteenth and eighth days of the half-month. Then, Ānanda, at the end of many years, many hundreds of years, many thousands of years, King Nimi addressed his barber, saying: . . . (*as above, reading* King Nimi) . . . [**82**] . . . He, having developed the four Brahma-abidings, was one who at the breaking up of the body after dying reached the Brahma-world.

But, Ānanda, King Nimi's son was called Kaḷārajanaka. He did not go forth from home into homelessness. He broke that lovely custom; of those (who observed it) he was the last man. It may be that this occurs to you, Ānanda: 'At that time King Makhādeva by whom that lovely custom was founded was someone else.' But this, Ānanda, must not be understood thus. I, at that time, was King Makhādeva; I founded that lovely custom; the folk that came after maintained that lovely custom founded by me. But that lovely custom, Ānanda, did not conduce to turning away from, nor to dispassion, stopping, tranquillity, super-knowledge, self-awakening or nibbāna—only to reaching the Brahma-world. But this lovely custom founded by me now, Ānanda, conduces to absolute turning away from, to dispassion, stopping, tranquillity, super-knowledge, self-awakening and nibbāna. And what, Ānanda, is the lovely custom founded by me now that conduces to absolute turning away from . . . nibbāna? It is this ariyan eightfold Way itself, that is to say, perfect view, perfect thought, perfect speech, perfect action, perfect mode of livelihood, [**83**] perfect endeavour, perfect mindfulness, perfect concentration. It is this lovely custom founded by me now, Ānanda, that conduces to absolute turning away from . . . nibbāna. I, Ānanda, speak about it thus: This lovely custom founded by me you should maintain; do not you be the last man after me. Ānanda, while two persons exist and there is a breaking of such a lovely custom, whichever one of these (breaks it), he is the last man. In regard to this, I, Ānanda, speak to you thus: This lovely custom founded by me you should maintain; do not you be the last man after me."

[1] Here: *evaṁ bhaddan tava;* above *evaṁ hotu bhaddan tava. MA.* iii. 314 says: *evaṁ hotu bhaddakan tava vacanan ti vatvā.*

Thus spoke the Lord. Delighted, the venerable Ānanda rejoiced in what the Lord had said.

Discourse on Makhādeva:
The Third

84. DISCOURSE AT MADHURĀ

(Madhurasutta)

THUS have I heard: At one time the venerable Kaccāna the Great was staying near Madhurā in the Gundā Grove.[1] Avantiputta,[2] king of Madhurā, heard that the recluse Kaccāna was staying near Madhurā in the Gundā Grove and that of that revered Kaccāna a lovely report had gone forth thus: 'He is clever, experienced, wise, one who has heard much, a brilliant speaker, of lovely intelligence, senior as well as being a perfected one. Good is the sight of perfected ones like this.' Then Avantiputta, king of Madhurā, having had many splendid vehicles harnessed, having mounted a splendid vehicle, set out from Madhurā with the many splendid vehicles and with great royal pomp so as to see the venerable Kaccāna the Great. He went by vehicle as long as the ground was passable, then, having dismounted from the vehicle, he approached the venerable Kaccāna the Great on foot; having approached, [**84**] he exchanged greetings with the venerable Kaccāna the Great; and having conversed in a friendly and courteous way, he sat down at a respectful distance. As he was sitting down at a respectful distance, Avantiputta, king of Madhurā, spoke thus to the venerable Kaccāna the Great:

"Good Kaccāna, brahmans speak thus: 'Only brahmans form the best caste, all other castes are low; only brahmans form the fair caste, all other castes are dark; only brahmans are pure, not non-brahmans; brahmans are own sons of Brahmā, born of his mouth, born of Brahmā, formed by Brahmā, heirs to Brahmā.'[3] What does the revered Kaccāna say to this?"

"Sire, this is merely a sound in the world, that 'Only brahmans

[1] As at *A.* i. 67. This Madhurā is on the Jumna.

[2] *MA.* iii. 319: the son of the daughter of the king of Avanti.

[3] As at *M.* ii. 148; *D.* iii. 81.

form the best caste . . . heirs to Brahmā.' This is a way in which it can be said, sire, that this is merely a sound in the world, that 'Only brahmans form the best caste . . . heirs to Brahmā.' What do you think about this, sire? Even if a noble were to thrive in wealth or corn or gold or silver, could he have as his obedient servant another noble to get up earlier than he would, to go later to rest, carrying out his pleasure, speaking affably,[1] or could he have a brahman or could he have a merchant or could he have a worker to get up earlier than he would, to go later to rest, carrying out his pleasure, speaking affably?"

"Good Kaccāna, if a noble were to thrive in wealth or corn or gold or silver he could have as his obedient servant a noble . . . a brahman . . . a merchant . . . a worker to get up earlier than he would, to go later to rest, carrying out his pleasure, speaking affably."

"What do you think about this, sire? If a brahman were to thrive in wealth . . . could he have another brahman . . . or a merchant or could he have a worker [**85**] or could he have a noble . . . speaking affably?"

"Good Kaccāna, if a brahman were to thrive . . . he could have as his obedient servant a brahman . . . a merchant . . . a worker . . . a noble to get up earlier than he would . . ."

"What do you think about this, sire? If a merchant were to thrive in wealth . . . could he have another merchant . . . or a worker or could he have a noble or could he have a brahman . . . speaking affably?"

"Good Kaccāna, if a merchant were to thrive . . . he could have as his obedient servant a merchant . . . a worker . . . a noble . . . a brahman . . . speaking affably."

"What do you think about this, sire? If a worker were to thrive in wealth . . . could he have another worker . . . or a noble or could he have a brahman or could he have a merchant . . . speaking affably?"

"Good Kaccāna, if a worker were to thrive in wealth or corn or gold or silver, he could have as his obedient servant another worker to get up earlier than he would, to go later to rest, carrying out his pleasure, speaking affably; and he could have a noble and he could have a brahman and he could have a merchant as his obedient servant, to get up earlier than he would, to go later to rest, carrying out his pleasure, speaking affably."

---

[1] *Cf. D.* i. 60; *A.* iii. 37.

" What do you think about this, sire ? This being so, are these four castes exactly the same or not ? Or how does this seem to you ?"

[**86**] " Indeed, good Kaccāna, this being so, these four castes are exactly the same; I do not see any difference between them in this respect."

" This is a way in which it can be said, sire, that this is merely a sound in the world, that ' Only brahmans form the best caste . . . heirs to Brahmā.' What do you think about this, sire ? If a noble made onslaught on creatures here, took what had not been given, wrongly enjoyed pleasures of the senses, were a liar, of slanderous speech, of harsh speech, a gossip, covetous, malevolent in mind, of wrong view—would he at the breaking up of the body after dying arise in the sorrowful way, the bad bourn, the Downfall, Niraya Hell ? Or not ? Or how does this seem to you ?"

" If a noble, good Kaccāna, made onslaught on creatures, took what had not been given . . . at the breaking up of the body after dying he would arise in . . . Niraya Hell. This is how it seems to me, and thus have I heard it from perfected ones."

" It is good, it is good, sire; it is good that it seems thus to you, sire, and it is good that you have heard this from perfected ones. What do you think about this, sire ? If a brahman, if a merchant, if a worker made onslaught on creatures here . . . at the breaking up of the body after dying would he arise in . . . Niraya Hell ? Or not ? Or how does this seem to you ?"

" If (a brahman, a merchant), a worker, good Kaccāna, made onslaught on creatures . . . at the breaking up of the body after dying he would arise in . . . Niraya Hell. [This is how it seems to me][1] and thus have I heard it from perfected ones."

" It is good, it is good, sire; it is good that it seems thus to you, sire, and it is good that you have heard this from perfected ones. What do you think about this, sire ? This being so, are these four castes exactly the same or not ? Or how does this seem to you ?"

[**87**] " Indeed, good Kaccāna, this being so, these four castes are exactly the same; I do not see any difference between them in this respect."

" This is a way in which it can be said, sire, that this is only a sound in the world, that ' Only brahmans form the best caste . . . heirs to Brahmā.' What do you think about this, sire ? If a noble refrained from onslaught on creatures here, from taking what had

---

[1] Omitted in the text, in error judging from the king's response.

not been given, from wrong enjoyment of the sense-pleasures, from being a liar, from slanderous speech, from harsh speech, from being a gossip, were not covetous, were benevolent in mind and of right view—would he at the breaking up of the body after dying arise in a good bourn, a heaven world ? Or not ? Or how does this seem to you ?"

" If a noble, good Kaccāna, refrained from onslaught of creatures . . . at the breaking up of the body after dying he would arise in a good bourn, a heaven world. This is how it seems to me, and thus have I heard it from perfected ones."

" It is good, it is good, sire; it is good that it seems thus to you, sire, and it is good that you have heard this from perfected ones. What do you think about this, sire ? If a brahman, if a merchant, if a worker refrained from onslaught on creatures here . . . would he at the breaking up of the body after dying arise in a good bourn, a heaven world ? Or not ? Or how does it seem to you ?"

" If (a brahman, a merchant), a worker, good Kaccāna, refrained from onslaught on creatures . . . at the breaking up of the body after dying he would arise in a good bourn, a heaven world. This is how it seems to me, and thus have I heard it from perfected ones."

" It is good, it is good, sire; it is good that it seems thus to you, sire, and it is good that you have heard this from perfected ones. What do you think about this, sire ? This being so, are these four castes exactly the same or not ? Or how does this seem to you ?"

[**88**] " Indeed, good Kaccāna, this being so, these four castes are exactly the same; I do not see any difference between them in this respect."

" This is a way in which it can be said, sire, that this is merely a sound in the world, that ' Only brahmans form the best caste . . . heirs to Brahmā.' What do you think about this, sire ? If a noble were to break into a house, or carry off loot, or commit a robbery, or make an ambush, or commit adultery,[1] and if men who had captured him were to show him to you, and say: ' This, your majesty, is the thief who is doing evil to you, decree what punishment you like for him '—what would you do to him ?"

" Good Kaccāna, we should kill him or ruin him or banish him or deal with him as we liked.[2] What is the cause of this ? Good Kaccāna, the designation of ' noble ' that he once had has now disappeared for him, and he is reckoned simply as ' thief.' "

---

[1] As at *M*. i. 87.

[2] Various punishments are named at *M*. i. 87.

"What do you think about this, sire? If (a brahman, a merchant), a worker were to break into a house . . . what would you do to him?"

"Good Kaccāna, we should kill him . . . he is reckoned simply as 'thief.'"

"What do you think about this, sire? This being so, are these four castes exactly the same or not? Or how does this seem to you?"

"Indeed, good Kaccāna, this being so, these four castes are exactly the same; I do not see any difference between them in this respect."

"This is a way in which it can be said, sire, that this is merely a sound in the world, that 'Only brahmans form the best caste **[89]** . . . heirs to Brahmā.' What do you think about this, sire? If a noble, having cut off his hair and beard here,[1] having donned saffron robes, should have gone forth from home into homelessness, and is one that refrains from onslaught on creatures, from taking what has not been given, from lying speech, is a one-meal-man, a Brahma-farer, virtuous, of lovely character—what would you do to him?"

"Good Kaccāna, we should salute him or rise up before him or offer him a seat or invite him to the requisites of robe-material, almsfood, lodgings and medicines for the sick, or we should have proper watch and ward and guard provided for him.[2] What is the cause of this? Good Kaccāna, the designation of 'noble' that he once had has now disappeared for him, and he is reckoned simply as 'recluse.'"

"What do you think about this, sire? If a brahman, a merchant, a worker, having cut off his hair and beard here . . . what would you do to him?"

"Good Kaccāna, we should salute him . . . and he is reckoned simply as 'recluse.'"

"What do you think about this, sire? This being so, are these four castes exactly the same or not? Or how does this seem to you?"

"Indeed, good Kaccāna, this being so, these four castes are exactly the same; I do not see any difference between them in this respect."

"This is a way in which it can be said, sire, that this is merely a

---

[1] The following passage down to "guard provided for him" also occurs at *M*. ii. 101.

[2] *Cf. D.* i. 61. "Proper" or "legitimate," *dhammika*, here seems to mean "recognised or understood as being customary." *MA*. iii. 321 says the arrangement would be like that (traditional one) where gatherers of sticks and leaves do not enter the *vihāra* of a Naked Ascetic, or where hunters and trappers do not catch animals or fish within the boundary of a *vihāra*.

sound in the world, that ' Only brahmans form the best caste, all other castes are low; only brahmans from the fair caste, all other castes are dark; only brahmans are pure, not non-brahmans; brahmans are own sons of Brahmā, born of his mouth, born of Brahmā, formed by Brahmā, heirs to Brahmā.' "

[**90**] When this had been said, Avantiputta, king of Madhurā, spoke thus to the venerable Kaccāna the Great: " Excellent, good Kaccāna, excellent, good Kaccāna. It is as if one might set upright what had been upset,[1] or might disclose what was covered, or show the way to one who had gone astray, or bring an oil-lamp into the darkness so that those with vision might see material shapes—even so in many a figure has *dhamma* been made clear by the good Kaccāna. Thus I am going to the revered Kaccāna for refuge and to *dhamma* and to the Order of monks. May the revered Kaccāna accept me as a lay-disciple going for refuge from today forth for as long as life lasts."

" But do not you, sire, go for refuge to me. You must go for refuge only to that Lord to whom I have gone for refuge."

" But where, good Kaccāna, is this Lord staying now, perfected one, fully Self-Awakened One ?"

" Sire, this Lord, perfected one, fully Self-Awakened One, has now attained final nibbāna."

" Good Kaccāna, if we should hear that that Lord were ten . . . twenty . . . thirty . . . forty . . . fifty *yojana* distant we should go the fifty *yojana* so as to see that Lord. And, good Kaccāna, even if we heard that the Lord were a hundred *yojana* distant, we should go the hundred *yojana* so as to see that Lord, perfected one, fully Self-Awakened One. But, good Kaccāna, since the Lord has attained final nibbāna, we are going for refuge to that Lord who has attained final nibbāna and to *dhamma* and to the Order of monks. May the revered Kaccāna accept me as a lay-disciple going for refuge from today forth for as long as life lasts."

Discourse at Madhurā:
The Fourth

---

[1] From here to the end of this Discourse, compare with *M*. ii. 162-163.

85. DISCOURSE TO PRINCE BODHI

(Bodhirājakumārasutta)

[91] THUS have I heard: At one time the Lord was staying among the Bhaggas in Suṁsumāragira in Bhesakaḷā Grove in the deer-park. At that time Prince Bodhi had a palace named Kokanada[1]; it had not long been built and had had not (yet) been inhabited by a recluse or brahman or by any human being. Then Prince Bodhi addressed the brahman youth Sañjikā's son, saying: "Come you, good Sañjikā's son, approach the Lord; having approached, in my name salute the Lord's feet with your head, and ask whether he is well, not indisposed, of bodily vigour, strong, abiding in comfort, and say: 'Lord, Prince Bodhi salutes the Lord's feet with his head and asks whether he is well . . . abiding in comfort.' And speak thus to him: 'Revered sir, may the Lord, together with the Order of monks, consent to (accept) a meal on the morrow with Prince Bodhi.'"

"Yes, sir," and the brahman youth Sañjikā's son, having answered Prince Bodhi in assent, approached the Lord; having approached, he exchanged greetings with the Lord, and having conversed in a friendly and courteous way, he sat down at a respectful distance. As he was sitting down at a respectful distance, the brahman youth Sañjikā's son spoke thus to the Lord: "Good Gotama, Prince Bodhi salutes with his head the good Gotama's feet and asks whether he is well . . . abiding in comfort. And he speaks thus: 'May the revered Gotama, together with the Order of monks, consent to (accept) a meal on the morrow with Prince Bodhi.'" The Lord consented by becoming silent. Then the brahman youth Sañjikā's son, having understood the Lord's consent, rising from his seat approached Prince Bodhi; having approached, he spoke thus to Prince Bodhi:

"I spoke in your name, good sir, to the Lord Gotama, saying: 'Good Gotama, Prince Bodhi [92] salutes with his head the good Gotama's feet and asks whether he is well . . . abiding in comfort. And he speaks thus: 'May the good Gotama, together with the Order of monks, consent to (accept) a meal on the morrow with

[1] As far as p. 280 below: "Prince Bodhi . . . sat down at a respectful distance," occurs also at *Vin.* ii. 127 *f.* For notes see *B.D.* v. 176 *ff.* See also opening of *M.* Sta. No. 53.

Prince Bodhi.' And the recluse Gotama consented." Then, after Prince Bodhi had had sumptuous foods, solid and soft, prepared in his own dwelling towards the end of that night, and had had the Kokanada palace spread with white cloths as far as the last[1] flight of stairs, he addressed the brahman youth Sañjikā's son, saying: "Come you, good Sañjikā's son, approach the Lord; having approached, announce the time to the Lord, saying: 'It is time, revered sir, the meal is ready.'"

"Yes, good sir," and the brahman youth Sañjikā's son, having answered Prince Bodhi in assent, approached the Lord; having approached, he announced the time to the Lord, saying: "It is time, revered sir, the meal is ready." Then the Lord, dressing in the morning and taking his bowl and robe, approached Prince Bodhi's dwelling. At that time Prince Bodhi, while he was waiting for the Lord, was standing at the porch of the outside gateway. And Prince Bodhi saw the Lord coming in the distance; having seen him and gone to meet him, he greeted and honoured the Lord and approached the Kokanada palace. Then the Lord stood leaning against the last flight of stairs. And Prince Bodhi spoke thus to the Lord:

"Revered sir, let the Lord step on the cloths, let the Well-farer step on the cloths so that for a long time it may be for my welfare and happiness." When this had been said, the Lord was silent. And a second time . . . And a third time Prince Bodhi spoke thus to the Lord: "Revered sir, let the Lord step on the cloths . . . for my welfare and happiness." Then the Lord looked towards the venerable Ānanda. And the [**93**] venerable Ānanda spoke thus to Prince Bodhi:

"Prince, have the cloths packed away. The Lord will not tread upon a cloth carpeting; the Tathāgata looks towards[2] the folk that come after."

Then Prince Bodhi had the cloths packed away, and had a seat made ready upstairs in the Kokanada palace. Then the Lord having ascended the Kokanada palace, sat down on the seat made ready together with the Order of monks. Then Prince Bodhi with his own hand served and satisfied the Order of monks with the Lord at its head with sumptuous foods, solid and soft. Then when the Lord had eaten and had withdrawn his hand from his bowl, Prince Bodhi, having taken a lower seat, sat down at a respectful distance.

---

[1] Or, western.

[2] *apaloketi*, but *Vin.* ii. 128 reads *anukampati*.

As he was sitting down at a respectful distance, Prince Bodhi spoke thus to the Lord: " Lord, it has occurred to me thus: Happiness is not to be achieved through happiness; happiness is to be achieved through suffering."[1]

" To me too, Prince, before my Awakening, while I was still the *bodhisatta*, not fully awakened, it occurred: Happiness is not to be achieved through happiness; happiness is to be achieved through suffering. Then I, Prince, after a time, being young, my hair coal-black . . . (*as in M.L.S.* i, p. 207 *to* p. 211, *reading* Prince *for* monks) . . . thinking, Indeed this does well for striving. Moreover, Prince, three similes occurred to me . . . (*as in M.L.S.* i, p. 295 *to* p. 303 *reading* Prince *for* Aggivessana) . . . even as I abided diligent, ardent, self-resolute.[2]

Then, Prince, it occurred to me: This *dhamma*, won to by me, is deep . . . (*as in M.L.S.* i, p. 211 *to* p. 217, *reading* Prince *for* monks) . . . [**94**] Whatever the two monks who had walked for almsfood brought back, that the group of six lived on. Then, Prince, the group of five monks, being thus exhorted, thus instructed by me, soon realising here and now by their own super-knowledge that matchless goal of the Brahma-faring for the sake of which young men of family rightly go forth from home into homelessness, entering on it abided in it."

When this had been said, Prince Bodhi spoke thus to the Lord: " After how long, revered sir, does a monk taking the Tathāgata as a leader, and having by his own super-knowledge realised here and now that matchless goal . . . entering on it, abide in it ?"

" Well then, Prince, I will ask you a question about this in return. As it may please you, so should you answer it. What do you think about this, Prince ? Are you skilled in elephant-riding, in the art of handling a goad ?"

" Yes, I, revered sir, am skilled in elephant-riding, in the art of handling a goad."

" What do you think about this, Prince ? A man might come along here, and think: ' Prince Bodhi knows how to ride elephants and the art of handling the goad. I will train myself in elephant-riding and the art of handling the goad under him.' But had he no faith he could not attain whatever is to be won by faith; and had he

---

[1] As at *M.* i. 93 (*M.L.S.* i. 123).

[2] *I.e.* read as far as the second occurrence of this phrase on p. 303 of vol. i. The sentence, " the pleasurable feeling, arising in me, persisted without impinging on my mind," found in vol. i, does not occur in Discourse No. 85.

poor health he could not attain whatever is to be won by good health; and if he were fraudulent and deceitful he could not attain whatever is to be won by honesty and the absence of deceit; and if he were lazy he could not attain whatever is to be won by the output of energy; and if he were poor in wisdom he could not attain whatever is to be won by one of wisdom. What do you think about this, Prince? Could that man train himself in elephant-riding and the art of handling the goad under you?"

"Assuredly, revered sir, if that man were possessed of (such) qualities, he could not train himself in elephant-riding and the art of handling the goad under me. But who speaks of five qualities?"

"What do you think about this, Prince? A man might come along here, and think: **[95]** "Prince Bodhi knows how to ride elephants and the art of handling the goad. I will train myself in elephant-riding and the art of handling the goad under him.' And if he had faith he could attain whatever is to be won by faith; and if he had good health ... and if he were not fraudulent or deceitful ... and if he had an output of energy ... and if he were one of wisdom he could attain whatever is to be won by one of wisdom. What do you think about this, Prince? Could that man train himself in elephant-riding and in the art of handling the goad under you?"

"Assuredly, revered sir, if that man were possessed of (such) qualities, he could train himself in elephant-riding and the art of handling the goad under me. But who speaks of five qualities?"

"Even so, Prince, are these five qualities for striving.[1] What five? As to this, Prince, a monk has faith; he has faith in the awakening of the Tathāgata, and thinks: 'Indeed this is the Lord, perfected one, fully Self-Awakened One, endowed with knowledge and (right) conduct, Well-farer, knower of the worlds, incomparable charioteer of men to be tamed, teachers of *devas* and men, the Awakened One, the Lord.' He is well, in good health, endowed with a good digestion, not over-cool, not over-hot, but of a middle kind suitable for striving. He is not fraudulent, not deceitful, but shows himself as he really is to the Teacher or the learned among his fellow Brahma-farers. He dwells with energy stirred up[2] for getting rid of unskilled states, for arousing skilled states, steadfast, firm in advance, persevering amid skilled states. He is one of wisdom endowed with wisdom[2] leading to (the cutting off of) rise and fall, with ariyan[3]

---

[1] As at *M*. ii. 128; *A*. iii. 65; *D*. iii. 237. [2] As at *M*. i. 356.

[3] *MA*. iii. 326 explains as "pure," *suddha*.

discrimination leading to the complete destruction of anguish. These, Prince, are the five qualities for striving. If, Prince, a monk is possessed of these five qualities for striving, taking the Tathāgata for leader, having by his own super-knowledge realised here and now that matchless goal of the Brahma-faring for the sake of which young men of family rightly go forth from home into homelessness, entering on it [**96**] he may abide in it within seven years. Let be the seven years, Prince. If a monk is possessed of these five qualities for striving . . . he may abide in it in six years . . . five years, four years, three years, two years, one year. Let be the one year, Prince. If a monk is possessed of these five qualities for striving . . . he may abide in it in seven months. Let be the seven months, Prince. If a monk is possessed of these five qualities for striving . . . he may abide in it in six months . . . five months, four months, three months, two months, one month, half a month. Let be the half month, Prince. If a monk is possessed of these five qualities for striving . . . he may abide in it in seven days and nights. Let be the seven days and nights, Prince. If a monk is possessed of these five qualities for striving . . . he may abide in it in six days and nights . . . five, four, three, two days and nights, one day and night. Let be the one day and night, Prince. If a monk is possessed of these five qualities for striving, taking the Tathāgata as leader, if he is instructed in the evening he will attain eminence in the morning; if he is instructed in the morning he will attain eminence in the evening."

When this had been said, Prince Bodhi spoke thus to the Lord: "O what an Awakened One,[1] O what a *dhamma*, O what a good teaching of *dhamma* in that if one is instructed in the evening he will attain eminence in the morning, if instructed in the morning he will attain eminence in the evening."

When this had been said, the brahman youth Sañjikā's son, spoke thus to Prince Bodhi: "So this revered Bodhi speaks thus: 'O what an Awakened One, O what a *dhamma*, O what a good teaching of *dhamma*,' but then he does not say: 'I am going to that revered Gotama for refuge and to *dhamma* and to the Order of monks.'"

"Do not, good Sañjikā's son, speak thus; do not, good Sañjikā's son, speak thus. Face to face with my mother, good Sañjikā's son, have I heard this, [**97**] face to face have I learnt it. There was a time, good Sañjikā's son, when this Lord was staying at Kosambī in Ghosita's monastery. Then my mother, who was with child,

---

[1] *aho buddho*, etc.; *cf. Thag.* 201, where *aho* is translated as "All hail."

approached the Lord; having approached, having greeted the Lord, she sat down at a respectful distance. As she was sitting down at a respectful distance my mother spoke thus to the Lord: 'Revered sir, my unborn child, whether a boy or a girl, is going to the Lord for refuge and to *dhamma* and to the Order of monks. May the Lord accept this layfollower who is going for refuge from this day forth for as long as life lasts.' There was the time, good Sañjikā's son, when the Lord was staying here itself among the Bhaggas in Suṁsumāragira in Bhesakaḷā Grove in the deer-park. Then my nurse, carrying me on her hip, approached the Lord; having approached and having greeted the Lord, she stood at a respectful distance. As she was standing at a respectful distance, my nurse spoke thus to the Lord: 'This, revered sir, is Prince Bodhi who is going for refuge to the Lord and to *dhamma* and to the Order of monks. May the Lord accept this layfollower who is going for refuge from this day forth for as long as life lasts.' Now I, good Sañjikā's son, am going for the third time to the Lord for refuge and to *dhamma* and to the Order of monks, thinking: 'May the Lord accept me as a layfollower going for refuge from this day forth for as long as life lasts.' "

Discourse to Prince Bodhi:
The Fifth

86. DISCOURSE WITH AṄGULIMĀLA

(Aṅgulimālasutta)

THUS have I heard: At one time the Lord was staying near Sāvatthī in the Jeta Grove in Anāthapiṇḍika's monastery. Now at that time, in the realm of King Pasenadi of Kosala[1] there was a robber named Aṅgulimāla,[2] a hunter, bloody-handed, bent on death and destruction, merciless to living creatures. Through him villages were depopulated[3] and [98] market towns were depopulated and country

[1] As this king is frequently mentioned in Suttas 86-90, I have almost always abbreviated his designation to: King Pasendi.

[2] Meaning "Garland of Fingers." The *Sutasoma-jātaka* (No. 537) was preached concerning him.

[3] *gāmā pi agāmā katā*, villages were rendered not-villages.

districts were depopulated. From his constant killing of people he wore a garland of fingers. Then the Lord, having dressed in the morning, taking his bowl and robe, entered Sāvatthī for almsfood; having walked for alms in Sāvatthī, returning from the almsgathering after the meal, having packed away his lodging, taking his bowl and robe, he set out along a highway towards the robber Aṅgulimāla. Cowherds, goatherds, yeomen farmers and travellers saw the Lord as he was setting out along the highway towards the robber Aṅgulimāla. Having seen the Lord, they spoke thus to him:

"Do not, recluse, set out along this road. There is a robber on this road called Aṅgulimāla, a hunter, bloody-handed . . . Through him villages are depopulated . . . he wears a garland of fingers. This is a road, recluse, along which ten or twenty or thirty or forty men set out only after they have collected together, and even they are at the mercy of the robber Aṅgulimāla."

When this had been said, the Lord, having become silent, went on. And a second time . . . And a third time the cowherds, goatherds . . . spoke thus to the Lord: "Do not, recluse, set out along this road . . . (*as above*) . . . even they are at the mercy of the robber Aṅgulimāla." Then the Lord, having become silent, went on.

The robber Aṅgulimāla saw the Lord coming in the distance; on seeing him, it occurred to him: "Indeed it is wonderful, indeed it is marvellous. This is a road along which ten or twenty [**99**] or thirty or forty men set out only after they have collected together, and even they are at my mercy. And now this recluse is coming along alone, without a companion, it seems from choice.[1] Suppose I were to deprive this recluse of life?"

Then the robber Aṅgulimāla, having grasped his sword and shield, having armed himself with bow and quiver, followed close after the Lord. Then the Lord performed such a wonder of psychic power that the robber Aṅgulimāla, although walking with all his strength, was not able to catch up with the Lord who was walking at an ordinary pace. Then it occurred to the robber Aṅgulimāla: 'Indeed

---

[1] *pasayha*. As this usually means "by force, forcibly," there may be in the word some allusion here to the Teacher's refusal to listen to all the pleadings and warnings which he encountered. The meaning here may however be that Aṅgulimāla thinks: it seems that by using force (*pasayha maññe*) suppose I were to deprive him of life. But the syntax is against this. *CPD*. s.v. *appasayha* gives "irresistible," *cf.* Monier-Williams, who for *prasahya* gives 1. to be resisted, conquered or defeated; 2. having withstood, overpowered or conquered; forcibly, violently, by force.

it is wonderful, indeed it is marvellous. Although formerly I could attack and seize a running elephant . . . a running horse . . . a running chariot . . . a running deer, now I, although walking with all my strength, am not able to catch up with this recluse who is walking at an ordinary pace." Standing still, he said to the Lord: " Stand still, recluse, stand still, recluse."

" I am standing still, Aṅgulimāla, you too stand still."

Then it occurred to the robber Aṅgulimāla: " These recluses, sons of the Sakyans, are truth-speakers, approving of truth. But yet this recluse, while he is walking, says: ' I am standing still, Aṅgulimāla, you too stand still.' Suppose I were to question this recluse ?" Then the robber Aṅgulimāla spoke out to the Lord in verses:[1]

" While you are walking, recluse, you say: ' I am standing still,' and you tell me, who am standing still, that I am not standing still.
I ask you, recluse, about this matter: How is it that *you* are standing still, yet *I* am not standing still ?"

" I, Aṅgulimāla, am standing still, having for all beings everywhere laid aside the stick,
But you are unrestrained regarding creatures; therefore *I* am standing still, *you* are not standing still."

[**100**] " Long it is since a great sage was honoured by me, yet this recluse is penetrating the Great Grove.
I will soon get rid of evil, hearing *dhamma* in a verse of yours."

When the robber had spoken thus, he hurled his sword and weapons down a cliff, into a pit, a chasm.
The robber honoured the Well-farer's feet; there he asked for the going forth.

The Awakened One and compassionate great sage who is the Teacher of the world with its *devas*,
Thereupon said to him: " Come, monk." This itself was monk's status for him.

Then the Lord set out on tour for Sāvatthī with the venerable Aṅgulimāla as his attendant. In due course, walking on tour, he

---

[1] The verses ascribed to Aṅgulimāla are at *Thag.* 866 *ff.*

arrived at Sāvatthī. While he was there the Lord stayed near Sāvatthī, in the Jeta Grove in Anāthapiṇḍika's monastery. Now at that time, a great concourse of people, having gathered together at the gate of King Pasenadi's palace, were making a loud noise, a great noise, saying: " There is a robber in your realm, sire, called Aṅgulimāla, a hunter, bloody-handed . . . Through him villages are depopulated . . . he wears a garland of fingers. Let the king drive him out."

Then King Pasenadi, with as many as five hundred horses, left Sāvatthī early in the morning and started for the monastery. Having gone by vehicle as far as the ground permitted, he dismounted from his vehicle and approached the Lord on foot; having approached, [**101**] having greeted the Lord, he sat down at a respectful distance. The Lord spoke thus to King Pasenadi as he was sitting down at a respectful distance: " What is it, sire ? Is King Seniya Bimbisāra of Magadha angry with you, or the Licchavis of Vesālī, or some hostile king ?"

" Revered sir, it is not that King Seniya Bimbisāra of Magadha is angry with me, or the Licchavis of Vesālī, or any hostile king. There is a robber in my realm, revered sir, named Aṅgulimāla, a hunter, bloody-handed . . . Through him villages are depopulated . . . he wears a garland of fingers. I, revered sir, shall never drive him out."

" But[1] if you, sire, were to see the robber Aṅgulimāla, having had his hair and beard cut off, having donned saffron robes, having gone forth from home into homelessness, refraining from onslaught on creatures, refraining from taking what has not been given, refraining from lying speech, a one-meal-man, a Brahma-farer, virtuous, of lovely character—what would you do to him ?"

" Revered sir, we would salute him or rise up before him or offer him a seat or invite him to the requisites of robe-material, almsfood, lodgings and medicines for the sick, or we would have a proper watch and ward and guard provided for him. But whence could there be, revered sir, such control in moral habit for one of bad morality, of evil character ?"

Now at that time the venerable Aṅgulimāla was sitting near the Lord. Then the Lord, stretching out his right arm, spoke thus to King Pasenadi: " This, sire, is Aṅgulimāla."

Then King Pasenadi was afraid, alarmed and his hair stood on end.

---

[1] For this paragraph and the next, see also *M.* ii. 89.

Then the Lord, knowing King Pasenadi's terror and agitation and that his hair was standing on end, spoke thus to King Pasenadi: "Do not be afraid, sire, do not be afraid, sire; you have no cause for fear here." Then King Pasenadi's fear [**102**] and alarm and the standing of his hair on end all abated. Then King Pasenadi approached the venerable Aṅgulimāla; having approached, he spoke thus to the venerable Aṅgulimāla:

"Revered sir, is the master really Aṅgulimāla?"

"Yes, sire."

"Of what clan was the master's father? Of what clan his mother?"

"Gagga was my father, sire, Mantāṇī my mother."

"Revered sir, let the master, the son of Gagga and Mantāṇī, be of good cheer. I will make an effort in the matter of the requisites of robe-material . . . and medicines for the sick for the master, the son of Gagga and Mantāṇī."

Now at that time the venerable Aṅgulimāla was a forest-dweller, an almsman, a rag-robe wearer, one who wore the three robes. So the venerable Aṅgulimāla spoke thus to King Pasenadi: "No, sire, I am complete as to the three robes."

Then King Pasenadi approached the Lord; having approached, having greeted the Lord, he sat down at a respectful distance. As he was sitting down at a respectful distance, King Pasenadi spoke thus to the Lord: "It is wonderful, revered sir, it is marvellous, revered sir, how this Lord, revered sir, tames the untamed, calms the uncalmed, helps to quell completely those that are not completely quelled.[1] Him, revered sir, that I was unable to tame with stick and sword, the Lord has tamed without stick or sword. Well, I am going now, revered sir, I am very busy, there is much to be done."

"You do now, sire, that for which you deem it the right time." Then King Pasenadi, rising from his seat, having greeted the Lord, departed keeping his right side towards him.

Then the venerable Aṅgulimāla, having dressed in the morning, taking his bowl and robe, entered Sāvatthī for almsfood. And as the venerable Aṅgulimāla was walking in Sāvatthī on an uninterrupted round for almsfood, he saw a woman in difficult and dangerous labour. On seeing her, [**103**] it occurred to him: "Beings are indeed impure, beings are indeed impure."

Then the venerable Aṅgulimāla, having walked in Sāvatthī for

---

[1] Or, "is a helper to final nibbāna (*parinibbāpetā*) of those who have not reached final nibbāna." *Cf. M.* i. 235; *D.* iii. 54.

almsfood, on returning from the almsgathering after the meal, approached the Lord; having approached, having greeted the Lord, he sat down at a respectful distance. As he was sitting down at a respectful distance, the venerable Aṅgulimāla spoke thus to the Lord: " Now, I, revered sir, having dressed in the morning . . . And as I was walking in Sāvatthī . . . I saw a woman . . . it occurred to me: ' Beings are indeed impure, beings are indeed impure.' "

" Well then, do you, Aṅgulimāla, approach Sāvatthī; having approached, speak thus to that woman: ' I, sister, am not aware of having intentionally deprived any living thing of life since I was born. By this truth may there be well-being for you, well-being for the unborn child.' "

" But would not this be deliberate lying on my part, revered sir ? For, revered sir, many living things have been intentionally deprived of life by me."

" Well then, do you, Aṅgulimāla, approach Sāvatthī; having approached, speak thus to that woman: ' I, sister, am not aware of having intentionally deprived any living thing of life since I was born of the ariyan birth. By this truth may there be well-being for . . . the unborn child.' "

" Yes, revered sir," and the venerable Aṅgulimāla, having answered the Lord in assent, approached Sāvatthī; having approached, he spoke thus to that woman: " I, sister, am not aware of having intentionally deprived any living thing of life since I was born of the ariyan birth. By this truth may there be well-being for . . . the unborn child."

Then the venerable Aṅgulimāla, living alone, aloof, diligent, ardent, self-resolute, having soon realised here and now by his own super-knowledge that matchless goal of the Brahma-faring for the sake of which young men of family rightly go forth from home into homelessness, entering on it, abided in it. And he knew: Destroyed is birth, brought to a close the Brahma-faring, done is what was to be done, there is no more of being [**104**] such or so. And so the venerable Aṅgulimāla was one of the perfected ones.

Then the venerable Aṅgulimāla, having dressed in the morning, taking his bowl and robe, entered Sāvatthī for almsfood. Now at that time a clod of earth thrown by one man fell on the venerable Aṅgulimāla, also a stick thrown by another and gravel thrown by a third.[1] Then the venerable Aṅgulimāla, with a broken head

[1] *MA.* iii. 338 explains that these were thrown at marauding crows, dogs and pigs, but fell on the Elder.

streaming with blood, his bowl smashed, and his outer cloak in tatters, approached the Lord. The Lord saw the venerable Aṅgulimāla coming in the distance; seeing him, he spoke thus to the venerable Aṅgulimāla: "Do you endure it, brahman,[1] do you endure it, brahman. You are experiencing here and now the ripening of that *kamma* through the ripening of which you would (otherwise) boil in Niraya Hell for many years, many hundreds of years, many thousands of years." Then the venerable Aṅgulimāla, as he was meditating in private, experienced the bliss of freedom,[2] and at that time uttered this solemn utterance:

"He[3] who formerly was slothful but afterwards is diligent
Illumes this world like the moon when freed from a cloud.
He whose evilly done *kamma* is closed by what is skilled
Illumes this world like the moon when freed from a cloud.
Indeed, he who, a young monk, cleaves to the Awakened One's Dispensation
Illumines this world like the moon when freed from a cloud.
Let my foes but hear talk on *dhamma*, let my foes but cleave to the Awakened One's Dispensation,
Let those men, my foes, but follow *dhamma*—and, calmed, only it will they accept.
[105] Let my foes, from speakers on forbearance and commenders of gentleness
Hear *dhamma* from time to time and act in conformity with it.
Such a one would not harm me nor yet any other at all—
He would attain the uttermost peace and guard those who have craving and those who have none.[4]
As[5] ditchers lead the water, as fletchers shape the shaft,
As joiners shape the timber, so do the wise tame themselves.
Some[6] are tamed by the stick, goads or whips;
I, without stick, without weapon, was tamed by Him who is 'Such.'

---

[1] *MA.* iii. 339 says he was so called because his *āsavas* were destroyed.

[2] As Gotama is recorded to have done at *Vin.* i. 1, etc.

[3] The verses ascribed to Aṅgulimāla continue at *Thag.* 871 *ff.* The first two are also found at *Dhp.* 172, 173.

[4] *tasathāvara.* *MA.* iii. 341 and *ThagA.* say that *tasā* means those with craving (*sataṇhā*) while *thāvarā* means those without (*nittaṇhā*). The word also occurs at *Khp.* IX. 4 (*KhpA.* 245 giving a slightly fuller explanation than *MA.* or *ThagA.*) and at *Sn.* 146.

[5] This verse also at *Dhp.* 80, 145.

[6] With this verse *cf.* *Vin.* ii. 196.

My name is 'Harmless,'[1] though once I harmful was.
Today I am truly named,[2] for I harm no thing at all.
Once I was the notorious robber Aṅgulimāla;
Being swept away by the great flood, I came to the Awakened One for refuge.
Once I was the notorious bloody-handed Aṅgulimāla—
O see my going for refuge, becoming's cord[3] removed!
Me who had wrought such *kamma* as leads to many a woeful bourn,
When touched by the ripening of *kamma*,[4] debtless I enjoy an owner's state.[5]
Fools,[6] folk poor in wisdom, pursue slothfulness;
A wise man guards diligence as wealth supreme.
Pursue[7] not slothfulness, be not acquainted with sensual delights—
Meditating with diligence one attains abundant joy.
Well[8] was (my) coming,[9] there is no departing, nor was I ill-advised—
Among various truths[10] that which I follow is supreme.

---

[1] According to *MA*. iii. 329 Ahiṁsaka was his name while he was a student. *ThagA*. on the other hand says that Hiṁsaka was his original name. See *Pss. Breth.*, p. 323, *n*. 3.

[2] *saccanāmo 'mhi.* Although Saccanāma, as "He whose name is Truth," is among the epithets of the Buddha, it is not being used as an epithet here as is clear from the context.

[3] *bhavanetti,* explained at *MA*. iii. 342 as *bhavarajju,* the cord, called *taṇhā* (craving): "Creatures are bound in their hearts like cattle with a cord tied to their necks, and are led on (*nīyanti*) to this or that becoming." *Bhavanetti* is therefore the cord, lead or conduit tying to or leading to "becoming."

[4] *kammavipāka* is called *maggacetanā*, determination in or will for the Way. Inasmuch as *kamma* is boiled and destroyed by this means, this means is therefore called *kammavipāka*.

[5] *bhuñjāmi bhojanaṁ.* Also at *Thag*. 789. *MA*. iii. 343, *Vism*. 43, *Jā*. v. 253 distinguish four kinds of *paribhoga*, enjoyment, use. Here *sāmiparibhoga* is meant: that of a master or owner, one whose *āsavas* are destroyed. *Bhojana* might therefore be translated here as "usage," "status" or even "privilege," "right."

[6] Verse also at *Dhp*. 26, *S*. i. 25.

[7] Verse also at Dhp. 27 (reading *vipulaṁ sukhaṁ*, "abundant joy," as *M*. above), and *Thag*. 884 and *S*. i. 25 (both reading *paramaṁ sukhaṁ*).

[8] This verse also at *Thag*. 9.

[9] *ThagA*. i. 55 says *svāgataṁ* means either: this coming of mine was beautiful; or, well was the coming on my part, *i.e.* to the Buddha's presence.

[10] *dhammā* could mean either "truths, teachings," as it appears to do at

Well was (my) coming, there is no departing, nor was I ill-advised—
Won is the threefold knowledge, done is the teaching of the Awakened One."

Discourse with Aṅgulimāla:
The Sixth

87. DISCOURSE ON "BORN OF AFFECTION"

(Piyajātikasutta)

[**106**] THUS have I heard: At one time the Lord was staying near Sāvatthī in the Jeta Grove in Anāthapiṇḍika's monastery. Now at that time the dear and beloved little only son of a certain householder had passed away. After he had passed away he (the father) had no inclination for work or for food. Going constantly to the cemetery, he wailed: "Where are you, little only son? Where are you, little only son?" Then that householder approached the Lord; having approached, having greeted the Lord, he sat down at a respectful distance. The Lord spoke thus to that householder as he was sitting down at a respectful distance:

"Have not you, householder, controlling faculties for stilling your own mind? There is a change in your faculties."

"But how could there be no change in my faculties, Lord? For, Lord, my dear and beloved little only son has passed away. Since he passed away I have no inclination for work or food. Going constantly to the cemetery, I wail: 'Where are you, little only son? Where are you, little only son?' "

"That is just it, householder. For, householder, grief, sorrow, suffering, lamentation and despair are born of affection, originate in affection."

"But for whom, Lord, could this hold good in this way: 'Grief . . . and despair are born of affection, originate in affection?' For, Lord, bliss and happiness are born of affection, originate in affection."

ThagA. i. 55; or "states of mind" which, as nibbāna, it appears to mean at *MA*. iii. 343. There are a number of variant readings for the preceding and qualifying word; in the *M*. text it is *paṭibhattesu*.

Then the householder, not rejoicing in what the Lord had said, repudiating it, rising from his seat, departed.

Now at that time a number of gamblers were playing dice not far from the Lord. Then that householder approached these gamblers; having approached, he spoke thus to these gamblers: "Now, I, sirs, approached the recluse [**107**] Gotama; having approached, having greeted the recluse Gotama, I sat down at a respectful distance. Then, sirs, the recluse Gotama spoke thus to me as I was sitting down at a respectful distance: 'Have not you, householder, controlling faculties . . ., . . . (*as above*) . . .' Then I, sirs, not rejoicing in what the Lord had said, repudiating it, rising from my seat, departed."

"That is just it, householder, that is just it, householder; for, householder, bliss and happiness are born of affection, originate in affection."

Then the householder, thinking: "There is agreement between me and the gamblers," departed. Then this subject of conversation[1] gradually penetrated the royal palace. And King Pasenadi of Kosala spoke thus to Queen Mallikā: "This was said to these, Mallikā, by the recluse Gotama: 'Grief, sorrow, suffering, lamentation and despair are born of affection, originate in affection.'"

"If this, sire, was said by the Lord, it is so."

"As the recluse Gotama speaks so does Mallikā because she is much delighted with him: 'If this, sire, was said by the Lord, it is so.' It is just as when a teacher speaks to his pupil and the pupil is so much delighted with him that he says 'It is just so, teacher, it is just so, teacher.' Even so do you, Mallikā, because you are so much delighted with what the recluse Gotama says, say: 'If this, [**108**] sire, was said by the Lord, it is so.' Be off, Mallikā, go away."

Then Queen Mallikā summoned the brahman Nāḷijaṅgha, and said: 'Come you, brahman, approach the Lord; having approached, in my name salute the Lord's feet with your head and ask whether he is well, not indisposed, of bodily vigour, strong, abiding in comfort; and say: 'Lord, Queen Mallikā salutes the Lord's feet with her head, and asks whether he is well . . . abiding in comfort,' and then say: 'Revered sir, were these words spoken by the Lord: Grief, sorrow, suffering, lamentation and despair are born of affection, originate in affection?' And when you have mastered well what the Lord

---

[1] *kathāvatthu*, matter, topic of talk, as at *M.* ii. 127, 132. Also the name of one of the Abhidhamma books.

explains to you, you must tell me. For Tathāgatas do not speak against the truth."[1]

"Yes, madam," and the brahman Nāḷijaṅgha, having answered Queen Mallikā in assent, approached the Lord; having approached, he exchanged greetings with the Lord; having conversed in a courteous and friendly way, he sat down at a respectful distance. As he was sitting down at a respectful distance, the brahman Nāḷijaṅgha spoke thus to the Lord: "Good Gotama, Queen Mallikā with her head salutes the good Gotama's feet and asks whether he is well . . . abiding in comfort. And she speaks thus: 'Revered sir, were these words spoken by the Lord: Grief, sorrow . . . originate in affection?'"

"It is just so, brahman, it is just so, brahman. For, brahman, grief, sorrow . . . originate in affection. And this is a way, brahman, in which it can be said that grief, sorrow . . . originate in affection: Once upon a time, brahman, in this very Sāvatthī a certain woman's mother had passed away. Since her passing away, she (the daughter), unbalanced and unhinged, went from street to street, from cross-road to cross-road, saying: 'Have you not seen my mother? Have you not seen my mother?'

[**109**] This too is a way, brahman, in which it can be said that grief, sorrow . . . originate in affection: Once upon a time, brahman, in this very Sāvatthī a certain woman's father . . . brother, sister, son, daughter, husband had passed away. Since his (her) passing away, she . . . went . . . from cross-road to cross-road, saying: 'Have you not seen my husband? Have you not seen my husband?'

This too is a way, brahman, in which it can be said that grief, sorrow . . . originate in affection: Once upon a time, brahman, in this very Sāvatthī a certain man's mother . . . father . . . brother, sister, son, daughter, wife passed away. Since her (his) passing away, he, unbalanced and unhinged, went from street to street, from cross-road to cross-road, saying: 'Have you not seen my wife? Have you not seen my wife?'

This too is a way, brahman, in which it can be said that grief, sorrow . . . originate in affection: Once upon a time, brahman, in this very Sāvatthī, a certain woman went to her relation's family. Those relations of hers, having forcibly taken her from her husband, desired to give her to another, but she did not want him. Then that woman spoke thus to her husband: 'These relations of mine, master, having forcibly taken me from you, want to give me to

---

[1] *vitathaṁ*, as at *D*. ii. 73.

another, but I do not want him.' Then that man, having cut that woman in two, [**110**] destroyed himself, thinking: ' We will both come to be hereafter.' This too is a way, brahman, in which grief, sorrow, suffering, lamentation and despair are born of affection, originate in affection."

Then the brahman Nāḷijaṅgha, having rejoiced in what the Lord had said, having given thanks, rising from his seat approached Queen Mallikā; having approached, he recounted to her the whole of the conversation he had had with the Lord. Then Queen Mallikā approached King Pasenadi; having approached, she spoke thus to King Pasenadi: " What do you think about this, sire ? Is your daughter Vajīrī dear to you ?"

" Yes, Mallikā. My daughter Vajīrī is dear to me."

" What do you think about this, sire ? From an alteration and otherness in your daughter Vajīrī would there arise in you grief, sorrow . . . despair ?"

" From an alteration and otherness, Mallikā, in my daughter Vajīrī there would be a change for me, even for life. How should there not arise in me grief, sorrow . . . and despair ?"

" It was in reference to this, sire, that it was said by the Lord, who knows, who sees, perfected one, fully Self-Awakened One: ' Grief, sorrow, suffering, lamentation and despair are born of affection, originate in affection.' What do you think about this, sire ? Is the noble lady Vāsabhā[1] dear to you ?"

" Yes, Mallikā, the noble lady Vāsabhā is dear to me."

" What do you think about this, sire ? From an alteration and otherness . . . would there arise in you grief . . . and despair ?"

" From an alteration . . . there would be a change for me, even for life. How should there not arise in me grief . . . and despair ?"

" It was in reference to this, sire, that it was said by the Lord . . .: ' Grief, sorrow . . . originate in affection.' What do you think about this, sire ? Is the General Viḍūḍabha[2] dear to you ?" [**111**] . . .[3] Am I dear to you ?[3] . . . What do you think about this, sire ? Are the peoples of Kāsi and Kosala dear to you ?"

" Yes, Mallikā, the peoples of Kāsi and Kosala are dear to me. Because of their might we obtain sandal wood from the country of Kāsi and use sweet-smelling garlands and perfumes."

" What do you think about this, sire ? From an alteration and

---

[1] According to *MA*. iii. 345 she was one of the King's consorts.

[2] Son of Pasenadi and Vāsabhā.

[3] The text repeats in full the whole conversation as in the case of Vajīrī.

otherness in the peoples of Kāsi and Kosala would there arise in you grief . . . and despair ?"

"From an alteration and otherness, Mallikā, in the peoples of Kāsi and Kosala there would be a change for me, even for life. How should there not arise in me grief, sorrow, suffering, lamentation and despair ?"

"It was in reference to this, sire, that it was said by the Lord, who knows, who sees, perfected one, fully Self-Awakened One: 'Grief, sorrow, suffering, lamentation and despair are born of affection, originate in affection.' "

"It is wonderful, Mallikā, it is marvellous, Mallikā, how much [112] the Lord, penetrating through wisdom, sees by means of wisdom.[1] Come, Mallikā, let me wash (ceremonially)."[2]

Then King Pasenadi, rising from his seat, having arranged his upper garment over one shoulder, having saluted the Lord with joined palms, three times uttered this solemn utterance: "Praise to the Lord, the perfected one, the fully Self-Awakened One."

Discourse on "Born of Affection":
The Seventh

88. DISCOURSE ON THE FOREIGN CLOTH

(Bāhitikasutta)

THUS have I heard: At one time the Lord was staying near Sāvatthī in the Jeta Grove in Anāthapiṇḍika's monastery. Then the venerable Ānanda, having dressed in the morning, taking his bowl and robe entered Sāvatthī for almsfood. When he had walked for almsfood in Sāvatthī, returning from the alms-gathering after the meal, he approached the palace of Migāra's mother and the Eastern

---

[1] *Cf. M.* i. 480, ii. 173; *A.* ii. 115-116.

[2] *ācāmehi.* The commentarial *ācamehi* is to be preferred, unless *ācāmehi* is a causative form; at *Jā.* vi. 8 we get *ācamāpeti*, which the sense of *MA.* iii. 346 seems to suggest, for it implies that although Pasenadi, and not Mallikā, was to perform the ceremonial ablution, she was enjoined to make this possible for her husband by providing him with rinsing water. His ablution would then consist in rinsing ceremonially, *ācamitvā*, washing his hands and feet and rinsing out his mouth before he paid his respects to the Teacher.

monastery for the day-sojourn. At that time King Pasenadi of Kosala, having mounted the bull-elephant Ekapuṇḍarīka (One-Lotus), set forth from Sāvatthī in the early morning. King Pasenadi saw the venerable Ānanda coming in the distance; seeing him, he addressed the chief minister, Sirivaḍḍha, saying: " Dear Sirivaḍḍha, is not this the venerable Ānanda ?"

" Yes, sire, this is the venerable Ānanda." Then King Pasenadi addressed another man, saying: " Come you, my good man, approach the venerable Ānanda; in my name salute the venerable Ānanda's feet with your head, saying: ' Revered sir, King Pasenadi salutes the venerable Ānanda's feet with his head,' and then say: ' If, revered sir, there is really nothing urgent to be done by the venerable Ānanda, please, revered sir, let the venerable Ānanda wait [**113**] for a moment out of compassion.' "

" Yes, sire," and this man having answered King Pasenadi in assent, approached the venerable Ānanda; having approached and having greeted the venerable Ānanda, he stood at a respectful distance. As this man was standing at a respectful distance, he spoke thus to the venerable Ānanda: " Revered sir, King Pasenadi of Kosala salutes the venerable Ānanda's feet with his head, and speaks thus: ' If there is really . . . out of compassion.' " The venerable Ānanda consented by becoming silent. Then King Pasenadi, having gone by the bull-elephant as far as the ground was possible for the elephant, having dismounted, approached the venerable Ānanda on foot; having approached, having greeted the venerable Ānanda, he stood at a respectful distance. As he was standing at a respectful distance, King Pasenadi spoke thus to the venerable Ānanda: " If, revered sir, there is nothing urgent to be done by the venerable Ānanda, it were good, revered sir, that the venerable Ānanda should approach the bank of the river Aciravatī out of compassion." And the venerable Ānanda consented by becoming silent.

Then the venerable Ānanda approached the bank of the river Aciravatī; having approached, he sat down on a seat made ready at the root of a tree. Then King Pasenadi, having gone by bull-elephant as far as the ground was possible for the elephant, having dismounted, approached the venerable Ānanda on foot; having approached . . . (*as above*) . . . spoke thus to the venerable Ānanda: " Now, revered sir, let the venerable Ānanda sit down on this elephant-rug."[1]

---

[1] See above, p. 259, *n*. 3.

"No, sire; you sit down, I am sitting on a seat of my own." King Pasenadi sat down on the prepared seat. As King Pasenadi was sitting down, he spoke thus to the venerable Ānanda: "Revered Ānanda, would the Lord engage not in such bodily conduct[1] as was offensive to[2] intelligent recluses and brahmans?"

"No, sire, the Lord would not engage in such bodily conduct as was offensive to intelligent recluses and brahmans."

[**114**] "But, revered Ānanda, would the Lord engage not in such conduct of speech . . . conduct of thought . . . ?"

"No, sire, the Lord would not engage in such conduct of speech . . . conduct of thought as was offensive to intelligent recluses and brahmans."

"It is wonderful, revered sir, it is marvellous, revered sir—what I was not able to convey fully in a question has been, revered sir, fully conveyed by the venerable Ānanda in answer to the question. Revered sir, when those who are ignorant and inexperienced speak in praise or dispraise of others without test or scrutiny,[3] we do not fall back on that as the pith (of the matter). But, revered sir, when those who are wise, experienced, clever, speak in praise or dispraise of others after test and scrutiny, we fall back on that as the pith (of the matter). But what, revered Ānanda, is the bodily conduct that is offensive to intelligent recluses and brahmans?"

"Whatever the bodily conduct, sire, that is unskilled."

"But what, revered sir, is unskilled bodily conduct?"

"Whatever the bodily conduct, sire, that has a blemish."

"But what, revered sir, is the bodily conduct that has a blemish?"

"Whatever the bodily conduct, sire, that is injurious."

"And what, revered sir, is the bodily conduct that is injurious?"

"Whatever the bodily conduct, sire, that is ill in result."

"And what, revered sir, is the bodily conduct that is ill in result?"

"Whatever bodily conduct, sire, conduces to torment of self and conduces to torment of others and conduces to torment of both, and of which the unskilled states increase much, the skilled states dwindle away—bodily conduct such as this, sire, is offensive to intelligent recluses and brahmans."

"And what, revered Ānanda, is the conduct of speech . . . the conduct of thought that is offensive to intelligent recluses and

---

[1] As at *Vin*. ii. 248.

[2] Or, a slur on, *opārambha*. *MA*. iii. 346, explaining as *uparambhaṁ dosam āropanaraho*, refers to the story of the murderous wanderers at *Ud*. IV. 8.

[3] *Cf*. *A*. i. 89, ii. 3, 84.

brahmans ?" . . . [115] . . . (*As above, reading* (1) conduct of speech (2) conduct of thought *for* bodily conduct) . . . ". . . conduct of thought such as this, sire, is offensive to intelligent recluses and brahmans."

"Revered Ānanda, does not the Lord praise the getting rid of precisely all unskilled states ?"

"The Tathāgata, sire, has got rid of all unskilled states and is endowed with skilled states."[1]

"But which, revered Ānanda, is the bodily conduct that is not offensive to intelligent recluses and brahmans ?"

"Whatever the bodily conduct, sire, that is skilled."

"But what, revered sir, is skilled bodily conduct ?"

"Whatever the bodily conduct, sire, that has no blemish."

"But what, revered sir, is the bodily conduct that has no blemish ?"

"Whatever the bodily conduct, sire, that is non-injurious."

"And what, revered sir, is the bodily conduct that is non-injurious ?"

"Whatever the bodily conduct, sire, that is joyous in result."

"And what, revered sir, is the bodily conduct that is joyous in result ?"

"Whatever bodily conduct, sire, does not conduce to the torment of self and does not conduce to the torment of others and does not conduce to the torment of both, and of which the unskilled states dwindle away, the skilled states increase much—bodily conduct such as this, sire, is not offensive to intelligent recluses and brahmans."

"And what, revered Ānanda, is the conduct of speech . . . the conduct of thought that is not offensive to intelligent recluses and brahmans ?" . . . [116] . . . (*As above, reading* (1) conduct of speech (2) conduct of thought *for* bodily conduct) . . . " . . . conduct of thought such as this, sire, is not offensive to intelligent recluses and brahmans."

"But, revered Ānanda, does the Lord praise the acquiring of precisely all skilled states ?"

"The Tathāgata, sire, has got rid of all unskilled states and is endowed with skilled states."

"It is wonderful, revered sir, it is marvellous, revered sir, how well spoken is this, revered sir, by the venerable Ānanda; and we, revered sir, are delighted and satisfied with the venerable Ānanda's well spoken words. Being thus delighted and satisfied, revered sir, with the venerable Ānanda's well spoken words, we would give a

---

[1] A reference is intended here to: *yathākārī tathāvādī*, as he does so he speaks (*D.* iii. 135).

valuable elephant to the venerable Ānanda if this, revered sir, were allowable to the venerable Ānanda, likewise a valuable horse, likewise the boon of a village if these, revered sir, were allowable to the venerable Ānanda. But then we know this, revered sir: This is not allowable to the venerable Ānanda. This piece of foreign cloth,[1] revered sir, inserted into the shaft of a sunshade, has been sent to me by King Ajātasattu of Magadha, the son of (the lady) Videhī; in length it is equal to sixteen (hands[2]), in breadth to eight (hands). Revered sir, let the venerable Ānanda accept it out of compassion."

"No, sire, I am complete as to the three robes."

[117] "Revered sir, after a great storm has rained down on the high mountain slopes, both you and I have seen how at such a time the river Aciravatī rushes along overflowing both its banks[3]—even so, revered sir, the venerable Ānanda can make a set of three robes for himself from this piece of foreign cloth; and the venerable Ānanda can distribute his old set of three robes among his fellow Brahma-farers. So will this gift of faith of ours go on with an overflow, methinks. Revered sir, let the venerable Ānanda accept this piece of foreign cloth."

And the venerable Ānanda accepted the piece of foreign cloth. Then King Pasenadi spoke thus to the venerable Ānanda: "If it please you, we are going now, revered sir, we are very busy, there is much to be done."

"You must do now, sire, that for which you deem it the right time."

Then King Pasenadi, having rejoiced in what the venerable Ānanda had said, giving thanks, rising from his seat and greeting the venerable Ānanda, departed keeping his right side towards him. Then not long after King Pasenadi had departed, the venerable Ānanda approached the Lord; having approached, having greeted the Lord, he sat down at a respectful distance. As he was sitting down at a respectful distance the venerable Ānanda told the Lord the whole of the conversation he had had with King Pasenadi, and he handed that piece of foreign cloth to the Lord. Then the Lord addressed the monks, saying: "Monks, it is a gain for King Pasenadi,

---

[1] *bāhitikā*. *MA*. iii. 347 says it is the name of a cloth or garment, *vattha*, produced outside the kingdom.

[2] So *MA*. iii. 347 and *cf*. *Miln*. 317. *Hattha* is more correctly hand and forearm.

[3] *Cf*. *Miln*. 36.

it is well gotten by King Pasenadi that he achieved a sight of Ānanda, that he achieved a paying of homage to him." Thus spoke the Lord; delighted, these monks rejoiced in what the Lord had said.

Discourse on the Foreign Cloth:
The Eighth

89. DISCOURSE ON TESTIMONIES TO DHAMMA

(Dhammacetiyasutta)

[118] THUS have I heard: At one time the Lord was staying among the Sakyans. Medaḷumpa[1] was the name of the market town belonging to the Sakyans. At that time King Pasenadi of Kosala had arrived at Naṅgaraka[2] on some business or other. Then King Pasenadi addressed Dīgha Kārāyana,[3] saying: "Good Kārāyana, harness some lovely vehicles; we are going to the garden of the pleasaunce to see its beauties."

"Yes, sire," and Dīgha Kārāyana, having answered King Pasenadi in assent, having had many lovely vehicles harnessed, announced to King Pasenadi: "Many lovely vehicles are harnessed for you, sire. You may deem it is now the right time for that." Then King Pasenadi, having mounted one of the lovely vehicles, set forth from Naṅgaraka with the many lovely vehicles and with great royal pomp, and drew near the park. When he had gone by vehicle as far as the ground was possible, dismounting from the vehicle, he entered the park on foot. As King Pasenadi was pacing up and down in the park and roaming about on foot he saw charming and attractive roots of trees, quiet and silent, without folk's breath, far from the haunts of men, suitable for solitary meditation.[4] Seeing them, he began to remember the Lord, thinking: "It is at these charming and attractive roots of trees . . . suitable for solitary meditation, that we

---

[1] *MA*. iii. 348: Medataḷumpa; *DhA*. i. 356=*Jā*. iv. 151: Uḷumpa.

[2] According to *M*. iii. 104 and *MA*. iii. 348 this was a market-town, *nigama*, of the Sakyans.

[3] Nephew of Bandhula, the commander-in-chief of the Mallas, *MA*. iii. 349.

[4] As at *Vin*. i. 39, ii. 158, etc.

can pay homage to that Lord, perfected one, fully Self-Awakened One." Then King Pasenadi addressed Dīgha Kārāyana, saying: "It is, good Kārāyana, at these charming and attractive roots of trees . . . that we can pay homage to this Lord . . . fully Self-Awakened One. Where, good Kārāyana, [**119**] is this Lord staying at present, perfected one, fully Self-Awakened One ?"

"Sire, there is a market town of the Sakyans called Medaḷumpa. The Lord, perfected one, fully Self-Awakened One, is staying there at present."

"Now, how far, good Kārāyana, is Medaḷumpa, the market town of the Sakyans, from Naṅgaraka ?"

"It is not far, sire; it is three *yojanas*. It is possible to get to it in what remains of the day."

"Well then, good Kārāyana, harness many lovely vehicles, we will go to see this Lord, perfected one, fully Self-Awakened One."

"Yes, sire," and Dīgha Kārāyana, having answered King Pasenadi in assent, having had many lovely vehicles harnessed, announced to King Pasenadi: "Many lovely vehicles are harnessed for you, sire, You may deem it is now the right time for that." Then King Pasenadi, having mounted one of the lovely vehicles, set forth from Naṅgaraka with the many lovely vehicles and drew near Medaḷumpa, the market town of the Sakyans, arriving there in what remained of that day, and approached the park.[1] When he had gone by vehicle as far as the ground was possible, dismounting from the vehicle, he entered the park on foot. Now at that time several monks were pacing up and down in the open air. Then King Pasenadi approached these monks; having approached, he spoke thus to these monks: "Where, revered sirs, is the Lord staying at present, perfected one, fully Self-Awakened One ? We are anxious to see the Lord . . . Self-Awakened One."

"Sire, this is the dwelling-place; the door is closed. Having approached quietly, having entered the verandah (but) not crossing it, having coughed, tap on the door-bolt. The Lord will open the door to you."[2] Then King Pasenadi immediately handed his sword and turban[3] to Dīgha Kārāyana. Then it occurred to Dīgha Kārāyana: "The King wants to be alone now; must I now remain just where I am ?" Then King Pasenadi having quietly approached

---

[1] *Cf. A.* v. 65-66, several of the details of which vary however from the *M.* account.

[2] As at *Vin.* i. 248. See *B.D.* iv. 342 for notes.

[3] Two of the five emblems of royalty, see *e.g. Jā.* v. 264.

that dwelling-place with its closed door, having entered the verandah (but) not crossing it, coughed and tapped on the door-bolt. The Lord opened the door. Then King Pasenadi, [120] having entered the dwelling-place,[1] having inclined his head to the Lord's feet, kissed the Lord's feet on all sides with his mouth and stroked them on all sides with his hands, and he made known his (own) name: "I, revered sir, am King Pasenadi of Kosala; I, revered sir, am King Pasenadi of Kosala."

"But for what special reason do you, sire, pay such deep respect to this body[2] and display such tokens of friendship?"

"Revered sir, for me there is a logical consequence[3] of the Lord's *dhamma*: 'The fully Self-Awakened One is the Lord, well taught is *dhamma* by the Lord, the Lord's Order of disciples fares along well.' I, revered sir, see some recluses and brahmans here, faring a restricted Brahma-faring for ten, twenty, thirty and forty years. After a time these, well washed,[4] well anointed, with their hair and beards trimmed, parade about in the full possession and enjoyment of the five strands of sense-pleasures. On the other hand I, revered sir, see monks here faring a perfectly fulfilled, perfectly purified Brahma-faring all their lives long until their last breath. And outside this, revered sir, I behold no other Brahma-faring so perfectly fulfilled and perfectly purified. This, revered sir, is a logical consequence of the Lord's *dhamma*: 'The fully Self-Awakened One is the Lord . . . fares along well.'

And again, revered sir, kings quarrel with kings, and nobles quarrel with nobles, and brahmans quarrel with brahmans, and householders quarrel with householders, and a mother quarrels with a child, and a child quarrels with the mother, and a father quarrels with a child, and a child quarrels with the father, and a brother quarrels with a brother, and a brother quarrels with a sister, and a sister quarrels with a brother, and friend quarrels with friend. But I, revered sir, see monks here living on friendly terms and harmonious, not quarrelling, like milk and water blending, [121] regarding one another with the eye of affection. But outside this, revered sir, I

---

[1] It was at this juncture that Dīgha Kārāyana made Viḍūḍabha king instead of Pasenadi, *MA*. iii. 352, *Jā*. iv. 151-152, *DhA*. i. 356.

[2] *Cf*. *S*. iii. 120, "What is there in seeing this vile body of mine?"

[3] *dhammanvaya*, as at *M*. i. 69. The *A*. account breaks off here, and Pasenadi gives, as recorded there, quite different reasons for his deep respect.

[4] *sunhāta*. This and the next two words also at *S*. i. 79, iv. 343, and *cf*. *D*. i. 104. *Sunhāta* probably refers to ceremonial washing rather than to the bathing at fortnightly intervals allowed to monks at *Vin*. iv. 117.

behold no other such harmonious company. And this too, revered sir, is for me a logical consequence of Lord's *dhamma*. 'The fully Self-Awakened is the Lord . . . fares along well.'

And again, I, revered sir, pace up and down and roam about from one park to another, from one pleasaunce to another. And there I see some recluses and brahmans who are thin, wretched, their colour bad, yellowish, their veins standing out on their limbs, methinks not at all pleasing to behold. So it occurs to me thus, revered sir: Undoubtedly these venerable ones are faring the Brahma-faring displeased, or there is some evil *kamma* done by them and concealed,[1] and that is why these venerable ones are thin, wretched . . . not at all pleasing to behold. So, approaching these venerable ones, I speak thus: 'How is it that you, venerable ones, are thin . . . wretched . . . not at all pleasing to behold?' They say: 'It is an illness that runs in our families,[2] sire.' On the other hand I, revered sir, see monks here who are very joyful, very exultant, looking contented and cheerful, living unconcerned, unruffled, dependent on others,[3] with a mind become as a wild creature's. So it occurs to me, revered sir: Undoubtedly these venerable ones recognise a high excellence in the Lord's teaching, a gradual accomplishing,[4] and that is why these venerable ones are very joyful, very exultant . . . living . . . with a mind become as a wild creature's. And this too is for me, revered sir, a logical consequence of the Lord's *dhamma*: 'The fully Self-Awakened One is the Lord . . . fares along well.'

And again, revered sir, I, a noble anointed king, [**122**] am able to execute one deserving execution, to fine one deserving to be fined, to banish one deserving banishment. But when I am sitting on a case, people sometimes speak interrupting (me). And I get no chance to say: 'While I am sitting on the case do not, good sirs, speak interrupting (me). Let the good sirs wait until I have finished speaking.' But I, revered sir, see monks here at a time when the Lord is teaching *dhamma* to various assemblies, and at that time there is no sound of expectorating among the Lord's disciples, no

---

[1] *Cf. Vin.* ii. 40 *ff.*, where an offence that has not been confessed is still 'concealed,' hidden or covered, *paṭicchanna*.

[2] *bandhukaroga*. *Bandhu* is of course kinsman, and although a v.l. is *paṇḍuka-* (jaundice), *MA*. iii. 353 explains by *kularogo amhākaṁ*, a family illness of ours, of hereditary nature.

[3] *paradavutta*, see *B.D.* v. 259, *n.* 2.

[4] *pubbenâpara visesa*, from *kasiṇa*-meditation through *vipassanā* (insight, a higher form of meditation) to arahantship, *MA*. iii. 353.

sound of coughing.[1] Once upon a time, revered sir, when the Lord was teaching *dhamma* to various assemblies a certain disciple of the Lord coughed; one of his fellow Brahma-farers tapped his knee and said: ' Let the venerable one be quiet, let the venerable one make no noise; the Lord, our Teacher, is teaching *dhamma*.'[1] In connection with this it occurred to me, revered sir: ' Indeed, it is wonderful, indeed it is marvellous; assuredly, how well trained—without stick,[2] without sword—must be such an assembly.' And outside this, revered sir, I see no other assembly well trained thus. And this too is for me, revered sir, a logical consequence of the Lord's *dhamma*: ' The fully Self-Awakened One is the Lord . . . fares along well.'

And again, revered sir, I see here some clever nobles,[3] subtle, practised in disputing with others, skilled in hair-splitting, who go about, methinks, breaking to pieces in their wisdom the views (of others). These hear: ' Undoubtedly the recluse Gotama will visit a certain village or market town.' They construct a question, thinking: ' Having approached the recluse Gotama, we will ask him this question of ours. If, on being asked by us thus, he answers thus, we will refute him thus; and if, on being asked by us thus, he answers thus, we will refute him thus.' These hear: ' It is certain that the recluse Gotama is visiting a certain village or market town.' So they approach the Lord. The Lord gladdens, rouses, incites, **[123]** delights them with talk on *dhamma*. These, gladdened . . . delighted by the Lord with talk on *dhamma*, do not ask the Lord the question at all—whence can they refute him ? On the contrary, they become the Lord's disciples. This too is for me, revered sir, a logical consequence of the Lord's *dhamma*: ' The fully Self-Awakened One is the Lord . . . fares along well.'

And again, revered sir, I see here some clever brahmans[4] . . . clever householders . . . clever recluses . . . (*as above*) . . . whence can they refute him ? On the contrary, they ask leave of the Lord himself for the going forth from home into homelessness. The Lord lets them go forth. These, gone forth like this, living alone, aloof,

---

[1] *Cf. M.* ii. 4-5.

[2] *daṇḍa* here possibly means more specifically " punishment," to balance the punishments meted out by the king, above; but we have not infrequently had the pair: (without) stick and (without) sword.

[3] *Cf.* following passage with *M.* i. 176 *f.*

[4] At *M.* i. 176 the brahmans are like the nobles who " on the contrary, become the Lord's disciples." Thus a pair is formed to balance the other pair—householders and recluses—who ask for the going forth. The reading at *M.* i. 176 is to be preferred.

diligent, ardent, self-resolute, having by their own super-knowledge soon realised here and now that matchless goal of the Brahma-faring for the sake of which young men of family rightly go forth from home into homelessness, entering on it, abide in it. These speak thus: 'Indeed we were nearly lost, indeed we were nearly lost, for while we were formerly not (true) recluses, we claimed that we were, saying: We are recluses. Not being (true) brahmans, we claimed that we were saying: We are brahmans. Not being (true) perfected ones, we claimed that we were saying: We are perfected ones. But now we really are recluses, now we really are brahmans, now we really are perfected ones.' This too is for me, revered sir, a logical consequence of the Lord's *dhamma*: 'The fully Self-Awakened One is the Lord . . . fares along well.'

And again, revered sir, I see here the equerries[1] Isīdatta and Purāṇa[2] whose food is mine, whose vehicles are mine,[3] for whom I provide a livelihood and to whom I bring fame. But yet they do not [**124**] pay me respect as they do the Lord. Once upon a time, revered sir, while marching against an army, in order to test these same equerries, Isīdatta and Purāṇa, I took up my quarters in some cramped habitation. Then, revered sir, these equerries, Isīdatta and Purāṇa, having passed the greater part of the night in talk on *dhamma*, lay down with their heads directed towards where they had heard that the Lord was, their feet towards me. In connection with this, revered sir, it occurred to me: 'Indeed it is wonderful, indeed it is marvellous. These equerries, Isīdatta and Purāṇa, whose food is mine, whose vehicles are mine, for whom I provide a livelihood and to whom I bring fame, yet do not pay me respect as they do the Lord. Undoubtedly these venerable ones recognise a high excellence in this Lord's teaching, a gradual accomplishing.' And this too is for me, revered sir, a logical consequence of the Lord's teaching: 'The fully Self-Awakened One is the Lord; well taught is *dhamma* by the Lord; the Lord's Order of disciples fares along well.'

And again, revered sir, the Lord is a noble, I too am a noble; the Lord is a Kosalan, I too am a Kosalan; the Lord is round about eighty years of age, I too am round about eighty years of age. It is because the Lord is a noble and I am a noble, because the Lord is a

---

[1] A translation of *thapatayo* suggested at *K.S.* v. 303, *n.* 1.

[2] For the two see *S.* v. 348 *ff.*, *A.* iii. 348, 351, 451, v. 139, 143, and *DPPN.*

[3] *mama bhattā mama yānā. MA.* iii. 354 says *mama santakaṁ bhattaṁ* (. . . *yānaṁ* . . .) *etesaṁ*, their food (vehicles) is due to me. There is little support for Chalmers' "who make my carriages."

Kosalan and I am a Kosalan, because the Lord is round about eighty years of age and I am round about eighty years of age that I am disposed, revered sir, to pay deep respect to the Lord and display tokens of friendship. Please, revered sir, I must be going now, I am very busy, there is much to be done."

"Do now, sire, that for which you deem it to be the right time."

Then King Pasenadi, rising from his seat, having greeted the Lord, departed keeping his right side towards him. Soon after King Pasenadi had departed, the Lord addressed the monks, saying:

"Monks, that is King Pasenadi of Kosala who, having spoken testimonies to *dhamma*,[1] rising from his seat, is departing. Learn, monks, the testimonies to *dhamma*; master, [125] monks, the testimonies to *dhamma*; remember, monks, the testimonies to *dhamma*. Connected with the goal, monks, are the testimonies to *dhamma*, fundamental to the Brahma-faring."

Thus spoke the Lord. Delighted, these monks rejoiced in what the Lord had said.

Discourse on Testimonies to Dhamma:
The Ninth

90. DISCOURSE AT KAṆṆAKATTHALA

(Kaṇṇakatthalasutta)

THUS have I heard: At one time the Lord was staying near Ujuññā[2] in the deer-park at Kaṇṇakatthala. At that time King Pasenadi

---

[1] *MA*. iii. 355 explains *dhammacetiyāni* as "words of respect for the *dhamma*. To whichever one of the Three Jewels respect is paid, it is paid to all. Therefore, if paid to the Lord, it is paid to *dhamma*, and so the Lord spoke of 'testimonies to *dhamma*.'" *Cetiya* usually means a (sepulchral) monument, from a root meaning to pile up, and in this Discourse Chalmers renders by "monuments" and Neumann by "Denkmale." The memorial monuments of India are, however, also in the nature of testimony to the virtues, etc. of the deceased person in whose honour they are erected. I hope the use of this word here does not take us too far from the meaning intended. "Attestations" might also have been chosen.

[2] Mentioned at *D*. i. 161. According to *MA*. iii. 356 it was both a district and a town; here the town is meant.

of Kosala had arrived at Ujuññā on some business or other. Then King Pasenadi addressed a certain man, saying: "Come you, my good man, approach the Lord; having approached, in my name salute the Lord's feet with your head and ask whether he is well, not indisposed, of bodily vigour, strong, abiding in comfort, and say: 'Revered sir, King Pasenadi salutes the Lord's feet with his head, and asks whether he is well . . . abiding in comfort'; and then speak thus: 'Revered sir, today after the meal when he has had breakfast, King Pasenadi is expecting to come to see the Lord.'"

"Yes, sire," and that man, having answered King Pasenadi in assent, approached the Lord; having approached, having greeted the Lord, he sat down at a respectful distance. As he was sitting down at a respectful distance, that man spoke thus to the Lord: "Revered sir, King Pasenadi salutes the Lord's feet with his head, and asks whether he is well . . . abiding in comfort. And he speaks thus: 'Revered sir, today after the meal . . . King Pasenadi is expecting to come to see the Lord.'"

The sisters Somā and Sakulā[1] heard: "Today [**126**] after the meal when he has had breakfast, King Pasenadi is expecting to go to see the Lord." Then the sisters Somā and Sakulā, having approached the place where King Pasenadi was eating,[2] spoke thus: "Well then, sire, in our names salute the Lord's feet with your head and ask whether he is well . . . abiding in comfort, saying: 'Revered sir, the sisters Somā and Sakulā salute the Lord's feet with their heads and ask whether he is well . . . abiding in comfort.'"

Then after the meal when King Pasenadi had eaten his breakfast, he approached the Lord; having approached, having greeted the Lord, he sat down at a respectful distance. As he was sitting down at a respectful distance, King Pasenadi spoke thus to the Lord: "Revered sir, the sisters Somā and Sakulā with their heads salute the Lord's feet and ask whether he is well . . . abiding in comfort."

"But how is it, sire, that the sisters Somā and Sakulā were not able to send another messenger?"

"Revered sir, the sisters Somā and Sakulā heard: 'Today after the meal when he has had breakfast, King Pasenadi is expecting to go to see the Lord.' Then, revered sir, the sisters Somā and Sakulā, having approached me in the place where I was eating, spoke thus:

---

[1] *MA*. iii. 356 says that these two sisters were wives of Pasenadi.

[2] *bhattâbhihāre*, as at *S*. i. 82. "The place where the rice (food) was brought," *MA*. iii. 356.

'Well then, sire, in our names salute the Lord's feet with your head and ask whether he is well . . . abiding in comfort.' The sisters Somā and Sakulā, revered sir, are saluting the Lord's feet with their heads and asking whether he is well, not indisposed, of bodily vigour, strong, abiding in comfort."

"May the sisters Somā and Sakulā be happy, sire."

Then King Pasenadi spoke thus to the Lord: "I have heard this about you, revered sir: 'The recluse Gotama speaks thus: There is neither a recluse nor a brahman who, all-knowing, all-seeing, can claim all-embracing knowledge-and-vision—this situation does not exist.' Revered sir, those who speak thus: 'The recluse Gotama [127] speaks thus: There is neither a recluse nor a brahman . . . this situation does not exist'—I hope that these, revered sir, speak what was spoken by the Lord, that they do not misrepresent the Lord by what is not fact, that they explain *dhamma* according to *dhamma*, and that no reasoned thesis gives occasion for contempt ?[1]

"Those, sire, who speak thus: 'The recluse Gotama speaks thus: There is neither a recluse nor a brahman who, all-knowing, all-seeing, can claim all-embracing knowledge-and-vision—this situation does not exist.'—these do not speak as I spoke but are misrepresenting me with what is not true, with what is not fact."

Then King Pasenadi addressed the commander-in-chief, Viḍūḍabha, saying: "Now, who was it, commander-in-chief, that brought this subject of conversation into the palace ?"

"The brahman Sañjaya of the Ākāsa clan, sire."

Then King Pasenadi summoned a man and said: "Come you, my good man, in my name summon the brahman Sañjaya of the Ākāsa clan, saying: 'King Pasenadi, revered sir, is summoning you.'"

"Yes, your majesty," and when this man had answered King Pasenadi in assent he approached the brahman Sañjaya of the Ākāsa clan; and having approached, he spoke thus to the brahman Sañjaya: "King Pasenadi is summoning you, revered sir."

Then King Pasenadi spoke thus to the Lord: "Could it be, revered sir, that people might have transferred to quite another topic something (originally) said by the Lord in reference to something else ? In regard to what, revered sir, does the Lord claim to have spoken the words ?"

"I, sire, claim to have spoken the words thus: There is neither a

---

[1] *Cf. M.* i. 368, ii. 77, 222, 243.

recluse nor a brahman who at one and the same time[1] can know all, can see all—this situation does not exist."

"Revered sir, the Lord speaks causally,[2] and it is in reference to cause,[2] revered sir, that the Lord says: 'There is neither a recluse nor a brahman [**128**] who at one and the same time can know all, can see all—this situation does not exist.' These, revered sir, are the four castes: nobles, brahmans, merchants and workers. Now, revered sir, could there be any distinction, any difference, between these four castes?"

"These are, sire, the four castes: nobles, brahmans, merchants and workers. Among these four castes, sire, two are pointed to as chief: the nobles and the brahmans, that is to say in the way of addressing them, rising up from one's seat for them, saluting them with joined palms and rendering them service."

"I, revered sir, am not asking the Lord about the here and now; revered sir, I am asking the Lord about a future state. These, revered sir, are the four castes: nobles, brahmans, merchants and workers. Now, revered sir, could there be any distinction, any difference between these four castes?"

"Sire, there are these five qualities for striving.[3] What five? As to this, sire, a monk has faith . . . with ariyan discrimination leading to the complete destruction of anguish. These, sire, are the five qualities for striving. These, sire, are the four castes: nobles, brahmans, merchants and workers. These might be possessed of the five qualities for striving. For a long time that would be for their welfare and happiness."

"These, revered sir, are the four castes: nobles, brahmans, merchants [**129**] and workers; and these might be possessed of the five qualities for striving. But, revered sir, might there be among them here any distinction, any difference?"

"I, sire, here speak of a divergence in striving. It is as if[4] there might be, sire, among elephants or horses or oxen to be tamed two elephants, two horses or two oxen that were well tamed, well trained and two that were not tamed, not trained. What do you think about

---

1 *sakideva*. *MA*. iii. 357 says "who, with one 'adverting' (of the mind), one thought, one 'impulsion,' can know and see the whole past, future and present."

2 *heturūpaṁ* . . . *saheturūpaṁ*.

3 As at *M*. ii. 95; see above, p. 282, and fill up the omission in this paragraph from there.

4 *Cf*. *M*. iii. 130.

this, sire? Would those two elephants or horses or oxen that were to be tamed and that were well tamed, well trained—would these, on being tamed, reach tamed capacity, would they, being tamed, attain tamed rank?"

"Yes, revered sir."

"But those two elephants or horses or oxen that were to be tamed but that were neither tamed nor trained—would these, not being tamed, reach tamed capacity, and would they, not being tamed, attain tamed rank as do the two elephants or horses or oxen to be tamed that were well tamed, well trained?"

"No, revered sir."

"Even so, sire, that which may be achieved by faith, by good health, by honesty and absence of deceit, by output of energy, by wisdom—that one of no faith, of poor health, fraudulent and deceitful, lazy, weak in wisdom could attain it—this situation does not exist."

"Revered sir, the Lord speaks causally, and it is in reference to cause, revered sir, that the Lord speaks. These, revered sir, are the four castes: nobles, brahmans, merchants and workers. These might be possessed of the five qualities for striving, and if they made the proper efforts would there be between them, revered sir, any distinction, any difference?"

"I, sire, here speak of no difference, that is to say in freedom as against freedom. It is as though a man, sire, bringing dry sticks from a teak tree[1] were to produce a fire and heat were to result. Then another man, bringing dry sticks from a sāl-tree **[130]** . . . another man, bringing dry sticks from a mango-tree . . . another man, bringing dry sticks from a fig tree were to produce a fire and heat were to result. What do you think about this, sire? Because of the different woods used for the fires, would there be any difference in what is produced, in flame as against flame, in hue as against hue, in brilliance as against brilliance?"

"No, revered sir."

"Even so it is, sire, with heat created by energy, produced by striving. I do not speak of any difference there, that is in freedom as against freedom."

"Revered sir, the Lord speaks causally, and it is in reference to cause that the Lord speaks. But, honoured sir, are there *devas*?"[2]

---

[1] *sāka* is probably teak, Tectonia grandis. *Cf.* four (or five) fires at *M.* ii. 152, and *M.* ii. 183.

[2] *Cf. M.* ii. 212. *MA.* iii. 359 quotes a passage giving a list of *devas*—see *A.* i. 210, iii. 287, 313, 316, v. 331, 334.

" How can you, sire, speak thus: 'But, revered sir, are there *devas* ?' "

" Be it that these *devas*, revered sir, are returners to a state of being such or so,[1] or be it that they are not returners to a state of being such or so ?"

" Sire, whatever *devas* have been malevolent are returners to a state of being such or so; whatever *devas* have not been malevolent are not returners to a state of being such or so."

When this had been said, the commander-in-chief, Viḍūḍabha, spoke thus to the Lord: " Revered sir, can those *devas* that are malevolent and are returners to a state of being such or so drive away or banish from that place those *devas* that have not been malevolent and are not returners to a state of being such or so ?"

Then it occurred to the venerable Ānanda: " This Viḍūḍabha, the commander-in-chief, is a son of King Pasenadi; I am the Lord's son. This is a time when son might confer with son." So the venerable Ānanda addressed Viḍūḍabha, the commander-in-chief, saying: " Well now, commander-in-chief, on this point I will ask you something in return. Answer exactly as it seems right to you. What do you think about this, commander-in-chief ? As far as the realm of King Pasenadi (extends), and there where King Pasenadi [**131**] holds dominion and sway, is King Pasenadi able to drive away or banish from that place a recluse or a brahman whether he is meritorious or not meritorious, whether he is a Brahma-farer or not a Brahma-farer?"

" Good sir, as far as the realm of King Pasenadi (extends) and there where King Pasenadi holds dominion and sway, King Pasenadi is able to drive away or banish from that place a recluse or a brahman whether he is meritorious or not, a Brahma-farer or not."

" What do you think about this, commander-in-chief ? As far as the realm of King Pasenadi does not (extend), and there where King Pasenadi holds no dominion or sway, is King Pasenadi able to drive away or banish from that place a recluse or a brahman whether he is meritorious or not meritorious, whether he is a Brahma-farer or not a Brahma-farer ?"

" Good sir, as far as the realm of King Pasenadi does not (extend) . . . King Pasenadi is not able to drive away or banish from that place a recluse . . . or not a Brahma-farer."

" What do you think about, this, commander-in-chief ? Have you heard of the *devas* of the Thirty-Three ?"

---

[1] *itthatta*, being such and such; such or so.

"Yes, good sir, I have heard of the *devas* of the Thirty-Three and the good King Pasenadi has also heard of the *devas* of the Thirty-Three."

"What do you think about this, commander-in-chief? Is King Pasenadi able to drive away or banish from that place the *devas* of the Thirty-Three?"

"Good sir, King Pasenadi is not even able to see the *devas* of the Thirty-Three. How then could he drive them away or banish them from that place?"

"Even so, commander-in-chief, those *devas* that have been malevolent and are returners to a state of being such or so are not even able to see those *devas* that have not been malevolent and are not returners to a state of being such or so. So how could they drive them away or banish them from that place?"

Then King Pasenadi spoke thus to the Lord: "What, revered sir, is this monk's name?"

"His name is Ānanda, sire."

"Bliss[1] indeed, indeed blissful![1] [132] Revered sir, the venerable Ānanda speaks causally and it is in reference to cause, revered sir, that the venerable Ānanda speaks. But now, revered sir, is there a Brahmā?"

"How can you, sire, speak thus: 'Is there a Brahmā?'"

"Be it that this Brahmā, revered sir, is a returner to the state of being such or so, or be it that he is not a returner to a state of being such or so?"

"Sire, whatever Brahmā has been malevolent is a returner to a state of being such or so; but whatever Brahmā has not been malevolent is not a returner to a state of being such or so."

Then a certain man spoke thus to King Pasenadi: "The brahman Sañjaya of the Ākāsa clan has arrived, sire." Then King Pasenadi spoke thus to the brahman Sañjaya of the Ākāsa clan: "Now, who was it, brahman, that brought this subject of conversation into the palace?"

"Viḍūḍabha, sire, the commander-in-chief."

"The commander-in-chief, Viḍūḍabha, speaks thus: 'The brahman Sañjaya, sire, of the Ākāsa clan.'"

Then a certain man spoke thus to King Pasenadi: "It is time for the vehicle, sire." Then King Pasenadi spoke thus to the Lord: "We, revered sir, questioned the Lord about omniscience; the Lord

---

[1] *ānanda . . . ānandarūpaṁ.*

explained omniscience, and because it was pleasing to us and approved we are delighted. Revered sir, we questioned the Lord about the purity of the four castes; the Lord explained the purity of the four castes, and because it was pleasing to us and approved we are delighted. Revered sir, we questioned the Lord about the *devas*; the Lord explained the *devas*, and because it was pleasing to us . . . we are delighted. Revered sir, we questioned the Lord about Brahmā; the Lord explained about Brahmā, and because it was pleasing to us and approved we are delighted. And, revered sir, whatever it was we questioned the Lord about, that very thing the Lord explained, and because it was pleasing to us and approved we are delighted. [**133**] And now, if it please you, revered sir, we are going; we are very busy and there is much to be done."

"You must do now, sire, that for which you deem it the right time."

Then King Pasenadi of Kosala, delighted at what the Lord had said, having given thanks, rising from his seat, having greeted the Lord, departed keeping his right side towards him.

Discourse at Kaṇṇakatthala:
The Tenth

The Royal Division:
The Fourth

V. THE DIVISION ON BRAHMANS

(Brāhmaṇavagga)

91. DISCOURSE WITH BRAHMĀYU

(Brahmāyusutta)

THUS have I heard: At one time the Lord was walking on tour in Videha together with a large Order of monks, with as many as five hundred monks. Now at that time the brahman Brahmāyu was living in Mithilā. He was worn, old, full of years, he had lived his span and was at the close of his life, a hundred and twenty years of age; he was master[1] of the three Vedas,[2] versed in the vocabularies and rituals together with the phonology and exegesis[3] and the legendary tradition as the fifth; he was learned in idioms, a grammarian, proficient in popular philosophy and the marks of a Great Man.[4] The brahman Brahmāyu heard: "Verily the recluse Gotama,[5] son of the Sakyans, having gone forth from the Sakyan clan, is walking on tour in Videha together with a large Order of monks, with as many as five hundred monks. The most lovely report has gone abroad thus concerning this revered[6] Gotama: He is indeed Lord, perfected one, fully Self-Awakened One, endowed with knowledge and (right) conduct, Well-farer, knower of the worlds, the matchless charioteer of men to be tamed, teacher of *devas* and mankind, the Awakened One, the Lord. Having realised through his own super-knowledge, he makes known this world together with *devas* including the Māras and the Brahmās; creatures together with recluses and brahmans, with *devas* and mankind. He teaches

---

[1] This is a stock description of a learned brahman. "Master," *pāragū*, is a goer to the beyond in, and so one who has come to finality or culmination. *Cf. M.* ii. 210; *D.* i. 88; *A.* i. 163, 166; *Sn.* p. 105, ver. 1019 *f.*

[2] *MA.* iii. 362, *DA.* 247, *AA.* ii. 261 and *SnA.* 447 all give Iru, Yaju and Sāma Vedas (Rig, Yajur and Sāman Vedas).

[3] See *Dial.* i. 109, *n.* 2, where it is said: "It is quite unnecessary to suppose a silent reference to it (the Atharva Veda) here," as *DA.* 247=*MA.* iii. 362=*AA.* ii. 261=*SnA.* 447 suggest.

[4] See *Ambaṭṭha Suttanta* (*D.* i. 87, and see *Dial.* i. 110, *n.* 2 and 131, *n.* 2). Also the *Lakkhaṇa Suttanta* (D. iii. 142), *Mahāpadāna Sta.* (*D.* ii. 1 *ff.*), *Mahāpurisa Sta.* (*S.* v. 158) and *Vassakāra Sta.* (*A.* ii. 35 *f.*). The last two give the Buddhist, as against the pre-Buddhist interpretation of the Great Man. See also *Mhvu. Transln.* i. 180 *f.*

[5] This too is a stock clause.

[6] *bhavantaṁ.*

dhamma that is lovely at the beginning, lovely in the middle and lovely at the ending; he explains with the spirit and the letter the Brahma-faring completely fulfilled and wholly purified. Good indeed is the sight of perfected ones such as this."

[**134**] Now at that time the brahman Brahmāyu had the brahman youth Uttara as pupil; he was master of the three Vedas . . . proficient in . . . the marks of a Great Man. Then the brahman Brahmāyu addressed the brahman youth Uttara, saying: "Dear Uttara, this recluse Gotama, son of the Sakyans . . . explains with the spirit and the letter the Brahma-faring completely fulfilled and wholly purified. Good indeed is the sight of perfected ones such as this. Come you, dear Uttara, approach the recluse Gotama; having approached, find out whether the recluse Gotama is in fact that revered Gotama of whom the report has gone abroad or whether he is not, and whether the revered Gotama is such a one or not such a one. Through you will we know that revered Gotama. So will I, in virtue of what you say, find out whether that revered Gotama is in fact the revered Gotama of whom the report has gone abroad or whether he is not, and whether the revered Gotama is such a one or not such a one. Dear Uttara, in our *mantras*[1] the thirty-two marks of the Great Man are traditional.[2] For a Great Man possessed of these only two courses[3] are open, not another: If he settles in the household state he becomes a king[4] who is a wheel-turner,[5] a *dhamma*-man,[6] a king under *dhamma*,[7] the ruler of the whole world, one who

---

[1] *manta*. *MA*. iii. 364 explains by *veda*. *Cf*. *Sn*. 1000*ff*. On the word *mantra*, as "prayer" (for the classes of poets, priests and warriors) and as "magical formula or incantation" (for the masses), see R. N. Dandekar, "Cultural Background of the Veda," *Univ. of Ceylon Review*, vol. XI, Nos. 3 and 4, 1953, p. 141*ff*. Whatever a *mantra* is it is not necessarily a Rig-Vedic hymn as such. There are 1,028 of these while, according to Dandekar, there are "about 10,560 (Rig-Vedic) *mantras*."

[2] *āgatāni*, have come down, been handed down.

[3] *gati*, bourn, going, procedure. *MA*. iii. 364 explains by *niṭṭhā*, goal or conclusion.

[4] *MA*. iii. 365, he is a king delighting the world with the four wonderful aspects of protection (given at *D*. iii. 232, *A*. ii. 32).

[5] *MA*. iii. 365, he rolls on the wheel-treasure; if he govern with the four wheels of prosperity, *sampatti* (*cf*. *A*. ii. 32), and if he govern others with these, he is doing his duty, *vatta*, for the good of others.

[6] *dhammika*, he walks by *dhamma*.

[7] *dhammarājā*. Having succeeded to the throne through *dhamma* (*i.e.* legitimately, rightly), he is the 'natural,' *jāta*, king. Or, he is *dhammika* because of his 'rightness,' *dhamma*, in regard to the good of others, just as he is *dhammarājā* because of his 'rightness' in regard to his own good, *attahita*.

brings stability to his realm; and he is possessed of the seven Treasures. These seven Treasures of his are the wheel-treasure, the elephant-treasure, the horse-treasure, the jewel-treasure, the woman-treasure, the householder-treasure, the adviser-treasure as the seventh. He will have more than a thousand sons, valiant, built on heroic lines,[1] able to crush opposing armies. He dwells conquering this sea-girt land by *dhamma*,[2] not by stick, not by sword. But, if he goes forth from home into homelessness he becomes a perfected one, a fully Self-Awakened One, a lifter of the world's veil.[3] Now I, dear Uttara, am an imparter[4] of *mantras*, you are a recipient[4] of *mantras*."

"Very well, sir," and the brahman youth Uttara, having answered the brahman Brahmāyu in assent, rising from his seat, having greeted the brahman Brahmāyu, keeping his right side towards him, set out on tour (to find) the Lord in Videha. [**135**] Walking on tour, he gradually approached the Lord; having approached, he exchanged greetings with the Lord; having conversed in a friendly and courteous way, he sat down at a respectful distance. As he was sitting down at a respectful distance the brahman youth Uttara looked for the thirty-two marks of a Great Man on the Lord's body. And the brahman youth Uttara saw all the thirty-two marks of a Great Man on the Lord's body except two. About these two marks of a great man he was in doubt, perplexed, uncertain, not satisfied—whether what was cloth-hid was sheath-cased and whether the tongue was large. Then it occurred to the Lord: "This brahman youth Uttara sees on me all the thirty-two marks of a Great Man except two. About these two marks of a Great Man he is in doubt, perplexed, uncertain, not satisfied: whether what is cloth-hid is sheath-cased

---

[1] *MA*. iii. 366: their bodies are like *devas;* they are called 'heroes' because of their uttermost valour, as though their bodies were made of energy.

[2] *MA*. iii. 367 identifies *dhamma* with *sīla* here, the moral conduct of keeping the five precepts.

[3] *MA*. iii. 367 shows that these three attainments follow one from another. *Vivattacchadda*, the lifter of the veil, refers to removing the seven darknesses of the defilements: attachment, hatred, confusion, pride, false views, ignorance and wrong-doing.

[4] *dātā . . . paṭiggahetā*, as at *D*. i. 89. For the following note I am indebted to Mr. P. Mehta: "The guru conveys or imparts a new mantra when he sees the pupil is ready for it. When the pupil sounds (pronounces) it correctly then the guru teaches him the meaning. Correct sounding influences the mental receptivity of the pupil and induces a state of consciousness which is most appropriate for learning the meaning. The 'mantra' as sound is imparted or conveyed; the 'mantra' as meaning or significance is taught."

and whether my tongue is large." Then the Lord contrived such a contrivance of psychic power[1] that the brahman youth Uttara saw that that which the Lord had cloth-hid was sheath-cased. Then the Lord, having put out his tongue, stroked it backwards and forwards over both his ears and he stroked it backwards and forwards over both his nostrils and he covered the whole dome of his forehead with his tongue.[2]

Then it occurred to the brahman youth Uttara: "The recluse Gotama is possessed of the thirty-two marks of a Great Man. Suppose I were to follow the recluse Gotama closely so as to watch his conduct ?" Then for seven months the brahman youth Uttara, like a constant shadow,[3] followed the Lord closely. After the lapse of the seven months the brahman youth Uttara set out on tour for Mithilā in Videha; walking on tour he gradually approached Mithilā and the brahman Brahmāyu; having approached and having greeted the brahman Brahmāyu, he sat down at a respectful distance. Brahmāyu the brahman spoke thus to the brahman youth Uttara as he was sitting down at a respectful distance: "I suppose, dear Uttara, that the report spread abroad about the revered Gotama was truly so [**136**] and not otherwise ? I suppose that the revered Gotama is such a one and not of another kind ?"

"Sir, the report spread abroad about the revered Gotama was truly so and not otherwise; this revered Gotama is such a one and not of another kind. And this revered Gotama is possessed of the thirty-two marks of a Great Man:[4]

The revered Gotama has feet with a level tread[5]—the good Gotama, a Great Man, has this mark of a Great Man.

On the soles of the good Gotama's feet wheels appear with a thousand spokes, with rims and hubs, in every way complete.

---

[1] *Cf. Miln.* 167-169. [2] *Cf. Sn.* 1022.

[3] As at *Dhp.* 2, *Thag.* 1041-1043, etc.

[4] For more notes on the thirty-two marks or signs, see *Dial.* ii. 13 *ff.* and *Mhvu. Translation,* i. 180*ff.*, where the order in which the marks are given differs now and again from the *M.* version. See also Lamotte, *Mppś.* i. 285-288, notes, where it is said that these 32 marks ornament the bodies both of Buddhas and of wheel-turning kings, and again, either all or some of the marks adorn the bodies of some other persons besides. Some of these men and women are known to the Pali Canon, for example the brahman Bāvarin, who had three of the marks (*Sn.* 1022). Like Brahmāyu he was 120 years old (*Sn.* 1019). *Cf.* also *Kvu.* 283 where the point of controversy is whether a *bodhisatta* is fully or partially possessed of the 32 marks.

[5] He puts the whole foot down on the ground with a single movement—neither the big toe first nor the heel.

The revered Gotama has projecting heels.

The revered Gotama has long fingers (and toes).[1]

The revered Gotama has soft and tender hands and feet.

The revered Gotama has (the fingers and toes) of his hands and feet evenly spaced.[2]

The revered Gotama has ankles that are midway in the leg.[3]

The revered Gotama has legs like (those of) antelopes.[4]

The revered Gotama, while standing erect and not bending, can stroke and rub his knees with the palms of both hands.

The revered Gotama has sheath-cased what is cloth-hid.

The revered Gotama is the colour of gold.[5]

The revered Gotama has a golden[6] coloured skin, a smooth complexion. Because of his smooth complexion no dust or dirt adheres to his body.

The revered Gotama has hairs that are separate. The separate hairs grow (one) to each pore.

The revered Gotama has hairs that grow upward. The upward growing hairs are dark blue, the colour of collyrium, curling in rings, curling to the right.

The revered Gotama has a divinely straight body.[7]

The revered Gotama has the seven convex surfaces.[8]

---

[1] *dīghaṅguli*. *Aṅguli* usually mean only the fingers. *MA*. iii. 376 includes the toes as well, and says that the *aṅguli* are thick at the roots and taper off gradually to slender points.

[2] *jālahatthapādo*. See "The Webbed Finger of the Buddha," by A. K. Coomaraswamy, *IHQ*. VII, 1931, p. 20. It is better to take this as does Buddhaghosa at *MA*. iii. 376, etc., as: "the four fingers of the Tathāgata's hands and the five toes of his feet are of an equal measure"—spaced as evenly apart (with no swellings) as is the "netting" or network, *jāla*, of a particular kind of latticed window when made by a skilled carpenter. A person whose fingers are "webbed" (*i.e.* grown together) like a snake's hood is not even fit to go forth (*Vin*. i. 71, quoted *MA*. iii. 376). So how could a "webbed finger" be a mark of a Great Man? "With hands and feet like a net" (*Dial*. ii. 14) explains nothing.

[3] Not towards the heels as in other people, *MA*. iii. 377. The Pali word is *ussaṅkhapādo*. *Cf*. also *BHSD*. s.v. *ucchaṅkha*.

[4] *I.e.* with flesh all round, not in a lump at one side. The notion is "straight-limbed." *Cf*. *Sn*. 165; *S*. i. 16.

[5] The traditional colour-symbol for immortality; *suvaṇṇa*.

[6] *kañcana* here; bright, shining.

[7] A straight tall body, like Brahmā's. Most creatures bend at the shoulders, hips and knees; but the Tathāgata, rising up tall, is like a high golden gateway in a city of the *devas*, *MA*. iii. 378.

[8] *sattussada*, omitted in Chalmers' text, but referred to in this textual

The revered Gotama has a body the front part of which is like a lion's.[1]

The revered Gotama has no hollow between his shoulders.[2]

The revered Gotama has the symmetrical proportions of a banyan tree—as is the height of his body so is the length of his arms when stretched out; as is the length of his arms when stretched out so is the height of his body.

The revered Gotama has a bust that is evenly rounded.

The revered Gotama has an exquisite sense of taste.

The revered Gotama has jaws like a lion's.

[**137**] The revered Gotama has forty teeth.[3]

The revered Gotama has even teeth.

The revered Gotama has teeth without spaces between them.

The revered Gotama has very lustrous eye-teeth.

The revered Gotama has a long tongue.

The revered Gotama has a voice like Brahmā's;[4] he speaks like a *karavīka* bird.[5]

The revered Gotama has eyes of an intense blue.

The revered Gotama has eyelashes like a cow's.

The hair that the revered Gotama has growing between the eyebrows is white and soft like cotton-down.

The revered Gotama has a head shaped like a (royal) turban.[6] The good Gotama, a Great Man, has also this mark of a Great Man.[7] The revered Gotama is possessed of these thirty-two marks of a Great Man.

If the revered Gotama is walking he leads off with his right foot; he does not put the foot too far (forward), he does not place the foot too short; he does not walk too quickly; he does not walk too slowly; he does not walk knocking knee against knee or ankle against ankle;

---

[1] *I.e.* curving, *paripuṇṇa*. Although the back portion of a lion's body does not curve, the whole of the Tathāgata's body curves, *MA*. iii. 379.

[2] From the small of the back up to the shoulders, the fleshy covering is like a smooth golden slab.

[3] twenty in each jaw, *MA*. iii. 381.

[4] *brahmassara*, a sublime voice. It is like a Great Brahmā's, *MA*. iii. 382. See *Kvu*. 467.

[5] Famed for its sweet note, the Indian cuckoo.

[6] *I.e.*, absolutely symmetrical.

[7] No doubt this refrain should occur after the naming of each mark; while omitted in our text it occurs in *D*. ii. 17-19.

---

position at *MA*. iii. 378 as meaning that on the four limbs, on both shoulders and on the back there is a protuberance of flesh.

while he is walking he does not bend his thighs up, he does not bend his thighs down, he does not bend his thighs in, he does not bend his thighs out.[1] As the revered Gotama walks he moves only with the lower part of his body and does not walk with his (full) bodily strength.[2] When he is looking around, the revered Gotama looks round with his whole body,[3] he does not look up, he does not look down, and he does not walk without observing,[4] for he looks (ahead) a plough's length;[5] further than that his knowledge and insight become unobstructed.[6]

On entering into a house[7] he does not bend his body up, he does not bend his body down, he does not bend his body in, [**138**] he does not bend his body out. He turns round not too far from his seat, not too near it, and he does not sit down on the seat clutching hold of it with his hand, nor does he fling his body (in a slovenly way[8]) on to the seat.[9] When he is seated in a house he does not fall into unseemly behaviour with his hands,[10] he does not fall into unseemly

---

[1] These words for "bending up, down, in, out," *unnāmeti, onāmeti, sannāmeti, vināmeti,* occur several times later in this Discourse. *Cf.* also *Miln.* 117.

[2] *MA.* iii. 388, sweat pours from the body if one keeps on flinging out one's arms.

[3] This is called the "elephant look," *M.* i. 337. See *MA.* ii. 420, iii 133 (the latter referred to at *MA.* iii. 388).

[4] *na ca vipekkhamāno gacchati.* The passage is somewhat corrupt. *MA.* iii. 388: he walks without looking from this side to that as though not seeing the elephants, horses, etc. So this phrase may mean: "he walks without staring (about)." On the other hand, the next phrase: *yugamattañ ca pekkhati,* seems to develop the idea of "not without observing." In walking as in the other "postures," there is to be not only mindfulness but also clear consciousness.

[5] *Cf. Sn.* 410. *MA.* iii. 388 says he fixes his eyes as little as nine *vidatthi* (ahead) when he is walking.

[6] *anāvaṭaṁ,* as at *S.* i. 52. "Irresistible" at *K.S.* i. 75. *MA.* iii. 388: "It could not be said that he does not see beyond a plough's length, since no wall or door or bush or creeper is able to obstruct him. Thus because of his unobstructed (all-pervading, *anāvaraṇa*) knowledge, various thousands of groups of world-systems are reckoned as one," *i.e.* he can see and know them all together and all at once, with 'open,' unhindered, *anāvaṭa,* insights.

[7] Here, according to *MA.* iii. 388 *antaraghara* means from the threshold, *ummāra,* of a house, in distinction to the *indakhīla* which, at *Vin.* iv. 160, is identified with the *ummāra.* The *indakhīla* is a (village) post.

[8] *pakkhipati. MA.* iii. 389, he does not first settle either his lower or upper limbs, but sits down *saṇikaṁ,* slowly, gently or gradually.

[9] See the Sekhiyas on walking and sitting "amid houses," *Vin.* iv. 186 *ff.*, 199.

[10] He does not twirl round his bowl or throw out a drop of water or split the leaf cover of a fly-whisk or fan.

behaviour with his feet;[1] he does not sit down crossing knee over knee or ankle over ankle, nor does he sit down holding his jaw in his hand. When he is seated in a house he is not afraid, does not tremble, shake or quiver—and so is the revered Gotama when he is sitting in a house unafraid, untrembling, not shaking, not quivering, unruffled, intent on aloofness.

When he is receiving water for the bowl he does not turn the bowl up, he does not turn the bowl down, he does not turn the bowl inwards, he does not turn the bowl outwards; he receives neither too little nor too much water for the bowl. He washes the bowl without making it clatter,[2] he washes the bowl without twirling it round; not until he has put the bowl down on the ground does he wash his hands; by the time the hands are washed the bowl is washed; by the time the bowl is washed the hands are washed. He throws away the water for the bowl not too far, not too near, and without scattering it.

When he is receiving boiled rice, he does not turn the bowl up, he does not turn the bowl down, he does not turn the bowl inwards, he does not turn the bowl outwards; he receives neither too little nor too much boiled rice. The revered Gotama eats the proper proportion of curry (to rice[3]) and he does not neglect (the rice) with each mouthful of curry. The revered Gotama swallows each mouthful only after having turned it round two or three times in his mouth; there is not a single grain of boiled rice that enters his body without having been broken up, and not a single grain of boiled rice remains in his mouth before he proceeds to the (next) mouthful. The revered Gotama eats food experiencing its flavour but not experiencing greed for the flavour. The revered Gotama eats food that is possessed of the eight characteristics[4] but not for fun or indulgence or personal charm or beautification, but just enough for the support of his body and keeping it going, for keeping it unharmed, for furthering the Brahma-faring, thinking: [**139**] 'Thus will I crush out an old feeling and not allow a new feeling to arise, and then there will be subsistence for me and blamelessness and abiding in comfort.'[5]

When he has eaten and is accepting water for the bowl, he does not

---

[1] He does not grind them on the ground.

[2] *na khulukhulukāraka*, not commented upon in *MA*. Chalmers translates: "he does not swish the water about"; Neumann: "ohne zu plätschen." See *PED. s.v. gala*, and *cf. BHSD. s.v. khurukhuru-*.

[3] Three portions of rice to one of curry.

[4] *MA*. iii. 392 refers to *M*. Sta. 2 and *Vism*. 31.

[5] As at *M*. i. 355, ii. 10, and also at e.g. *S*. iv. 104, *A*. iii. 388, iv. 167; and see *Vism*. 31.

turn the bowl up . . . down . . . inwards . . . outwards. He receives neither too little nor too much water for the bowl. He washes the bowl without making it clatter (*as above in last paragraph but one*) . . . He throws away the water for the bowl not too far, not too near, and without scattering it. When he has eaten, he places the bowl on the ground, not too far, not too near, for he is not without concern for the bowl[1] yet he is not over-protective of the bowl. When he has eaten, he sits silent for a moment, but he does not let pass the time for giving thanks. When he has eaten, he gives thanks. He does not decry that meal, he does not hope for another meal; on the contrary he delights, rouses, inspires, gladdens that assembly with talk on *dhamma*. When he has delighted . . . gladdened that assembly with talk on *dhamma*, rising from his seat, he departs. He does not walk too quickly, he does not walk too slowly, he does not walk (as if) anxious to get free (of that assembly).[2]

The revered Gotama's robe is not pulled up too high on his body, it is not pulled down too low[3]; and neither does it stick to his body,[4] nor is it drawn away from his body,[5] and neither does the wind blow the revered Gotama's robe about on his body,[6] nor do dust and dirt cling to the revered Gotama's body.

When he has gone to a monastery he sits down on an appointed seat and while sitting down he cleanses his feet[7]—but the revered Gotama does not live intent on the practice of beautifying his feet. When he has cleansed his feet he sits down cross-legged, holding the body erect and arousing mindfulness in front of him. He does not strive after hurt of self, he does not strive after hurt of others, he does not strive after hurt of both.[8] The revered Gotama sits down striving only after weal of self, weal of others, weal of both, weal of the whole world. [**140**] When, in a monastery, he is teaching *dhamma* in an assembly, he does not exalt that assembly, he does not disparage that assembly; on the contrary he delights, rouses, inspires,

---

[1] Not indifferent to it and taking care of it—not like someone who once he has put his bowl on a stand (for bowls) does not pour water into it but watches indifferently while dust falls into it.

[2] He does not hurry away, *MA*. iii. 393.

[3] Not as high as his jaw or as low as his ankles, *MA*. iii. 393.

[4] Because he does not sweat as other people do.

[5] It does not stand free like a *khali* cloak.

[6] Reading *kāyasmiṁ* with Siamese instead of text's *kāyamhā*. The wind cannot make his robe stir, *MA*. iii. 393.

[7] As at *Vin*. i. 9.

[8] *Cf*. *M*. i. 414, iii. 23; *A*. i. 157; *S*. iv. 339.

gladdens that assembly with talk on *dhamma*. The sound that issues from the revered Gotama's mouth[1] is possessed of eight characteristics: it is distinct and intelligible and sweet and audible and fluent[2] and clear and deep and resonant. Wherefore when the revered Gotama instructs an assembly by voice the sound does not carry beyond that assembly. These, after being delighted . . . gladdened by the revered Gotama with talk on *dhamma*, rising from their seats, depart reluctantly, keeping their gaze on him.

We, sir, have seen that revered Gotama walking, we have seen him standing still, we have seen him sitting silent within a house, we have seen him eating in a house, we have seen him sitting silent after he has eaten, we have seen him giving thanks after he has eaten, we have seen him going to a monastery, we have seen him sitting silent in a monastery, we have seen him in a monastery teaching *dhamma* in an assembly. This revered Gotama is like this and like that and even more so."[3]

When this had been said, Brahmāyu the brahman, rising from his seat, having arranged his upper robe over one shoulder, having saluted the Lord with joined palms, three times uttered this solemn utterance: "Praise to that Lord, perfected one, fully Self-Awakened One . . . Praise to that Lord, perfected one, fully Self-Awakened One. Perhaps somewhere, sometime we might meet this revered Gotama, perhaps there might be some conversation between us."

Then the Lord, walking on tour in Videha, in due course arrived at Mithilā. While he was there the Lord stayed near Mithilā in Makhādeva's Mango Grove. Brahmans and householders of Mithilā heard: "Verily the recluse Gotama, [**141**] son of the Sakyans, having gone forth from the Sakyan clan, is walking on tour in Videha together with a large Order of monks, with as many as five hundred monks. The most lovely report has gone abroad thus concerning the revered Gotama . . . (*as in the first paragraph*) . . . Good indeed is the sight of perfected ones such as this." Then the brahmans and householders of Mithilā approached the Lord: some, having approached and having greeted the Lord, sat down at a respectful distance; some, after they had exchanged greetings with the Lord and had conversed in a friendly and courteous way, sat down at a

---

[1] *Cf. D.* ii. 211, 227 of Brahmā Sanaṁkumāra's voice.

[2] *bindu. MA.* iii. 394 gives *sampiṇḍita*, brought together, connected.

[3] "His excellent virtues that I have not spoken of are more than those I have spoken of—like the great earth, the great ocean, unending, boundless, wide as the sky," *MA.* iii. 395.

respectful distance; some, after saluting the Lord with joined palms, sat down at a respectful distance; some, having made known to the Lord the name of their clan, sat down at a respectful distance; some, becoming silent, sat down at a respectful distance.

The brahman Brahmāyu heard: "Verily the recluse Gotama, son of the Sakyans, gone forth from the Sakyan clan, has arrived at Mithilā and is staying near Mithilā in Makhādeva's Mango Grove." Then Brahmāyu the brahman together with a number of brahman youths approached Makhādeva's Mango Grove. When Brahmāyu the brahman was near the Mango Grove it occurred to him: "It is not suitable in me that I should approach to see the recluse Gotama without being announced first." So Brahmāyu the brahman addressed a certain brahman youth, saying: "Come you, brahman youth, approach the recluse Gotama; having approached, in my name ask the recluse Gotama whether he is well, not indisposed, of bodily vigour, strong, abiding in comfort, saying: 'Good Gotama, Brahmāyu the brahman is asking whether the revered Gotama is well, not indisposed, of bodily vigour, strong, abiding in comfort'; and then speak thus: 'Good Gotama, Brahmāyu the brahman is worn, old, full of years, he has lived his span and is at the close of his life, a hundred and twenty years of age; he is master of the three Vedas, versed in the vocabularies and rituals together with the phonology and exegesis and the legendary tradition as the fifth; he is learned in idioms, a grammarian, proficient in popular philosophy and the marks of a Great Man. Of all the brahmans and householders, sir, who live in Mithilā, Brahmāyu the brahman is pointed to as chief in respect of wealth, Brahmāyu the brahman is pointed to as chief in respect of *mantras*, **[142]** Brahmāyu the brahman is pointed to as chief in respect of longevity as well as of renown. He is anxious to see the good Gotama."

"Very well, sir," and the brahman youth, having answered the brahman Brahmāyu in assent, approached the Lord; having approached, he exchanged greetings with the Lord, and having conversed in a friendly and courteous way, he stood at a respectful distance. As he was standing at a respectful distance, the brahman youth spoke thus to the Lord: "Good Gotama, the brahman Brahmāyu is asking whether the revered Gotama is well, not indisposed, of bodily vigour, strong, abiding in comfort. The brahman Brahmāyu, good Gotama, is worn, old, full of years . . . proficient in popular philosophy and the marks of a Great Man. Of all the brahmans and householders who live in Mithilā, Brahmāyu the brahman is pointed to as chief in respect of wealth . . . in repect of *mantras* . . . in respect of longevity as well as of renown. He is anxious to see the good Gotama."

"Brahmāyu the brahman must now do that for which he deems it the right time, brahman youth."

Then that brahman youth approached Brahmāyu the brahman; having approached, he spoke thus to Brahmāyu the brahman: "Permission has been given,[1] revered sir, by the recluse Gotama. Revered sir, you may now do that for which you deem it the right time."

Then Brahmāyu the brahman approached the Lord. His assembly saw the brahman Brahmāyu coming in the distance. Having seen him, they, standing each at his own side,[2] made room for him because he was well known and renowned. Then Brahmāyu the brahman spoke thus to that assembly: "No, good sirs, you sit down each on your own seat, I will sit here near the recluse Gotama." Then Brahmāyu the brahman approached the Lord; having approached, he exchanged greetings with the Lord; having conversed in a friendly and courteous way, he sat down at a respectful distance. As he was sitting down at a respectful distance, Brahmāyu the brahman [**143**] looked for the thirty-two marks of a Great Man on the Lord's body. And Brahmāyu the brahman saw all the thirty-two marks of a Great Man on the Lord's body except two. About these two marks of a Great Man he was in doubt, perplexed, uncertain, not satisfied—whether what was cloth-hid was sheath-cased and whether the tongue was large. Then Brahmāyu the brahman addressed the Lord in verses:

"Of these thirty-two marks of a Great Man of which I have heard
There are two that I do not see on your body, Gotama.
I wonder whether what is cloth-hid is sheath-cased, Supreme of men ?
Or is it female ? I wonder whether the tongue is not short ?
I wonder whether you have a long tongue. So that I might know this,
Put forth this tongue, dispel our doubt, Seer.
For welfare here and now, and for bliss in a future state
We ask for permission (to see) that which we long (to know)."

---

[1] *katāvakāsa.*

[2] *oram atha* or *oram attha.* *MA.* iii. 396 says: "getting up quickly, having divided into two, they made room for him." See *JPTS.*, 1887, p. 154 *ff.*

Then it occurred to the Lord: "This brahman Brahmāyu sees on me all the thirty-two marks of a Great Man except two. About these two marks of a Great Man he is in doubt, perplexed, uncertain, not satisfied—whether what is cloth-hid is sheath-cased and whether my tongue is large." Then the Lord contrived such a contrivance of psychic power that the brahman Brahmāyu saw that that which the Lord had cloth-hid was sheath-cased. Then the Lord, having put out his tongue, stroked it backwards and forwards over both his ears and he stroked it backwards and forwards over both his nostrils and he covered the whole dome of his forehead with his tongue.

Then the Lord responded in verses to the brahman Brahmāyu:

"Those thirty-two marks of a Great Man of which you have heard
Are all on my body. Do not you doubt them, brahman.
What[1] is to be known is known by me, and to be developed is developed,
What is to be got rid of has been got rid of—therefore, brahman, am I Awake.[2]
[**144**] For welfare here and now and for bliss in a future state
Do ask for permission (to see) that which you long (to know)."

Then it occurred to the brahman Brahmāyu: "Permission has been given me by the recluse Gotama. Suppose I were to ask the recluse Gotama about the goal either of the here and now or of a future state?" But then it occurred to the brahman Brahmāyu: "I myself am skilled in the goals of the here and now, and others ask me about the goal of the here and now. Suppose I were to ask the recluse Gotama simply about the goal of a future state?" Then Brahmāyu the brahman addressed the Lord in verses:

"How is one a brahman? How does one become master of knowledge?
How is one a threefold knowledge-man? Who is called learned?
How is one perfected? How does one become whole?
And how is one a sage? Who is called Awake?"

Then the Lord responded in verses to the brahman Brahmāyu:

---

[1] *Sn.* 558; and below, p. 337. This and the next line are quoted at *VinA.* i. 115; *ItA.* 149; *UdA.* 84; *PṭsA.* i. 215; *Vism.* 201.

[2] *tasmā buddho 'smi;* also below, p. 337=*Sn.* 558, *A.* ii. 39; *cf. M.* i. 171, *Vin.* i. 8.

"Who knows his former habitations and sees heaven and the sorrowful ways,
Who has attained destruction of births,[1] accomplished by super-knowledge, a Sage is he.
Who knows his mind is quite pure, freed from every attachment,
Who has got rid of birth and dying, in the Brahma-faring Whole is he.[2]
Who is master of all states of mind,[3] such a one Awake is called."

When this had been said, Brahmāyu the brahman, rising from his seat, arranging his upper robe over one shoulder, having inclined his head to the Lord's feet, kissed the Lord's feet on all sides with his mouth and stroked them on all sides with his hands, and he made known his (own) name:[4] "I, good Gotama, am Brahmāyu, the brahman." Then that company was filled with wonder and marvel, and said: "Indeed it is wonderful, indeed it is marvellous how great is the psychic power and the majesty of the recluse in virtue of which this Brahmāyu the brahman, well known and renowned, pays such deep respect."

Then the Lord spoke thus to Brahmāyu the brahman: [**145**] "Enough, brahman, rise up; do sit down on your own seat since your mind was pleased with me." Then the brahman Brahmāyu, having risen up, sat down on his own seat. Then the Lord gave a talk to Brahmāyu the brahman on various topics:[5] talk on giving, talk on moral habit, talk on heaven; he explained the peril, the vanity, the depravity of the pleasures of the senses, the advantage in renouncing them. When the Lord knew that the mind of Brahmāyu the brahman was ready, malleable, devoid of the hindrances, uplifted, pleased, then he explained to him that teaching on *dhamma* that the Awakened Ones have themselves discovered: anguish, uprising, stopping, the Way. And as a clean cloth without black specks will easily take dye, even so as Brahmāyu the brahman was (sitting) on that very seat did *dhamma*-vision, dustless and stainless, arise in him: that "whatever is liable to origination all that is liable to stopping." Then Brahmāyu the brahman, having seen *dhamma*, attained *dhamma*, known *dhamma*, plunged into *dhamma*, having crossed over doubt,

---

[1] *Iti.* p. 100; *A.* i. 165; *S.* i. 167; *Thīg.* 63 *f.* *Cf.* *Dhp.* 423; *Sn.* 647, of a brahman.

[2] This line also occurs at *A.* ii. 23.

[3] See also *A.* ii. 23.

[4] *As at M.* ii. 120. *Cf.* *S.* i. 178, 193. See Intr. p. xxv. above.

[5] *Cf.* *Vin.* i. 15, ii. 155 *ff.*; *D.* i. 110; *M.* i. 379, etc.

put away uncertainty and attained without another's help to full confidence in the Teacher's instruction, spoke thus to the Lord:

"It is excellent, good Gotama; it is excellent, good Gotama. Even, good Gotama, as one might set upright what had been upset, or disclose what was covered, or show the way to one who had gone astray, or bring an oil-lamp into the darkness thinking that those with vision might see material shapes, even so is *dhamma* made clear in many a figure by the good Gotama. So I am going to the revered Gotama (for refuge)[1] and to *dhamma* and to the Order of monks. May the revered Gotama accept me as a lay-disciple going for refuge from this day forth for as long as life lasts. And may the revered Gotama consent to a meal with me on the morrow together with the Order of monks."

The Lord consented by becoming silent. Then Brahmāyu the brahman, having understood the Lord's consent, rising up from his seat, having greeted the Lord, departed keeping his right side towards him. Then the brahman Brahmāyu having had sumptuous foods, solid and soft, prepared in his own dwelling towards the end of that night, had the time announced to the Lord, saying: "It is time, good Gotama, the meal is ready." **[146]** Then the Lord, having dressed in the morning, taking his bowl and robe, approached the dwelling of Brahmāyu the brahman; having approached, he sat down on the appointed seat together with the Order of monks. Then did Brahmāyu the brahman for seven days with his own hand serve and satisfy the Order of monks with the Awakened One at its head with sumptuous foods, solid and soft. Then at the end of the seven days the Lord set out on tour in Videha.

Not long after the Lord had set out Brahmāyu the brahman passed away. Then a number of monks approached the Lord; having approached, having greeted the Lord, they sat down at a respectful distance. As they were sitting down at a respectful distance, these monks spoke thus to the Lord: "Revered sir, Brahmāyu the brahman has passed away. What is his bourn, what his future state?"

"Clever,[2] monks, was the brahman Brahmāyu; he followed after *dhamma* according to various parts of *dhamma*,[3] and he did not

---

[1] *saraṇaṁ* not in Chalmers' text; probably omitted by an oversight.

[2] For this paragraph *cf. M.* iii. 247, 270; *S.* iv. 63, v. 346; *Ud.* 8, 50. In all these passages other men are concerned, and other bourns.

[3] *paccapādi dhammassânudhammaṁ. MA.* iii. 398 says: "In this Discourse *dhamma* means the Way of perfection (*arahattamagga*); *anudhamma* means

annoy me[1] with questionings about *dhamma*. Monks, Brahmāyu the brahman, by the complete destruction of the five fetters binding to this lower (shore), is of spontaneous uprising, one who attains nibbāna there, not liable to return from that world."

Thus spoke the Lord. Delighted, these monks rejoiced in what the Lord had said.

Discourse with Brahmāyu:
The First

92. DISCOURSE WITH SELA

(Selasutta)[2]

THUS have I heard: At one time the Lord walking on tour among the people of Anguttarāpa,[3] together with a large Order of monks, [*Sn.* **103**] with twelve hundred and fifty monks, arrived at the market town called Āpaṇa belonging to the people of Anguttarāpa. Keṇiya the matted hair ascetic[4] heard: "Verily the recluse Gotama, son of the Sakyans, having gone forth from the Sakyan clan, walking on tour among the people of Anguttarāpa together with a large Order of monks, with twelve hundred and fifty monks, has reached Āpaṇa.

---

[1] *M.* text reads *navamaṁ vihesesi*, instead of *na ca maṁ*, as in two variant readings of the text, in the parallel contexts, and at *MA.* iii. 398. This *navamaṁ* has misled Chalmers, although it might be argued that his "difficulty with the ninth stage" (of meditation ?) is borne out to some extent by the fact that Brahmāyu is not said to have achieved arahantship, being spoken of in words descriptive only of a non-returner. But this is far-fetched, and nothing is said in this Discourse about Brahmāyu attempting any of the "stages" in meditation or of becoming proficient in them.

[2] The text of this Sutta is not given in *M.* ii. "as it is identical with that of the same name in the Suttanipāta, printed at p. 99 of Prof. Fausböll's edition for the P.T.S." This Sutta is also printed at p. 102 *ff.* of Dines Andersen and Helmer Smith's edn. of the *Sn.*, likewise a P.T.S. publication. *Cf. Vin.* i. 245 *ff.*, *D.* i. 87 *ff.*

[3] As in *M.* Sta. 54. [4] For notes and references see *B.D.* iv. 336, *n.* 10.

---

the three lower Ways and the fruits of recluseship. The meaning is that he acquired these in successive order."

The most lovely report has gone abroad thus concerning this revered Gotama . . .[1] Good indeed is the sight of perfected ones such as this." Then Keṇiya the matted hair ascetic approached the Lord; having approached, he exchanged greetings with the Lord; having conversed in a friendly and courteous way, he sat down at a respectful distance. As the matted hair ascetic Keṇiya was sitting down at a respectful distance the Lord delighted, roused, inspired, gladdened him with talk on *dhamma*. Then Keṇiya the matted hair ascetic, delighted . . . gladdened by the Lord with talk on *dhamma*, spoke thus to the Lord: "May the good Gotama together with the Order of monks consent to a meal with me on the morrow."[2] When this had been said, the Lord spoke thus to Keṇiya the matted hair ascetic:

"But, Keṇiya, great [*Sn.* **104**] is the Order of monks, twelve hundred and fifty monks, and you are favourably disposed towards[3] the brahmans." And a second time did Keṇiya the matted hair ascetic speak thus to the Lord:

"Although, good Gotama, the Order of monks is large, twelve hundred and fifty monks, and although I am favourably disposed towards the brahmans, (yet) may the good Gotama consent to a meal with me on the morrow together with the Order of monks." And a second time did the Lord speak thus to Keṇiya the matted hair ascetic:

"But, Keṇiya, great is the Order of monks, twelve hundred and fifty monks, and you are favourably disposed towards the brahmans." And a third time did Keṇiya the matted hair ascetic speak thus to the Lord:

"Although, good Gotama, the Order of monks is large, twelve hundred and fifty monks, and although I am favourably disposed towards the brahmans, (yet) may the good Gotama consent to a meal with me on the morrow together with the Order of monks." The Lord consented by becoming silent. Then Keṇiya the matted hair ascetic, having understood the Lord's consent, rising from his seat, approached his own hermitage; having approached, he addressed his friends and acquaintances, his kith and kin, saying: "Let my good friends and acquaintances, my kith and kin, hear that the recluse Gotama together with the Order of monks has been invited

---

[1] As in Sta. 91 (*M*. ii. 133).

[2] *Cf. Vin.* i. 246 for Keṇiya's invitation to a meal.

[3] *abhippasanna*, with the *loc*. The meaning really amounts to: being well enough pleased with to believe in; feeling very serene with.

by me for a meal on the morrow. So would you do personal service for me ?"

"Yes, good sir," and when the friends and acquaintances, the kith and kin of Keṇiya the matted hair ascetic had answered him in assent, some dug pits (for the fire), some chopped sticks, some washed pots, some put out jars of water, and some got ready the seats, while Keṇiya himself prepared a pavilion.[1]

Now at that time Sela the brahman was living in Āpaṇa. [*Sn.* **105**] He was master of the three Vedas,[2] versed in the vocabularies and the rituals together with the phonology and exegesis and the legendary tradition as the fifth; he was learned in idioms, a grammarian, proficient in popular philosophy and the marks of a Great Man. He instructed three hundred brahman youths in *mantras*. At that time Keṇiya the matted hair ascetic was favourably disposed towards the brahman Sela. Then as Sela the brahman, surrounded by the three hundred brahman youths, was pacing up and down and roaming about on foot he approached the hermitage of Keṇiya the matted hair ascetic. And in the hermitage of Keṇiya the matted hair ascetic Sela the brahman saw some people digging pits . . . some getting ready seats, and Keṇiya the matted hair ascetic himself preparing a pavilion. So he spoke thus to Keṇiya the matted hair ascetic:

"How now, is there to be a marriage[3] at the good Keṇiya's or a giving in marriage, or is a great oblation arranged, or has King Bimbisāra of Magadha been invited for the morrow together with his troops ?"

"No, Sela, there is to be no marriage with me nor giving in marriage, nor has King Seniya Bimbisāra of Magadha been invited for the morrow together with his troops. But I have arranged a great oblation: the recluse Gotama, son of the Sakyans, gone forth from the Sakyan clan, who has been walking on tour among the people of Anguttarāpa, together with a large Order of monks, with twelve hundred and fifty monks, has arrived at Āpaṇa. [*Sn.* **106**] The most lovely report has gone abroad thus concerning the recluse Gotama . . . the Awakened One, the Lord. He has been invited by me for the morrow together with the Order of monks."

---

[1] *maṇḍalamāla*. *MA*. iii. 400 calls it *dussamaṇḍala*, a cloth (covered) pavilion (?). *SnA*. ii. 447 says "he made a pavilion with a canopy" (or awning).

[2] As at *M*. ii. 133.

[3] From here to "hard to come by in the world" below, *cf*. with *Vin*. ii. 155.

"Keṇiya, did you say 'Awakened One'?"
"I did say 'Awakened One,' Sela."
"Keṇiya, did you say 'Awakened One'?"
"I did say 'Awakened One,' Sela."

Then it occurred to the brahman Sela: "Even this sound 'Awakened One' is hard to come by in the world. But in our *mantras* the thirty-two marks of a Great Man are traditional. For a Great Man endowed with these, only two courses are open, not another . . .[1] But if he goes forth from home into homelessness he becomes a perfected one, a fully Self-Awakened One, a lifter of the world's veil. And where, good Keṇiya, is this revered Gotama, perfected one, fully Self-Awakened One, staying at present?"

When this had been said, Keṇiya the matted hair ascetic, stretching out his right arm, spoke thus to Sela the brahman: [*Sn.* **107**] "There, good Sela, by that dark blue line of forest." Then Sela the brahman with the three hundred brahman youths approached the Lord. Then Sela the brahman addressed these brahman youths, saying:

"Come quietly, good sirs, (carefully) placing foot after foot; for, like lone-faring lions,[2] these Lords are hard to approach. So if I should hold converse with the recluse Gotama, do not interrupt me, good sirs; but wait for me until the end of the conversation."

Then Sela the brahman approached the Lord; having approached, he exchanged greetings with the Lord; having conversed in a friendly and courteous way, he sat down at respectful distance. As he was sitting down at a respectful distance Sela the brahman looked for the thirty-two marks of a Great Man on the Lord's body . . .[3] [*Sn.* **108**] Then the Lord, having put out his tongue, stroked it backwards and forwards over both his ears and he stroked it backwards and forwards over both his nostrils and he covered the whole dome of his forehead with his tongue.

Then it occurred to Sela the brahman: "The Lord is endowed with the thirty-two marks of a Great Man in full, not partially, but yet I do not know whether he is an Awakened One or not. All the same, I have heard it said by aged brahmans, full of years, teachers of teachers: 'When their own praises are being spoken, those that are perfected ones, fully Self-Awakened Ones reveal the self.[4] Suppose

---

[1] As in Sta. 91 (*M.* ii. 134).

[2] *MA.* iii. 401, the solitary lion is watchful and diligent, *appamāda*. It is to mark the diligent dwelling that this simile is made.

[3] As in Sta. 91 (*M.* ii. 135).

[4] *attānaṁ pātukaronti; cf. Vin.* ii. 186, *A.* iii. 123, *i.e.* manifest, or make

that I, face to face with the recluse Gotama were to praise him in suitable verses?" Then Sela the brahman, face to face with the Lord, praised him in suitable verses:

Sela "Your[1] body is complete,[2] gleaming, finely proportioned,[3]
beautiful to behold;
you are the colour of gold, the Lord; lustrous your teeth,
you are heroic.
Indeed those distinguishing signs of a finely proportioned
man—
all these marks of a Great Man are on your body.
Your eyes are clear, the face is full,[4] you are well grown,[5]
straight, splendid;
in the midst of an Order of recluses you shine like the sun.
Lovely to see is a monk with a golden coloured skin;
but for this recluseship what use is such supremacy of
colour?[6]
You should be a king, a wheel-turner, a bull of charioteers,[7]
victor over the whole world, chief of the Rose-apple Grove.[8]
[*Sn.* **109**] Nobles and wealthy kings will be your vassals;
you are king of kings, the lord of men; rule, O Gotama."

---

[1] *Cf. Thag.* 818-837, the verses ascribed to Sela, and the responses as below.

[2] *I.e.* with the full complement of "marks," *MA.* iii. 402.

[3] *sujāta.* I have taken this as does Bu.: "well born in regard to excellence of height to breadth, to excellence of form," so as to keep a reference to the "mark" that is "symmetry."

[4] "Like the face of the full moon," *MA.* iii. 402. *Cf. e.g. Suvarṇaprabhāsa Sūtra,* Ch. XII (as given in R. Robinson's *Chinese Buddhist Verse,* London, 1954): "The countenance of the Buddha is like the clear full moon." This is only one of many examples of this simile.

[5] *brahā.* This also refers to the symmetrical development of height to breadth when the arms are stretched out. The next refers to the limbs being as straight as Brahmā's.

[6] *uttamavaṇṇino.*

[7] *rathesabho. MA.* iii. 402 explains by *uttamarathī,* with v.l. *uttamasārathī-sārathī,* charioteer, occurring in the stock description of the Buddha. *ThagA.* ii. 44 (*SHB*) explains by *rathesu ājāniya-usabhapuriso mahārathiko,* in regard to chariots he is a thoroughbred bull of a man, a great charioteer.

[8] The same as Jambudīpa, India. *ThagA.* ii. 44 (*SHB*) says that a wheel-turner is not merely Lord of Jambudīpa but of the four great "continents" or "islands" as well.

---

visible, exhibit, bring to light, "betray" (*G.S.* iii. 98) the self. But in the Buddha's Teaching this is what a foolish person does, *e.g.* Devadatta, not arahants, and, at *D.* iii. 115 not the Tathāgata.

Gotama " I am a king, Sela," said the Lord,
" a matchless king under *dhamma*;
I turn the wheel by *dhamma*,[1]
the wheel that cannot be turned back."

Sela " Self-Awakened do you profess to be," said Sela the brahman,
" ' A matchless king under *dhamma*;
I turn the wheel by *dhamma* '—thus, Gotama, you speak.
But who is the revered one's captain,
the disciple second to the Teacher ?
Who turns on this wheel of *dhamma*
That was set turning by you ?"

Gotama " The wheel set turning by me,
Sela," said the Lord,
" The matchless wheel of *dhamma*—
Sāriputta[2] turns it on;
he is heir born[3] to the Tathāgata.
What is to be known is known by me, and to be developed developed is,
what is to be got rid of has been got rid of—therefore, brahman, am I Awake.[4]
Dispel your doubt in me, have faith, brahman.
Ever difficult to come by is the sight of Self-Awakened Ones.
[*Sn.* **110**] Ever difficult to come by is their appearance in the world.
But I, brahman, am Self-Awakened, a physician without peer,
Brahma-become, without compare, crushing Māra's hosts;
having mastered all foes I rejoice, with no fear from anywhere."

---

[1] Beginning with the four peerless arousings of mindfulness. The wheel of command is: get rid of this, make that arise. The wheel of *dhamma* is, beginning with *dhamma*, as learning, *pariyattidhamma*: ' This, monks, is the ariyan truth of anguish,' *MA*. iii. 403.

[2] According to the Comys. Sāriputta was sitting nearby.

[3] *anujāta*, " taking after " or "born equal to." See *Iti*. p. 63 for three kinds of children: *avajāta*, *anujāta*, *atijāta*. Here no physical relationship to the Tathāgata is meant, simply " heir in dhamma " as in *M*. Sta. 12.

[4] This line and the preceding one are also found at *M*. ii. 143.

Sela " Attend to this, good sirs. As speaks the Visioned One,
physician, great hero, so roars the forest-lion.
Seeing him, Brahma-become, without compare, crushing Māra's hosts,
who should not have faith—even a base-born black ?
Who wishes, let him follow me; or, who wishes it not, let him depart;
but I will go forth here under Him of Excellent Wisdom."

Brahmans " If this teaching of the fully Self-Awakened One is agreeable to your reverence,
we too will go forth under Him of Excellent Wisdom."

Sela " These three hundred brahmans, their palms joined in salutation, are asking
to fare the Brahma-faring under you, O Lord."

Gotama " Well taught[1] is the Brahma-faring, Sela," said the Lord,
" It is self-realised, it is timeless.
The going forth in it is nothing vain for him who trains diligently."

Sela the brahman and his company received the going forth under the Lord, they received ordination.

Then towards the end of that night, Keṇiya the matted hair ascetic, having had sumptuous foods, solid and soft, prepared in his own hermitage, [*Sn* **111**] had the time announced to the Lord, saying: " It is time, good Gotama, the meal is ready." Then the Lord, dressing in the morning, taking his bowl and robe, approached the hermitage of the matted hair ascetic Keṇiya; having approached, he sat down on the appointed seat together with the Order of monks. Then Keṇiya the matted hair ascetic with his own hand served and satisfied the Order of monks with the Awakened One at its head with sumptuous foods, solid and soft. When the Lord had eaten and had withdrawn his hand from the bowl, Keṇiya the matted hair ascetic, taking a low seat, sat down at a respectful distance. As Keṇiya the matted hair ascetic was sitting down at a respectful distance, the Lord thanked him in these verses:

" Sacrifice is chief in fire-worship,[2]
Sāvitrī chief of Vedic metres,

[1] *MA.* iii. 406 says that the use of this phrase means Sela and the three hundred brahmans went forth by the ' Come, bhikkhu ' formula.

[2] For notes on these verses, which occur at *Vin.* i. 246, see *B.D.* iv. 340.

A king is chief of men,
The ocean chief of waters.

The moon is chief of the lamps of night,
The sun the chief of luminaries,
For those giving alms, desiring merit,
The Order is indeed the chief."

When the Lord had thanked the matted hair ascetic Keṇiya in these verses, rising from his seat, he departed.

Then the venerable Sela and his company, dwelling alone, aloof, diligent, ardent, self-resolute, [*Sn.* **112**] having soon realised here and now by their own super-knowledge that matchless goal of the Brahma-faring for the sake of which young men of family rightly go forth from home into homelessness, entering on it abided therein; and they knew: " Destroyed is birth, brought to a close the Brahma-faring, done is what was to be done, there is no more of being such or so." And the venerable Sela and his company became perfected ones. Then the venerable Sela and his company approached the Lord; having approached, having arranged his upper robe over one shoulder, having saluted the Lord with joined palms, he addressed the Lord in verses:[1]

" Eight days ago, O Visioned One, we came to you for refuge;
Lord, through your teaching we were tamed in seven nights.
You are the Wake, you the Teacher, you the Seer who is Māra's victor;
Having cut out latent tendencies, you, crossed over, help this mortality to cross.
The basis (for rebirth) has been transcended by you, the cankers shattered by you.
A lion are you, without attachment, who has got rid of fear and dread.
These three hundred monks are standing with joined palms—
Stretch forth your feet, O Hero, let great beings[2] honour the Teacher."

Discourse with Sela:
The Second

---

[1] As at *Thag.* 838-841.

[2] *nāga*, as in *M.* Stas. 5, 24 (*M.* i. 32, 151).

93. DISCOURSE WITH ASSALĀYANA

(Assalāyanasutta)

[147] Thus have I heard: At one time the Lord was staying near Sāvatthī in the Jeta Grove in Anāthapiṇḍika's monastery. Now at that time at least five hundred brahmans from a number of districts were residing at Sāvatthī on some business or other. Then it occurred to these brahmans: "This recluse Gotama lays down the purity of the four castes. Now, who is capable of arguing about this saying with the recluse Gotama?" At that time the brahman youth Assalāyana was residing at Sāvatthī. He was young, his head shaven, sixteen years of age from his birth; he was master of the three Vedas . . .[1] . . . proficient in . . . the marks of a Great Man. Then it occurred to these brahmans: "This brahman youth Assalāyana is residing at Sāvatthī. He is young, his head shaven . . . proficient in . . . the marks of a Great Man. He is capable of arguing about this saying with the recluse Gotama." Then these brahmans approached the brahman youth Assalāyana; having approached, they spoke thus to the brahman youth Assalāyana:

"Good Assalāyana, this recluse Gotama lays down the purity of the four castes; you go, good Assalāyana, and argue about this saying with the recluse Gotama."

When this had been said, Assalāyana the brahman youth spoke thus to those brahmans: "Truly, sirs, is the recluse Gotama a speaker on *dhamma* but speakers on *dhamma* are difficult to argue with. *I* am not able to argue about this saying with the recluse Gotama." And a second time these brahmans spoke thus to the brahman youth Assalāyana: "Good Assalāyana, this recluse Gotama lays down the purity of the four castes; you go, good Assalāyana, [148] and argue about this saying with the recluse Gotama. A wanderer's (life) is led by the good Assalāyana."

And a second time Assalāyana the brahman youth spoke thus to those brahmans: "Truly, sirs, is the recluse Gotama a speaker on *dhamma* but speakers on *dhamma* are difficult to argue with. *I* am not able to argue about this saying with the recluse Gotama."

---

[1] As in Sta. 91 (*M*. ii. 133).

And a third time these brahmans spoke thus to the brahman youth Assalāyana: "Good Assalāyana, this recluse Gotama lays down the purity of the four castes; you go, good Assalāyana, and argue about this saying with the recluse Gotama. A wanderer's life is led by the good Assalāyana. Let not the good Assalāyana be defeated in a defeat without resistance."[1] When this had been said, Assalāyana the brahman youth spoke thus to those brahmans:

"Sirs, truly the recluse Gotama is a speaker on *dhamma* but speakers on *dhamma* are difficult to argue with. *I* am not able to argue about this saying with the recluse Gotama. All the same, I will go at the bidding of the reverend ones."

Then Assalāyana the brahman youth together with a large concourse of brahmans approached the Lord; having approached, he exchanged greetings with the Lord; having conversed in a friendly and courteous way, he sat down at a respectful distance. As he was sitting down at a respectful distance, Assalāyana the brahman youth spoke thus to the Lord:

"Good Gotama, brahmans speak thus: 'Only brahmans form the best caste, all other castes are low; only brahmans form the fair caste, all other castes are dark; only brahmans are pure, not non-brahmans; only brahmans are own sons of Brahmā, born of his mouth, born of Brahmā, formed by Brahmā, heirs to Brahmā.'[2] What does the good Gotama say about this?"

"But, Assalāyana, brahman wives of brahmans are known[3] to have their seasons and to conceive and to give birth and to give suck. Yet these brahmans, born of woman like everyone else, speak thus: 'Only brahmans form the best caste . . . heirs to Brahmā.'"

[149] "Although the good Gotama speaks thus, yet brahmans still consider it thus: 'Only brahmans . . . heirs to Brahmā.'"

"What do you think about this, Assalāyana? Have you heard that in Yona[4] and Kamboja[5] and other adjacent districts there are only two castes, the master and the slave? And that having been

---

[1] Wanderers preserve the *mantras* and behave as they have learnt and been taught. Therefore Assalāyana will not be defeated, but will be the victor. *MA*. iii. 408.

[2] As at *M*. ii. 84.

[3] Brahman women are seen being led to weddings so as to provide brahmans with sons, *MA*. iii. 408.

[4] See *DPPN*. where "probably the Pali equivalent for Ionians, Bactrian Greeks. . . . In later times, the name Yavanā or Yonā seems to have included all westerners living in India."

[5] A Mahājanapada belonging not to the Middle Country but to Uttarāpatha.

a master one becomes a slave; having been a slave one becomes a master ?"[1]

" Yes, I have heard this, sir. In Yona and Kamboja . . . having been a slave one becomes a master."

" In reference to this then, Assalāyana, on what strength and authority do brahmans speak thus: ' Only brahmans form the best caste . . . heirs of Brahmā ' ?"

" Although the good Gotama speaks thus, yet brahmans still consider it thus: ' Only brahmans form the best caste . . . heirs to Brahmā.' "

" What do you think about this, Assalāyana ? If a noble made onslaught on creatures, took what had not been given, wrongly enjoyed pleasures of the senses, were a liar, of slanderous speech, of harsh speech, a gossip, covetous, malevolent in mind, of wrong view—would only he at the breaking up of the body after dying arise in the sorrowful way, the bad bourn, the Downfall, Niraya Hell, and not a brahman ? Nor yet a merchant ? And would a worker if he made onslaught on creatures . . . were . . . of wrong view—would he at the breaking up of the body after dying, arise in the sorrowful way . . . Niraya Hell, and not a brahman ?"

" This is not so, good Gotama. If a noble, good Gotama, made onslaught on creatures, took what had not been given . . . at the breaking up of the body after dying he would arise in . . . Niraya Hell. And so would a brahman, good Gotama, and so would a merchant, good Gotama, and so would a worker, good Gotama—so, good Gotama, if they made onslaught on creatures, [**150**] took what had not been given . . . were . . . of wrong view, all the four castes at the breaking up of the body after dying would arise in the sorrowful way, the bad bourn, the Downfall, Niraya Hell."

" In reference to this then, Assalāyana, on what strength and authority do brahmans speak thus: ' Only brahmans form the best caste . . . heirs of Brahmā ' ?"

" Although the good Gotama speaks thus, yet brahmans still consider it thus: ' Only brahmans form the best caste . . . heirs to Brahmā.' "

" What do you think about this, Assalāyana ? If a brahman

---

[1] *MA*. iii. 409 says that if a brahman and his wife go trading in adjacent districts he may die there leaving no son, and the wife may have intercourse with a slave or workman. Any son born is a slave, although " pure " on his mother's side. If this son goes to trade in the Middle Country and marries a brahman girl, any son born will be " pure " only on his mother's side.

refrained from onslaught on creatures, from taking what had not been given, from wrong enjoyment of the sense-pleasures, from being a liar, from slanderous speech, from harsh speech, from being a gossip, were not covetous, were benevolent in mind and of right view—would only he at the breaking up of the body after dying arise in a good bourn, a heaven world, and not a noble, nor a merchant, nor a worker ?"

"That is not so, good Gotama. If a noble refrained from onslaught on creatures . . . were benevolent in mind and of right view, at the breaking up of the body after dying he would arise in a good bourn, a heaven world. And so would a brahman, good Gotama, and so would a merchant, good Gotama, and so would a worker, good Gotama—so, good Gotama, if they refrained from onslaught on creatures, from taking what had not been given . . . were benevolent in mind and of right view, all the four castes at the breaking up of the body after dying would arise in a good bourn, a heaven world."

"In reference to this then, Assalāyana, on what strength and authority do brahmans speak thus: 'Only brahmans form the best caste . . . heirs to Brahmā' ?"

"Although the good Gotama speaks thus, yet [**151**] brahmans still consider it thus: 'Only brahmans form the best caste . . . heirs to Brahmā.'"

"What do you think about this, Assalāyana ? Is it only a brahman who, on this supposition,[1] is capable of developing a mind of friendliness that is without enmity, without malevolence ? And not a noble, not a merchant, not a worker ?"

"That is not so, good Gotama. On this supposition, a noble too, good Gotama, is capable of developing a mind of friendliness that is without enmity, without malevolence; and also a brahman, good Gotama, and also a merchant, good Gotama, and also a worker, good Gotama—so, good Gotama, on this supposition all the four castes are capable of developing a mind of friendliness that is without enmity, without malevolence."

"In reference to this then, Assalāyana, on what strength and authority do brahmans speak thus: 'Only brahmans form the best caste . . . heirs to Brahmā' ?"

"Although the good Gotama speaks thus, yet brahmans still

---

[1] *asmiṁ padese.* The meaning of *padesa* as "showing, pointing out, decision, appealing to precedent" seems unknown to the Pali Dictionaries. But see Monier-Williams under *pra-diś*, "to point out, show, announce, communicate," etc.

consider it thus: 'Only brahmans form the best caste . . . heirs to Brahmā.' "

"What do you think about this, Assalāyana? Is it only a brahman who, taking a back-scratcher and bath-powder[1] and going to a river, is capable of cleansing himself of dust and mud? And not a noble, not a merchant, not a worker?"

"That is not so, good Gotama. A noble too, good Gotama, who, taking a back-scratcher and bath-powder and going to a river, is capable of cleansing himself of dust and mud. And so is a brahman . . . and so is a merchant . . . and so is a worker, good Gotama—so, good Gotama, all the four castes, taking a back-scratcher and bath-powder and going to a river, are capable of cleansing themselves of dust and mud."

"In reference to this then, Assalāyana, on what strength and authority do brahmans speak thus: 'Only brahmans form the best caste . . . heirs to Brahmā?"

"Although the good Gotama speaks thus, yet brahmans still consider it thus: 'Only brahmans form the best caste . . . heirs to Brahmā.' "

"What do you think about this, Assalāyana? If[2] a noble anointed king [**152**] were to assemble a hundred men of varying origins, saying to them: 'Let the good sirs come; and let those who are of noble, priestly and royal families, bringing an upper piece of fire-stick[3] of teak[4] or sāl or of a sweet-scented tree[5] or of sandal or lotus, light a fire and get it to give out heat. But let the good sirs come; and let those who are from a despised family, a trapper family, a bamboo-plaiter family, a cartwright family, a scavenger family,[6] bringing an upper piece of fire-stick from a dog's trough or a pig's trough or from a trough for dyeing or dry sticks from a castor-oil shrub, light a fire and get it to give out heat.' What do you think about this, Assalāyana? Is the fire that is lit and the heat that is got by someone—no matter whether he be from a noble, priestly or royal family, and no matter whether he bring an upper piece of fire-stick of teak or sāl or of a sweet-scented tree or of sandal or lotus—

---

[1] *Cf. M.* ii. 46, 182; and *cf. MA.* iii. 280 with *Vin.* ii. 106.

[2] As at *M.* ii. 183.

[3] *Cf. M.* i. 240.

[4] *sākassā vā*, as in two versions, and as at *M.* ii. 183. *Cf.* also *sākakaṭṭhaṁ* . . . *sālakaṭṭhaṁ* at *M.* ii. 129.

[5] *salaḷa* as at *e.g. Budv.* II. 51. Translators (*Min. Anth.* iii. p. 11) say this is probably a pine tree, Pinus Devadara.

[6] For notes on these five kinds of "low birth" see *B.D.* ii. 173 *f.*

is it a fire that has flame and hue and brightness[1] and, being this fire, is it able to serve the purposes of a fire? But is the fire that is lit and the heat that is got by someone—no matter whether he be from a despised family, a trapper family, a bamboo-plaiter family, a cartwright family, a scavenger family, and no matter whether he bring an upper piece of fire-stick from a dog's trough or a pig's trough or from a trough for dyeing or dry sticks from a castor-oil shrub—is it a fire that has neither flame nor hue nor brightness and, being this fire, is it unable to serve the purposes of a fire?"

"That is not so, good Gotama. Whoever from a noble, priestly or royal family, bringing an upper piece of fire-stick of teak or sāl or of a sweet-scented tree or of sandal or lotus, lights a fire and gets it to give out heat—this fire has flame and hue and brightness and is able to serve the purposes of a fire. And too, whoever from a despised family, a trapper family, a bamboo-plaiter family, a cartwright family, a scavenger family, bringing an upper piece of fire-stick from a dog's trough or a pig's trough or a trough for dyeing or dry sticks from a castor-oil shrub, lights a fire and gets it to give out heat—this fire too has flame and hue and brightness and is able to serve the purposes of a fire. So, good Gotama, all these fires have flame **[153]** and hue and brightness and are able to serve the purposes of a fire."

"In reference to this then, Assalāyana, on what strength and authority do brahmans speak thus: 'Only brahmans form the best caste, all other castes are low; only brahmans form the fair caste, all other castes are dark; only brahmans are pure, not non-brahmans; only brahmans are sons of Brahmā, born of his mouth, born of Brahmā, formed by Brahmā, heirs to Brahmā'?"

"Although the good Gotama speaks thus, yet brahmans still consider it thus: 'Only brahmans form the best caste . . . heirs to Brahmā.'"

"What do you think about this, Assalāyana? Suppose a noble youth were to consort with a brahman girl and as a result a son were born to them.[2] Would that son of the noble youth and the brahman girl be like his mother and also like his father, and should he be called 'noble' and also 'brahman'?"

"Whatever son, good Gotama, were born to a noble youth and a brahman girl, he would be like his mother and also like his father, and he should be called 'noble' and also 'brahman.'"

---

[1] *pabhassara* here; *ābhā* at *M*. ii. 130.

[2] *Cf. D*. i. 97.

" What do you think about this, Assalāyana ? Suppose a brahman youth were to consort with a noble girl and as a result a son were born to them.[1] Would that son . . . and should he be called ' noble ' and also ' brahman ' ?"

" Whatever son, good Gotama, were born to a brahman youth and a noble girl, he would be like his mother and also like his father, and he should be called ' noble ' and also ' brahman.' "

" What do you think about this, Assalāyana ? Suppose a mare were mated with an ass and as a result a foal[2] were born of this mating. Would that foal of the mare and the ass be like the mother and also like the father, and should it be called ' horse ' and also ' ass ' ?"

" Because of its crossed birth,[3] good Gotama, it is a mule. This, [**154**] good Gotama, is a difference that I see for it, but elsewhere, for the others, I see no difference at all."

" What do you think about this, Assalāyana ? There might be two brahman youths here, uterine brothers, the one skilled (in the Vedas), educated (in them), the other unskilled, uneducated. To which of these would brahmans first serve offerings for the dead[4] or cereals or oblations or meals for guests ?"

" Good Gotama, brahmans would first serve offerings for the dead or cereals or oblations or meals for guests to that brahman youth who is skilled (in the Vedas), educated (in them). For, good Gotama, what great fruit could there be of a gift to an unskilled, uneducated (person) ?"

" What do you think about this, Assalāyaṇa ? There might be two brahman youths here, uterine brothers, the one skilled (in the Vedas), educated (in them), but of bad moral habit, of evil character, and the other not skilled, uneducated, but of moral habit, lovely in character. To which of these would brahmans first serve offerings for the dead . . . or meals for guests ?"

" Good Gotama, brahmans would first serve offerings for the dead . . . or meals for guests to that brahman youth who is not skilled (in the Vedas), uneducated (in them), but who is of moral habit, lovely

---

[1] *Cf. D.* i. 97.

[2] *kisora*, with v. ll. *kissero, kissaro.* Childers gives " colt." *Kiśora* in Sanskrit.

[3] *vekurañjāya*, with v. ll *kuṇḍaṁ, kumāraṇḍu.* Neumann (II. 554) says: read *vekuranvāya=vaikriyānvayāya.*

[4] These four kinds of offerings also mentioned at *D.* i. 97. The first, " a gift for departed relatives," is *saddha.*

in character. For, good Gotama, what great fruit could there be of a gift to (a person of) bad moral habit, of evil character ?"

" First you, Assalāyana, went on about birth; leaving birth you went on about *mantras*; leaving *mantras* you arrived at the purity of the four castes which is just what *I* lay down."

When this had been said, the brahman youth Assalāyana sat silent, ashamed, his shoulders drooped, his face cast down, overcome with disappointment, at a loss for an answer. Then the Lord, understanding why Assalāyana the brahman youth was silent, ashamed, his shoulders drooped, his face cast down, overcome with disappointment, at a loss for an answer, spoke thus to Assalāyana the brahman youth:

" Once upon a time,[1] Assalāyana, while seven brahman seers were living in leaf huts in a stretch of forest a pernicious view like this arose in them: ' Only brahmans form the best caste, [**155**] all other castes are low . . . heirs to Brahmā.' And, Assalāyana, the seer Asita Devala[2] heard: ' Indeed seven brahman seers are living in leaf huts in a stretch of forest and a pernicious view like this has arisen in them: " Only brahmans form the best caste . . . heirs to Brahmā." ' Then, Assalāyana, the seer Asita Devala, having trimmed his hair and beard, having clothed himself in a pair of crimson coloured cloths, having put on sandals with many linings[3] and taking a staff made of gold, appeared in a cell in a hall[4] of the seven brahman seers. And then, Assalāyana, as the seer Asita Devala was pacing up and down in the cell in a hall of the seven brahman seers, he spoke thus: ' Now, where have these revered brahman seers gone ? Now, where have these revered brahman seers gone ?' Then, Assalāyana, it occurred to the seven brahman seers: ' Who is it who, while pacing up and down like a village lad[5] in a cell in a hall of the seven brahman

---

[1] Before Gotama's birth, *MA.* iii. 411.

[2] *Cf. Jā.* iii. 466. *MA.* iii. 411 says Asita was Kālaka, Devala was his name, and at that time the Lord was he. The name Kālaka probably identifies Asita with Kāla (or Asita) Devala of the *Indriya-jātaka, Jā.* iii. 463 *ff.* At *Mhvu.* ii. 37 the seer Asita, who prophesied that the infant Gotama would become a Buddha, calls himself Kāla.

[3] *ataliyo,* also at *S.* i. 226; explained at *MA.* iii. 411, *SA.* i. 346 by *gaṇaṅgaṇa,* for which see *Vin.* i. 185.

[4] *patthaṇḍila; MA.* iii. 411 explains by *paṇṇasālapariveṇa,* a cell in a leaf hall.

[5] *gāmaṇḍala,* as at *Thag.* 1143. *MA.* iii. 411 explains by *gāmadāraka,* a village youngster; *cf. ThagA.* on ver. 1143. There is probably also a hidden idea of " an ox (*go*) walking round and round on a threshing-floor."

seers, speaks thus: "Now, where have these revered brahman seers gone? Now, where have these revered brahman seers gone?"' Then, Assalāyana, the seven brahman seers put a curse on the seer Asita Devala, saying: 'Become a vile cinder.'[1] But, Assalāyana, the more the seven brahman seers cursed the seer Asita Devala, the more lovely became the seer Asita Devala, the more good to look upon and the more charming. Then, Assalāyana, it occurred to the seven brahman seers: 'Vain is austerity[2] for us, fruitless the Brahma-faring. Formerly when we put a curse on anyone, saying: Become a vile cinder, he became as a cinder; but the more we put a curse on this one the more lovely he becomes, the more good to look upon, the more charming.'

'Austerity is not vain for the revered ones, nor fruitless the Brahma-faring. But, revered sirs, please get rid of your misapprehension about me.'

[**156**] 'We will get rid of whatever misapprehension there is. But who is the revered sir?'

'Is the seer Asita Devala known to the revered sirs?'

'Yes, sir.'

'I, sirs, am he.' Then, Assalāyana, the seven brahman seers approached the seer Asita Devala in order to honour him. Then, Assalāyana, the seer Asita Devala spake thus to those seven brahman seers: 'I have heard this, good sirs: While seven brahman seers were living in leaf huts in a stretch of forest a pernicious view like this arose in them: "Only brahmans form the best caste, all other castes are low; only brahmans form the fair caste, all other castes are dark; only brahmans are pure, not non-brahmans; only brahmans are own sons of Brahmā, born of his mouth, born of Brahmā, formed by Brahmā, heirs to Brahmā."'

'Yes, sir.'

'But do you, sirs, know whether their mothers consorted only with brahmans, not with non-brahmans?'

'No, sir.'

'And do you, sirs, know whether their mothers' mothers back through seven generations consorted only with brahmans, not with non-brahmans?'

---

[1] Or, "become a cinder, vile one."

[2] *tapo*, perhaps magical heat produced by ascetic practice. As this was used to reduce one's enemies or opponents to cinders, so here *tapo* may have the double meaning of austerity (balancing the Brahma-faring) and of power to burn up others.

'No, sir.'

'And do you, sirs, know whether their fathers consorted only with brahman women, not with non-brahman women?'

'No, sir.'

'And do you, sirs, know whether their fathers' fathers back through seven generations consorted only with brahman women, not non-brahman women?'

'No, sir.'

'But do you, sirs, know how there is conception?'

'We do know, sir, how there is conception. [**157**] There is here a coitus of the parents, it is the mother's season and the *gandhabba* is present; it is on the conjuction of these three things that there is conception.'[1]

'But do you, sirs, know whether that *gandhabba* is a noble or brahman or merchant or worker?'

'We do not know, sir, whether that *gandhabba* is a noble or a brahman or a merchant or a worker.'

'This being so, do you know, sirs, who you are?'

'This being so, sir, we do not know who we are.'

Assalāyana, these seven so called brahman seers, on being questioned, cross-questioned and pressed for an answer by the seer Asita Devala concerning their own claims to lineage were not able to explain. So how can you, on being questioned, cross-questioned and pressed for an answer by me now explain your own claims to lineage —you who have the same teacher as they have, but not Puṇṇa the holder of the oblation-ladle?"[2]

When this had been said, Assalāyana the brahman youth spoke thus to the Lord: "It is excellent, good Gotama, it is excellent, good Gotama. May the good Gotama accept me as a lay-disciple going for refuge from this day forth for as long as life lasts."[3]

Discourse with Assalāyana:
The Third

---

[1] See *M.* i. 265-266.

[2] *dabbigāha. MA.* iii. 412: "Puṇṇa was the name of a benefactor of those seven seers; he took a ladle and cooked *paṇṇa*, leaves. He knew the art of handling the ladle. But he is not one of their teachers whom you (Assalāyana) also have; therefore you do not even know the art of handling a ladle."

[3] The usual formula for asking to become a lay disciple does not appear to occur here in full. The text does not even give abbreviation or omission marks.

94. DISCOURSE WITH GHOṬAMUKHA

(Ghoṭamukhasutta)

THUS have I heard: At one time the venerable Udena was staying near Benares in the Khemiya Mango Grove. Now at that time the brahman Ghoṭamukha had arrived at Benares on some business or other. Then while the brahman Ghoṭamukha [**158**] was pacing up and down and roaming about on foot he approached the Khemiya Mango Grove. Now at that time the venerable Udena was pacing up and down in the open. Then the brahman Ghoṭamukha approached the venerable Udena; having approached, he exchanged greetings with the venerable Udena, and having conversed in a friendly and courteous way, he spoke thus, while still pacing up and down, to the venerable Udena while he was still pacing up and down:[1] "My good recluse, there is no going forth under *dhamma*,[2] or so it seems to me; but then is this through not seeing revered men like yourself, or that which, in this matter, is *dhamma*?"

When this had been said, the venerable Udena came down from the place for pacing up and down, entered a dwelling-place and sat down on an appointed seat. And the brahman Ghoṭamukha also coming down from the place for pacing up and down and entering the dwelling-place stood at a respectful distance. The venerable Udena spoke thus to the brahman Ghoṭamukha as he was standing at a respectful distance: "Brahman, there are seats; do sit down if you like."

"While waiting for the good Udena we do not sit down. For how could one like me presume to sit down on a seat before being invited?" Then the brahman Ghoṭamukha, having taken a low seat, sat down at a respectful distance. As he was sitting down at a respectful distance, the brahman Ghoṭamukha spoke thus to the venerable Udena: "My good recluse, there is no going forth under *dhamma*, or so it seems to me; but then, is this through not seeing revered men like yourself, or that which, in this matter, is *dhamma*?"

---

[1] Following the v.l. *caṅkamantaṁ*, instead of text's *ekamantaṁ*.

[2] *dhammiko paribbājo*, explained by *dhammikā pabbajjā* at *MA*. iii. 412.

"But if you, brahman, could allow what is approved by me, and could reject what should be rejected, and should you not know the meaning of what is said by me were to question me further about it, saying: 'What is this, good Udena, what is the meaning of that?'—having arranged it like this we might have some conversation."

"I will allow what is approved by the good Udena, and I will reject what should be rejected, and if I [**159**] do not know the meaning of what is said by the good Udena I will question the honoured Udena further about it, saying: 'What is this, good Udena, what is the meaning of that?'—having arranged it like this let there be some conversation between us."

"Brahman, these four kinds of persons are found existing in the world . . .[1] [**160**] . . . But, good Udena, whatever person is neither a self-tormentor, intent on the practice of self-torment, nor a tormentor or others, intent on the practice of tormenting others, he, neither a self-tormentor nor a tormentor of others, is here-now allayed, quenched, become cool, an experiencer of bliss that lives with self Brahma-become. He does not mortify or torment either himself or others—(all of them) yearning for happiness and recoiling from pain. Therefore this person appeals to my mind."

"Brahman, there are these two companies.[2] Which two? Here, brahman, some company, inflamed with a passion for gems and jewelry,[3] looks about for a wife and children, men and women slaves, fields and sites, gold and silver. But here, brahman, some company, not inflamed with a passion for gems and jewelry, getting rid of wife and children, men and women slaves, fields and sites, gold and silver, goes forth from home into homelessness. This person, brahman, neither torments himself nor is intent on the practice of self-torment, he is not a tormentor of others nor intent on the practice of tormenting others. He, neither a self-tormentor nor a tormentor of others, is here-now allayed, quenched, become cool, an experiencer of bliss that lives with self Brahma-become. In which company do you, brahman, mostly see that man—in that company that is inflamed with a passion for gems and jewelry and looks about for a wife and children, men and women slaves, fields and sites, gold and silver; or in that company that is not inflamed with a passion for gems and

[1] As at *M.* i. 341, above, p. 5 *ff.*

[2] *Cf. A.* i. 70-76.

[3] *maṇikuṇḍalesu;* perhaps jewelled earrings; *cf. M.* ii. 64. Also see *S.* i. 77=*Dhp.* 345, 346=*Jā.* ii. 140 for the sentiment expressed in the first half of this paragraph, and *Thag.* 187.

jewelry and that, getting rid of wife and children, men and women slaves, fields and sites, gold and silver, goes forth from home into homelessness ?"

[161] " This man, good Udena, who is neither a tormentor of self intent on the practice of tormenting self, who is not a tormentor of others intent on the practice of tormenting others, and who, neither a self-tormentor nor a tormentor of others, is here-now allayed, quenched, become cool, an experiencer of bliss that lives with self Brahma-become—I mostly see that man in that company that is not inflamed with a passion for gems and jewelry and that, getting rid of wife and children, men and women slaves, fields and sites, gold and silver, goes forth from home into homelessness."

" But this was said by you just now, brahman: ' We understand thus, good recluse, there is no going forth under *dhamma*, or so it seems to us; but then is this through not seeing revered men like yourself, or that which, in this matter, is *dhamma* ?' "

" Good Udena, these words spoken to me are certainly helpful. There is a going forth under *dhamma*, or so it (now) seems to me, and so may the good Udena understand me. But it would be good if, out of compassion, the good Udena would explain to me in full these four kinds of persons that he has spoken of in brief but not explained in full."

" Well then, brahman, listen, attend carefully and I will speak."

" Yes, sir," the brahman Ghoṭamukha answered the venerable Udena in assent. The venerable Udena spoke thus:

" And which, brahman, is the person who torments self and is intent on the practice of self-torment ? Here, brahman, some person is unclothed, flouting life's decencies . . .[1] **[162]** . . . This, brahman, is called the person who is neither a self-tormentor intent on the practice of tormenting self, nor a tormentor of others intent on the practice of tormenting others. He, neither a self-tormentor nor a tormentor of others, is here-now allayed, quenched, become cool, an experiencer of bliss that lives with self Brahma-become."

When this had been said Ghoṭamukha the brahman spoke thus to the venerable Udena:

" Excellent, good Udena, excellent, good Udena. It is as if one might set upright what had been upset,[2] or might disclose what was covered, or show the way to one who had gone astray, or bring an

---

[1] As at *M*. i. 343 to 349; see above, p. 7 to p. 14.

[2] From here to the second request to be accepted as a lay disciple, *cf*. *M*. ii. 90.

oil-lamp into the darkness so that those with vision might see material shapes—even so in many a figure has *dhamma* been made clear by the revered Udena. Thus I am going to the revered Udena for refuge and to *dhamma* and to the Order of monks. May the revered Udena accept me as a lay-follower going for refuge from today forth for as long as life lasts."

"But do not you, brahman, go for refuge to me. You must go only to that Lord for refuge to whom I have gone for refuge."

"But where, good Udena, is this revered Gotama staying now, perfected one, fully Self-Awakened One?"

"Brahman, this Lord, perfected one, fully Self-Awakened One, has now attained final nibbāna."

"Good Udena, if we should hear that that honoured[1] Gotama were ten . . . twenty . . . thirty . . . forty . . . fifty *yojana* distant, we should go the fifty *yojana* so as to see that honoured Gotama, perfected one, fully Self-Awakened One. And, **[163]** good Udena, even if we heard that the honoured Gotama, perfected one, fully Self-Awakened One were a hundred *yojana* distant, we should go the hundred *yojana* so as to see that honoured Gotama, perfected one, fully Self-Awakened One. But, good Udena, since that revered[2] Gotama has attained final nibbāna, we are going for refuge to that honoured Gotama who has attained final nibbāna and to *dhamma* and to the Order of monks. May the revered Udena accept me as a lay-follower going for refuge from today forth for as long as life lasts. And, good Udena, the king of Aṅga daily gives me a regular supply of alms,[3] so I am giving the good Udena one of these regular supplies of alms."

"But what, brahman, does the king of Aṅga give you daily as a regular supply of alms?"

"Five hundred *kahāpaṇa*, good Udena."

"But, brahman, it is not allowable for us to receive gold and silver."[4]

"If it is not allowable to the good Udena, I will have a dwelling-place built for the good Udena."

"If you, brahman, wish to have a dwelling-place built for me, do have an assembly hall built for the Order at Pāṭaliputta."

"I am even more delighted and pleased with the good Udena that he urges me to make a gift to the Order. So I, good Udena, will

[1] *bhavantaṁ*. [2] *bhavaṁ*.

[3] *niccabhikkhā*, alms as a permanent or constant gift.

[4] Nissag. XVIII, see *Vin*. iii. 236 *ff*.

have an assembly hall built for the Order at Pāṭaliputta from this regular supply of alms and from subsequent supplies of alms."

Then Ghoṭamukha the brahman from this regular supply of alms and from subsequent supplies of alms had an assembly hall built for the Order at Pāṭaliputta. At the present time it is called Ghoṭamukhī.

Discourse with Ghoṭamukha:
The Fourth

95. DISCOURSE WITH CAṄKĪ[1]

(Caṅkīsutta)

[**164**] Thus have I heard: At one time the Lord, walking on tour among the Kosalans together with a large Order of monks, arrived at a brahman village of the Kosalans called Opasāda. While he was there near Opasāda the Lord stayed to the north of Opasāda in the Devas' Grove, the Sāl Grove.[2] At that time in Opasāda—a place teeming with life, (a place of) grass, wood and water and of corn, in fief to the King—there dwelt the brahman Caṅkī as overlord, on a royal gift, a gift with full powers[3] that had been made to him by King Pasenadi of Kosala. Then the brahman householders of Opasāda heard: "Verily the recluse Gotama . . .[4]. . . Good indeed is the sight of perfected ones such as this." Then the brahman householders of Opasāda, having set forth from Opasāda, went in companies, crowds and groups by the northern entrance to the Devas' Grove, the Sāl Grove. At that time the brahman Caṅkī was lying down in the upper part of the palace during the heat of the day. And the brahman Caṅkī saw the brahman householders of Opasāda who,

---

[1] This Discourse, which should be compared with the *Soṇadaṇḍa Suttanta* at *D.* i. 111 *ff.*, might be called "prompted by Caṅkī," the main part being delivered not to him but to Kāpaṭhika. *Cf. M.* Sta. 51.

[2] *MA.* iii. 414: it is said that oblations were offered here to the *devas.*

[3] *brahmadeyya. MA.* iii. 455 explains as *seṭṭhadeyya,* the best gift; and then says: "having raised the parasol, it was to be enjoyed as if he were a king; once given, this gift could not be taken back again." *Cf. D.* i. 87 for this description of a royal gift, and see *Dial.* i. 108, *n.* 1.

[4] As at *M.* ii. 54-55 (above, p. 251), substituting Opasāda for Thullakoṭṭhita.

having set forth from Opasāda, were going in companies, crowds and groups by the northern entrance to the Devas' Grove, the Sāl Grove; and seeing them, he addressed an adviser, saying:

"Why, good adviser, do the brahman householders of Opasāda, having set forth from Opasāda, go in companies, crowds and groups by the northern entrance to the Devas' Grove, the Sāl Grove?"

"There is, good Caṅkī, the recluse Gotama, a son of the Sakyans, gone forth from a Sakyan family . . .[1]. . . an Awakened One, a Lord. These are approaching this honoured Gotama."

"Well then, good adviser, approach the brahman householders of Opasāda; having approached, speak thus to the brahman householders of Opasāda: 'Sirs, the brahman Caṅkī speaks thus: Please let the revered ones wait; Caṅkī the brahman will also approach to see the recluse Gotama.'"

"Yes, sir," and when that adviser had answered the brahman Caṅkī [**165**] in assent, he approached the brahman householders of Opasāda; having approached, he spoke thus to the brahman householders of Opasāda: "Sirs, the brahman Caṅkī speaks thus: Please let the revered ones wait; Caṅkī the brahman will also approach to see the recluse Gotama."

Now at that time at least five hundred brahmans from various brahman districts[2] were residing at Opasāda on some business or other. These brahmans heard that the brahman Caṅkī would approach to see the recluse Gotama. Then these brahmans approached the brahman Caṅkī; having approached, they spoke thus to the brahman Caṅkī: "Is it indeed true that the good Caṅkī will approach to see the recluse Gotama?"

"That is my intention,[3] sirs; I will approach to see the recluse Gotama."

"Do not, good Caṅkī, approach to see the recluse Gotama. It is not right[4] that the good Caṅkī should approach to see the recluse Gotama; it is right that the recluse Gotama should himself approach to see the honoured Caṅkī. For the good Caṅkī is of pure birth on both sides, of pure descent from his mother and father back through seven generations, unchallenged, irreproachable in respect of birth.[5] And because the good Caṅkī is of pure birth on both sides . . .

---

[1] As at *M*. ii. 55, above, p. 251.

[2] Lit. kingdoms, *rajja; MA*. iii. 416 instances Kāsi and Kosala.

[3] *evaṁ kho me bho hoti*, lit. it is thus by me.

[4] *na arahati*, not fit.

[5] Stock. See under *akkhitta* (unchallenged) in *PTC*. *Cf. D*. i. 120 for five things that brahmans declare make a brahman.

irreproachable in respect of birth, this is a reason why it is not right for the good Caṅkī to approach to see the recluse Gotama; it is right that the recluse Gotama should himself approach to see the honoured Caṅkī. For the good Caṅkī is prosperous, very wealthy, very rich. Then the good Caṅkī is master of the three Vedas, versed in the vocabularies and rituals together with the phonology and exegesis and the legendary tradition as the fifth; he is learned in idioms, a grammarian, proficient in popular philosophy and the marks of a Great Man. Then the good Caṅkī is lovely, good to look upon, charming, possessed of the greatest beauty of complexion, of a sublime colour,[1] a sublime stature,[2] stately in appearance. Then the good Caṅkī is of moral habit, one who has grown in moral habit, he is possessed[3] of a moral habit that has grown.[4] Then the good Caṅkī has a lovely voice, a lovely [**166**] delivery, he is possessed of urbane speech, distinct, not mumbling, he is able to make his meaning clear. Then the good Caṅkī, the teacher of many teachers, instructs three hundred brahman youths in *mantras*. Then the good Caṅkī is respected, revered, esteemed, venerated by King Pasenadi of Kosala. Then the good Caṅkī is respected . . . venerated by the brahman Pokkharasāti.[5] Then the good Caṅkī dwells as overlord in Opasāda —a place teeming with life, (a place of) grass, wood and water . . . on a royal gift, a gift with full powers that has been made to him by King Pasenadi of Kosala. And because the good Caṅkī dwells as overlord . . . on a gift with full powers that has been made to him by King Pasenadi of Kosala, this is a reason why it is not right for the good Caṅkī to approach to see the recluse Gotama; it is right that the recluse Gotama should himself approach to see the honoured Caṅkī."

When this had been said, the brahman Caṅkī spoke thus to those brahmans:

" Well then, sirs, hear from me why it is right that we ourselves should go to see the honoured Gotama and why it is not right that the revered Gotama should himself come to see us. Indeed, sirs, the recluse Gotama is of pure birth on both sides, of pure descent

---

[1] *brahmavaṇṇī*, with the best golden colour of the pure castes, *MA*. iii. 418.

[2] *brahmavaccasī*. *MA*. iii. 418 says his body is like that of Mahā-Brahmā—one of the marks of a Great Man (see Sta. 91).

[3] *MA*. iii. 418 gives *yutta*, intent on, in explanation of text's *samannāgata*, possessed of.

[4] *MA*. iii. 418 says that these last two attributes are synonymous.

[5] A very rich brahman, evidently also of spiritual integrity. See *M*. Sta. 99.

from his mother and father back through seven generations, unchallenged, irreproachable in respect of birth. And because the recluse Gotama is of pure birth on both sides . . . irreproachable in respect of birth, this is a reason why it is not right for the good Gotama to come to see us, while it is right that we ourselves should go to see the honoured Gotama. Indeed the recluse Gotama has gone forth giving up an abundance of unwrought and wrought gold[1] both in the ground and above it.[2] Indeed, sirs, the recluse Gotama while he was a young man with lovely coal-black hair, endowed with radiant youth, in the prime of his life, went forth from home into homelessness. Indeed, sirs, although his parents were unwilling and tears poured down their cheeks the recluse Gotama, having cut off his hair and beard and donned saffron robes, went forth from home into homelessness. Indeed, sirs, the recluse Gotama is lovely, good to look upon, charming, possessed of the greatest beauty of complexion, [**167**] of a sublime colour, a sublime stature, stately in appearance. Indeed, sirs, the recluse Gotama is of moral habit, one who is ariyan in moral habit, one who is skilled in moral habit, possessed of a moral habit that is skilled. Indeed, sirs, the recluse Gotama has a lovely voice, a lovely delivery, he is possessed of urbane speech, distinct, not mumbling, he is able to make his meaning clear. Indeed, sirs, the recluse Gotama is the teacher of many teachers. Indeed, sirs, the recluse Gotama has destroyed attachment to sense-pleasures, has put away frivolity.[3] Indeed, sirs, the recluse Gotama teaches *kamma*, teaches effective *kamma*,[4] desiring no evil for the brahman race.[5] Indeed, sirs, the recluse Gotama has gone forth from a distinguished family, a leading noble family.[6] Indeed, sirs, the recluse Gotama has gone forth from a prosperous family, very wealthy, very rich. Indeed, sirs, (people) come from distant kingdoms, distant regions to question the recluse Gotama. Indeed, sirs, various thousands of *devatās* have gone to the recluse Gotama for refuge for breathing things. Indeed, sirs, a lovely report has gone abroad concerning the recluse Gotama: He

---

[1] On *hiraññasuvaṇṇa* see *B.D.* i. 28, *n.* 1. [2] See *B.D.* i. 79, *n.* 6.

[3] *cāpalla.* At *M.* i. 470, *Vbh.* 351, *Vism.* 106 *cāpalya.*

[4] *kammavādī kiriyavādī.*

[5] *MA.* iii. 422 says that Sāriputta, Moggallāna, Mahākassapa and so on belong to this race. 'Brahman' is therefore taken in the Buddhist sense above.

[6] *ādīnakhattiyakulā.* On *ādīna* in this compound see *Dial.* i. 148, *n.* 2. *Cf. ādīnamānaso* at *S.* v. 74 and see *K.S.* v. 61, *n.* 5.

is indeed Lord, perfected one, fully Self-Awakened One, endowed with knowledge and (right) conduct, Well-farer, knower of the worlds, the matchless charioteer of men to be tamed, teacher of *devas* and mankind, the Awakened One, the Lord. Indeed, sirs, the recluse Gotama is endowed with the thirty-two marks of a Great Man. Indeed, sirs, King Seniya Bimbisāra of Magadha with his wife and children has gone to the recluse Gotama for refuge for breathing things. Indeed, sirs, King Pasenadi of Kosala with his wife and children has gone to the recluse Gotama for refuge for breathing things. Indeed, sirs, the brahman Pokkharasāti with his wife and children has gone to the recluse Gotama for refuge for breathing things. Indeed, sirs, the recluse Gotama has arrived at Opasāda and is staying near Opasāda, to the north, in the Devas' Grove, the Sāl Grove. Whatever recluses and brahmans come to our villages or fields, they are our guests. And guests must be revered, reverenced, esteemed, honoured by us. So, sirs, because the recluse Gotama has arrived at Opasāda and is staying near Opasāda, to the north, in the Devas' Grove, the Sāl Grove, the recluse Gotama is our guest. The guest must be revered, reverenced, esteemed and honoured by us. [**168**] This too is a reason why it is not right that the revered Gotama should come and see us. But it is right that we ourselves should go and see the honoured Gotama. To this extent I, sirs, know the good Gotama's splendour,[1] but this is not the (full) extent of the good Gotama's splendour—immeasurable is the splendour of the good Gotama. It is not right that the good Gotama, possessed as he is of each one of these qualities, should come to see us. But it is right that we ourselves should go to see the honoured Gotama. Well then, sirs, all of us will go ourselves to see the recluse Gotama."

Then the brahman Caṅkī together with a large group of brahmans approached the Lord; having approached, he exchanged greetings with the Lord; and having conversed in a friendly and courteous way, he sat down at a respectful distance. Now at that time the Lord was sitting down talking in a courteous way on this topic and that with a number of venerable brahmans. Now at that time a brahman youth called Kāpaṭhika, young, with shaven head, sixteen years of age since his birth, master of the three Vedas, versed in the vocabularies and rituals together with the phonology and exegesis with the legendary tradition as the fifth, learned in the idioms, a grammarian, proficient in popular philosophy and the marks of a Great Man, was

---

[1] *vaṇṇa* as at end of *M*. Sta. 56.

sitting down in that company. At intervals he interrupted the conversation that the Lord was holding with the venerable brahmans. Then the Lord reprimanded the brahman youth Kāpaṭhika, saying: "Do not let the venerable Bhāradvāja interrupt at intervals the conversation being held with the venerable brahmans: let the venerable Bhāradvāja wait until the end of the conversation." When this had been said the brahman Caṅkī spoke thus to the Lord:

"Do not let the good Gotama reprimand the brahman youth Kāpaṭhika. The brahman youth Kāpaṭhika is a young man of a respectable family, and the brahman youth Kāpaṭhika is very learned, and the brahman youth Kāpaṭhika has a lovely delivery, and clever is the brahman youth Kāpaṭhika, and the brahman youth Kāpaṭhika is capable of arguing about this speech together with the good Gotama."

Then it occurred to the Lord: "Certainly, **[169]** the brahman youth Kāpaṭhika must be 'finished'[1] in the threefold Vedic lore since brahmans honour him." Then it occurred to the brahman youth Kāpaṭhika: "If the recluse Gotama catches my eye, then I will ask the recluse Gotama a question." Then the Lord, knowing with his mind the reasoning in the mind of the brahman youth Kāpaṭhika, caught his eye. Then it occurred to the brahman youth Kāpaṭhika: "The recluse Gotama is paying respect to me. Suppose I were to ask the recluse Gotama a question?" Then the brahman youth Kāpaṭhika spoke thus to the Lord: "Good Gotama, that which is an ancient *mantra*[2] of the brahmans according to hearsay and tradition, according to the authority of the collections[3] and in regard to which brahmans inevitably come to the conclusion: 'This alone is the truth, all else is falsehood'—what does the good Gotama say about this?"

"But, Bhāradvāja, is there even one brahman among them who speaks thus: 'I know this, I see this: this alone is the truth, all else is falsehood'?"

"No, good Gotama."

"But, Bhāradvāja, is there even one teacher of brahmans, even

---

[1] *kataṁ*, in the sense of perfect, finished, and therefore master; *cf. kataṁkaraṇīyaṁ* where *kataṁ* means both 'ended' or 'concluded' and 'concluded well or properly"; thus finished (as ended) and finished (as in "a finished product").

[2] *mantapada. MA.* iii. 424 says this as well as *mantā* means Veda. Some of the seers mentioned below have Vedic verses traditionally ascribed to them. See *B.D.* iv. 337.

[3] *Cf. M.* i. 520.

one teacher of teachers back through seven generations of teachers who speaks thus: ' I know this, I see this; this alone is the truth, all else is falsehood ' ?"

" No, good Gotama."

" But, Bhāradvāja, those who were formerly seers of the brahmans,[1] makers of *mantras*, preservers of *mantras*, whose ancient *mantras*[2] as sung, taught and composed the brahmans of today still sing, still speak; they still speak what was spoken, they still teach what was taught—that is to say (by) Aṭṭhaka, Vāmaka, Vāmadeva, Vessāmitta, Yamataggi, Aṅgirasa, Bhāradvāja, Vāseṭṭha, Kassapa, Bhagu—do even these speak thus: ' We know this, we see this: this alone is the truth, all else is falsehood ' ?"

[**170**] " No, good Gotama."

" So it comes to this, Bhāradvāja: there is not a single brahman who speaks thus to a brahman: ' I know this . . . all else is falsehood.' There is not a single teacher of brahmans, not a single teacher of teachers back through seven generations of teachers who speaks thus: ' I know this . . . all else is falsehood.' And those who were formerly seers of the brahmans, makers of *mantras* . . . that is to say (by) Aṭṭhaka . . . Bhagu, not even these speak thus: ' We know this, we see this: this alone is the truth, all else is falsehood.' Bhāradvāja, it is like a string of blind men[3] holding on to one another—neither does the foremost one see, nor does the middle one see, nor does the hindmost one see. Even so, methinks, Bhāradvāja, do the words of the brahmans turn out to resemble a string of blind men: neither does the foremost one see nor does the middle one see nor does the hindmost one see. What do you think about this, Bhāradvāja ? This being so, does not the faith of the brahmans turn out to be groundless ?"

" But, good Gotama, brahmans do not merely go by[4] faith in this matter; brahmans also go by report."

" First you, Bhāradvāja, set off about faith, now you are speaking of report. These five things, Bhāradvāja, have a twofold maturing[5] here-now. What five ? Faith, inclination, report, consideration of reasons, reflection on and approval of an opinion.[6] These, Bhārad-

[1] Down to the name Bhagu *cf. Vin.* i. 245; *D.* i. 104, 238, 242; *A.* iii. 224, 229; *M.* ii. 200.

[2] See note 2 on previous page.

[3] As at *M.* ii. 200, *D.* i. 239.

[4] *payirūpāsanti*, to pay homage, usually with the acc.

[5] *MA.* iii. 426 says a maturing that has been and that has not (yet) been.

[6] On the five also see *S.* ii. 115, iv. 138. *Cf. A.* i. 190, ii. 191.

vāja, are the five things having a twofold maturing here-now. Moreover, Bhāradvāja, even although something be thoroughly believed in, it may be empty, void, false; on the other hand, something not thoroughly believed in may be fact, truth, not otherwise. Moreover, [**171**] Bhāradvāja, even although something may be thoroughly inclined towards . . . well reported . . . well considered . . . well reflected upon, it may be empty, void, false; on the other hand, even although something is not well reflected upon, it may be fact, truth, not otherwise. Preserving a truth, Bhāradvāja, is not enough for an intelligent man inevitably to come to the conclusion: 'This alone the truth, all else is falsehood.' "

"But to what extent, good Gotama, is there preservation of a truth? To what extent does one preserve a truth? We are asking the honoured Gotama about preservation of a truth."

"Bhāradvāja, if a man has faith and says: 'Such is my faith,' speaking thus he preserves a truth, but not yet does he inevitably come to the conclusion: 'This alone is the truth, all else is falsehood.' To this extent, Bhāradvāja, is there preservation of a truth, to this extent does one preserve a truth, and it is to this extent that we lay down the preservation of a truth; but not yet is there awakening to truth. And if, Bhāradvāja, a man has an inclination . . . a report . . . a consideration of reasons . . . a reflection on and approval of an opinion and says: 'Such is my reflection on and approval of the opinion,' speaking thus he preserves a truth, but not yet does he inevitably come to the conclusion: 'This alone is the truth, all else is falsehood.' To this extent, Bhāradvāja, is there preservation of a truth, to this extent does one preserve a truth, and it is to this extent that we lay down the preservation of a truth; but not yet is there awakening to truth."

"To this extent, good Gotama, is there preservation of a truth, to this extent one preserves a truth, to this extent do we behold the preservation of a truth. But to what extent, good Gotama, is there awakening to truth? To what extent does one awaken to truth? We are asking the honoured Gotama about awakening to truth."

"As to this, Bhāradvāja, suppose a monk is living depending on a village or market town; a householder or a householder's son, having approached him, examines him concerning three states: [**172**] states of greed, states of aversion and states of confusion.[1] He thinks: 'Does the venerable one have such states of greed that, his mind obsessed by

[1] *Cf. A.* i. 190 *f.*

such states of greed, although not knowing, he would say, "I know," or although not seeing, he would say, "I see," or would he incite another to such a course as for a long time would be for his woe and ill?' While examining him, he knows thus: 'This venerable one does not have such states of greed that, his mind obsessed by such states of greed, while not knowing he would say, "I know," or while not seeing he would say, "I see," nor would he incite another to such a course as would be for a long time for his woe and ill.' As is that venerable one's conduct of body, as is his conduct of speech, so is it not that of a greedy person. And when this venerable one teaches *dhamma*, that *dhamma* is deep, difficult to see, difficult to understand, peaceful, excellent, beyond dialectic, subtle, intelligible to the wise; it is not a *dhamma* that could be well taught by a greedy person.

After examining him and beholding that he is purified of states of greed, then he examines him further on states of aversion. He thinks: 'Now, does this venerable one have such states of aversion that, his mind obsessed . . . or would he incite another to such a course as for a long time would be for his woe and ill?' . . . As is that venerable one's conduct of body . . . of speech, so is it not that of a person with aversion. And when this venerable one is teaching *dhamma* . . . it is not a *dhamma* that could be well taught by a person with aversion.

After examining him and beholding that he is purified of states of aversion, [**173**] then he examines him further on states of confusion. He thinks: 'Now, does this venerable one have such states of confusion that, his mind obsessed . . . it is not a *dhamma* that could be well taught by a confused person.'

After examining him and beholding that he is purified of states of confusion, then he reposes faith in him; with faith born he draws close;[1] drawing close he sits down near by; sitting down near by he lends ear; lending ear he hears *dhamma*; having heard *dhamma* he remembers it; he tests the meaning of the things he remembers; while testing the meaning the things are approved of; if there is approval of the things desire is born; with desire born he makes an effort; having made an effort he weighs it up; having weighed it up he strives; being self-resolute he realises with his person the highest truth itself; and penetrating it by means of intuitive wisdom, he

[1] The text reads *saddhājāto upasaṁkamanto payirūpāsati*. But to agree with the manner of the wording in the rest of the passage, I think *upasaṁkamati* should be inserted after *saddhājāto* as at *M*. i. 480. Otherwise these two passages are similar.

sees. It is to this extent, Bhāradvāja, that there is an awakening to truth; it is to this extent that one awakens to truth; it is to this extent that we lay down an awakening to truth; but not yet is there attainment of truth."

"To this extent, good Gotama, is there awakening to truth, to this extent does one awaken to truth, and to this extent do we behold an awakening to truth. But to what extent, good Gotama, is there attainment of truth? To what extent does one attain truth? We are asking the honoured Gotama about attainment of truth."

[174] "There is attainment of truth, Bhāradvāja, by following, developing and continually practising these things themselves. To this extent, Bhāradvāja, is there attainment of truth, to this extent does one attain truth, and to this extent do we lay down the attainment of truth."

"To this extent, good Gotama, is there attainment of truth, to this extent does one attain truth, and to this extent do we behold the attainment of truth. But what thing, good Gotama, is of much service in the attainment of truth? We are asking the honoured Gotama about a thing that is of much service in the attainment of truth."

"Striving, Bhāradvāja, is of much service in the attainment of truth; for whoso should not strive after truth would not attain it; but if he strives, then he attains truth; therefore striving is of much service in the attainment of truth."

"But what thing, good Gotama, is of much service to striving? We are asking the honoured Gotama about a thing that is of much service to striving."

"Weighing (things up), Bhāradvāja, is of much service to striving; for whoso should not weigh (things up) would not strive; but if he weighs up, then he strives; therefore weighing up is of much service to striving."

"But what thing, good Gotama, is of much service to weighing up? We are asking the honoured Gotama about a thing that is of much service to weighing up."

"Making an effort, Bhāradvāja, is of much service to weighing up; for whoso should not make an effort would not weigh up; but if he makes an effort, then he weighs up; therefore making an effort is of much service to weighing up."

"But what thing, good Gotama, is of much service to making an effort? We are asking the honoured Gotama about a thing that is of much service to making an effort."

" Desire, Bhāradvāja, is of much service to making an effort; should desire for it not be born, one could not make an effort for it; but if desire is born, then he makes an effort; therefore desire is of much service to making an effort."

" But what thing, good Gotama, is of much service to desire ? [**175**] We are asking the honoured Gotama about a thing that is of much service to desire."

" Approving of the things, Bhāradvāja, is of much service to desire; should the things not be approved of, desire for them could not be born; but if there is approval of the things, then desire is born; therefore approval of the things is of much service to desire."

" But what thing, good Gotama, is of much service to (reflection on and) approval of the things ? We are asking the honoured Gotama about a thing that is of much service to (reflection on and) approval of the things."

" Testing the meaning, Bhāradvāja, is of much service to reflection on and approval of the things. If one did not test that meaning, the things could not seem right for this reflection; but if one tests the meaning, then the things seem right for reflection; therefore testing the meaning is of much service to reflection on and approval of the things."

" But what thing, good Gotama, is of much service to testing the meaning ? We are asking the honoured Gotama about a thing that is of much service to testing the meaning."

" Remembering *dhamma*, Bhāradvāja, is of much service to testing the meaning; for whoso should not remember that *dhamma* could not test that meaning; but if he remembers *dhamma*, then he tests the meaning; therefore remembering *dhamma* is of much service to testing the meaning."

" But what thing, good Gotama, is of much service to remembering *dhamma* ? We are asking the honoured Gotama about a thing that is of much service to remembering *dhamma*."

" Hearing *dhamma*, Bhāradvāja, is of much service to remembering *dhamma*. Whoso should not hear that *dhamma* could not remember that *dhamma*; but if he hears *dhamma*, then he remembers *dhamma*,[1] therefore hearing *dhamma* is of much service to remembering *dhamma*."

" But what thing, good Gotama, is of much service to hearing

---

[1] Text reads: *yasmā ca kho dhammaṁ dhāreti*, instead of, as would seem more correct, *yasmā ca kho dhammaṁ suṇāti tasmā dhammaṁ dhāreti*.

dhamma ? We are asking the honoured Gotama about a thing that is of much service to hearing *dhamma*."

"Lending ear, Bhāradvāja, is of much service to hearing *dhamma*; [**176**] for whoso should not lend ear to it could not hear this *dhamma*; but if he lends ear, then he hears *dhamma*; therefore lending ear is of much service to hearing *dhamma*."

"But what thing, good Gotama, is of much service to lending ear ? We are asking the honoured Gotama about a thing that is of much service to lending ear."

"Drawing close, Bhāradvāja, is of much service to lending ear; for whoso should not draw close to him could not lend ear to him; but if he draws close, then he lends ear; therefore drawing close is of much service to lending ear."

"But what thing, good Gotama, is of much service to drawing close ? We are asking the honoured Gotama about a thing that is of much service to drawing close."

"Approaching, Bhāradvāja, is of much service to drawing close; for whoso should not approach him could not draw close to him; but if he approaches, then he draws close; therefore approaching is of much service to drawing close."

"But what thing, good Gotama, is of much service to approaching ? We are asking the honoured Gotama about a thing that is of much service to approaching."

"Faith, Bhāradvāja, is of much service to approaching; for should faith in him not be born, one could not approach him; but if faith is born, then he approaches; therefore faith is of much service to approaching."

"We asked the honoured Gotama about the preservation of truth; the good Gotama explained the preservation of truth; and we approved of it and were pleased, and so we are delighted. We asked the honoured Gotama about awakening to truth; the good Gotama explained . . . we are delighted. We asked the honoured Gotama about the attainment of truth . . . We asked the honoured Gotama about a thing that is of much service to the attainment of truth . . . [**177**] we are delighted. Whatever it was that we asked the honoured Gotama, that very thing the good Gotama explained; and we approved of it and were pleased, and so we are delighted. For, formerly, good Gotama, we used to know (a distinction) thus: 'And who are these little shaveling recluses, menials, black, off-scourings of our Kinsman's heels ?[1] And who are the knowers of

[1] As at *M*. i. 334; see *M.L.S.* i. 397.

dhamma ?'[1] Indeed the good Gotama has aroused in me a recluse's regard[2] for recluses, a recluse's satisfaction in recluses, a recluse's respect for recluses. It is excellent, good Gotama, it is excellent, good Gotama . . . May the revered Gotama accept me as a lay-disciple going for refuge from this day forth for as long as life lasts."

Discourse with Caṅkī:
The Fifth

96. DISCOURSE WITH ESUKĀRĪ

(Esukārisutta)

THUS have I heard: At one time the Lord was staying near Sāvatthī in the Jeta Grove in Anāthapiṇḍika's monastery. Then the brahman Esukārī approached the Lord; having approached, he exchanged greetings with the Lord, and having conversed in a friendly and courteous way, he sat down at a respectful distance. As he was sitting down at a respectful distance, Esukārī the brahman spoke thus to the Lord:

"Brahmans, good Gotama, lay down four (types of) service: they lay down service for a brahman, they lay down service for a noble, they lay down service for a merchant, they lay down service for a worker. As to this, good Gotama, brahmans lay down service for a brahman, saying: 'A brahman may serve a brahman, or a noble may serve a brahman, or a merchant may serve a brahman, or a worker may serve a brahman.' This is the [**178**] service, good Gotama, that brahmans lay down for a brahman. As to this, good Gotama, brahmans lay down service for a noble, saying: 'A noble may serve a noble or a merchant may serve a noble or a worker may serve a noble.' This is the service, good Gotama, that brahmans lay down for a noble. As to this, good Gotama, brahmans lay down service for a merchant, saying: 'A merchant may serve a merchant or a worker may serve a merchant.' This is the service, good Gotama, that brahmans lay down for a merchant. As to this, good Gotama, brahmans lay down service for a worker, saying: 'A worker may serve a worker. For who else could serve a worker?' This is the

[1] *Cf. M.* i. 480.

[2] *pema*, liking, affection.

service, good Gotama, that brahmans lay down for a worker. Brahmans, good Gotama, lay down these four (types of) service. What does the good Gotama say about this ?"

"But, brahman, does everyone agree with the brahmans when they lay down these four (types of) service ?"

"No, good Gotama."

"Like a poor needy destitute man[1] on whom they might force a morsel (of meat although) he did not want it, saying: 'You must eat this meat, my good man, and you must hand over a price for it as well'—even so, brahman, do the brahmans—and moreover without the assent of recluses and brahmans—lay down these four (types of) service. I, brahman, do not say that everyone should serve. But, brahman, I do not say that everyone should not serve. For if, brahman, there is a servitor who is worse for his service, not better, I do not say that he should serve. But if, brahman, there is a servitor who is better for his service, not worse, I say that he should serve. And if, brahman, one should ask a noble, saying: 'Is your servitor worse, not better, as a result of his service; or is your servitor, better, not worse, as a result of his service ? And so which one should you be served by ?'—then the noble, [**179**] brahman, in replying rightly would reply thus: 'The servitor who is worse, not better, as a result of serving me—I should not be served by him. But the servitor who is better, not worse, as a result of serving me —I should be served by him.'

And if, brahman, one should ask a brahman . . . a merchant . . . a worker, saying: 'Is your servitor worse . . . (*as above*) . . .' '. . . But the servitor who is better, not worse, as a result of serving me—I should be served by him.'

I, brahman, do not speak of 'better' because of birth in a high-class family.[2] But, brahman, I do not speak of 'worse' because of birth in a high-class family. I, brahman, do not speak of 'better' because of splendour of complexion.[3] But, brahman, I do not speak of 'worse' because of splendour of complexion. I, brahman, do not speak of 'better' because of splendour of possessions.[4] But I, brahman, do not speak of 'worse' because of splendour of possessions. For, as to this, brahman, someone from a high-class

---

[1] As at *A*. iii. 384. See also *M*. i. 450.

[2] *MA*. iii. 428, noble and brahman.

[3] *MA*. iii. 428, even a merchant has a splendid complexion.

[4] *MA*. iii. 428, even a worker, indeed even a member of a despised class, may have splendid possessions.

family makes onslaught on creatures, takes what has not been given, wrongly enjoys pleasures of the senses, is a liar, of slanderous speech, of harsh speech, a gossip, covetous, malevolent in mind, of wrong view. Therefore I do not speak of 'better' because of birth in a high-class family. But, as to this, brahman, someone from a high-class family may refrain from onslaught on creatures, from taking what has not been given, from wrongly enjoying pleasures of the senses, from lying, from slanderous speech, from harsh speech, from gossiping, and be not covetous, not malevolent in mind, of right view. Therefore I do speak of 'worse' because of birth in a high-class family. As to this, brahman, someone with splendour of complexion . . . with splendour of possessions makes onslaught on creatures . . . is of wrong view. Therefore I do not speak of 'better' because of splendour of possessions. But, as to this, brahman, someone with splendour of possessions refrains from onslaught on creatures . . . is of right view. Therefore [**180**] I do not speak of 'worse' because of splendour of possessions. I, brahman, do not say that everyone should serve. But, brahman, I do not say that everyone should not serve. That servitor, brahman, in whom as a result of his service faith grows, moral habit grows, learning grows, renunciation grows, wisdom grows,[1] I say of him that he should serve."

When this had been said, Esukārī the brahman spoke thus to the Lord:

"Brahmans, good Gotama, lay down four (types of) treasure:[2] they lay down a brahman's wealth,[3] they lay down a noble's wealth, they lay down a merchant's wealth, they lay down a worker's wealth. In regard to this, good Gotama, brahmans lay down that a brahman's wealth is walking for alms.[4] But, on despising the wealth of walking for alms, a brahman is one who does not meet his obligations and is like a guardian taking what has not been given. This, good Gotama, is how brahmans lay down a brahman's wealth. In regard to this, good Gotama, brahmans lay down that a noble's wealth is the bow and quiver. But, on despising the wealth of bow and quiver, a noble is one who does not meet his obligations and is like a guardian taking what has not been given. This, good Gotama, is how brah-

---

[1] At *A.* iii. 80=*S.* iv. 250 these five ways of growing constitute ariyan growth.

[2] *dhana.*

[3] *sandhana*, assets, resources, belongings.

[4] Even if a brahman is very rich he should walk for alms as did at one time the rich brahmans of old, *MA.* iii. 428.

mans lay down a noble's wealth. In regard to this, good Gotama, brahmans lay down that a merchant's[1] wealth is agriculture and cow-keeping.[2] But, on despising the wealth of agriculture and cow-keeping, a merchant is one who does not meet his obligations and is like a guardian taking what has not been given. This, good Gotama, is how brahmans lay down a merchant's wealth. In regard to this, good Gotama, brahmans lay down that a worker's wealth is the sickle and pingo. But, on despising the wealth of sickle and pingo, a worker is one who does not meet his obligations and is like a guardian taking what has not been given. This, good Gotama, is how brahmans lay down a worker's wealth. Brahmans, good Gotama, lay down these four (types of) treasure. What does the good Gotama say about this ?"

"But, brahman, does everyone agree with the brahmans when they lay down these four (types of) treasure ?"

[**181**] "No, good Gotama."

"Like a poor needy destitute man on whom they might force a morsel . . . (*as above*) . . . even so do brahmans . . . lay down these four (types of) treasure. Now I, brahman, lay down that a man's wealth is *dhamma*, ariyan, supermundane. On recollecting his ancient family lineage on his maternal and paternal sides,[2] wherever it is that there is the production of an individuality,[3] it is reckoned in accordance with that. So, if there is the production of an individuality in a noble family, it is reckoned as a noble. If there is the production of an individuality in a brahman family, it is reckoned as a brahman. If there is the production of an individuality in a merchant family . . . in a worker family, it is reckoned as a merchant . . . a worker. As a fire, brahman, no matter on account of what condition it burns, is reckoned precisely as that: if the fire burns because of dry sticks it is reckoned as a dry stick fire; if the fire burns because of chips . . . grass . . . cowdung it is reckoned as a fire of chips . . . grass . . . cowdung—even so, brahman, do I lay down that a man's wealth is *dhamma*, ariyan, supermundane. On recollecting his ancient family lineage on his maternal and paternal sides, wherever it is that there is the production of an individuality, it is reckoned in accordance with that. So, if there is the production of an individuality in a noble . . . brahman . . . merchant . . . worker

---

[1] *vessa*, which I have translated throughout by "merchant" could only be a merchant-trader if he first provided himself with something to sell, mainly grains and the products of the cow.

[2] *Cf. D.* i. 93.

[3] *attabhāvassa abhinibbatti*, two very complex words.

family, it is reckoned precisely as noble . . . brahman . . . merchant . . . worker. But if, brahman, one who has gone forth from home into homelessness from a noble family, owing to the *dhamma* and discipline promulgated by the Tathāgata refrains from onslaught on creatures, from taking what has not been given, from unchastity, lying, slanderous speech, harsh speech, gossiping, is not covetous, not malevolent in mind and is of right view, he is accomplishing the right path, *dhamma*, what is skilled.[1] [182] And if, brahman, one who has gone forth from home into homelessness from a brahman family . . . a merchant family . . . a worker family, owing to this *dhamma* and discipline promulgated by the Tathāgata refrains from onslaught on creatures . . . and is of right view, he is accomplishing the right path, *dhamma*, what is skilled. What do you think about this, brahman ? On this supposition, is it only a brahman who is capable of developing a mind of friendliness that is without enmity, without malevolence ? And not a noble, not a merchant, not a worker ?"[2]

" That is not so, good Gotama. For on this supposition a noble too is capable of developing a mind of friendliness that is without enmity, without malevolence, and so is a brahman, good Gotama, and so is a merchant, good Gotama, and so is a worker, good Gotama —so, good Gotama, on this supposition all the four castes are capable of developing a mind of friendliness that is without enmity, without malevolence."

" Even so, brahman, if one who has gone forth from home into homelessness from a noble family, owing to the *dhamma* and discipline promulgated by the Tathāgata refrains from onslaught on creatures . . . he is accomplishing the right path, *dhamma*, what is skilled. And if, brahman, one who has gone forth from home into homelessness from a brahman family . . . a merchant family . . . a worker family, owing to this *dhamma* and discipline promulgated by the Tathāgata refrains from onslaught on creatures . . . he is accomplishing the right path, *dhamma*, what is skilled. What do you think about this, brahman ? Is it only a brahman who, taking a back-scratcher and bath-powder[3] and going to a river, is capable of cleansing himself of dust and mud ? And not a noble, not a merchant, not a worker ?"

" That is not so, good Gotama. A noble too, good Gotama,

---

[1] *Cf. M.* i. 502 (above, p. 182), *M.* ii. 197 (below, p. 386).

[2] *Cf. M.* ii. 151 (above, p. 343). [3] *Cf. M.* ii. 151.

taking a back-scratcher and bath-powder and going to a river, is capable of cleansing himself of dust and mud. And so is a brahman, good Gotama, and so is a merchant, [**183**] good Gotama, and so is a worker, good Gotama—so, good Gotama, all the four castes, taking a back-scratcher and bath-powder and going to a river, are capable of cleansing themselves of dust and mud."

"Even so, brahman, if one who has gone forth from home into homelessness from a noble family, owing to this *dhamma* and discipline promulgated by the Tathāgata refrains from onslaught on creatures . . . he is accomplishing the right path, *dhamma*, what is skilled. And if, brahman, one who has gone forth from home into homelessness from a brahman family . . . a merchant family . . . a worker family, owing to this *dhamma* and discipline promulgated by the Tathāgata refrains from onslaught on creatures . . . he is accomplishing the right path, *dhamma*, what is skilled. What do you think about this, brahman? If[1] a noble anointed king were to assemble a hundred men of varying origins . . . (*as above, p.* 344 *to p.* 345 *reading* brahman *for* Assalāyana) . . ." [**184**] ". . . So, good Gotama, all these fires have flame and hue and brightness and all are able to serve the purposes of a fire."

"Even so, brahman, if one who has gone forth from home into homelessness from a noble family, owing to this *dhamma* and discipline promulgated by the Tathāgata refrains from onslaught on creatures . . . he is accomplishing the right path, *dhamma*, what is skilled. And if, brahman, one who has gone forth from home into homelessness from a brahman family . . . a merchant family . . . a worker family, owing to this *dhamma* and discipline promulgated by the Tathāgata refrains from onslaught on creatures . . . he is accomplishing the right path, *dhamma*, what is skilled."

When this had been said the brahman Esukārī spoke thus to the Lord:

"It is excellent, good Gotama, it is excellent, good Gotama . . . May the revered Gotama accept me as a lay-disciple going for refuge from this day forth for as long as life lasts."

Discourse with Esukārī:
The Sixth

[1] As at *M.* ii. 151-152.

97. DISCOURSE WITH DHĀNANJĀNI

(Dhānañjānisutta)

THUS have I heard: At one time the Lord was staying near Rājagaha in the Bamboo Grove at the squirrels' feeding-place. Now at that time the venerable Sāriputta was walking on tour near the Northern Mountain[1] together with a large Order of monks. Then a certain [185] monk who had spent the rains near Rājagaha approached the Northern Mountain and the venerable Sāriputta; having approached, he exchanged greetings with the venerable Sāriputta, and having conversed in a friendly and courteous way he sat down at a respectful distance. The venerable Sāriputta spoke thus to this monk as he was sitting down at a respectful distance: "I hope, your reverence, that the Lord is well and strong?"

"The Lord is well and strong, your reverence."

"And I hope, your reverence, that the Order of monks is well and strong?"

"The Order of monks is also well and strong, your reverence."

"There is there, your reverence, a brahman named Dhānañjāni near the Taṇḍulapāla Gateway.[2] I hope, your reverence, that the brahman named Dhānañjāni is well and strong?"

"Your reverence, the brahman Dhānañjāni is also well and strong."

"I hope, your reverence, that the brahman Dhānañjāni is being diligent?"

"How could the brahman Dhānañjāni be diligent, your reverence? Under the king's patronage, your reverence, the brahman Dhānañjāni plunders brahman householders; and under the patronage of the brahman householders he plunders the king. His wife who had faith and whom he had married from a family that has faith has died, and he has married another wife who has no faith and who comes from a family that has no faith."

"This is indeed bad hearing, your reverence; indeed, your

---

[1] Dakkhiṇāgiri. *MA*. iii. 429 says *giri* is the mountain slope, and that this was the name of the northern part of the mountainous country surrounding Rājagaha.

[2] One of the lesser gateways of Rājagaha, *MA*. iii. 429.

reverence, it is bad hearing that we hear the brahman Dhānañjāni is negligent. Perhaps sometime, somewhere we might meet the brahman Dhānañjāni, perhaps there might be some conversation."

Then the venerable Sāriputta, having stayed near the Northern Mountain for as long as he found suitable, set out on tour for Rājagaha. Walking on tour he gradually arrived at Rājagaha. While he was there the venerable Sāriputta stayed near Rājagaha in the Bamboo Grove at the squirrels' feeding-place. Then the venerable Sāriputta, dressing in the morning, taking his bowl and robe, entered Rājagaha for almsfood. [**186**] Now at that time the brahman Dhānañjāni was having cows milked in a cow-pen outside the town. When the venerable Sāriputta had walked for alms in Rājagaha and was returning from the alms-gathering after the meal, he approached the brahman Dhānañjāni. The brahman Dhānañjāni saw the venerable Sāriputta coming in the distance; seeing him, he approached the venerable Sāriputta; having approached, he spoke thus to the venerable Sāriputta: "Drink some of this milk, good Sāriputta, until it is time for a meal."

"No, brahman, I have finished with eating for today. I will take my day-sojourn at the root of a tree—you could come there."

"Yes, sir," the brahman Dhānañjāni answered the venerable Sāriputta in assent. Then when the brahman Dhānañjāni had had breakfast, he approached the venerable Sāriputta; having approached he exchanged greetings with the venerable Sāriputta, and having conversed in a friendly and courteous way, he sat down at a respectful distance. The venerable Sāriputta spoke thus to the brahman Dhānañjāni as he was sitting down at a respectful distance: "I hope that you are being diligent, Dhānañjāni?"

"How could I be diligent, good Sāriputta, when there are my parents to support, my wife and children to support, my slaves, servants and work-people to support, when there are services to perform[1] for friends and acquaintances, services to perform for kith and kin, services to perform for guests, rites to perform[1] for the ancestors, rites to perform for the *devatās*, duties to perform[1] for the king—and this body too must be satisfied and looked after."

"What do you think about this, Dhānañjāni? Suppose someone were a non-*dhamma*-farer, an uneven-farer because of his parents; because of his non-*dhamma*-faring, uneven-faring the guardians of Niraya Hell might drag him off to Niraya Hell. Would he gain

---

[1] *karaṇīyaṁ kātabbaṁ.*

anything by saying: 'I was a non-*dhamma*-farer, an uneven-farer because of my parents—do not let the guardians of Niraya Hell (drag) me off to Niraya Hell?' [187] Or would his parents gain anything for him by saying: 'It was because of us that he was a non-*dhamma*-farer, an uneven-farer—do not let the guardians of Niraya Hell (drag) him off to Niraya Hell'?"

"No, good Sāriputta, for the guardians of Niraya Hell would hurl him wailing into Niraya Hell itself."

"What do you think about this, Dhānañjāni? Suppose someone were a non-*dhamma*-farer, an uneven farer because of his wife and children[1] ... his slaves, servants and work-people ... his friends and acquaintances ... his kith and kin ... his guests ... [188] ... his ancestors ... the *devatās* ... the king; because of his non-*dhamma*-faring, uneven-faring the guardians of Niraya Hell might drag him off to Niraya Hell. Would he gain anything by saying ... '... do not let the guardians of Niraya Hell (drag) him off to Niraya Hell'?"

"No, good Sāriputta, for the guardians of Niraya Hell would hurl him wailing into Niraya Hell itself."

"What do you think about this, Dhānañjāni? Suppose someone were a non-*dhamma*-farer, an uneven-farer because of satisfying and looking after his body; because of his non-*dhamma*-faring, uneven-faring the guardians of Niraya Hell might drag him off to Niraya Hell. Would he gain anything by saying: 'I was a non-*dhamma*-farer, an uneven-farer because of satisfying and looking after my body—do not let the guardians of Niraya Hell (drag) me off to Niraya Hell'? Or would others gain anything for him by saying: 'He was a non-*dhamma*-farer, an uneven-farer because of satisfying and looking after his body—do not let the guardians of Niraya Hell (drag) him off to Niraya Hell'?"

"No, good Sāriputta, for the guardians of Niraya Hell would hurl him wailing into Niraya Hell itself."

"What do you think about this, Dhānañjāni? Which is the better: he who, because of his parents, is a non-*dhamma*-farer, an uneven-farer; or he who, because of his parents, is a *dhamma*-farer, an even-farer?"

"He is not the better, Sāriputta, who because of his parents is a non-*dhamma*-farer, an uneven-farer; but he who, good Sāriputta, because of his parents is a *dhamma*-farer, an even-farer, he is indeed

---

[1] As above paragraph mutatis mutandis.

the better. *Dhamma*-faring, even-faring, good Sāriputta, is better than non-*dhamma*-faring, uneven-faring."

"There are, Dhānañjāni, other causally effective rightful actions[1] by which one is able to support one's parents and not make evil *kamma* but proceed on a course that is good.[2] What do you think about this, Dhānañjāni? Which is the better: he who, because of his wife and children is a non-*dhamma*-farer, an uneven-farer; or he who, because of his wife and children is a *dhamma*-farer, an even-farer?"

[**189**] . . . (*Question and answer repeated for* slaves, servants and workpeople; friends and acquaintances; kith and kin; [**190**] guests; ancestors; *devatās*; . . . [**191**] . . . king; . . . satisfaction and care of the body . . .)

"He who, good Sāriputta, because of satisfying and caring for his body, is a non-*dhamma*-farer, an uneven-farer—he is not the better; but he who, good Sāriputta, because of satisfying and caring for his body is a *dhamma*-farer, an even-farer, he is indeed the better. *Dhamma*-faring, even-faring, good Sāriputta, is better than non-*dhamma*-faring, uneven-faring."

"There are, Dhānañjāni, other causally effective rightful actions by which one is able to satisfy and care for the body and not make evil *kamma* but proceed on a course that is good."

Then Dhānañjāni the brahman, having rejoiced in what the venerable Sāriputta had said, having given thanks, rising from his seat departed.

Then after a time the brahman Dhānañjāni was ill, in pain, grievously afflicted. Then the brahman Dhānañjāni summoned a man, and said: "Come you, my good man, [**192**] approach the Lord; having approached, in my name salute the Lord's feet with your head, saying: 'Revered sir, Dhānañjāni the brahman is ill, in pain, grievously afflicted; he salutes the Lord's feet with his head'; and then approach the venerable Sāriputta; having approached, in my name salute the venerable Sāriputta's feet with your head, saying: 'Revered sir, Dhānañjāni the brahman is ill, in pain, grievously afflicted; he salutes the venerable Sāriputta's feet with his head'; and then say: 'It would be good indeed, revered sir, if the venerable Sāriputta would approach the dwelling of the brahman Dhānañjāni, out of compassion.'"

"Yes, revered sir," and this man, having answered the brahman

---

[1] *sahetukā dhammikā kammantā.*

[2] *puññaṁ paṭipadaṁ.* Here, as frequently, *puñña* as the opposite of *pāpa*, evil, is "good" rather than "merit."

Dhānañjāni in assent, approached the Lord; having approached, having greeted the Lord, he sat down at a respectful distance. As he was sitting down at a respectful distance, this man spoke thus to the Lord: " Revered sir, Dhānañjāni the brahman is ill . . . he salutes the Lord's feet with his head." And then he approached the venerable Sāriputta; having approached, having greeted the venerable Sāriputta, he sat down at a respectful distance. As he was sitting down at a respectful distance, this man spoke thus to the venerable Sāriputta: " Revered sir, the brahman Dhānañjāni is ill . . . It would be good indeed, revered sir, if the venerable Sāriputta would approach the dwelling of the brahman Dhānañjāni, out of compassion."

Then the venerable Sāriputta, having dressed in the morning, taking his bowl and robe, approached the dwelling of the brahman Dhānañjāni; having approached, he sat down on the appointed seat. As he was sitting down the venerable Sāriputta spoke thus to the brahman Dhānañjāni: " I hope that you, Dhānañjāni, are better, I hope you are keeping going. I hope the painful feelings are decreasing, not increasing, and that a decrease in them is apparent, not an increase ?"

" No, good Sāriputta, I am no better, I am not keeping going. My grievously painful feelings are increasing, not decreasing, an increase in them is apparent, not a decrease. Good Sāriputta, as[1] [**193**] a strong man might cleave one's head with a sharp-edged sword, even so, good Sāriputta, do exceedingly loud winds rend my head. I am no better, good Sāriputta, I am not keeping going. My grievously painful feelings are increasing, not decreasing, an increase in them is apparent, not a decrease. As, good Sāriputta, a strong man might clamp a turban on one's head with a tight leather strap, even so, good Sāriputta, do I have very bad headaches. I am no better . . . an increase in them is apparent, not a decrease. As, good Sāriputta, a skilled cattle butcher or his apprentice might cut through the stomach with a sharp butcher's knife, even so, good Sāriputta, do very strong winds cut through my stomach. I am no better . . . an increase in them is apparent, not a decrease. As, good Sāriputta, two strong men, having taken hold of a weaker man by his limbs, might set fire to him, might make him sizzle up over a charcoal pit, even so, good Sāriputta, there is a fierce heat in my body. I am no better, good Sāriputta, I am not keeping going.

---

[1] This and the following similes as at *M.* i. 243-244, etc.

My grievously painful feelings are increasing, not decreasing, an increase in them is apparent, not a decrease."

"What do you think about this, Dhānañjāni? Which is better: Niraya Hell or an animal womb?"

"An animal womb is better than Niraya Hell, good Sāriputta."

"What do you think about this, Dhānañjāni? Which is better: an animal womb or the realm of the departed?"

"The realm of the departed is better . . ."

"What do you think about this, Dhānañjāni? Which is better: the realm of the departed or human-kind?

"Human-kind is better . . ."

[194] "What do you think about this, Dhānañjāni? Which is better: human-kind or the Four Great Regent *devas*[1]?"

"The Four Great Regent *devas* . . ."

". . . Which are better: the Four Great Regent *devas* or the *devas* of the Thirty-Three?"

"The *devas* of the Thirty-Three . . ."

". . . Which are better: the *devas* of the Thirty-Three or Yama's *devas*?"

"Yama's *devas* . . ."

". . . Which are better: Yama's *devas* or the Tusita *devas*?"

"The Tusita *devas* . . ."

". . . Which are better: the Tusita *devas* or the *devas* of creation?"

"The *devas* of creation . . ."

". . . Which are better: the *devas* of creation or the *devas* that have power over the creations of other?"

"The *devas* that have power over the creations of others are better than the *devas* of creation, good Sāriputta."

"What do you think about this, Dhānañjāni? Which is better: the *devas* that have power over the creations of others or the Brahma-world?"

"The revered Sāriputta said 'Brahma-world,' the revered Sāriputta said 'Brahma-world.'"

Then it occurred to the venerable Sāriputta: "These brahmans are very intent on the Brahma-world. Suppose I were to show the brahman Dhānañjāni the way to companionship with Brahmā?—Dhānañjāni, I will show you the way to companionship with Brahmā. Listen to it, attend carefully, and I will speak."

---

[1] *Cf.* with the longer list of *devas* at *M.* i. 289.

"Yes, sir," the brahman Dhānañjāni answered the venerable Sāriputta in assent. [**195**] The venerable Sāriputta spoke thus: "And which, Dhānañjāni, is the way to companionship with Brahmā? As to this, Dhānañjāni, a monk dwells, having suffused the first quarter with a mind of friendliness, likewise the second, likewise the third, likewise the fourth; just so above, below, across; he dwells having suffused the whole world everywhere, in every way, with a mind of friendliness that is far-reaching, wide-spread, immeasurable, without enmity, without malevolence. This, Dhānañjāni, is a way to companionship with Brahmā. And again, Dhānañjāni, the monk dwells, having suffused the first quarter with a mind of compassion . . . sympathetic joy . . . equanimity . . . that is far-reaching, wide-spread, immeasurable, without enmity, without malevolence. This, Dhānañjāni, is a way to companionship with Brahmā."

"Well then, good Sāriputta, in my name salute the Lord's feet with your head, and say: 'Lord, the brahman Dhānañjāni is ill, in pain, grievously afflicted; he salutes the Lord's feet with his head.'"

Then, although there was something further to be done, the venerable Sāriputta established the brahman Dhānañjāni (only) in the less, in a Brahma-world[1] and, rising from his seat, he departed. Soon after the venerable Sāriputta had gone, the brahman Dhānañjāni passed away, and arose in the Brahma-world.[2]

Then the Lord addressed the monks, saying: "Monks, although there was something further to be done, this Sāriputta established the brahman Dhānañjāni (only) in the less, in the Brahma-world, and rising from his seat, he is departing."

Then the venerable Sāriputta approached the Lord; having approached, having greeted the Lord, he sat down at a respectful distance. As he was sitting down at a respectful distance, the venerable Sāriputta spoke thus to the Lord: "Lord, the brahman Dhānañjāni is ill, in pain, grievously afflicted; he salutes the Lord's feet with his head."

---

[1] The idea no doubt is that Sāriputta missed an opportunity of telling the brahman about *dhamma* and spoke only of *hīna Brahmaloka*, a "low" world instead of the *lokuttara dhamma*, the supermundane *dhamma* (see Sta. No. 96, above, p. 369), towards the winning of which the teaching of the Buddha is directed.

[2] No mention of *hīna*, low or lesser, Brahma-world here. This raises the problem of whether Dhānañjāni profited more from Sāriputta's teaching than the latter knew or had attempted.

"But why did you, Sāriputta, although [**196**] there was something further to be done, having established the brahman Dhānañjāni (only) in the less, in the Brahma-world, rising from your seat, depart ?"[1]

"It occurred to me, Lord: 'These brahmans are very intent on the Brahma-world. Suppose I were to show the brahman Dhānañjāni the way to companionship with Brahmā ?'"

"Sāriputta, the brahman Dhānañjāni has died and has uprisen in the Brahma-world."

Discourse with Dhānañjāni:
The Seventh

98. DISCOURSE TO VĀSEṬṬHA

(Vāseṭṭhasutta)[2]

[*Sn*.**115**] THUS have I heard: At one time the Lord was staying near Icchānaṅkala in a forest glade near Icchānaṅkala. Now at that time many wealthy and distinguished brahmans were living in Icchānaṅkala, such as the brahman Cankī,[3] the brahman Tārukkha, the brahman Pokkharasāti, the brahman Jāṇussoṇi, the brahman Todeyya, and other wealthy and distinguished brahmans.[4] Then as the brahman youths Vāseṭṭha and Bhāradvāja were pacing up and down and roaming about on foot, this chance conversation arose: "How is one a brahman ?" The brahman youth Bhāradvāja spoke thus: "If one is of pure birth on both the mother's and the father's side,

---

[1] A rebuke recorded to have been given by Gotama to Sāriputta, "the beloved disciple," is of rare occurrence. See above, p. 131 and Intr. p. xxvi.

[2] The text of this Discourse is not given in *M*. ii. It is the same as the *Vāseṭṭhasutta* at *Sn*. p. 115 *ff*. The Comys (*SnA*. 462 *ff*. and *MA*. iii. 431 *ff*.) show several interesting variations. *Cf*. also *D*. i. 235 *ff*.

[3] *MA*. iii. 431 says that Caṅkī and the four others were priests of King Pasenadi.

[4] *MA*. iii. 431: "every six months they gather together in two places: if they want to purify (their) birth (*jātiṁ sodhetukāmā*), then for this purpose they gather together at Ukkaṭṭhā under Pokkharasāti. If they want to purify the *mantras*, then they gather together at Icchānaṅkala. At this time they gathered together there for purifying the *mantras*." *SnA*. 462 says that they were there for meditating upon and thoroughly examining the Vedas.

and is of pure descent back through seven generations, unchallenged and irreproachable in respect of birth, then is one a brahman." The brahman youth Vāseṭṭha spoke thus: "If one is of moral habit and right practice,[1] then is one a brahman." But neither was Bhāradvāja the brahman youth [*Sn*. **116**] able to convince Vāseṭṭha the brahman youth, nor was Vāseṭṭha the brahman youth able to convince Bhāradvāja the brahman youth. Then Vāseṭṭha the brahman youth spoke thus to Bhāradvāja the brahman youth: "Bhāradvāja, this recluse Gotama, the son of the Sakyans, gone forth from a Sakyan clan, is staying near Icchānaṅkala in a forest glade near Icchānaṅkala. And a lovely report has gone abroad about the recluse Gotama thus: '. . . the Awakened One, the Lord.' Let us go, good Bhāradvāja; we will approach the recluse Gotama, and having approached we will ask the recluse Gotama about this matter, and as the recluse Gotama explains it to us, so will we accept it."

"Yes, sir," the brahman youth Bhāradvāja answered the brahman youth Vāseṭṭha in assent. Then the brahman youths Vāseṭṭha and Bhāradvāja approached the Lord; having approached, they exchanged greetings with the Lord; having conversed in a friendly and courteous way, they sat down at a respectful distance. As he was sitting down at a respectful distance, Vāseṭṭha the brahman youth addressed the Lord in these verses:

Vāseṭṭha "Both of us have been recognised as[2] and we claim to be three-Veda-(men),
I, of Pokkharasāti (a pupil), this brahman youth of Tārukkha. (594)[3]
In what is pointed out of the three Vedas—in that we are whole:
We are versed in the *pada-pāṭha*,[4] grammarians, in speaking we are like teachers. (595)

---

[1] *MA*. iii. 432=*SnA*. 463, in explanation of *kammanā* (*Sn*. 596) say: "to say one 'is of moral habit' (*sīlavā*) refers to the sevenfold ways of skilled *kamma* in gesture and speech; referring to the threefold *kamma* of mind, one says 'endowed with right practice' (*vat(t)a-sampanna*)". See *M*. Sta. 41 for this tenfold way of skilled action.

[2] By their teachers.

[3] These numbers refer to *Sn*. verse numbers. For passages parallel to these verses see the Concordance in *Wov. Cads*., p. 199 *f*.

[4] An educated brahman who can pronounce each word in a *mantra* separately "without coalescence or *saṁdhi* and with its own specific accent" is a *padaka*,

[*Sn.* **117**] There is contention between us, Gotama, in respect of birth:
'By birth one is a brahman'—so speaks Bhāradvāja;
But I say, 'By doing'[1]—let the Visioned One know it thus. (596)
As we are each unable to convince the other,
We come to ask the revered Self-Awakened One, widely famed. (597)
As people salute the moon when it has come to the full,
So, in the world, honouring him, do they thus praise Gotama. (598)
We are asking Gotama, the Eye risen in the world:
Is one by birth a brahman or does one (so) become by doing?
Tell us this who know not, that a brahman we may know." (599)

Gotama[2] "Vāseṭṭha," said the Lord, "I will expound
To you in gradual and very truth
Division in the kinds[3] of living things; (600)
For kinds divide.[4] Behold the grass and trees!
They reason not, yet they possess the mark
After their kind, for kinds indeed divide. (601)
[*Sn.* **118**] Consider then the beetles, moths and ants:
They after their kind too possess the mark . . . (602)
And so four-footed creatures, great and small . . . (603)
The reptiles, snakes, the long-backed animals . . . (604)

---

[1] *kammanā*, see above, p. 380, *n.* 1. It therefore appears to mean by accomplished training, that is in *sīla* and mind development; and thus has no pronounced reference to past *kamma* working in the present. *PED.* gives "by character." In the following verses, *e.g.* 650 *ff.*, I follow E. M. Hare in translating as "deeds." *Cf. Sn.* 136: *kammanā vasalo hoti kammanā hoti brāhmaṇo*, which *SnA.* 183 explains as: "he is an outcaste from thriving on impure *kamma*, a brahman from driving out what is impure by means of pure *kamma*" (or, "doing," *kammunā*, where *kammunā* is but a variant of the instrumental *kammanā*).

[2] From here to the end of the verses I give E. M. Hare's translation in *Woven Cadences.*

[3] *jāti*, kind or birth.

[4] There is a diversity of kind.

---

i.e. versed in Vedic lines and words. See R. N. Dandekar, *Cultural Background of the Vedas, UCR.* vol. XI, Nos. 3 and 4, July-October, 1953, p. 139.

Fish and pond-feeders, water-denizens . . . (605)
Birds and the winged creatures, fowls o' the air,
They after their kind all possess the mark; (606)
For kinds divide. Each after his kind bears
His mark; in man there is not manifold.[1] (607)
Not in the hair or head or ears or eyes,
Not in the mouth or nose or lips or brows, (608)
Not in the throat, hips, belly or the back,
Not in the rump, sex-organs or the breast, (609)
Not in the hands or feet, fingers or nails,
Not in the legs or thighs, colour or voice,
Is mark that forms his kind as in all else. (610)
[*Sn.* **119**] Nothing unique[2] is in men's bodies found:
The difference in men is nominal. (611)

The man forsooth who earns his livelihood
By minding cows and fields, know, Vāseṭṭha,
He is a farmer, not a brahmana ! (612)
Who works at diverse crafts, know him to be
An artisan and not a brahmana ! (613)
Who plies a trade for livelihood, know him
To be a trader, not a brahmana ! (614)
Who toils in service for another man,
Know as a servant, not a brahmana ! (615)
Who lives by taking things not giv'n, know him
To be a thief and not a brahmana ! (616)
Who lives indeed by archery, know him
To be a soldier, not a brahmana ! (617)
Who lives by priestly craft, know him to be
A celebrant and not a brahmana ! (618)
And he who owns the village, countryside,
Know him as a rajah and no brahmana ! (619)

I call none ' brahman ' from mere parentage,
Tho' he be ' Sir '-ed and wealthy too: the man
Of naught, who grasps not, brahman him I call ! (620)

Who cuts all fetters, thirsting not, fears not,
Fetter-free, bondless, brahman him I call. (621)

[*Sn.* **120**] Who cuts thong, halter, strap, and cord, throws off

---

[1] *I.e.* no variety of native marks.

[2] Or specific.

The bar,[1] has woken, brahman him I call. (622)

Who, blameless, bears blows, bonds, abuse, well armed
With strength of patience, brahman him I call. (623)

Him wrathless, spotless, moral, free of pride,[2]
Last body bearing, tamed, I brahman call. (624)

As water on a leaf, as seed on awl,
Who to lust clings not, brahman him I call. (625)

Who knows here now that ill for self is quenched,
Burden-dropped,[3] bondless, brahman him I call. (626)

Him of deep wisdom, sage, skilled in all ways,
Won to the goal supreme, I brahman call. (627)

Who not with homeless nor with householder sorts,
Frugal, resort-less, brahman him I call. (628)

Who rod lays by 'gainst weak and strong, slays not,
To slay incites none, brahman him I call. (629)

Him cool[4] mid violence, mid foes no foe,
Mid grasping grasping not, I brahman call. (630)

From whom hate, passion, pride, and guile have fall'n,
As seed from needle, brahman him I call. (631)

[*Sn.* **121**] Who teaches gently, utters words of truth,
And none offendeth, brahman him I call. (632)

Who here takes naught, long, short, small, large, good, bad,
Nothing not given, brahman him I call. (633)

In whom no hopes are found for here or yon,
Fetter-free, hope-free, brahman him I call. (634)

In whom no grooves are found, gone doubt, who knows,
Won to depths deathless,[5] brahman him I call. (635)

Who here has passed bond of both good and ill,
Griefless, cleansed, dustless, brahman him I call. (636)

---

[1] Or, lifts the barrier, *ukkhittapaligha*, as at *M.* i. 139.
[2] *anussadaṁ.*
[3] *pannabhāra*, as at *M.* i. 139.
[4] *nibbuta.*
[5] *amatogadha*, the plunge into deathlessness.

Him spotless, cleansed, unclouded, clear as moon,
With 'life '[1] and pleasure quenched, I brahman call. (637)

Who hath this bog, false, painful round, passed o'er,
Crossed and yon-fared, a muser, doubt gone, still,
Cool[2] in detachment, brahman him I call. (638)

Who pleasures here forsakes and homeless fares,
Lust and 'life '[1] ended, brahman him I call. (639)

Who craving here forsakes and homeless fares,
Craving, 'life '[1] ended, brahman him I call. (640)

Him rid of human yoke, passed *deva*-yoke,
Fetterless, free of yokes, I brahman call. (641)

Him rid of likes and dislikes, cool,[3] detached,
Vigorous, world-conqueror, I brahman call. (642)

[*Sn.* **122**] Who knows of all men the rise and fall, uncaught,
Awake, well-faring, brahman him I call. (643)

Whose lot men, *devas*, *gandharvas* know not,
Cankerless, worthy,[4] brahman him I call. (644)

Him for whom present, future, past, holds naught,
Who grasps not, man-of-naught, I brahman call. (645)

The bull, elect, the hero, victor, sage,
Awake, still, washen, brahman him I call. (646)

Who knows his former life, sees heav'n and hell,
Won to birth's ending, brahman him I call. (647)

What the world holds as 'name' and 'lineage'
Is indeed nominal, terms risen here
And there by popular opinion, (648)

Adhered to long, views of the ignorant!
The ignorant declare: 'A brahman is (649)

By birth.' None is by birth a brahman; none
By birth no brahmana; by deeds is one
A brahmana, by deeds no brahmana! (650)

---

[1] *bhava*. [2] *nibbuta*. [3] *sītibhūta*, cooled, become cool. [4] *arahantaṁ*.

By deeds one is a farmer and by deeds
An artisan, by deeds a trader too; (651)

By deeds one is a servant and a thief,
By deeds a soldier and a celebrant,
And even so a rajah is by deeds. (652)

[*Sn.* **123**] ' Tis thus in truth the wise perceive the deed,
Seers of origin by way of cause,[1]
Men expert in result of deeds. The world (653)

Revolves by deeds, mankind revolves by deeds;
As pin holds fast the rolling chariot's wheel,
So beings are in bondage held by deeds. (654)

A brahman one becomes by Brahma-faring,
By temperance, austerity, restraint:
This is indeed supreme for brahmanhood. (655)

Who by three Vedas is accomplished,
With no more coming here, and man-of-calm,
Know thou, Vāseṭṭha, even thus of him:
He is of knowers Sakka[2] and Brahmā !" (656)

When this had been said, the brahman youths Vāseṭṭha and Bhāradvāja spoke thus to the Lord: " It is wonderful, good Gotama . . . we are going to the revered Gotama for refuge[3] and to *dhamma* and to the Order of monks. May the revered Gotama accept us as lay-disciples going for refuge from today forth for as long as life lasts."

Discourse to Vāseṭṭha:
The Eighth

---

[1] *paṭiccasamuppādadasā.*

[2] Note at *Wov. Cads.* p. 97 reads: " *Sn. Index* suggests word-play; so perhaps ' best possible of knowers.' *Tīhi vijjāhi* may refer to the ' triple lore ' given in verse 647 above, see *K.S.* i. 208 and *G.S.* i. 149."

[3] According to *DA.* 406 this was their first time of going for refuge. The second was after they had heard the *Tevijja Suttanta* (*D.* Sta. 13); a few days afterwards they " went forth ", were ordained and attained arahantship. DA. 406 refers to the *Aggañña Sutta* (*D.* Sta. 27) for this event, which *DA.* 872 states to be the case.

99. DISCOURSE WITH SUBHA

(Subhasutta)

THUS have I heard: At one time the Lord was staying near Sāvatthī in the Jeta Grove in Anāthapiṇḍika's monastery. Now at that time the brahman youth Subha, Todeyya's son[1] was residing in Sāvatthī in a householder's dwelling on some business or other. Then the brahman youth Subha, Todeyya's son, who was staying in that householder's dwelling, spoke thus to that householder: "I have heard, householder, that Sāvatthī is not unfrequented by perfected ones. Could we today pay our respects to a recluse or brahman ?"[2]

"Revered sir, this Lord is staying near Sāvatthī in the Jeta Grove in Anāthapiṇḍika's monastery. You could pay respects to this Lord, revered sir."

[197] When the brahman youth Subha, Todeyya's son, had answered that householder in assent, he approached the Lord; having approached, he exchanged greetings with the Lord; having conversed in a friendly and courteous way, he sat down at a respectful distance. As he was sitting down at a respectful distance, the brahman youth Subha, Todeyya's son, spoke thus to the Lord:

"Good Gotama, brahmans speak thus: 'A householder is accomplishing the right path, *dhamma*, what is skilled;[3] one who has gone forth is not accomplishing the right path, *dhamma*, what is skilled.' What does the good Gotama say to this ?"

"On this point I, brahman youth, discriminate,[4] on this point I do not speak definitely.[5] I, brahman youth, do not praise a wrong course in either a householder or one who has gone forth. If, brahman youth, either a householder[6] or one who has gone forth is faring along wrongly, then as a result and consequence of his wrong

---

[1] The *Subhasutta* at *D.* i. 204 *ff.* records a conversation between Subha and Ānanda soon after the Buddha's death. See also *M.* Sta. 135, the real name for which, according to Bu., is also *Subhasutta*. See *DA.* 384 *f.* Todeyya was a rich brahman, overlord of a village named Tudi not far from Sāvatthī.

[2] *Cf. D.* i. 47.

[3] *Cf. M.* i. 502 (above, p. 182).

[4] *vibhajjavādo*, speak analysing.

[5] *na ekaṁsavādo*, do not make a definite assertion, do not speak one-sidedly.

[6] *Cf. A.* i. 69.

course he is not accomplishing the right path, *dhamma*, what is skilled. But I, brahman youth, praise a right course both for a householder and for one who has gone forth. If, brahman youth, either a householder or one who has gone forth is faring along rightly, then as a result and consequence of his right course he is accomplishing the right path, *dhamma*, what is skilled."

"Good Gotama, brahmans speak thus: 'Having a great deal to do: many duties, a large administration, great problems—this occupation[1] of householders is of great fruit. Not having a great deal to do:[2] few duties,[3] a small administration, small problems—this occupation of those who have gone forth is of small fruit.' What does the good Gotama say to this?"

"On this point too I, brahman youth, discriminate, on this point I do not speak definitely. There is, brahman youth, an occupation where there is a great deal to do: many duties, a large administration, great problems—which if failed of is of small fruit. There is, brahman youth, an occupation where there is a great deal to do: many duties, a large administration, great problems—which if succeeded in is of great fruit. There is, brahman youth, an occupation where there is not a great deal to do: few duties, a small administration, small problems—which if failed of is of small fruit. There is, brahman youth, an occupation where there is not a great deal to do: few duties, a small administration, small problems—which if succeeded in is of great fruit. And what, [**198**] brahman youth, is an occupation where there is a great deal to do: many duties, a large administration, great problems—which if failed of is of small fruit? Agriculture, brahman youth, is an occupation where there is a great deal to do: many duties, a large administration, great problems—which if failed of is of small fruit. And what, brahman youth, is an occupation where there is a great deal to do: many duties . . . which if succeeded in is of great fruit? Agriculture, brahman youth, is an occupation . . . which if succeeded in is of great fruit.

And what, brahman youth, is an occupation where there is not a great deal to do: few duties, a small administration, small problems—which if failed of is of small fruit? Trading, brahman youth, is an occupation where there is not a great deal to do: few duties, a small administration, small problems—which if failed of is of small fruit. And what, brahman youth, is an occupation where there is not a

---

[1] *kammaṭṭhāna.* [2] *appaṭṭha; cf. A.* iii. 120.

[3] *appakiccha; cf. A.* iii. 120; *It.* p. 72; *Sn.* 144.

great deal to do: few duties . . . which if succeeded in is of great fruit? Trading, brahman youth is an occupation where there is not a great deal to do . . . which if succeeded in is of great fruit. As, brahman youth, agriculture is an occupation where there is a great deal to do: many duties, a large administration, great problems—which if failed of is of small fruit, even so, brahman youth, an occupation of a householder where there is a great deal to do: many duties . . . is one which if failed of is of small fruit. As, brahman youth, agriculture is an occupation where there is a great deal to do . . . which if succeeded in is of great fruit, even so, brahman youth, an occupation of a householdei where there is a great deal to do: many duties, a large administration, great problems—is one which if succeeded in is of great fruit. As, brahman youth, trading is an occupation where there is not a great deal to do: few duties, a small administration, small problems, which if failed of is of small fruit, even so, brahman youth, an occupation of one who has gone forth where there is not a great deal to do: few duties, a small administration, small problems—is one which if failed of is of small fruit. As, brahman youth, trading is an occupation where there is not a great deal to do: few duties, a small administration, small problems—which if succeeded in is of great fruit, even so, [**199**] brahman youth, an occupation of one who has gone forth where there is not a great deal to do: few duties, a small administration, small problems—is one which if succeeded in is of great fruit."

"Brahmans, good Gotama, lay down five things[1] for the doing[2] of good, for success in what is skilled."

"If it were not burdensome to you, brahman youth, it would be good if you would speak in this company about those five things that the brahmans lay down for the doing of good, for success in what is skilled."

"It is not burdensome to me, good Gotama, where there may be a revered one or ones like revered ones."

"Well then, brahman youth, do speak."

"Truth, good Gotama, is the first thing that brahmans lay down for the doing of good, for success in what is skilled. Austerity, good Gotama, is the second thing . . . Chastity,[3] good Gotama, is the third

---

[1] *pañca dhamme.*

[2] *kiriyāya,* or causally effecting, hence Gotama's question, just below, whether any result (*vipāka,* ripening) is declared.

[3] *brahmacariya.* *MA.* iii. 448 gives chastity. *Cf. MA,* iii. 443, *VbhA.* 504, *SnA.* 317, 387.

thing . . . Study of the (Vedic) hymns,[1] good Gotama, is the fourth thing . . . Renunciation, good Gotama, is the fifth thing that brahmans lay down for the doing of good, for success in what is skilled. Brahmans, good Gotama, lay down these five things for the doing of good, for success in what is skilled. What does the good Gotama say to this ?"

"But what, brahman youth ? Is there even a single brahman who speaks thus: 'I, having realised by[2] super-knowledge, declare the result of these five things' ?"

"No, good Gotama."

"So what, brahman youth ? Is there a single teacher of brahmans, even a single line of teachers back through seven generations of teachers, who speaks thus: 'I, having realised by my own super-knowledge, declare the result of these five things' ?"

"No, good Gotama."

[200] "So what, brahman youth ? Even those who were formerly seers of the brahmans,[3] makers of *mantras*, preservers of *mantras*, whose ancient *mantras* as sung, taught and composed the brahmans of today still sing, still speak; they still speak what was spoken, they still teach what was taught—that is to say (by) Aṭṭhaka, Vāmaka, Vāmadeva, Vessāmitta, Yamataggi, Aṅgirasa, Bhāradvāja, Vāseṭṭha, Kassapa, Bhagu—do even these speak thus: 'We, having realised by our own super-knowledge, declare the result of these five things' ?"

"No, good Gotama."

"So what you are really saying, brahman youth, is that among the brahmans there is not even a single brahman who speaks thus . . . not even a single teacher of brahmans, not even a single line of teachers back through seven generations of teachers who speaks thus: 'I, having realised by my own super-knowledge, declare the result of these five things.' And also that even those who were formerly seers of the brahmans . . . not even these speak thus: 'We, having realised by our own super-knowledge, declare the result of these five things.' Brahman youth, it is like a string of blind men[4] holding on to one another—neither does the foremost one see, nor does the middle one see, nor does the hindmost one see. Even so, methinks, brahman youth, do the words of the brahmans turn out to

---

[1] *ajjhena; MA.* iii. 448 says *mantagahaṇa*, perhaps "reciting."

[2] *sayaṁ* omitted here, probably in error.

[3] As at *M.* ii. 169.

[4] As at *M.* ii. 170.

resemble the string of blind men: neither does the first one see nor does the middle one see nor does the last one see."

When this had been said, the brahman youth Subha, Todeyya's son, angry and displeased at being spoken to by the Lord with the simile of the string of blind men, scorning even the Lord, despising even the Lord, and saying even of the Lord: "The recluse Gotama will be disgraced,"[1] spoke thus to the Lord: "A brahman, good Gotama, Pokkharasāti, of the Upamañña (clan, incumbent)[2] of the Subhaga forest glade,[3] speaks thus: 'Even thus do some recluses and brahmans claim states of further-men, the excellent knowledge and vision befitting the ariyans. This speech of theirs [**201**] proves merely ridiculous, it proves merely worthless, it proves merely empty, it proves merely void. For how could a man know or see or realise states of further-men, the excellent knowledge and vision befitting the ariyans?'—such a situation does not exist."

"But, brahman youth, does the brahman Pokkharasāti of the Upamañña (clan, incumbent) of the Subhaga forest glade, comprehend with his mind the reasoning in the mind of absolutely all recluses and brahmans?"

"Good Gotama, the brahman Pokkharasāti of the Upamañña (clan, incumbent) of the Subhaga forest glade, does not even comprehend with his mind the reasoning in the mind of Puṇṇikā, his slave woman. So how could he comprehend with his mind the reasoning in the mind of absolutely all recluses and brahmans?"

"Brahman youth, it is like[4] a man blind from birth who could not see dark or bright shapes, who could not see green . . . yellow . . . red . . . crimson shapes, who could not see what is even or uneven, who could not see the stars, who could not see the moons and the suns. He might speak thus: 'There are no dark and bright shapes, there is no one who sees dark and bright shapes . . . there are no moons and suns, there is no one who sees the moons and the suns. I do not see this, therefore it does not exist.' Would he, brahman youth, in speaking rightly speak thus?"

"No, good Gotama. 'There are dark and bright shapes, there is one who sees dark and bright shapes; there are green shapes, there is one who sees green shapes . . . there are moons and suns, there is one who sees the moons and the suns. I do not [**202**] know this, I do not

---

[1] *Cf. M.* ii. 43.
[2] *MA.* iii. 447, *issara,* lord, master.
[3] Near Ukkaṭṭhā, *MA.* iii. 447. Pokkharasāti was a resident of this place, *DA.* 399.
[4] *Cf. M.* i. 509.

see this, therefore it does not exist'—in speaking rightly he would not speak thus, good Gotama."

"In the same way, brahman youth, the brahman Pokkharasāti of the Upamañña (clan, incumbent) of the Subhaga forest glade, is blind, he is without vision. This situation certainly does not exist—that he might know or see or realise states of further-men, the excellent knowledge and vision befitting the ariyans. What do you think about this, brahman youth? Which is better for those wealthy brahmans of Kosala, such as the brahman Caṅkī,[1] the brahman Tārukkha, the brahman Pokkharasāti, the brahman Jāṇussoṇi, and your father the brahman Todeyya— that the speech they should utter be conventional[2] or unconventional?"

"Conventional, good Gotama."

"Which is better for them, that the speech they should utter be thought out[3] or not thought out?"

"Thought out, good Gotama."

"Which is better for them, that the speech they should utter be considered[4] or not considered?"

"Considered, good Gotama."

"Which is better for them, that the speech they should utter be connected with the goal[5] or not connected with the goal?"

"Connected with the goal, good Gotama."

"What do you think about this, brahman youth? This being so, is the speech uttered by the brahman Pokkharasāti of the Upamañña (clan, incumbent) of the Subhaga forest glade, conventional or unconventional?"

"Unconventional, good Gotama."

"Is the speech uttered thought out, or not thought out?"

"Not thought out, good Gotama?"

"Is the speech uttered considered or not considered?"

"Not considered, good Gotama."

"Is the speech uttered connected with the goal or not connected with the goal?"

"Not connected with the goal, good Gotama."

---

[1] These five brahmans are also mentioned at the beginning of Sta. 98.

[2] *sammusā=samuccā*, as what is agreed upon by the opinion of the world; by common consent.

[3] *mantā;* at *MA*. iii. 447 explained by *tulayitvā*, weighed, and by *parigaṇhitvā*, examined.

[4] *patisaṅkhāya=jānitvā, MA*. iii. 447.

[5] *atthasaṁhitā=kāraṇanissitā*, dependent on action (?).

[203] " These five, brahman youth, are hindrances. What five ? The hindrance of desire for sense-pleasures, the hindrance of malevolence, the hindrance of sloth and torpor, the hindrance of restlessness and worry, the hindrance of doubt. These, brahman youth, are the five hindrances. Brahman youth, the brahman Pokkharasāti, of the Upamañña (clan, incumbent) of the Subhaga forest glade, is veiled, obstructed, covered and enveloped by these five hindrances. This situation certainly does not occur that he should know or see or realise states of further-men, the excellent knowledge and vision befitting the ariyans. These five, brahman youth, are the strands of pleasures of the senses: What five ? Material shapes cognisable by the eye, agreeable, pleasant, liked, enticing, connected with sensual pleasures, alluring. Sounds cognisable by the ear . . . Smells cognisable by the nose . . . Tastes cognisable by the tongue . . . Touches cognisable by the body, agreeable, pleasant, liked, enticing, connected with sensual pleasures, alluring. These, brahman youth, are the five strands of sense-pleasures. Brahman youth, the brahman Pokkharasāti of the Upamañña (clan, incumbent) of the Subhaga forest glade, is enslaved and infatuated by these five strands of sense-pleasures, he is addicted to them, and enjoys them without seeing the peril (in them), without knowing the escape (from them). This situation certainly does not occur that he should know or see or realise states of further-men, the excellent knowledge and vision befitting the ariyans. What do you think about this, brahman youth ? Which of these fires would have flame and hue and brightness: the fire that one could kindle from fuel of grass and dry sticks or the fire that one could kindle without fuel of grass and dry sticks ?"

" If it were possible, good Gotama, to kindle a fire without fuel of grass and dry sticks, that fire would have flame and hue and brightness."

" That is impossible, brahman youth, it cannot come to pass, that one should kindle a fire without fuel of grass and dry sticks—except through pyschic power.[1] I, brahman youth, say of this delight which is a delight on account of the five strands of sense-pleasures, that it is like the fire that burns on account of fuel of grass and dry sticks. **[204]** I, brahman youth, say of this delight which is a delight apart from pleasures of the senses, apart from unskilled

---

[1] As at the *pāṭihāriya* when Gotama kindled the matted-hair ascetics' firewood at *Vin.* i. 31.

states of mind, that it is like the fire that burns because it is without fuel of grass and dry sticks. And what, brahman youth, is delight apart from pleasures of the senses, apart from unskilled states of mind? As to this, brahman youth, a monk aloof from pleasures of the senses, aloof from unskilled states of mind, entering on the first meditation, abides therein. This, brahman youth, is delight apart from pleasures of the senses, apart from unskilled states of mind. And again, brahman youth, a monk, by allaying initial and sustained thought . . . entering on the second meditation, abides therein. This too, brahman youth, is delight apart from pleasures of the senses, apart from unskilled states of mind. Brahman youth, those brahmans who lay down five things for the doing of good, for success in what is skilled—what is the thing of greatest fruit that these brahmans lay down for the doing of good, for success in what is skilled?"

"Good Gotama, those brahmans who lay down five things for the doing of good, for success in what is skilled—renunciation is the thing of greatest fruit that these brahmans lay down for the doing of good, for success in what is skilled."

"What do you think about this, brahman youth? Suppose a great sacrifice to be prepared here by a certain brahman, and that two brahmans should come along, thinking: 'We will enjoy the great sacrifice of the brahman so-and-so,' and that one brahman should think: 'O may I myself get the best seat in the refectory,[1] the best drinking water, the best food; may that (other) brahman not get the best seat in the refectory, the best drinking water, the best food—the other brahman is getting the best seat in the refectory, the best drinking water, the best food, I am not getting the best seat in the refectory, the best drinking water, the best food;' thinking thus [**205**] he is angry and discontented—what result do brahmans lay down for him, brahman youth?"

"But, as to this, good Gotama, brahmans do not give a gift, thinking: 'Let the other be angry and discontented with this.' For, as to this, brahmans give a gift simply out of compassion."

"This being so, brahman youth, is this the sixth method of brahmans for doing good, that is to say compassion?"

"This being so, good Gotama, this is the sixth method of brahmans for doing good, that is to say compassion."

"Brahman youth, those brahmans who lay down five things for

---

[1] *Cf. M.* i. 28 (*M.L.S.* i. 35).

the doing of good, for success in what is skilled—where do you observe these five things abundantly: among householders or among those who have gone forth ?"

"Good Gotama, these five things that brahmans lay down for the doing of good, for success in what is skilled—I observe these five things abundantly in those who have gone forth, little among householders. For a householder, good Gotama, having a great deal to do: many duties, a large administration, great problems—is not constantly and consistently a truth-speaker. But one who has gone forth, good Gotama, having not a great deal to do: few duties, a small administration, small problems—is constantly and consistently a truthspeaker. A householder, good Gotama, having a great deal to do . . . is not constantly and consistently a man of austerity, a chaste man, intent on study, intent on renunciation. But one who has gone forth, good Gotama, having not much to do: few duties, a small administration, small problems— is constantly and consistently a 'burner-up,'[1] a Brahma-farer,[2] intent on study, intent on renunciation. Those five things, good Gotama, that recluses and brahmans lay down for the doing of good, for success in what is skilled—I observe these five things abundantly among those who have gone forth, little among householders."

"Those five things, brahman youth, that brahmans lay down for the doing of good, for success in what is skilled, [**206**] I say that these are equipments[3] of the mind, that is to say for developing a mind that is without enmity, without malevolence. Here, brahman youth, a monk is a truth-speaker. He, thinking, 'I am a truth-speaker' acquires knowledge of the goal,[4] acquires knowledge of *dhamma*, acquires the rapture which is connected with *dhamma*. I say of that rapture which is connected with what is skilled[5] that it is an equipment of the mind, that is to say for developing a mind that is without enmity, without malevolence. Here, brahman youth, a monk is a burner-up, he is a Brahma-farer, he is intent on study, he is intent on renunciation. He, thinking, 'I am intent on renunciation' acquires knowledge of the goal, acquires knowledge of *dhamma*, acquires the rapture which is connected with *dhamma*. I say of that rapture which is connected with what is skilled that it is an equip-

---

[1] *tapassin*, burning up wrong states of mind; "man of austerity" better suits the brahman mode of life.

[2] *brahma-cārin* also means chaste.

[3] *parikkhāra; cf. cittaparikkhāra* at *A*. iv. 62.

[4] *Cf. M*. i. 37.

[5] *kusalūpasaṁhita*, as at *S*. ii. 220.

ment of the mind, that is to say for developing a mind that is without enmity, without malevolence. I say that those five things, brahman youth, that brahmans lay down for the doing of good, for success in what is skilled, are equipments of the mind, that is to say for developing a mind that is without enmity, without malevolence."

When this had been said, the brahman youth Subha, Todeyya's son, spoke thus to the Lord: "I have heard, good Gotama, that the recluse Gotama knows the way to companionship with Brahmā."[1]

"What do you think about this, brahman youth? Is Naḷakāra village near here? Is Naḷakāra village not far from here?"

"Yes, sir, Naḷakāra village is near here, Naḷakāra village is not far from here."

"What do you think about this, brahman youth? Suppose a man had been born and bred here in Naḷakāra village, and that someone were to ask him who had never up to that time left Naḷakāra village the way to Naḷakāra village—would that man who had been born and bred in Naḷakāra village hesitate or be at a loss when asked the way to Naḷakāra village?"

"No, good Gotama. What is the reason for this? It is that that man was born and bred in Naḷakāra village; so all the roads to Naḷakāra village are well known to him."

"Yet, brahman youth, there might be hesitation or being at a loss for that man who was born and bred in Naḷakāra village on being asked the way to Naḷakāra village. [**207**] But for the Tathāgata there is neither hesitation nor being at a loss when he is asked about the Brahma-world or the course leading to the Brahma-world. And I, brahman youth, comprehend Brahmā and the Brahma-world and the course leading to the Brahma-world; and that according to the faring is the uprising in the Brahma-world, that too I comprehend."

"I have heard, good Gotama, that the recluse Gotama teaches the way to companionship with Brahmā. It would be good if the revered Gotama would teach me the way to companionship with Brahmā."

"Well then, brahman youth, listen and attend carefully, and I will speak."

"Yes, sir," the brahman youth Subha, Todeyya's son, answered the Lord in assent. The Lord spoke thus:

"And what, brahman youth, is the way to companionship with

---

[1] *Cf. M.* ii. 194; *D.* i. 249.

Brahmā? As to this, brahman youth, a monk dwells having suffused the first quarter with a mind of friendliness, likewise the second, likewise the third, likewise the fourth; just so above, below, across; he dwells, having suffused the whole world everywhere, in every way with a mind of friendliness that is far-reaching, wide-spread, immeasurable, without enmity, without malevolence. When, brahman youth, the freedom of mind that is friendliness has been developed thus, that deed which is done in a limited range does not rest there, does not remain there.[1] Brahman youth, as a stout conch-blower informs the four quarters without any difficulty, so, brahman youth, when the freedom of mind that is friendliness has been developed thus, that deed which is done in a limited range does not rest there, does not remain there. This, brahman youth, is a way to companionship with Brahmā.

And again, brahman youth, a monk dwells having suffused the first quarter with a mind of compassion . . . with a mind of sympathetic joy . . . with a mind of equanimity, likewise the second, likewise the third, likewise the fourth; just so above, below, across; he dwells having suffused the whole world everywhere, in every way, with a mind of equanimity that is far-reaching, wide-spread, [**208**] immeasurable, without enmity, without malevolence. When, brahman youth, the freedom of mind that is equanimity has been developed thus, that deed which is done in a limited range does not rest there, does not remain there. Brahman youth, as a stout conch-blower informs the four quarters without any difficulty, so, brahman youth, when the freedom of mind that is equanimity has been developed thus, that deed which is done in a limited range does not rest there, does not remain there. This too, brahman youth, is a way to companionship with Brahmā."

When this had been said, the brahman youth Subha, Todeyya's son spoke thus to the Lord: "It is excellent, good Gotama, it is excellent, good Gotama. It is as if one might set upright what had been upset, or disclose what was covered, or show the way to one who had gone astray, or bring an oil lamp into the darkness so that

---

[1] See also *D.* i. 251; *S.* iv. 322; *A.* v. 299; and *cf. Jā.* ii. 61 *f.*, which regards *pamāṇa* as equivalent to *paritta*, small. All the Comys. (except *Jā.* ii. 62) take *pamāṇakata kamma* as equivalent to *kāmâvacara*, "that which pertains to the senses and their corresponding objects." It seems that the small deed or the deed done in the limited range (such as is being thought of in this context) cannot remain and give its own result unless it is "covered" (*ajjhottharitvā*) by a large deed.

those with vision might see material shapes—even so in many a figure has *dhamma* been made clear by the good Gotama. I myself am going to the honoured Gotama for refuge and to *dhamma* and to the Order of monks. May the revered Gotama accept me as a lay-disciple going for refuge from today forth for as long as life lasts. But, please, good Gotama, we are going now, we are very busy and there is much to be done."

"You must do now, brahman youth, that for which you deem it to be the right time."

Then the brahman youth Subha, Todeyya's son, having rejoiced in what the Lord had said, having given thanks, rising from his seat, having greeted the Lord, departed keeping his right side towards him.

Now at that time the brahman Jāṇussoṇi was leaving Sāvatthī early in the day in a chariot (drawn by) all-white mules. The brahman Jāṇussoṇi saw the brahman youth Subha, Todeyya's son, coming in the distance; and seeing him, he spoke thus to the brahman youth Subha, Todeyya's son: "Now, where is the good Bhāradvāja coming from so early in the day?"

"I, sir, am coming from the recluse Gotama."

"What do you think about this, good Bhāradvāja? Has the recluse Gotama lucidity of wisdom? Do you think him clever?"[1]

[209] "But who am I, sir, that I should know whether the recluse Gotama has lucidity of wisdom? Surely only one like him could know whether the recluse Gotama has lucidity of wisdom?"

"Undoubtedly it is with lofty praise that the revered Bhāradvāja praises the recluse Gotama."

"But who am I that I should praise the recluse Gotama? Praised by the praised is the revered Gotama, chief among *devas* and men. And, sir, the recluse Gotama speaks of those five things that brahmans lay down for the doing of good, for success in what is skilled, as equipments of the mind, that is for developing a mind that is without enmity, without malevolence."

When this had been said, the brahman Jāṇussoṇi, having got down from his chariot (drawn by) all-white mules, having arranged his upper cloth over one shoulder, having saluted the Lord with joined palms, uttered this solemn utterance: "It is a gain for King Pasenadi of Kosala, it is well gotten by King Pasenadi of Kosala

---

[1] This passage, to "*devas* and men," also at *M.* i. 175.

that the Tathāgata, perfected one, fully Self-Awakened One, is staying in his kingdom."[1]

Discourse with Subha:
The Ninth

100. DISCOURSE TO SANGĀRAVA

(Saṅgāravasutta)[2]

THUS have I heard: At one time the Lord was walking on tour among the Kosalans together with a large Order of monks. Now at that time the brahman lady called Dhānañjānī,[3] who had confident belief in the Awakened One, in *dhamma* and in the Order, was residing in Caṇḍalakappa.[4] Then the brahman lady Dhānañjānī, having tripped,[5] three times uttered this solemn utterance: "Praise to that Lord, perfected One, fully Self-Awakened One. Praise to that Lord, perfected one, fully Self-Awakened One. Praise to that Lord, perfected one, [**210**] fully Self-Awakened One." Now at that time the brahman youth Saṅgārava was residing in Caṇḍalakappa; he was master of the three Vedas,[6] versed in the vocabularies and rituals together with the phonology and exegesis and the legendary tradition as the fifth; he was learned in idioms, a grammarian, proficient in popular philosophy and the marks of a Great Man. The brahman youth Saṅgārava heard what the brahman lady

---

[1] Such a "gain" is karmic in its nature.

[2] Six other *Saṅgāravasuttas* are given in *DPPN.*, but probably not all were addressed to the Saṅgārava of this *M.* Sta.

[3] See *S.* i. 160; and *K.S.* i. 199, *n.* 1, 2.

[4] There are several v.ll, for this name, *MA.* iii. 451 for example reading Maṇḍalakappa. It was a little village.

[5] The text reading is *upakkhalitvā*, which means having tripped or stumbled; *S.* i. 160 (in a rather different context) reads *upakkamitvā*, having approached or gone on to, with v.l. *upakkhalitvā*; *MA.* iii. 451 reads *pakkhalitvā*, which can mean either "having washed" or "having stumbled." Brahmans often wash before a ceremonial event, but I have chosen to render by "tripped" in conformity with the textual meaning. The *udāna* (solemn utterance) would then be an expression used for warding off the ill-luck which might otherwise ensue after stumbling. *Cf. Mhvu.* iii. 223.

[6] As at *M.* ii. 133.

Dhānañjānī was saying; on hearing it he spoke thus to the brahman lady Dhānañjānī: "This brahman lady Dhānañjānī is mean, this brahman lady Dhānañjānī is disgraced in that, while there are brahmans in existence, she speaks in praise of this little shaveling recluse."

"But do not you, dear learned friend,[1] know this Lord's moral habit and wisdom[2]? If you, dear learned friend, were to know this Lord's moral habit and wisdom, you, dear learned friend, would not consider that this Lord should be abused and reviled."

"Well then, lady, if the recluse Gotama arrives in Caṇḍalakappa, you might let me know."

"Yes, learned friend," the brahman lady Dhānañjānī answered the brahman youth Saṅgārava in assent.

Then as the Lord was walking on tour among the Kosalans he gradually arrived at Caṇḍalakappa. While he was there the Lord stayed in the mango grove of the brahmans of Tudi.[3] Then the brahman lady Dhānañjānī heard that the Lord had arrived at Caṇḍalakappa and was staying in the mango grove of the brahmans of Tudi. Then the brahman lady Dhānañjānī approached the brahman youth Saṅgārava; having approached, she spoke thus to the brahman youth Saṅgārava: "Dear learned friend, this Lord has arrived at Caṇḍalakappa and is staying in the mango grove of the brahmans of Tudi. Dear learned friend, you must do now that for which you think it the right time."

"Yes, lady," and the brahman youth Saṅgārava, having answered the brahman lady Dhānañjānī in assent, approached the Lord; having approached, he exchanged greetings with the Lord; having [**211**] conversed in a friendly and courteous way, he sat down at a respectful distance. As he was sitting down at a respectful distance, Saṅgārava the brahman youth spoke thus to the Lord:

"There are, good Gotama, some recluses and brahmans who claim that, in regard to the fundamentals of the Brahma-faring,[4] they

---

[1] *bhadramukha*, as at *M*. ii. 53. See above, p. 249, *n*. 1.

[2] *sīlapaññāṇa*, as at *D*. i. 124. See note at *Dial*. i. 156.

[3] *Todeyyānaṁ brāhmaṇānaṁ*. These brahmans were so-called because they lived in Tudi (-gāma). Only the one was called Todeyya because he was the head of these; see above, p. 386, *n*. 1.

[4] *MA*. iii. 453 says of *ādibrahmacariyaṁ: brahmacariyassa ādibhūtā uppādakā jānakâ ti*, which seems to mean that they were producers and generators of the Brahma-faring; but the grammar is against this. I think it more likely that the "fundamentals of the Brahma-faring" refer to "the practices that have been pointed out by me for disciples," enumerated in *M*. Sta. 77.

have attained here-now to excellence and to going beyond through super-knowledge.[1] Among those recluses and brahmans, good Gotama, who claim that, in regard to the fundamentals of the Brahma-faring, they have attained here-now to excellence and to going beyond through super-knowledge—of which (sort) is the revered Gotama ?"

" I, Bhāradvāja, say that there is a difference among those who claim that, in regard to the fundamentals of the Brahma-faring, they have attained here-now to excellence and to going beyond through super-knowledge. There are, Bhāradvāja, some recluses and brahmans who depend on report;[2] these claim that it is through report that, in regard to the fundamentals of the Brahma-faring, they have attained here-now to excellence and to going beyond through super-knowledge —such as the three-Veda-brahmans. But there are, Bhāradvāja, some recluses and brahmans who with only mere faith claim that, in regard to the fundamentals of the Brahma-faring, they have attained here-now to excellence and to going beyond through super-knowledge—such as reasoners and investigators.[3] There are, Bhāradvāja, some recluses and brahmans who by fully understanding *dhamma* of themselves only,[4] although these truths had not been heard before,[5] claim that, in regard to the fundamentals of the Brahma-faring, they have attained here-now to excellence and to going beyond through super-knowledge. Now, Bhāradvāja, I am one of those recluses and brahmans who by fully understanding *dhamma* of themselves only, although these truths had not been heard before, claim that, in regard to the fundamentals of the Brahma-faring, they have attained here-now to excellence and to going beyond through super-knowledge. You must understand it in this way, Bhāradvāja, that I am one of those recluses and brahmans who by fully understanding *dhamma* of themselves only, although these truths had not been heard before, claim that, in regard to the fundamentals of the Brahma-faring, they have attained here-now to excellence and to going beyond through super-knowledge.

As to this,[6] Bhāradvāja, before my Self-awakening while I was still

---

[1] *abhiññāvosānapāramippatta. Cf. M.* ii. 11 *ff.* (see above, p. 211, *n.* 2).

[2] *Cf. M.* i. 520, *anussavika.* [3] *Cf. M.* i. 520, *takkī-vīmaṁsī.*

[4] *I.e.* not learning it or hearing it from others; *cf. Vin.* i. 8, *na me ācariyo atthi,* " I have no teacher."

[5] As at *A.* iii. 9; *cf. D.* ii. 33; *S.* ii. 9, 105. " Truths " is *dhammesu,* which *AA.* iii. 225 explains as *catusaccadhammesu. Dhammā* can also mean things; or mental states, elements or ultimates. [6] As at *M.* i. 240.

the *bodhisatta*, not fully awakened, it occurred to me: Narrow is the household life, a path of dust, going forth is in the open, nor is it easy while dwelling in a house to lead the Brahma-faring completely fulfilled, completely purified, polished like a conch-shell. Suppose now that I, having cut off hair and beard, having donned saffron garments, should go forth from home into homelessness? So I, Bhāradvāja, [212] after a time, being young, my hair coal-black, possessed of radiant youth, in the prime of my life . . . (*repeat from M.* i. *p.* 163, *l.* 28 *to p.* 167, *l.* 8—*M.L.S.* i. *p.* 207 *to p.* 211; *for* monks *read* Bhāradvāja) . . . So I, Bhāradvāja, sat down just there, thinking: 'Indeed this does well for striving.'

Moreover, Bhāradvāja, three similes occurred to me . . . (*repeat from M.* i. *p.* 240, *l.* 29 *to p.* 247, *l.* 16—*M.L.S.* i. *p.* 295 *to p.* 302, *but omitting* "But yet that painful feeling . . . persisted without impinging on my mind, *on pp.* 297, *etc., and* 299) . . . saying: 'The recluse Gotama lives in abundance, he is wavering in his striving, he has reverted to a life of abundance.'

But when I, Bhāradvāja, had taken some material nourishment,[1] having picked up strength, aloof from pleasures of the senses . . . I entered on and abided in the first meditation . . . By allaying initial and discursive thought, with the mind subjectively tranquillised and fixed on one point, I entered and abided in the second meditation . . . I entered and abided in the third meditation.[2]

With the mind composed thus, quite purified, quite clarified, without blemish, without defilement, grown soft and workable . . . (*repeat from M.* i. *p.* 248, *line* 19 *to p.* 249, *line* 21—*M.L.S.* i. *p.* 302 *to p.* 303, *substituting* Bhāradvāja *for* Aggivessana, *and omitting* "But yet that pleasurable feeling . . . persisted without impinging on my mind") . . . even as I abided diligent, ardent, self-resolute."

When this had been said, the brahman youth Saṅgārava spoke thus to the Lord:

"Indeed the good Gotama's striving was steadfast,[3] indeed it was that of a true man[4] such as that of a perfected one, a fully Self-Awakened One. But now, good Gotama, are there *devas*?"[5]

"Certainly, Bhāradvāja, it is known to me that there are *devas*."

---

[1] As at *M.* i. 247.

[2] The fourth meditation, not mentioned here, is I think omitted in error.

[3] *aṭṭhita*. This is a case of tmesis, for *aṭṭhita* is to be taken with *padhāna*. The meaning may more properly be that the striving was that of (or, worthy of) a steadfast man.

[4] *sappurisa*, also a case of tmesis.

[5] *Cf. M.* ii. 130 (above, p. 311).

" But why do you, good Gotama, on being asked if there are *devas* say that it is certainly known to you that there are *devas* ? Even if this is so, good Gotama, is it not a vain falsehood ?"

" If on being asked, Bhāradvāja, ' Are there *devas* ?' [**213**] one should say: ' There are *devas* ' and should say: ' Certainly they are known to me,' then the conclusion to be reached by an intelligent person is indubitable, namely that there are *devas*."

" But why did not the revered Gotama explain this to me at the beginning ?"

" It is commonly[1] agreed in the world, Bhāradvāja, that there are *devas*."

When this had been said, the brahman youth Saṅgārava spoke thus to the Lord:

" It is excellent, good Gotama, it is excellent, good Gotama. It is as if, good Gotama, one might set upright what had been upset, or might disclose what was covered, or might show the way to one who had gone astray, or bring an oil-lamp into the darkness so that those with vision might see material shapes—even so in many a figure has *dhamma* been made clear by the good Gotama. I am going to the Lord[2] Gotama for refuge and to *dhamma* and to the Order of monks. May the revered Gotama accept me as a lay-disciple going for refuge from this day forth for as long as life lasts."

Discourse to Saṅgārava:
The Tenth

Division on Brahmans:
The Fifth

TOLD ARE THE MIDDLE FIFTY

---

[1] *ucce*. *MA*. iii. 454 says *uccena saddena sammataṁ* (v.l. *samma*) *pākaṭaṁ mataṁ lokasmiṁ*, with a loud noise agreed upon by the usual thought of the world.

[2] Reading here is *bhagavantaṁ*.

INDEXES

I—TOPICS

World: beyond, 71 *ff.*; exclusively happy, 232 *ff.*; instable, no refuge, not one's own, lacks, 261 *ff.*; 'is (not) eternal', *etc.*, xxii, 97, 162 *ff.*; 's veil, 319, 355; -ly life (*gehasita*), 149 *n.*

Wrong (*daṇḍa*), 36 *f.*, 39, 41 *f.*

Youth, radiant (*bhadra yobbana*), 136, 260, 281, 357, 401

II—SIMILES

ARROW and reed, 217

baby boy, 62, 102, 223, 238
ball of thread, 198
bath attendant, 216
belle of the countryside, 230, 237
Benares muslin, 214 *f.*
bird on the wing, 11
blind men, 360, 389
borrowed wealth, 30

calf, 130
cattle-butcher, 376
clean cloth, 45, 330
conch blower, 219, 396

distiller, 39
ditchers, fletchers, joiners, 290
dream, 30
drops of water, 125
drunkard, 39
dyed monkey, 49

earth, water, fire, air, wind, 94 *f.*
elephant-bonds, 122
elephant playing, 39
elephant-riding, 281
elephant's trunk, 88
elephants, horses, oxen to be tamed, 310 *f.*
emerald jewel, 217, 231

fire and fuel, 165 *f.*, 311, 369, 392
flax blossom, 214
fruits of a tree, 30 *f.*

Ganges to sea, 172
gelder, gouger, 48
grass torch, 29

heap of flowers, 53
hen and eggs, 23
house with eleven doors, 18
hungry dog, 28

iron hook, 61 *f.*

leper, 185 *ff.*
lotus-pond, 216
lump of flesh, 28

man blind from birth, 188, 190, 390
man crossing Ganges, 104 *f.*
man fully clothed, 217
man going from village to village, 220
man pressing out honey, 206
man with hands and feet cut off, 202
man with one eye, 115
milk and water, 66, 303
mirror, 88
moon, 290
morning star, 215

palm-tree, 137
pit of glowing embers, 29
pith, 104
poisoned arrow, 99
pool of water, 216, 221
poor man, 367, 369
poor man's bonds, 123
potter, ivory worker, goldsmith, 218

quail, 121

reflection in a mirror, 219
rich householder, 184
rich householder's bonds, 124
river in spate, 300

sāl-timber, 166
seeds, 130
setting upright, *etc.*, 32, 58, 64, 83, 167, 172, 180, 191, 236, (239), 278, 331, 352, (366), (385), 396, 402
snake and slough, 218
strong man, 39, 130
strong man torturing, 376
sword and scabbard, 218

thoroughbred colt, 117
treasure, 17
two houses, 221
two strong men, 376

water and water-vessel, 87 *f.*
water-pot, 236

III—NAMES

IV—SOME PALI WORDS IN THE NOTES